Location of culture groups referred to in text

NORTH AMERICA

1 Abnaki (U.S.A.)
2 Apache (U.S.A.)
3 Arapaho (U.S.A.)
4 Aztec (Mexico)
5 Blackfeet (U.S.A. and Canada)
6 Cherokee (U.S.A.)
7 Cheyenne (U.S.A.)
8 Chilcat (U.S.A.)
9 Cree (Canada)
10 Creek (U.S.A.)
11 Delaware (U.S.A.)
12 Eskimo
    a Alaskan (U.S.A.)
    b Caribou (Canada)
    c Greenland (Denmark [Greenland])
    d Labrador (Canada)
13 Flathead (U.S.A.)
14 Fox (U.S.A.)
15 Haida (Canada)
16 Hopi (U.S.A.)
17 Hupa (U.S.A.)
18 Iroquois (Huron, Mohawk, Seneca) (U.S.A.)
19 Ixcatec (Mexico)
20 Kiowa (U.S.A.)
21 Kwakiutl (Canada)
22 Massachuset (U.S.A.)
23 Maya (Quiché, Tzeltal, Zinacantan) (Mexico and Guatemala)
24 Mazatec (Mexico)
25 Menomini (U.S.A.)
26 Micmac (Canada)
27 Miskito (Nicaragua and Honduras)
28 Natchez (U.S.A.)
29 Navajo (U.S.A.)
30 Nootka (Canada)
31 Northern Paiute (U.S.A.)
32 Ojibwa (U.S.A.)
33 Penobscot (U.S.A.)
34 Sioux (Dakota, Oglala) (U.S.A.)
35 Tlingit (Chilcat) (U.S.A.)
36 Washo (U.S.A.)
37 Yana (U.S.A.)
38 Yaqui (U.S.A. and Mexico)
39 Zapotec (Mexico)
40 Zuñi (U.S.A.)

SOUTH AMERICA

41 Alacaluf (Chile)
42 Chono (Chile)
43 Inca (Peru)
44 Nambicuara (Brazil)
45 Ona (Argentina)
46 Siriono (Bolivia)
47 Yaghan (Chile)
48 Yanomamö (Venezuela and Brazil)

All references in parentheses are to countries. In some cases, a group straddles the boundaries of two countries; this is indicated by listing them both.

HUMANITY
AND
CULTURE

HUMANITY AND CULTURE
An Introduction to Anthropology

ORIOL PI-SUNYER
University of Massachusetts, Amherst

ZDENEK SALZMANN
University of Massachusetts, Amherst

HOUGHTON MIFFLIN COMPANY   BOSTON

DALLAS
GENEVA, ILLINOIS
HOPEWELL, NEW JERSEY
PALO ALTO
LONDON

PART OPENER CREDITS

David Horr/Anthro-Photo (Part One)
David Horr/Anthro-Photo (Part Two)
Irven De Vore/Anthro-Photo (Part Three)
E. Carella/Semitic Museum (Part Four)
Owen Franken/Stock Boston (Part Five)

COVER AND TITLE PAGE PHOTO CREDITS

by Steve R. Lorton, Courtesy of Sunset *Magazine*
(a market place in Korea)
Owen Franken/Stock Boston
(Pompidou Art Center)

PRINTED IN THE U.S.A.

Library of Congress Catalog Card Number:
77–76336

ISBN: 0–395–25051–X

Contents

PART TWO

HUMAN SOCIETIES:
LEVELS OF
COMPLEXITY *129*

PART THREE

HUMAN SOCIETIES: FRAMEWORKS AND INSTITUTIONS

PART FOUR

COMMUNICATION: THE
PIVOT OF CULTURE *343*

Preface

All books have their distinctive histories. This one evolved several years ago from informal discussions between ourselves and with our colleagues and students. Initially, we were less concerned with writing yet another textbook than with considering how the existing ones served the needs of students seeking an exposure to anthropology. It seemed to us then—and perhaps the situation has not changed much since —that there was a place for a more broadly based introduction to the study of humanity and culture than those that were available.

While we recognized that the general field of anthropology was well served by some exceptionally fine authors of talent, insight, and expressive ability, we found the vast majority of their works addressed to readers assumed to be equipped with sufficient background to place the points made and opinions voiced in the proper perspective. Our experience has been that the typical undergraduate student lacks such a background and, more likely than not, tends to become lost when turning to the classics of the discipline or the discussions of contemporary issues in scholarly journals.

If most anthropologists write for other anthropologists, it was also our impression that a great many introductory textbooks do not do justice to the intellectual capacities of today's undergraduates. Rather than accepting the prevalent opinion that the average student will not read a "demanding" text, we maintain that a distinction should be made between unnecessarily technical writing on the one hand and mental fare that requires some intellectual effort and input on the other. But while respecting the intellect of our potential readers, we fully recognize that they are new to anthropology and that it would be false to assume prior knowledge on their part of what anthropology is all about. For this reason we have tried to give this book a format that would encourage a steady growth in factual and theoretical knowledge about humanity.

Following an introductory discussion of the nature and scope of anthropology, the book is organized into five parts whose component chapters may be read and reread independently but which also represent a carefully considered progression. Part One establishes a framework for the study of humanity and culture. Although the textbook is primarily designed to acquaint students with the social and cultural aspects of the human species, our point of departure is that there are not several separate and distinct "anthropologies," but one unified field concerned with and dedicated to the study of the human condition—"the science of man," as some of the older texts phrase it. We are convinced that the maintenance of sharp intra- as well as interdisciplinary boundaries runs counter to the reality of an experience and a history that are distinctly human, and only human. Thus, we offer a concise introduction to the biocultural aspects of human evolution and devote several chapters to the archaeological perspective and to culture history.

The final chapter of Part One requires a brief explanation. Coming after a discussion of New World culture history, it examines the Native American experience of recent centuries. While it might simply have been included as an expression of the debt American anthropology owes to American Indian societies, we feel that such a chapter is especially appropriate in a book that will be read mainly by American students. We believe that an understanding of the struggle of the earliest Americans can offer us wisdom and insight particularly relevant to our time.

Part Two is a presentation, according to broad levels of social complexity, of the major categories of human cultures. The sequence does not imply a formal progression from simple to complex societies, for the process of cultural evolution is much more than a step-by-step development from hunter-gatherers to citizens of modern industrial states. Rather, it represents our desire to emphasize the fact that degrees of organizational complexity help to define the scope and nature of institutions found in different cultures. The organizational variety characterizing human societies has been placed into what we hope is a meaningful and justifiable typology. As is the case with typological arrangements in the social sciences in general, some simplification has been inevitable: the real world of humans and the kaleidoscopic evidence that bears upon it are not susceptible to neat divisions

into a limited number of conceptual categories. Nevertheless, we hope that our scheme will be found neither arbitrary nor unduly abstruse.

Part Three consists of an examination of the major institutional structures that in one guise or another manifest themselves in all cultures, for societies everywhere must cope with a number of like fundamental needs. In Part Four the pivotal component of all human culture—language, and communication in general—receives more than just cursory attention. Finally, Part Five deals with selected topics in theory and application, and with some observations on the future of both anthropology and humankind.

Throughout the book, we have endeavored to avoid several pitfalls that might easily have resulted in a skewed picture of what cultural anthropology, broadly conceived, is about. Anthropologists have taken many approaches to the subject ranging from the traditional to the highly polemical. In our turn, we have tried to draw on the best that all of these have to offer. Anthropology began as a study of "exotic" peoples but in recent years has shifted its attention increasingly to modern complex societies. For our many examples, we have tapped all societies and cultures, present and past, our own and distant ones; for, after all, there is but one humanity. Last but not least, we have tried to keep technical terms to a minimum except in those several chapters where such restraint would have significantly impaired the presentation of relevant subject matter.

It remains for us to thank the many colleagues, students, and friends who have helped us in our task. To begin with, we would like to note the following colleagues to whom we are grateful for reviewing various drafts of the manuscript: Francisco E. Aguilera, McGill University; Milton Altschuler, East Carolina University; William Bright, University of California, Los Angeles; Eugene N. Cohen, Baruch College,

City University of New York; Edward O. Henry, San Diego State University; Dell Hymes, University of Pennsylvania; William G. Lockwood, The University of Michigan, Ann Arbor; Marjorie Nam, Tallahassee Junior College; Hampton Rowland, Jr., Florida State University, Tallahassee; and Carl Trubschenck, Sacramento City College.

At the University of Massachusetts, Amherst, several of our colleagues gave us their valuable comments on drafts of individual chapters: George J. Armelagos, Joan M. Chandler, Ralph H. Faulkingham, Sylvia H. Forman, David H. Fortier, Alfred B. Hudson, Samuel Jay Keyser, Jean E. Ludtke, Donald A. Proulx, and Richard B. Woodbury. Jessica Kelly, now with the National Park Service, helped to research several chapters of the book while an undergraduate research assistant in the Department of Anthropology.

Finally, meriting special mention is Joy Salzmann, who has read and commented on every line of the several drafts through which the manuscript has gone. Without her moral support and editorial help, the book would have taken longer to complete and would have lacked a certain clarity and insight.

O.P–S.
Z.S.

HUMANITY
AND
CULTURE

Chapter 1
Anthropology: its nature and scope

We begin with a series of questions:

Did Neanderthals speak?

Why was the domestication of plants and animals the single most important revolution in human history?

Are the practices of child training reflected in the typical personality of an adult member of a society?

How does a society without formal laws and police maintain social controls?

Can witchcraft kill?

Why are sexual relations between brother and sister universally forbidden?

Is a "killer instinct" built into human nature?

What do all of these and many other similarly intriguing questions have in common besides their question marks? They are the sort of queries anthropologists make it their business to answer.

WHAT IS ANTHROPOLOGY?

Anthropology may very simply be defined as the study of humankind. This definition is fair enough, but it raises some points.

Certainly, anthropology is not the only discipline concerned with the study of humans. The various social and behavioral sciences—economics, political science, psychology, sociology, and others—deal with the institutions and the functioning of human societies and seek generalizations regarding human behavior. Among the biological sciences, anatomy, genetics, and physiology—again to mention only a few—contribute to our knowledge of the structure, variation, and functioning of the human organism. History provides us with a careful and orderly record of past human events and an explanation of their origins and causes. Linguistics endeavors to lay bare the nature of that peculiarly human trait, the gift of language. And how much our understanding and appreciation of humanity would suffer without the study of art, literature, and music and without contributions of philosophy, theology, and other disciplines.

Considering the existence of these disciplines that touch on the many aspects of the human condition, one is surely entitled to ask at this point: What is the need for anthropology? Is it perhaps largely a science of leftovers? Or, if one takes the opposing view: Is it simply a platform for those making the claim that they are the only ones who can hope to "put it all together"?

A brief history

In this country, in fact, anthropology did begin as a study of subjects unclaimed by others. During the 1800s, there were a number of areas that other disciplines had not looked into—the little-known "primitive" peoples in particular—and it was to this gap in knowledge that the early anthropologists turned their attention. The popular conception of anthropology as the academic equivalent of a curio shop continues to linger to the present day, as does the notion that the anthropologist's main goal is to excavate for arrowheads and bones.

In the United States, the oldest anthropological organization is the American Ethnological Society, established in 1842. In 1873 Major John Wesley Powell, known primarily for his early explorations of the Grand Canyon, founded the Anthropological Society of Washington, D.C., and six years later he organized the Bureau of (American) Ethnology as part of the Smithsonian Institution. Toward the end of the nineteenth century it was thought that anthropology had gained sufficient respectability to be admitted into the halls of academe. The first university position in anthropology was set up in the late 1880s at Clark University in Worcester, Massachusetts, and the first doctorate in the subject was awarded there in 1892. As a growing field of scholarship, anthropology steadily matured during the early part of the twentieth century and then received added impetus during and after World War II, when contacts with the most remote parts of the world and its peoples became commonplace for a great many Americans. Only in the last few years has the growth of anthropology begun to level off.

Some characteristics

The scope and general orientation of anthropology became defined in the early part of the 1900s under the influence of some of its most distinguished representatives. The hallmark of anthropology, in brief, is its insistence that humankind must be studied comprehensively and from a comparative viewpoint. This means that the scope of anthropology must be universal: the members of a remote Indian group of the Amazonian tropical rain forest are no less deserving of serious consideration than are their sophisticated compatriots in Rio. It further means that the concerns of anthropology know no time limitations: the story of humankind reaches several million years into the past and in a certain sense much beyond. And finally it means that the many strands of human biological and social development are so inextricably interwoven that none can be traced without examining the entire fabric.

Another characteristic that has marked anthropological work from its beginnings and that sets it apart from the other social sciences is a strong field-work component. While it is true that the administration of questionnaires, the application of statistics, and the use of other more or less impersonal methods of research have become the necessary tools for understanding modern populous societies, a prolonged and usually repeated exposure to those whom anthropologists study remains the most desirable goal. This practice of sharing, even if to a limited extent, in the lifeways of other groups not only leads to the establishment of a close relationship between anthropologists and those whom they study but also gives their writings a special flavor of intimacy that is generally absent from the other disciplines.

Now it is only fair to mention that, just

like scientists in every other field of knowledge, anthropologists too are becoming rapidly overspecialized. As a result, the professed unity of their discipline is not always visible, and it would be an exaggeration to claim such unity for much of their scholarly output, if not in fact misleading. What anthropology is in practice may best be ascertained by reviewing what those who call themselves anthropologists are actually doing. An examination of the program of a recent annual meeting of the American Anthropological Association reveals an astonishing assortment of subjects. To give an example, at the Seventy-first Annual Meeting of the association the subjects ranged all the way from a comparison of human and chimpanzee chromosomes to the distribution of deities among the figurines found at the pre-Aztec ceremonial center of Teotihuacán; from methods of curing gonorrhea in the Cook Islands to aspects of transitive verbs in the language of the Micmac Indians; from marriage by capture among the Tzeltal Indians of Mexico to a program for the study of the future in education; and from prime-time television programming as a source of mythology in complex societies to the pricing of eggs in rural southeastern Ohio. Some anthropologists find these tendencies of ever-broadening scope disconcerting, and one prominent member of the profession, Dell H. Hymes, has recently gone so far as to preface a book with the statement: "If anthropology did not exist, would it have to be invented? If it were reinvented, would it be the anthropology we have now? To both questions, the answer, I think, is no" (1972:3).

The fact that the accomplishments of anthropology thus far, its thrust, and its right to independent existence are currently being questioned by various members of the profession may be taken as an indication of a fundamental weakness. We prefer to consider such questioning a sign of vigor and viability. Nevertheless, we would agree with Hymes, and others, that regarding the future direction of the discipline, two cautions are clearly in order.

One has to do with the unifying approach to the study of our species— the touchstone of anthropology at its best. This approach not only must be preserved but must be strengthened still further. Anthropology may not be equipped to compete with some of the specialized disciplines that study humankind; but as an integrative inquiry into the many-sided nature of our species, it has a distinctive contribution to make by offering the possibility of discovering significant connections between the results of very diverse investigations.

The second caution concerns the purpose, or the needs, to which future anthropological research should be applied. Playing the game of anthropology on the fields of convention halls, museums, and college campuses is not enough. If people are to be studied seriously and responsibly, then anthropologists need to address themselves to the issues and problems of our times and of the generations to come. If anthropology is truly about all humankind, then it must serve and belong to all humankind.

THE SCOPE OF ANTHROPOLOGY

A brief discussion of the overall scope of anthropology may best be introduced by the following propositions:

1 Homo sapiens is a biological organism, and the study of human beings must therefore be grounded in the recognition and understanding of their animal origins and nature.

2 In transcending their animal heritage, human beings had to embark on a cumulative series of innovations as they strove to adapt or adjust to an ever-growing variety of natural and self-made conditions.

3 In the course of a remarkable evolution during the past several million years, human beings have been immeasurably aided by the development of a uniquely effective means of communication—language.

4 In its astonishing variety of lifeways, humanity displays a multiplicity of solutions to problems that though ostensibly different are nevertheless rooted in the indivisible oneness of the human condition throughout the ages and the world over.

Accordingly, practicing anthropologists tend to cluster into four subfields, commonly designated as biological anthropology, archaeology, linguistic anthropology, and cultural-social anthropology (including ethnography and ethnology).

The overarching concern of *biological* (or of *physical*) *anthropology* has long been with the ultimate origins and subsequent development of the human species. More specifically, this concern has centered on the tantalizing problems of discovering when in the course of biological evolution the initial steps were taken that eventually led to the emergence of our species; what innovations, both physical and cultural, must have occurred that marked this extraordinary course of events; and how the physical variations among human populations of the present and of the recent past can best be accounted for. In the earlier stages of biological anthropology, scholars either were busily engaged in comparative study of the fossil record in their search for the so-called missing links or were preoccupied with variations among living forms and racial classifications based on the observable or measurable physical traits. With the occurrence of major developments in the natural sciences, their research and priorities changed correspondingly. The rediscovery of Mendel's laws of inheritance in the early 1900s, for instance, stimulated research in human genetics.[1] Some of the advances made in biochemistry since World War II, especially in the field of molecular biology, are being applied to the measuring of the evolutionary "distance" between two related species. And new ingenious methods of dating fossil remains have provided opportunity for a thoroughgoing revision of the calendar of events of human paleontology.

Among the last major trends in biological anthropology has been the opening up of the study of primates. To be sure, research on the anatomy, evolution, and genetics of our nearest biological relatives, the primates, has a respectable history; but a dramatic shift has taken place during the past dozen or so years with the upsurge of interest in the study of primate behavior. The unmistakable evidence of varying degrees of social life in monkeys and apes—for example, the year-round association of the two sexes, the prolonged infant dependency on adults, and the natural inclination among some species to communicate or even to use tools—has led to the recognition that primate social behavior is part of the same

Biological anthropology

The study of nonhuman primates in their natural environment allows physical anthropologists to investigate differences and similarities in behavior and social organization between human groups and other members of the primate order. (From Jane van Lawick-Goodall, Grub the Bush Baby, *Houghton Mifflin Company, Boston and Collins Publishers, London, 1972)*

[1]Gregor Johann Mendel (1822–1884) was an Augustinian monk whose scientific fame rests on long years of botanical experimentation in the gardens of his monastery in the Moravian city of Brno. Using garden peas for hybridization experiments, he was able to demonstrate with precision how inherited characteristics are transmitted from generation to generation. He may aptly be regarded as the founder of scientific genetics, although the importance of his research was not recognized during his lifetime.

general evolutionary process that culminated in humankind. In the words of Jane Goodall, a pioneer in the study of the chimpanzee:

It is my belief that a better understanding of the behavior of man's closest living relative will suggest new lines of inquiry into the biological basis of certain aspects of human behavior—especially problems connected with child-raising, adolescence, aggression and some mental disorders (Edey 1972:148).

Interestingly enough, especially for cultural anthropologists, these lines of inquiry represent a significant departure from a tradition of purely biological concerns to something akin to the descriptive study of the life styles of human groups. Research of this kind, exploring the interplay of inherited biological and acquired behavioral traits, is particularly worthy of note: its aim is to come closer to the vision of anthropology as able to bridge the gap that most other disciplines dealing with humans avoid altogether.

If one can project from ongoing research interests the future course of biological anthropology, one may anticipate a greater emphasis on the need for thoughtful understanding of contemporary humankind. Especially significant among current concerns are inquiries into the nature and structure of breeding populations framed in terms of population genetics: for example, studies of the relationship between marriage patterns and gene distribution; investigations of the relationship between human groups and aspects of their natural environments that may tend to limit or enhance their future development; and explorations of genetic, environmental, and social factors affecting diseases or their prevention. The applications of these and similar findings to medicine and to enlightened population control may well be of real significance. We do not wish to seem to be claiming that progress in biological anthropology is the key to human survival. We do assert that

A physical anthropologist with equipment used to measure oxygen intake under strenuous work conditions. (Zdenek Salzmann)

some of the current trends give promise of an anthropology committed to serve and not merely to describe and explain.

Archaeology

To the extent that biological anthropology deals with humankind's more remote past, it complements *archaeology*, another subfield of anthropology. In fact, the two dovetail very neatly at the threshold of humanity, a period of a million-odd years when the feedback between biological and social developments must have been exceptionally constant and direct.

Archaeology began as the collecting of antiquities in Italy during the Renaissance. Originally it served and contributed to the revival of interest in the extraordinary accomplishments of ancient Greece and Rome. Later it also came to embrace the other great civilizations of the ancient Mediterranean world and the Middle East. All these civilizations possessed many attributes in common, among them monumental architecture, exquisite art, and—above all—writing. In a way, then, the kind of archaeology

An international team of archaeologists and engineers dismantled and moved to a safe location the huge sandstone monuments of Abu Simbel in Nubia, Egypt, before the area was flooded by the waters of the Aswan High Dam. The magnificent monument's Great Temple again faces the same direction as before: the first rays of the morning sun will penetrate its innermost sanctuary on two days of the year, just as the original architects planned it in the thirteenth century B.C. (UNESCO/Nonadovic)

Subway construction in Mexico City exposed the remains of important Aztec ceremonial structures. Modern urban growth and other large-scale construction pose a danger to all manner of archaeological sites, but destruction can be minimized through protective legislation designed to foster salvage archaeology. (Wide World Photos)

The return of ceremonial objects to their places of origin represents a heightened sensitivity to the symbolic values of other cultures. Shown here is the revered statue of the Afo-A-Kom, which had been stolen in 1966, after its return in 1973 to the Kom people of Cameroon. (Tom Johnson/New York Times Pictures) that we have thus far referred to must be seen as rather closely linked to the history of a limited period and particular part of the world. Today, scholarly interest in the material achievements of ancient civilizations of the Old World continues unabated under the designation *classical archaeology*, and in the yellow pages of academia it is most likely to be found together with art history or classics.

Ancient though the finds of classical archaeology are, their antiquity pales when compared to that of some of the material evidences left behind by preliterate peoples the world over. The systematic study of these remains is the concern of *prehistoric archaeology*, or archaeological anthropology, now marking roughly the first centennial of its existence. An unhurried discussion of prehistoric archaeology is presented in a later chapter, but a few brief remarks are in order now. By necessity, prehistoric archaeologists tend to be less specialized than their classical colleagues. Dealing as they must with a time depth several hundred times greater, they provide anthropology with the necessary time perspective for the understanding of the very remote past. The need for such perspective developed, once emphasis began to shift from painstaking classification of the numerous items of material evidence of early cultures to the interpretation of the functions that these items must have served among their users. A stone tool or garbage deposit is seen as the tangible manifestation of an economic system, and an assemblage of tools provides some understanding of population size and structure as well as of some of the major preoccupations of the people who left them behind. In short, the modern approach holds that the level and form of material achievements are far less significant than the understanding they can give of a group's ability to adjust to and shape its natural and social environment.

Finally, mention must be made of *salvage archaeology*, an effort on the part of archaeologists to obtain as much information as possible from sites threatened by destruction as a result of either natural causes or human activity. The need for salvage archaeology grows correspondingly with our technical ability and increasing penchant for changing the face of the land to suit our own immediate purposes. Until awareness is created that the supply of archaeological evidence still underground (or underwater) is both finite and irreplaceable—very much like some of the raw materials that have recently become scarce—emergency research and excavation afford our heritage at least some protection against the growing specter of complete and needless destruction. A people who are respectful of their past tend to value themselves and their present more highly and to show more thoughtful, urgent concern for their future. If for no other reason than this, it is of the utmost importance that both professional and amateur archaeologists should understand that all antiquities belong to the peoples and countries where they are found.

Linguistic anthropology

Since human language represents one of the most crucial adaptive advantages that characterize our species, it is no wonder that anthropologists give it its full share of attention. While the study of the structure of languages forms the separate discipline of linguistics, with a tradition reaching back to the work of ancient grammarians in India several centuries before Christ, *linguistic anthropology* is a relatively recent field. It is concerned with language in its human context, both biological and social.

Quite appropriately, one of the questions that linguistic anthropologists have been trying to answer has to do with the origins of language. Because languages change slowly and systematically, study of their history provides many important clues to the migrations and contacts of their earlier speakers. Because all peoples typically talk about matters of immediate concern to them, language vocabularies serve as excel-

Anthropology has always had a potential for varied applications. Here a linguistic anthropologist works in an educational program.

lent indices of a group's material, social, and conceptual universe. And because the study of any nonliterate people would not be complete without attention to their communicative behavior, American anthropologists have been particularly instrumental in contributing to our knowledge of a great many unwritten languages, those of the American Indians in particular.

The most recent emphases in linguistic anthropology are on primate communication and the nature of speech use in different cultures, the former following a biological line of inquiry, the latter a social one. While the findings of linguistic anthropology do not have the practical applications that the research results of the rest of anthropology do, linguistic theories and methodologies have repeatedly served as models for the study of human nonverbal behavior. Like prehistoric archaeology, linguistic anthropology is customarily thought of as being more closely related to cultural than to biological anthropology, and indeed both these subfields are considered by some (including

the authors of this book) to be specialized extensions of cultural anthropology.

Interdisciplinary research

The steadily increasing specialization of all scholarship is being partly offset by the growing volume of interdisciplinary research. The latter tendency is particularly strong in anthropology, which touches on so many aspects of the human condition. From the beginning, anthropologists of whatever subfield repeatedly came to make use of findings and methods of such widely separate fields as geology on the one hand and psychology on the other. This borrowing was not a one-way affair, as two examples from among many will demonstrate. For his *Totem and Taboo* (1913), in which he discusses the resemblances between the psychic lives of "savages" and neurotics, Sigmund Freud (1856–1939) drew heavily on available anthropological literature. Karl Marx (1818–1883) kept notebooks on ethnology and acknowledged his intellectual debt to the American lawyer-anthropologist Lewis Henry Morgan (1818–1881), whose

Ancient Society (1877) also inspired a book by Friedrich Engels (1820–1895).

More recently, as anthropologists have begun increasingly to be attracted away from the study of small preliterate tribal groups to an examination of complex societies, interdisciplinary contacts and research have intensified and new areas of inquiry such as economic, legal, maritime, medical, nutritional, political, psychological, and urban anthropology have received professional recognition. Sociology and cultural anthropology have always been sister disciplines, one difference between them being, as Clyde Kluckhohn wryly used to observe, that sociologists have no museums. Inasmuch as sociologists neither excavate nor collect specimens of material culture, this point still holds. However, the emphasis on collecting among contemporary cultural anthropologists is less than it was in the past, in part because modern techniques of documentation (photography, film, and audiotape) offer alternatives that were not readily available formerly.

TO SUM UP Anthropology is the study of humankind in a broad sense. It is concerned with both biological aspects of the human species and the behavior of people as members of societies, and its coverage extends over all periods and parts of the world. The comprehensive subject matter of anthropology is apportioned among several subdisciplines: biological anthropology—the study of the biological variation and evolution of the human species; archaeology—the study of past cultures based on their material remains; linguistic anthropology—the study of language in both its biological and social contexts; and *cultural-social anthropology* (or *cultural anthropology* as it is commonly referred to in the United States)—the study of cultural variation in human societies. Because the scope and content of cultural anthropology is the subject matter of this book, we will limit our discussion here to a clarification of the key concepts of culture and society.

The concept of culture

Broadly speaking, the term *culture* takes in all human behavior that is learned and, by extension, all the tangible and intangible results of such behavior. In this sense, then, wiping one's feet before entering a house is just as much an instance of cultural behavior as is performing open-heart surgery; a pull-open beer can is just as much a cultural product as is a powerful radio telescope; and planning a picnic is just as much a cultural preoccupation as is designing a supersonic airplane. We do not wish to imply that these activities or material products are of equal weight: a radio telescope is the end product of centuries of scientific development, while a pull-open beer can is only a recent trivial invention catering to our desire for ease in enjoying a beverage whose history exceeds that of the telescope. Nevertheless, they all are manifestations of culture.

The examples above have been taken from a setting with which all of us are completely familiar. As such, they are representative of only one particular cultural tradition, not of humanity as a whole. Clearly, then, it is necessary to draw a distinction between *a culture*—the complex of typical behavior and manufactured environment peculiar to a specific group or society—and *culture* in its general sense—all of human behavior and its products, whether encountered in the world's busy metropolises or the Australian bush. To observe that particular cultures vary, some slightly and others profoundly, hardly comes as a surprise. Less commonly appreciated is the fact that no matter what these differences may be, they are all reducible to an attribute that all members of the human species share to the fullest extent—the possession of culture. A concept powerful enough to link in one grand view all living humans and the billions of those who came before them requires careful consideration.

The fact that very few social scientists would take exception to such a broad definition does not mean that the concept of

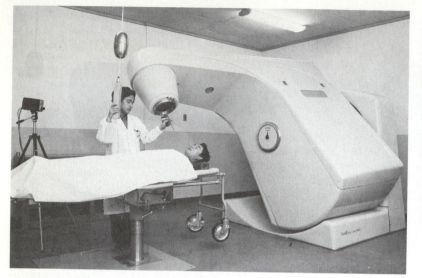

Modern medicine tends to be dependent on complex technology for diagnosis and treatment. Curing is a highly specialized profession often performed in special locations—clinics or hospitals. Shown here are a patient and staff member of the National Cancer Center in Tokyo. (Consulate General of Japan, N.Y.)

(right) !Kung Bushman healers attending a sick woman. In this culture, patients and healers may enter a state of trance during ritual curing situations. (Richard Lee/Anthro-Photo)

culture is not susceptible to a great multiplicity of views. Ever since Edward B. Tylor defined culture in 1871 as "that complex whole which includes knowledge, belief, art, morals, law, custom, and any other capabilities and habits acquired by man as a member of society" (1871:1), hundreds of definitions or characterizations have been proposed, and their number continues to grow steadily. In reviewing a few from this impressive list, we do not suggest that a concept of such crucial importance in the study of humans inevitably becomes blurred when dissected by generations of scholars. Rather, it is our intent to show how different emphases have tended to illuminate

the unique comprehensiveness of culture and to chart different approaches to the understanding of its nature.

Some approaches to the concept of culture

In many definitions of culture a very common emphasis is on social heritage or tradition. Thus, according to Talcott Parsons, culture consists "in those patterns [of] behavior and the products of human action which may be inherited, that is, passed from generation to generation independently of the biological genes" (1949:8). Two important features of culture are brought out in this definition. Culture is not genetically transmitted as are general body build, color and texture of hair, blood group, or susceptibility to certain diseases. Instead, it is handed down by some members of a particular society to other members of that society—typically, in an informal manner by parents and more experienced peers, and in more formal settings, by other, specially trained individuals. Growing up, then, is nothing but a long succession of innumerable time-tested lessons in how to cope with the specific social, ideological, and material circumstances into which an individual has been born. This aspect of long apprenticeship to which all new members of any society necessarily are subject has been succinctly expressed by Clyde Kluckhohn, according to whom culture "consists in all transmitted social learning" (1942:2). Taken from this point of view—that the acquisition of culture amounts to learning how to cope—culture is essentially a problem-solving device. Quite recently, Ralph L. Holloway, Jr., has suggested the inclusion in the traditional definitions of culture of two attributes that he phrases as "the *imposition* of *arbitrary form* upon the environment" (1969:395, emphasis added). He argues that definitions so amended would uniquely specify human culture and would cut across the fuzzy area where the behavior of humans and that of other social and/or teachable animals may seem to overlap. To use a simple example, taking a pebble (a piece of environment) and shaping it into a hand ax or spear point (imposing an arbitrary form upon it) is cultural behavior, while the riding of a bicycle by a chimpanzee is not.[2]

During the past twenty or so years, the status of the culture concept has undergone a great deal of rethinking. The challenge has been, in the words of Roger Keesing, "to narrow the concept . . . so that it includes less and reveals more" (1974:73).[3] One widely accepted theory, influenced by evolutionary perspective and ecological orientation, sees

cultures as adaptive systems. In this view, any particular culture is a complex pattern of socially transmitted behavior which helps a group (community, society) make do within the ecological constraints to which it is subject. Because the balance that is approached between cultures and their social and natural environment in the broadest sense tends to become disturbed as a result of changes from a variety of sources, adaptation (cultural change) is an ongoing process. Central to this process are readjustments in technology, subsistence economy, and production-oriented aspects of social organization.

Besides the different versions of the adaptationist, or cultural-ecological, conception of culture, which is materialistic in a philosophical sense, there are several approaches that view cultures as systems of ideas. One of these approaches, most prominently represented by Ward Goodenough, is commonly referred to as the cognitive conception of culture. According to Goodenough, culture is not material, it does not consist of things, people, or behavior. Rather,

culture . . . consists of standards for deciding what is, standards for deciding what can be, standards for deciding how one feels about it, standards for deciding what to do about it, and standards for deciding how to go about doing it (Goodenough 1963:258–259).

Whereas in the approaches discussed thus far anthropologists act as outsiders to the culture they happen to study—looking into a society from outside it, as it were, and describing what they see there—the proponents of the cognitive view place importance on what members of the society see *themselves* as doing. They have frequently spoken of the necessity for field workers to "get inside the heads" or "skin" of those whom they study in order to discover how these people construe their cultural universe and how they have "mapped" it. In doing so, the

[2]Some of the following definitions, both formal and informal, throw additional light on the concept of culture. According to these, culture may be said to be "all those historically created designs for living, explicit and implicit, rational, irrational, and nonrational, which exist at any given time as potential guides for the behavior of men" (Kluckhohn and Kelly 1945:97); "the rationalization of habit" (Tozzer n.d.); "that which distinguishes men from animals" (Ostwald 1907:510); "*what* a society does and thinks [and, we might add, says]" (Sapir 1921:233); "a product of human association" (Groves 1928:23); and "all behavior mediated by symbols" (Bain 1942:87). Those cited here are but a small selection from a survey made by Kroeber and Kluckhohn (1952), which is useful for the study of the concept up through the early 1950s.

[3]Throughout our discussion we draw on Keesing's (1974) perceptive review article.

cognitive anthropologists have come up with formal descriptions for various societies of several rather well-defined cultural domains in terms of explicit rules governing their religious behavior, their litigation, drinking behavior, weddings, and the like. Yet they have failed to live up to the promise of integrating their analyses into the overall design of culture.

This goal is being achieved with greater success by those, like Clifford Geertz, who view cultures as symbolic systems. For Geertz, to analyze culture amounts to "a searching out of significant symbols, clusters of significant symbols, and clusters of clusters of significant symbols." Culture, according to him, can be likened neither to a "spider web" nor to a "pile of sand."

It is rather more [like] the octopus, whose tentacles are in large part separately integrated, neurally quite poorly connected with one another and with what in the octopus passes for a brain, and yet who nonetheless manages both to get around and to preserve himself, for a while anyway, as a viable if somewhat ungainly entity (Geertz 1973:407–408).

The goal of an ethnographic account, as Geertz conceives of it, is not to be able

to capture primitive facts in faraway places and carry them home like a mask or a carving, but . . . to clarify what goes on in such places, to reduce the puzzlement— what manner of men are these?—to which unfamiliar acts emerging out of unknown backgrounds naturally give rise. . . . It is not worth it, as Thoreau said, to go round the world to count the cats in Zanzibar (Geertz 1973:16).

How an anthropologist thinks about culture (what one's theory of culture is) is usually reflected in the manner in which he or she describes the society being studied. The views that we have presented here must serve for the time being, but we shall return to the subject when we discuss theory and

method in anthropology. Like their colleagues in the other subdisciplines of anthropology, cultural anthropologists may either describe a society's culture, or some aspect of it, or take up the more demanding task of classifying, comparing, and interpreting available data. In the first instance, they are engaged in *ethnography*, or the descriptive study of a culture; in the latter, in *ethnology*, or the comparative and analytical study of cultures. Good ethnographic accounts logically come first, since accurate, detailed descriptions are a necessity if one is to make useful and meaningful comparisons and analyses.

The concept of society

Throughout this book we will make frequent reference to society as well as to culture, and it is important that the manner in which we use the two concepts be clearly understood. The term *society*, which is applied by anthropologists to human aggregations ranging in size from hunting and gathering bands to large industrialized nations, stresses the organizational and structural aspects that unite a group by common patterns of relationships and overarching institutions. Although this term, very much like *culture*, is not easily reducible to a sharp and concise definition, the members of a typical society may be said to share a common habitat, to be characterized by a relative self-sufficiency, and to maintain a continuity of existence across generations. The goals and expectations that bind such a group in mutual interdependence are imparted to its new members through the process of socialization, that is, training for assuming an adult status. Whereas the word *culture* brings to mind time depth and tradition, learned behavior, common values, and blueprints for living, the word *society* emphasizes the importance of links and networks that join individuals and groups to other individuals and groups within a common framework. The two concepts may be joined conveniently in the term *sociocultural* whenever the properties of both are to be considered.

If the anthropological approach is to be of value in understanding the manner in which societies work and the ways individuals behave within given cultural contexts, it must have application to all societies and all cultures, simple or complex, past or present. For a number of reasons, including the relatively recent Western exposure to other societies (the Age of Exploration began in the late fifteenth century) and the fact that established fields of knowledge had little to say about so-called primitives, the major interest of anthropological inquiry has traditionally been non-Western simple societies. This interest is eminently valid: it stems from a recognition on the part of anthropologists that every culture is worthy of examination and that the human mosaic is left with many gaps when attention is solely fixed on literate societies and what are sometimes referred to as civilizations.

Because human societies are scarcely if ever isolated from contacts with other peoples, the task of arriving at an adequate description of a society's culture is never an easy one. An approach widely used by American anthropologists during the early part of the twentieth century may serve as a good example. With no written records preceding the arrival of Europeans in North America, anthropologists have made great efforts to reconstruct aboriginal cultures as of the time of initial white contacts, relying in part on recorded observations by early explorers, traders, missionaries, and others. The time of such contacts varied from one part of the continent to another, sliding upward over a period of more than two centuries as the Europeans steadily pushed westward. Until fairly recently, the standard practice was to arrive at a description of Indian cultures for this variable time line and—as if time were standing still—to couch it in the present tense, a hypothetical time frame known as the *ethnographic present*.

This practice is questionable for two reasons. Cultures are constantly changing, and to attempt to freeze a slice of an earlier

The ethnographic present

cultural period by the use of the ethnographic present not only can be misleading but tends to distort the history of culture contacts and the view of culture as a dynamic entity. What is more, the practice is likely to create the impression that native cultures are being described in their pristine state, untouched and unshaped by any external influences. From the cultures of the Great Plains we can easily draw an example of just how false such an impression can be. There a number of so-called typical buffalo-hunting societies pivoted their cultural activities on the use of the horse—itself introduced to the Western Hemisphere only a short time earlier by the Spaniards. Elsewhere, the bumping effect of one tribe against another as those directly exposed to the encroachment of the Europeans receded westward and even the peaceful trading of Europeans with Indians in the interior must have resulted in marked changes in the Indian way of life long before firsthand knowledge of these societies became available. In short, the shadows must have been cast upon Indian cultures by the newcomers from the East before their actual arrival.

Anthropology and the study of American culture

Finally, it would be entirely wrong to think that anthropology is by definition the study of tribal societies or peasant peoples. Although in many ways much more complex than a tribe in South America or a peasant community in India, the culture of the United States can also be approached anthropologically. Allowances have to be made for factors of scale and much internal heterogeneity; it can in fact be argued that there is not just one American culture, but rather a variety of American subcultures, each with fairly distinct attributes. There is, however, a substantial core of shared cultural beliefs, institutional forms and values, that constitute a cultural complex that is distinctly American.

It is a paradox that while countless volumes have been published on American history, government, economics, and geography, we know less about American culture in

Race, as commonly understood, is a variable independent of culture. In this photograph spectators of different "races" watch a sporting event. (Andrew Sacks from Editorial Photocolor Archives)

Cross-cultural interaction often takes place in rather specific contexts. Here Arabs and Jews mingle in a bedouin market. (Owen Franklin/Stock, Boston)

an anthropological sense than about the culture of many small communities and tribal societies in distant parts of the world. The paradox is made all the more intriguing when we consider how much anthropological research has been conducted by American anthropologists abroad.

Some may question the objective reality of American culture. True, the United States is in no sense as homogeneous a society as a tribal group, a village community, or even some long-established modern states. The nation, as we all are aware, is composed of people who trace their descent from many parts of the world, and not only Europe but also Africa and Asia. To these must be added Native Americans, who were the first to settle this continent. Granted this variety, and the fact that it is in part a characteristic of the American scene, there remains a common factor that joins ethnic groups, classes, regions, and generations. This shared element is perhaps brought into sharpest focus when Americans are abroad. Regardless of background, Americans in foreign countries, in particular those who must reside there for some period of time, typically express clear feelings of loss at their severance from the United States, and not just in terms of personal and family contacts, but a more generalized cultural loss. An American business executive in Paris or a G.I. in Japan may have very different perceptions of "home," but that they all in their different ways experience what has been termed *culture shock* cannot be doubted.

Clearly, learning about or experiencing the ways of another society brings into sharper focus the many aspects of one's own culture that tend so casually to be taken for granted. Here, too, anthropology plays an important role by providing a mirror in which individuals and groups can better see themselves as they are.

REFERENCES

BAIN, READ
1942 A definition of culture. *Sociology and Social Research* 27:87–94.

EDEY, MAITLAND A.
1972 *The missing link*. New York: Time-Life Books.

GEERTZ, CLIFFORD
1973 *The interpretation of cultures*. New York: Basic Books.

GOODENOUGH, WARD HUNT
1963 *Cooperation in change*. New York: Russell Sage Foundation.

GROVES, ERNEST RUTHERFORD
1928 *An introduction to sociology*. New York: Longmans, Green.

HOLLOWAY, RALPH L., JR.
1969 Culture: a *human* domain. *Current Anthropology* 10:395–412.

HYMES, DELL H., ED.
1972 *Reinventing anthropology*. New York: Pantheon Books.

KEESING, ROGER M.
1974 Theories of culture. In *Annual review of anthropology*, vol. 3. Bernard J. Siegel and others, eds. Palo Alto, Cal.: Annual Reviews. Pp. 73–97.

KLUCKHOHN, CLYDE
1942 Report to the Sub-subcommittee on Definitions of Culture. Committee on Conceptual Integration. Mimeographed.

KLUCKHOHN, CLYDE, AND WILLIAM H. KELLY
1945 The concept of culture. In *The science of man in the world crisis*. Ralph Linton, ed. New York: Columbia University Press. Pp. 78–106.

KROEBER, A. L., AND CLYDE KLUCKHOHN
1952 *Culture: a critical review of concepts and definitions*. Papers of the Peabody Museum of American Archaeology and Ethnology, Harvard University, vol. 47, no. 1. Cambridge, Mass.

OSTWALD, WILHELM
1907 The modern theory of energetics. *The Monist* 17:481–515.

PARSONS, TALCOTT
1949 *Essays in sociological theory, pure and applied*. Glencoe, Ill.: The Free Press.

SAPIR, EDWARD
1921 *Language; an introduction to the study of speech*. New York: Harcourt, Brace.

TOZZER, ALFRED MARSTON
n.d. Unpublished lectures.

TYLOR, SIR EDWARD BURNETT
1871 *Primitive culture; researches into the development of mythology, philosophy, religion, language, art, and custom*. 2 vols. London: J. Murray.

PART
ONE

DIMENSIONS
OF
THE
PAST

INTRODUCTION

For an understanding of human society and culture, careful examination of the past is indispensable. The anthropological perspective stresses that the past is more than a prologue to the present, for in many ways culture is the precipitate of history or past experience. All cultures should be viewed as moving through a temporal frame, a continuum of elapsed time that allows the lessons of history to be applied to current situations and problems. Those who do not learn from the errors of the past are destined to repeat them, an observation that holds for cultural systems as well as for nations and individuals. History and tradition offer established guidelines for current action, but these guidelines must always meet the test of relevance; for while culture is transmitted from one generation to the next, the problems are never exactly replicated. Successful cultural adaptation thus calls for regulated change, a process that steers a course between the totally new and a mechanical acceptance of old designs.

This view of cultural adaptation has been strongly influenced by our appreciation of the biological history of the human species. Humankind evolved as part of the natural order that embraces all life. As a species, we have managed to survive with the aid of both biological and cultural mechanisms, but biology and culture are not two different entities; rather, they are two different facets of the same adaptive system.

The concern of anthropologists with the past is understandable on intellectual grounds as well: anthropologists typically study societies that are spatially distant from their own, while historians study societies that are removed in time. In both instances, the results of their researches are interpretations of culture, a complex of events and beliefs as seen through the prism of the investigator's mind.

The following five chapters share a certain unity of perspective. The broad outlines of human evolution are traced with special emphasis on the factors that impinge on adaptation and selectivity; then the past is examined from the archaeological perspective. Next, the trends of cultural progression in the Old and New Worlds are considered, and since this book is primarily designed for a North American readership, it seems appropriate that particular attention be given to American Indians. This choice is dictated not by theoretical considerations — a valid case could be made for other continents or regions whose inhabitants have had to cope with similar stresses and dislocations — but by the belief that a certain virtue may be found in examining historical events that, directly or indirectly, continue to touch all of us.

Chapter 2

Human biology
and human culture

In 1863 Thomas H. Huxley (1825–1895) published a book which was to become one of the classics of modern science dealing with the human condition. Entitled *Evidence as to Man's Place in Nature,* the book was a defense of Charles Darwin and of Darwinian evolution at a time when both the man and the theory were under attack from those who refused to consider that the human species forms part of the natural order and that it evolved in essentially the same manner as other biological entities. More than this, Huxley asks the same kind of general questions that have been with us ever since and will no doubt remain valid for years to come:

The question of questions for mankind — the problem which underlies all others, and is more deeply interesting than any other — is the ascertainment of the place which Man occupies in nature and of his relations to the universe of things. Whence our race has come; what are the limits of our power over nature, and of nature's power over us; to what goal we are tending; are the problems which present themselves anew and with undiminished interest to every man born into the world (Huxley 1863:71).

The quotation eloquently points up what all anthropologists today are agreed upon — that humankind has both biological and sociocultural attributes, and that these attributes are inseparable one from the other.

The biocultural nature of humankind

Every culture that we know of attempts to define the place of humans in the total universe. Included in this speculation is the question of human origins. According to most religious-mythological explanations, humans were created by supernaturals who granted them certain attributes, including the gift of what we now term *culture.* The impression is created that at one time the universe lacked people and subsequently fully human ancestors entered the scene.

Western cultures are in this sense no different from others, for our own religious traditions also imply that we were created as the consequence of a specific supernatural act — "and man became a living soul," as it is phrased in Genesis. Obviously, if humans were created at a given instant of time and in the form they now possess, the possibility of change, or evolution, is unlikely. The scientific study of our species certainly could not progress within such a static mold.

Historically speaking, the break with tradition is very recent. Barely a century ago, great controversy and much acrimony surrounded scientists who claimed that the study of human origins could be approached in essentially the same manner as the study of other plant and animal species—that is, that humankind had a biological history. Without doubt, the individual who contributed most to bringing "man himself, his origin and constitution, within that unity"[1] that joins other living forms was the English naturalist Charles Darwin (1809–1882). In 1859 he published *On the Origin of Species by Means of Natural Selection*, a carefully argued statement explaining the development and diversification of life, and twelve years later *The Descent of Man*, the capstone of his lifework.

The fact that we exist both as biological organisms and as beings endowed with culture gives rise to a situation in which human biology necessarily impinges on human culture, and vice versa. It also means that there are many questions touching on the human condition that, directly or indirectly, must be answered with reference to our biological heritage. All of the central questions that were posed by Huxley have a biological dimension: What is a human being? What is the nature of the relationship between human beings and other creatures that inhabit this earth? What are the origins of humankind? And how different, or how similar, are the physical varieties of human beings? In short, what are we, and what kinship do we share with our brothers and

[1]This quotation is taken from a review of Darwin's *The Descent of Man*, written by his son (Darwin 1892:289). By this date, a dozen years after *Origin* had caused so much turmoil, most leading scientists had been won over to the evolutionary view.

The publication of Darwin's The Descent of Man *in 1871 brought forth dozens of cartoons in contemporary English magazines. In this drawing from* The Hornet *(1871), Darwin's theory is caricatured by depicting its proponent as an ape.*

sisters and with other living things?

This two-sided nature of humanity has proved to be not only a unique advantage but a source of special and burdensome obligation. If we have found it hard to live in harmony with nature—as we are reminded with increasing frequency—we have also found it difficult to live with others of our own kind. Many reasons can be cited in explanation, but in this country a major source of friction has been racism, the second main subject of discussion here. Racism is false biology, a doctrine that cannot be defended on scientific grounds. Nevertheless, it is a powerful force and one needs to understand its origin and its dangers.

HUMANKIND AND THE NATURAL ORDER

And God said, Let us make man in our image, after our likeness: and let them have dominion over the fish of the sea, and over the fowl of the air, and over the cattle, and over all the earth, and over every creeping thing that creepeth upon the earth.

In these words, the Book of Genesis describes the creation of human beings and defines the relationship between humans and the universe: creatures formed in the image of God and holding dominion "over all the earth." We can think of this ancient story as the Judeo-Christian origin myth. For our purpose, its importance rests less on how many twentieth-century Westerners believe it in a literal sense than on the fact that it establishes the position of humans in the natural order as one of superiority and control.

All cultures assign a very special place to their own members and to their mythological first ancestors. For this reason the names that many societies use to designate themselves can most simply be translated as *people* or *the people*, the understanding being that while there may be many other peoples, they themselves stand in a special relationship to the divine forces of creation. This uniqueness, however, does not necessarily imply that the human species occupies a position of absolute privilege and total separation from the nonhuman world. For instance, the relationship of the Navajo Indians to nature is one that stresses accommodation with a universe that is always difficult and often dangerous:

Contrary to the common white conception of nature as something that needs to be mastered for human ends, the Navaho view is that man must adjust himself to the demands of nature. Technological instruments are highly valued, not to master the natural environment, but to enable man to live with a minimum of security in the difficult Navaho habitat (Vogt 1951: 36–37).

In many cases, not even the supernaturals are perceived as all-wise and all-powerful.

In the origin myth of the Quiché Maya of Guatemala, we learn that gods can and do make errors. In the beginning, they are said to have experimented with a number of human creations, most of which turned out to be failures. There were attempts to make humans out of clay (they fell apart on getting wet) and out of wood (they lacked the proper human feelings), and success was achieved only when the gods modeled the first ancestors out of life-giving maize. However, from one of the early attempts there escaped some creatures that gave rise to the monkeys of the tropical forest—an event that acknowledges the close kinship of humans with nature.

The Western view of this relationship to nature has changed remarkably little since the Book of Genesis. Medieval cosmology placed humans in an intermediate position between heaven and earth, between God and nature. The closer they came to God, the farther they moved from nature. Prior to the scientific and industrial revolutions, this perception could have only a limited impact on the environment, although it explicitly gave sanction to human exploitation of the natural world. Nature, after all, was there for humans to use.

We should note that there is no discontinuity, no contradiction, between Western religious values and modern scientific-technological attitudes towards nature. In the sixteenth and seventeenth centuries, the formative period of modern science, the study of science and its practical utilization were important attributes of Christian "good works." The linkage of science and religion is clearly demonstrated in the writings of Francis Bacon (1561–1626), who claimed that "the further proficience and augmentation of all sciences" was "ordained by God." Bacon, often regarded as the father of modern science, believed that the end of knowledge should be utility ("knowledge itself is power") and saw his work as furthering the establishment of the reign of humans over nature.

The commanding position over nature attributed to humans in the Western cultural tradition is reflected in Dürer's 1504 engraving of Adam and Eve (right). Contrast this view with one stressing man's insignificance, as portrayed (below) in the tenth-century Chinese engraving of a landscape dwarfing the Buddhist hermit priest seen in the lower center. ([right] Courtesy, Museum of Fine Arts, Boston. Centennial Gift of Landon Clay; [below] Courtesy of the Fogg Art Museum, Harvard University. Purchase from Richard C. Rudolph Daly Fund, Higginson Fund, Hyatt Fund)

The perception of the place of humankind in the order of the universe has undoubtedly provided one of the major value orientations underlying the idea of progress. Progress, which is often equated with greater mastery over nature and with dependence on technological and scientific solutions to what are basically social problems, is the common heritage of Western societies and as much a cornerstone of the ideology of capitalism as of contemporary socialism. Furthermore, doctrines of progress, often phrased in the idiom of technological development, are now virtually universal among the directing classes of all complex societies. Among the traditionally non-Western societies, the transfer of Western technology and economics has been most conspicuous in Japan.

HUMAN EVOLUTION

The core of Darwin's theory has the simplicity and neatness typical of major scientific discoveries. In the words of his contemporary Hermann von Helmholtz, it contains "an essentially new creative thought" (Darwin 1892:287). Darwin begins on the foundation that all life is related and that there has been an increase in the number of species through time. These two hypotheses, while not entirely novel,[2] are for the first time integrated into a logically consistent whole, supported with unprecedented detail, and argued with clarity and a scholarly

[2]By the mid-nineteenth century paleontologists (experts in the study of fossil remains) had amassed a sufficient body of evidence that left little doubt as to the antiquity of life and its great diversity through the passage of time. Among other scholars who contributed to the theory of evolution, special mention must be made of Alfred Russel Wallace (1823–1913), who proposed a virtually identical theory in the same year that *Origin* was published. Darwin always recognized Wallace as a codiscoverer (they were close friends and frequent correspondents), but history has been less kind. Evolutionary theory should be recorded as a Wallace-Darwin contribution, although they came to the same conclusions quite independently.

respect for evidence. The result is an explanatory concept of biological change that is both dynamic (nonstatic) and processual (having direction).

Variation, Darwin maintained, is inherent in nature, for one of the characteristics of breeding populations is that they do not reproduce themselves identically from generation to generation. This variation between and within species should be considered against a backdrop of variation in the natural environment and change in the environment through time. Under most circumstances, nature is generous—that is, organisms multiply geometrically well beyond the requirements of replacement. In this scenario, some organisms will be "fitter" than others: more capable of obtaining food, better able to survive the rigors of climate, and better able to evade their enemies. These better-adapted organisms will tend to survive and reproduce in greater numbers than forms that are less well adapted; hence selection is built into the system or, in Darwin's terminology, it is "natural."

The principle by which each slight variation, if useful, tends to be preserved was seen by Darwin as part of a master plan common to all nature. He saw nature as a force working constantly for improvement through competition. Hence biological evolution is clearly a theory that fits nineteenth-century ideologies (one may point to competition as the key element in capitalist economic theory), and it was not Darwin, but the English philosopher Herbert Spencer (1820–1903), who coined the phrase "the survival of the fittest." Darwin, on the other hand, viewed competition not only as beneficial in the long run, but even as benign:

When we reflect on this struggle, we may console ourselves with the full belief, that the war of nature is not incessant, that no fear is felt, that death is generally prompt, and that the vigorous, the healthy, and the happy survive and multiply (Darwin 1859:79).

This may be an overly optimistic assessment, and one that, if moved from the biological to the cultural plane, is not automatically applicable. Yet it should be noted that in his *Origin of Species*, Darwin not only avoided the question of cultural conflict but even abstained from issues having to do with human evolution, a matter that he addressed himself to only in *The Descent of Man* (1871).

Granted that the theory of evolution can be grossly misapplied when the subject is human populations—it continues to be one of the favorite "scientific" arguments used by racists—Darwinian evolutionary theory simply links two processes, change and continuity in nature. The thread of life goes back to the very beginnings of organic presence on earth, millions of years before the appearance of the first complex organisms; and from that time on to the present we can trace a continuity, not in the context of stability, but of variation between species and among populations.

When we turn our attention to *Homo sapiens*, modern humans, we have to recognize that the species emerges late but clearly as a product of the same forces and circumstances that influenced the evolution of other living forms. What is peculiar to humankind is that a level of biological development made possible, and later indispensable, the attribute that we refer to as culture.

We should view culture not as a sudden acquisition but as the end product of a process going back to pre-*sapiens* forms—our *hominid* (humanlike, but not fully human) fossil ancestors. At first, biological development and cultural capacity are inextricably linked together. With the appearance of *Homo sapiens*, an evolutionary plateau was reached at which culture, in substantial measure, substituted social solutions for biological evolution.

Although rooted in biology, culture is situated outside it. In no sense does this assertion mean that all biological constraints are dispensed with, but simply that humans and human societies, while indubitably part of the natural order, respond as both biological organisms and as culture-bearing entities. Biology establishes limits; culture works within them. Another way of phrasing this issue of the interfaces of biology and culture is that our species is like no other. At birth we have few instincts and certainly no built-in mechanism for survival. Hence there is no "human nature" outside of culture.

FOSSILS AND ANCESTORS

We have already acknowledged that humans are a product, even though very recent, of the planet on which they live. Yet the life-generating process began as much as some 3.5 billion years ago. At least, there is fossil evidence of single-celled organisms, resembling algae and bacteria, whose existence may be traced back through about three-fourths of the earth's life span. For some 3 billion years, life was confined to the sea. Once the green plants and invertebrate animals invaded the land, however, the pace of evolution quickened markedly. By about 200 million years ago, the earliest mammals had become established, and some 120 million years later the first primates appeared. Halfway between the appearance of the primates and the present, two lineages became differentiated—one leading to ancestral Old World monkeys and a second to ancestral *hominoids* (Hominoidea),[3] the

[3]Taxonomically, humans belong to the order of primates (Primates), suborder of anthropoids (Anthropoidea), superfamily of hominoids (Hominoidea), family of hominids (Hominidae), genus *Homo*, and species *sapiens*. Gibbons, orangutans, gorillas, and chimpanzees are separated from hominids at the level of family, together forming the family Pongidae. *Ramapithecus* (by virtue of its dentition) and *Australopithecus* are considered by most anthropologists as genera of the hominid family, biologically coordinate (but not contemporaneous) with *Homo*.

group that came to comprise the apes and both recent and fossil humanlike creatures. In turn, the subsequent evolution of the hominoids appears to have taken several paths. One development has come to be represented in our times by the orangutan, gorilla, and chimpanzee, and man.

Ramapithecus

Sometime during the Miocene, an epoch extending roughly from twenty-five million to ten million years ago, a creature branched off from the ape line. Known as *Ramapithecus* and attested by fossil evidence from India and Kenya dating back ten to fourteen million years, it may well be the earliest direct human ancestor. The consensus of anthropologists, at any rate, is that *Ramapithecus* was a creature not yet human but unmistakably on the march toward humanity. Exciting as this may sound, the evidence for such a momentous assertion is admittedly skimpy—several loose teeth and less than a dozen jaw fragments.

Nevertheless, for the investigators of human origins, the ramapithecine finds hold some important clues. Foremost among them is the reduction in the size of the front teeth, suggesting that these man apes may have had to use their forelimbs to grasp and tear their food (mostly plants) before it reached their mouths. The inference that anthropologists draw from such an interpretation is that here at last was a creature beginning to place reliance on hind legs for locomotion or, more technically, one that exhibited incipient bipedalism.

From man apes to ape-men

There is a widespread notion, deriving probably from such phrases as "the appearance of man," that at some vaguely specified time in the distant past the first unmistakably human creatures stepped out of the woods and into an Old World forest clearing, ushering in the first act of the human drama. While it is true that in the long history of our planet the total period of human occupancy has thus far been but an episode, close

examination of the circumstances of humankind's emergence strongly suggests a succession of countless selective tests in the demanding laboratory of nature.

The adaptations that marked the transformation of ancestral forms from man apes to ape-men and ultimately to full-fledged humans were exceedingly numerous and complex. They must have been strongly influenced by the pressures of a natural environment that was itself constantly undergoing change. Moreover, the many strands of the evolutionary progression leading to humans were unfolding concurrently and in mutual interaction. The earlier simplistic accounts, positing a straightforward sequence of well-defined stages apart from the environment, have yielded to an ecological approach and to the recognition of the important part that mutual interaction and reinforcement—feedback—must have played in human evolution.

The innovations contributing to the process of hominization were of two basic kinds—physical and behavioral. Physical, or biological, innovations were effecting changes in the anatomical development of the ancestors of our species. Among the crucial biological adaptations were those associated with the adoption of a bipedal gait, ultimately culminating in fully erect posture; the attendant reshaping of the pelvis, which occurred without an adequate widening of the birth canal to match the growing size of the infant's skull, thus limiting the maturity of the newborn; reduction in size of the masticatory apparatus, the parts of the head used for chewing; changes in the structure and function of the brain; and modification of the hand, which eventually made a precision grip possible.

Other innovations were behavioral, altering the life style of both individuals and groups. Primarily individual adaptations included the employment of natural objects as tools, with a progressive shift to toolmaking; a change in eating habits from exclusive dependence on vegetable food to an omnivorous diet; and a recognition of the value of, and the need for, solving simple problems and profiting from past mistakes—in short, learning. Among social innovations, one can hypothesize patterned techniques of food sharing, various improvements in intragroup communication and in cooperative hunting of large game, and perhaps a rudimentary division of labor.

By the standards of our rapidly changing world, these and other innovations must seem rather unimpressive, and singularly so when we realize that the amount of time needed to accomplish them was on the order of about one million generations—that is, if we choose *Ramapithecus* as a starting point. In this sense, then, our species took a long time to evolve, a circumstance that alone should make us regard our responsibility for the course of its future development with utmost seriousness. With this time depth in mind, a highly compressed reconstruction of the highlights leading from the humble ramapithecine beginnings to fully developed humanhood might take the following form.

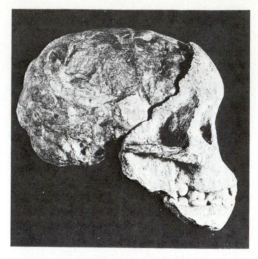

Cast of the skull of an adult Australopithecus africanus. *Although only about one-third the size of a modern human skull, it belonged to a creature clearly foreshadowing our genus. (Courtesy of The American Museum of Natural History)*

The initial setting was East Africa during the late Miocene, some fifteen million years ago. A period of decreasing precipitation probably had set in, which began to reduce the abundant tropical forests, converting them slowly to extensive stretches of grassland with an occasional clump of trees here and there, mostly along watercourses. Some of the tree-dwelling primates clung to their shrinking forest habitat. Others were able to maintain themselves in exposed areas, in all likelihood pre-adapted in some manner to the new environment, and managed to make do with what little refuge the shrinking groves could afford them. Among the latter, those who were forced by the keen competition for the remaining tree cover to adapt to existence on the ground might seem to have been the losers. Yet they were the ones who would become our ancestors.

Reconstruction of Australopithecus. *Living in the grasslands of South Africa during Lower Pleistocene times, the australopithecines obtained meat by scavenging and most likely also by hunting small game and young animals. (Trustees of The British Museum [Natural History])*

Adapting to life on the ground

Like some of the other primates, these early hominids must have lived in bands, averaging possibly a score or so. For safety at night, they may have used trees unclaimed by other animals, but the daytime was undoubtedly spent on the ground looking for food. The tall grass through which they moved worked to their advantage, but it also served to conceal their predators. Their primary mode of locomotion, to begin with, was most likely knuckle walking—that is, resting the weight of the front part of the body on the knuckles. On frequent occasions they must have stood up on their hind legs in order to survey the surrounding savanna. After all, vigilance and curiosity are traits far from limited to humans.

The occasional but steadily growing reliance on the hind limbs for locomotion invited a trait that was to have significant consequences—hand carrying. No doubt, as these early hominids became more and more adept at shuffling—a stage intermediate between knuckle walking and a fully erect gait—their arms and hands were increasingly freed for a variety of new tasks. The ever more complex demands placed on the hands furthered anatomical adaptations that ultimately led to what is known as the *precision grip*. Characterized by the pulp-to-pulp contact that can be easily established between the thumb and any finger, such a grip was an indispensable prerequi-

site to all but the most primitive toolmaking and tool-using activity.

It seems likely that the early hominids initially armed their newly freed hands with a suitable stick, bone, or stone only to defend themselves against predators. Although omnivorous in principle, they probably first scavenged for animal flesh out of necessity rather than by design. But judging from some of the present-day large primates who clearly enjoy an occasional meal of animal flesh, an appetite for meat should not have been difficult to acquire. In any case, the change in diet is reflected in the dentition of the various fossil forms. In the course of time the early hominids came to use their

The human hand is an "instrument" of great refinement and flexibility that lends itself to such diverse tasks as the manufacture of fine decorative items or modern surgery. ([left] Mel Konner/Anthro-Photo; [right] Leonard Freed/Magnum Photos, Inc.)

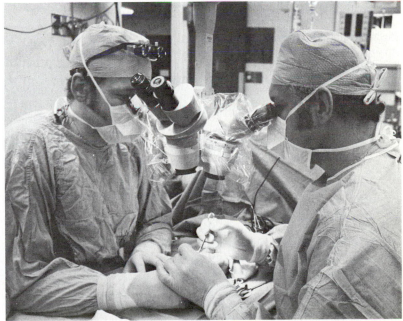

crude weapons habitually to kill animals for the sake of their meat, thus tapping a new source of food that was in plentiful supply. Moreover, they had unwittingly struck upon a diet rich in valuable amino acids and vitamins.

The adoption of the bipedal gait was associated with a great many anatomical changes, affecting the hominid skeleton and musculature virtually from head to foot. For example, bipedalism, in part through liberating the forelimbs from their original locomotive function and in part through the added height that it gave to the body (the world looks very different viewed at five feet from the ground that it does at an elevation of two or three feet), further stimulated the already complex primate brain and the central nervous system. One of the consequences was the disproportionate increase in the size of the head compared with the rest of the body. This change also meant that head size was large in relation to the female pelvis, a potential birth hazard for the infant and mother. The evolutionary solution to this difficulty was fraught with risks: to have the infant leave the mother's uterus at a relatively early stage of its development, when its head could still fit through the pelvic ring, and then complete its growth in the inhospitable outside world. The way to overcome this initial handicap was to extend correspondingly the dependence of the child on its mother and on the group in general, with the result that maturation takes a long time.

We have already passed the point at which our reconstruction becomes increasingly difficult to sustain without losing some of the many strands of the ongoing hominizing process: the sharing of food from a successful hunt, the slow but constant improvement of techniques designed to make better use of the natural environment, the pressures to make the existing communicative system ever more responsive to the steadily growing needs, and the like. But one more discovery that marks humanity's ascendancy over the natural environment does bear

mentioning—the control of fire. What for millennia must have been a source of awe and danger was turned into an indispensable servant: it protected early humans from nocturnal predators, made the flesh of the game more palatable and easier to digest, and provided warmth for creatures ill-equipped to cope with the chilling nights of the temperate regions they were entering. By this time, some three quarters of a million years ago, the right of these hunters and collectors to full-fledged humanity can no longer be questioned.

As we follow human development over the past million-odd years, the dominant theme throughout is that of exceptional adaptability. To begin with, the long-term adaptations were chiefly biological, enabling human groups to make permanent and successful homes under great extremes of natural conditions, ranging from steaming tropical forests and parched deserts to fiercely inhospitable arctic regions. Yet the undisputed uniqueness of our species among the world's living creatures rests solidly on cultural adaptability, an evolutionary development of the greatest consequence. It was this growing capacity for rapid and flexible learned adjustments to meet changed conditions that more than compensated for a remarkable lack of specialization in humans, compared with that in most other animals.

THE SCOPE OF BIOLOGICAL
ANTHROPOLOGY

Contemporary biological (physical) anthropology has developed into a highly specialized subdiscipline. It concerns itself with various areas of inquiry, which we can sketch out only in the briefest terms. While interest in human fossils and biological variation remains strong, new discoveries and methods of research have posed further problems or restated existing ones. Fifty years ago, or even as recently as twenty-five years ago, fossil hominids could be fitted into a relatively simple evolutionary frame.

Today, with many more specimens available for study, the temporal horizons have been pushed back millions of years, and the number of alternative hypotheses concerning the ancestry of *Homo sapiens* and the relationship of various finds to one another have multiplied. Perhaps it is enough to note that this is a highly dynamic area of research that is constantly shedding new light on human origins and attempting to integrate a growing body of data; there are many new answers, but these in turn raise many new questions.

Although perhaps lacking some of the spectacular qualities of the discovery of a hominid fragment dating back two or three million years, the studies of modern humans have made considerable progress during the last few generations. Of particular importance has been research that examines the relationship between biology and environment, not only physical environment but sociocultural environment as well.

Environment and human biology

Central to such studies is the concept of a population as the unit of study. Unlike the arbitrary and unwieldy categories of "race," which differentiate a species on the basis of visible (phenotypical) physical characteristics, populations are specific entities ranging in size from as little as fifty individuals to several hundred thousand or more. Typically, they are breeding entities evidencing a degree of genetic homogeneity and occupying a particular cultural-ecological niche. Whether the unit under consideration is a band of hunter-gatherers or the long-established residents of an agricultural region, it is possible to demarcate geographic and environmental gradients, or clines,[4] that allow the investigator to hold some factors constant.

[4]In the clinal approach, the variation or the frequency of each trait or gene is examined in terms of its environmental or geographic distribution. Maps showing the graded series of physical differences among population groups should serve as a particularly fruitful starting point for the study of genetic evolution of the human species.

For example, it can be demonstrated that in the course of many generations the native inhabitants of high-altitude regions have undergone a systematic physical adaptation involving lungs, muscles, and blood circulation that permits the utilization of habitats well above ten thousand feet. These physical characteristics are essentially similar in a variety of comparable environmental niches, such as the high Andes, the Himalayas, and the Ethiopian highlands.

But it is not only altitude and physical environment, the heat of tropical deserts or the cold of the arctic tundra, that impinge on human biology. Nutrition is a cultural as well as environmental variable. There is now a substantial body of information that in some nonindustrialized societies, where nutritional levels are low, growth and maturation progress at a considerably slower pace than in societies with more adequate and balanced diets. Such slow growth of children, often coupled with quite short adult stature, may at least in part be due to a process of natural selection favoring slow growth and short adult height in populations with a long history of poor nutrition. Biologically, the most is being made of an inadequate food base—the maturation period is stretched out and average adult stature is kept short.

One should also take into consideration individual life experiences. Even in the course of one or two generations, improvements in diet can lead to demonstrable increases in adult height and accelerate the onset of physical maturity. Severe and constant malnutrition in many parts of the world and the growing imbalance between food resources and population can have a very damaging effect on intellectual development. What is more, evidence indicates that poor nutrition in the early childhood years cannot be made up by improvements later on in life.

Studies of human genetics

Perhaps the major recent developments in biological anthropology have been in the field of genetics. There is now a fairly extensive list of genetic characteristics that can be linked to the presence of a single gene. These include blood group systems, various blood enzymes, color vision characteristics, and taste sensitivity. Some of these traits, at least in our current state of knowledge, do not appear to offer any advantage or disadvantage in terms of natural selection, but in other instances a case can be made for environmental "fit." Thus, one can posit that individuals with red-green color blindness (a sex-linked gene) would be at a disadvantage in situations where color differentiation is important for hunting and collecting. In fact, the rates for color blindness are substantially lower among hunters and gatherers than among long-settled agricultural and urban populations. But regardless whether an individual trait is advantageous or otherwise, studies of frequency distributions help to delimit genetic pools. For example, the Basques, a long-established population in northern Spain and southwestern France, are characterized by a high incidence of the gene for blood group O, an unusually low frequency of the gene for blood group B, and the highest value of Rh-negative factor in the world. These rates are in marked contrast to those found among their French and Spanish neighbors and are indicative of a long period of relative genetic isolation. The peculiarities of Basque blood group frequencies thus permit the geneticist to delimit with some assurance the genetic boundaries of a population that has occupied a particular geographic location for several thousand years. In this instance, the genetic evidence parallels linguistic evidence, for unlike their neighbors, the Basques speak a non–Indo-European language of unknown origin or affiliation.

Genetic studies not only help to demarcate populations in a much more objective manner than the traditional categories of race but also offer some insights into the interrelationships between environment and human biology. Sometimes a genetic trait that under given environmental conditions is harmful may be advantageous in other contexts. The sickle-cell trait (hemoglobin S) apparently offers some protection against malaria. The frequency of this gene correlates positively with locations of high malarial incidence, such as much of equatorial Africa. The long-established tribal peoples of southern Asia also have a high incidence of the sickle-cell trait, and again one must assume a selective advantage in terms of protection against malaria. With the eradication of malaria, or with the movement of populations to nonmalarial regions, the sickle-cell trait no longer serves this useful function.

The sickling phenomenon was first recognized among American blacks as a gene that when received from only one parent (heterozygous), usually presents no medical problem for the individual. However, when an individual receives the sickling gene from *both* parents (homozygous), the consequences are a severe and often fatal anemia. Obviously, any advantage that the sickling trait might have conferred on the inhabitants of malarial regions is totally out of place in a different environmental context. In fact, sickle-cell anemia is one of the major health problems of American blacks and other populations of African origin.

It is not always possible, given the present state of knowledge, to link the incidence of particular diseases in a population to specific genetic traits. Furthermore, we do not know enough about the influence of environment on populations to determine to what degree the incidence of a disorder or condition is a function of genetics or the general conditions of life, in short, of physical and cultural environment. What we do know is that some major diseases occur with greater frequency in some contexts than in others. The populations of developing areas evidence disease profiles quite distinct from those of populations in developed regions. We have mentioned malnutrition and its consequences as a condition found throughout much of the Third World. To this one could add malaria, tuberculosis, various

Within the range of possibilities, culture rather than human biology primarily determines modes of environmental adaptation. These African villagers dispense with protective clothing, as do American vacationers at a popular beach resort. The traditional Arab response to heat and strong sunlight, on the other hand, calls for enveloping garments. ([right] George Roger/Magnum Photos, Inc.; [below right] Ed Johnson from Leo de Wys, Inc.; [below] George Rodger/Magnum Photos, Inc.)

types of gastrointestinal disorders, trachoma, and leprosy. The relationship between these conditions and such factors as poor diet and bad sanitation is evident. Industrialized societies have managed to minimize the impact of many of these diseases, especially the communicable diseases that can be controlled by preventive medicine, readily available medical facilities, and adequate nutrition. However, modern industrial societies face health problems that are at least in part attributable to an increasingly urban-industrial life style. It is possible that there may be some genetic foundation for the high incidence of some diseases found in the industrialized West, conditions like cancer, heart disease, and susceptibility to respiratory virus ailments. Again, though, it would seem that overall environment and such factors as the greatly extended life span are the most important variables.

TO SUM UP   In this section, we have done no more than give a sample of the type of problems and the sort of questions that biological anthropologists address themselves to. Basically, they are concerned with the interplay of three variables: human biology, including the genetic make-up of populations, culture, and environment. None of these is static.

In this tripartite systemic arrangement, the genetic variation presented by the human species may be viewed as an account that can be drawn upon now and in the future. We know that the species has proved highly flexible in accommodating to an extraordinarily wide range of environmental settings. We can expect that the future will not be static and that adaptive responses to new physical and social environments will in part be genetic. To make this assumption is not to deny that the biological significance of diversity as a mechanism for species survival has decreased as the capacity of human culture to buffer the pressures of environment has grown. But this trend has been in operation for tens of thousands of years and it is simplistic to try to equate human culture with the termination of natural selection as an adaptive mechanism.

RACISM: A MODERN MYTH

Earlier we examined some of the factors responsible for the attitudes of most members of Western societies towards nature, or more broadly, the whole universe. These attitudes are rooted in ancient religious and philosophical traditions: hence the idea of mastery or dominion over nature did not have to await the scientific and technological development of the last several centuries. The result has been that ours as well as other complex societies have tended to view nature as an antagonist, or at the least as a resource to be exploited. Very simply, we have failed to recognize the necessity of living in harmony with the universe and are now beginning to pay the price for the delusion that nature is an inexhaustible treasure house open to our rapacious demands.

This attitude of superiority and exploitation is not limited to our perception of the nonhuman world. It is paralleled by doctrines that insist that some societies, some countries, or some races[5] are inherently superior to others. Such superiority and inferiority are taken to be innate in the groups in question, a matter of higher or lower capacity, not a question of greater or

[5]From the early attempts by Carolus Linnaeus (1707–1778) to classify humankind up until the present, the concept of race has been one of the prickliest subjects in physical anthropology. In the numerous controversies that have arisen, discussions have focused primarily on the differences among the various classifications (the numbers of races proposed have ranged from two to as many as two hundred), but the validity of the concept of race itself has been seriously questioned. As the term *race* is used today by anthropologists, there is general agreement that it refers to a distinct population sharing genetic traits as a result of a common origin. To go beyond this simple but serviceable definition would take us outside the scope of our discussion.

lesser success (however defined) based on different historical experience or variation in opportunity, education, and so forth.

The analytical distinction we have made between the exploitation of the nonhuman world and those attitudes that support the exploitation of some populations by others is often blurred. Natural resources—land, water, minerals, and the like—seldom lack human ownership, for in the majority of cases environments supported human groups prior to their being defined as available for exploitation by the agents of more powerful societies. It is perhaps sufficient to recall that the opening up of the Plains meant not only the decimation of animal populations and, more recently, environmental degradation from the strip mining of coal, but also resulted in the destruction of traditional indigenous communities and the tragedy of reservation life. Many other examples could be cited from different parts of the world: long before *bikini* brought to mind a bathing suit, it was an atoll in the Pacific with its own distinct culture; so that Bikini could be used as a proving ground for atomic weapons in 1946, its inhabitants were removed from their homeland.

Yet we generally view racism and related attitudes in terms of interpersonal and intergroup relations. In many cases, it is rationalized by totally false quasi-scientific theories that give an aura of respectability to the exploitation of the weak by the strong and deny that all human groups share the same capacity for culture, the same potentials, and the same limitations.

During the formative years of modern anthropology, a period that covers the terminal decades of the nineteenth century to the early 1920s, much popular, as well as scientific, interest was shown in the interrelationships between culture and biology. This interest stemmed in substantial measure from the conditions of the time, in particular the social, political, and the economic domination of classes and societies of European descent over non-European groups.

Racism and imperialism

Most Westerners of the period insisted on the superiority not only of European and American culture but of Western genes as well. The two variables of culture and biology were not always clearly differentiated. In fact, they tended to become hopelessly scrambled in popular usage: there were superior cultural traditions that coincided with superior biological stocks; conversely, there were peoples possessing less viable cultures and in all probability inferior biological attributes.

The apologists for Western imperialism utilized these notions to rationalize and validate policies of colonialism and neocolonialism. Popularizers of imperialism such as Rudyard Kipling (1865–1936) held that it was not only the right but in fact the duty of Englishmen to carry the "white man's burden," the obligation to manage the affairs of the nonwhite colonies of the British Empire. Very similar philosophies were current in the United States. It was maintained, for instance, that the United States had a manifest destiny—an inherent right—to be the dominant power in the Western Hemisphere. The French, for their part, insisted that France had a civilizing mission to carry out in its overseas possessions. It would be a distortion to claim that all Westerners were imbued with identical attitudes. Certainly there were critics of imperialism in the heyday of empire, as well as those who insisted on universal kinship among all humans and racial equality among peoples.

However, attitudes of cultural and racial superiority were clearly an important element in Western thought. It would otherwise be hard to understand how a person of such stature as Alfred Tennyson (1809–1892) could put forth the claim, "Better fifty years of Europe than a cycle of Cathay." In one line, the antiquity of Chinese culture and the accomplishments of Chinese civilization were devalued and made to appear irrelevant. For that matter, Westerners were not alone in judging other cultures as inferior to theirs. Similar attitudes toward

Europeans characterized Eastern civilizations as well.

Racism and slavery

The question of the relative superiority of peoples and cultures had bearing not only on imperialism and national expansion but also on attitudes toward nonwhite or non–Western European components in national cultures. This matter is of special relevance for an understanding of the origins of racism and prejudice in the United States, whose population, in terms of national origins, was much more heterogeneous than most of Europe.

It should come as no surprise that doctrines of racism were initially used to rationalize slavery and the low socioeconomic condition of blacks. In its simplest form, the argument was that slavery was justifiable on biological grounds. Some argued, in fact, that it was most fortunate for the blacks—given their inherent inequality—to be "protected" by the institution of slavery and not forced to compete on the open market. Of the voluminous literature that came out of the antebellum South, one example of the genre will suffice. In 1854 George Fitzhugh, a Virginia lawyer, wrote *Sociology for the South,* an attempted defense of slavery on humanitarian grounds. One typical passage stresses the "humanity" of slave owners and the unsuitability of free institutions for black people:

Now, it is clear the Athenian democracy would not suit a negro nation, nor will the government of mere law suffice for the individual negro. He is but a grown up child, and must be governed as a child. . . . The master occupies towards him the place of parent or guardian. . . .

Secondly. The negro is improvident; will not lay up in summer for the wants of winter; will not accumulate in youth for the exigencies of age. He would become an insufferable burden to society. Society has the right to prevent this, and can only do so by subjecting him to domestic slavery. In the last place, the negro race is inferior to the white race, and living in their midst, they would be far outstripped or outwitted in the chase of free competition. Gradual but certain extermination would be their fate. . . .

We would remind those who deprecate . . . negro slavery, that his slavery here relieves him from a far more cruel slavery in Africa, or from idolatry and cannibalism, and every brutal vice and crime that can disgrace humanity; and that it christianizes, protects, supports and civilizes him (Fitzhugh 1960:88–89).

While slavery as a legal institution was terminated by the Emancipation Proclamation, theories of black racial inferiority were to remain current for a long time. They are still with us today as the most common form of racial prejudice.

Racism and European immigration

Prejudice against blacks was part of the American reality, and very similar preconceptions governed the American attitude toward the waves of immigrants from southern and eastern Europe. From the turn of the century, literature is replete with such titles as *The Passing of the Great Race, The Revolt Against Civilization,* and *The Conquest of New England by the Immigrant.* Most of these books were written for a general rather than a scientific audience and for this reason were even more influential. A cursory examination of this literature reveals its similarity to that devoted to examining the "Negro problem." In the preface to the second edition of *The Passing of the Great Race,* its author observes:

Whatever may be its intellectual, its literary, its artistic or its musical aptitudes, as compared with other races, the Anglo-Saxon branch of the Nordic race is again showing itself to be that upon which the nation must chiefly depend for leadership, for courage, for loyalty, for unity and harmony of action, for self-sacrifice and devotion to an ideal. . . . in no other human stock which has come to this country is

there displayed the unanimity of heart, mind and action which is now being displayed by the descendants of the blue-eyed, fair-haired peoples of the north of Europe (Grant 1918:xi).

Lothrop Stoddard, author of *The Revolt Against Civilization,* in commenting on the results of World War I United States Army intelligence tests, which compared the responses of native-born Americans to those of foreign-born immigrants, sounds a very similar note:

Of course, these tables refer merely to the intelligence of foreign-born groups *in America;* they may not be particularly good criteria for the entire home populations of the countries mentioned. But they *do* give us a good indication of the sort of people America is getting by immigration from those countries, and they indicate clearly the intelligence levels of the various foreign-born groups in America. And, once more we see a confirmation of those biological, sociological, and psychological researches which we have previously mentioned; viz., that the intelligence level of the racial elements which America has received from northern Europe is far above that of the south and east European elements (Stoddard 1922:72).

Here, two comments are in order. First, it is important to recognize that poorly educated and culturally and socially disadvantaged immigrants were being compared not only with citizens who had lived all of their lives in the United States but with those who were products of the American educational system and felt perfectly at home in the context of American institutions. That immigrants scored lower in tests is not surprising, but at the time, evidence of this nature seemed proof positive of the superiority of northern European peoples—the "old stock"—to those whose national origins were to be traced to southern and central Europe.

Second, intelligence tests measure with

deceptive precision a quantity that is not only poorly understood but incapable of being defined across the wide range of varying cultural experience. Even within one and the same society (for example, the United States), the joint effect of cultural and psychological experiences, achievable aspirations, and conditions under which IQ is measured may be of sufficient variance to render the validity of any IQ score highly questionable. It is more appropriate to approach an IQ score as an indication of the lowest boundary for a particular individual of what such tests purport to gauge. Then, too, estimates of the size of the genetic component of intelligence are equally subject to a variety of errors, and no reliable methods of measuring it have yet been devised.

THE ANTHROPOLOGICAL
RESPONSE TO RACISM

It is with this general background in mind that we must examine the response of American anthropologists to claims of superior and inferior races and national origins. The first solid challenge to these racist doctrines was very much the work of Franz Boas (1858–1942), a brilliant scholar in all fields of anthropology and, if any single individual deserves claim to the title, the founder of the holistic approach that has remained the one firm goal of American anthropology from the turn of the century to the present day.

In 1908 Boas and his assistants began a study of immigrants and their children for the United States Immigration Commission. Apparently, the commission was concerned that the influx of immigrants might result in a deterioration of the physique of the American population. The study was biometrical—it plotted such variables as stature, head length and breadth, and weight—and compared a total of nearly eighteen thousand persons to determine

what differences, if any, existed in the physical characteristics of immigrants and their American-born children. A half-dozen different national groups were analyzed in this manner and the main report was issued in book form in 1912 under the title *Changes in Bodily Form of Descendants of Immigrants.*

Boas's main finding, and a critically important one for the period, was that the children of immigrants approach the uniform type for their country of birth, that is, the United States, rather than that of the country of origin of their parents. Bodily constitution was evidently very plastic, easily susceptible to change even in one generation.

These conclusions, directly striking at the doctrine of immutability of biological characteristics, and indirectly at the very idea of race as a valid biological concept, made Boas unpopular with all who maintained that physical types were in some manner linked to cultural attributes and mental or psychological capacities. Boas's interest in race and racism continued to the very end of his life; in fact, he died of a heart attack while in the middle of a sentence: "I have a new theory about race. . . ." While we will never know what he was going to say, we do know that more than fifty years of research convinced him that each individual is the product of his or her own particular biological heredity, a heredity shaped by life experience and culture. This comes through clearly in his many popular and professional writings, including *The Mind of Primitive Man* (1911), *Anthropology and Modern Life* (1928), and *Race, Language and Culture* (1940).

His students and colleagues continued the tradition, and maintained the legacy. We see this clearly in the work of Ruth Benedict, who in a prophetic statement written in 1947 observed:

Our race prejudice is the great enemy within our gates, and these postwar years will be a fateful testing ground of how far we will let this enemy advance. . . . We can only stand our ground if we are willing to make open admission that the patient— our whole country—is very sick, and that the cure is a matter in which we have an incomparable stake. Then perhaps we can use all possible resources wisely and win through to a happier day (Mead 1959:367–368).

To these and other statements of individual anthropologists, the members of the profession collectively added their voices at the Sixtieth Annual Meeting of the American Anthropological Association in 1961, when they passed unanimously a resolution publicly affirming their position on race. In it they asserted:

There is no scientifically established evidence to justify the exclusion of any race from the rights guaranteed by the Constitution of the United States. The basic principles of equality of opportunity and equality before the law are compatible with all that is known about human biology. All races possess the abilities needed to participate fully in the democratic way of life and in modern technological civilization.[6]

Nevertheless, a few influential scholars from other professional quarters continued to cast doubts on the position that existing populations are genetically equivalent. The American Anthropological Association, in its Sixty-eighth Annual Meeting in 1969, felt it necessary to reassert its earlier conclusion and to add a specific repudiation of "any suggestion that the failure of an educational program could be attributed to genetic differences between large populations." Yet no amount of resolutions or scholarly rejoinders is sufficient to set matters straight. In the last analysis, the breeding ground for prejudice and inequality is social indifference, and each of us is part of the problem.

[6]*Fellow Newsletter of the American Anthropological Association*, vol. 2, no. 10 (December 1961), p. 1.

REFERENCES

BOAS, FRANZ
1911 *The mind of primitive man.* New York: Macmillan.
1912 *Changes in bodily form of descendants of immigrants.* New York: Columbia University Press.
1928 *Anthropology and modern life.* New York: W. W. Norton.
1940 *Race, language and culture.* New York: Macmillan.

DARWIN, CHARLES
1859 *On the origin of species by means of natural selection.* London: John Murray.
1871 *The descent of man, and selection in relation to sex.* New York: D. Appleton.

DARWIN, SIR FRANCIS, ED.
1892 *Charles Darwin; his life told in an autobiographical chapter and in a selected series of his published letters.* New York: D. Appleton.

FITZHUGH, GEORGE
1960 Sociology for the South. In *Antebellum writings of George Fitzhugh and Hinton Rowan Helper on slavery.* Harvey Wish, ed. New York: Capricorn Books.

GRANT, MADISON
1918 *The passing of the great race* (rev. ed.). New York: Charles Scribner's Sons.

HUXLEY, THOMAS H.
1863 *Evidence as to man's place in nature.* London and Edinburgh: Williams and Norgate, and New York: D. Appleton.

MEAD, MARGARET, ED.
1959 *An anthropologist at work; writings of Ruth Benedict.* Boston: Houghton Mifflin.

STODDARD, LOTHROP
1922 *The revolt against civilization.* New York: Charles Scribner's Sons.

VOGT, EVON Z.
1951 *Navaho veterans; a study of changing values.* Papers of the Peabody Museum of American Archaeology and Ethnology, Harvard University, vol. 41, no. 1. Cambridge, Mass.

Chapter 3
Archaeology as anthropology

At first sight, the field of archaeology may appear to be deceptively easy, not with respect to such intricate techniques as radiocarbon dating or computer mapping, but in terms of its underlying aims. Inquire of almost anyone what archaeologists do, and the answer is likely to be given with little or no hesitation: archaeologists "dig up the past," "uncover the remains of ancient civilizations," or, more simply, "collect artifacts."

It is worth considering how few individuals, unless they had spent long years of training and study, would judge themselves ready to engage in research in cultural anthropology, biological anthropology, or linguistics. Yet the world is full of people who with little or no prior education or background are ready enough to excavate the past. Even today, there are a number of states in this country where no license is needed, no academic degree is required, to dig for the material remains of vanished Indian societies. In every state of the Union and in many coun-

Archaeology: the popular image

ties, there are clubs and associations of dedicated weekend diggers. While some do their work with care and are valuable allies of the professional excavator, many are relic collectors and pothunters. This situation gives rise to the belief that all one needs in order to be an archaeologist is a bit of free time, a few simple tools, and the consent of a friendly local farmer. Yet as we shall see, there is much more to archaeology than digging up and collecting ancient artifacts.

The popular image of the professional archaeologist is also far from accurate. In 1960, the archaeologist Robert Ascher published a short survey of all the articles on archaeology that had come out in *Life* magazine over the ten-year period 1946–1955. Assuming that *Life*, as a mass circulation magazine, reflected fairly accurately the public perception of what archaeologists do, Ascher concluded that this image was composed of four main themes: the chance nature of archaeological discoveries, the emphasis on technical knowledge and skill, the role of the archaeologist as an expert readily available to authenticate finds (something akin to an art expert being asked to give his opinion on a doubtful Rembrandt), and the heavy use of superlatives emphasizing "the earliest, the biggest, the most" (Ascher 1960:403). Associated with these themes are the beliefs that almost anyone, if fortunate, can come upon an archaeological find, and that such a discovery achieves both a scientific goal and the more personal adventure of archaeology.[1]

As is true of many popular images, this one suffers from a misplaced emphasis and a failure to consider a number of central, if somewhat less glamorous, elements. No ar-

[1]Books on archaeology and related topics have for many years enjoyed wide popular appeal. Such books come in two categories: serious archaeological works written for the nonspecialist and highly fanciful books that purport to explain the origins of ancient civilizations. The reader should be warned that there is more fiction than science in this latter category of writing, and that fantastic and cataclysmic interpretations of the rise and fall of ancient societies (Atlantean colonists, visitors from another planet, and the like) can be discounted as having no basis in serious research, even though they may indeed make good bedtime reading.

Archaeological perspective

chaeologist (if he or she is honest) is likely to deny that there is a component of adventure in the archaeologist's work—the same kind of adventure that is likely to be found in other areas of scientific research. But as is true of other scientific research and discovery, archaeology also requires day-to-day labor that is always painstaking and often even routine. To be sure, now and again chance does play an important part: a scuba diver may discover a Spanish treasure ship wrecked off the Florida Keys, or a bedouin herdsman may accidentally stumble upon the entrance to a pharaoh's tomb—or find a cave with the Dead Sea Scrolls, as in fact happened in 1947. Most archaeological discoveries, however, are not the result of chance, but of careful surveying and testing. There is also no question that archaeologists are interested in any find that pushes back the furthermost limits of time, or reveals some unexpected facet of life in ancient societies. But granted an element of chance and the desire to increase our knowledge of early periods, most archaeology is aimed at the steady reconstruction of cultures, some old, others less so, that have left behind material remains.

The principle of stratigraphy was illustrated as early as 1850 in this idealized painting based on the excavation of a mound of the prehistoric Mississippian cultural tradition. (The St. Louis Art Museum. Eliza McMillan Trust Fund)

In the 1960s one of the authors worked with other archaeologists on the excavation of early agricultural villages in southern Ohio. Because of the evidence of long-distance trade, craft specialization, and substantial burial mounds (all of which required individuals free from time-consuming food production), he and his colleagues had long suspected that the Indian cultures of the region must have had an economy based on agriculture. Yet up to that time no village settlements in the general area had been fully excavated. They surveyed a number of sites and then chose to excavate one that gave promise of a village (a high density of potsherds was the main surface indication). It was their good fortune to find not only the remains of a village but some corncobs that, thanks to a minor culinary accident several centuries ago, had been burnt and thus had not decomposed. The local press hailed this as the "discovery of the earliest agricultural village in Ohio," a description that was probably an over statement.

The finding of a few cobs of burnt corn, however, did establish the presence of agri-culture. Equally important was the fact that botanists were able to compare the corn with the remains of corn from other archaeological sites in North America. In this manner, the evidence from Ohio could be fitted into the broader frame of agricultural evolution in the New World. This is basically how archaeology progresses—another settle-ment to compare, a slightly different assem-blage of tools to contrast with those recov-ered from neighboring or more distant sites.

What we have explained thus far is only part of the archaeological perspective. Ma-terial remains are important and deserve to be treated with respect because they are often all that is left of prehistoric societies. However, these objects are important not in themselves but rather for what they are able to disclose about the societies that produced them. As the noted British archaeologist Sir Mortimer Wheeler expressed it, "the ar-chaeological excavator is not digging up

things, he is digging up *people;* however much he may analyse. . . , the ultimate appeal across the ages . . . is from mind to intelligent mind, from man to sentient man" (1956:17). This is the reason why ar-chaeology is anthropology and why the em-phasis is on the varieties of culturally or-dered human experience rather than on antiquities as such.

HISTORICAL OVERVIEW

The origins of archaeology are to be found in the curiosity that people have about the material remains of the past. We know, for example, that although ancient Greeks and Romans never engaged in anything ap-proaching scientific excavation, they did recognize that some items were produced before their times and for this reason were worthy of being kept and admired. Modern archaeologists have also noted that in more than a few instances excavations reveal not only artifacts from the period being exca-vated but much older pieces as well that were either passed down generation by gen-eration or found accidentally and kept by the finders.

Archaeological excavation showing work in progress. (Richard Moseley/Anthro-Photo)

It is this concern with the curious and the old that triggered the first formal attempts at digging up the past; but long before the first would-be archaeologist dug the first trench, there was a flourishing interest in rare and exotic items. It can be said that cultural anthropology has its origins in travelers' tales and the reports written by sea captains during the Age of Discovery, and archaeology began under somewhat similar circumstances. The same Renaissance gentlemen who filled their libraries with descriptions of new lands and peoples were in all likelihood also collectors of strange artifacts, although not always old ones.   While material objects from the far corners of the earth were necessarily quite rare, a voyage in time was easier to undertake once some rudimentary techniques of excavation had been mastered. Europe, and later other continents, proved to be full of ancient remains. Antiquities were held to have a historic value, but for long the main interest was aesthetic and antiquarian. The items themselves were collected primarily for display and decoration, to dress up a *salon* or fill a glass-topped cabinet of curiosities. We may take as fairly typical of the enlightened gentleman-collector the British diplomat Sir William Hamilton (1730–1803), who was for many years the ambassador to the Court of Naples. He is described by Goethe, his friend and contemporary, as a "connoisseur and student of Art and Nature," although history knows him best as the husband of Lady Hamilton, mistress of Horatio Nelson. As an archaeologist, Hamilton initiated the excavations of the Roman city of Pompeii (buried by an eruption of Mount Vesuvius in A.D. 79) and wrote several monographs on Roman and Etruscan antiquities.

Early archaeologists were given to great flights of fancy. Since the past, especially what we would now call prehistory, was very much a void, they tended to attribute their finds to the few known groups for which they had names, often names culled from the Bible or from the writings of classical authors. With respect to the New World, they interpreted the remains of American high civilizations as due to Egyptian or Phoenician colonists, or equally unlikely peoples.

Nevertheless, some progress was being made. Slowly at first, archaeology and more broadly the study of material culture changed from a dilettante pursuit to a recognized field of scholarship. Archaeologists—the term enters the standard vocabulary early in the nineteenth century—were still, in the main, auxiliary historians interested in the description of traits and the analysis of styles; and archaeology, much like human evolution, long remained shackled by a narrow temporal perspective. Scholarship was made to fit a conceptual straitjacket woven from a hazy knowledge of ancient history and the dictates of the Scriptures. As a case in point, much effort was expended in trying to prove the universality of the Flood.

Part of the problem is that the stock in trade of the archaeologist, material remains, gives no direct answers. The historian has texts and inscriptions that tell of past events, and the cultural anthropologist can observe people and customs directly. But the archaeologist has no informants and is forced to squeeze information from material objects and the context in which they are found. We can perhaps understand the despair of the early nineteenth-century Danish archaeologist Rasmus Nyerup, who wrote that

everything which has come down to us from heathendom is wrapped in a thick fog; it belongs to a space of time which we cannot measure. We know that it is older than Christendom, but whether by a couple of years or a couple of centuries, or even by more than a millennium, we can do no more than guess (Nyerup 1806, quoted by Daniel 1967:91).

The writer stresses chronology, and he has a point: for much of the time span covered by archaeology, historical records are silent.

The sources available to scholars in the eighteenth and early nineteenth centuries—the Scriptures, the works of Greek and Roman writers—were more often than not misleading. In short, there was no body of information relevant to the distant past of the West or the ancient societies of other regions.

ARCHAEOLOGY AND THE RECONSTRUCTION OF A MEANINGFUL PAST

The task of archaeology is first to describe and then to explain social and cultural variety and similarity through time and space—the same job, in short, that cultural anthropology sets out to do. The difference lies in the data available to archaeologists and the operational procedures and techniques that they use.

Since archaeology attempts to draw meanings and conclusions from the material remains of vanished societies, it has often been defined as the history of those who have no history. This definition stresses the common ground between archaeologists and historians—an interest in the past—but fails to give sufficient weight to archaeology's anthropological orientation. An evolutionary perspective is necessary, for some of the questions archaeology asks are intimately linked with the passage of time and with aspects of cultural adaptation and culture change in the broadest sense of these terms. But just as archaeologists study artifacts not for their own sake but as clues to the societies that fashioned them, time is also important as the dimension through which cultures pass and in which they evolve viable solutions to the problems of survival or else disappear from the face of the earth.

Archaeology starts from a very simple premise that could be phrased as follows: wherever people have been, they have left behind clues of their existence; these clues constitute a body of information amenable to scientific inquiry. They include mortal remains—since, typically, human beings treat the dead with special care and reverence—tools, the remains of houses and other shelters, and all the things that are discarded as useless and worn-out in this life—broken pottery, blunted implements, even the leftovers from yesterday's lunch, should these survive.

An archaeological problem may be likened to a giant jigsaw puzzle with many missing pieces. Archaeologists must put together the picture as well as they are able and then explain its meaning. To aid them in this task, a variety of experts may be called upon, but, in the last analysis, archaeological interpretation relies heavily on the excavator's skill and the care with which the evidence revealed by the spade is evaluated.

Time may be the archaeologists' domain, but it is also one of their most formidable enemies. The material evidence of human activity is usually inversely proportional to the age of a site: the older the site, the less representative the sample. Wood decays before bone does; pottery, as a rule, survives longer than bone, while stone items may remain in essentially mint condition thousands of years after they were fashioned. When we speak of the Stone Age, it should not be thought that people then living used nothing but flint artifacts. Rather, it is simply that after tens of thousands of years virtually nothing else remains. Climate, temperature, the acidity and moisture of the soil, and many other variables will hasten or delay the deterioration of artifacts. It is the fortunate archaeologist who excavates in a desert environment, where such otherwise ephemeral objects as seeds, straw mats, wooden beams, and even food or feces may survive for centuries. Similar high levels of preservation are found in arctic regions and such special (and unusual) locations as peat bogs.

Nevertheless, we have said that archaeologists assume that sites are amenable to logical interpretation. This means more than that tools had a function, that houses were built to be lived in, or that temples were used as places of worship. The size of dwellings can often tell us something about family size and domestic arrangements, while differences in the quality of housing units may serve as an indication of class differences and the allocation of economic and political power within a community. In the past, just as today, social distinctions had their material manifestations.

At what might be called the primary level of analysis, archaeologists concern themselves with inferences that may be drawn from the spatial arrangements of materials within the site. A pioneer example of such interpretation is Thomas Jefferson's excavation of a Virginia Indian burial mound. In the course of his studies, Jefferson (1743–1826) became interested in certain "barrows, of which many are to be found all over this country" (Jefferson 1964:93) and decided to open and thoroughly examine one near his home. In particular, he wanted to satisfy himself about current opinions regarding their function. The report of his excavation, first published in 1785 in his *Notes on the State of Virginia*, testifies to his careful observation:

Appearances certainly indicate that it [the mound] has derived both origin and growth from the accustomary collection of bones, and deposition of them together; that the first collection had been deposited on the common surface of the earth, a few stones put over it, and then a covering of earth, that the second had been laid on this, had covered more or less of it in proportion to the number of bones, and was then also covered with earth; and so on (Jefferson 1964:95).

It will be noted that Jefferson accomplished substantially more than the excavation of a mound. He recognized the importance of what we would now term *stratigraphy*—the tendency for older materials to be buried deeper than more recent ones—and in other passages traced the sources of raw materials for the mound and

recorded features of the skeletal remains. Jefferson also assumed that material remains found together were contemporaneous, thus making use of what a professional archaeologist would term the principle of association.

Careful and observant as Jefferson was in his excavations, he could do little more than describe a single archaeological episode. There was no comparative material, no chronological information to serve as background. Since Jefferson's time, archaeology has matured as a discipline to the degree that careful observation gives way to detailed description, and description in turn leads to sophisticated sociocultural interpretation.

ARCHAEOLOGY AND
CULTURAL ANTHROPOLOGY:
SOME CONTRASTS

The Sutton Hoo ship burial

As a case in point, let us consider the excavation in 1939 of a large mound located about 100 miles northeast of present-day London at a site known as Sutton Hoo. This mound was found to be the burial place of an East Anglian king who probably died in battle in the year A.D. 665 and was buried inside a longship, a large undecked boat. As was the custom of the times, the dead king was placed inside the boat (which had been pulled onto dry land) together with a collection of items, some precious, others more utilitarian. His subjects then built a long earth mound to cover the ship and its royal occupant (Green 1963; Bruce-Mitford 1972).

Had an early nineteenth-century archaeologist discovered this burial, it is quite possible that he would have placed it roughly between the fall of the Roman Empire and the establishment of fairly secure medieval kingdoms around A.D. 1000—a period generally referred to as the Dark Ages. From literary sources, if not from archaeology, he might have known that Viking chieftains were often buried in this fashion (for a

description of Viking ship burials see Sjøvold 1958). However, it is most unlikely that even with this knowledge, our hypothetical discoverer could have done much more than make some rough guesses as to the significance of the find.

As an exercise, let us consider how we would approach the same archaeological problem today. The steps that follow have been greatly simplified and expressed sequentially; obviously, archaeologists in the field will not neatly compartmentalize their thinking to fit such a scheme, for this is not how the human mind works. Any major find, such as an especially interesting artifact, will move the mind simultaneously along several interpretative channels: What is it? Who made it? What are its uses?

We are presenting here, however, a logical sequence that runs from concrete observation to interpretation of function:

Observation Under this heading we include the ship itself, various military trappings (helmet, iron sword and scabbard, the remains of a metal-embossed shield), what has been interpreted as a royal scepter, and various objects of wealth, such as a purse with gold coins, several silver bowls, and items of jewelry.

Description Some objects are utilitarian, others are obviously luxury items. The workmanship of some pieces indicates that they were turned out by local artisans (a beautifully enameled purse lid of gold, a couple of hinged golden clasps). These Anglo-Saxon valuables are found side by side with precious items that are not of local derivation. Among the foreign objects are a couple of silver spoons with Greek writing, gold coins struck by the Merovingian kings of France prior to A.D.650, and a set of silver bowls crafted in the eastern Mediterranean.

Interpretation A royal grave, but a rather special one. To understand it, we have to keep in mind the nature of the times and the kind of societies then present on the shores of western Europe. Geographically and culturally, these were societies on the edge of the known world that nevertheless maintained contact with the decaying remains of ancient Mediterranean civilization. It is not by chance that the Anglo-Saxons, like the Vikings a few centuries later, buried their great men in ships. They had few permanent settlements and tended to make their living from a combination of piracy and trade. This life style also helps to explain the nature of the materials found on board. The Mediterranean artifacts were probably acquired by a combination of trade and plunder and ended up in England after passing through several hands.

The Sutton Hoo treasure is not the only one of its kind that can be attributed to the Anglo-Saxon period of English history. Historical sources and literary references—few inhabitants were literate—dealing with the Anglo-Saxons are scant but sufficient to

indicate that the accumulation of treasure was very much part of the cultural ethos of the people, or at least of those in control.[2] A poem of the period describes a prince as "he [who] lacks not what he wants,/ Horses or treasures or the joys of hall,/ Or any noble treasure in this world," while *Beowulf*, the greatest Anglo-Saxon epic, contains a description of a sea burial that is part of the same tradition as the Sutton Hoo ship burial:

[2]While Anglo-Saxon poems such as *Beowulf* depict a society rich in gold and other precious objects, there was little reason to consider these verses much more than poetic license. The Sutton Hoo ship burial confirmed with startling accuracy the detailed descriptions of Anglo-Saxon poets and chroniclers. The situation here is very similar to the descriptions contained in the Homeric epics (especially the *Iliad*), which were only confirmed by excavations at Troy and other Mycenaean sites at the turn of the century.

When at length the fated hour was come, Scyld, the valiant, departed unto the keeping of the Lord. Then his dear companions bore him down to the ocean-flood, even as he himself had bidden them. . . . There at the harbor stood a ship with curving prow, all icy, eager to depart—meet for a prince. And in the ship's bosom, hard by the mast, they laid their dear lord, the giver of treasure, that famous hero. Many treasures were there, abundance of ornaments brought from afar. Never have I heard men tell of a ship more splendidly laden with battle-weapons and war-harness, with swords and coats of mail. Upon his breast lay many precious things which were to go far out with him into the realm of the waters (Cook and Tinker 1902:10).

From specifics to generalizations

In addition, though, archaeologists, in their role as students of cultural comparison, can ask how typical burials of this nature were for societies of the same type. The answer would be that, while the details of mortuary practices are likely to vary, it was not at all unusual in chiefdoms and petty kingdoms to honor the departed ruler with sumptuous grave offerings: the king was expected to maintain his station in the hereafter in a manner befitting his condition on earth.

A burial of this kind also raises a number of interesting questions regarding the society that gave rise to it. What, for instance, can be learned about trading networks or raiding territories? What was the pattern of wealth allocation—if kings were buried in such splendor, how did the common people fare? What information can be gleaned concerning the social and political systems? We do not imply that all this information is immediately available from a single burial, splendid though it may be, but rather that material objects can be approached as sources of information about the society which fashioned or acquired them.

The goals of modern archaeology, in fact, can be seen as in no essential way different from those of cultural anthropology; only the methods and the sources of information vary. It is perhaps instructive to compare the aims of these two branches of anthropology, as has been done by the archaeologists Gordon R. Willey and Philip Phillips (1958:4). They have looked at the two subdisciplines in terms of their respective levels of organization. Their approach can be rendered diagrammatically as shown below.

On the observational level, cultural anthropology concerns itself with group behavior and cultural constructs. Archaeology, for its part, observes primarily the material products of a society. Behavior itself must be inferred, as we have done in the case of burial practices.

As used by Willey and Phillips, the term *culture-historical integration*

covers almost everything the archaeologist does in the way of organizing his primary data: typology, taxonomy, formulation of archaeological "units," investigation of their relationships in the contexts of function and natural environment, and determination of their internal dimensions and external relationships in space and time (Willey and Phillips 1958:5).

The aim is primarily to describe what happens to specific cultural units, typically sites, in terms of chronology and spatial relationships. No attempt is made at this level to develop generalizations from these observations and descriptions. Ethnography is the cultural anthropological equivalent for this level of analysis. Just as the archaeologist describes sites, typically the remains of communities, the cultural anthropologist is generally concerned with descriptions of such units as tribes, villages, or more complex social structures.

At the explanatory level, the aims of archaeology and cultural anthropology meet in that they both strive to establish regularities concerning the nature of culture and the organization of social systems. The processual interpretation of Willey and Phillips is intended to cover not only the *how* of social and cultural systems, but also the *why*. It may be thought that this is a tall order for archaeology. However, archaeologists should be particularly qualified to study the process of evolutionary change, especially processes that are relatively slow and thus unfold over a long time span.

THE INTERPLAY OF ARCHAEOLOGY
AND CULTURAL ANTHROPOLOGY

Although this chapter is not primarily concerned with archaeological techniques, focusing instead on the goals of archaeology

	ARCHAEOLOGY	CULTURAL ANTHROPOLOGY
Observation	Field work	Field work
Description	Culture-historical integration	Ethnography
Explanation	Interpretation of process	Ethnology

and the way in which archaeology fits into the general frame of contemporary anthropology, it is necessary to say something about the orientation of archaeological research and how it influences the conduct of field work.

First of all, it should be understood that archaeology has never operated in a vacuum. As a social science, it has consciously borrowed theoretical concepts from sister disciplines, most obviously from cultural and social anthropology. Since archaeologists start with the premise that they are studying societies, it is natural that they project contemporary concepts on the nature of society into their deliberations. For instance, an archaeologist who excavates the remains of hunting and gathering societies is well advised to be aware of research on groups of this type—their social organization, the density of population of contemporary or historical hunting bands, the nature of their economic base, their influence on the environment, and so forth. The same holds true for whatever level of cultural complexity the archaeologist directs attention to, whether the subject of his or her investigation is associated with subsistence agriculture, archaic state systems (such as the high civilizations of Mesoamerica, ancient Egypt, or Mesopotamia), or even a settlement from a well-documented historical period.

It is worth stressing that this borrowing of concepts and information is not a one-way street. In recent years, archaeologists, as well as other anthropologists, have devoted considerable effort to delineating *culture types*, in part from archaeological remains, in part from historical sources, and to some degree from ethnographic reports. The culture type concept (Braidwood 1960; Steward 1955; Willey 1960) stresses the structural similarities common to a number of distinct cultures. A case in point might be the parallels observable in early civilizations in both the Old and New Worlds. According to Julian H. Steward:

The parallels are striking and undeniable. They include the independent develop-

ment . . . of an impressive list of basic features: domesticated plants and animals, irrigation, large towns and cities, metallurgy, social classes, states and empires, priesthoods, writing, calendars, and mathematics (Steward 1955:25).

Archaeology not only offers broad temporal and spatial perspectives for cross-cultural comparison, but one of its virtues is that it often brings to light the kinds of information that are not readily available other than through archaeological work. This unique quality permits a mutually beneficial association: archaeology in its relationships to the rest of anthropology may be likened to a mutually supporting system of feedbacks.

The archaeologist can and does make use of analogy. For instance, projectile points are identified as such because similar objects are known from ethnographic contexts. The same holds true for most material objects dug up by the archaeologist: house remains, pottery, ceremonial objects, temples, and the like. The archaeologist assumes—generally rightly—that there is an association of form and function. A harpoon head does not proclaim its identity, but we can assume with some degree of security that an object of this form was used to hunt or fish in a particular manner. Analogy is not limited to objects; it may be applied to the societies that made them. Obviously, there is an element of danger in the use of analogy, and archaeologists must be careful that deductive logic does not get the better of them. For instance, axes may be used to chop trees, or hit enemies over the head, or as purely ceremonial objects; similarly, not all pre-agricultural societies roamed around in bands and lived in temporary dwellings.

The other side of the coin from ethnographic analogy is archaeological inference—the degree to which archaeology can fill gaps in the record. For example, James F. Deetz points out that excavations of seventeenth-century house sites in old Plymouth Colony reveal that "approximately 98 percent of the meat consumed was from domesticated animals. Hunting was an insignificant factor" (1970:124). How different this finding is from the Thanksgiving-derived picture of sturdy Pilgrim men moving into the forest with muskets at the ready in search of the wild turkey! And yet, the explanation is perfectly reasonable and culturally valid. According to Deetz:

Legislation governing hunting rights in their native England was so restricted on the yeomanry [small farmers] that they endured food shortages . . . without resorting to hunting on any significant scale. . . . This reluctance to hunt would appear to result from a retention of attitudes toward hunting engendered prior to colonization, combined with an unfamiliarity with the use of firearms in hunting (1970:124).

In this instance, archaeology gives us an insight into early New England history—even a quantitative measure of subsistence patterns—and history in turn, in the form of English legislation and the practices which it generated, helps to explain why men in the wilderness made such little use of game animals.

THE NEW ARCHAEOLOGY

One of the most significant developments in contemporary anthropology has been the re-emergence of evolutionary theory in the study of cultural process. During the second half of the nineteenth century—from about the publication of Darwin's *Origin of Species* (1859)—the archaeological, ethnographic, and geological evidence all appeared to confirm a basic hypothesis: just as there had been an evolutionary sequence that led to the emergence of *Homo sapiens*, evolutionary forces had been at work in cultural transformation.

As we noted earlier, the concept of evolution was not invented or discovered by Darwin; his claim to fame lies in presenting

Cultural evolution and anthropology

a scientifically logical and consistent explanatory model. With respect to cultural evolution, the idea that human societies had progressed along certain determined lines is also very old. What is now termed the concept of cultural evolution may be found in the writings of classical Greek thinkers, the speculations of ancient Chinese scholars and, more recently, in the theories of eighteenth-century humanist philosophers who posited a sequential development from "natural man" to humans living in complex state systems. However, such theorizing and speculation lacked a base of material evidence until the nineteenth century. Nineteenth-century scholars contributed a great deal to establishing the antiquity of humankind and, on the basis of excavation and the collection of material remains, framed out a basic sequence in terms of ages—the Stone Age, the Bronze Age, and the Iron Age.

The interpretation of these discoveries must be understood in the context of the times. In the preceding chapter we have already noted how early thinkers proposed theological and mythological models of the past that fitted the prevailing climate of thought; similarly, interpretations of cultural evolution were heavily influenced by the work of naturalists and the then prevailing notions of cultural and racial superiority. Until late in the nineteeth century, knowledge of simple societies was very scant, and it was generally believed that so-called primitives were inferior to civilized people in both cultural and biological endowments. It seemed logical enough to assume that prehistoric peoples—the ancient inhabitants of Western Europe who had fashioned tools and weapons of stone thousands of years prior to the rise of civilization—could be equated with living hunters and gatherers, and that both the ancestors of modern humans and primitive contemporaries had been, or were, decidedly inferior in mental capacity to modern Western populations.

Nineteenth-century cultural evolution was therefore permeated with racism and false biological analogies. These very real shortcomings stimulated a strong reaction on the part of a new generation of anthropologists, especially in the United States. As is often the case with theories that become unfashionable, a price had to be paid for an uncritical rejection of everything associated with cultural evolution: a potentially valuable explanatory model was discarded because it embodied flaws in interpretation. Evolutionary theory had another strike against it that added to its burden of unpopularity. In developing his theory of dynamic social change (dialectical materialism), Karl Marx (1818–1865) was strongly influenced by Charles Darwin (1809–1882) and the cultural evolutionists of the second half of the nineteenth century, Lewis Henry Morgan (1818–1881) in particular. Marx was a brilliant political theoretician but a rather unsophisticated reader of anthropological materials. For those with a firmer knowledge of anthropology (writing one or two generations after Marx) it was easy enough to point out a number of glaring errors, both in source materials and in matters of interpretation. As a result, cultural evolution was altogether out of favor in the formative years of American anthropology, in part because of early ties with racism and in part for ideological reasons.

Until recent years, archaeologists tended to emphasize description and classification and on the whole shied away from interpretation and the building of theoretical models of sociocultural development. There are some notable exceptions to this general observation. We have already commented on the work of Julian H. Steward, and mention should also be made of the researches of the British anthropologist V. Gordon Childe. But while these and other scholars were important precursors of the new archaeology, they spoke for a minority of professionals and their impact on American archaeological thinking was limited. The new archaeology is, more than anything else, a revitalization of cultural evolution, and if a single individual can be said to be responsi-

Cultural evolution and archaeology

ble for its development, the candidate would be Lewis R. Binford.

In 1962, Binford published an article in *American Antiquity*, the leading archaeological journal in the United States, aptly titled "Archaeology as Anthropology." He noted that most archaeological research was concerned with descriptions of material culture, the classification of artifacts, and the reconstruction of culture history (the description of societies known from the archaeological record), whereas very little attention was paid to broad questions of comparative sociocultural process. He then proceeded to define the goals of what would later be known as the new archaeology:

Archaeology must accept a greater responsibility in the furtherance of the aims of anthropology. Until the tremendous quantities of data which the archaeologist controls are used in the solution of problems dealing with cultural evolution or systemic change, we are not only failing to contribute to the furtherance of the aims of anthropology but retarding the accomplishment of these aims (Binford 1962:224).

Only two years later, Eric R. Wolf, a social anthropologist whose thinking tended to parallel that of the new archaeologists, heralded recent developments in somewhat more strident tones:

A new archaeology, freeing itself from both the collector's madness of obtaining show pieces and from the infantile wish to restore the lost splendor of ruins long covered by earth or jungle, turned to the recovery of entire settlements of past populations. It just began to look beyond the mechanical gathering of isolated bits of material culture to the reconstruction of past communities, attempting to grasp the archaeological equivalent of the ecologists' group and the social anthropologist's organization-bearing unit (Wolf 1964: 68–69).

Most significantly, the new archaeologists are genuinely holistic in their orientation.

They take the total society as the unit of analysis, not simply selected elements. This change of focus is very important since, historically, archaeologists have devoted a disproportionate amount of effort to unearthing those remains of past cultures that make good museum exhibits or sumptuous ruins. The result has been that even the aims of cultural reconstruction have been hindered by an unbalanced data base. It is as if social anthropologists devoted the bulk of their energies to studying elites without reference to the peasant masses that provide the work, time, and economic surpluses that alone allow those in control to enjoy luxury and power.

Binford and his followers insist that archaeological problems can be solved through the proper utilization of information derived from archaeology alone—if only the right questions are asked.

We assert that our knowledge of the past is more than a projection of our ethnographic understanding. The accuracy of our knowledge of the past can be measured; it is this assertion which most sharply differentiates the new perspective from more traditional approaches. The yardstick of measurement is the degree to which propositions about the past can be confirmed or refuted through hypothesis testing (Binford 1968:17).

The questions that are posed by the new archaeologists are fundamental and have to do with the limitations and potentialities of societies operating within specific sociocultural and environmental frames. In particular, they examine different modes of subsistence and production (economics), political organization, and sociocultural complexity. One may ask, therefore, such questions as: What are the underlying factors common to early civilizations? What are the requirements for plant and animal domestication? What are the inherent limitations on sociocultural complexity in societies that depend on hunting and food collecting? This list is not meant to be exhaustive, but simply illustrative. What we should note is the shift in focus from isolated elements (individual sites, specific traits, or artifacts, and the like) to sociocultural systems as dynamic entities.

Central to this approach is the conceptualization of cultures as ecologically based and composed of a number of interacting subsystems. Accordingly, environment and culture are viewed not as two separate and different entities but as a complex whole, which in turn is part of the ecological system ("ecosystem"). Human societies are thus approached as part of the totality of nature.

The evolutionary perspective recognizes that cultural systems change through time. Changes in one subsystem (social, economic, ideological, and so on) cause changes in other subsystems and thus in the total culture. Similarly, changes in the environment result in culturally adaptive responses or in disequilibrium between environment and society, while the process of culture change typically has an impact on the environment.

This process of transformation is guided by the internal structure of a culture, its past historical experience, and its interrelationships with other cultures and the environment. The new archaeologists claim that there is a directional quality, or trajectory, to the process of culture change, although we should not mistake this claim for the laws of cultural evolution that were so fashionable in the nineteenth century. What is involved here is statements of probability rather than deterministic models.

CHRONOLOGICAL CONTROLS

As we pointed out earlier in this chapter, there are very good reasons why archaeologists have long been concerned with establishing a firm temporal frame for the societies and cultures that they investigate. These reasons go much deeper than a desire to affix a date to a particular site or other material remains, for time is less important as a mere measure of antiquity (How old is it?" is perhaps the first question that the layperson asks the archaeologist) than as a temporal context in which all societies and cultures can be ordered.

It is difficult to reconstruct the conditions that prevailed in a particular ancient society without reference to *when* the remains formed part of a functioning sociocultural unit. The environment and the resource base of a region (the hinterland tapped by a community) may change greatly over time, either as the result of human action or through factors, such as climatic change, over which people have little control. Even more rapid may be the changes in the socio-cultural context within which a society operates. As a case in point, a community of Carib Indians that flourished some years prior to 1492 is something very different from a village of the same group that can be dated to twenty years after the establishment of Spanish colonial control and the brutal exploitation of native labor. As another example, the whole organizational structure of hunting communities in a given region is likely to vary enormously with the availability of big game, and once such big game disappears, as did mammoths and mastodons on the North American plains, new patterns of social organization are likely to arise.

Chronology is important also in studies whose primary goal is to interpret and explain culture process—the dynamics of change. The direction and rate of change (What aspects of a culture are especially prone to change under given conditions? What is the pace of change?) may be studied for a locality or geographical area or in order to frame out the regularities in the evolution of several similar but geographically separate cultures. Thus, regardless of the specific goals of a particular archaeological research project, good time controls are highly desirable and often indispensable.

Chronology, for the archaeologist, is of two kinds: absolute and relative. *Absolute chronology* is the kind we are most familiar with. It positions events—some of longer, others of shorter, duration—along an agreed-upon temporal yardstick divided into recognized units of measurement (hours, days, months, years, and so forth). Thus, Britain was under Roman occupation from A.D. 43 until the early 400s; on July 4, 1776, the Second Continental Congress declared the American colonies to be free and independent of Great Britain; or to use a specifically archaeological example, the ancient Indian farmers of the Mesa Verde region in Colorado were forced to abandon their cliff villages soon after the twenty-four-year drought first struck in 1276.

Archaeologists also measure time in a relative manner rather than according to precise dates. In many instances, these estimates were the only measures available, particularly in an earlier generation when archaeologists had to work without the techniques of absolute dating recently developed in the physical sciences. *Relative dating*, or *chronology*, is a statement of greater or lesser antiquity of two or more archaeological phenomena. Again, the temporal span will vary greatly depending on what is being measured. For example, nineteenth-century archaeologists recognized that, prior to the advent of classical civilization in Europe, three ages had run their course. They knew that the Stone Age had preceded the Bronze Age, and that the Iron Age had followed the Bronze Age, but it was extremely difficult to assign absolute time spans to these developments. Relative dating is always attempted in any excavation, regardless of how modest. The archaeologist works on the assumption that, all things being equal, older material will be found farther down in the ground and more recent material nearer to the surface. A well-stratified site with clearly defined occupational levels tells its own story if carefully dug, but unless the levels can be tied to absolute dates, one has to speak of relative relationships: this artifact is relatively older than that one; this layer of occupation follows an earlier one encountered farther down. Both forms of dating, absolute and relative, are means of controlling the dimension of time, and typically both are used in combination if feasible.

Most of the recent developments in dating techniques fall into the category of absolute dating. In the brief survey we are undertaking, only a few of the more important techniques can be considered. There are many in use and still others are in an experimental stage. It is important to realize how new most of these techniques are and what extraordinary impact they have had on archaeology. In large measure, these new tools have made possible many of the innovative approaches to the interpretation of the past that contemporary archaeologists engage in; for to the degree that temporal questions can be more easily answered, energies have been released to tackle complex questions having to do with the structure of societies in time past and long-term patterns of sociocultural development.

The natural sciences began to make their impact on archaeology early in the nineteenth century. It was geology and related studies that first established that the deposits in which Old Stone Age tools were recovered belonged to the Ice Age (or were "antediluvian" [before the flood], in the quaint terminology of the period). The conclusion that people had inhabited the earth at the same time as long-extinct Pleistocene animals pushed back by many thousands of years the threshold of human history.

By the turn of the century, the geologic-climatic record for Europe was known in some detail, especially for areas that had been glaciated during the last Ice Age and from which the ice had subsequently receded. When the ice sheets that had covered much of northern Europe (and much of North America) slowly retreated northwards, they left behind lakes and ponds at the bottom of which were fine deposits of silt or clay. These deposits form a series of superimposed layers, or *varves*, each layer representing the sediment for a single year.

Techniques of absolute dating

This layering effect was caused by differential rates of ice melting during the year: coarse grains were deposited during the summer melt, while finer materials settled to the bottom much more slowly during fall and winter. Although the retreat of the ice sheets was steady, it did not proceed at the same pace each year. For some years, the varves are very thin, indicating that the ice retreat progressed very slowly owing to cold conditions; in warmer years more ice melted and consequently the deposited layers are thicker.

As a result, the varves give us a year-by-year climatic profile. No single body of water is deep enough or large enough to contain a sequence covering the whole retreat of the ice. But since varves faithfully display minor fluctuations in climate, it is possible to match the evidence from several lakes with overlapping sections in order to establish a full chronology. The result is a geochronological calendar going back to early postglacial times (about 10,000 B.C.) to which cultural remains can be linked. Obviously, this dating process is applicable only to those areas that have been glaciated, such as northern Europe and the geographically equivalent regions of North America.

Tree-ring dating (dendrochronology) is based on a very similar principle, in this case the observation that tree rings record yearly growth and that this growth reflects climatic fluctuations (see Figure 3-1). But just as no lake tells more than part of the climatic story of the retreat of the northern ice sheets, the life span of a tree is generally limited to a few score years. It is possible to determine the age of a felled tree by counting the rings in a cross section, but then these cross sections must be matched with older and younger specimens in order to develop a continuous record.

Tree-ring dating was first applied to establishing an absolute chronology for the Southwest, where the dry climate has preserved many ancient beams and logs. We now have an absolute chronology for the

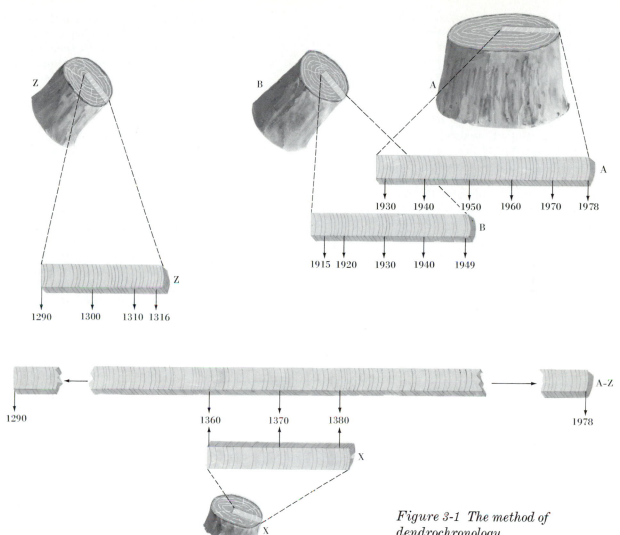

Figure 3-1 The method of dendrochronology

In this diagram, a chronology has been developed by matching the oldest growth rings of a contemporary tree (A) with tree-ring patterns of successively older beams from the same general area (B through Z) back to the year 1290. An unknown specimen (X) can now be dated by finding where its tree-ring pattern is identical with that of the master chart (A–Z).

Southwest that stretches back two thousand years, and local sequences have also been established for other areas, including Alaska, the Great Plains, and parts of Europe. Obviously, having a dendrochronological sequence is not the same as being able to date everything that falls within the span of time covered by the interlocking record of tree rings. Archaeological materials must be in association with wooden objects or structures that can then be matched with a dendrochronological calendar. There is also the problem that people living in the past made use of wood that had been cut long before their lifetime—just as we might use the beams of a ruined colonial house in a modern dwelling. But these and similar stipulations aside, dendrochronology has proved to be a very valuable dating technique. As in all other archaeological dating procedures, *cross dating* extends the scope of this method. A firm association between a dendrochronological date and a particular class of artifacts—say, pottery vessels with distinct stylistic features—is established for site A; site B, with no wooden materials amenable to dendrochronological analysis, contains artifacts of the same type. Under such circumstances it is reasonable to hypothesize that the two sites are more or less contemporary.

The original research on varves goes back to the late nineteenth century. Dendrochronology was initially developed in the early part of the current century by A. E. Douglass, an American astronomer interested in the effects of sunspots on climate. More recent breakthroughs in dating are in large measure a by-product of relatively new scientific disciplines. The best-known means of absolute dating is by radiocarbon, or carbon 14. The *carbon-14 method* was developed by the physicist Willard F. Libby and first announced by him in 1949. While this technique of dating is complex—it demands precise instrumentation and highly trained personnel—the principles behind radiocarbon dating are not hard to grasp. Neutrons produced by cosmic radiation enter the atmosphere and react with the nitrogen isotope N 14 to produce a heavier isotope of carbon, C 14, which is radioactive and conveniently long-lived. Carbon-14 atoms, in carbon dioxide molecules, ultimately enter into all living things as part of the familiar plant-animal carbon cycle. While the organism is alive, the proportion of carbon 14 to the stable carbon 12 remains constant; but after the organism dies, carbon-14 atoms decay, or disintegrate, at a fixed rate. In the language of the physicists, C 14 has a half-life of 5,730 ± 40 years. The half-life in this case is the time required for half of the radiocarbon atoms present to be eliminated. The " ± " is an error factor known as the standard deviation and it follows all radiocarbon dates. In the figure for the half-life of carbon 14, it means that there is a two-in-three chance that the true length of carbon 14 half-life falls within the span of 40 years before or 40 years after 5,730.

It follows that, if all living things contain a fixed amount of carbon 14, and if carbon 14 decays at a steady rate, any organic materials recovered from an archaeological site can be tested for radiocarbon content and an absolute date attributed to them on the basis of this content. Easy as this theory is in principle, there are problems in practical application. Organic material must be available for the test, and it is typically organic material (wood, natural fiber, human and animal remains, and so forth) that tends to decompose first and disappear from the archaeological record. It is in part for this reason that burned materials—such as the corncobs mentioned with reference to the Ohio excavation—are especially valuable, because partial burning (as in charcoal) acts to preserve specimens that might otherwise not have survived the passage of time. It is also important that the samples used for dating not be contaminated by organic materials that are older or younger than the sample, for otherwise the radiocarbon reading becomes skewed.

Radiocarbon dating can measure materials up to 70,000 years old, although the most secure dates are from specimens several thousand years younger. Unlike dendrochronology and varve analysis, radiocarbon dating has the advantage that it is tied neither to localities that have experienced glacial recession nor to a dendrochronological sequence that, by necessity, is closely related to the climatic history of a region.

Several other dating techniques are based on the radioactive decay of elements.

Potassium-argon dating measures the decay of potassium 40 into argon 40. By determining the ratio of potassium to argon, one can estimate the age of rocks. The value of this method is that it is applicable to rocks laid down by natural means (such as in volcanic eruptions) that have been found in association with archaeological deposits. The method is useful for very early sites and it has been successfully applied to dating fossil finds. Very old fossil hominid bones from East Africa that have been found in deposits of consolidated volcanic ash have successfully been dated by this method.[3]

Because of the search for even the most minute clues that might lead to the discovery of hidden answers, the archaeologist has frequently been likened to a detective. The professional archaeologist is concerned not only with the temporal sequences of cultural materials in a given locality but also with the comparison of these materials as they may relate with remains uncovered in other sites nearby or distant. And like the detective, the archaeologist must piece together the story with both patience and ingenuity. It is no wonder that archaeology has never failed to captivate the imagination of the insatiably curious—laypersons and scholars alike.

TO SUM UP   The new archaeology is asking new questions, and these new questions have stimulated new methods of analysis and interpretation of the fascinating record of humanity's past.

---

[3]Among the techniques that have remained unmentioned are pollen analysis and the fluorine test. The former involves the identification and determination of frequency of pollen grains in peat bogs and other preservative situations, the latter is based on the fact that the fluorine content of fossil bones and teeth buried in earth tends to increase through time at a rate particular to a given locality.

Other techniques that promise to be important in the future, but that are still in an experimental stage (it is always necessary to test such techniques in different contexts in order to eliminate "bugs" and establish limitations and potentials), include measures of obsidian hydration and thermoluminescence (TL). For an up-to-date review and bibliography, the interested reader is referred to Michels 1972.

REFERENCES

ASCHER, ROBERT
1960 Archaeology and the public image. *American Antiquity* 25:402–403.

BINFORD, LEWIS R.
1962 Archaeology as anthropology. *American Antiquity* 28:217–225.
1968 Archeological perspectives. In *New perspectives in archeology*. Sally R. Binford and Lewis R. Binford, eds. Chicago: Aldine. Pp. 5–32.

BRAIDWOOD, ROBERT J.
1960 Levels in prehistory: a model for the consideration of the evidence. In *Evolution after Darwin,* vol. II: *The evolution of man.* Sol Tax, ed. Chicago: The University of Chicago Press. Pp. 143–151.

BRUCE-MITFORD, RUPERT
1972 *The Sutton Hoo ship-burial; a handbook* (2nd ed.). London: The Trustees of the British Museum.

CHILDE, VERE GORDON
1951 *Social evolution.* New York: H. Schuman.

COOK, ALBERT S., AND CHAUNCEY B. TINKER
1902 *Select translations from Old English poetry.* Boston: Ginn.

DANIEL, GLYN EDMUND
1967 *The origins and growth of archaeology.* Baltimore, Md.: Penguin Books.

DEETZ, JAMES
1970 Archeology as a social science. In *Current directions in anthropology.* Ann Fischer, ed. Bulletins of the American Anthropological Association, vol. 3, no. 3, part 2, pp. 115–125. Washington, D.C.: American Anthropological Association.

GREEN, CHARLES
1963 *Sutton Hoo; the excavation of a royal ship-burial.* London: Merlin Press.

HAMER, RICHARD, COMP.
1970 *A choice of Anglo-Saxon verse.* London: Faber and Faber.

JEFFERSON, THOMAS
1964 *Notes on the state of Virginia.* New York: Harper and Row.

MICHELS, JOSEPH W.
1972 Dating methods. In *Annual review of anthropology.* Bernard J. Siegel et al., eds., vol. 1. Palo Alto, Cal.: Annual Reviews. Pp. 113–126.

SJØVOLD, THORLEIF
1958 A royal Viking burial. *Archaeology* 11:190–199.

STEWARD, JULIAN H.
1955 *Theory of culture change; the methodology of multilinear evolution.* Urbana: University of Illinois Press.

WHEELER, SIR MORTIMER
1956 *Archaeology from the earth.* Harmondsworth, Middlesex: Penguin Books.

WILLEY, GORDON R.
1960 Historical patterns and evolution in native New World cultures. In *Evolution after Darwin,* vol. II: *The evolution of man.* Sol Tax, ed. Chicago: The University of Chicago Press. Pp. 111–141.

WILLEY, GORDON R., AND PHILIP PHILLIPS
1958 *Method and theory in American archaeology.* Chicago: The University of Chicago Press.

WOLF, ERIC R.
1964 *Anthropology.* Englewood Cliffs, N.J.: Prentice-Hall.

Chapter 4

The Old World: culture history and culture process

Until late in the fifteenth century the Atlantic Ocean had served as an effective barrier to geographical explorations, with the result that the opening up and conquest of the Western Hemisphere by European kingdoms were accomplished only in relatively recent times. The term *Old World*, which is used to refer to the Eastern Hemisphere, derives from the fact that in 1503 an Italian navigator, Amerigo Vespucci,[1] wrote

[1] In this connection it is of interest to note that a bare dozen years prior to Vespucci's letter, Columbus had set sail from Palos, Spain, in search of a shorter route to the Orient with its spices and silks, precious stones and metals, which at that time reached Europe only by means of costly and dangerous overland caravans from the Orient. In preparing for his anticipated destination, Columbus armed himself with a letter of introduction to the "Great Khan of Cathay" that he expected to present upon his arrival in China. It is ironic that in his search for a better route by which to obtain and then transport the Orient's goods and riches from one point to another in the "old world," he found instead a "new world," whose vast treasures lay as yet unrecognized.

a widely read letter in which he claimed that he had discovered a "new world" beyond the sea, thereby relegating what up to that time had been the only world to "old world" status.

But the Old World was old in a still more basic sense. It had served as the cradle of humanity several million years before the European expansion—and long before members of the modern human species, *Homo sapiens*, had unwittingly entered the "new world" some thirty or forty thousand years ago by crossing into North America from northeast Asia by way of the Bering Strait.

Our concern in the present chapter will be the analysis of the archaeological evidence for culture history and culture process in the Old World, with consideration given to the ecological factors that influenced man's cultural adaptation. As an adaptive mechanism, culture may be viewed as comprising three major aspects: technology, social organization, and ideology. Not only are all three closely interrelated, but their presence is essential for the long-range survival of any human group. In earlier archaeological research, technological evidence received an inordinate amount of attention, and for good reason. Not only had the material items recovered been directly involved at one time in exploiting the environment, but they were virtually all that remained from the distant past. Yet we have seen that tools, shelters, burials, and the other elements of material culture that the archaeologist is likely to uncover are but a partial index of the total pattern of a society's lifeway. A carefully finished, half-million-year-old hand ax or a well-preserved hearth of a Stone Age cave dweller may indeed be exciting pieces of archaeological evidence, but what is even more important is that behind them are human beings, with much the same pleasures and anxieties that we experience today — giving life to offspring, protecting them as they grow to maturity, struggling to obtain the necessities of daily living, and working out the problems that come from being a member of a group. If one is to understand the adaptation of a group, then, it is necessary to analyze the manner in which its members organized themselves into social units. The survival of individuals is dependent upon the survival of the group, for only as members of a collectivity can humans utilize effectively what nature has to offer and at the same time meet their psychological and social needs. In this respect, settlement patterns and physical features of dwellings often provide important insights into the social life of prehistoric populations. The reconstruction of the ideological bases of a culture is the most difficult problem, but some aspects of ritual activities and associated beliefs may be gleaned from such evidence as burial practices.

THE PLEISTOCENE EPOCH

Before we sketch out the broad outline of prehistoric cultural adaptations in the Old World, it is necessary to preface the discussion with a few comments concerning some of the drastic physical and climatic changes that, although independent of any human activity, nevertheless influenced significantly the environment in which humankind was coming of age. The dawn of culture dates back to the beginning of the *Pleistocene epoch*, some three million years ago. This geological epoch was characterized by a succession of vigorous glaciations that advanced southward from the North Pole. So much of the earth's waters periodically became locked up in glacial ice that the seas must have dropped several hundred feet below their present level each time, exposing a good deal of additional land. Every glacial stage was followed by a period of moderately warm weather and melting, resulting in a relatively ice-free interglacial phase. Greenland, northwestern Europe, northern Siberia, and the upper half of North America were particularly affected by the glacial advances, four of which customarily have been singled out for both the Old and the New World. The European glaciations have been traditionally designated after Alpine localities in which the effects of the ice sheets have been especially prominent. Nevertheless, agreement of scholars on the chronology of the Pleistocene and the cultural stages during this epoch is far from complete. For this reason, Figure 4-1, which is designed to provide a convenient summary of about three million years, must be taken as an approximation of scholarly concensus, particularly in its lower portion, dealing with the earlier phases of the Pleistocene.

The geological epoch of the Pleistocene corresponds rather closely with the long cultural period of the Stone Age, characterized by remains consisting principally of stone (lithic) artifacts. Utilizing a typological approach in their analysis of stone technology, early students of prehistory established a sequence of three major subdivisions of the Stone Age: *Paleolithic* (Old Stone Age), *Mesolithic* (Middle Stone Age), and *Neolithic* (New Stone Age). The Paleolithic, in turn, is divided into Lower, Middle, and Upper Paleolithic periods. The cultural activities of the Lower Paleolithic are dated from Basal, Lower, and Middle Pleistocene, spanning a period of perhaps as much as three million years. Middle and Upper Paleolithic periods are usually associated with Upper Pleistocene deposits that have been dated from about 130,000 years ago to the end of the last glaciation (Würm III), about 11,000 years ago. The greatest advances in culture occurred during the last 12,000 years, beginning with the Mesolithic.

TOOLS AND TOOLMAKING IN THE PALEOLITHIC AGE

Although nearly all of the artifacts obtained from early Paleolithic sites were manufactured from stone, one must assume that other, more perishable materials would also have made ideal tools. Wood, for example, was plentiful in many areas of the Old World and was easily workable. In addition, some of the skeletal parts of animals likewise would have provided a source of suitable implements. Raymond A. Dart (1949) is convinced that the earliest tools were made from the bones, teeth, and horns of animals. On the basis of an analysis of materials left behind by extinct southern African hominids, belonging to the now well-documented genus *Australopithecus*, he argues that the long bones from the upper part of antelopes' forelimbs would have made ideal clubs, and their horns excellent punches. A number of scholars have questioned whether many of the bone tools identified by Dart were in fact tools, for given the crudity of all australopithecine implements, it is difficult to arrive at firm identifications. However, we need not doubt that bone and other workable materials were utilized by many early prehistoric groups. The chief advantage of animal skeletal remains is that they do not need much if any modification to serve as tools.

The earliest stone tools found in Paleolithic sites were either ready-made or at best were fashioned haphazardly. The experienced archaeologist can generally detect certain characteristics that mark them as used or produced by humans rather than naturally formed and deposited. For example, when such primitive tools are found to be of stone that does not occur naturally at or in the proximity of the site, it is most likely that they were brought in by those who made use of them. In some cases, such early tools may be found associated with other evidence that tends to corroborate further their human use. Almost invariably, these earliest modified stone tools were fashioned from river-worn pebbles ranging in size from a small egg to a human fist.

The earliest stone tools, made from pebbles, served as crude choppers. Flakes were struck off a stone until the core approximated the desired shape. (Courtesy of The American Museum of Natural History)

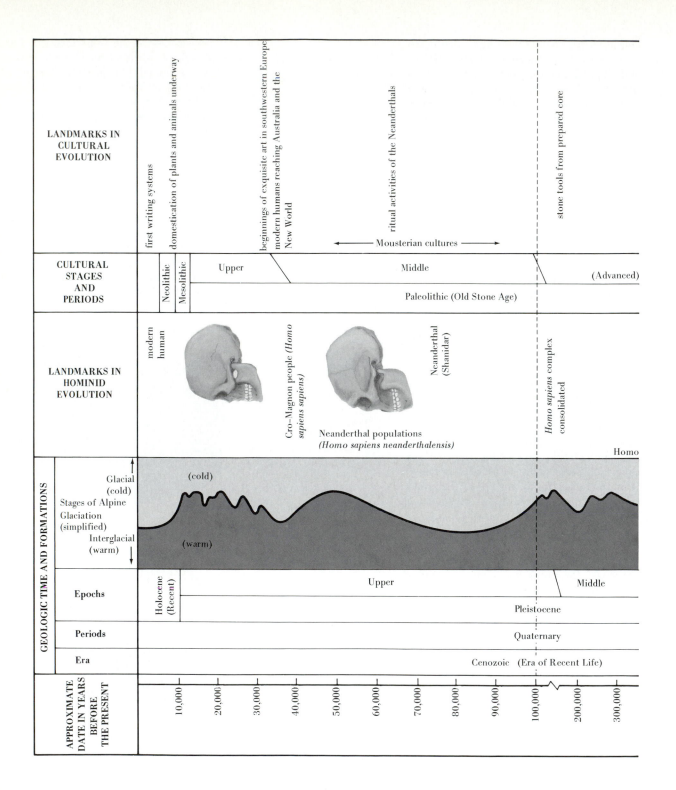

| | | | | | | | | | | | | | | | | |

LANDMARKS IN CULTURAL EVOLUTION

first writing systems

domestication of plants and animals underway

beginnings of exquisite art in southwestern Europe

modern humans reaching Australia and the New World

ritual activities of the Neanderthals

stone tools from prepared core

← Mousterian cultures →

CULTURAL STAGES AND PERIODS

Neolithic | Mesolithic | Upper | Middle | (Advanced)

Paleolithic (Old Stone Age)

LANDMARKS IN HOMINID EVOLUTION

modern human

Cro-Magnon people (*Homo sapiens sapiens*)

Neanderthal (Shanidar)

Homo sapiens complex consolidated

Neanderthal populations (*Homo sapiens neanderthalensis*)

Homo

GEOLOGIC TIME AND FORMATIONS

Glacial (cold)
Stages of Alpine Glaciation (simplified)
Interglacial (warm)

(cold)

(warm)

Epochs

Holocene (Recent) | Upper | Middle

Pleistocene

Periods

Quaternary

Era

Cenozoic (Era of Recent Life)

APPROXIMATE DATE IN YEARS BEFORE THE PRESENT

10,000 20,000 30,000 40,000 50,000 60,000 70,000 80,000 90,000 100,000 200,000 300,000

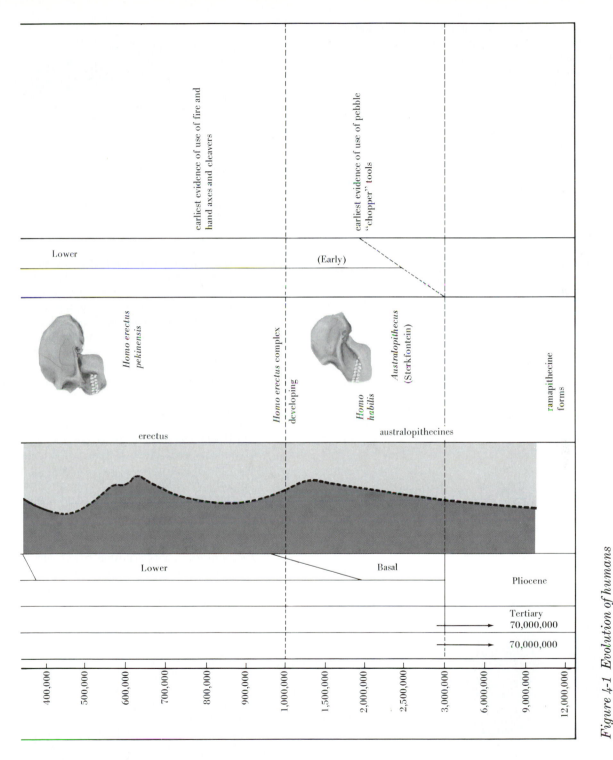

Figure 4-1 Evolution of humans

*The beginning of the Mesolithic aligns with 12,000 B.P. (before the present), the beginning of the Neolithic with 10,000 B.P., and the beginning of the Holocene with 11,000 B.P. But it must be emphasized that these dates are only approximate. The main problem is that the onsets of the Mesolithic and the Neolithic were later in the northern regions than in the south, and whatever dates are chosen for a table of this sort are therefore inevitably arbitrary.

earliest evidence of use of fire and hand axes and cleavers

earliest evidence of use of pebble "chopper" tools

Lower

(Early)

Homo erectus pekinensis

Homo erectus complex developing

Homo habilis

Australopithecus (Sterkfontein)

ramapithecine forms

erectus

australopithecines

Lower

Basal

Pliocene

Tertiary 70,000,000

70,000,000

| 400,000 |
| 500,000 |
| 600,000 |
| 700,000 |
| 800,000 |
| 900,000 |
| 1,000,000 |
| 1,500,000 |
| 2,000,000 |
| 2,500,000 |
| 3,000,000 |
| 6,000,000 |
| 9,000,000 |
| 12,000,000 |

Of the two common methods of shaping stone, the one that involves *percussion* is unquestionably the older. Using either a fixed rock or boulder as an anvil to strike a suitable pebble against or a hammerstone to strike such a pebble, early humans produced rather crude all-purpose implements (see Figure 4-2). Referred to as *core tools*, because they were produced by striking flakes from a stone until the original lump approximated the desired shape and size, these earliest recognizable manufactured implements in all probability served as choppers. Such chopping tools have been found in early Pleistocene deposits in Africa, but specimens of lesser age have also been uncovered in temperate parts of Europe, Southeast Asia, and China. Tools of the same general kind have been found in New World deposits and may well represent a basic toolmaking technique introduced into the New World across the Bering Strait.

Figure 4-3 Baton technique

A baton or billet of bone or wood permits greater control in striking off flakes as the desired core tool is shaped.

A greater degree of control was achieved by a later variant of *percussion flaking*, in which the striking was done by means of a cudgel of wood or bone. Some specimens produced by this method—frequently referred to as the *baton technique* (see Figure 4-3)—date back to at least a half-million years ago. The numerous massive hand axes and cleavers, both core tools produced by either the anvil or the baton technique and usually found together, range in time from about 750,000 years ago up until the onset of the Upper Paleolithic; and below 45° north latitude they are widely distributed throughout the Old World as far east as the Bay of Bengal (see Figure 4-4). To improve the cutting edge of the hand axes, their makers eventually began to flatten the core by trimming it on both sides, producing what the archaeologists refer to as a *bifacial core tool*, or *biface*. There is no doubt that some of the flakes struck off the core turned out to be a handy size and of sufficient sharpness to be put to use for more delicate activities than the substantial axes or cleavers had been designed for.

By about 150,000 years ago, another innovation began to contribute significantly to the improvement of stone tools—the method of preparing a core for the crucial final blow by carefully trimming it to resemble a tortoise shell. A brisk blow then removed a distinctive flake, which was used

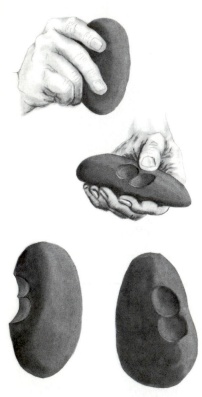

Figure 4-2 Percussion method

The oldest and simplest method of fashioning tools is by direct stone-on-stone percussion. This technique does not permit much control over the form of the finished product.

Chopping-tool
tradition

Hand-axe
tradition

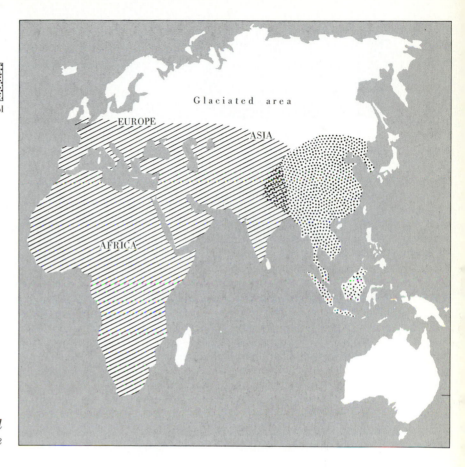

Glaciated area

EUROPE

ASIA

AFRICA

*Figure 4-4 Distribution of tool
traditions during the Pleistocene*

*Two typical forms of a bifacial core tool,
commonly known as a hand axe, from
the ancient quarries of St. Acheul in
northern France. (Courtesy of The
American Museum of Natural History)*

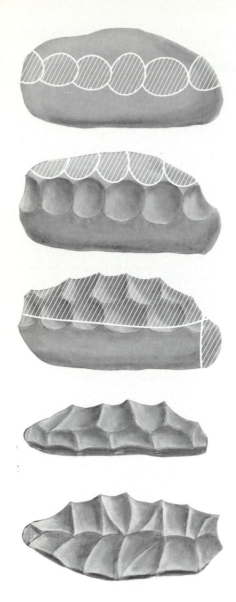

Figure 4-5 Levalloisian method

Distinctive tools were produced by early humans from carefully prepared tortoise-shaped cores by the Levalloisian technique. The main stages in the manufacture of a point are shown here, with the broken lines indicating the areas where the original stone has been trimmed and struck.

as a point for hunting weapons. This technique, known as *Levallois(ian)*, yielded some of the earliest manufactured items of delicate beauty and may well have been the first attempt at mass production (see Figure 4-5).

The second general method of stone toolmaking was an innovation most likely dating back to at least fifty thousand years ago and foreshadowing the elaborate tool kit of the Upper Paleolithic hunters. Known as *pressure flaking*, it consisted of pressing a pointed implement of bone, wood, or stone against a stone until a flake of desired shape was forced off. The greater degree of precision and control attainable with this method of flaking resulted in both more differentiated and more finely made tools.

AUSTRALOPITHECINES:
THE FIRST TOOLMAKERS

The stoneworking traditions that we have briefly surveyed provide a general background for the consideration of the subsistence patterns forming the basis of the technological system. Following Braidwood (1960a), Karl W. Butzer has classified these adaptive patterns into three broad subsistence levels: unspecialized food collecting, specialized hunting and food gathering, and primary food producing (1971:405–406).

The Lower Paleolithic was characterized by a pattern of unspecialized food collecting. At the lowest level of subsistence in this category, frequent shifting of camp must have been necessary as the immediate environment was exploited, and the technology must have evidenced little if any standardization of tools. The adaptation of the australopithecines would fall within the range of this subsistence pattern. J. Desmond Clark has summarized their adaptation thus:

The picture that now emerges . . . is one of small-brained, bipedal tool-makers, spread widely across the continent [of

Africa] and living in small but variable, highly social, open groups existing by collecting vegetable foods and by organized hunting, the proceeds of which were shared with the other members of the group. The success of this behavioural adaptation lay in the way the learned skills of tool-making were transmitted from parent to offspring and the increasing experimental use to which the tools were put (Clark 1970:75).

The evidence for such a reconstruction of the australopithecine life style has been reinforced by the productive excavations of Mary and Louis S. B. Leakey at Olduvai Gorge in East Africa. Clark is convinced that the testimony of the Olduvai finds suggests tool kits designed for domestic activities rather than for use as weapons. Undoubtedly, sticks and stones would have been used for protection, but this may not have been their primary function. At one particular Olduvai site a small concentration of cultural debris, covering an oval area about 300 square feet, distinctly marks such a living space. The location of the site and the distribution of the debris within and around it suggest the possibility of its use as a home base. The objects uncovered and the availability of resources such as vegetation, water, and game indicate that the site was frequently occupied for several days or possibly even a more extended period of time.

The debris, consisting of a variety of bashing stones, choppers, and flake scrapers, provides clear evidence that the australopithecines possessed a basic knowledge of stoneworking techniques. The evidence is so

Our understanding of the evolution of the genus of modern humans has been greatly enhanced by the excavations of Louis Leakey in Tanzania's Olduvai Gorge. (Mohamed Amin/Keystone)

astounding, in fact, that some scholars have labeled the late form of the gracile *Australopithecus africanus* as belonging to a separate species, *Homo habilis*, or "handy" human. Their artifacts could have served a variety of uses. The bashing stones would have been effective for smashing bone, working skin, opening nuts, and preparing fibrous plant material that would otherwise have been inedible. The chopper tools could well have provided an excellent means for sharpening a digging stick, essential in gathering roots and catching burrowing animals (Clark 1970:69–70).

The social unit of the australopithecines, according to Clark, very likely consisted of two or three families. A home base would have been a necessity for these hominids, whose young required a longer period of care and nurture than those of other higher primates. Some division of labor may have been present, and sharing of food was undoubtedly an important aspect of their rudimentary social life. Nevertheless, the impact of australopithecine technology on the environment must have been minimal.

THE COMING OF TRUE HUMANS

A second phase in the cultural evolution of the Lower Paleolithic is reflected in the adaptation of *Homo erectus* and, toward the end of the period, of early *Homo sapiens* populations. Remains of both species, uncovered in tropical and temperate zones of Africa, Europe, China, and Java, show significant advancement from the adaptation of the australopithecines, who appear to have been restricted to tropical and semi-tropical areas. Although this second phase is also characterized by unspecialized food collecting, there is convincing evidence for such group activity as selective gathering of plants and selective hunting of large game animals. Technologically, tools became standardized, with the increasing employment of flaking techniques playing an important role. For example, flake tools, with their sharp cutting edges, would have greatly increased efficiency in butchering animals. Various locations within a campsite must have been used for specific activities, such as toolmaking, butchering, constructing crude shelters for temporary occupation, and so on.

Early humans in China   Among the best-known sites documenting the cultural process of hominization are those in the People's Republic of China, Spain, and France. Excavations in the caves near the village of Choukoutien, about twenty-five miles southwest of Peking, began in 1921 and have since then produced a wealth of evidence for the subsistence patterns of one variety of *Homo erectus*. It appears that this early true human, formerly referred to as Peking man (*Sinanthropus pekinensis*), arrived in the area from Southeast Asia at least 400,000 years ago. The Choukoutien caves, conveniently located near a river and overlooking a grassy plain, were used as shelter for several hundred thousand years. In mental capacity and cultural complexity, *Homo erectus*, "upright" human, clearly surpassed the ancestral australopithecines.

That these cave dwellers had been making use of fire for a very long period of time is attested by ashes piled 22 feet high over one particular hearth. The bottoms of their caves were found to be thickly littered with many thousands of stone tools and tool fragments, charred bones of animals, and fire-hardened tips of antlers and points of wooden spears, some of the deposits well over 150 feet deep. The tools found belong to a crude chopper tool industry and were made largely from brought-in quartz and greenstone. Extensive faunal remains have been recovered, including insectivores, numerous rodents, both small and large carnivores, and rhinoceroses. But the Choukoutien cave dwellers' favorite fare would seem to have been deer meat, bones from deer being by far the most numerous found there. Since many of these animals do not naturally live in or frequent caves, the cave dwellers must have been proficient hunters. Whether they depended mainly on weapons, pitfalls, or the use of fire, or a combination of all of these methods, we cannot tell.

An intriguing question is posed by the presence of crushed or charred long bones and human skulls bashed in at the base, all indicating the practice of cannibalism. Whether this practice was ritualistic or was forced upon the cave dwellers by occasional famine (or whether they simply found human flesh to their liking), is impossible to ascertain.

A second set of sites is at Torralba and nearby Ambrona, about 100 miles northeast of Madrid, Spain. Some ninety years ago, while digging a trench for a water main near Torralba, workers uncovered several huge animal bones a few feet below the surface of a valley slope. In the early 1900s, a local nobleman who also happened to be an amateur archaeologist made an excavation and in the course of several years gathered a collection of fossils, among them the remains of at least two dozen elephants. More important, the site also proved to contain implements of stone, bone, and wood, as well as other indications of human activity. Yet

*Early humans
in the
Mediterranean*

not until 1961 was a systematic excavation of Torralba begun, this time by an American team of archaeologists led by F. Clark Howell. Although the explorations at Torralba, and at a second site about a mile away at Ambrona, are far from complete, the importance of these sites is already established. Even though no human fossils have as yet been found in either locality, careful reconstruction of past events on the basis of the technological level characteristic of the sites and the dates established for them gives us a surprisingly good picture of the activities of a *Homo erectus* group operating in the area at least 300,000 years ago.

At the time we are considering, the climate of central Spain was considerably cooler and wetter than it is now. The valley bottom of Torralba was a swampy meadow bordered by pine-covered slopes. As such it served as a natural seasonal migration route for herbivorous animals—elephants, horses, cattle, and deer.

The rich assemblages of stone tools from Torralba and Ambrona were developed from cores, flakes, and chips. The tool inventories include bifaces, notably hand axes and cleavers, chopping tools, different types of scrapers, notched and toothed artifacts

Elephant bones from the Homo erectus *site of Ambrona, Spain. Although no human fossils have yet been discovered from this locality, the people who once lived here employed a variety of stone tools, hunted large game, and used fire. (F. Clark Howell)*

made from flakes, borers, and hammerstones (Howell 1966). Stone tools were produced from a variety of materials, in particular quartzite, limestone, and flint. Several hundred bone fragments and tusk tips of elephants, chipped or trimmed into pointed forms, were found among the stone tools. About three dozen pieces of wood, some showing signs of wear or pointing, were scattered about the sites, as were also several pieces of charcoal. In addition, thousands of fossil bones have been recovered. One small region alone contained the broken remains of about thirty elephants, some two dozen wild horses and red deer, and a number of wild oxen and rhinoceroses.

The association of such quantities of animal bones with a wide assortment of tools is interesting enough, but there are some tantalizing bits of additional evidence. For example, in one of the excavated areas, much of the left side of a large elephant lies with what would have been the skin side up, but the right side, which one could have expected to find directly beneath, is missing. Thus, although the bones at first sight appeared to be in their natural position, the intriguing possibility exists that these prehistoric hunters went to the trouble of reassembling part of an elephant skeleton. If this was not the case, what had happened to the bones of the right side, which could logically have been expected to lie beneath those of the exposed left side? If the bones were indeed reassembled, for what reason would this have been done? Moreover, at one Ambrona site, massive elephant leg bones and tusks were uncovered that had been placed end to end to form a straight row some twenty feet in length, with additional elephant bones laid at right angles to this row. The fact that artifacts recovered from neighboring excavation sites are significantly different adds still another facet to the enigma, suggesting that different activities took place in the two areas.

What all of this evidence points to is that these must have been big-game hunters who went about their business very efficiently and systematically. The distribution of charcoal suggests that they may have made deliberate use of fire in hunting, either lighting torches or setting grass afire to stampede elephants into the swamp in order to render them defenseless for the kill. Butchering and meat processing may have taken place in separate areas. The significance of the row of bones will probably remain a mystery. One hypothesis that was initially suggested is that it might have served as a bridge across a swampy area, but this theory was later discarded when it was established that no swamp had ever existed there. An expression of a ritual practice cannot be excluded; but a practical function, such as a structure supporting a shelter, is probably more likely.

One is led to extrapolate even further. Hunting elephants under the circumstances just described required not only a fair amount of planning but a great deal of human energy. A small band of fifty-odd people—roughly the size of many documented groups that derive subsistence from hunting and collecting—would probably have been incapable of staging a slaughter of such magnitude unless several bands had joined together. Making plans for such an enterprise would have been difficult without a fairly serviceable means of communication, indicating that the hunters possessed at least a full-blown gestural language if not a rudimentary oral one. In short, there seems to be no question that the early humans at Torralba and Ambrona must have employed considerable forethought in pursuing their rather specialized activity of wholesale big-game hunting.

The most recent discovery, and in many ways the most revealing, was made in France at Nice in the mid-1960s (de Lumley 1969). It came about by accident as bulldozers began to excavate for the foundations of a fashionable new apartment house on Terra Amata, a dead-end street overlooking the Mediterranean. As the evidence was analyzed, it became increasingly clear that a *Homo erectus* band of about two dozen individuals enjoyed an annual sojourn on the Riviera some 350,000 years ago. There are indications that for eleven consecutive seasons the group spent a brief period at this particular location on the top of a sand dune below a limestone cliff, with a view of the sea. They appear to have arrived in June (the fossilized feces of the visitors contain the pollen of plants blossoming at that time of the year) and proceeded to erect an oval-shaped dwelling, with walls made of saplings reinforced by stones, and then to light a fire on the floor of their temporary shelter.

Near the site of the original discovery, remains of additional huts were found at two separate locations. Altogether, nearly thirty-five thousand objects have been recovered from the area, but unfortunately no human bones were among them. We can be sure, though, that the visitors ate in a style appropriate to their choice campsite, for their menu included elephant, deer, wild boar, birds, turtles, fish, oysters, and other animals. With the remains of these feasts were found an assortment of cleavers, choppers, scrapers, spear points, and tools made from bones.

A special bonus, in addition to the clear evidence of huts, was the discovery of several pieces of red ocher, the preserved footprint of an adult human, and a spherical imprint of some object that may well have been a vessel of some sort. If our speculations concerning Torralba and Ambrona may seem almost a flight of fancy, the Terra Amata site serves as solid confirmation that the march toward modern humanity was indeed proceeding.

THE NEANDERTHALS

Although the Middle Paleolithic humans continued to subsist by selective hunting and gathering, there is the suggestion of the beginning of regional specialization in the exploitation of resources. This change in subsistence patterns and the tendency to-

ward semisedentary settlements herald a third phase in the adaptation of unspecialized hunting and gathering populations. Improved habitation sites were occupied for extended periods, abandoned when resources of an area diminished, and then reoccupied if a group returned to the same locality.

There is also evidence of specialization in the manufacture of stone tools. The inventory of tools in Middle Paleolithic sites increases, with over sixty distinct types of artifacts put to as many specialized uses. In addition, regional specialization may be seen in that contemporaneous sites exhibit distinctive tool kits, reflecting their occupants' adaptation to different microenvironments within a particular region or from one region to another.

The reconstruction of the general features of Middle Paleolithic cultural traditions is based on the interpretation of Mousterian sites, associated between ninety thousand and forty thousand years ago with the well-known Neanderthals, members of the species *Homo sapiens* (subspecies *neanderthalensis*).[2] The term *Mousterian* refers to a tool tradition first described for Le Moustier, a cave site in Dordogne, France, and characterized by the extensive use of flake tools struck from cores prepared by the Levalloisian technique and then retouched into the desired shape. This method of manufacture made it possible to fabricate a variety of tools using a single core. However, bifaces made in the earlier, the so-called *Acheulean*, tradition continue to be found alongside. While most of the known Neanderthal sites are in Europe, some have been discovered as far away as in China and central Africa.

The quality of Mousterian tools has been questioned by some prehistorians who felt that they represented a deterioration in stoneworking techniques. This judgment was in part based on comparisons with

[2]The name derives from the Neander Valley (*Neandert[h]al*) near Düsseldorf, Germany, where remains were discovered in 1856.

Tools of the advanced Mousterian industry found at Neanderthal sites have carefully retouched edges. The points shown here were made from flakes. (Courtesy of The American Museum of Natural History)

highly refined Acheulean bifacial tools from the Middle Pleistocene. Yet the development of an industry based on flake tools must be recognized as a significant advancement. In the words of Grahame Clark and Stuart Piggott:

Even the most perfectly finished hand-axe represented no more than the culmination of a process of refining on the primitive chopper-tool. By contrast, the production of complete implements at a single blow from cores previously prepared so as to ensure that flakes when detached conformed to desired patterns was something new, something which marked a further extension of human foresight. Moreover, since it was possible to strike off a series of flakes by rejuvenating the same core, the technique was economical both of labour and of raw material. Even more important, the flakes so formed could easily be shaped by a simple retouch into a variety of forms, so that in place of the all-purpose hand-axe it was a simple matter to fabricate a whole range of tools adapted to specific functions (Clark and Piggott 1965:55).

The abundance of specialized tools such as sidescrapers in European Neanderthal sites strongly supports the contention that Middle Paleolithic hunters had developed techniques for cleaning and working skins, which would have been essential in the preparation of covers for shelters as well as of the necessary clothing for survival in the colder regions. We know that the sites of these hunters have an accumulation of bones from such large animals as the woolly mammoth, an excellent source of meat and skin. Their proficiency in hunting is also indicated by the bones of fish and of fowl.

In addition to hunting excursions from semisedentary settlements, Middle Paleolithic populations exploited marginal areas of Europe by following hunted animals on their seasonal migratory paths. In Africa, the success of these hunters and gatherers is attested to by the fact that much of the continent had been occupied by this time. Even the fringes of the tropical rain forests, which prior to this period had been impenetrable, were being exploited.

Beginnings of ritual behavior

One of the most intriguing topics of speculation about the Middle Paleolithic cultures has centered on the evidence for magical-religious ritual behavior among the Neanderthals. One is the bear cult, documented in numerous caves but most dramatically in the tunnellike cavern of Drachenloch in the Swiss Alps, explored some sixty years ago. Several stone chests of carefully arranged skulls and leg bones of cave bears were found, but the most astonishing was a rock-lined pit, sunk into the cave floor and covered by a massive stone slab, that contained seven bear skulls, all facing the cave entrance. The full significance of this and similar discoveries is left to our imagination—the Neanderthals must have found these large and ferocious bears, who also dwelled in caves and stood on their hind legs, exceedingly awesome. It is likely that the hunting of this animal, now extinct, was associated with some sort of widespread and powerful magic.

That the Neanderthals were contemplating matters far removed from the material aspects of their hunting way of life is even more convincingly revealed by their elaborate funeral practices. Once again, the evidence is readily available. In a cave near La Ferrassie in France, the remains of two adults and four children were found buried in shallow graves. The head of the man had been protected by a stone slab; the woman's body was tightly flexed. The skull of one of the children had been placed several feet from the body and overlaid by a slab of limestone. The underside of the slab was marked with scattered pairs of roughly hemispherical indentations deliberately ground into the stone.

A still more unexpected find was made at Shanidar cave in the mountains of northern Iraq. Some sixty thousand years ago, a male whose skull had been badly crushed was buried there, with wild flowers placed both under the body and around it. Microscopic analysis of the fossil pollen was able to tell us even the species of flowers with which the mourners had bidden him a final farewell.

Findings of this sort along with others—a variety of grave goods buried with the dead, even half a dozen pairs of goat horns surrounding a child—have helped to revise sharply the earlier image of the Neanderthals as slumped and hairy brutes whose existence did nothing at all to grace human ancestry. Quite the contrary, the evidence clearly shows that the Neanderthals were people with well-formed beliefs in an afterlife and an abiding concern for those among their fellows who were claimed by death. "No longer," wrote the discoverer of the Shanidar funeral flowers, Ralph S. Solecki, "can we deny the early men the full range of human feelings and experience" (1971:250).

THE CRO-MAGNONS

The Cro-Magnons derive their name from a rock-shelter near Les Eyzies in a limestone plateau of southwestern France, where some of the best-known sites left by these groups are located. But it would be a mistake to conclude that southwestern Europe has a special claim on Cro-Magnons. By around 16,000 B.C., there was no continent that would not have been well-traveled by the bands of humans of this type—fully modern in the same sense we consider ourselves modern (*Homo sapiens sapiens*). They managed to adapt fully to arctic as well as tropical regions, and the distinctive varieties of their different populations foreshadowed the physical variations of more recent and contemporary mankind.

The Cro-Magnons appear to have supplanted the European Neanderthals about thirty-five thousand years ago, but the exact geographic and biological whereabouts of their origin are still the subject of unresolved scholarly debate. There are several possibilities. One hypothesis holds that fully modern humans developed in the Near East and then migrated to Europe. Recent fossil finds in the Near East indeed attest to the presence of hybrid or transitional Neanderthals there some forty thousand to forty-five thousand years ago. According to other theories, these Cro-Magnons evolved simultaneously in several locations of the Old World, including Europe and the Near East. Regardless of the hypothesis preferred, other questions remain: did the Cro-Magnons displace the European Neanderthals forcibly, or did they absorb them by interbreeding?

Be this as it may, they ushered in a cultural period now known as the Upper Paleolithic, dating roughly from thirty-five thousand to ten thousand years ago. Their subsistence derived from specialized hunting and food gathering, closely tuned to the seasonal and local resources of their far-flung habitation sites.

The Cro-Magnons were superb hunters and master stoneworkers. To increase the range and velocity of their spears, they made use of a device known as a spear-thrower. With the help of their effective weapons, traps, fire, and above all their quick minds, they hunted a variety of animals both singly and on a gigantic scale, as fossil bones of hundreds of mammoths in central European sites and of about ten thousand wild horses at the bottom of a high cliff in east-central France eloquently testify. Their specialties were what are called *blades*—very thin flakes produced in many varieties by the technique of chisel flaking—and *burins*—implements characterized by strong chisel points. Burins were evidently used as cutting and engraving tools for work with wood, bone, antler, and ivory. Cro-Magnons used needles and awls for a variety of domestic tasks, including sewn skin clothes, and—as indicated in a central European open-air site—they burned coal in ovens in order to fire clay figurines as early as twenty-six thousand years ago. It is more than likely that they began to use bows and arrows and to weave baskets, even though the intervening millennia have not been kind to the perishable materials from which these would have been made. But it is their exquisite art that has earned them an incontestable place in the history of the finest human accomplishments.

To do even partial justice to the representative examples of Upper Paleolithic works of art would require an entire book of photographs and text. These prolific artists left an incredibly rich record of their efforts, including pieces of both portable art and art permanently attached in place; art geometric, abstract, naturalistic, and daringly stylized; painted, carved, engraved, and sculpted; in stone, clay, bone, ivory, and antler; both delicate and monumental (for example, a forty-foot-long frieze portraying animals of the hunt).

Especially striking among the portable objects are the so-called Venuses, which were modeled in stone, clay, or ivory. Generally only a few inches high, they are female figures with greatly exaggerated breasts, bellies, and thighs. A widely held assumption is that they served as fertility symbols. Equally stunning are delicate carvings of animals, many ingeniously captured in characteristic motion that also happened to fit the lines of a reindeer antler or an ivory tusk.

Paintings on walls or ceilings of caves

*Upper
Paleolithic art*

were done with mineral pigments, various hues of brown predominating. What is especially interesting is that many of the paintings were executed in places difficult of access and submerged in total darkness. Vessels hollowed out of stone to hold grease were used to illuminate the recesses of caves so that the artist, assisted by helpers, could depict leaping cows and boars, running horses, fleeing deer, and charging bisons—sometimes tens of such animals, life-sized, on a single "canvas."

There is obviously no longer any question that beliefs concerning the supernatural among the Cro-Magnons were elaborate and complex. But even in this case, the lack of direct evidence must inevitably lead to speculation. If the numerous representations of animals were not intended for the public eye—as they obviously could not be—their function must have been ritual, magical. Drawing on ethnographic evidence available for recent groups deriving their subsistence from the hunt, the animals portrayed as pierced by spears and darts were almost certainly executed in the hope of achieving similar success in future hunting forays. Such a practice, based on the belief that a desired end can be brought about by imitating it beforehand, is labeled imitative magic. A similar magical purpose was probably served by the carving of the Venus figurines. The most dramatic example of magical art, one that has particularly excited the imagination of archaeologists, is a painting discovered in Les Trois-Frères Cave in the French Pyrenees. This painting, commonly referred to as "The Sorcerer," depicts a creature that is part human and part a combination of animals. The figure, which appears to be dancing, has the beard, legs, and feet of a human, the antlers of a stag, and the ears, face, front limbs, and tail of several other animals. Whether "The Sorcerer" was meant to represent a masked shaman during a hunting ritual, a god of the hunt, or some other being in touch with supernatural powers, we cannot say with any certainty.

The Venus of Willendorf, now at the Museum of Natural History in Vienna, is probably one of the best known pieces of Upper Paleolithic sculpture. Many other small female figures have been found in Europe, and some authorities have surmised that they were associated with fertility beliefs or rituals. (Museum of Natural History, Vienna)

Two bull bisons from the cave of Lascaux, France. In the deep recesses of caves, skillful Upper Paleolithic artists painted the various animals that they hunted. The location of these exquisite works of art has been a great aid to their preservation. (© Archives Photographique Paris/S.P.A.D.E.M.)

During the terminal phase of the Pleistocene, significant climatic changes occurred that profoundly altered the natural environment. Pollen analyses for various localities in Europe indicate a change in plant cover, with an increase in woodlands at the expense of the tundra. A number of species of large animals appear to have become extinct during this period—the woolly mammoth, the steppe bison, and the cave bear among them. Climatic factors without question played a part in the extinction of the large fauna, but efficient hunting techniques may have accelerated the process both directly and indirectly.

All of these environmental transformations have been suggested as the root cause of the impending shift from intensified food collecting to the development of a subsistence based on food production. This shift did not come about abruptly. The transitional period between the (late Upper) Paleolithic and the Neolithic is referred to as the Mesolithic and, for Europe, its characteristic features have been summarized by Lewis R. Binford as follows: a recession in the growth of the population centers of western Europe; a major change in the form of stone tools, favoring small geometric flints, the so-called *microliths;* a greater geographic variety in cultural remains suggesting more specific responses to local environmental conditions; a marked increase in the exploitation of aquatic resources and wild fowl; a trend toward the hunting of small game; and cultural degeneration, especially when compared to the manifestations of the exquisite art of the Upper Paleolithic (1968:317–318).

Not all scholars have agreed with Binford's characterizations. Karl Butzer, for example, is convinced that several features listed by Binford are but a continuation of trends well underway during the late Upper Paleolithic (1971:536–537). There is no question, however, that the specialized hunters of Europe began facing a major food crisis with the disappearance or out-migration of

The Mesolithic transition

the large game that had been in such plentiful supply in the times of their forebears. Yet interestingly enough, the revolutionary shift from food procurement to food production, which changed the pattern of adaptation that had existed for several million years, did not occur in Europe but in the Near East.

THE NEOLITHIC REVOLUTION

Although the cultural revolution we are about to discuss was utterly peaceful, its consequences have been nothing short of stupendous. The domestication of plants and animals provided the basis for exponential rates of technological, social, and ideological changes. A self-sufficient economy with a potential for generating large food surpluses, expanding sedentary populations, and stratified social organizations all have been linked to the development of farming during the Neolithic. The Neolithic also marks ever more profound changes in the relationship between humans and their natural environment. In short, for countless thousands of years human beings had accepted the capricious hospitality of the land; now they were about to take control of it.

Much of what we know about the origin of agriculture is based on recent excavations. Although the Near East has provided the major source of information on agricultural developments, there are reports of an independent center in Burma and adjacent areas. Further work in Asia should provide important comparative data. New World agriculture, of course, developed independently with quite different crop staples.

Earlier theories of the origins of domestication drew largely on environmental factors. Some scholars suggested that drying (desiccation), which occurred following the last glaciation, may have provided the necessary stimulus toward the adoption of a food-producing economy and forced human populations to concentrate in oases or by the banks of ever more precarious springs and streams. . . . Animals and men would be herded together round pools and wadis [gullies] that were growing increasingly isolated by desert tracts, and such enforced juxtaposition might almost of itself promote that sort of symbiosis between man and beast that is expressed in the word "domestication" (Childe 1928:42).

Recent excavations have convincingly disproved this desiccation, or oasis, theory, putting the inquiry on a more empirical basis.

The main challenge came from Robert J. Braidwood, whose patient work in the hilly flanks of the Fertile Crescent—an area in the Near East arching from the Mediterranean coast in the west around the Syrian Desert to Iraq in the east—produced valuable new clues. In his opinion, the causes were entirely cultural:

There is no need to complicate the story with extraneous "causes." The food-producing revolution seems to have occurred as the culmination of the ever increasing cultural differentiation and specialization of human communities. Around 8000 B.C. the inhabitants of the hills around the fertile crescent had come to know their habitat so well that they were beginning to domesticate the plants and animals they had been collecting and hunting (Braidwood 1960b:134).

While Braidwood may have put to rest the desiccation theory, he nevertheless did not address himself to the motivation that led to the changing of a subsistence basis that for countless thousands of years had served the hunting and gathering peoples so well. According to Binford (1968), the crucial selective pressure may have come from population shifts. The increase of population in a number of the areas of the Near East would have forced some groups to move into marginal areas where the additional demand for food strained already taxed resources.

Transplanting wild grains from their original homes could have provided the bare minimum necessary for the survival of the migrants in their new environment. On the other hand, such a manipulation of plants is unlikely to have occurred in those localities where the wild varieties of grains grew abundantly. According to this hypothesis, the first steps in domestication combined experimentation with types of seeds, and the development of methods of sowing. Sowing, of course, changes natural patterns of plant distribution and concentrates plants of the same species in a reduced area. Tilling, weeding, and guarding the plots against whatever factors endanger the potential yield would have come next.

The evidence for domestication of animals is more difficult to interpret, since skeletal changes in animals undergoing domestication are not as distinct as the genetic changes that occur in domesticated plants (especially large seed size). One might surmise that young animals captured during hunting were taken back to the village and raised either as pets or as a reserve food supply. Experience shows that many animals are capable of aiding in their own domestication. For instance, dogs—undoubtedly descended from the wolf—probably followed the moving bands as early as the Mesolithic or even before. They were tolerated in exchange for their services as sentinels and scavengers, which kept the camps guarded from unwanted visitors and free from disagreeable vermin attracted by meat caches and rotting discards. In time dogs would develop a close symbiotic relationship with humans.

Once the principle of domestication had been recognized—independently in various places—it was applied to many additional species. There is evidence that between 8500 and 1000 B.C. at least a score of animal species were domesticated. During the same period the list of plants that made their way into the human larder became even longer. Among the latter, einkorn and emmer (kinds of wheat) and barley were the first to be used.

JARMO: A NEOLITHIC FARMING COMMUNITY

The search for the origins of agriculture has centered in the nuclear area of the Near East, but as a result of the recent discoveries of Neolithic sites in adjacent regions, the boundaries may have to be extended as far west as Greece and eastward toward Afghanistan. Evidence of incipient cultivation and domestication, dated between 9500 and 7000 B.C., has been uncovered in sites attributed to the Natufian culture in the area bordering the eastern Mediterranean, where, in addition to the expected inventory of implements, there have been finds of flint sickle blades and grinding stones. By about 7000 B.C. food production by dry farming must have been well established in several

areas of the Near East, and the first farmers had settled in numerous small but permanent villages.

One such was Jarmo, a village in the eastern foothills of the Zagros Mountains of Iraq, which was excavated by a team led by Braidwood. The results of his investigations permit us to reconstruct a fairly complete picture of an early Neolithic village and the economy and life style of its inhabitants at about 7000 B.C. (Braidwood 1960b).

Some 150 people may have once lived at Jarmo in about two dozen rectangular houses. Walls were made of mud with straw used as a binder. The houses were surprisingly spacious, each containing several rooms and an open walled courtyard. They were equipped with doors, and each had an oven. Among the equipment uncovered were mortars and pestles, hoelike implements, and sickle blades not only of flint but also of obsidian, the nearest source of which was some 200 miles distant.

Charred seeds of wheat and barley provided not only a reliable means of dating but also evidence of fairly advanced domestication of cereals. In addition to remains of wild animals, snails, and wild plants— indicating that hunting and gathering continued to play a part in the villagers' daily round—bones of sheep and goats show that domesticated animals were kept. Crude weaving and the making of coarse pottery were among the villagers' activities. Their pottery would have supplemented handsome cups and bowls made of ground stone.

But not all of the objects were utilitarian. A great variety of figurines representing animals and pregnant women were found, as well as ornaments of stone and bone, and decorative shells suggesting trade reaching to the Persian Gulf.

The example of the inhabitants of Jarmo and like villages was not lost on the semi-sedentary groups with whom they came into contact. Agricultural food production spread from the well-watered uplands to the low-land steppes where irrigation began to be employed about 5500 B.C. and continued to

Jarmo, an early Neolithic settlement, shows that village life, including houses with mud walls and ovens, was well established in parts of the Middle East as early as 7000 B.C. (Wide World Photos)

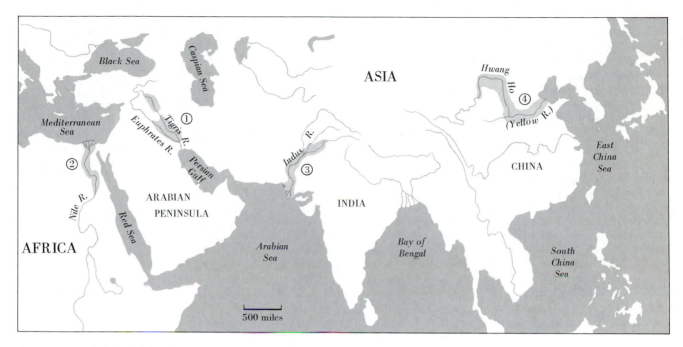

Figure 4-6 Old World urban civilizations, c. 4000–1000 B.C.

The main centers of ancient Old World urban civilizations arose in river valleys. While clusters of settlements were not limited to major river systems, it was the organizational potential of the state that made possible the complex forms of irrigation found in the locations indicated. Shown on the map are (1) the region between the Tigris and Euphrates rivers, where the first Mesopotamian city-states began to develop between 4000 B.C. and 3500 B.C.; (2) the valley of the Nile, where the ancient Egyptian cities rose soon after 3000 B.C.; (3) the valley of the Indus, with its Harappan civilization dating back to about 2500 B.C.; and (4) the Shang Dynasty civilization along the Yellow River, which began to flourish around 1600 B.C.

be used with increasing frequency and success.

As the Neolithic was reaching its climax, a new material began to make its appearance. First worked by cold-hammering and later melted and cast, copper ushered in both a new technological age and, more important, the incipient era of urbanization, with the first city-states developing in Sumer (see Figure 4.6). Although technically these were still prehistoric times—the art of writing, also a Near Eastern invention, was not to appear until about 3000 B.C.—the human world had now embarked on an inexorable course of ever-increasing social and cultural complexity.

REFERENCES

BINFORD, LEWIS R.
1968   Post-Pleistocene adaptations. In *New perspectives in archeology*. Sally R. Binford and Lewis R. Binford, eds. Chicago: Aldine. Pp. 313–341.

BRAIDWOOD, ROBERT J.
1960a Levels in prehistory: a model for the consideration of the evidence. In *Evolution after Darwin*, vol. II: *The evolution of man*. Sol Tax, ed. Chicago: The University of Chicago Press. Pp. 143–151.

1960b The agricultural revolution. *Scientific American* 203:3:130–148 (September).

BUTZER, KARL W.
1971 *Environment and archeology; an ecological approach to prehistory* (2nd ed.). Chicago: Aldine-Atherton.

CHILDE, V. GORDON
1928 *The most ancient East; the oriental prelude to European prehistory*. London: K. Paul, Trench Trubner.

CLARK, J. DESMOND
1970 *The prehistory of Africa.* London: Thames and Hudson.

CLARK, GRAHAME, AND STUART PIGGOTT
1965 *Prehistoric societies.* New York: Alfred A. Knopf.

DART, RAYMOND A.
1949 The predatory implemental technique of *Australopithecus. American Journal of Physical Anthropology* (n.s.) 7:1–38.

DE LUMLEY, HENRY
1969 A Paleolithic camp at Nice. *Scientific American* 220:5:42–50 (May).

HOWELL, F. CLARK
1966 Observations on the earlier phases of the European Lower Paleolithic. *American Anthropologist* 68:2 (Part 2):88–201.

SOLECKI, RALPH S.
1971 *Shanidar, the first flower people*. New York: Alfred A. Knopf.

Chapter 5

The New World:
culture history and
culture process[1]

In an early chapter of his history of the Aztec nation, the sixteenth-century Spanish chronicler Fray Diego Durán gives his opinion that

It also seems to me that it will be impossible to tell everything that has occurred in this New World, as it is such a large country. There are so many kingdoms, cities, and villages here, so many large towns where innumerable people lived, divided into many nations, ways of life, and languages, as well as dress and customs. The good and bad fortunes that befell a single one of these nations would be enough for one painstaking historian (Durán 1964:14).

[1]It is simply not possible in a chapter of this length to deal in equal detail with all the temporal and spatial manifestations of New World archaeology and culture history. Rather than provide a very superficial overview, we felt it wiser to stress some selected themes. In keeping with a central consideration throughout the book, we emphasize the regularities of process and cultural transformation in the New World, in particular such major shifts as the development of agriculture, the establishment of sedentary life, and the evolution of complex political and social structures.

If this was true of a portion of the New World shortly after its discovery, we can hardly hope to do much more than introduce the reader to the Native American past. The temporal and spatial frame of New World culture history taxes the imagination. We start with a length of human occupation of approximately thirty thousand years, time enough to allow for a broad range of cultural adaptations. In geographic terms, the area is immense: well over one-fourth of the earth's land surface spread over almost 140 degrees of latitude. The two continents offer virtually every variety of climate habitable by humans. Estimates on population at the time of first European contact vary considerably, but by the end of the fifteenth century the New World must have supported at least several million residents, according to some scholars as many as twenty-five million. The vast majority were concentrated in those areas where agriculture and sedentary life were well established—the high-culture areas of Mesoamerica (the southern half of Mexico and

Central America) and the central Andes. Taking the Western Hemisphere as a whole, we have to imagine thousands of different societies speaking a corresponding multitude of languages and organized in levels of complexity ranging from the simplest hunting and gathering bands to highly sophisticated states and empires (see Figure 5-1).

It may be thought that this conglomerate of tribes and nations hardly lends itself to a common approach. But granting all the diversity and complexity of New World cultures, the history of humankind in the Americas is a phenomenon of a special type. In contrast to the Old World, the New World is a region of relatively recent human occupation, allowing us to dispense with considerations of pre-*sapiens* humans, as well as with nearly three million years of cultural evolution referred to as the Lower Paleolithic in the Old World.

The earliest Americans were of East Asian origin, primitive hunting and gathering people who most likely crossed the Bering Strait when its floor lay temporarily exposed some thirty-five thousand years ago. We must assume that they were initially attracted to the new territories in the pursuit of game. The evidence points to multiple migrations by small bands over a substantial period of time rather than to a single massive population shift. Although some of these population movements and cultural influences are subject to the re-evaluation that always follows new findings, the Asian ancestry of American populations is not seriously in doubt. At the same time, we should recognize that the Arctic hardly constituted an easy passageway for people and ideas; it would be more valid to think of the northern wastes as serving as a sort of cultural filter.

This generalization held true for all the prehistoric bands who entered the New World via the northern route. While their technologies must of necessity have been sufficiently sophisticated to permit the exploitation of harsh arctic and subarctic en-

Peopling of the New World

vironments, for a long time their economic organization—geared to such exploitation—did not lend itself to the creation of complex societies. Phrased somewhat differently, the major human achievements in the New World—the domestication of plants and animals, the establishment of permanent settlements, the evolution of intricate political and economic systems—owe little, if anything, to external influences.

Seen in this light, the single most important phenomenon of New World culture history is that, once established in their new home, the inhabitants of the New World developed their distinctive styles of life essentially from their own resources. In order to maintain such a position it is not necessary to espouse a kind of anthropological Monroe Doctrine. One can even accept some degree of transoceanic contacts before 1492. However, it is important to consider such contacts in their proper perspective, that is, not as migrations or even as planned expeditions, but as an occasional boatload of men blown off course and driven onto an alien shore. That such luckless mariners would be allowed much of a say in local affairs is highly doubtful.[2]

[2]In recent years, a number of scholars have examined the archaeological, botanical, and cultural evidence for transpacific and transatlantic contacts between the Old World and the New World at different times from the Bering Strait migrations to Columbus's first voyage of discovery in 1492. Most professionals would now agree to the possibility of such contacts, and with respect to Norse contacts there need be no doubt; more problematic is the impact of such influences on New World cultures. Even if we grant that Chinese or Japanese sailors, Polynesian navigators, or Norse adventurers may have reached American shores, it is still necessary to evaluate the importance of these contacts. The test must be that of significant influence on the indigenous populations, and for this the evidence is scant, although in part the lack of decisive evidence may reflect gaps in our archaeological knowledge. Needless to say, anthropologists do not waste much time in debating whether it was Leif Ericson or Christopher Columbus who first discovered America or, for that matter, some unknown captain of a Chinese junk.

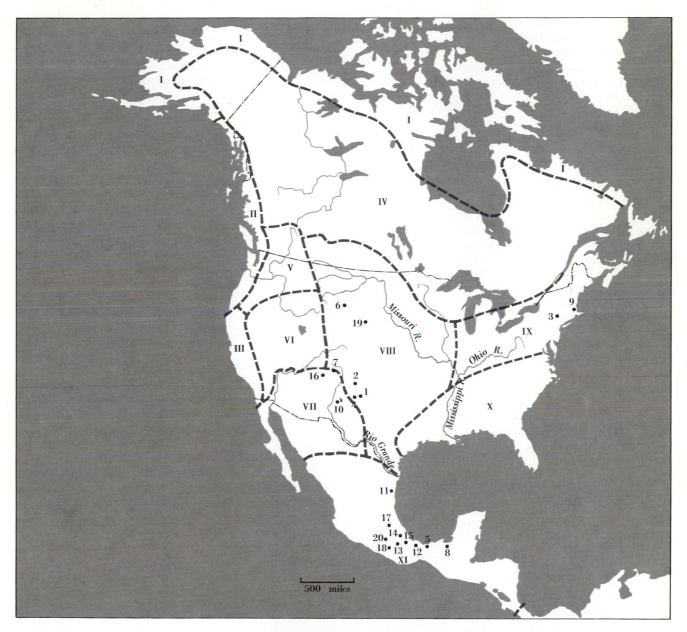

Figure 5-1 North American culture areas and selected locations

I Arctic	VII Southwest	1 Clovis, N.M.	8 Palenque, Mex.	15 Tlatelolco, Mex.
II Northwest Coast	VIII Great Plains	2 Folsom, N.M.	9 Plymouth Colony, Mass.	16 Tsaile, Ariz.
III California	IX Eastern Woodlands	3 Fort Orange (Albany), N.Y.	10 Sandia Cave, N.M.	17 Tula, Mex.
IV Subarctic	X Southeast	4 Fort Sumner, N.M.	11 Tamaulipas, Mex.	18 Tzintzuntzan, Mex.
V Plateau	XI Mesoamerica	5 La Venta, Mex.	12 Tehuacán Valley, Mex.	19 Wounded Knee, S.D.
VI Great Basin		6 Little Bighorn, Wyo.	13 Tenochtitlán, Mex.	20 Zamora, Mex.
		7 Mesa Verde, Colo.	14 Teotihuacán, Mex.	

Source: Robert F. Spencer and Elden Johnson, *Atlas for Anthropology* (Dubuque, Iowa: Wm. C. Brown Company, 1960) and Harold E. Driver and William C. Massey, "Comparative Studies of North American Indians," *Transactions of the American Philosophical Society*, n.s., vol. 47, pt. 2 (Philadelphia, 1957).

Given this isolation, the New World can be approached somewhat as a controlled experiment in cultural dynamics—an experiment of great complexity and long duration. It was common humanity and common needs that in the main accounted for the similarities between New World cultures and those from other continents.

THE NEW WORLD: EARLY ACCOUNTS AND INTERPRETATIONS

The isolation of the New World from the mainstream of Old World cultural development was far from evident to early European scholars. From the time of Columbus well into the nineteenth century, speculation on American origins was rife. While much of this speculation was fanciful, it is not so much the search for linkages and similarities that makes a great deal of the earlier scholarship barren, but rather the underlying assumption that the natives of the Americas lacked the capacity to develop their own civilizations. We may take as typical of this approach the early nineteenth-century theories on the origins of the Ohio Valley earthworks. The supposition was that an ancient and gifted race, the Mound Builders, quite distinct from the contemporary Indian tribes, had been responsible for building the ceremonial centers reported by settlers. In 1834 Josiah Priest asked in his *American Antiquities and Discoveries in the West:*

Who would believe for a moment, that the common Indians of the West, who are derived in part from the wandering hordes of the northern Tartar race of Asia, were the authors of these works; bearing the marks of so much labor and scientific calculation in their construction? It cannot be (Priest 1834:161).

At about the same time, Patrick Walker, the leader of the British expedition to the ancient Maya site of Palenque in Mexico, gave as his strong impression

Aerial view of the Great Serpent Mound, Ohio. This mound, clearly depicting the form of a serpent, belongs to the Hopewell cultural tradition, which flourished in the American Midwest more than one thousand years ago. (Photograph Courtesy of Museum of the American Indian, Heye Foundation)

that the ruins had been "constructed according to one undeviating model"—that of ancient Egyptian architecture (Pendergast 1967:175).

In penetrating American prehistory it was necessary not only to overcome such initial narrowness of vision but also to develop a whole range of new techniques and approaches. John L. Stephens, a pioneer observer and explorer of ancient Central American civilizations, was certainly correct in observing that "the ground was entirely new; there were no guide-books or guides; the whole was a virgin soil" (1841:119). While Stephens's reference was to a specific site, the statement was valid for the field as a whole; for unlike the pioneer Old World archaeologists who could count on some historical reference points, "history" was silent with respect to the New World.

A great deal of what we know today about the culture history of the Western Hemisphere has been learned in the course of the last hundred years. While scholars from various fields can claim credit for contributing to this expansion in knowledge, a critically important role has been played by archaeologists. Whenever possible, archaeologists use as the starting point of their investigations reports and chronicles of native societies at the time of their initial contact with Europeans. The period of initial contact with native American cultures is of particular importance in that it represents the first, and in some instances the last, opportunity for recording a way of life unaffected by European colonists. The information (which obviously must be handled with considerable care) is valuable not only because of what it tells us about the societies in question at a particular moment of time but as a baseline for interpretation of cultures known only from the archaeological record.

The chronicles and accounts written by the adventurers and colonists who first came into contact with the Indians were eagerly received in Europe. There is in much of the literature of discovery a quaint combination of the factual and the fantastic. Even Hernando Cortés (1485–1547), a man little given to fantasy, instructed his relative Francisco Cortés to press on with the conquest of the lands bordering the Pacific

because I am informed that down the coast . . . there are many provinces thickly inhabited by people and containing, it is believed, great riches, and that in these parts of it there is one which is inhabited by women, with no men, who procreate in the way which the ancient histories ascribe to the Amazons (Bolton 1952:3).

This quixotic flavor, especially pronounced in the Spanish chronicles, caused later scholars to question the validity of early European observers. The problem is that speculation and firsthand observation are often intermixed in the same volume.

Some scholars did shy away from wild speculation. José de Acosta, a Spanish missionary, hypothesized in 1590 that the inhabitants of the New World had originally crossed into America by way of northeast Asia, an opinion shared some two hundred years later by Thomas Jefferson, who pointed out that "if the two continents of Asia and America be separated at all, it is only by a narrow strait" (Jefferson 1964:96).

Without doubt, what most puzzled Europeans was the high cultures of Mesoamerica and the Andes. Other areas were initially less well known and, in any case, raised fewer problems. The Indians of eastern North America or the inhabitants of the Amazonian forests could be characterized as "savages" and were interesting merely as curiosities. In contrast, the civilizations of Mexico and Peru were not so easily explained away. They stirred both the imagination and the intellect and gave rise to a literature that for its vividness has seldom been surpassed. In part the quality of these writings (reasonably accurate on matters of observation) reflects the scholarship of the men who followed on the heels of conquest: the administrators and officials, the judges,

This representation of Tenochtitlán, the Aztec capital, by the Mexican painter Diego Rivera captures much of the grandeur of the Aztec Empire at its peak: the temple-topped pyramids, the warriors and courtiers around the emperor, and the bustling activity of the great market. (Editorial Photocolor Archives)

and perhaps most important of all, the missionaries. But even common soldiers were impelled to write down their experiences and record for posterity the wonders of this new world. Putting pen to paper some fifty years after the conquest of Mexico, the old soldier Bernal Díaz del Castillo could still conjure up all the awe and wonder of his first impression of the Aztec capital of Tenochtitlán. A party of Spaniards, in the company of the Aztec ruler Moctezuma, had climbed to the top of the highest temple of the city.

So we stood looking about us . . . and we saw the three causeways which led into Mexico . . . and we saw the bridges on the three causeways which were built at certain distances apart through which the water of the lake flowed in and out from one side to the other, and we beheld on that great lake a great multitude of ca-

noes, some coming with supplies of food and others returning loaded with cargoes of merchandise; and we saw that from every house of that great city and of all the other cities that were built in the water it was impossible to pass from house to house, except by drawbridges which were made of wood or in canoes; and we saw in those cities Cues [temples] and oratories like towers and fortresses and all gleaming white, and it was a wonderful thing to behold. . . .

After having examined and considered all that we had seen we turned to look at the great market place and the crowds of people that were in it, some buying and others selling, so that the murmur and hum of their voices and words that they used could be heard more than a league off. Some of the soldiers among us who had been in many parts of the world, in Constantinople, and all over Italy, and in Rome, said that so large a market place and so full of people, and so well regulated and arranged, they had never beheld before (Díaz del Castillo 1956:218–219).

This huge city set in the midst of a lake was the center of an empire stretching from the Gulf of Mexico to the Pacific. It was the focal point of trade with outlying provinces and tribute paid by subject populations, an administrative capital and religious center, the residence of thousands of artisans and specialists, and the court city and home of the ruler whom the Spaniards referred to as the "Emperor" of Mexico.

Virtually all Spanish commentators on Mexico described in considerable detail the great markets, elaborate trading networks, and specialist merchant classes. Aztec religious practices, including human sacrifice, were seldom neglected. For Peru, the picture is somewhat different. More than anything else it was the capacity of the Incas to control vast territories, in short their administrative skills and techniques of imperial organization, that impressed European observers. The territory of the Inca Empire was considerably larger than the lands under Aztec dominion, and while the Aztecs depended primarily on a system of indirect rule to control outlying areas (local princes were not deprived of their power so long as they accepted their dependence and were not tardy with tribute payments), the Inca system was much more centralized. Moreover, Inca policy favored the assimilation of conquered peoples, a goal that some early Spanish administrators also worked for. Pedro de Cieza de León, another Spanish soldier turned chronicler, writes of the Inca system with evident approval:

It should be well understood that great prudence was needed to enable these kings to govern such large provinces, extending over so vast a region, parts of it rugged and covered with forests, parts mountainous, with snowy peaks and ridges, parts consisting of deserts of sand, dry and without trees or water. These regions were inhabited by many different nations, with varying languages, laws and religions, and the kings had to maintain tranquillity and to rule so that all should live in peace and in friendship towards their lord (Cieza de León 1883:36).

These two New World superstates—those of the Incas and the Aztecs—had a number of features in common. They were both

The city of Machu Picchu guarded the eastern frontier of the Inca Empire. The site contains some exceptionally well-preserved terraces and fortifications. (Richard W. Wilkie)

conquest states, the most powerful political and military organizations in their respective areas. Economically, the whole edifice of empire—the administrative and ceremonial centers, the structure of classes, the specialists catering to the nobility and the state—rested on agricultural surpluses produced by hundreds of thousands of peasant farmers. At the apex of power stood the ruler: in Peru a living deity, in Mexico a monarch hedged about by taboos and not far short of divinity.

The ruling classes of both the Aztecs and the Incas indulged in the erection of temples and other monumental structures so typical of ancient empires. Architects designed, artisans decorated, and thousands of laborers hauled and carried stone blocks and other building materials in order to enshrine gods or provide fitting residences for kings, priests, and the nobility. Other arts besides architecture were well developed. Of particular interest to the Spaniards was the work in precious metals. But in contrast to the Old World, utilitarian metallurgy was rare, especially in the case of Mesoamerica, where work in metal was largely restricted to the production of decorative items.

The peoples of Mesoamerica were heirs to a long tradition of picture writing. While no such system was in use in the Andes, Inca officials used an elaborate system of numeration and accounts. In both areas, intellectual pursuits, including theology and astronomy, had a recognized place and were put to the service of the state. As one might expect, education was restricted to the upper levels of society.

DEVELOPMENTAL STAGES
OF NEW WORLD
CIVILIZATIONS

In order to facilitate interpretation and analysis, it is useful to organize the extensive data on the precontact New World in such a manner that two goals are met: the classification of phenomena of the same order or type for purposes of contrast and comparison, and the arrangement of the distinct types in such a manner as to shed light on the course of historical development—in short, to permit the tracing out of cultural evolution.

The idea that culture is evolutionary, that it follows a certain progression, is not novel. With respect to the New World, it appears as early as 1777 in William Robertson's *History of America*. The early evolutionary thought tended to be conceptually rigid (all societies were viewed as having passed through identical stages) and was not based on research in the field. Contemporary archaeologists utilize a more refined set of concepts, generally referred to as *developmental stages*. These are generalizations about stages of evolution based on archaeological and sociocultural evidence from a large variety of sites.

A number of factors enter into the definition of a stage, but, typically, emphasis is placed on such criteria as technology, economic base, political and social organization, and the degree of intellectual and artistic development. Clearly, since archaeologists must necessarily work mainly with material remains, information on all relevant factors is not always directly available. To give an example, we know much about the stone tools and weapons used by the earliest hunting groups in the Americas but have little direct evidence concerning their religious life. This is not to say that we must be satisfied with a collection of projectile points and other artifacts made of stone. The societies in question were necessarily small-scale and could not have had much in the way of social stratification or division of labor: everyone strong and healthy enough had to hunt or collect; there was no place for high priests or kings.

While authors vary somewhat in the terms that they apply to developmental stages, the following five, running in order from the earliest to the most recent, have a wide acceptance and embrace all of the Americas: Lithic, Archaic, Formative, Classic, and Postclassic (Caso 1953; Willey and

Figure 5-2 Development of New World civilizations

Chart showing the developmental stages of New World civilizations, with their approximate temporal ranges and geographic distribution.

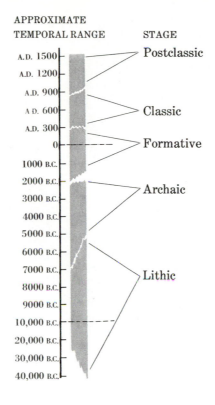

APPROXIMATE TEMPORAL RANGE	STAGE	NOTES
A.D. 1500	Postclassic	Terminates at the time of the Spanish Conquest. Applicable only to Mesoamerica and Peru.
A.D. 1200		
A.D. 900		
A.D. 600	Classic	Applicable only to Mesoamerica and Peru.
A.D. 300		
0	Formative	Terminal date of around A.D. 300 applies to Mesoamerica and Peru.
1000 B.C.		
2000 B.C.	Archaic	Became clearly established by 5000 B.C. In some areas, plant and animal domestication started during the second half of the Archaic.
3000 B.C.		
4000 B.C.		
5000 B.C.		
6000 B.C.		
7000 B.C.	Lithic	Terminated around 7000–5000 B.C., depending on the locality.
8000 B.C.		
9000 B.C.		
10,000 B.C.		May have begun as early as 40,000 B.C., but conservative authorities prefer a starting date of around 30,000–20,000 B.C.
20,000 B.C.		
30,000 B.C.		
40,000 B.C.		

Phillips 1958). The *Lithic* stage is characterized by chipped-stone technology. For this stage, archaeologists assume small nomadic groups without permanent settlements or agriculture. The beginning of the *Archaic* stage was marked by the introduction of other stoneworking techniques—polishing and grinding—and the establishment of somewhat larger and more stable communities. In some localities at least, a gradual shift occurred from hunting and gathering to more specialized collecting and the beginnings of agriculture. With the *Formative* stage we enter the period of settled village life and a fully integrated agricultural economy. The late Formative witnessed the advent of complex ceremonialism, including some grandiose temple building, and was preparatory—hence the term *formative*—to further developments. The *Classic* stage is defined by great ceremonial architecture, monumental art, intellectual accomplish-ments, and the establishment of states and kingdoms. The *Postclassic* stage is predicated on the emergence of large-scale territorial states and of militarism, a shift in emphasis from technology to political and social manipulation, and perhaps a greater incidence of urban life. The last two stages, the Classic and Postclassic, were represented only in the Mesoamerican and the Peruvian culture areas. Figure 5-2 gives the generally accepted chronological time ranges for the different stages. It should be understood that this is a very simplified breakdown of a complex problem.

The concept of developmental stages as outlined above has been subject to criticism. Some of the stages are conceptually linked to particular regions. The Formative stage, for instance, makes sense as a precursor to the Classic, but in areas where there is no Classic stage it is somewhat awkward to postulate a Formative. But this is not the only objection that has been raised. The criteria for stage definitions vary considerably from stage to stage and some scholars feel that a certain uniformity would be helpful.

In recent years, an effort has been made to establish descriptive and developmental categories of wide applicability that focus on the key characteristics of social systems. The idea is to identify the level of technological mastery and the complexity of social organization at each level of cultural evolution. The emphasis is therefore put on the mode of adaptation to the environment (for example, hunting and gathering, horticulture) and the degree of economic and social elaboration. These are then related to the economic surplus that the economy can generate and the society can utilize. Running from simple to more complex—from societies of minimal or no surpluses to those with considerable margins above subsistence— the hierarchy of evolution proceeds from band through tribe and chiefdom to state (Steward 1955; Sahlins and Service 1960; Service 1962).

In a broad sense, these categories can be equated with the developmental stages of Lithic, Archaic, Formative, Classic, and Postclassic, the last two being subsumed under the heading of "state." The taxonomy based on the degree of complexity of social systems has a flexibility not present in the more traditional format. Like the developmental stages from Lithic to Postclassic, it can be used to pace out the broad course of cultural evolution, but it raises far fewer problems as a descriptive tool. For the purposes of this chapter, we shall make use of both the archaeologically derived concept of stage-period and the ecologically oriented levels of sociocultural integration.

EARLY HUMANS IN THE AMERICAS

Early in the twentieth century, most anthropologists were unwilling to consider the idea that human populations had inhab-

Figure 5-3 Big-game hunting tools

Projectile points characteristic of prehistoric big-game hunters of North America: *a* Folsom, *b* Clovis, *c* Sandia, and *d* Plano (Scottsbluff type). Drawn about one-half of their average size. Note the fluting of *a* and *b*, the "weak shoulder" at bottom left of *c*, and the elongated form of *d*.

ited the New World during the Ice Age. In the Americas, as in Europe a century earlier, it was the discovery of manufactured tools together with skeletal remains of extinct animals that finally resolved the matter.

The event that opened intensive investigation on early humans was the chance discovery in 1926 of a flint spear point lodged in the rib cage of an extinct species of giant bison, *Bison antiquus*, an animal known to have roamed the Great Plains some ten thousand years ago, at the end of the last major, or Wisconsin, glaciation. The discovery took place near the community of Folsom in northeastern New Mexico. The association of a manufactured tool with an extinct species was remarkable enough, but the characteristics of the weapon were even more surprising. It was by no means a crude artifact, but rather a well-made, carefully flaked implement exhibiting a peculiar fluting on both of its sides, or faces. As a tool type, it shared little in common with points found in Eurasian sites of comparable age. In the years following the Folsom discovery, many similar points came to light, mostly in the high plains of North America and the northern portion of the Southwest. A number of radiocarbon dates indicate that Folsom points fit a time slot of several centuries, clustered around 8000 B.C. With further research and excavation, it became apparent that points of the Folsom type constituted but one class of a family of related artifacts, some more recent than Folsom, others of greater antiquity. These were attributed to the earliest human occupation in the Americas and came to be designated as characteristic of the Paleo-Indian period[3] (see Figure 5-3).

[3]The Paleo-Indian period is sometimes referred to as the Paleo-Indian tradition. We prefer to use the term *tradition* to designate a cultural complex of some time depth characterized by a number of common features, for instance, the Big-Game Hunting tradition in North America and Mesoamerica. The concept of tradition stresses shared cultural elements (social organization, technology, economic base, and the like), often developed within the framework of a given environment. Thus, one can distinguish a number of Paleo-In-

The earliest projectile-point type falling within this tradition is known as Clovis, from Clovis in eastern New Mexico. Clovis points are quite similar to Folsom points, but somewhat larger and less well made. They share with Folsom the characteristics of fluting, but Clovis fluting is generally much more restricted, covering a half or less of the length of the artifact measuring from the base. Clovis points date back as far as 10,000 B.C. by radiocarbon determinations, and some may be several thousand years older. In terms of distribution, the type is found not only in the Plains and the Southwest but also in the eastern United States and northern Mexico. Clovis points are usually associated with the remains of the mammoth (*Mammuthus columbi*), which apparently became extinct somewhat earlier than *Bison antiquus*.

More elusive is a nonfluted point type known as Sandia, named after Sandia Cave in central New Mexico. Sandia points are shaped like a lance head and are often distinguished by a weak shoulder on one side of the base. At Sandia Cave, they were found lodged beneath Folsom deposits, a fact that indicates that they are old, but exactly how old remains to be determined. Unfortunately, we lack reliable radiocarbon dates for Sandia. Sandia may be a strictly regional development: very few Sandia points have been found outside central New Mexico.

Much more widespread are a series of nonfluted points that now go by the name of Plano. Points of this general type have been recovered from Alaska to Mexico City and from the Atlantic to the Rockies. Plano points are of two broad subtypes, one resembling Clovis and Folsom points in shape but lacking the characteristic fluting, the other a more elongated form that is sometimes stemmed. Most archaeologists believe

that Plano points developed from Clovis-Folsom forms and that the many varieties of Plano reflect a process of local adaptation to the changing environments of the end of the Ice Age and post–Ice Age times. Plano points may be as early as 8000 B.C. in some localities and as late as 4000 B.C. in others. Where they have been found at kill sites, the typical association is not with extinct animals but with that staple of historic Plains Indian hunters, *Bison bison*, the buffalo.

The Big-Game Hunting tradition

The artifacts we have been dealing with—the fluted Clovis and Folsom points, the single-shouldered Sandia, and the Plano varieties—have a good deal in common. For the most part, they are too large and heavy to have been delivered by bow and arrow and must, therefore, have been attached to spears, either hand-held or propelled by the atlatl, or spear-thrower. Clearly, they were highly specialized hunting weapons, and in a good many instances we find the projectiles together with their victims, mostly extinct herbivores. A general similarity in typology and function allows us to group all these cultural remains as expressions of a particular mode of subsistence, or more broadly, a style of life. The archaeologist Gordon R. Willey has called this the "Big-Game Hunting tradition." In his words:

All these points compose an historically related series. All were integral parts of complexes which reflected a way of life primarily dependent on killing large game animals, many of the species now extinct (Willey 1966:38).

To understand better the way of life of the big-game hunters, one must try to visualize the natural setting of North America during the last major stage of the glacial advances. With ice sheets covering the northern half of this continent and in several places penetrating deep into the area of the present-day United States, the climate was considerably wetter and colder than it is today. On the other hand, large portions of the North American Southwest and present-day

dian traditions in the New World, some in North America, others in South America. The Desert tradition, mentioned later in the chapter, refers to a specific mode of life that evolved in the arid zones of the Southwest and northern Mesoamerica following the Big-Game Hunting tradition.

Mexico, which are now desert or semidesert, were then well-watered grasslands.

The magnificent animals of the Pleistocene that roamed these grasslands and adjacent forests were impressive in both number and variety. They included several species of mammoth and mastodon; bison, horses, and camels; antelopes, giant sloths, and the extinct peccary. To the list must be added the predators that lived off the game: extinct species of jaguars and other great cats, the dire wolf, and, of course, humans. Probably all kinds of game were hunted, large and small, species that subsequently became extinct and those that managed to survive. But it was the larger animals, especially the herbivores, that drew much of the hunters' attention, since they were likely to be found conveniently clustered in herds.

The disappearance of this fauna in such a remarkable short period of time—in North America a dozen large mammals became extinct between 8000 and 4000 B.C.—has long intrigued scientists. The drying up of the Plains as the ice sheets receded northward may have contributed to the debacle, but suspicion falls most heavily upon human hunting activities.

Reconstruction of cultural traditions on the basis of a limited sample of material remains is always difficult. For the time we are considering, so much of the archaeological evidence is in the form of artifacts associated with hunting that one is tempted to interpret the subsistence pattern of these groups as overwhelmingly dependent on the large mammals of the Pleistocene. However, recent studies of contemporary nonagricultural peoples indicate that a purely hunting economy is exceedingly rare.

But even if we assume a more diversified subsistence base, this does not preclude an important human factor in the extinction of Ice Age fauna. The matter is quite complex and involves a number of puzzles. Thus, while the extinctions are to some degree selective, the pattern is far from consistent. The dire wolf died out but not the timber wolf; *Bison antiquus* failed to survive, but

A kill site from near Folsom, New Mexico, dated at about 8000 B.C., showing the remains of extinct bison in association with chipped stone projectile points. (Courtesy of The American Museum of Natural History)

his cousin, *Bison bison*, roamed the Plains in the millions until a hundred years ago. A reasonable interpretation has to take these facts into account. Some animals, such as the mammoths and mastodons, may have been especially vulnerable because they were slow breeders and as herd animals lent themselves to mass slaughter.

It should also be noted that hunting-oriented societies sometimes make very irrational use of resources. John C. Ewers, for instance, has noted:

As early as 1754, Anthony Hendry observed that when buffalo were plentiful, the "Archithinue" of the Saskatchewan Plains took only the tongues and other choice pieces, leaving the rest to the wolves (Ewers 1955:169).

However, it is not necessary to assume that human activities were directly responsible

for the extinction of all Pleistocene fauna. Humans may have sufficiently disturbed the ecological balance to put some species in jeopardy. As the geologist Richard F. Flint points out, "Decimation of one element of a fauna may upset the ecological balance, with far-reaching results to the vital statistics of several races" (Flint 1957:420).

Thirty years ago, specialized big-game hunting tools were generally regarded as the earliest evidence of humans in the Western Hemisphere (Wormington 1947:20). The reconstruction of early prehistory was fairly straightforward: humans had entered North America around 12,000 B.C., established themselves south of the glaciers, and slowly made their way through Central America into South America to arrive finally at the southern tip of the continent, perhaps seven thousand years later (Bennett and Bird 1949:26). Current information is sufficient to indicate a much greater antiquity than was formerly assumed. Charcoal samples from Fell's Cave site show that people were in the region of the Strait of Magellan around 9000 B.C. (Bennett and Bird 1960:26), while other radiocarbon dates from Venezuela establish human occupation in northern South America as early as 14,500 B.C. These dates are compatible with radiocarbon dates from early cave and open-air sites in Peru (Lauricocha and Ayacucho).

In recent years, the evidence has been accumulating for what is generally termed a "preprojectile point period." At present, it is still something of a catchall category since the assemblages attributed to this technological level are chiefly distinguished by the absence of the highly specialized projectile points that are the hallmark of late Pleistocene hunters. Typologically, these assemblages fall into two broad categories. One group is characterized by crude and relatively large core tools. It would be difficult for the nonspecialist to recognize these artifacts as consciously made tools. The other category consists of large bifacially worked tools, at least some of which must have been used as points. These are the two most

characteristic artifact types, with other tools rounding out the respective "work kits." Since both core tools and bifaces are ancient forms in the Old World, there is certainly the possibility that they formed part of the tool inventories introduced into the Americas by early populations.

A reconstruction of the earliest periods of American prehistory along these lines has obvious advantages. Some scholars have long felt that the chronologies pegged to the Paleo-Indian Big-Game Hunting tradition in North America and different but parallel traditions in South America are unduly restrictive, a viewpoint that is supported by recent radiocarbon dates that lend weight to a much earlier human presence in the New World.

If we assume that the first American settlers crossed the Bering Strait around 35,000 B.C., or even earlier, this date would have allowed ample time for dispersal through the hemisphere and the evolution of specialized assemblages in both North and South America. In this light, the Sandia-Clovis-Folsom-Plano sequence of specialized hunting tools (so different from those in the Old World), can easily be explained as a native response to the New World environment. There was time enough for such an evolution and it is not necessary to look for antecedents in East Asia. The same would hold true for other specialized tool assemblages such as the willow-leaf-shaped points of the Pacific Northwest, dated at least 8000 B.C., and the distinctive stemmed projectile points found at the tip of South America.

ARCHAIC CULTURES AND THE ORIGINS OF AGRICULTURE

The end of the Pleistocene made necessary a substantial shift in the subsistence patterns of New World inhabitants. These changes are directly linked to the new ecological conditions that came into being with the northward contraction of the ice sheets.

Although it may be debated to what degree climate, rather than human action, was responsible for the disappearance of the Ice Age fauna, it is evident that changing patterns of precipitation and alternations in vegetation were, on the whole, not congenial to large herbivores.

Over much of the Plains, and most dramatically in the Great Basin area west of the Rockies, increased aridity dictated a generalized search for food—a search that involved collecting as well as hunting—at the expense of more specialized hunting procedures. It would be wrong to see this as some absolute or sudden shift; rather, it was a matter of priorities. In much the same way, eastern North America was witnessing a series of environmental changes, although in a different direction. Here, forest cover increased, game herds were reduced, and a premium was placed on the collection of plants and the exploitation of river and lake resources.

The Desert tradition

Archaeologists recognize what has been termed the *Desert tradition* as the major cultural successor of the Big-Game Hunting tradition in western United States, northern Mexico, and Mesoamerica proper, in short, those regions where a post-Pleistocene cycle of dry climate turned many formerly grassland areas into steppe and desert. Economically, the Desert way of life was structured around the hunting of small game and the collection of wild plants and, in particular, wild seeds. Where larger game happened to be available, it too was hunted.

The archaeological evidence would seem to favor a Great Basin origin for the Desert tradition, although the matter of cultural ancestry is still somewhat obscure (some of the tools show a similarity to artifacts from the Pacific Northwest). Be this as it may, sometime between 8000 and 7000 B.C. the inhabitants of the Great Basin caves and rock-shelters of Utah and Nevada initiated a series of cultural adaptations destined to influence not only the American West, but also the arid lands south of the Rio Grande.

The chief material characteristics of this tradition are basketry and milling stones. Fortunately, the people of the Desert tradition made ample use of caves and rock-shelters for both hunting stations and habitation sites. This tendency, as well as the fact that substantial portions of their hunting and gathering territories have remained arid zones to the present day, has greatly facilitated the preservation of items that in most cases would have disappeared. Although the Desert tradition is hardly flamboyant—the constant food quest can have left little time for leisure—archaeologists have recovered such an extensive range of artifacts that it is possible to document the life of Desert people in minute detail. Their sites have yielded not only basketry and grinding stones, but also an extensive complement of nets, mats and cordage, digging sticks, fire drills, spear-throwers, and projectile points.

While the assemblages are not identical throughout the Desert tradition domain, there is a definite similarity in economic patterns, whether the sites are located in the Great Basin and the Southwest, the caves of Tamaulipas in northeastern Mexico, or the Tehuacán Valley of the central Mexican highlands. But artifacts give us only part of the picture. The really striking finds from such sites are nonartifactual. Richard S. MacNeish has summarized the importance of the data for the Tehuacán phases, and his observations essentially hold true for other sites:

Because of the extreme dryness of the area, in over 55 of the floors in the five caves everything had been preserved: foodstuffs, feces, and other normally perishable human remains and artifacts. This type of refuse not only allows one to make an unusually complete reconstruction of the way of life of the ancient inhabitants, but gives considerable information about subsistence, food habits, diet, climatic changes, and, in many cases, even indicates which months of the year the floors were occupied (MacNeish 1964:531–532).

The Desert tradition can be viewed as an adjustment to an extremely demanding environment. It is interesting to consider what occurred once this adjustment had been achieved. In southern California, we can trace a succession of Desert-type cultures from around 7000 B.C. to the time of European contact. This is not to imply complete cultural stagnation over a span of nearly ten thousand years but rather to highlight the fact that the cultures that replaced the Desert tradition remained geared to a food-collecting and generalized hunting economy almost down to our own day.

The picture for Mesoamerica could not be more different. Here we can trace a gradual development over thousands of years, from gathering and hunting through more specialized collecting, to incipient agriculture, culminating finally in sedentary village life and establishment of elaborate civilizations.

Around 5000 B.C., a period of increased heat and aridity in these areas may have put a strain on natural resources and encouraged a diversification of subsistence activities. A product of this diversification was the practice of some rather casual agriculture. It would seem that squash was being domesticated at this time in the Tehuacán region. Wild rice added something to the diet, as did the collection of other edible plants: avocados, chili peppers, amaranth, and tepary beans. At approximately the same time, the inhabitants of the Tamaulipas caves were involved in the domestication of chili peppers, bottle gourds, pumpkins, and perhaps the yellow and red beans. The major agricultural breakthrough occurred with the domestication of maize. This took place sometime between 5000 and 3500 B.C. in central Mexico, although it is not possible to pinpoint the time and location exactly. The first evidence of corn in Tamaulipas is considerably later—around 2500 B.C.

Plant domestication is the work of centuries. Initially, yields from early forms of domesticated plants were extremely low. Thus, primitive domesticated maize bore

The origins of New World agriculture

Indian corn, or maize, is one of today's most important world food staples. First domesticated in Mesoamerica, the earlier varieties were small and unimpressive. Contrast the native eight-row flint corn from seventeenth-century Massachusetts (above) with a modern ear (Peabody Museum of Salem. Photo by M. W. Sexton)

cobs about the size of a strawberry, an output that could hardly have contributed much to the total diet. It is wrong, therefore, to imagine that plant domestication automatically and immediately leads to the production of substantial surpluses. Certainly, the archaeological and botanical evidence fails to indicate a revolutionary leap from hunting and gathering to established agriculture and sedentary life.

Societies dependent on agriculture for a substantial portion of their nutrition typically depend on a variety of crops. In part, this is a hedge against adversity, but such an arrangement also assures greater dietary balance. Consequently, the shift to agriculture involves the integration of a number of cultivated plants into a balanced subsistence pattern, a process that, like the gradual increase in yields from given species, has generally been slow and gradual. In the New World, as elsewhere, there were a number of centers of plant domestication. Maize, for example, appears early in central Mexico, while pumpkin, which was certainly domesticated in Tamaulipas by 5000 B.C., does not show up in the Tehuacán sequences for another two thousand years.

The earliest evidence of agriculture in Peru comes from a series of coastal desert sites dating to around 2500 B.C. The most thoroughly studied of these sites is Huaca

Prieta near the mouth of the Chicama River. The inhabitants of Huaca Prieta lived in single-roomed semisubterranean houses and subsisted on a diet made up in part of domesticated plants (squash, beans, and chili, but no maize) and in part of wild produce and seafood. However, it is debatable whether the coast of Peru was in fact a major locus of plant domestication. A number of important crops, later to become significant for the inhabitants of the Andean culture area, do not appear to be of coastal origin: the potato is a highland crop, tropical South America was the homeland of manioc and peanuts, while maize was first domesticated in Mesoamerica.

In contrast to the Old World, animal domestication in the Americas was not a cornerstone of agriculture and settled life. We have to envisage a situation where agriculture developed without cattle, pigs, or sheep, and where transportation was devoid of most pack and draft animals (horses, oxen, donkeys). Only in the Andes was this situation somewhat different, with the domestication of llamas, employed chiefly as pack animals, and alpacas, raised almost exclusively for their fine wool.

TO SUM UP By around 2000 B.C., agriculture was well established in both Mesoamerica and Peru. It was also at about this time that pottery began to make its appearance.

THE FORMATIVE STAGE
AND THE RISE OF CIVILIZATION

Up to this point in our discussion, we have followed the gradual transformation of some hunting and gathering societies into societies of simple agriculturalists. Although village agriculture remained the mainstay of a great number of New World societies until the period of European contact, and vast regions of both North and South America still continued to support hunting and gathering groups, Mesoamerica and Peru experienced, during the Formative, a series of cultural and economic shifts that in retrospect can be seen as the harbingers of civilization.

The earlier part of the Formative offers few clues of the shape of things to come. In Mesoamerica and Peru, as well as the intervening lands of Central America, the first thousand years of the Formative were an era of relative stability. Communities were small; ample land must have been available for all who wished to work it; and handicrafts, though certainly not crude and experimental, tended to be on the simple and utilitarian side. Modest burials attest to the consideration given to the dead, but in no way does one get the impression of complex social or religious systems.

By around 900 B.C., with maize cultivation serving as the economic mainstay, some societies in Peru and Mesoamerica had been transformed into prototype states. The exact nature and causes of this shift are open to debate; what is not in question is the precipitous reorganization that permitted the establishment of great ceremonial centers dedicated to complex religious undertakings. The hallmark of this transformation is the rise (probably independently) of two great artistic styles, one in Mexico, the other in Peru.

The rise of high cultures Before we examine the significance of these traditions and the localities in which they flourished, the following observations are in order:

1 Cultural manifestations of this type represent a reordering of economic priorities in which surpluses that would otherwise have been expended locally, or perhaps not even generated, were placed at the disposal of structures of higher order (such as religious institutions and state systems). An established agricultural base, with its long-range stability and productivity, made such a reallocation feasible. We do not imply that such a shift was inevitable; in fact, a very interesting question is why some regions experienced these changes while others, apparently equally endowed, did not.

2 While it is correct to emphasize the organizational breakthroughs that alone permitted the concentration of surpluses on which all else rested, an interpretation of middle and late Formative societies should not lose sight of the fact that much remained unchanged. The ceremonial center was clearly a novelty on the cultural landscape, but such centers were far from being true towns. Aside from a relatively small number of specialists and those directly catering to their needs, everyone lived in surrounding village communities under the control of a ceremonial center.

3 Just as true urbanism was absent at such early times, a number of other features associated with more developed New World cultures were either absent or only in their infancy. This is the case with writing, metallurgy, and calendric systems.

In short, we are concerned with cultural manifestations that appear early in the growth of American civilizations. It is in the realm of religion and its expression in art and architecture that the greatness of these ancient cultures is most evident. In the words of the archaeologist Gordon Willey:

These great pre-Columbian art styles of Mesoamerica and Peru are expressed monumentally; they occur in settings that were obviously sacred or important in the cultures which produced them; they are also pervasive, being reproduced in a variety of media and contexts; the products are rendered with the consummate skill of the specially and long-trained artist; they conform to strict stylistic canons; their subject matter tends to be thematic; and finally, the finest monuments or creations in these styles are truly powerful and awe-inspiring (Willey 1962:1–2).

We wish to stress that these works are the material manifestations of underlying social systems. The predominant themes are religious and, to us at least, esoteric. They bespeak of the integrative power of religion and are symbols of institutions and the attitudes that supported and maintained belief systems. At another level, they tell us much about cultural priorities and the ordering of society.

Peru   In Peru, the early great style is Chavín, named after the famous ceremonial site of Chavín de Huántar. This is a northern highland site, but sites sharing the same stylistic tradition are to be found across the whole northern half of Peru. The Chavín style was rendered in a variety of media—ceramics, stone, precious metals, textiles—but is perhaps best exemplified in relief carvings.

The style is based almost exclusively on the feline concept in which the feline is represented by the head or by a head and profile

Chavín artistic style typically makes use of surface reliefs and incisions to render highly stylized markings and figures. The feline motif, especially representative of this style, is illustrated by this jaguar-shaped mortar. (The University Museum, University of Pennsylvania)

body or by a zoomorphic front view. Appendages may be added to this basic feline figure which allow it to be identified as a condor, snake, or fish. Even the design detail is dominated by the feline elements (Bennett 1947:84).

Chavín is labyrinthine in complexity and there is little mastery of realism or naturalism. The Chavín artist abhorred free space and sought to fill it with a myriad of secondary detail.

Even at this early time, the inhabitants of the Andean region were establishing their reputation as consummate craftsmen in metal by producing earspools, rings, and headbands of gold, and developing techniques of soldering and welding. Rich funerary offerings of nonutilitarian pottery, jet mirrors, and shell and turquoise pendants and beads all attest to social stratification and reiterate the theme of pervasive religious ceremonialism. Terraced, stone-faced pyramids mark the religious sanctuaries.

Meanwhile, a similar trend of events was unfolding in Mesoamerica. During the earlier part of the Formative we can distinguish a pattern of village agricultural subsistence at a number of central Mexican sites. The picture changes quite radically around 900 B.C., at the site of Tlatilco in the valley of Mexico. Although Tlatilco can hardly be termed a major ceremonial center—it lacks substantial architecture and monumental art—it does present clear evidence of social stratification and developed ceremonialism.

Above all, it is the burials that offer us an insight into Tlatilco society. Grave goods include clay figurines (a common feature of most Mesoamerican Formative sites) in a variety of styles and some remarkably fine figurines, pendants, and earspools in jade. Some burials are far more sumptuous than others. Especially striking are those pieces produced in what is known as the Olmec style. In the words of Miguel Covarrubias, Olmec artists were

Olmec craftsmen were consummate sculptors in both monumental stone and fine jade pieces. As in this colossal head, the style is direct, powerful, and relatively unelaborated. (Inge Morath/ Magnum Photos, Inc.)

Mexico

mainly concerned with the representation of a peculiar type of human being made up of solid, ample masses, powerful and squat. . . . They handled these forms with architectural discipline and sensitivity. They delighted in the smooth, highly polished surfaces of their jades, broken occasionally by fine incised lines to indicate such supplementary elements as tattooing, details of dress, ornaments, and glyphs (Covarrubias 1957:54).

However, these were human figures of a very strange sort. In common with Chavín, there is a preoccupation with feline attributes. The central theme is one of transformation, of the subtle interweaving of human characteristics and jaguar traits. Figures that follow the Olmec canon are depicted as somewhat infantile or babyfaced, with snub noses and open downturned mouths—mouths, in fact, not unlike those of crying children. In many cases, it is difficult to tell where human characteristics end and jaguar motifs begin. Some figures are clearly human; in others, downturned mouths become fanged and snarling jaguar masks. Although the ware-jaguar (anthropomorphized jaguar) theme pervades all Olmec art, the properties of the style are realistic and nonabstract. The lines are sharp and precise and, in contrast to Chavín, the iconography is not filled with secondary detail.

Tlatilco artwork in the Olmec style is powerful and sophisticated, but apparently the site was little more than an Olmec outpost. The Olmec heartland lay to the east and south in the tropical lowland region of the Gulf of Mexico. A score of Olmec sites dotted the Gulf coast and surrounding regions, but most impressive of all must have been the ceremonial center of La Venta. La Venta boasted an architectural complex centered on a great mound, carved altars, stupendous tombs, and colossal stone heads.

With respect to intellectual accomplishments, the Olmec were the first people in the New World to invent the calendar, probe the secrets of astronomy, and make the initial advances in writing. In short, we find at major Olmec sites a foreshadowing of the great civilizations that came to full expression in the Classic period.

It is inevitable that, given the similarities in Olmec and Chavín great styles, and the temporal congruence of the two cultural manifestations (in both cases we are dealing with a time frame running from about 900 to 400 B.C.), the question of possible links arises. Direct contact is difficult to envisage; for one thing, while themes—in particular the jaguar motif—are similar, the forms of artistic expression are quite distinct. Much more likely is independent development founded on a similar base of effective village agriculture.

Such a hypothesis does not preclude an undercurrent of common belief that might have found somewhat different modes of expression in the form of the two great styles. Central America should be thought of not as an impenetrable barrier to cultural influence but as a corridor permitting the passage of broad concepts and basic techniques.

CLASSIC SPLENDOR

During the first thousand years of the Christian era, Mesoamerica and Peru experienced a period of great cultural florescence. In both regions, the potentials inherent in aboriginal technology, intellectual traditions, and social organization reached climactic proportions in the form of a series of regional cultures. If the Formative can be viewed as a time of incubation, Classic cultures are recognizable as fully formed civilizations. As William T. Sanders has noted:

Civilization is a special type of cultural growth that occurred only in a few regions of the world. Archeologists define civilizations in terms of excellence of technology, and especially by the presence of monumental architecture. More significant, however, are the social and economic implications of these technological achievements. They are always the product of a *large organized human society with marked occupational specialization and social stratification* (Sanders 1968:89–90).

Until quite recently, scholars tended to differentiate between the Classic and Postclassic on the basis of political structures, degree of centralization, and what may be termed proclivities toward empire building. Classic societies, it was thought, were essentially theocratic, a mosaic of city-states controlled from their respective ceremonial centers by priestly elites more concerned with theology than with territorial expansion. In contrast, Postclassic civilizations were militaristic empire states supported by loot and tribute and governed by warrior kings.

It is debatable whether this image ever fitted Andean reality since even early Classic civilizations appear to have been highly organized and aggressive states. In part, the rise of the early Andean polities may be related to an arid coastal environment where the requirements of irrigation imposed strict social controls. The pattern, once established, could then be applied to areas where similar ecological constraints were not present. The natural environment of southern Mesoamerica, on the other hand, favored extensive rather than intensive agriculture. Here, slash-and-burn shifting agriculture was, and continues to be, the norm. No doubt, this economic base imposed some limits on urban clustering and may have favored political decentralization. It is in this region, the homeland of the Classic Maya, that the traditional concept of the Classic is most appropriate. However, recent evidence does point to patterns of incipient urbanism at Tikal in Guatemala and other sites, and some authorities have interpreted hieroglyphic inscriptions as indicating the presence of royal lineages in a number of ceremonial centers. For central Mexico, and in particular the great metropolis of Teotihuacán, the evidence for large-scale urbanism, intensive agriculture (based, as in coastal Peru, on irrigation), and expansionist policies is quite conclusive.

Even if we grant that Postclassic civilization may carry some of these trends to their logical conclusion—we have in mind the huge conquest states described in much detail by the Spanish chroniclers—these nevertheless are phenomena that have their roots deep in the Classic. Another characteristic of the Postclassic is the rise and fall of a succession of states and empires. For this, too, there is a precedent in the cataclysmic disintegration of Classic civilizations.

The chronology of the Classic is firmest in southern Mesoamerica where it is anchored to the many Long Count dates inscribed on Maya monuments.[4] Using the generally ac-

cepted correlation, the Classic in this region begins around A.D. 300 and ends some six hundred years later. In central Mexico, Classic Teotihuacán civilization may have begun one or two centuries earlier, and it certainly terminated a few centuries prior to the Classic Maya collapse. It is hypothesized that the fall of Teotihuacán—the city was burned and abandoned and the empire disintegrated—set in motion a train of events that ultimately affected the stability of Maya civilization.

The chronological frame of the Peruvian Classic cultures is much more open to question. Part of the problem is archaeological—considerably less work has been done in Peru than in Mesoamerica—and part is a matter of definition. As we have noted, a high degree of centralization backed by intensive agriculture characterizes Peruvian cultures. The period from the first centuries of the Christian era to A.D. 600 witnessed the emergence of a number of regional states. By the end of the period, these regional states had reached the limits of growth in their respective areas and further expansion could have been achieved only at the expense of their neighbors. There followed a series of large imperial states with capitals in the Andean highlands. The last of these was the Inca Empire, which was overthrown by the Spaniards in the sixteenth century. In Peru,

<hr/>

[4]The Maya in Classic times made use of a number of calendars for different purposes, including a 260-day sacred calendar, a Venus calendar, and a

highly accurate solar year. What Mesoamericanists call the Maya Long Count was a consecutive count of elapsed days from a date fixed in the distant past, probably some occurrence in their mythology. Reconstructing back to this date, the start of the Long Count is 3113 B.C. in our system. Apparently, all Classic Maya ceremonial centers utilized an identical Long Count that gives Maya chronology a degree of internal control the like of which is found nowhere else in the New World. Long Count dates in the Maya area begin to be recorded around A.D. 300 (there are a few inscriptions in Olmec sites that appear to be older), and the whole system ceased to be used after the collapse of Maya civilization around A.D. 900. Since the Maya inscribed dates on a great number of monuments, it is relatively easy to cross-date Maya sites and plot the growth and decline of Maya ceremonial centers.

therefore, we have a tradition of imperial organization that goes back almost to A.D. 800. In much the same way, it would appear that the central Mexican empire of Teotihuacán served as the model for later empires, including the Aztec Empire. Thus, for both central Mexico and Peru it is difficult to distinguish the Classic from the Postclassic on the basis of organizational features.

In discussing the Classic in the two New World high-culture areas, we have put stress on developmental and functional similarities, in particular socioeconomic and political parallels. Nevertheless, in contrast to the Formative and Postclassic stages, the Classic shows considerable regional diversity. For Mesoamerica, two major patterns are recognizable, one with its locus in the central Mexican highlands, the other pertaining to

The Aztecs and the Maya

the tropical lowland regions of southern Mexico, northern Guatemala, and Honduras. It is from the Classic onward that the central Mexican subarea, with the valley of Mexico as its heart, dominates the rest of Mexico and strongly influences southern Mesoamerica. In Classic times the paramount city of central Mexico was Teotihuacán, an urban complex overshadowed by two enormous flat-topped pyramids surrounded by more than seven square miles of ceremonial structures, palaces, plazas, and

Teotihuacán, capital of a powerful empire, dominated the Mesoamerican scene during the early half of the Classic Period. A true urban center, its former wealth and power may still be gauged from the huge pyramids and other ceremonial structures. (Erich Hartmann/Magnum Photos, Inc.)

residential neighborhoods. Population estimates vary, but a figure of fifty thousand inhabitants does not seem extreme.

Obviously, this was much more than an imposing ceremonial and administrative capital holding sway over a limited geographic area. Only as the center of a vast empire could such a city thrive. We have to envisage a degree of political control and cultural influence very similar to that enjoyed by the Aztec capital of Tenochtitlán many centuries later. The rulers of Tenochtitlán received tribute both precious and utilitarian. According to Cortés' secretary, luxury items were kept in royal treasure houses.

The other tributes were used to feed the soldiers. . . . In Mexico, as I have said, there were storehouses and buildings in which the grain was kept, with a major-domo and assistants to receive it, distribute it in an orderly manner, and keep the records in picture books. Each town had its tribute collector. . . . He listed the goods and numbers of people in the towns and provinces of his district, and brought the accounting to Mexico. If any collector made an error or cheated, he died for it, and even the members of his family would be penalized as kinsmen of a traitor to the king (Gómara 1964:155).

Such was the way of empire at the turn of the sixteenth century and one can hardly doubt that similar methods were in vogue eight hundred years earlier.

In southern Mesoamerica a somewhat different pattern is discernible. There is little evidence that points to great territorial states or the dominance of the region by any single city. Certainly some sites are larger and more imposing than others, but the Maya region is dotted with major ceremonial centers. Insofar as urbanization is concerned, some sites probably achieved a degree of urbanization, but many others were evidently ceremonial centers catering to the needs of outlying hamlets.

Classic Maya art is one of the glories of

Temple One at Tikal, Guatemala, showing reconstruction in progress. The metropolis of Tikal was one of the most important Classic Maya population centers. The pyramids are exceptionally steep and the impression of great height is reinforced by the roof-combs on top of the temple structures. (Lee A. Parsons Milwaukee Public Museum)

pre-Columbian civilization. The Maya style is clearly of local inspiration and only a limited number of themes and motifs appear to be foreign imports. Artists expressed themselves in a variety of media—in full-round stone sculptures, in relief carvings in stone and on wooden lintels, in stucco sculptures, and in wall paintings. Most great Maya art revolves around the human figure and it is possible to identify representations of priests, kings, gods, soldiers, and captives. The figures are usually rendered realistically, but at the same time the style allows sufficient license to accentuate important details such as headdresses and ceremonial regalia. Typically, the effect is sumptuous, and monarchs and deities come through in all their glory.

Maya art was intimately linked to two other features of Classic Maya civilization—hieroglyphic writing and calendrical notations. One of the chief preoccupations of the Maya was the measurement and recording of time. Almost every monument was erected to mark the end of a discrete segment of time, usually the passage of a five- or ten-year period. This consuming interest in time and its passage was made possible by a scientific knowledge of astronomy, the presence of a suitable notation system, and a calendar involving the permutation of a series of name days and numbers.

EPILOGUE

Whatever the catalyst may have been that precipitated the collapse of Classic civilizations—internal strife, population pressures, and foreign invasions may in part or in whole have been contributory factors—the root cause of dissolution, as the archaeologist Sylvanus Morley indicated for the specific case of the Classic Maya, "must be sought within the society itself rather than in outside forces, either natural or human" (Morley 1956:438).

By and large, Classic societies touched the limits of a given technological system and forms of social control and human organization. Barring breakthroughs in these areas, it was impossible to improve productivity and translate this productivity into a more complex or more efficient social order. Such changes were not forthcoming and consequently we have to envisage the period from the late Classic to the Spanish Conquest as a kind of cultural plateau, with few significant changes; empires might rise and empires might fall, but the basic patterns of social organization changed little.

Although Postclassic cultures are certainly more than a pallid aftermath of the Classic, and native societies remained vital up to the time of European contact, the archaeological record identifies very few innovations. It is not surprising, therefore, that Postclassic history is essentially the history of the cyclical rise and fall of competing power centers.

In some regions, the developmental sequence from Classic times to the Spanish Conquest can be firmly established. Thus, Classic Teotihuacán provided the master model for the Toltec empire with its capital at Tula. This, the first Postclassic conquest state in Mesoamerica, offered a pattern for the aggressively militaristic Aztecs. The Aztec state, like the Inca Empire in Peru, was cut down at the peak of power by European invaders. The Spanish conquest of the Americas is a final episode that, interestingly enough, fits in quite well with Morley's observation. The overthrow of the empires of the Aztecs and the Incas was precipitated much less by European firepower or Spanish zeal than by the internal frailties of these states. Outwardly strong, but riven by factions and the discontents of subject peoples, they were never in a position to present a united front in the face of external danger. Hernando Cortés used these cleavages to full advantage:

I was not a little pleased to see this discord . . . because it appeared to me to strengthen my design, and later I would find means to subjugate them. . . . So I treated with the one, and the other, and privately I thanked both for the advice they gave me, giving to each the credit for more friendship, than to the other (Cortés 1908:212).

The end was quick and brutal. We may use as the epitaph for all American high cultures an Aztec lament composed while Spanish soldiery and their newfound Indian allies (many of them onetime subjects of the Aztec emperor) were concluding the siege of Tenochtitlán:

Broken spears lie in the roads;
We have torn our hair in our grief.
The houses are roofless now, and their walls
are red with blood.

Worms are swarming in the streets and
*   plazas,*
and the walls are splattered with gore.
The water has turned red, as if it were
*   dyed,*
and when we drink it,
it has the taste of brine.

We have pounded our hands in despair
against the adobe walls,
for our inheritance, our city, is lost and
*   dead.*
The shields of our warriors were its
*   defense,*
but they could not save it.[5]

(*icnocuicatl* [songs of sorrow],
quoted in León-Portilla 1962:137–138.)

Although the empires fell, never to be reconstituted, the people themselves endured. But that is another story.

[5]From Miguel León-Portilla, ed., *The Broken Spears: The Aztec Account of the Conquest of Mexico,* Lysander Kemp, trans. (Boston: Beacon Press, 1962), pp. 137–138. Copyright © 1962 by the Beacon Press. Originally published in Spanish under the title *Visión de los Vencidos;* Copyright © 1959 by Universidad Nacional Autonoma de Mexico. Reprinted by permission of Beacon Press.

REFERENCES

BENNETT, WENDELL CLARK
1947 The archeology of the Central Andes. In *Handbook of South American Indians*, vol. 2: *The Andean civilizations.* Julian H. Steward, ed. Bureau of American Ethnology, Bulletin 143. Washington, D.C.: Government Printing Office. Pp. 61–147.

BENNETT, WENDELL CLARK, AND JUNIUS B. BIRD
1949 *Andean culture history.* The American Museum of Natural History, Handbook series no. 15. New York
1960 *Andean culture history* (2nd and rev. ed.). Garden City, New York: The Natural History Press.

BOLTON, HERBERT EUGENE, ED.
1952 *Spanish exploration in the Southwest, 1542–1706.* New York: Barnes and Noble.

CASO, ALFONSO
1953 New World culture history: Middle America. In *Anthropology today.* A. L. Kroeber, ed. Chicago: The University of Chicago Press. Pp. 226–237.

CIEZA DE LEÓN, PEDRO DE
1883 *The second part of the Chronicle of Peru.* Clements R. Markham, trans. and ed. London: Hakluyt Society.

CORTÉS, HERNANDO
1908 *Letters of Cortés; the five letters of relation from Fernando Cortés to the Emperor Charles V.* Francis Augustus MacNutt, trans. and ed. New York: G. P. Putnam's Sons.

COVARRUBIAS, MIGUEL
1957 *Indian art of Mexico and Central America.* New York: Alfred A. Knopf.

DÍAZ DEL CASTILLO, BERNAL
1956 *The discovery and conquest of Mexico, 1517–1521.* A. P. Maudslay, trans. New York: Farrar, Straus and Cudahy.

DURÁN, DIEGO
1964 *The Aztecs; the history of the Indies of New Spain.* Doris Heyden and Fernando Horcasitas, trans. New York: Orion Press.

EWERS, JOHN C.

1955 *The horse in Blackfoot Indian culture.* Bureau of American Ethnology, Bulletin 159. Washington, D.C.: Government Printing Office.

FLINT, RICHARD FOSTER

1957 *Glacial and pleistocene geology.* New York: Wiley.

GÓMARA, FRANCISCO LÓPEZ DE

1964 *Cortés: the life of the conqueror by his secretary.* Lesley Byrd Simpson, trans. and ed. Berkeley: University of California Press.

JEFFERSON, THOMAS

1964 *Notes on the State of Virginia.* New York: Harper and Row.

LEÓN-PORTILLA, MIGUEL, ED.

1962 *The broken spears; the Aztec account of the conquest of Mexico.* Lysander Kemp, trans. Boston: Beacon Press.

MACNEISH, RICHARD STOCKTON

1964 Ancient Mesoamerican civilization. *Science* 143:531–537 (no. 3606, February 7).

MORLEY, SYLVANUS GRISWOLD

1956 *The ancient Maya* (3rd ed.). Rev. by George W. Brainerd. Stanford, Calif: Stanford University Press.

PENDERGAST, DAVID M., ED.

1967 *Palenque: the Walker-Caddy expedition to the ancient Maya city, 1839–1840.* Norman, Okla.: University of Oklahoma Press.

PRIEST, JOSIAH

1834 *American antiquities and discoveries in the West.* Albany: Hoffman and White.

ROBERTSON, WILLIAM

1777 *The history of America.* Dublin: Printed for Messrs. Whitestone.

SAHLINS, MARSHALL D., AND ELMAN R. SERVICE, EDS.

1960 *Evolution and culture.* Ann Arbor: University of Michigan Press.

SANDERS, WILLIAM T.

1968 Hydraulic agriculture, economic symbiosis and the evolution of states in central Mexico. In *Anthropological archeology in the Americas.* Betty J. Meggers, ed. Washington, D.C.: The Anthropological Society of Washington. Pp. 88–107.

SERVICE, ELMAN R.

1962 *Primitive social organization; an evolutionary perspective.* New York: Random House.

STEPHENS, JOHN LLOYD

1841 *Incidents of travel in Central America, Chiapas, and Yucatán,* vol. 1. New York: Harper and Brothers.

STEWARD, JULIAN HAYNES

1955 *Theory of culture change; the methodology of multilinear evolution.* Urbana: University of Illinois Press.

WILLEY, GORDON RANDOLPH

1962 The early great styles and the rise of the pre-Columbian civilizations. *American Anthropologist* 64:1–14.

1966 *An introduction to American archaeology,* vol. 1: *North and Middle America.* Englewood Cliffs, New Jersey: Prentice-Hall.

WILLEY, GORDON RANDOLPH, AND PHILIP PHILLIPS

1958 *Method and theory in American archaeology.* Chicago: The University of Chicago Press.

WORMINGTON, HANNAH MARIE

1947 *Prehistoric Indians of the Southwest.* Denver, Colorado: The Colorado Museum of Natural History.

Chapter 6
Native Americans: five centuries of struggle

The preceding chapter has brought the account of Native Americans up to the time of the "discovery" of the New World. This ethnocentric label, ignoring as it does the fact that the Western Hemisphere had been settled by Asian hunters many thousands of years prior to its "rediscovery," is indicative of the attitude of Europeans toward the peoples who much earlier had made these continents their home. Daniel J. Boorstin has described this attitude very aptly in his preface to Hagan's historical account of the relationship between whites and Indians:

It is common to explain one or another feature of American history by the peculiar fact that Europeans transferred their culture to an "empty" continent. The Indians are then recalled, in afterthought, as the people whose presence here prevented the continent from being entirely empty. They are often included with the inclement weather, the wild animals, and the unknown distances, among the half-predictable perils of a wilderness. We are taught to remember them as carrying off an un-

wary traveler, harassing a wagon train, or fighting the cowboys. The Indians thus seem nothing more than sand in the smoothly oiled gears of American progress (Hagan 1961:vii).

The casual disregard of perhaps as many as fifty million Indians who inhabited the Western Hemisphere at the end of the fifteenth century[1] has taken various forms. Cultural anthropologists, in particular, are aware of the oversimplification or gross distortion to which the image of the American Indian has been subjected throughout much of the history of this nation. Native Americans were commonly looked upon as savages or enemies who lacked "religion, or government," "[any] conception of right and

[1] Although estimating the size of the pre-Conquest aboriginal American population on a hemispheric scale involves a great many imponderables, scholars today appear to be in general agreement that the several earlier figures on the order of ten million have been too conservative. Our figure derives from recent calculations made by Dobyns 1966 and the discussion appended thereto.

In the view of many early European chroniclers, American Indians were "savages" capable of the most extreme atrocities. This perspective is reflected in an engraving of the period showing a group of Indians mutilating the enemy dead. (Courtesy of The American Museum of Natural History)

wrong," and "the smallest taste for the arts" (Forbes 1964:16, 19, 17). During much of the present century, motion pictures depicting the westward movement generally succeeded in creating yet another one-sided portrayal of the Indians: as mounted warriors given to hit-and-run harassment of God-fearing pioneers dedicated to the opening of the West and the taming of its wilderness. According to this stereotype, the Indians may have slightly delayed the establishment of new communities west of the Mississippi or the laying of the tracks for transcontinental rail routes, but the days of their power were numbered and their cultural fate was sealed.

While the attitude of the United States government toward the affairs of Native Americans changed during the interwar period (1918–1939), it was not until after World War II that substantial progress began to be made. These developments were aided by the growing determination on the part of the Indians to be heard. But it will no doubt take some time before the many

deep-seated misconceptions are finally cleared away and injustices are righted. With respect to the past, the simplistic notion of a generalized "primitive Indian culture" needs to be dispelled, for the cultural traditions of Native Americans are as varied as they are rich. Indians—repeatedly written off in the past as "assimilated" or "finished"—have not "vanished" as was predicted; instead, their numbers have recently been increasing rapidly. Today, they are searching for the roots of their identity with justifiable pride and determination. The present chapter is a recognition of the fact that even in the broad context of cultural anthropology, these first "Americans" merit special consideration.

CULTURAL VARIATION IN THE NEW WORLD

The aboriginal New World was a hemisphere of great diversity. Even if we use conservative estimates of the number of

Indian languages spoken in the Americas at the time of the first European contact, there must have been no fewer than four hundred separate Indian language groups in North America and well over six hundred in South America and the West Indies. The size of these groups varied enormously, ranging from hunting and gathering bands of several hundred individuals to populations of many millions in the elaborate civilizations of Mesoamerica and the Andean highlands. Taking a comprehensive hemispheric perspective, one can identify three broad economic types of aboriginal cultures according to the manner in which the bulk of their subsistence was derived: cultures based on hunting, gathering, and fishing; cultures characterized by an intermediate form of agriculture; and the civilizations based on advanced farming techniques.

As we have seen in the foregoing chapter, the advanced agriculturalists (the third category) were represented in two separate and rather well-defined areas of the New World. One was the Mesoamerican area of the southern half of present-day Mexico, together with Guatemala, Belize (formerly British Honduras), El Salvador, and parts of Honduras and Nicaragua. The other, the central Andean area of high culture, extended over the arid coastal region and rainy highland areas of present-day Peru and Bolivia.

Cultures of the second category—those employing agriculture of an intermediate level—were characteristic of the southeastern quarter of North America and regions adjacent to the Mesoamerican area, both to the north (the United States Southwest) and to the south. In South America, cultures of this general type covered the continent north of the Tropic of Capricorn, with the exception of the high-culture area of the Andes and several relatively small pockets in the tropical forests. The first category—hunters, gatherers, and fishers—occupied most of North America and were found in only minor portions of South America.

The concept of culture area

Within each of these three broad categories, one may further distinguish a pattern of aboriginal regional groupings, each exhibiting a significant measure of internal cultural similarity while differing from all the others. In the terminological shorthand of the anthropologist, adjacent societies that share a dominant cultural orientation are said to belong to a *culture area*.[2]

For example, extending over much of Alaska, northern Canada, and coastal Greenland was a culture area of highly specialized hunters who ingeniously exploited a limited range of resources—large sea mammals in the winter and caribou during the short summer. Directly south of them, in the coniferous forests broken here and there by treeless tundra, hunters in birch-bark canoes or on snowshoes followed caribou, moose, and other game. Along the Northwest coast lay a culture area rich in natural resources—salmon, in particular—that provided abundant support for societies emphasizing hereditary social rank and material wealth. By contrast, the small groups of the densely populated area covering more than two-thirds of today's California subsisted mainly on acorns, supplemented by seeds, deer, and small game.

Of the dozen or so culture areas of North America, discussion in this chapter will be limited to the buffalo hunters of the Plains and the societies of intermediate agricul-

[2]The concept of the culture area, which is especially applicable to the New World, was explicitly formulated more than fifty years ago by Clark Wissler, curator of anthropology at the American Museum of Natural History in New York. It took its form as Wissler faced the difficult task of attempting to do justice to the rich variety of material culture among the Indian peoples, given the limitations on the space available for a well-balanced museum display. The application of this concept to the North American continent received strong support in one of the major works of A. L. Kroeber (1939), a foremost American anthropologist. Our discussion of a few selected culture areas draws primarily on Driver 1969 and Driver and Massey 1957.

turalists in the East; both figure prominently in our subsequent discussion.

In the popular view, the North American Indians are typified by the tribes of the Great Plains. At the time of the first white contact, these Indians roamed a vast stretch of grassland extending from the Mississippi River westward to the Rocky Mountains, and from present-day Alberta and Saskatchewan to the Rio Grande border of Texas. Belonging to some two dozen different tribal societies, most of the Plains Indians were nomadic hunters, with the plentiful buffalo their primary source of meat as well as of materials for clothing, shelter (tepees), and tools. Their only domesticated animal was the dog.

The introduction of the horse into this hemisphere by the Spaniards during the sixteenth century stimulated a profound change in the life style of these people. By about the middle of the eighteenth century,

Indians of the Great Plains

horses had become common throughout the area and the Plains Indians were known as superb horsemen. The possession of horses revolutionized the hunting of buffalo, drew surrounding peoples into what had earlier been a rather sparsely populated region, and in a short time gave rise to a fairly uniform but distinctly vibrant way of life.

Some of the tribes directly to the east of the Plains proper, were semisedentary village dwellers, who divided their time between hunting and the tending of crops in fertile river valleys—primarily maize, beans, and squash. These tribes thus constituted a somewhat distinctive cultural subdivision, termed by some anthropologists the *Prairies culture area*.

During historic times, each of those tribes basing their subsistence on the buffalo hunt was organized in separate bands that usually camped together only once or twice during the year. There were no hereditary classes. Individuals gained social rank and

The various Eskimo groups of the far North have for thousands of years coped with a most inhospitable environment through fortitude and highly specialized cultural adaptation. This Eskimo seal hunter is on the point of launching a harpoon. (The Museum of Modern Art/Film Stills Archive)

The mounted hunters of the Great Plains are still regarded by many Americans and Europeans as "typical" Indians. George Catlin, an early nineteenth-century painter, has depicted here a somewhat romanticized version of the buffalo hunt. (Courtesy of Smithsonian Institution)

prestige by virtue of age, horse ownership, and—most important—the bravery displayed during small-scale raiding parties on neighboring tribes. The purpose of such exploits was to avenge the death of a tribesman or to obtain horses. Stealing a horse from inside the enemy's encampment or counting coups—that is, touching or striking one's adversary during combat with the hand or a short stick—were considered feats of the utmost distinction. For the male members of the Plains tribes, then, cultural emphasis was on individual achievement through activities that required bravery and endurance—hunting, raiding, and warfare.

Of special significance in the Plains area was belief in the efficacy of the *vision quest* as a source of supernatural power. Such quests were undertaken by fasting and praying in seclusion from others. During visions, or dreams, individuals would commonly experience visitation by a guardian spirit—an animal or a bird—and be given a

sacred song, afterward returning to their people spiritually strengthened. Ceremonial life was rich, culminating for almost all of the Plains tribes in a *sun dance* held during the summer in fulfillment of an individual's pledge to hold such a dance in return for supernatural assistance at a time of sickness or other urgent personal or family need. The entire tribe gathered for this ceremony, in which the pledger and other male participants danced and fasted and, in some cases, even engaged in self-torture. Lasting several days, the sun dance was an occasion of both ritual and social importance and did much to encourage a sense of tribal cohesion (Jorgensen 1972).

Indians of Eastern North America

In three regions of aboriginal North America—the Eastern Woodlands, the Southeast (these two occasionally lumped together), and the Southwest—intermediate agriculture was practiced. Corn (maize), together with beans and squash, provided the major source of subsistence for all of the

East and was supplemented by plentiful game and fish. Except for the dome-shaped wigwams of some groups in the north, the multifamily houses of the sizable villages or towns tended to be rectangular in their ground plan—for example, the large communal bark-covered long houses of the Iroquois (see Figure 6-1).

Throughout the East, work in the fields was the province of women, and the prevailing socioeconomic unit was an extended family located at the maternal residence and including all daughters, their husbands, and children. Dwellings and land for the most part were owned or used by a resident group of kin who reckoned their descent within the same maternal line. Although village chiefs and other officers were commonly selected by a male council, the succession of offices usually remained in the female line.

The East was further characterized by large and well-organized political institutions. Among the peoples of the Eastern Woodlands area, the best-organized and most powerful were the League of the Iroquois. However, it was in the Southeast that the richest and most complex cultures east of the Mississippi River were developing on the eve of European colonization. Prehistoric cultural contact with Mesoamerica and

the influence of that area were clearly evidenced in both the patterns of subsistence and the sociocultural elaboration of some of the Indian societies. Among them, the Natchez people, with their kingly rulers and complex system of social ranking, represented a notable cultural advance. Yet, despite the many favorable conditions for cultural development in the East, population was in part kept down by incessant warfare, which continued on into the early centuries of the colonial period.

TO SUM UP   Even this small sample of the great variety of cultural adaptations to the ecological spectrum of the hemisphere indicates how inadequate is the popular image of the Native Americans, whose uninvited guests we have all become. The general lack of awareness of how much our civilization is indebted to them is equally appalling.

THE CONTRIBUTION
OF THE INDIANS TO
WORLD CIVILIZATION

Whatever the origin of the phrase *Indian giver* may have been, history shows that the characterization is certainly not deserved. In

Figure 6-1 Iroquois long house

The traditional Iroquois long house, frequently well over 100 feet long, housed numerous related families. Each family unit occupied a stall and shared a fire in the central aisle with the family on the opposite side.

fact, it is easy to argue that the cultural traffic between Native Americans and the representatives of the "superior" European civilization has been remarkably one-sided, with the former the tragic losers. While the "culture-poor" Indians contributed a number of fundamental and lasting innovations to the material well-being of their conquerors, what they received in return—guns, alcohol, disease, and arrogant or inhuman treatment—stands as one of the great injustices of modern history.

Of the four major staple crops raised in the world today—wheat, rice, maize, and potatoes—two were originally domesticated by Native Americans. The potato was developed by the Indians of the central Andean culture area in pre-Columbian times and taken to Europe by Spaniards in the latter part of the sixteenth century. After gaining popularity in various countries of Europe during the seventeenth century, it made its way back to other parts of the Western Hemisphere.

Maize has been the principal food of Indians of the warmer regions for several millennia prior to the European conquest. About a century after it had been taken back by Columbus, it became known over much of Europe and was diffused to other parts of the Old World. Unlike the potato, it was popular with the early colonists from the very beginning and was used by them not only for food but as a medium of exchange. Among the other plant foods of New World origin are the peanut, squash, bean, cassava, and sweet potato and cacao, the source of cocoa and chocolate.

By contrast, nearly all of the important domesticated animals are of Old World origin. For one animal, however, we are indebted to the Indians—the turkey, which in addition to its tasty flesh has acquired a symbolic significance for a great majority of people in the United States.

Tobacco, a native American plant cultivated in pre-Columbian times, is today considered a mixed blessing, but a great many of the medicinal plants known to the Indi-

ans, or substances derived from them, proved invaluable to the early European settlers and for centuries figured prominently among the officially accepted drugs used to bring relief to millions of people. One of these, quinine, was the only effective remedy for the dreaded malaria until well into the twentieth century. Aztec medicine was so highly thought of by the Spanish conquerors that in the Imperial College of Santa Cruz, established by the Church in Tlatelolco in 1536, it was taught as a separate subject. Its empirical foundation is judged sound even by contemporary scientific standards (de Montellano 1975).

Although cotton was domesticated independently in both the Old World and the New World, commercial cottons grown today derive largely from the species and varieties cultivated in the Western Hemisphere before European contact. Rubber was used by some Indians of Mesoamerica and tropical South America for a variety of purposes, including the making of balls for their games and the waterproofing of their clothing. Samples of this remarkable plant product were taken back to Europe by the earliest visitors to the New World, although it was not until much later that rubber became commercially valuable. Obviously, the impact of these various new foods and industrial crops on the economy of Europe and other parts of the world has been of great significance.

PATTERNS OF CONTACT
AND CONQUEST:
LATIN AMERICA

The seeds of modern colonialism were planted during the fifteenth century, when European seafaring expeditions began exploring the waters and lands beyond the confines of the then known world. Technologically, the era of exploration and colonialism was ushered in by improvements in navigation and shipbuilding; politically and economically, it paralleled the rise of centralized national monarchies, which were eager to expand their dominions and find new sources of wealth. The experience of conquest, both for the conquerors and the conquered, was far from limited to the New World. There are parallels, for example, between the Russian consolidation of Siberia and central Asia and the territorial expansion in North America.

As elsewhere around the world, the nature of the initial contact and the subsequent pressure on the native populations in the Americas by the Europeans were far from uniform. They varied with the period and region, the colonizing policies of the several European governments, the perceptions and attitudes of colonists, and the characteristics of the different native societies.

The colonization of the Americas was initiated by the Spanish and Portuguese. At least in the early years of their incursion, the chief quest of Spanish colonists was for wealth and military renown. To the footloose conquistadors who opened up new territories, the Americas presented a welcome opportunity for acquiring personal fortunes and provided an unlimited adventure of historic uniqueness. Mines producing gold, silver, and other metals were opened with a minimum of delay, and Indians were put to forced labor to extract the riches demanded by the royal treasury. Taking advantage of the long tradition of native agricultural activity, the Spaniards introduced the institution of *encomienda*, a form of exploitation analogous in many respects to the feudal system of peasant servitude.

The supplanting of native religions

Realizing that Native America was a vast untapped reservoir of souls to be claimed for Christianity, the Catholic Church and the Spanish Crown wasted no time in dispatching numerous representatives of religious orders on overseas missions. Economic control and religious conversion were complementary aspects of a conquest policy that proved especially successful in the Mesoamerican and Andean regions.

In these areas, the sedentary populations—accustomed to agriculture, mining, construction of monumental public works, and payment of heavy tributes under the

Spanish soldiers attack the great temple of Tenochtitlán during the final phase of the siege of the Aztec capital. This illustration shows Aztec eagle and jaguar knights defending the temple while Spaniards and their Indian allies press home the attack. (Courtesy of The American Museum of Natural History)

efficient regimes of the native empires prior to the Spanish incursion—were simply forced to transfer their allegiance to the hierarchical order of their new masters. The supplanting of native supernaturalism by Christian ideology was likewise made possible by striking parallelisms between the two. Eric R. Wolf has provided us with an excellent summary of this aspect of the Spanish conquest:

> Both religions . . . believed in a structured and ordered supernatural world, in which more powerful, unseen, and unfathomable divinities stood above local supernatural mediators of lesser scope and power. . . . The Middle American peasant, like his Spanish counterpart, focused his religious interest on these lowlier supernatural helpers. . . . Where the Spanish peasant worshipped wooden saints, the Middle American peasant worshipped clay idols; both had recourse to the magical practices of folk medicine; both had a strong sense of omens; and both believed in the reality of witches (Wolf 1959:169).

Most astonishing, perhaps, were the ritual and institutional similarities between Catholicism and the religious doctrines of the Aztecs and other Mesoamerican peoples. Continuing with Wolf's comparison,

In Catholicism, the child was baptized and named. . . . The Mexica [Aztecs] similarly bathed and named the child in a religious rite, and the Maya celebrated with a ceremony the first time the child was carried astride the hip. Both religious traditions had a kind of confession. The Mexica and the inhabitants of the Gulf coast confessed their sexual transgressions to a priest of the earth goddess Filth-Eater; the Zapotec had annual public confessions; and the Maya confessed themselves either to priests or members of their families in case of illness. Both religious traditions possessed a ritual of communion. The Catholics drank wine and swallowed a wafer to symbolize their contact with the divine blood and body of Christ; the Mexica consumed images of the gods made of

This masked Guatemalan Indian dancer is dressed to impersonate a Spaniard of the colonial era. Note the hat, plume, and jacket. One way of responding to subjugation is to ridicule the conqueror (Mary Jane Pi-Sunyer).

amaranth and liberally anointed with sacrificial blood. Both people used incense in their churches; both fasted and did penance; both went on pilgrimages to holy places; both kept houses of celibate virgins. Both believed in the existence of a supernatural mother; and both believed in virgin birth (Wolf 1959:171–172).

Once having converted the native nobles, the Spanish missionaries turned their attention to the peasants, their individual efforts culminating in claims of as many as fourteen thousand baptisms on a single day. Such mass conversions should no doubt be understood as symbolic changes in allegiance rather than an abrupt change in religious beliefs.

Cultural crystallization

Unlike the Anglo-Americans to the north, most of the Spaniards, especially in the early period, came without families and freely intermarried with the native population to produce offspring of mixed European and American Indian ancestry. These unions were the origin of the *mestizos*, who today constitute the majority of the population of Mexico and of a number of other Latin American countries. Within the short span of less than a century, all the densely populated regions of the New World south of the Rio Grande (with the notable exception of present-day Brazil, colonized by the Portuguese) were actively shaped by the powerful forces of a strikingly different way of life. The high degree of contact between the native peoples and their conquerors was chiefly responsible for the uniformity of the emerging hybrid civilizations of Spanish America. The result has been the development of an overlying secondary culture area, characterized by the pre-eminence of the Spanish language, the dominance of the Catholic ethos, and numerous borrowings of Spanish material traits and a great many social patterns of European provenience, such as the ideal of family solidarity and a strong sense of individual uniqueness and personal dignity. This cultural homogenization was due only in part to the political and military control exerted by Spain over its vast overseas territories. It was heightened by a process of cultural selection and simplification of the varied regional traditions and practices imported from the mother country. This process of concentrating Spanish patterns in the New World serves as an excellent example of "conquest culture." The subsequent process of modification, once the colonial culture embarked on its own course, has come to be referred to as *cultural crystallization* (Foster 1960).

For the relatively sparse Indian population of what today is Brazil, Portuguese colonization had much direr consequences. By the second half of the sixteenth century, thousands of Indians found themselves serving as slaves in towns and on sugar plantations along the coast. Many had been captured by armed expeditions into the interior, during which entire villages were razed and massacred. Intertribal warfare and Old World diseases exacted heavy additional tolls. When, during the latter part of the seven-

Portuguese colonization

teenth century, African slaves became available in sufficient numbers to replace native-born laborers, the pressure on Indians subsided. By this time, however, their populations had already been reduced to a fraction of their original size.

Of those Indians who had been spared, most resided in mission-protected villages established by the Jesuit order. By the time the activities of the Jesuits were abruptly terminated in the second half of the eighteenth century, the majority of these Indians had been detribalized. Ready to be assimilated into colonial life, they became rural farmers, with no desire to reclaim their ancestral Indian identity. Some were subjected to involuntary labor once again when, more than a century ago, the demand for rubber created a feverish boom in the Amazon Valley region. Frequent raids on Indian villages to procure laborers for rubber fields created an international scandal.

Until the beginning of the twentieth century, Brazilian civilization had largely been limited to regions along the coast and such portions of the interior as the rubber-rich Amazon Valley. When the frontier began to move again, a bloody and protracted clash appeared inevitable between the Brazilian settlers and those native groups threatened with dispossession. Fortunately for the Indians, who stood no chance in what was to become another unequal contest, the Indian Protection Service (SPI) was established in 1910 by Cândido Mariano da Silva Rondon (1865–1958), himself of Indian ancestry. Rondon, whose motto was "Die if necessary, but never kill," had developed techniques during his army service for pacification of the interior forest tribes with no spilling of Indian blood. But even the SPI was unable to prevent the steady demise of aboriginal groups. Measles, influenza, and other imported diseases had devastating effects on most of the forest populations, and hunger and the relentless pressures of the modern frontier have done the rest.

After Rondon's death in 1958, the Indian Protection Service steadily deteriorated.

Perhaps most tragic of all, a report published in 1968 by the Brazilian Ministry of the Interior admitted that wholesale slaughter of Indians had been committed or condoned by members of the SPI. The finger was pointed not only at nearly all of the more than one thousand employees of the SPI but also at its head, who was accused of collusion in several murders, the illegal sale of land, and embezzlement. Apparently, as the opening up of the jungles of Amazonas continued apace, rich landowners—with the full knowledge of the SPI—were "clearing" new land of Indians with dynamite and machine-gun fire from the air, or by poisoned food and deliberate smallpox infection. Nor are the Brazilian excesses isolated. In the frontier regions of Colombia, Venezuela, Peru, and other countries, similar inhumanities are known to have occurred. One "Indian hunter," arrested in 1968, confessed to having killed thirty-two Indians in the course of eight years. It is no coincidence that as soon as the panic-stricken survivors fled their homelands, land speculators invariably moved in. Even today, despite the indignation aroused in world opinion, it appears doubtful that the economic exploitation of the interior regions of Brazil and other South American countries can be made compatible with the survival and preservation of what little is left of the heritage of the Indians of the tropical forest.

PATTERNS OF CONTACT AND CONQUEST: NORTH OF MEXICO

To say that Native Americans were defrauded of their homeland and almost exterminated by the European settlers in the New World is to reduce the interaction of a great many cultural forces to a mere shadow play between cowboys and Indians. Atrocities were committed by both sides, although the Indians were more often on the receiving end. Fundamentally, the ultimate settling of the continent by white colonists at the expense of the native peoples should be viewed, not as the consequence of a chain of criminal acts perpetrated by individual Europeans, but rather as the result of a complex process of cultural conflict. In the words of Bernard W. Sheehan, a historian:

In truth . . . the Indian disintegrated; as an Indian he was not annihilated but he faded culturally into another entity. . . . The inexorable breakdown of the native's cultural integrity [was] in part the result of conscious policy and in part the inevitable consequence of competition between two disparate ways of life. Rather than the singular clarity of one despicable act, the American aborigine was the victim of a process. . . .
It was not merely a question of a shortage of governmental or philanthropic goodwill but of a booming white America bursting out of the constrictions of its social bounds, causing the decline of a native society virtually devoid of the resources for serious competition (Sheehan 1969:269 and 284–285).

Some may object that such a view simply attempts to hide a profound continent-sized tragedy behind the smoke screen of scholarly rhetoric. We disagree. More appropriately, it calls for an analysis of the nature of the early contacts between the Indians and the whites so that the whys and hows of the conquest can be better understood. Here we can only sketch some of the elements of a very complex answer.

The fur trade A particular case may serve as an illustration. The Europeans not only seemed more inclined toward violence than were the Indians but were much better equipped to engage in it, and at lesser risk. One concrete reason was the superior firepower of the musket and later of the rifle. However, these weapons did not remain for long in the sole possession of the whites. In the brisk fur trade that developed along the early frontier, firearms were of great importance. In this early period of contact the Europeans were far more interested in trade than in the acquisition of land, and they supplied weapons to the Indians in great numbers, along with metal traps, blankets, and other items. In short, the fur trade was the economic mainspring of colonial North America, with beaver playing the dominant role.

As early as the first half of the seventeenth century, the Iroquois in what today is central New York had become so dependent upon a steady supply of European goods, firearms in particular, that they put their own basis of livelihood in jeopardy by depleting the supply of beaver, whose pelts served as the universal medium of exchange. When the Dutch at Fort Orange (later Albany) finally clamped down on traders who had been selling guns to the Iroquois, the Indians turned instead to the French and the Hurons. The Hurons were superior traders, exchanging goods supplied by the French with a number of tribes to the west for furs, which the French were anxious to obtain for the growing European market (beaver hats enjoyed a great vogue in Europe, where the animal by this time had been virtually wiped out). An agreement between the Five Nations of the strong Iroquoian Confederacy and the Hurons, concluded in 1645, was a dubious bargain for the Hurons: they agreed to deliver peltry to the Iroquois, who in return promised to refrain from raiding the Huron territory in quest of furs. When, later during the same year, the Hurons sent canoeloads of furs directly to Montreal in disregard of their agreement, the angered Iroquois responded with unbridled revenge. In the course of five short years, the Huron Nation of some thirty thousand individuals was decimated beyond restoration. In rapid succession a similar fate befell other Indian nations to the west of the Confederacy.

The point we wish to make is that from the very beginning the relationship the Europeans had established with Indian societies was by nature exploitative; and once it degenerated into strong economic and cultural dependence, several native populations were doomed without any direct involvement on the part of the whites.

Early contacts   Another source of large-scale disasters was the communicable diseases brought from the Old World—smallpox especially—against which the Indians lacked the immunity acquired by the whites over many centuries of exposure. The sizable villages of much of the aboriginal Eastern Woodlands and the Southeast made the native populations particularly vulnerable to epidemic diseases. As early as several years before the Pilgrims landed at Plymouth (there had been preliminary explorations and trading), one such epidemic swept the coastal area of present-day New England, taking many lives.

Although the Indians of the East were agriculturalists, a good portion, perhaps as much as half, of their subsistence derived from hunting and fishing. In contrast to Mesoamerica, the population density was relatively low, and cultivated land constituted a minute fraction of the total landscape. Unconcerned about or ignorant of the concepts that the Indians held with respect to rights to hunting territory or fishing sites, the English settlers considered free for the taking any land not explicitly claimed or visibly utilized. Even when land was clearly claimed by the Indians, settlers perceived native occupants as "savages" who could be dislodged or exterminated without scruple. From the skirmishes that inevitably followed such encroachment, the Indians invariably emerged the losers.

Whatever attempts were made by the early settlers to encourage Indian men to take up English-style farming usually met with little success, since work in the fields in most of the aboriginal East had long been the province of women. This cultural barrier to the availability of Indian males for agricultural labor on cotton and tobacco plantations in the coastal regions of the South, as well as the low dependability of their services—they were easy prey to a variety of imported diseases or prone to run away—did little to enhance the Indians' status in the eyes of the land-hungry settlers. The importation of slaves from Africa was in part designed to fill the growing need for an inexpensive labor force.

Despite the continued shrinking of their populations and their original homeland, some Indian tribes periodically managed to enjoy a measure of prosperity and bargaining power as long as France, England, and Spain vied for control of North America. However, once the ascendancy of the United States had become established at the beginning of the nineteenth century and the American frontier began to press steadily westward, the Indians were soon brought under control and were gradually forced to cede the land they still claimed for themselves.

Not even those few surviving Indian peoples in the Southeast—later known as the Five Civilized Tribes—who made considerable strides toward accommodation with the whites and their government were spared. They turned from hunting to agriculture, no doubt in part because the supply of game had become exhausted, and also tended cattle, learned crafts, and permitted their children to receive school instruction. In only two respects did they refuse to yield: they were unwilling to accept the white man's religion or his idea of holding land individually.

By the mid-1820s, it became clear that the rapid settlement of the territory east of the Mississippi was incompatible with the presence of even peaceful Indians—a sentiment that found its expression in the Indian Removal Act of 1830. Those Indian peoples who did not accept the terms and agree to their own removal were moved forcibly to Indian Territory (later Oklahoma). It is estimated that about half of the Creeks failed to survive the removal and the difficult adjustment to their new home in the

The nineteenth century

West, and that some four thousand Cherokees—about a fourth of those who set out from Georgia—perished in the winter of 1838–1839 during their trek under military escort along what was to be called the "Trail of Tears."

Well before 1850, then, the viability of Native American cultures east of the Mississippi had been virtually destroyed, and what remnants of their original populations had survived the impact of conquest had either been subdued or been moved westward. At the time, it must have seemed likely that the transfer to the "worthless" land beyond the Mississippi of perhaps as many as one hundred thousand Indians would launch a period of relative tranquility for both the conquerors and the dispossessed. However, the territory west of the Mississippi was not to escape the growing waves of immigrants for long. The discovery of gold in California in 1848 heralded the beginning of the end.

Encounters between the whites and the Indians during this last phase of the westward movement differed substantially from what they had been earlier. Except for the farming villagers of the Southwest, the Indians were largely nomadic hunters, fishers, and gatherers, and the nature of their contact with the frontiersmen was consequently elusive. On the other hand, the accelerating pace of white settlement was marked by a growing impatience with any obstacles. Before the century came to a close, the vast area west of the Mississippi had been brought under the full control of United States troops, and by 1890 the American "frontier" had officially ceased to be.

EFFECTS OF COLONIZATION
ON THE WESTERN INDIANS

The Great Plains

In the course of a few decades, the vast herds of buffalo that roamed the Plains were wantonly destroyed by the ever-increasing numbers of immigrants, adventurers, and soldiers. Some of the Indians themselves contributed to the slaughter, once they had succumbed to trading furs with the whites. The inevitable result was the collapse of the subsistence base on which these Indian cultures were built. The subjection of the Plains tribes was punctuated by a series of bloody battles. Tribes that had previously lived in hostility frequently united in defense against the intruders, and the effects of their brave resistance were felt repeatedly by the armed expeditions sent to subdue them. Nevertheless, by the end of 1890 the relentless pressure had forced the Indians of the Plains to submit and accept a listless existence on the reservations to which they had been assigned. Attempts by the government to convert them to farming were singularly unsuccessful. As a rule, the reservations were little suited for agriculture, the necessary capital for developing the land was not available, and for those used to hunting buffalo, the circumscribed life of farmers held little attraction. Just as in the East, smallpox, cholera, and other diseases contributed further to the decimation and demoralization of the once formidable warriors.

The remainder of the West had been made secure for the whites in relatively short order, long before the conquest of the Plains Indians. The frontier leaped over the arid Southwest and the intermountain culture areas of the Plateau and the Great Basin and swallowed California, whose numerous but small aboriginal groups were neither organized nor strong enough for effective defense. In the Northwest Coast culture area, the indiscriminate killing of animals by Indians who engaged for a period in a flourishing fur trade with the whites also eventually destroyed an important source of subsistence. In California, the disruption of native life and the rapid depopulation of the Pacific coastal area closely paralleled the fate of the Eastern Indians two centuries earlier.

It is not easy to generalize about the conquest of Native Americans within the bounds of the United States and the adjacent Canadian territory or about the impact of white civilization upon their cultures. Despite the overall uniformity of the cultural pressures to which Indian peoples were subject, their response varied from one culture area to another and even within them.

The Southwest   On the one hand, the several centuries of contact with the Spanish and the subsequent Anglo-American influence notwithstanding, some of the Pueblo Indians of the Southwest have managed to retain many of their traditional lifeways. While material and technological changes in their cultures have been in evidence since about the beginning of the century, indigenous sociopolitical institutions—especially the large extended family as the primary unit of socialization—and ceremonial organization have shown a strong tendency to persist side by side with a socioceremonial system of Spanish-Catholic derivation. This phenomenon, characteristic of the Eastern Pueblos (New Mexico), has been referred to by anthropologists as *compartmentalization*. In the words of Edward P. Dozier:

That the Catholic church and Catholic ritual were distinct and separate from native ceremonialism is . . . clear from the [eighteenth-century] reports of the missionaries. We may conclude that the Pueblos were already successfully concealing the esoteric rites of their [own] ceremonial life and that the Pueblo leaders were insisting on the purity of indigenous practices. . . . It is evident, therefore, that compartmentalization had been fully established by the latter part of the eighteenth century. Compartmentalization was an obvious accommodating device which permitted the Indians to carry on their indigenous cultural practices behind a façade of activities acceptable or at least tolerable to Spanish authorities (Dozier 1961:150–151).

Today, the question is not so much whether this compartmentalization will or

A Hopi Indian painting a kachina doll. Carved from cottonwood roots and decorated to resemble kachina dancers, these figurines serve primarily as ceremonial gifts to Hopi children. Like some of the Hopi baskets, which are woven by women, the kachina dolls are often of high artistic merit and have become objects much sought after by discriminating collectors. (Courtesy of the Santa Fe Railway)

to enhance the host's fame and social standing and to challenge the invited guests to reciprocity that might bring them to economic ruin and social disgrace. Since the end of the potlatch period, the rapid adaptation of the Kwakiutl has been marked by a substantial loss of institutional integrity, large-scale participation and specialization in the white economy (mostly fishing), and dominance of English—in short, thorough assimilation to Canadian-American culture has taken place. What ceremonials are still performed have assumed a different mean-

A Northwest Coast potlatch ceremony at the turn of the century, Fort Rupert, British Columbia. The speaker is praising the chief responsible for the distribution of these valuable goods. (Courtesy of The American Museum of Natural History)

will not continue to function but rather how such drastic economic changes as a shift from agricultural subsistence to wagework may affect the unity of Pueblo communities. Thus far, the strong element of conservatism characteristic of the Pueblos has not been seriously undermined. Among the Western Pueblos, the Hopi of Arizona represent an extreme case of indigenous cultural integrity, most of them having rejected white influence except for some superficial material expressions.

The Northwest Coast

On the other hand, among the Kwakiutl of the Northwest coast (on northern Vancouver Island and the adjacent British Columbia coast), virtually all aspects of their native culture have been subject to extensive replacement. A major break with their past practices came in the mid-1920s, when the Kwakiutl discontinued the competitive *potlatches*, dating back to the middle of the eighteenth century. These were ceremonial feasts featuring displays of wealth, ostentatious destruction of personal property, and lavish gift giving—all of these designed

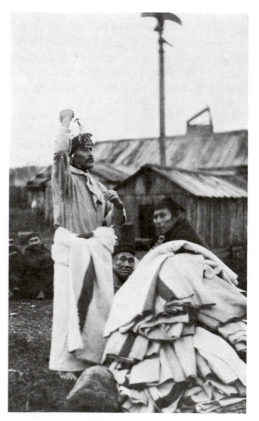

The Navajo Indians have been particularly successful in making effective use of elements of contemporary American culture while at the same time retaining many aspects of their native way of life. For example, their traditional houses, called hogans, are customarily reached today by pickups or jeeps. (Courtesy of the Museum of Northern Arizona)

ing in the changed context. The only aspect of traditional life that has persisted to the present is the interest of the Kwakiutl in profitable economic ventures, property, and the maximization of social status. In this respect, the old value orientations have proved helpful to them in their new circumstances, even if few have managed to achieve economic equality with the whites. The remarkably rapid and relatively painless substitution of the new culture for the indigenous one strongly suggests that, despite the conspicuous differences between the two, the old Kwakiutl way of life and the Canadian-American, which they have so readily assumed, must have shared some fundamental features.

In an intermediate position between the Pueblos and the Kwakiutl stand the Navajo. Ever since their appearance in the Southwest a few centuries prior to Francisco Coronado's expedition to the region in 1540–1541, they have been eager and prodigious cultural borrowers. From the Pueblos they learned to practice agriculture, weav-

The Navajo

ing, and probably the making of pottery and also adopted a number of socioceremonial concepts. By the mid-nineteenth century, they had fully integrated into their culture horses, sheep, and goats, all of which were earlier introduced by the Spanish. Still later, directly or indirectly influenced by the Mexicans, they became very proficient silversmiths. In the Anglo-American period, which began inauspiciously enough with their conquest by the United States troops and the "Long Walk" into captivity at Fort Sumner, New Mexico, between 1864 and 1868, the Navajo have increased their mobility by adding the pickup truck, made use of boarding schools and modern medical facilities on their reservation, and launched a variety of economically profitable tribal enterprises.

And yet, theirs is one of the most distinctive ways of life to be found in all of North America today. Far from creating a cultural patchwork of elements of various origins, the Navajo have managed to rework their many borrowings and mold or integrate them to fit the framework of their core institutions. In short, they combine a practical approach toward the potential and real contributions of other civilizations with a healthy respect for their own time-tested cultural values. A good illustration is the fact that the Navajo operate the Navajo Community College at Tsaile, Arizona, which is dedicated to the maintenance of a minority heritage and culture within the complex and changing world of which they are now a part.[3]

These three examples are meant not to exhaust the possible outcomes of culture contact situations experienced by North American Indians, but only to illustrate the variety of their responses. There still are Indian groups in northwestern Canada both north and south of the Arctic Circle who continue to hunt and trap game without appreciable encroachments upon their land or way of life. Some have experienced meaningful contact with a highly industrialized society only very recently, although at a precipitous rate. It is not difficult to find an Alaskan Eskimo who has flown in an airplane but has never seen an automobile.

TO SUM UP   The process of culture change — to be discussed on a global basis and in more detail in a later chapter — is affected by a great many variables. On the one hand, there is the society or community that comes to experience culture contact on its home grounds. The manner in which the contact evolves and becomes resolved is partly influenced by the vigor of the contending forces, but there are numerous other factors that help determine the nature of the process of mutual adjustment. Among them, as we have seen, are demographic conditions (for example, the high population density characteristic of parts of aboriginal Mesoamerica), ecological setting (such as the vast grassland areas of the Plains, replete with buffalo), type of subsistence (such as dependence on big-game hunting in the Plains), nature of sociocultural integration (for example, the tightly structured system of the Pueblos), emphases in value orientations (such as the materialistic outlook of the Kwakiutl). Also important are the identity and role of the agencies or brokers who mediate the contact: it does make a difference whether they are missionaries, traders, soldiers, settlers, or others. In each case, the initial contact stimulates a different kind of response and sets the stage for the course of subsequent relations. An additional circumstance in North America that contributed to the relatively rapid conquest of its vast area was the political fragmentation and cultural diversity of its indigenous peoples. Not only did this situation preclude a common stand against the invaders, but it also facilitated the sowing of dissension and strife between native societies.

FROM DESPAIR TO NEW HOPE:
INDIAN-GOVERNMENT RELATIONS
IN THE UNITED STATES

Legislation   From the beginning of white settlement until the middle of the eighteenth century, dealing with the Indians was at the discretion of the individual colonies. When, subsequently, attempts were made to find a joint approach to the management of Indian affairs and regulation of white-Indian relations, enforcement was usually all but nonexistent. The first important legislation affecting the relationship between the Indians and the United States government was the Indian Removal Act of 1830, which, as we have seen, provided for an exchange of lands with the Indians residing in any of the states or territories and for their removal west of the Mississippi River. Then in 1871, in the form of a simple rider to an appropriations act, Congress decreed that "hereafter no Indian nation or tribe within the territory of the United States shall be acknowledged or recognized as an independent nation, tribe, or power with whom the United

[3]For our discussion of the Kwakiutl, the Pueblo, and the Navajo Indians, we have drawn mainly on Spicer 1961. The concept of compartmentalization was introduced in Spicer 1954.

States may contract by treaty" (Washburn 1973:2183). To be sure, those Indian tribes that had earlier concluded treaties with the United States (389 treaties, according to one count) saw them repeatedly broken. The few Indian nations that had managed to retain nominal autonomy up until this time were now rapidly being brought under the existing reservation system of control. The ultimate objectives of government policy, however, were to eliminate reservations altogether and to further the assimilation of the Indians into the white rural populations.

Such assimilation was the intent of the General Allotment Act of 1887, also known as the Dawes Act. In brief, it authorized the President of the United States to allot reservation land to the Indians at his discretion, the land thus allotted to be held in trust for a period of twenty-five years for the sole use and benefit of the Indians. Full rights of citizenship were to accompany each individual allotment. The amount of land allottable to a family was set at one quarter of a section (160 acres), half that amount to single persons over eighteen years of age or to orphans, and one-fourth the amount to any person under eighteen born prior to the law's implementation. The "surplus" land, if any, was subject to release to the United States for sale to homesteaders. The act thus marked an important turning point in Indian history: prior to its enactment, Indians were generally dealt with as tribes; from its enactment on, the Indian was treated primarily as an individual. While some Indian groups were excluded from the Dawes Act— the Five Civilized Tribes, for example— these were soon subject to laws of similar effect. Between 1887 and 1934 Indians were dispossessed of some ninety million acres, or nearly two-thirds of their tribal land base.

Even legal ownership of land proved a questionable boon for the Indians, and subsequent amendments designed to protect such holdings were of little help. The taxes assessed were frequently excessive. Assuming guardianship for minor or "incompetent" Indians became a common technique used by enterprising whites to seize control of property. Problems of inheritance often frustrated the gainful use of the original allotments. In general, Indian holders became subject to pressure to sell and were victims of numerous schemes, both legal and illegal, to deprive them of what land had been left in their care.

The ghost-dance religious movement

With the old way of life in complete disarray but its dignity still within living memory, the last third of the nineteenth century became a period of the deepest cultural crisis and despair for the majority of the Western Indians. Decimated by disease and encounters with the military, their subsistence destroyed, and their homelands overrun or rapidly shrinking, they placed their hopes in supernatural deliverance. Tribal prophets and messianic movements were quite widespread in earlier times, having occurred both in the East and the West; but none developed the ardent following received in the latter part of the century by the ghost-dance religion.

There were two waves of this revitalization movement. Although both had their origin among the Northern Paiute in Nevada, the influence of the first was limited to northern California, lasting from about 1870 to 1872. The second wave, of much greater importance, began in 1889 and soon swept throughout most of the western United States. This time, the California Indians remained almost totally unaffected: their societies had by now been in shambles for two decades, and they still felt deep disillusionment because of the failure of their earlier attempts to bring about the return of their former condition.

The prophet of the second wave was Wovoka, known also as Jack Wilson, the name given him by the rancher for whom he had worked since early youth. Wovoka claimed to have had a vision in which he saw God and all the people who had died long ago. They were happy and at peace, living in a plentiful land and following the old ways of their tribes. In the vision, God instructed Wovoka

For the Indians of the Plains, the end of the last century was a period of the greatest despair and tragedy. In the photograph above, a group of these Indians are seen engaged in a ghost-dance ritual, the performance of which they believed would restore them to their proud cultural heritage. The Wounded Knee massacre of 1890 shattered all such hopes. The photograph on the left, taken shortly before the victims were buried in a communal grave, shows the body of an Indian leader lying in the bitter winter cold. (Smithsonian Institution, National Anthropological Archives)

to return to his people with a message of goodwill and a dance ritual that was to be performed for five consecutive days at frequent intervals. Wovoka was promised that if these instructions were followed, he and his brothers would live to see the return of the good life and would be reunited with their dead relatives and friends.

From the Paiutes, the ghost-dance religion spread to neighboring tribes, especially the Arapaho, the Cheyenne, the Dakota, and other Plains Indians, among whom visions were a traditional and integral part of the belief system. Along the way the ghost dance underwent various changes and additions. One of the elaborations was the idea of the impending destruction of the white man, who had taken away Indian lands and decimated the buffalo herds. The Plains Indians in particular were quick to embrace a religion that predicted the annihilation of the white intruders and the restoration of the good old days. Ghost dances were carried on with increasing fervor. The dancers would fall from exhaustion into trancelike states in which they would see their dead relatives and friends or relive the joys of a successful hunt. Some groups began to decorate their shirts with various symbols of the ghost dance in the belief that these symbols would make them safe from bullets (Mooney 1896).

On December 29, 1890, several hundred Sioux men, women, and children who had come together for the purpose of performing the ghost-dance rituals were slaughtered in an infamous "battle" with eight troops of the Seventh Cavalry at Wounded Knee, South Dakota.[4] The massacre proved a

deadly blow to the ghost-dance movement, which slowly faded away as the promised renewal failed to materialize. The Indians once again returned to the harsh realities of life on the reservations.

Widespread as the ghost-dance cult had become at its peak, the impression it made on the tribes of the Southwest was very limited. The Pueblos had little reason to perceive the white conquest of the West as threatening their existence. For the Navajo, on the other hand, the bitter experience of captivity at Fort Sumner was still fresh at the time of the first wave, and the subsequent two decades were marked by frequent clashes with both settlers and the government. One might therefore have expected the Navajo to prove avid followers of the ghost dance, but this was not the case. The reason for their total abstention from the movement can be understood from their beliefs concerning the supernatural. The Navajo believe that the most evil witch power resides in the dead, and for them the return of the dead—a principal element in the ghost-dance prophecy—would have represented a calamity of major proportions.

New hope for the future

In the opening years of the twentieth century it seemed only a question of time until the widely shared conception of the Indian as "the vanishing American" would have proved true. Instead, the situation was about to take a turn for the better. Among the first signs were the reversal of the declining population trend among Native Americans and the passing of the Indian Citizenship Act of 1924. Usually attributed to heightened respect for Indians in recognition of their distinguished service during World War I, the act declared all Indians born within the territorial limits of the United States to be citizens. While not uniformly applauded by Indians—citizenship carried not only privileges but obligations as well—the act nevertheless marked

[4]One of us (Pi-Sunyer) has had the opportunity to talk about this bloody event with Indians whose parents survived Wounded Knee. The experience, for which slaughter is not too strong a term, remains indelibly engraved in Sioux consciousness to the present day. The photographs taken after the atrocity show the frozen bodies of dead Indians, many shot while attempting to escape the deadly gunfire. For the Seventh Cavalry, Wounded Knee was not so much a military operation as an act of revenge for the defeat the unit suffered when General George Armstrong Custer

and his Seventh Cavalry command were wiped out by Sioux warriors on the Little Bighorn on June 25, 1876.

the beginning of a more constructive attitude toward Native Americans on the part of the government. Two years later, a careful study of Indian economic and social conditions was undertaken at the request of the secretary of the interior. When the findings were made public in 1928 in what was called the "Meriam Report," the bitter harvest of the policies of the previous forty years became undeniably evident. The report singled out the critical need for educational and medical improvements, urgently recommended personnel reforms in the Bureau of Indian Affairs, and pointed out that the policy of individual allotment, "not accompanied by adequate instruction in the use of property, . . . has largely failed in the accomplishment of what was expected of it. It has resulted [for the Indian] in much loss of land . . . without a compensating advance in . . . [his] economic ability . . . " (Meriam 1928:41). The impact of the report was chiefly responsible for the Wheeler-Howard (Indian Reorganization) Act of 1934, drafted and subsequently administered by Commissioner of Indian Affairs John Collier, who was deeply sympathetic to the Indian cause. The act tacitly acknowledged the mistakes of past Indian policy and provided for the strengthening of the tribal land base as well as for the Indians' participation in charting their own future. Unfortunately, the depression of the 1930s and World War II severely limited the congressional appropriations vital to the implementation of the act.

The experience of some twenty-five thousand young Indians in the armed forces and thousands of others working in war industries provided the impetus for Native Americans to seek a greater measure of human rights and the correction of past injustices. In 1946, by virtue of the Indian Claims Commission Act, tribal groups received a sweeping authorization to present not only "claims in law or equity arising under the Constitution, laws, treaties of the United States, and Executive orders of the President," but also "claims based upon fair

and honorable dealings that are not recognized by an existing rule of law or equity." More than six hundred such claims have been docketed, and awards made through the fiscal year ending June 30, 1973, amounted to over $484 million (representing only about 5 percent of the total amount claimed). More than fifty anthropologists were called as expert witnesses in these hearings, the majority of whom viewed the available evidence as supporting the Indian claimants. The high point of Indian involvement in the legislative process was reached in the Alaska Native Claims Settlement Act of 1971, which increased the amount of land reserved to the natives from ten to forty million acres and specified payment to them of $962.5 million.

NATIVE AMERICANS TODAY

With the exception of the several historic confederacies, Indian political units tended to splinter into new, and smaller, autonomous groups, incapable of standing up to the pressure of the white colonists. Only after virtually all Indian tribes had been brought under control and their viability stifled was there a reaction—the ghost-dance movement—that came close to being pan-Indian in scope. Its successor, known as the Native American Church, has remained active to the present day. It is a blend of Christian beliefs and Indian practices, especially the sacramental use of peyote.

The first deliberate effort to mobilize Indian resources on a nationwide basis resulted in the founding in 1926 of the National Council of American Indians. The chief aim of this organization and of its better-known successor, the National Congress of American Indians (NCAI, established in 1944), was to keep an eye on legislative developments and to make sure that the Indian viewpoint was put before the public.

The vigorous growth of activism among Native Americans dates back to the early

Mohawk high-steel workers. Many Native Americans from both sides of the United States–Canadian border work in the skilled and dangerous occupation of high-steel construction. This specialty calls for qualities and courage that have long been held in high esteem by the Mohawk people. (Bruce Davidson/ Magnum Photos, Inc.)

1960s. Dissatisfied and impatient with the work of the NCAI, some members of the young generation of college-trained Indians established the National Indian Youth Council. The American Indian Chicago Conference (1961), attended by nearly five hundred delegates representing some ninety North American tribes, issued a "Declaration of Indian Purpose" setting forth proposals that were to build upon and strengthen the principles of the Indian Reorganization Act of 1934. In addition, the Conference denounced in strong terms the termination bills enacted during 1954. These acts, which were designed to withdraw federal aid and protection from selected tribes ("free" them from federal jurisdiction), were hastily and arbitrarily implemented and proved generally unfavorable and even catastrophic to those affected. In most cases the acts brought disorganization to the management of tribal affairs and impoverishment to those individuals who chose to take their share of tribal assets on a per capita basis. In 1969 a series of activist efforts calculated to dramatize the plight of Native Americans began with the takeover of the island of Alcatraz in San Francisco Bay and continued with the occupation of the offices of the Bureau of Indian Affairs in Washington, D.C. (1972) and the seizure of the village of Wounded Knee, South Dakota (1973). It was during this period of surging activism that the American Indian Movement (AIM) emerged as the most militant organization seeking both radical reform of the relations between the Indians and the federal government and redress of historic injustices and current inequities.

By 1976 the activism of Native Americans appeared to have reached a crossroads. Is their progress to be gauged according to the non-Indian standards of the larger society, or does the answer to the future condition of Indian Americans lie in the strengthening of their collective ethnic identity or in the reaffirmation of their individual tribal heritage? The population of Native Americans is currently growing much faster than the general population, and their migration rate into cities exceeds their increase on the reservations. Seeking unskilled or temporary employment in metropolitan areas exposes them to the problems of urban adjustment common to those who are educationally, socially, and economically deprived and who lack access to strategic resources and political power (Waddell and Watson 1971). Is the loss of congenial family ties, a more relaxed atmosphere, and the psychologically supportive effect of the traditional base available on the reservation too high a price to pay for the uncertain prospects of employment and a higher standard of material living? Clearly, concerted efforts to improve opportunities on reservations and in the communities surrounding them would alleviate the present situation and also help to stem the Indian "brain drain,"—the movement of professional Native Americans away from reservations—which has been seriously weakening the quality of tribal leadership. But even this solution poses a potential conflict between growing ecological concerns and the inevitable consequences of technological development.

TO SUM UP   The basic alternatives that Native Americans seem to be facing today, then, are assimilation, detribalization resulting in only a general identity as Indians, or deliberate return to the sources of their individual tribal traditions. We have raised a number of questions to which at present there are no clear answers. To quote Vine Deloria, Jr., a well-known spokesman for the Indian cause:

In view of their amazing revival and determination to survive as Indians gradually reclaiming their homelands, they had at last become a group that could not be administered. Perhaps this is all that many people had wanted (Deloria 1973:579).

REFERENCES

DELORIA, VINE, JR.
1973 American Indians: the end of the fifth century of contact. In *Britannica Book of the Year 1973*. Chicago: Encyclopaedia Britannica. Pp. 577–579 (Special Report).

DE MONTELLANO, BERNARD ORTIZ
1975 Empirical Aztec medicine. *Science* 188:215–220 (no. 4185, April 18).

DOBYNS, HENRY F.
1966 Estimating aboriginal American population: an appraisal of techniques with a new hemispheric estimate. *Current Anthropology* 7:395–416, 425–444.

DOZIER, EDWARD P.
1961 Rio Grande Pueblos. In *Perspectives in American Indian culture change*. Edward H. Spicer, ed. Chicago: The University of Chicago Press. Pp. 94–186.

DRIVER, HAROLD E.
1969 *Indians of North America* (2nd rev. ed.). Chicago: The University of Chicago Press.

DRIVER, HAROLD E., AND WILLIAM C. MASSEY
1957 Comparative studies of North American Indians. *Transactions of the American Philosophical Society*, vol. 47 (n.s.), part 2, pp. 165–456.

FORBES, JACK D., ED.
1964 *The Indian in America's past*. Englewood Cliffs, N.J.: Prentice-Hall.

FOSTER, GEORGE M.
1960 *Culture and conquest; America's Spanish heritage*. Viking Fund Publications in Anthropology, no. 27. New York.

HAGAN, WILLIAM T.
1961 *American Indians*. Chicago: The University of Chicago Press.

JORGENSEN, JOSEPH G.
1972 *The sun dance religion; power to the powerless*. Chicago: The University of Chicago Press.

KROEBER, A. L.
1939 *Cultural and natural areas of native North America*. University of Califor-

nia Publications in American Archaeology and Ethnology, vol. 38. Berkeley and Los Angeles: University of California Press.

MERIAM, LEWIS, AND ASSOCIATES
1928 *The problem of Indian administration.* Baltimore, Md.: The Johns Hopkins Press.

MOONEY, JAMES
1896 The ghost-dance religion and the Sioux outbreak of 1890. *Fourteenth Annual Report of the Bureau of Ethnology,* part 2. Washington, D.C.: Government Printing Office. Pp. 641–1136.

SHEEHAN, BERNARD W.
1969 Indian-white relations in early America: a review essay. *William and Mary Quarterly* 26 (3rd series):267–286 (April).

SPICER, EDWARD H.
1954 Spanish-Indian acculturation in the Southwest. *American Anthropologist* 56:663–684.

SPICER, EDWARD H., ED.
1961 *Perspectives in American Indian culture change.* Chicago: The University of Chicago Press.

WADDELL, JACK O., AND O. MICHAEL WATSON, EDS.
1971 *The American Indian in urban society.* Boston: Little, Brown.

WASHBURN, WILCOMB E., COMP.
1973 *The American Indian and the United States,* vol. 3. New York: Random House.

WOLF, ERIC R.
1959 *Sons of the shaking earth.* Chicago: The University of Chicago Press.

CONCLUSIONS

The major purpose of Part One has been to trace human evolution from its primate origins and crude cultural beginnings to the rise of elaborate civilizations in several parts of the Old World and the New World. We have observed that although biological and cultural innovations were inseparable and mutually reinforcing during the earliest phases of human development, the weight of the cultural component has been rapidly increasing through time. As one approaches the emergence of Homo sapiens, *examination of the physical changes in our species steadily reveals the growing ability of human beings to cope with many different types of environments as they spread throughout most of the habitable world. Ultimately, as was the case with the Native Americans, some had to face an unprecedented situation— the need to adjust to the effects of wholesale culture contact brought about by European colonization.*

128

PART TWO

HUMAN SOCIETIES: LEVELS OF COMPLEXITY

INTRODUCTION

Controlled comparison, better known as the comparative method, *is one of the major analytical tools used by anthropologists in the study of sociocultural systems. Given the variety and scope of social and cultural phenomena that can be examined comparatively, it is imperative that the units or items under consideration be of the same type or order. Only then can important differences and similarities be thrown into sharp relief and valid generalizations made.*

One approach that anthropologists have used in examining human societies is to classify them according to their degree of complexity or, as it is often called, their level of social integration. Although this is a rough classificatory device, for it lumps the great many societies into a relatively few categories, it highlights some of the crucial continuities and discontinuities in methods of livelihood, social structure, and political organization.

The four chapters in Part Two are devoted to a consideration of sociocultural systems arranged in terms of organizational complexity. Chapter 7, "The Ecology of Hunting and Collecting," deals with societies that are dependent on the surpluses of the natural environment—for the most part edible plants and hunted animals. There are few of these societies left today, but for many tens of thousands of years the human species and its antecedents survived in just such a manner. In short, this was the original mode of human adaptation.

"Varieties of Tribal Experience," Chapter 8, is concerned with tribal groups. Tribes are larger than hunting and collecting bands and may incorporate many thousands of individuals. Nevertheless, the bonds that unite members of tribal societies tend to be those of custom and traditional usage rather than the codified legal systems and impersonal political arrangements found in state systems. As a rule, tribes are ethnically homogeneous in composition, and members of a given tribe often share the same language and the same set of religious beliefs and practices. Prior to the establishment of the state, tribes were autonomous and self-regulating units with mechanisms of internal jurisdiction and external defense. The economies of tribal societies are based on domesticated plants and an-

imals or, at the least, on highly predictable sources of subsistence.

Chapter 9, titled "The Peasant Condition," deals with the important rural
sector of some complex societies. Our
emphasis here is on the place and
condition of agriculturalists in pre-
industrial states and developing
nations. Peasants everywhere are
subordinate to higher-order structures and institutions, most commonly city-based elites and their
agents. Nevertheless, the life of peasants is very different from that of urbanites, and although peasants
constitute the majority of all pre-industrial state systems, their political
and economic power is highly circumscribed. Because peasants numerically comprise the majority of
humankind, they have received a

great deal of attention from anthropologists and other social scientists.
Peasants and peasant communities
survive within the constraints
imposed on them by the powerful
agencies of the larger world,
which they sustain with their labors
but over which they have little or no
control.

Chapter 10, "The Anthropology of
Complex Societies," examines the social organization of contemporary
states, in particular the life of urban
dwellers in industrial and industrializing societies. In such societies only
a portion—and sometimes a very
small portion—of the population lives
directly by agriculture. Many people
reside in cities, far removed from primary subsistence activities. Complex
societies are indeed very intricate in

their class composition, their high
level of organization and specialization, and the great variety of social
and cultural elements that are en-
compassed within the political orbit
of the state.

Chapter 7
The ecology of hunting and collecting

Although the foundations of human culture can be traced back two or three million years, only in the course of the last ten thousand years have human beings engaged in agriculture, lived in social units larger than a few hundred individuals, built permanent settlements, and elaborated complex systems of government and law. Even if we limit our consideration to *Homo sapiens*, people lived as hunters and collectors for well over fifty thousand years before there was significant change in their patterns of subsistence. One could phrase it differently and say that for the vast span of human history people survived in a manner not unlike other members of the animal kingdom—they lived off the country, gathering wild produce and killing game.

Today, only a tiny fraction of societies still hunt and collect, for the most part societies tucked away in inaccessible or marginal locations that are largely unsuited for agriculture.[1] Yet in the not too distant past, using the measure of human residence on earth, all viable locations and all environments were the domains of gatherers and hunters. We should also understand that while the hunting way of life began to

[1]Hunting and collecting societies are referred to in the anthropological literature by a variety of terms, *hunters and gatherers*, *hunter-gatherers*, *hunters and collectors*, and *prefarming societies* being the most common. These terms put the emphasis on subsistence and economies. The concept of *band-level societies* or, more simply, *bands*, directs attention to aspects of social organization. For the sake of simplicity, we will use the term *hunters*, except in contexts where it would not be appropriate. We must stress, however, that this is a term of convenience and does not imply that hunters obtain all or even most of their food from hunting. In virtually all cases, except where the environment does not permit it, collecting, rather than hunting is the mainstay of such societies.

change with the first domestication of plants and animals—itself a process that was gradual rather than revolutionary—as recently as a few hundred years ago vast areas that are today inhabited by more complex societies were peopled by bands of hunters and collectors (see Figure 7-1).

Hunting societies have fascinated civilized people since classical antiquity. In part, this curiosity can be attributed to the great contrast between the simple life of hunting groups and the social and economic complexity that is always present in state systems. Also, for many commentators over the centuries, hunters have appeared to represent what might be termed *humanity in the raw*—a life that is led close to nature and is rudimentary with respect to technology and social complexity. But regardless of this interest, contacts between highly complex and very simple societies have generally been sporadic. Furthermore, throughout history, the trend has been that more complex societies either eliminate or incoporate (and thus change) simpler ones and, in particular, the simplest.

One very important consequence of this assimilation is that actual knowledge of hunters has been scant. And where knowledge is lacking, speculation and fantasy take its place. We can distinguish two broad attitudes, or forms of interpretation, that civilized people have applied to hunters. One is positive in the sense that the simple way of life is admired as uncorrupted and "closer to nature." This viewpoint is exemplified by the eighteenth-century natural philosophers, such as Jean Jacques Rousseau (1712–1778), who praised "natural man" as one who, having met his needs for food, is at peace with all nature and the friend of all his fellow creatures. A very different, and essentially negative, interpretation of life in a state of nature is offered by Thomas Hobbes (1588–1679), who claimed that the natural condition of man "is a condition of war of everyone against everyone." From him also

Hunter-gatherers: a historical view

Hunters as a subject of anthropological interest

comes the often quoted opinion that the life of man stripped of the civilizing influences and the protection that is given by formal political and civil structures is "solitary, poor, nasty, brutish, and short." Both perspectives lack a factual base. Existence in simple societies is neither so idyllic nor so prone to danger and disharmony. In more recent times, simple societies have been viewed either as interesting anachronisms or as stumbling blocks in the way of "progress" that deserve to be swept away by the tide of civilization.

Hunter-gatherer societies are very limited in number when compared to tribal groups or peasant peoples, but they have nevertheless received a substantial amount of anthropological attention. Initially, it was the fact that such societies were in danger of being destroyed that stimulated field work and research among them. This concern with what some have termed *salvage ethnography*—the study and, if possible, the protection of endangered cultural forms—is still pressing and valid. But a new consideration has been added. Much current research is devoted to understanding hunting and gathering as a highly flexible form of subsistence economy that can be adapted to exploiting a wide range of environments and resources. This exploitation is accomplished by using a variety of technological and social arrangements that are finely tuned to the existing ecological system.

In this regard, there has come the recognition that hunting groups—so long as their economic base is not destroyed or badly impaired—constitute societies in equilibrium with the ecosystem. Much current research is thus directed at the central question of how hunters and gatherers make a living, the strategies of survival they utilize, and, more broadly, the proven ability of hunting sociocultural systems to endure and adapt over tens of thousands of years.

Modern research has laid to rest a number of myths. There is no question that in situa-

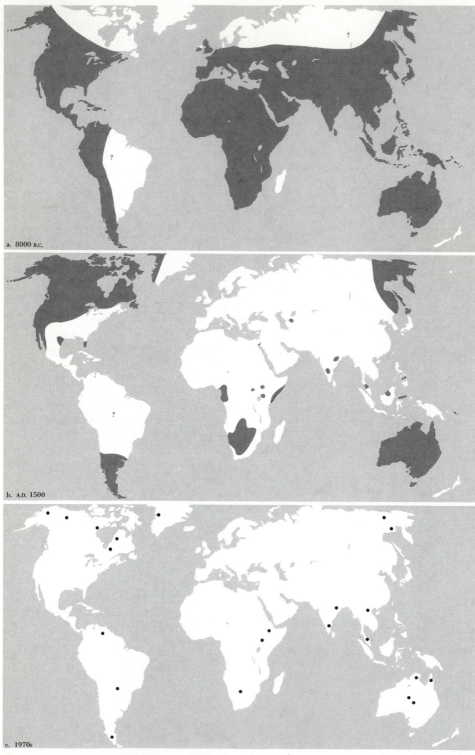

Figure 7-1 Approximate distribution of hunting populations, 8000 B.C. to the present

(a) The blank areas indicate uninhabitable glaciated northern regions, those parts of the world that in all probability were peopled later, and regions concerning which information is very scanty or completely lacking.

(b) The map shows the substantial reduction of hunter-gatherer territories by the period of early European exploration. Because for many parts of the world the available information for this period is insufficient, the distribution shown on the map should be viewed as approximate and schematic. (Reprinted by permission from Richard B. Lee and Irven DeVore *Man The Hunter* (Chicago: Aldine Publishing Company); copyright © 1968 by Wenner Gren Foundation for Anthropological Research.)

(c) Many recent hunter-gatherers have been forced to shift to a mixed subsistence with the result that today the few remaining hunting and gathering groups are found only in the most marginal areas. There is still no reliable information for parts of the tropical forest region of South America. This map, too, must therefore be viewed as schematic.

tions of competition with more complex cultures, hunters generally come out the losers. But aside from such intergroup conflict situations, hunters by and large do not live a precarious life. Given reasonable natural resources, hunters in the main live lives that are secure and relatively predictable. The social organization of hunting groups may lack many of the features that are to be found in larger-scale societies, but it would be wrong to suppose that there is a dearth of social interaction or such nonmaterial concerns or activities as mythology, ceremonialism, and ritual. In fact, since the food quest generally consumes but a small portion of available time, rich oral traditions and a good deal of human interaction are in no sense incompatible with subsistence patterns geared to hunting, fishing, and collecting. What is generally absent is an elaborate material culture, and it is perhaps this paucity of material goods that has led observers to assume, with a certain amount of prejudice, that hunting societies are "poor." Under no circumstances, however, should material poverty be equated with a precarious existence or a lack of nonmaterial cultural embellishments.

CONTEMPORARY HUNTING SOCIETIES: LOCATIONS AND ENVIRONMENTS

Hunting for sport, prestige, or as an inexpensive way of extending the food supply is commonplace. In almost all locations and environments where hunting can add variety to the diet, one will find people engaged in it, for the most part as a spare-time sport, but even, in some instances, as the major occupation of a few individuals. Much the same is true of collecting, for those who have grown up in the country know where wild edible plants or their fruits are likely to be found and when to gather them. In modern complex societies, the expense that goes into hunting in the form of guns, ammunition, transportation, gear, and licenses bears little relationship to the value as food of the game that may be bagged. In not a few societies, hunting is a prestige sport indulged in mostly by the rich, especially when the quarry is that of large game animals living in preserves. This kind of hunting is very different from hunting as a way of life. Similarly, while commercial fishing is very important to some communities and individuals in even the most technologically advanced societies, such societies do not subsist primarily by fishing.

Effects of culture contact

The cultures and societies that we are considering in this chapter are nonagricultural and nonindustrial. Their economies are the closest contemporary equivalent to those of pre-Neolithic populations, but we should bear in mind that even groups that made their living directly from nature have not

Sometimes the material rewards of hunting do not appear commensurate with the time and effort expended. This Bushman hunter has probably spent many hours tracking his small quarry, but there will be a story to tell on the return to camp. (Irven DeVore/Anthro-Photo)

In many complex societies, hunting is an upper-class sport involving distinct values and behavior patterns. This scene is from an elite shooting party; note clothes, equipment, and hunting dog. (Burt Glinn/Magnum Photos, Inc.)

Hunting in the United States and Canada is typically a popular rather than elite pastime. These American game bird hunters are dressed in a utilitarian fashion. (Bob Adelman/Magnum Photos, Inc.)

Modern gatherers? Almost all the food we eat is processed and packaged and sold in stores. Is it significant that the supermarket shoppers in this picture are women? (Dan O'Neill from Editorial Photocolor Archives)

escaped influences from the external, non-hunting world. The fact that hunters are in contact with, or surrounded by, more populous sedentary societies with resources and technologies that are far more advanced than those available to hunters has, in some instances, dramatically changed the economic and social structures of hunting groups. Thus, high-powered rifles began to enter the Eskimo arsenal in some quantity early in the twentieth century, and there are now few Eskimos who hunt with the compound bow. More recently, Eskimos have adopted snowmobiles and outboard motors. American Indian hunting societies began to make use of firearms in colonial times, and from that time to the present have exchanged furs for guns and ammunition. Today, we find that many of the remaining Indian hunters, most of whom are to be found in the Canadian north, are primarily fur hunters rather than food hunters, and they purchase a good deal of their food, paying for it from the sale of furs. But even in regions where hunters continue to live in greater isolation, some external influences are evident. The Pygmies of the Ituri Forest of central Africa take aspirin for their headaches when they can get it, and the Bushmen of the Kalahari Desert are not adverse to using plastic containers. Junk and throwaways from modern society are often refashioned into useful articles.

While for some hunting societies these changes and influences are relatively recent, hunting societies as a whole have been in retreat for thousands of years. Hunting territories have shrunk, as more powerful groups have steadily taken over regions that were previously the homelands of simpler societies. These trends are still observable today in many parts of the world. In the Amazon basin and on the eastern slopes of the Andes, simple societies of hunters and slash-and-burn agriculturalists are under extreme pressure from settlers and land speculators.

In many localities hunters have been totally exterminated (see Figure 7-1). This occurred in Tasmania during the nineteenth century, when white colonists tracked down and killed all the Tasmanians they could find. In many instances, planned genocide was not necessary to drive hunting peoples from their land. In the Plains of North America, the policy followed by settlers, the railroads, and often the government, ruined the economic base of hunting societies. Thus, between 1870 and 1890, literally millions of buffalo were slaughtered, with the result that Indian societies that were vital and dynamic around 1850 were in total disarray and cultural shock by 1890. Cultures that had been structured around the buffalo hunt were forced by a combination of military action and the indiscriminate slaughter of buffalo herds to sign treaties that penned them into small enclaves (reservations) where they had no option but to subsist on government handouts.

All too often the mere presence of outsiders in previously remote areas has proved sufficiently dangerous to kill all, or virtually all, the native inhabitants. This is exactly what occurred with the fishing and hunting groups at the extreme southern tip of South America. Collectively known as the Fuegians, the Alacaluf, Chono, Ona, and Yahgan depended primarily on shellfish collecting, fishing, and the hunting of aquatic mammals. Lacking immunity to measles, chicken pox, and a number of other diseases to which European populations had developed a degree of natural resistance, the Fuegians died out or became so reduced in numbers as to preclude independent sociocultural existence.

Marginal locations of surviving hunting societies

It should be evident by now that those hunting societies that have survived to the present are very much the exception. They are to be found for the most part in environments that would be highly inhospitable to other societies. This includes the Arctic, the Kalahari Desert in southern Africa, the central Australian desert, and regions of dense forest in Africa, Southeast Asia, and South and North America. Not all these

localities are impervious to exploitation by techniques other than hunting and collecting, but some hunting groups have survived because communications have been poor and the costs of opening up such lands to agriculture have thus far been prohibitive. However, given the growing scarcity of natural resources, very substantial inroads are being made into regions that had previously been left to hunting groups.

We should note, though, that hunting and gathering groups survive in widely different environments. In many cases, these environments constitute the least productive portions of previously much more extensive ranges. One result of this situation is that many hunting groups that are now ethnographic "classics"—well studied and thoroughly documented—are more correctly approached as societies that had retreated into inhospitable regions and were thus available to research when anthropologists came on the scene. We associate the Australian aborigines with a desert environment, but before contact Australian groups inhabited not only the desert but also other parts of Australia with a far more hospitable climate and more abundant resources. Archaeological and ethnographic evidence also indicates that several centuries ago the Bushmen were not restricted to the Kalahari but occupied substantial portions of southern Africa. It has also been estimated that before contact two-thirds of the Eskimo lived *south* of the Arctic Circle. It would be wrong, therefore, to jump to the conclusion that a hunting way of life is some kind of special adaptation to difficult environmental conditions. True, hunters survive in what we would think of as extremely harsh environments, but this has seldom been a matter of choice.

Although only a few contemporary hunter-gatherer societies live in rich environments, ethnographic reconstruction gives us some insight into the condition of such groups some generations ago when, for some groups, the situation was substantially different. For example, we have good reports on Eskimo culture written fifty years

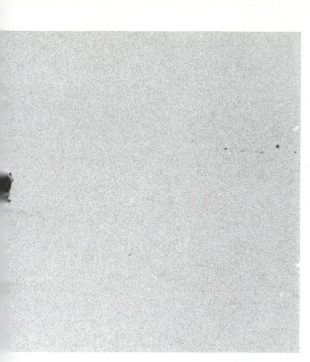

Traditional Eskimo subsistence patterns depended almost entirely on hunting and fishing. This Eskimo is on his way to his hunting grounds. (Marc Riboud/Magnum Photos, Inc.)

ago, when game was much more plentiful and most Eskimo still relied on native hunting techniques. We therefore wish to stress the fact that hunting as a culturally adaptive response fits the widest range of environmental situations. This may seem an elementary finding, but it is important if we are to make generalizations about hunters. We have, in short, great environmental variety against which we must project constants and regularities applicable to hunting cultures. It is not that all hunters are alike, but rather that the economic and organizational options open to hunters are fairly limited. Hunting as a form of subsistence establishes limits on the size of social and economic units and tends to structure social and economic relations along very similar lines.

MODES OF ADAPTATION

Living off nature may seem extremely risky, even under the most favorable circum-

stances. In part, popular ideas of the insecurity of hunting are due to misconceptions of the rigors and hazards inherent in hunting-based subsistence patterns. It is certainly true that some hunting activities entail an element of danger and that game animals have a will of their own and do not appear on demand. But while game animals must first be found and then killed before they can be turned into food, many follow patterned habits and activities. Animals must eat, and there are places where game is plentiful and other localities where it is scarce. Animals must drink, and the streams and water holes are not unlimited in number. Furthermore, there are times when given species of animals are more active and times when they are much less so. Again, we should remember that many of the larger game move around in herds and that these herds, unless frightened, move at a relatively slow pace that allows time for the organization of communal hunting procedures such as drives and ambushes. In some environments, the major game animals are migratory, and migrations are yearly events following a limited number of defined routes such as passes and fording places.

The Eskimo pattern

Diamond Jenness gives us the following vivid account of an Eskimo caribou hunt early in the century:

Lines of stones, with here and there a stick to which a coat or a flat resonant board is attached, are run down each side of the valley from the deer to the lake, where the hunters lie concealed in their kayaks. The women and children behind the deer howl like wolves *hu-u-u-u hu-u-u-u*, and the startled deer move down between the lines until they reach the water. There they stop irresolute, afraid to dash off to a flank on account of the barricade of stones and streamers. The "wolves" draw nearer and nearer until the frightened deer one after the other rush into the water and try to swim across the lake. Then the kayakers dash out, each man armed with a short knife lashed on the end of a pole. One after another the helpless caribou are stabbed in the nape of the neck, nooses are thrown over their horns and their carcasses dragged to the shore (Jenness 1922:149).

All these factors, while not assuring a successful hunt, reduce the element of chance. Game is not always available, for typically there are slack periods, but at least at some periods of the year or at some points in the animals' life cycle game is especially vulnerable. Some important species of fish run with an almost calendrical regularity, as anyone who has witnessed the upstream migration of salmon can attest, while many marine mammals congregate in fixed locations during the breeding and pupping season.

Because of their almost absolute reliance on hunting and fishing, the Eskimo cannot be regarded as typical of most hunting and collecting cultures. The almost complete absence of vegetable foods in the Eskimo environment means that successful hunting is imperative to survival. But until very recent times, the Eskimo could count on fairly predictable food supplies, often substantially more food than could be consumed. Eyewitness reports made some fifty years ago indicate that during most years food was plentiful. Kaj Birket-Smith, describing the caribou herds that were mustering around Baker Lake in northern Canada for the migration south in the summer of 1922, observed that "the whole of the south shore seemed to be alive with animals. There were caribou in thousands, as far as the eye could see" (Birket-Smith 1929:56). During a period of less than three months in 1923, an Eskimo community on Southampton Island numbering fourteen adults, six children, and forty dogs consumed ninety-eight caribou. This was regarded as a lean period and some of the dogs died of hunger (Mathiassen 1928:61). Speaking of the Central Eskimo of the period we have referred to, Asen Balikci recently made the observation that "with the exception of occasional cases of people getting lost in traveling or

getting caught in bad weather . . . widespread starvation of a magnitude required to induce culture loss, is a very rare phenomenon" (Balikci 1968:84).

We have gone into some detail on Eskimo subsistence, in part because the documentation is good, but also because the Eskimo are something of an exception among the world's hunters. The arctic environment in which they live precludes any adaptive response other than some combination of hunting and fishing, the mix of these two variables for any given Eskimo group at any given time being determined by locality and the season of the year. Translated into subsistence terms, this reliance on hunting and fishing means that the Eskimo either are successful hunters or face starvation. That they have managed to survive under these conditions shows that pure hunting economies—given the right ecological circumstances and highly specialized hunting technologies—are viable, although it seems unlikely that a heavy reliance on hunting has ever characterized more than a minority of nonagricultural societies.

The typical pattern

The typical hunting economy is in reality underpinned by collecting. The food that the hunter brings to the camp is highly valued—in part, no doubt, because it is scarce. Meat also provides animal protein that, in combination with other foods, makes for a balanced and nutritious diet. Hunted food, however, except in the highest latitudes, seldom makes up more than 35 percent of the total intake, and the figure can be considerably lower.

Collected foods are a far more secure source of supply than game animals. Typically, such foods can be gathered within a short distance of temporary camps and without the expenditure of effort that goes into hunting expeditions, which not infrequently may bring the hunter home empty-handed. While gathering is vital, it lacks the excitement (in part a function of the gamble involved) that goes into hunting. Gathering is typically women's work and in most societies it lacks the prestige of hunting activities. We could express it differently and say that women provide the essentials, and men (sometimes) furnish the delicacies. As Richard Lee has observed of the !Kung Bushmen:

The essence of their successful strategy seems to be that while they depend primarily on the more stable and abundant food sources (vegetables in their case), they are nevertheless willing to devote considerable energy to the less reliable and more highly valued food sources such as medium and large mammals. The steady but modest input of work by the women provides the former, and the more intensive labors of the men provide the latter. It would be theoretically possible for the Bushmen to survive entirely on vegetable foods, but life would be boring indeed without the excitement of meat feasts. The totality of their subsistence activities thus represents an outcome of two individual goals; the first is the desire to live well with adequate leisure time, and the second is the desire to enjoy the rewards, both social and nutritional, afforded by the killing of game. In short, *the Bushmen of the Dobe area eat as much vegetable food as they need, and as much meat as they can* (Lee 1968:41).

Lee's analysis of Bushman subsistence patterns can be applied to most other hunting societies. We wish to stress, however, that even in inhospitable environments such as the Kalahari there is a substantial degree of security. This security is the result of a number of factors, including a detailed knowledge of what the environment has to offer. The small size of economic units—the low density of population—also assures that resources will not be easily depleted.[2]

Hunters, who seldom have stores of food to fall back upon, simply cannot afford to strain ecological limits. A further hedge against adversity is a set of attitudes common to most hunting groups that stress the necessity—it is more than a virtue—of generosity. We will examine these factors later, but perhaps enough has been said to indicate that it would be incorrect to view hunters and collectors as living on the razor's edge of survival.

Historically, the breakdown of hunting cultures has more commonly been caused by external influences, in particular the encroachment of more powerful groups, than by resource mismanagement on the part of hunters. This does not mean that we have to subscribe to a theory that hunters are imbued by some kind of natural ecological insight. We know that species became extinct long before the advent of agriculture and settled life, and at least one of the causative factors may well have been the hunting of some species to the point that regeneration of the herds was extremely difficult.[3] A reasonable assumption is that Pleistocene extinctions were caused by a combination of overhunting and climatic/environmental changes. As a result, the size of some animal populations were reduced enough so that kill rates that had previously not interfered with the natural replacement

---

[2]Compared to sedentary peoples, the population density of hunting societies is very low. With the exception of some habitats extremely rich in food resources, hunter densities rarely exceed one person per square mile and may run as low as one person per hundred square miles. While a major determinant of population density is the availability (and predictability over substantial periods of time) of food resources, social and cultural factors also influence the size and distribution of hunter groups. Although the evidence is still inconclusive and fragmentary in some cases, it would appear that most hunting groups use child-spacing techniques to maintain the population in equilibrium with and generally well below the natural carrying capacity of the environment.

[3]Even with respect to contemporary species, what kill rates constitute a dangerous depletion of animal populations is a matter of debate. For example, the whaling industry, made up in large part of Japanese and Russian interests, insists that whale populations are not on the point of extinction. Independent marine biologists are of the opinion that many species of whale have reached such low numbers that a total cessation of commercial whaling is necessary if they are to be saved.

A Bushman woman gathers ostrich eggs to take home in her bag. Her stick is used to dig out edible tubers. (Richard Lee/Anthro-Photo)

Paiute women with baskets for collecting and carrying wild foodstuffs. In most hunter-gatherer societies, collected foods constitute the bulk of the diet. The photograph was taken in Arizona at the turn of the century. (Photograph Courtesy of Museum of the American Indian, Heye Foundation)

of these populations were no longer biologically acceptable.

We make this point because there is no need to romanticize the hunting peoples of the world, past and present. We mentioned earlier that Eskimos often came across more game than they could reasonably utilize at a given time. We know also that Eskimo hunters often killed more animals than were necessary to meet their food needs. Citing an official government report, Jenness gives the following example of Eskimo overhunting:

In November, 1917, a Royal North West Mounted Police patrol visited the mouth of a small river that flows into Gordon bay, and found deer [caribou] carcasses strewn all along its banks under the snow. Evidently the natives has speared them that summer and taken only the skins, leaving the meat to be devoured by the wolves and ravens (Jenness 1922:149).

Ernest Hawkes, writing about the Labrador Eskimo early in the present century, comments that "the idea of restricting the pursuit of game is repugnant to the Eskimo, who hold that food belongs to everyone" (Hawkes 1916:25). As is true of many other hunting societies, the Eskimo believe that "the spirits of the animals cannot be destroyed simply by killing the animals" (Weyer 1932:333).

While it is not valid to extrapolate from the Eskimo to all other hunters with respect to attitudes toward game, the Eskimo perspective is fairly typical. There are good reasons why hunter-collectors, of whatever type, seldom disturb the ecological balance to the point where irrevocable damage is done. Such peoples must generally find food on a daily basis, and while it is true that periods of plenty will alternate with periods of relative scarcity, a feast-or-famine existence is simply not a viable way of life.[4] A

[4]A feast-or-famine existence may not be viable, but we should note that some hunters and part-hunters seem to survive on the borderlines of famine. The Ik, a group on the borders of northern

person or a group cannot survive by eating their fill for nine months of the year and going without food for the other three. Although disasters *are* possible—as they are for all societies regardless of their economic base—the practical result of this iron law of survival is that hunters generally live well within the food-bearing capacity (plants and animals) of the particular environments they inhabit. Ecologically, they have no alternative.

THE CASE FOR PRIMITIVE AFFLUENCE

We have tried to lay to rest the myth of hunting and collecting societies as surviving at the very edge of subsistence. Recent research on the diet of hunting groups, the time and effort involved in the food quest, and the degree of leisure that hunters enjoy has led to some fascinating new insights on the hunting way of life. Apparently, for at least many hunters, existence is the very opposite of "solitary, poor, nasty, brutish, and short" and could be better characterized, within the limitations inherent in the social and economic structures of hunting cultures, as rewarding, not overly demanding, and perhaps even "affluent," if by the latter we understand a condition of plenty as this would be defined by hunting people.

To begin with, we should dismiss the notion that obtaining food from the wild is a dangerous thing. Little danger is involved in the gathering of nuts and berries, the hunting of small game, the collection of shellfish, and most fishing. Even big-game hunting is not as risky as one might think. All these tasks, however, do require skill and an intimate knowledge of the natural environment. It is mostly white hunters, professional and amateur, who are responsible for depicting the hunt as fraught with danger. Field research indicates that this element is minimal. Lions, renowned in folklore for their bravery and ferocity, will normally trot away from animals they have killed rather than face a confrontation with humans. The major problem that hunters face is getting close enough to their targets to kill or disable them, not contesting with their quarry the question of who is the more powerful adversary.

If hunting, by and large, is not a high-risk occupation, neither are hunting environments especially dangerous or unhealthy. The functional groups in hunting societies are small and widely dispersed, and while not all hunters are nomadic, semipermanent camps are characteristic of most hunting groups. These patterns of settlement and dispersal are a built-in protection against the spread of disease. Shifts in settlement also improve the hygienic situation: water supplies are likely to be relatively free from human contamination and a pattern of mobility keeps camps from becoming too fouled by human and animal excrement, rotting food, and other pollutants. We do not imply that hunters consciously follow "good health habits," but rather that hunters are likely to be healthy as a consequence of the dictates imposed by their economic conditions. Agriculturalists, who often live in compact settlements and generally continue to live in the same locations generation after generation, are likely to pay a price in health for village life. This at least was certainly the case prior to the introduction of modern medicine. What we know of urban life in premodern times hardly warrants the conclusion that towns were ever healthy places.

Uganda, have been described by Colin M. Turnbull in *The Mountain People* (1972), perhaps one of the most disturbing and thought-provoking ethnographies ever written. The Ik subsist by agriculture, and when agriculture fails, which it does periodically, they turn to hunting and collecting. The environment is ruthless and the people respond to one another in like manner. Allan R. Holmberg's book, *Nomads of the Long Bow* (1950), a study of the Siriono of eastern Bolivia, also describes a hunting society beset with hunger, frustration, anxiety, and an unconcern of one individual for another that "never ceased to amaze" the anthropologist and "is manifested on every hand" (Holmberg 1950:98).

We have noted that in the course of western expansion many indigenous peoples, hunters included, succumbed to newly introduced diseases. The lack of resistence of "primitives" to a host of infections previously unknown to them should be attributed not to poor health or physical weakness, but rather to the fact that the barriers that had served them so well were breached by outsiders who were equipped not only with superior technologies but also with the "secret weapon" of the infections they carried. In fact, the very health of many populations—their lack of exposure to certain diseases and hence failure to develop mechanisms of natural resistance against them—has been their undoing. Historically, many conditions that did not threaten Europeans and descendants of Europeans proved catastrophic to native peoples. Although some hunters are still vulnerable to infections brought in by outsiders, the raging epidemics that formerly followed culture contact seem to be a thing of the past.

A number of attitudinal and behavioral characteristics that are widespread among hunters can also be easily misinterpreted as evidence of harsh conditions. *Infanticide*—the killing, often by exposure, of some newborn children—is culturally sanctioned in a number of hunting societies. The reasons for this practice are twofold: the difficulty of a mother to breast-feed and look after closely spaced children, and the more general concern that the population of a group should be kept well within the limits of available food sources. As a method of population control, infanticide will strike many of us as cruel, but one could argue that it is far less cruel to destroy an infant or young child than to permit it to live with reduced chances of survival. We should note that infanticide is resorted to only in cases of necessity, and that where normal infant mortality rates keep the population from overexpanding, the practice is absent or discontinued.

The same underlying reasons—the chances of individual survival and the capacity of a group to operate effectively—account for the killing or abandonment of the very old, except that in this case it is typically the person in question who decides that he or she constitutes an unacceptable burden to the collectivity. Both infanticide and *senilicide* (killing of old people) are unusual occurrences. It is probably the strangeness of these practices to Westerners, rather than a numerically high incidence, that accounts for the attention they have received in anthropological literature.

Actually, many hunting groups contain a very substantial percentage of older people who often exercise a good deal of political authority and enjoy respect as ceremonial leaders. Although not as economically active as young and middle-aged adults, the senior citizens of most hunting cultures are senior not only in age but also in the affairs of the group. In some hunting and collecting societies, powerful older males are in a position of dominance, which is manifested by their tendency to have more than one wife, *polygyny*. Among the Australians, politically important males tend to marry women a generation or more younger than themselves. This practice leads to the concentration of a number of women—the major food producers—around key older males. Polygyny and extreme age differentials at marriage are not features of all hunting groups, but the fact that these patterns are possible is evidence that individuals in hunting societies may continue to exercise power long after their middle years.

Diversified subsistence base

We have been developing an argument that hunting cultures generally tap only a portion of the available surpluses produced by the natural environment. It is worth keeping in mind that under native conditions—before the massive encroachment on hunting habitats by outsiders—the range of plant and animal species available to hunters was generally considerably more extensive than in the "ethnographic present," the period of anthropological reporting. But even when pushed into marginal localities, hunters enjoy the advantage of a diversified subsistence base. Unlike simple agriculturalists who are totally dependent on a limited number of crops, often one staple and a few supplementary foods, hunters can pick and choose. If an animal species is scarce at a particular season or during a given year, the option is always open to rely more heavily on other animals. And what is true of hunted game is equally true of wild plants.

This diversification is an extremely important feature of most hunting ecologies. Thus, the Siberian hunters (notably Voguls, Ostyaks, Samoyed, and Tungus) make use of more than thirty kinds of mammals, some for meat and some for fur, and about the same number of bird species. Clearly, not all these birds and animals are of equal economic importance; many have migratory habits, and they inhabit a variety of ecological niches. Nevertheless, this spread represents a diversified resource base, which can be tapped according to fluctuations in the animal population. The Siberians may be primarily hunters and fishers, but in other parts of the world collecting is the backbone

of the native economy. The Arunta of central Australia, who inhabit a very forbidding desert and semidesert environment, eat almost all kinds of animal or plant life, unless the taking of particular species is prohibited on religious grounds. The men hunt the larger animals, such as the kangaroo and the related wallaby, and the emu, a large ostrichlike terrestrial bird, and also kill smaller animals and birds. Women and children collect seeds and bulbs, eggs of both reptiles and birds, witchetty grubs (the larvae of a species of moth), and such "slow game" as lizards and snails. They also collect all kinds of insects and dig up burrowing rodents. While this may not strike us as gourmet fare, the Arunta and other Australian groups enjoy a balanced diet that is often available in quantity.

Northwest coast: the life of plenty

Ethnographic reports make it clear that some hunting groups favored with especially productive environments live what can only be called a life of plenty. Among recent hunters, the inhabitants of the Northwest coast (Nootka, Kwakiutl, Tlingit,

Fishing is often a specialized hunter-gatherer adaptation. These men are tending fish traps on the Congo River. (United Nations/FAO)

Haida, and others), living between the mountains and the sea along a strip of land stretching from northern California to southern Alaska, enjoyed an extremely rich environment. The area was, and to some degree continues to be, inhabited by different groups, speaking a number of languages and dialects but sharing a hunting and fishing economy and many similarities in culture.

The Northwest coast environment has been described as

an area where one could find, on a single occasion, quite literally tons of food. Salmon ran into the smaller streams by the thousands and into larger streams by the tens and hundreds of thousands. Waterfowl came to the marshes by the tens and hundreds of thousands. A single sturgeon can weigh nearly a ton, a bull sea lion more than a ton, a whale up to thirty tons (Suttles 1968:58).

True, we should not forget the operative phrase "on a single occasion," for such abundance was not a constant. Still, the picture is one of great plenty, and it is perhaps not surprising that with this abundance of resources, a major concern of Northwest Coast cultures was coping with abundance. Wealth was displayed, goods were consumed conspicuously in great competitive giveaway feasts, the material culture (huge totem poles, massive wooden houses) was elaborate, and slavery was part of the structure of prestige.

We mention the Northwest coast not because the groups in question are typical of hunting-level societies, but to indicate the high complexity of cultural elaboration possible for nonagricultural groups in very favorable ecological contexts. In the Old World, we have the case of various Upper Paleolithic populations that apparently could count on sufficient surpluses to devote time and energy to extensive cave art and the production of sculpture in bone and stone, not to mention extremely fine weapons and tools. Somewhat different is the case of Plains Indian cultures following the introduction of the horse and firearms, but the ceremonial, political, and military activities

of Plains cultures were also greatly facilitated by the success of mounted hunters.

It is only fair to recognize that these are all somewhat exceptional examples, and that just as a balanced evaluation of hunting economies should not be entirely based on the situation of remnant groups living in the most difficult natural environments, generalizations on hunting societies should not be made from a consideration of groups living in optimum environments. The case for relative affluence, however, can be elaborated on the basis of societies residing in regions endowed with relatively modest resources.

First of all, it is pertinent to ask what *affluence* or *wealth* means to most hunters. Aside from cultures like those of the North-

Time for leisure

west coast, whose members lived in permanent settlements and could accumulate quantities of material objects, most hunters, of necessity, live in a world characterized by a paucity of possessions. Hunters must be mobile and, in most cases, everything they own must be carried with them. The result is that there is no feasible manner by which wealth can be accumulated. To be burdened by many possessions would be clearly a disadvantage for a nomadic way of life.

The affluence we are concerned with is thus very different from what one is likely to find among some segments of the population in permanently settled societies. It is affluence in the restricted sense of having a secure food supply obtained without much effort, with the resulting enjoyment of regular periods of leisure. While hunting societies vary in their methods of food procurement and the distribution of this food once it is obtained, the food quest is seldom very demanding. James Woodburn, writing of the Hadza, a group of nomadic hunters and collectors living in Tanzania, makes the following general observation:

In spite of the fact that the Hadza make scarcely any attempt to conserve the food resources of their area, that they rapidly eat all the food which comes into camp without preserving it, that they do not cooperate very much or coordinate their food gathering activities with each other, that they make hunting difficult for themselves by using their arrows for gambling, that a high proportion of men are failures at hunting, they nonetheless obtain sufficient food without undue effort. Over the year as a whole probably an average of less than two hours a day is spent obtaining food (Woodburn 1968:54).

The Hadza live in an environment rich in game animals and wild foods, but a very similar picture emerges when we consider Bushman work and leisure. According to Richard B. Lee:

In all, the adults of the Dobe camp worked about two and a half days a week. Since the average working day was about six hours long, the fact emerges that !Kung Bushmen of Dobe, despite their harsh environment, devote from twelve to nineteen hours a week to getting food (Lee 1968:37).

Granted that different societies generate different "needs" in their members, we would all agree that a nineteen-hour week is not even a hypothetical goal for trade unionists or the most reform-minded legislators in complex industrial societies. Hunters have something that has been lost since the dawn of the Neolithic—spare time. This leisure may be spent playing games, sleeping, telling stories, or weaving intricate mythologies, to cite but some of the alternatives available to different groups.

THE SOCIAL ORGANIZATION OF HUNTING SOCIETIES

Hunters have often been described as band-level societies. A *band* is a rather concrete term for a loose assemblage of people. For our immediate purposes, we can define a band as an aggregate, larger than the basic family group, that shares in the performance of economic, social, and ritual activities. Most of the information available on band size is approximate, but it would appear that band size is a function of both general environmental conditions—all things being equal, the more productive the environment, the larger the size of the band—and of such specifics as the economic requirements of particular seasonal rounds. Bands of less than twenty individuals are seldom reported in the literature, while the upper limit of band size is in the order of 200 individuals. To be sure, such large aggregates are likely to come together only under very favorable circumstances. For example, as many as 120 Ona, a Fuegian group, might gather briefly to consume a beached whale.

Bands are characterized by their fluidity. Individuals and families come and go at will, some to join other bands, others to form bands of their own. This flexibility permits bands to wax and wane in a manner designed to take advantage of fluctuating food sources. Many units that have been described as bands in the literature are probably nothing more permanent than a cluster of a few families joined for purposes of temporary cooperation.

Some anthropologists prefer to use the term *local group* rather than *band*, since the former does not seem to carry the implication of a closed system. In societies of greater complexity, structures tend to be more permanent and membership in them more clearly delineated. The reasons for this are that in such societies, social units tend to work as corporate entities—that is, ownership of some valuable resource is vested in the unit and its members share the benefit of this ownership. However, although

In many societies hunting is more than an economic activity. The thrill of the chase is captured in this photograph of a Giriama bowman (northern Kenya) at the instant of releasing an arrow. (Africapix from Peter Arnold)

among hunters each local group tends to be associated with a geographical range, in few instances can it be said that bands have a developed sense of resource ownership. Similarly, geographical boundaries do not take the form of rigid demarcations. Among herders and agriculturalists, on the other hand, the ownership of land and other resources is a very important matter, and social units function to define economic rights and obligations.

Some years ago, when the ecology of hunting groups was less well understood, a number of anthropologists, in particular Julian H. Steward (1955), hypothesized that the basic social unit of hunting societies was what he termed the *patrilocal* band. The principle of *patrilocality* is that women marry out and men stay put. The postulated reason behind this type of band organization is that a knowledge of the hunting territory is something that a young male learns over a long period of time by accompanying his father or other older males on hunting expeditions. The argument is that it would be clearly dysfunctional for a male

trained to know the habits of game in one locality to be forced to make a livelihood in an area he does not know equally well.

Patrilocal bands are, in fact, a feature of some hunting societies, but they are far from universal. With respect to adaptive functions, the economic value of patrilocality does not give sufficient weight to two features common to many hunting societies: first, the important contribution of collecting, performed, as we have seen, mainly by women; second, the tendency of many bands to live a nomadic style of life. Not all bands range over vast territories, but often the same resource base of plants and animals is used by more than one band.

The broad outlines of social structures among hunters are quite simple and it is to this organizational simplicity that reference is made when we speak of "simple" societies. The local units form part of a larger breeding population and linguistic community that can be said to share a culture. Contact between bands is often maintained by frequent visiting, which acts to keep the separate components of the larger cultural unit in touch with one another. Patterns of visiting also assure that individuals know not only the people but also the resources of areas beyond their immediate hunting and collecting territories. A consequence of all this mobility and fluidity is that it prevents any one group, or any individual within the group, from developing unduly strong attachments to any single area. For the same reasons, individual mobility tends to limit the attachment that a person has to his or her local group.

The small size of the functional economic groups in hunting societies does not mean that other facets of social organization are necessarily on the same scale. Kinship structures in band-level societies may be highly elaborate and, in fact, the Australian aborigines are organized in terms of such intricate kinship systems that a whole body of anthropological literature has been devoted to their analysis. The result is that in Australian society an individual may recognize several hundred kin, all of whom may potentially form part of reciprocal networks of aid and exchange. Although the Australian case is extreme, hunters can typically call on the services of many friends or kinfolk.

Reciprocity and egalitarianism

Hunters generally live in the context of a system that codifies the rights and obligations of reciprocity. This emphasis on reciprocity acts as a built-in safeguard against adversity. It is backed by values emphasizing the importance of sharing and the antisocial qualities of private ownership. Not only is food shared, but often even the few material goods that hunters possess circulate freely from one person to another. It is as if hunters recognize that the survival of all is best assured by strong sanctions against individual claims to ownership. From the point of view of survival, an economic base—which from the individual perspective is not highly predictable (a hunter is fortunate one day, the next he will return without game; a collector may come back with a nearly empty basket, while a neighbor finds an especially rich source of

food)—is made much more secure when the highs and lows are evened up.

A socioeconomic system of this type has to be egalitarian in nature. This means, not that status differences are absent—people will be respected for their skill and knowledge—but rather that no individual or group of individuals within the band is in a position to wield economic power over others. In such small-scale societies there is little evidence of institutionalized social and economic hierarchies.

In the political sphere, vital decisions are group decisions. There are no chiefs, nor are there any judges. Those who transgress cultural codes feel the impact of group sanctions rather than the power of officials and headmen. As is true of every society, there are people of importance, people with greater knowledge and experience. Their advice is heeded not because of any office they hold, but because it represents the consensus of the group.

In some hunting groups the intensity of social life is accelerated during periods of plenty. A temporary surfeit of food in a certain location, such as might occur when economically important plants or animals are available in quantity, will bring about a concentration of people. This occurred with the acorn harvest among California Indians and is still the case among some Eskimo during the winter months following a successful hunting season. Marcel Mauss, a well-known French anthropologist, went so far as to state that religion, as an organized activity, is limited to the winter—*il n'y a pas de religion en été* ("there is no religion in the summer") (1906:96)—which is something of an exaggeration but makes a useful point.

SOME OBSERVATIONS
ON EXTERNAL AND
INTERNAL RELATIONS

In one of the early chapters we had occasion to note that for the most part simple societies are not aggressive societies. The point

we were making is that few societies at the
band level of social organization are structured on the basis of dominance and aggression. This absence of aggressiveness is
true of person-to-person interaction and
holds also for relations between groups. In
societies that are not controlled by dominant
individuals, there is little opportunity for
organized conflict—warfare. This lack of
intergroup conflict is no doubt associated
with the emphasis on cooperation and sharing that seems to permeate many hunting
groups: to take from others by force is
psychologically and culturally incompatible
with a situation in which survival depends in
the long run on amicable relations between
groups and individuals.

An examination of the ethnographic literature indicates that institutionalized
group conflict among hunters is likely to be
found in situations where the transference
of resources is possible. Thus, the mounted
hunters of the Great Plains were great

*Australian aborigines, painted with colored
clay, participate in a corroboree. These
feasts may last several days and bring together substantial numbers of people. (Wide
World Photos)*

warriors, and one of the major objects of
warfare was the horses that were vital both
in the hunt and in war. The wealth of an
individual was counted in terms of the
string of ponies that he kept for his use.
Similarly, warfare was elaborated among
the Northwest Coast peoples, but again, the
successful soldier could expect to reap
rewards in the form of goods and slaves. We
claim, therefore, not that hunters are intrinsically gentle people, but rather that
subsistence hunting and collecting seldom
fit a cultural pattern that emphasizes aggression and conflict.

It is also worth noting that hunting societies seldom display patterns of dominance

and submission based on sexual demarcation. Men and women may perform different economic tasks, and hunting may be a prestige occupation; but the rigid sexual cleavages that one often encounters among sedentary peoples are typically absent. The tasks of child rearing are usually shared by both sexes, and we should remember that most hunters have time enough to devote to their children. Similarly, one can make the general observation that children in hunting societies enjoy a good deal of freedom and that they slowly, rather than abruptly, move into adult roles.

To all of the above generalizations one will find exceptions, but our aim has been to draw broad outlines applicable to the majority of hunting societies as we know them from field reports and as we extrapolate from historical and archaeological sources.

REFERENCES

BALIKCI, ASEN
1968 Discussions, part II. In *Man the hunter*. Richard B. Lee and Irven DeVore, eds. Chicago: Aldine. Pp. 83–95.

BIRKET-SMITH, KAJ
1929 *The Caribou Eskimos: material and social life and their cultural position.* Reports of the fifth Thule expedition 1921–24, vol. 5, part 1. Copenhagen: Gyldendalske boghandel.

HAWKES, ERNEST W.
1916 *The Labrador Eskimo.* Geological Survey of Canada, Memoir 91 (Anthropological series, no. 14). Ottawa: Government Printing Bureau.

HOLMBERG, ALLAN R.
1950 *Nomads of the long bow: the Siriono of eastern Bolivia.* Smithsonian Institution, Publications of the Institute of Social Anthropology, no. 10. Washington, D.C.: Government Printing Office.

JENNESS, DIAMOND
1922 *The life of the Copper Eskimos.* Report of the Canadian Arctic Expedition, 1913–1918, vol. 12, part A. Ottawa: F. A. Acland.

LEE, RICHARD B.
1968 What hunters do for a living, or, how to make out on scarce resources. In *Man the hunter*. Richard B. Lee and Irven DeVore, eds. Chicago: Aldine. Pp. 30–48.

MATHIASSEN, THERKEL
1928 *Material culture of the Iglulik Eskimos.* Reports of the fifth Thule expedition 1921–24, vol. 6, part 1. Copenhagen: Gyldendalske boghandel.

MAUSS, MARCEL
1906 *Essai sur les variations saisonnières des sociétés Eskimos: étude de morphologie sociale.* L'Année Sociologique 9:39–132.

STEWARD, JULIAN H.
1955 *Theory of culture change; the methodology of multilinear evolution.* Urbana: University of Illinois Press.

SUTTLES, WAYNE
1968 Coping with abundance: subsistence on the Northwest coast. In *Man the hunter*. Richard B. Lee and Irven DeVore, eds. Chicago: Aldine. Pp. 56–68.

TURNBULL, COLIN M.
1972 *The mountain people.* New York: Simon and Schuster.

WEYER, EDWARD MOFFAT, JR.
1932 *The Eskimos; their environment and folkways.* New Haven: Yale University Press.

WOODBURN, JAMES
1968 An introduction to Hadza ecology. In *Man the hunter*. Richard B. Lee and Irven DeVore, eds. Chicago: Aldine. Pp. 49–55.

Chapter 8
Varieties of
tribal experience

In the preceding chapter, we examined hunting and collecting, or band-level, societies as a distinct sociocultural type. We observed that the cultures in question are unique because they represent a mode of adaptation that can be traced back to Paleolithic times. To say this, of course, is not the same as to claim that modern hunters are identical in technology, economic base, or even social structure with those ancient hunters that roamed the earth prior to plant and animal domestication and the establishment of sedentary life. Our chief concern was simply to delimit broad areas of similarity that are identifiable in cultures widely scattered in time and space.

The present chapter is similar in perspective. The social and cultural units we shall be dealing with can be referred to as *tribes*. Within this category there is considerable room for variation, but just as hunters represent a level of generalization applicable to groups that typically subsist by economic strategies associated with collecting and hunting, tribespeople organize themselves around a stable and relatively predictable economic base. In the majority of cases, tribal economies are underpinned by agriculture, but the important consideration is not the specifics of the livelihood, but the fact that resources are sufficiently plentiful and stable to permit more elaborate forms of social organization than are found in band-level societies.

Tribal societies defined

A definition of tribal societies that is adequate to cover the range of variation present among such units is not easy to formulate: if the definition is too sharply drawn, it will not apply to some societies; if too general, there is the danger that it may fail to bring out important characteristics that distinguish tribes from other anthropological units of analysis. Nevertheless, we offer an initial working definition that will be elaborated in the course of the chapter. We can begin by emphasizing that it is primarily shared culture—the recognition of a common cultural heritage—that gives cohesion to the tribe and its various components.

Typically, there is also a unity of language and of territorial homeland. Thus a *tribe* can be viewed as an aggregate of smaller groups held together by the links of kinship and common heritage rather than by the force of a strong and self-perpetuating political organization. Social and political organization of tribal societies relies strongly on custom and the influence of powerful and influential individuals.

While virtually everywhere the cultivation of plants is the mainstay of tribal groups, animal domestication has commonly formed part of the agricultural complex. Some tribes depend heavily on large domesticated animals—cattle, camels, horses, sheep, and so forth—but such herding societies, often migratory or seminomadic in nature, are typically linked to sedentary agricultural groups by symbiotic economic

ties. Thus, "pure" pastoralism is probably as exceptional as total dependence on hunting.[1]

Dependence on regular crops does not automatically assure greater security from want than that enjoyed by hunters. True, some domesticated plants, in particular the grain staples, can be stored for long periods and may thus offer a protection against want, but the main benefits of agriculture accrue not so much to individuals as to society. Agriculture greatly facilitates permanent settlement (hamlets, villages, and later towns), a more centralized control of economic surpluses, and the elaboration of

[1]Some pastoral groups are found in environments that are far removed from settled agricultural people. This is the case with the reindeer herders of northern Eurasia, who live in arctic and subarctic environments.

Nomad pastoralists passing the ancient ruins of Persepolis, Iran. Pastoral groups are generally found on the borders of settled agricultural regions. (Inge Morath/Magnum Photos, Inc.)

The bulk of the diet of the Yąnomamö of northern South America comes from cultivated plants, plantains in particular. Gardening requires that brush and trees be cleared and then burned during the dry season. Women help with weeding and planting. (Napoleon Chagnon/Anthro-Photo)

social structures no longer geared to such small units as families or bands.

Tribal societies can be distinguished from band-level societies not only on the basis of economics and population size but also in terms of social organization. It is, in fact, the social organization of tribes that has received the most attention from anthropologists. Band organization is—has to be—very flexible in order to permit a ready response to changes in food supplies and related factors.

What one finds in tribal groups—and from this springs much of the interest of anthropologists—is the articulation of local ties, in particular kinship links, into structures that join the component units of the group. In most tribal societies the bond of common descent, especially as manifested in *lin-*

Kinship as the major organizing principle

eages, is the major structuring principle. For the moment, it is sufficient to recognize that a lineage is composed of individuals who reckon their descent from a common ancestor. Descent may be traced through either the father (*patrilineage*) or the mother (*matrilineage*), but some societies do not limit themselves to one descent line exclusively. Needless to say, a tribe is invariably composed of several lineages, since an individual is not allowed to marry within his or her own lineage. Lineages are often clustered into larger units that claim a common distant ancestry, even if this ancestry cannot always be demonstrated. Such lineage clusters are generally referred to as *clans*.

The importance of lineages goes well beyond the regulation of marriage, for in tribal societies lineages are corporate entities that function as the major economic, legal, and religious institutions. The structure of the whole society thus becomes based on the interlocking rights and obligations of kinship.

Despite the great importance of kinship as the major principle of organization in tribal societies, there is little uniformity among these societies with respect to the kinds of lineage systems utilized. What matters is that within any given tribe there are clearly recognized criteria for establishing group membership and, with group membership, a designated place in society. The social life of hunters revolves primarily around band membership, which is in large measure a matter of individual choice; in tribal society it is kinship and in particular lineage membership that determine the place of the individual.

STRUCTURE AND PROCESS

It seems reasonable to hypothesize that tribes became the dominant form of social integration in the wake of the plant and animal domestication that occurred during the Neolithic. This is something of a simplification since alterations in the social structure very likely paralleled, rather than followed, these changes in subsistence. Furthermore, although developments in food production made possible the elaboration of lineage systems, agriculture or pastoralism should not be seen as a necessary condition of tribal life.

The building blocks of social life in tribal groups are highly elaborated versions of simple kinship regulations that must have long antedated the first experiments in food growing. All kinship systems are anchored in some fundamental attributes of the human family, and more broadly, human biology. Among these are the universality of the *nuclear family* (a family group consisting of father, mother, and their children), the long period of dependence of the young on parents and other adults, and the universal regulation that marriages must be con-

tracted with individuals falling outside the immediate kin group—although what "outside" means varies enormously from culture to culture.[2] All of these features are present in band-level societies. Regulations pertaining to marriage are founded more on cultural and social necessities than on biology, and for good social reasons the universal rule is—and long must have been—marry out or die out.

The link between food production and social organization rests on the fact that crops and domesticated animals generally permit more complex forms of sociocultural integration than is commonly the case with hunting and collecting. Also, with crops or domesticated animals the kind of open ownership system so typical of hunting groups can no longer function and there must be stricter regulations pertaining to property. Property is often a matter of definition, but it is likely to cover crops, domesticated animals, land, and various other disposable resources generated by fairly complex economic systems.

We should also note that much the same problems may arise when hunters and collectors live in an especially bountiful natural environment, for in such cases there is also the possibility of allocating surpluses to special purposes. As we have already seen, this apparently occurred on the Northwest coast of North America, where the rich coastal environment allowed marine hunters and fishermen to operate at a tribal

[2]Most anthropologists would agree that all systems of kinship proceed from the family as the base, although there is no single, universal, family unit. It should be noted, however, that some communities have managed to survive and for a time even flourish without benefit of families. A variety of nineteenth-century utopian communities, some modern communes, and Israeli kibbutzim organize one or more of the customary family functions along nonfamilial lines. In every case that we know of, however, such communities form part of larger sociocultural units in which family structures are the norm. For a more detailed examination of the various kinds of family organization, the reader is referred to Chapter 12, "The Powerful Bond of Relationship."

level. Some authorities have postulated that Upper Paleolithic hunters in Europe, also blessed with plentiful natural resources, might well have evolved forms of social organization of a tribal nature. With the development of agriculture, patterns that had been possible in only a very few regions became the rule rather than the exception.

In time, pressure on land and resources was bound to rise, and with it the incidence of conflict. We have indicated that warfare is generally little developed among hunters: the social units tend to be too small for this kind of specialized venture. Furthermore, since war is often closely linked to economic factors, hunters have little to fight about and little to defend, in particular from other hunters. We would not wish to perpetuate a simplistic equation that identifies tribespeople with warriors, but on the whole there appears to be a relationship between the military potential of a society and the degree to which it can harness human and natural resources for purposes of culturally approved armed conflict. In some tribal societies, especially those in which a considerable degree of power and influence devolves

Sources of conflict and cohesion

on lineage and clan leaders, war is far from a peripheral interest. We should thus understand a tribal level of sociocultural integration not only as characterized by the articulation of a substantial number of individuals and considerable resources for internal purposes but also as heralding the use of armed power for the pursuit of group goals. Within the context of group combat, war also tends to offer opportunities for individual achievement and, hence, prestige and social mobility.

War might seem desirable for a variety of reasons, including the pressure of population on resources. For instance, slash-and-burn agriculturalists equipped with wood and stone tools would find it much harder to clear primary forest than to clear second growth. In such circumstances, the temptation would be high to take over land previously cultivated by another group. Warfare among the Maori of New Zealand, who lived in a hard-to-clear true rain-forest environment, has been interpreted in this light (Vayda 1960).

Having made these observations, we must caution the reader not to jump to the conclusion that organizationally tribes are

Papuans in war canoes, West Irian, Indonesia. While the men in this photograph are not on their way to raid, the picture gives a good idea of the size and organization of village war parties. (George Holton/ Photo Researchers, Inc.)

nothing but petty states. While the distinctions between band and tribe are significant, both quantitatively and qualitatively tribal societies are in some respects like band societies. Thus, although tribal societies are characterized by a greater degree of specialization, a member of a tribe is not only an agriculturalist or a herder but usually also a warrior, an active member in judicial councils, and an active participant in the ceremonial and religious life of the group.

TO SUM UP   What is absent in tribal societies, then, is specialization approaching professionalization. There are those few who possess more extensive religious knowledge than the average individual, but there are no true priests; there are important war leaders

An Indian woman from southern Mexico clearing a field before planting corn. Trees and shrubs have been cut and burned (slash-and-burn agriculture) prior to this operation. Note the steepness of the hillside, a factor that may later aggravate soil erosion. (Arthur Tress/Magnum Photos, Inc.)

selected for their bravery, but they do not constitute a military class. For the most part it is the lineage, and beyond the lineage the clan, that integrates individuals into a working whole. Lineages, like bands, are thus essentially self-sufficient sociocultural components, each encompassing a wide range of functions.

The structures we have outlined lack the permanence and stability of states. The advantages of flexibility are offset by potential disunity whenever lineages within the same tribe find themselves in conflict or when the tribe as a whole faces aggression from without. In short, the price of lineage autonomy is the specter of tribal disharmony. The very nature of lineages is that they split and differentiate over time. What we have, therefore, in tribal societies is structures with an inherent brittleness. In leadership functions, what generally matters is the authority of the individual as representing group consensus (lineage, clan, or tribe), not the "office" as such. This is one of the major distinctions between tribes and states.

THE ECONOMIC DIMENSION

While there are substantial differences in the economic structures of tribal societies, we can isolate a number of factors that are characteristic of most tribal situations. Subsistence may be based on agriculture, pastoralism, or a combination of the two; fishing may be important, as in the case of many Polynesian societies, and even hunting and collecting may continue to play a significant economic role. But regardless of how a livelihood is obtained, technologies are typically rather simple and skills tend to be generalized. Even when tribal technologies are more developed, these capacities are not backed up by organizational structures designed to maximize production. Thus the emergence of the state in the Near East, as well as in many other localities, was

The large quantities of yams harvested in this New Guinea village are likely to enhance the prestige of the individual who displays them and who will later host a big feast for his supporters. (Kal Muller/ Woodfin Camp & Assoc.)

heralded, not by the introduction of new crops or even new basic techniques of cultivation, but by new patterns of sociopolitical organization. These new patterns not only helped centralize government in much more formal and explicit ways than is the case with tribal societies, past and present, but made possible large-scale irrigation projects that boosted the productivity of Neolithic farming methods (Adams 1966; Braidwood and Willey 1962).[3]

[3]Historically, the transition from subsistence food production to food production generating "surpluses" for the maintenance of hierarchically organized political and territorial units (states) was a process rather than an event. It is thus somewhat misleading to speak of such long-term developments as "revolutions"; the consequences were to prove revolutionary indeed, but the changes developed gradually. Ecologically and culturally, the domestication of plants and animals permitted the broadening of ecological niches available to ancestral plants and animals: through conscious seeding, weeding, clearing, and selection, the habitats of food plants and animals were enormously extended, allowing much greater population densities in suitable areas.

Disposition of surpluses

In most tribal societies, therefore, the productive capacities of the individual or of the family unit are restricted. And even where productivity is high, problems of transportation and storage limit the use to which surpluses may be put. In most tribal contexts, there is also an absence of markets, both in the specific sense of trading centers and in the sense of organized outlets for production, although goods, including agricultural products, are exchanged. Again, these limitations are a function of relatively simple forms of organization. It should not surprise us, therefore, that in a number of tribal societies surpluses that cannot be consumed are used for display, destruction, or competitive gift giving. The best-documented example of such conspicuous consumption is undoubtedly the potlatch custom of the Northwest Coast Indians—"fighting with property," to use a term that has been made into the title of a classic study of economic behavior among the Kwakiutl (Codere 1950). Phenomena of much the same kind may be encountered in other parts of the globe as well, especially in Melanesia. Douglas L. Oliver (1955), who has worked in the Solomon Islands society of Siuai, examines in great detail the competitive feasts that important men, backed by kinsmen and friends, throw for one another as a means of acquiring prestige. The hope is that the individual to be so "honored" will not be able to escalate the "gift" of the feast and will be rendered what the Siuai call "near-death"—in short, knocked out of action as a feast-giver and individual of commanding position. Prestige comes from more than simple largess for, as Oliver notes:

renown is more than accumulating and giving away wealth. Renown comes from utilizing capital in such a way that loyalties are mobilized, obligations created, prestige enhanced, and authority exercised *in traditionally acceptable ways*—above all, in the staging of special kinds of feasts (Oliver 1955:362).

Important Siuai feasts involve much ritualized behavior including ceremonial speeches that are self-deprecatory in tone, everyone understanding, of course, that this is nothing more than a formula and that the feast-giver (host) has strained every resource to provide a sumptuous banquet. One of the speech exchanges collected by Oliver goes as follows:

Host's spokesman: I want to tell you something.
Guest's spokesman: I listen to what you have to say.
Host's spokesman: You made me very happy when you ended my mourning. You overwhelmed me with the huge feast you prepared for me, and with the great sums of shell-money you gave me.
Guest's spokesman: Actually, I was very ashamed of the pitifully small feast and the bagatelle of a gift.
Host's spokesman: Now I am ashamed by the pitifully small gift which I must give you in return. Alas, there have been many

deaths among my relatives, and all my resources have gone into providing cremations.
Guest's spokesman: But that small feast I gave to you was little enough for me to give to such a leader as you; such a taovu-partner [a relationship involving economic exchange and credit] as you. And now you shame me by the size of the feast you give to me in return. Et cetera (Oliver 1955: 369–370).

The point we wish to make is not that the Siuai are affluent (actually, like not a few tribesmen, they often go hungry), nor that individuals and groups in tribal societies necessarily engage in competitive gift giving and similar activities, but simply that the economics of tribal societies, together with the organizational structures typical of them, make activities of this kind one of the available options. However, even in tribes characterized by patterns of conspicuous consumption, efforts in this direction do not preclude trade and barter.

If we look at the matter of the disposal of surpluses in terms of sociocultural discontinuities, bands generally deal with temporary surpluses in ways that are not competitive, whereas in states such institutions as taxes, rents, and market networks provide an economic foundation geared to the collection and disposal of food and other commodities. In this frame of reference, tribes occupy the middle ground: they command surpluses but do not manipulate them in the bureaucratized manner typical of state systems.

Exchange and redistribution The transactional principles governing the distribution of goods in tribal societies include exchange and systems of redistribution. As George Dalton notes:

The integrative patterns which do exist widely in primitive economy are (1) reciprocity, that is, material gift and counter gift-giving induced by social obligation derived, typically, from kinship . . . and (2) redistribution, the channeling upward

of goods or services to socially determined allocative centers (usually king, chief, or priest), who then redistribute either to their subordinates at large by providing community services, or in specific allotments to individuals in accordance with their political, religious, or military status (Dalton 1961:9).

Generally, economic relations in tribal society function within the kinship framework. This is as true of exchange as it is of systems of redistribution that are in the main geared to lineage structures. The dignitaries that Dalton refers to are in most cases lineage heads. Although, as we have noted, productivity tends to be low (in large measure because production is geared to family subsistence needs), what surpluses remain are often shunted upward where they are utilized by lineage or tribal heads to underwrite ritual events and other undertakings of importance to the community. Writing of the situation in the Trobriand Islands, Bronislaw Malinowski observes that "the chief on the one hand has the power to accumulate agricultural produce and to control the live-stock and the palms of the district, while on the other hand, he is the

one who has both the right and duty to use this accumulated wealth effectively" (1935:1:47). In a more general context, he notes that "the chief, everywhere, acts as a tribal banker, collecting food, storing it, and protecting it, and then using it for the benefit of the whole community" (1937:232).

Such systems of redistribution are linked to the presence of some socially recognized center—usually a chief or lineage head—who reallocates a portion of what he receives to provide for community services (such as defense or feasts) and the maintenance of retainers. Reciprocity, on the other hand, is much less dependent on formalized structures of rank, for—as we have noted in the case of the Siuai—prestige may be derived from successful transactions. What we have to keep in mind is that the principle of reciprocity entails obligatory giving of gifts and countergifts, a concept that may be difficult for us to grasp. Reciprocity plays a relatively minor role in Western societies, and although it is probably fair to assume that we expect some return (children are urged to write "thank-you notes" indicative of appreciation; birthday and wedding gifts carry implicit reciprocal obligations, and so forth), gift giving is of little importance economically in societies with developed systems of market exchange.

Market exchange is present in tribal societies, but production for purposes of exchange seldom is a central feature of tribal economies. Exchange lacks the obligatory character of redistribution and reciprocity and is in the main a feature of more complex socioeconomic systems. Another way of phrasing the situation is that market exchange seldom interlinks with the moral, religious, and juridical dimensions of tribal life; there is much greater play for haggling and chicanery than is the case in redistribution and reciprocity.

THE SOCIAL ORGANIZATION OF TRIBES

We have stressed that an understanding of tribal social organization requires some knowledge of kinship structures. All such structures are basically conventions for determining group membership—another way of saying that kinship systems are a cultural overlay on biology. That there are generations and kinspeople of two sexes is indeed a biological fact, but that an individual traces his or her descent through either the maternal or the paternal line alone is a cultural arrangement. The reckoning of descent defines social relations for an individual and has little to do with the fact that genetically a person is beholden to both parents, and by extension to parents' parents, and so on.

Since the reckoning of descent strictly through one line is foreign to Western European cultures and to cultures derived from European colonists, we sometimes find it difficult to appreciate the implications of such an arrangement. Simply stated, for purposes of social relations one of the two biological lines is disregarded. In Western systems, biology and culture come closer

together, although they do not perfectly overlap. It is perhaps sufficient to note that in American society children normally take their father's surname and not their mother's, and that in Western monarchies and aristocracies titles and offices normally pass from male bearer to eldest son. As a result, our history books contain many kings but very few reigning queens. Furthermore, the English language blurs the distinction between social and biological relations. We use one word, *father*, to cover two related but analytically distinct functions: biological father and social father. However, the duties of a social father—the person who performs the culturally recognized father role—may be undertaken by an individual biologically unrelated to the son or the daughter. This is the case with adopted children, and it highlights the essential difference between biological ties and social ties. The Romans made the distinction considerably clearer than we do and referred to the biological father as *genitor* and the social father as *pater*.

This digression may seem to have carried us some distance away from tribal societies, but it should make us more comfortable with kinship systems very different from our own. Also, it stresses a point that is often forgotten: all kinship systems address themselves to social relations and roles.

The segmentary lineage principle

Unilineal descent—descent reckoned through either the maternal or paternal line—is not limited to tribal societies, nor are all tribal societies structured on the basis of unilineal principles. But the phenomenon is so closely associated with such a range of tribal societies that it can be approached as a mechanism commonly utilized to integrate tribal-level societies.

The unilineal principle has some very definite organizational advantages. It neatly and conveniently assigns an individual to one particular group. Also, membership in the lineage is restricted to those individuals who are recognized as being born into the

Figure 8-1 The segmentary principle

Lineages *a* through *h*, occupying respective territories (*a'* through *h'*) are the result of segmentation over time from the original lineages *A* and *B*. (Adapted from Paul Bohannan, "The Migration and Expansion of the Tiv," *Africa*, 1954, International African Institute, No. 3)

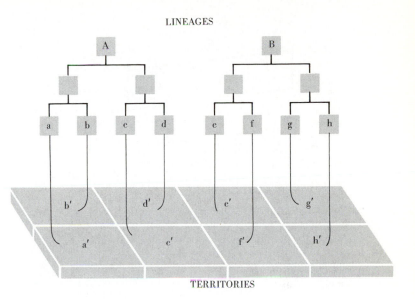

TERRITORIES

social unit. This exclusiveness precludes conflicts as to membership: one either is or is not a member of a lineage and, in unilineal situations, one cannot be a member of more than one lineage. As a result, conflicts of interest are reduced, for the rules of descent clearly stipulate where one's loyalties lie and who one's kinspeople are.

As we have noted, the lineage principle typically entails segmentation, a process of periodic splitting that results in the formation of *segmentary lineages* (see Figure 8-1). Thus a lineage may divide into two headed by two brothers (in a patrilineal system), and these may in turn segment once again in a subsequent generation. This "hiving-off" process is perhaps especially advantageous when a need arises to establish new lineages in territories coming under the control of an expansionist tribe.

We have to bear in mind that while segmentary lineages are autonomous, they are still joined by recognized bonds of kinship into clusters of related lineages. The framework is thus highly flexible and allows for both segmentation and mobilization. The component tribal units remain at a size that

is not unwieldy, and yet these components can, as necessity requires, "mobilize" for common action such as warfare. According to Marshall D. Sahlins:

The segmentary lineage system is an institution appearing at the tribal level of general cultural evolution; it is not characteristic of bands, chiefdoms, or the several forms of civilization. It develops among societies with a simple neolithic mode of production and a correlative tendency to form small, autonomous economic and political groups. The segmentary lineage system is a social means of temporary consolidation of this fragmented tribal polity for concerted external action. It is, in a sense, a substitute for the fixed political structure which a tribal society is incapable of sustaining (Sahlins 1961:341–342).

In the above quotation, Sahlins differentiates between tribes and chiefdoms, a distinction that for the purposes of this chapter is too fine. As in segmentary lineages, the organizational principle remains that of kinship, but kinship so ordered as to allow for ranking and hierarchy.

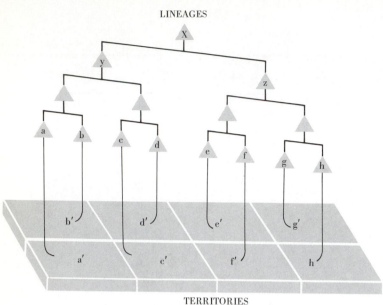

LINEAGES

TERRITORIES

Figure 8-2 The principle of the conical clan

In this diagram, priority goes to the firstborn (older) son (here indicated by a slightly elevated position). Among the eight local lineage chiefs (*a* through *h*), Chief *a* occupies the highest rank, that of paramount chief. The hierarchy among the eight lineage chiefs is as follows:

paramount chief *a*: over *a* through *h*
territorial chiefs: *a* over *a* through *d*, and *e* over *e* through *h*
district chiefs: *a* over *a* and *b*, *c* over *c* and *d*, *e* over *e* and *f*, and *g* over *g* and *h*
local lineage chiefs: *a*,*b*,*c*, and so forth, over their respective lineages and the associated localities *a'*, *b'*, *c'*, and so forth

X designates the ancestral clan founder; *y* and *z* the original lineage heads (chiefs), the older and the younger son respectively. (Marshall D. Sahlins, *Tribesman*, © 1968, p. 25. Adapted by permission of Prentice-Hall, Inc., Englewood Cliffs, New Jersey.)

The main strategy of chiefdom organization is a structure referred to as the *conical clan* (see Figure 8-2), a common-descent group divided into a number of lineages. These lineages, however, are not separate and equal but are organized into a hierarchy of senior and junior lineages. The organizing principle of conical clans is genealogical seniority, with all lineages and individuals ranked according to the distance from the lineage founder and, within a lineage, by order of birth. Thus, in patrilineal conical clans priority goes to the firstborn son of first born sons, other sons having lesser rank in accordance with order of birth.

The organizational advantages of conical clans are easy enough to grasp: by joining the principle of seniority to that of descent, all individuals can be sorted out as closer to, or further away from, a recognized first ancestor. If to seniority and descent is added a unilineal principle, so that only one sex is recognized as being able to transmit the major attributes of position, the system is further simplified in terms of numbers.

It is understandable that in conical lin-

The conical clan

eage systems (or conical clans) considerable effort is devoted to tracing out genealogical links and maintaining as much of a monopoly on rank and position as the system permits—hence the tendency of high chiefs to marry eligible close relatives, a feature that has often also characterized the marriage patterns of European royal families. It would be incorrect, however, to perceive chiefdoms based on conical clan arrangements as petty states. There are ranking and hereditary roles, but these positions are not backed by the coercive and, in large measure impersonal, power of the state. There is no state machinery, as such, and no specialized trappings of central government. Even the highest and most important chiefs depend directly on the support of their lineage, and senior lineages must be able to count on the continuing support of junior lineages. In practice, a "strong chief" is likely to be an individual who not only commands respect by virtue of his position in the genealogical order but who also knows well the usages of persuasion, the duties of reciprocity, and the value of personal charisma. The success of chiefs depends greatly on what we might term "effective leadership." It should be kept in mind that even in ranked tribal societies, the political order rests on a large measure of consensus, and there is often an option for the component groups, in particular junior lineages, to go their own way and disregard the ideal structure of genealogically based authority. For these reasons, tribal and lineage councils—mechanisms for ironing out conflicting viewpoints and establishing consensus—tend to be key institutions in tribal society.

Conical clans are found in different parts of the world, but the best-documented examples come from Oceania and central Asia. Conical clan systems, as is true of other chiefdoms, may evolve into true states, but this transformation involves a considerable reorganization of the sociopolitical structure. It is also possible for a conical clan organization to develop very substantial political and military momentum, but when this occurs it is usually the result of exceptionally astute and successful leadership.

Some societies emphasize territoriality rather than descent, and while they may have recognized lineages, these are relatively unimportant. In the New Guinea highlands, for instance, the clan claims and defends a given territory, and leadership is exercised by local "big-men." Lineages are present, but they do not act as the major organizational units, either as autonomous segmentary units or as ranked components of a conical clan. The big-men achieve their position by consummate wheeling and dealing and by personal alliances.

The segmentary lineage and the conical clan do not exhaust the organizational possibilities of tribal societies of the world, at least a third of which are not unilineal. In nonunilineal societies, an individual is related to a number of other persons through both mother and father. This spread of kinfolk is commonly referred to as a *kindred*. We should understand such a system as being composed of persons related to a given individual. It follows that the members of a kindred network need not themselves be related to one another but are like the spokes of a wheel with a particular individual at its hub. Many Plains Indian tribes used this principle of organization, the overall effect being a constellation of alliances gravitating around important personages, some with more allies, others with fewer. The "war party" that has become so enshrined in the folklore of the West would in most instances rely heavily on kindred ties, although a successful leader might well attract individuals other than those related to him by marriage or line of descent.

LIMITS OF TRIBAL INTEGRATION

We have examined a sample of the most common patterns of tribal organization. That tribal structures of whatever type suffer from built-in limitations is evident from the fact that as a political structure, a tribe is at a clear disadvantage when confronted with the routinized and specialized institutions of a state system, primarily because a tribe is much more a cultural category than a social one. Typically, tribespeople share a common language and a common culture and recognize what we might now term a shared ethnic membership. But the members of a tribe seldom work in unison, except perhaps when faced by powerful outside forces. Even in such instances, tribes are not organized to carry out with any ease policies that demand unity and endurance.

The amorphous and shifting quality of tribal structures sometimes makes it difficult to determine where the social boundaries of a given tribe should be drawn. It is easy enough to delimit lineages, and even clans tend to possess substantial cohesiveness, but as E. E. Evans-Pritchard notes with respect to the Nuer of southern Sudan:

It is evident that when we speak of a Nuer tribe we are using a relative term, for it is not always easy to say, on the criteria we have used, whether we are dealing with a tribe with two primary segments or with two tribes. The tribal system as defined by sociological analysis can, therefore, only be said to approximate to any simple diagrammatic presentation (Evans-Pritchard 1940a:283–284).

It is true that on occasion spatial boundaries give tribal organizations firmer contours, as is the case with tribal societies inhabiting some of the smaller Pacific islands, but Evans-Pritchard's discussion of the Nuer fits the more common situation where physical borders are not as firmly delimited and where segmentation and competition are the norm. As a generalization, it is correct to say that the political order of tribes is very much influenced by chance and situational factors. A dynamic leader, the fortunes of war, the discontent of subordinate lineages or conquered tribes can all help to elevate a subordinate group or subdue a dominant one. The political or military success of an individual is likely to raise those associated with him, in particular other lineage members, to positions of influence. As Max Gluckman observes for the Zulu in the nineteenth century:

A notable feature of Zulu political organization throughout Zulu history is the creation of new groups as people moved about, settled and increased, and the heads of all these groups were minor political officers who might in time achieve prominence (Gluckman 1940:45).

We mention the Zulu because for a period the Zulu nation—a federation of tribes—managed to put up a stiff and successful resistance against the British and the Boers in South Africa. But even the powerful Zulu kings were limited in their overlordship, and the "nation" was not so much a unitary body as a series of semiautonomous groups, each with separate identity and its own chief, prone to follow their own course and engage in internal conflicts.

Under the influence of a successful military and political leader, a relatively loose assemblage of lineages, clans, or tribes have on occasion been welded into a powerful force. Perhaps the historically most striking example of this phenomenon was the unification of Mongol tribes under the leadership of Genghis Khan (1162–1227), a feat that for generations assured these mounted nomads from Asia mastery over every battlefield.

The Mongol case is illuminating in a number of respects. Genghis Khan rose to power by able political and military maneuvering, but Mongol power, once institutionalized, needed the organizational support of Chinese bureaucrats, and in due course the Mongol leadership became transformed into another Chinese dynasty.

Without such transformations—sometimes successful, at other times not—the leaders of large tribal confederacies have had to rely on a combination of personal power and a fairly constant supply of plunder and tribute to redistribute to lesser chiefs. Obviously, as the boundaries of such a system expand, internal cohesion diminishes. Success is necessary to keep the system together, but there are limits to expansion, whether by forced alliance or conquest.

We might say that there is a self-liquidating aspect to large political and social aggregates put together from lineages, clans, and tribes. In part, the problem is technological and economic—the difficulty of generating surpluses to maintain the system by means other than conquest and tribute—but in the last analysis the flaw is organizational. Control has to remain personal and charismatic and there are no built-in institutional structures to tide such systems over periods of mediocre leadership.

MAINTENANCE OF
TRIBAL STRUCTURES

In the preceding section we have focused on the limitations inherent in tribal structures as political organizations. Our point was that in the absence of formalized higher-order institutions—the kinds of institutions that we associate with complex societies—the maintenance of social cohesion devolves on units with a propensity to break down into their component elements.

But if this is the case, then how do tribes manage to maintain any kind of social order? The fact is that we have been addressing ourselves to only a portion of the total picture. Historically, tribal federations may be short-lived, but it does not follow that a condition of anarchy is the rule in tribal society. There are definite pressures in the direction of cleavage and segmentation, but there are also forces that work in the direction of cohesion, even if there are clear organizational ceilings to what may be achieved in a tribal context.

Alliance through marriage

We should understand that the basic units of tribal society are not self-maintaining. The only way that a lineage can perpetuate itself over time is through an exchange with other lineages of marriageable partners, and in tribal societies marriage is very much a group concern. Individuals must, because of incest regulations, select their spouses from outside their own lineage, but this is phrasing it at a very personal level: it would be more correct to say that lineages must acquire from other lineages suitable partners for those ready to marry. Marriage, then, is the key to all kinds of cooperative arrangements. While in tribal society it seldom fails to take into account the preferences of the would-be spouses, these are of secondary importance. What is vital is the function of marriage as a compact between two groups of persons, generally lineages in their corporate capacity. In brief, a marriage is an alliance. It symbolizes the coming together not only of two people but of the two social units of which they are members. This point was made as early as 1889 by Edward B. Tylor when he observed that "among tribes of low culture there is but one means known of keeping up permanent alliance, and that means is intermarriage" (1889:267).

If we see marriage in this light, much else falls into place. The "marriage payment" given in many tribal societies by the groom and the groom's kin to the wife's kin is not, as many Westerners—in particular, missionaries—believe, a purchase price on the bride but a transaction that formalizes the alliance and legitimizes the union and the offspring that may come from it. Indicative of the importance of the bride, it sets into motion further reciprocal arrangements between the two groups. Far from demeaning the bride, it establishes her worth as a representative of her own lineage.

The significance of marriage patterns rests on the fact that they establish an orderly "flow" of individuals between distinct social entities. In some cases, this exchange is directly reciprocal, in others it is more circular. For instance, lineage (or clan) A may with regularity provide brides to lineage B, which in turn does the same to lineage C, which finally is a source of brides for lineage A. Clearly, whether reciprocal or circular, such arrangements establish an interaction sphere that, in the interests of those concerned, should remain free of conflict. Marriages constitute only one level of exchange. Reciprocity may also be established through the exchange of goods or valued services. More often than not, however, marriage is the cement that binds social groups together, with other cooperative ventures complementing the exchange of spouses.

Age-grades

The institution of the marriage alliance in its various guises, with the social and psychological devices that have evolved to protect it, is only one of the means that help integrate tribal society. Religious, military, and *age-grade* associations crosscut lineages and clans in many tribes, joining individuals of similar status for common action and common affective relationships. Age-grade systems, which group together individuals of the same sex and approximately the same age, apparently have evolved independently in many parts of the world as a response to

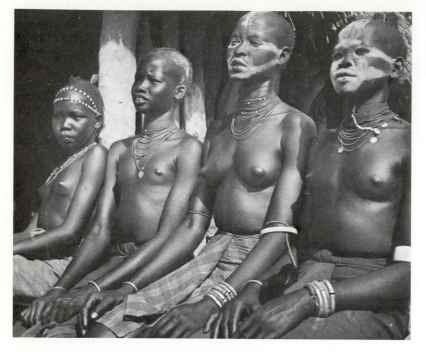

Young Nuer women. Many tribal societies utilize the organizational principle of age-grades. Members of such sets belong to the same culturally defined generation. (George Rodger/Magnum Photos, Inc.)

the segmentary principle. They are especially well represented in Africa, the Pacific, and among Native Americans. As is true of marriage patterns, age-grades do not conflict with the web of kinship but rather act as linkages or strands that give greater cohesion to the social fabric.

Age-grades may be more or less marked, more or less developed, but the principle is simple: people of the same general age are clustered into sex-specific aggregates. Thus males may fall into three categories—boys, warriors, and elders—or there may be a general concept of unity linking those who have come of age at the same time, or the system may be highly elaborated into many grades with distinct functions. The underlying principle is the unity of the generational group, and as such it has something in common with age demarcations found in Western societies—graduating classes, for example. However, while generational ranking is not limited to tribal societies, it takes on a functional importance seldom

found in either more complex or simpler sociocultural systems.

The solidarity of age-grade companions is often reinforced by shared experiences beginning with initiation ceremonies designed to demarcate initiates from noninitiates and one group of initiates from another. Among the Nuer of the Sudan, all males mark the transition from boyhood to adulthood by a very severe operation that involves deep incisions in the forehead running from ear to ear. The Nuer believe that "were a boy to be initiated by himself he would be lonely and might die. Also, it is easier to cater for the boys and to give them the care and attention they require during convalescence if they are initiated in batches" (Evans-Pritchard 1940b:249). Among the Zulu, a decidedly martial people, age-grades formed the basis of regiments, each male fighting in company with his age-mates.

Because they are structured according to age, age-grades lack the capacity for self-

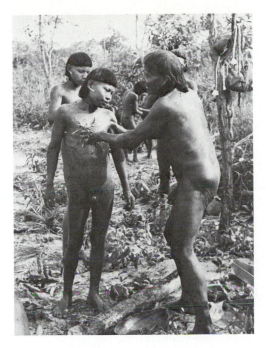

Critical periods in the lifetime of a society's members are commonly marked by ritual activity, the so-called rites of passage. Shown here are youths of the Xavante people, in South America, during their initiation into adult status. (Maybury-Lewis/Anthro-Photo)

perpetuation that one finds in lineages and many other corporate entities. Any given age-grade is only one interlinking strand that is preceded by similar strands and followed by others. Hence, while the grade itself is fixed in membership, it should be viewed as part of an ongoing system that is constantly being replenished and just as constantly moving through the normal life cycle until death finally extinguishes the last representatives of a given grade.

Usually less formalized and less inclusive are other associational arrangements, such as trading partnerships between individuals from different social units. In some societies, stress is placed on organizations that group together individuals engaged in trade, war, or ritual activities. The "war societies" of the Plains Indians fall into this category.

Tribal structures are also reinforced in a variety of ways that we may term ideological and religious. Tribes generally occupy fairly fixed geographical areas that tribal

Attachment to homeland

members regard as their homeland. A homeland is a location that engenders strong positive feelings; it is the ancestral land often characterized or bounded by specific geographical features such as mountains, streams, and forests that are not only a backdrop to present tribal life but the scene of past actions, whether historical or mythological. This strong attachment is manifested in different ways, but they all have in common a linkage between individuals and the land of their birth. The story is told, and it may well be true, that not one of the Mohawk steelworkers, whose skill and courage helped build the George Washington Bridge, the Empire State Building, and most of the other high structures in New York, has ever been buried in New York City. If they die outside their homeland or are killed in the performance of their hazardous duty, they are sent back home by their Indian co-workers to be buried in the soil of their reservations in upstate New York or across the border in Canada.

This linkage of people to land is reinforced not only by human ties and early experience but by strong cultural bonds that include shared language and shared religious practices. Religion fuses with every aspect of tribal life. Ritual helps maintain lineages and gives cohesion to most other associations. At a more general level, religion is intimately tied to areas and localities. There are places sacred to worship and features of the landscape associated with important mythological figures. The sacred and the nonsacred are thus part of the same physical world. One hundred years ago, the old chief Standing Bear of the Sioux observed that white people did not understand this relationship between land and its inhabitants, for they were still alien to the land.

But in the Indian the spirit of the land is still vested. It will be until other men are able to divine and meet its rhythm. Men must be born and reborn to belong. The bodies must be formed of dust of their forefathers' bones (quoted by Steiner 1968:167).

This complex of symbols and relationships effectively functions without the structure of the state and without a belief system that has been formalized into a theology. As such, it cuts across internal cleavages and special interests and helps make tribes something more than a random collection of smaller social units.

REFERENCES

ADAMS, ROBERT MCCORMICK
1966   *The evolution of urban society: early Mesopotamia and prehistoric Mexico.* Chicago: Aldine.

BRAIDWOOD, ROBERT J., AND GORDON R. WILLEY, EDS.
1962   *Courses toward urban life: archeological considerations of some cultural alternates.* Viking Fund Publications in Anthropology, no. 32. New York: Wenner-Gren Foundation for Anthropological Research.

CODERE, HELEN
1950   *Fighting with property; a study of Kwakiutl potlatching and warfare, 1792–1930.* New York: J. J. Augustin.

DALTON, GEORGE
1961   Economic theory and primitive society. *American Anthropologist* 63: 1–25.

EVANS-PRITCHARD, E. E.
1940a The Nuer of the southern Sudan. In *African political systems.* Meyer Fortes and E. E. Evans-Pritchard, eds. London: Oxford University Press. Pp. 272–296.

1940b   *The Nuer, a description of the modes of livelihood and political institutions of a Nilotic people.* Oxford: Clarendon Press.

GLUCKMAN, MAX
1940   The kingdom of the Zulu of South Africa. In *African political systems.* Meyer Fortes and E. E. Evans-Pritchard, eds. London: Oxford University Press. Pp. 25–55.

MALINOWSKI, BRONISLAW
1935   *Coral gardens and their magic.* London: George Allen and Unwin Ltd. 2 vols.

1937   Anthropology as the basis of social science. In *Human affairs.* Raymond B. Cattell, J. Cohen, and R. M. W. Travers, eds. London: Macmillan. Pp. 199–252.

OLIVER, DOUGLAS L.
1955   *A Solomon Island society; kinship and leadership among the Siuai of Bougainville.* Cambridge: Harvard University Press.

SAHLINS, MARSHALL D.
1961   The segmentary lineage: an organization of predatory expansion. *American Anthropologist* 63:322–345.

STEINER, STAN
1968   *The new Indians.* New York: Harper and Row.

TYLOR, EDWARD BURNETT
1889   On a method of investigating the development of institutions; applied to laws of marriage and descent. *Journal of the Anthropological Institute of Great Britain and Ireland* 18:245–269.

VAYDA, ANDREW P.
1960   *Maori warfare.* Wellington, New Zealand: The Polynesian Society.

Chapter 9
The peasant condition

Since World War II, a growing number of anthropologists have turned their attention to the study of peasants. While tribal and band-level societies, the more traditional subjects of anthropological research, are becoming an ever-diminishing portion of the world population, most of the inhabitants of the technologically less advanced countries may be classified as peasants. Furthermore, many modern industrial nations include a substantial peasant conponent.[1] On num-

bers alone, therefore, peasants would seem to merit attention. But the importance of peasant studies rests on more than the fact that there are many peasants or that anthropologists have developed an interest in peasant societies. Above all, there is the growing realization that the world as a whole is confronted with a critical food-to-population imbalance.

The problems of food, population, and resources are closely interrelated, but it is evident that part of the answer must be sought in the rural regions of the world. Production of foodstuffs and other agricultural commodities takes place in both the developed and the developing (or underdeveloped) lands, but poor peasants constitute the majority of cultivators. In a very real sense, then, the future of us all is intimately tied to the conditions of life and the productive capacity of the peasant majority.

Peasants may be the majority of mankind, but our knowledge of them is still far from adequate. Most anthropological research on peasants has been conducted during the past thirty years, and considering

[1]The industrial revolution had a profound effect upon the lives of European peasantries. However, neither industrialization nor social and political change led to the disappearance of peasants in Western Europe—although agriculturalists did become a proportionately smaller segment of the total population. Sometimes the modernization of social structures has worked to reinforce peasant elements. As a case in point, in Britain only 12 percent of the agricultural land was farmed by owner-occupiers in 1908, but by 1957 the duties and taxes on large estates had become so heavy that 50 percent of the land was farmed by those who owned it. The English case may be exceptional, but peasants remain very much in evidence in such highly industrialized countries as France, Germany, and Japan and in such rapidly industrializing countries as Poland.

The work of the agriculturalist in pre-industrial societies is often very demanding, while the productivity from this effort is generally low. An Ethiopian farmer guides his ox team. (Paul Conklin)

that peasants have been the mainstay of states and empires for thousands of years, good historical information is surprisingly scarce, being limited to a few areas such as Japan, Western Europe, and China. Although anthropologists, historians, and sociologists are paying increasing attention to peasants past and present, reliable information often must compete with a wealth of hearsay and stereotyped beliefs about how peasants think and act.

THE PEASANT WAY OF LIFE

A number of features characterize peasant life. First and most obviously, peasants are farmers.[2] But they are farmers in a particular and total sense. Peasants, as Eric Wolf points out, view agriculture as a means of livelihood, not as a business for profit (Wolf 1966:2). It is not so much that peasants lack an interest in selling a portion of their crops but rather that such sales are not an end in themselves. These sales can be best understood as transactions that help maintain a given style of life and permit the acquisition of basic necessities. Consequently, farming is less a business enterprise than a key attribute of the peasant condition. Peasants are primarily concerned with subsistence production and generally consume a major portion of the food and other articles they produce. It is very exceptional for peasants

[2]A strong case can be made for considering many herdsmen and fishermen as subtypes of peasantry. It has also been suggested that groups such as miners in Appalachia and some agriculturalists in the southern United States (sharecroppers, small tenant farmers, and the like) represent American versions of peasant societies.

(unlike modern commercial agriculturalists) to concentrate on the cultivation of cash crops for an external market.

Typically, peasants are village inhabitants who are known to one another through shared experience in work, ritual, and leisure activities. This close association entails a social system based on face-to-face relationships. Villagers may also have personal ties with individuals outside the community in contrast to the more limited or specialized relationships found in modern industrial society.

As a rule, the technology used by peasants is antiquated—in some cases it has changed little since Neolithic times—and the productivity of peasant agriculture is low. There are in fact many features of peasant economy that remind one of tribal economies: reliance on agriculture, simple technology, an emphasis on subsistence production, a limited range of items produced, and a direct dependence on the environment (weather, plant diseases, and so forth). The hazards that peasants continually face have often been held responsible for the poverty, distrust, and anxiety that seem to be found so often in peasant societies.

Sources of insecurity

While there is little question that peasants would generally feel more secure if a way could be found to improve the output from their fields, peasant anxieties are not based solely on low productivity and related matters. Unlike tribal peoples, who were essentially autonomous before they came under colonial control, peasants are now—and have been for centuries—a subordinate element in the societies of which they form a part. This dependent relationship to non-peasant governing classes chiefly distinguishes peasants as a social and cultural type and is primarily responsible for the climate of insecurity and deprivation characteristic of so many peasant societies.

Given their subordinate position, their lack of power, peasants may have sound reasons to fear that production much above

In contrast to the methods of small peasant landholders, large-scale agribusiness employs machinery and wage labor. Shown here are harvesters and ten-ton trailers used in harvesting a tomato crop in California. Afterwards, the plants are plowed under and a different crop planted (U.S.D.A. Photo)

subsistence level will ultimately be siphoned off in the form of higher taxes and other governmental requirements. Regardless of whether or not peasants evaluate the situation correctly, attitudes born of such expectations become woven into the fabric of peasant life and guide their social and economic behavior.

In this light a number of peasant traits become easier to understand. Fear of powerful outsiders, as well as the desire not to provoke the envy of one's neighbors, can establish a psychological barrier to wealth. The same is true of conservative attitudes in general. Peasants have survived for thousands of years through a series of techniques designed to make them less tempting targets. It is difficult to convince peasants that they can now discard these defenses with impunity. Peasants, it is said, "make the economists sigh, the politicians sweat, and the strategists swear . . . all over the world—Moscow and Washington, Peking and Delhi. . ." (Shanin 1966:5). Yet, unless this peasant sector—more than two billion strong—can be assured that major benefits will accrue to those willing to risk change, all the economic and social programs in government ministries and international agencies will in the end be worth little more than the paper they are written on. Hard as it may be for some to understand, it is not bureaucrats, or social scientists, who grow the crops but farmers. And most farmers are peasants.

THE PEASANT AND ECONOMIC BEHAVIOR

Demands of ceremonialism

While peasant communities are always linked to external power structures, much that has to do with economic and social behavior in peasant life is best approached, at least initially, from the perspective of the village. In many peasant societies, great effort is directed at meeting the material demands of religious observance and social position. Consider, for example, the manner in which traditional obligations influence economic activities in the Indian peasant village of Panajachel in western Guatemala. Panajacheleños sell a portion of their agricultural produce to the national capital and other urban centers. Some of the profits from this trade are used to buy articles and manufactured goods that are not available in the community. Transactions of this type are economically "rational": coffee beans or vegetables are sold for so many quetzales, and the currency is then used to purchase machetes, salt, needles, or perhaps a young pig for fattening.

But this is only part of the economic picture. A community of some eight hundred inhabitants must also find the surpluses to support a total of fifty-two offices in the village's political and religious hierarchy. What ceremonialism entails in terms of expenditure can be gauged by the importance of alcohol in the family budgets. We are told that the amount spent for this item, a key ingredient in virtually all ceremonial activities, represents "about a fourth of that spent on clothing; it is more than that for any item of food excepting corn or meat; and it is almost as much as is spent on all tools and household utensils and supplies" (Tax 1953:177). Additional expenditures are necessary for such other items as fireworks, incense, candles, and festive food.

Not all peasant societies allocate so much capital to what one writer has called the "ceremonial fund" (Wolf 1966:7). It remains true, however, that peasants generally establish priorities and earmark surpluses in a manner likely to puzzle Western economists. It is not that the dictates of custom inhibit rational calculation—even the shortest visit to a peasant market offers ample evidence of a keen sense of price and value. Rather, the peasants believe that in the long run such economic considerations as making the largest possible profit are secondary to the maintenance and preservation of community or family structures.

Peasant economic behavior is far from uniform. Many peasant societies are characterized by what economists would call a "lack of deferred gratification"—the tendency to spend rather than to save, to spend now rather than tomorrow. Such patterns of immediate consumption may in part be founded on the philosophy that what one enjoys today cannot be taken away tomorrow. Furthermore, as we shall note later, it is generally difficult for the peasant to hold on to unencumbered resources once family, friends, and neighbors become aware of their existence.

These patterns of consumption can be contrasted with what we may term the theme of the frugal peasant. Here the emphasis is on delayed consumption and often the slow and steady accumulation of cash or crops. We learn, for instance, that the Basseri of southern Iran, a "peasantized" pastoral group, evidence "an almost obsessive desire to postpone every incident of consumption—to let each lamb gain weight one more day, or week, or season, to have one more lamb from an old sheep, to make a worn-out pair of shoes last till the next market town, or till arrival in the summer area" (Barth 1964:79). In much the same way, many European peasants will purchase a suit to be married in, wear it for ceremonial occasions the rest of their life, and finally be buried in it—perhaps half a century later.

To some degree, both thrift and rapid consumption may be seen as attempts to come to terms with the unpredictability of life. One option stresses that since the future cannot be relied upon it is wiser to spend while the opportunity presents itself; the other, that some element of security may be gained by watching every penny. Which alternative is chosen depends much less on individual tastes than on the demands and restrictions established by the culture.

Obviously, a tendency to delay consumption and accumulate capital is potentially a factor of considerable economic importance,

Immediate versus deferred gratification

but much depends on how the capital is used. It can, of course, be used to underwrite ceremonialism, and in such instances—as in the case of the Guatemalan community we mentioned—it may literally go up in the smoke of fireworks and incense. Again, capital kept for a rainy day under the cottage thatch is not much help to the owner, except psychologically. For a variety of reasons, peasants, frugal or otherwise, seldom use their limited capital resources to improve output. To understand why this is so it is necessary to examine the values and motivations underlying behavior.

PEASANT ATTITUDES

Emphasis on personal relationships

Peasants have a profound distrust of whatever is distant and impersonal. Relationships within the framework of the village community and, where possible, beyond it are characterized by an emphasis on individual agreements, on negotiations and adjustments arrived at for specific purposes. Each peasant is like the hub of a wheel from which radiate a number of spokes, each spoke a bond to another individual, each contact a potential source of aid and cooperation.

Relationships of this type are subject to a good deal of mutual accommodation. The rules that matter are the rules agreed upon, backed though they may be by traditional concepts of fair dealing. Other codes of ethics and conduct—the law as understood by judges and policemen and, by extension, all official agencies—are either discarded or little heeded.

Distrust

Through such contacts and relationships, villagers search for ways to improve their security, but security is hard to find and agreements are often entered into with the suspicion that for any one individual to gain by some arrangement another person must necessarily be the loser. Related to this belief is the assumption that each individual

Peasants paying dues to a landlord, as depicted in a fifteenth-century woodcut. The relationship of peasant and landlord involved economic and social obligations and was based on the institutionalized subordination of the peasantry. (Library of Congress, Rosenwald Collection)

is motivated by self-interest or the interests of family, caste, or similar grouping. This element of distrust is especially evident when one of the parties is rich, powerful, or influential. It is generally assumed that all individuals in controlling positions have gotten there by deceit, trickery, and the exploitation of the less powerful. In the words of a villager from northern India:

When we see a police constable or deputy's assistant in the village we know that someone is going to be threatened and will have to part with some of his money. Who are the men who own watches and live in brick houses? Not one of us here thinks that he can afford a watch, it is in the luxury class. But the minor officers all own watches. . . . Who pays for all this? We do! (Wiser and Wiser 1963:220).

A characteristic closely related to distrust, fear, and envy is the tendency of peasants to regard all that is good in the world as strictly limited in quantity. According to George M. Foster:

The concept of limited good

Peasants view their social, economic, and natural universes—their total environ-

ment—as one in which all of the desired things in life such as land, wealth, health, friendship and love, manliness and honor, respect and status, power and influence, security and safety, *exist in finite quantity* and *are always in short supply*, as far as the peasant is concerned. Not only do these and all other "good things" exist in finite and limited quantities, but in addition *there is no way directly within peasant power to increase the available quantities* (Foster 1965:296; his emphasis).

This theory of how peasants view the world they live in has not escaped criticism, and one may validly question the universality of a perceptual frame that covers such a broad range of desired things. Much depends on the degree to which individual peasant societies exercise effective control over resources and technological skills. Where such control is present, the social and physical environment is less likely to be perceived as absolutely fixed in quantity.

Nevertheless, we should recognize that what might be termed *autonomous peasantry*—peasants linked to external structures but not dominated by them—is something of a historical rarity, a product of frontier conditions or the erosion of traditional institutions (such as happened in Europe with the decay of the feudal system). In contrast, peasants living in feudal and semifeudal subordination manifest attitudes very similar to those described by Foster.

Two related elements are involved in the peasant's perception of a limited good. There is the belief, already noted, that the good things of life have been unfairly divided between peasants and the nonpeasant directing classes, or as it was expressed by an English peasant in the fourteenth century, "Their satiety was our famine; their merriment was our wretchedness; their jousts and tournaments were our torments" (Cohn 1957:214). But it is not only the rich and the powerful who pose a danger. One's neighbors, it is assumed, are constantly seeking ways to improve their position, and consequently one must make an effort to do the same. In the words of a student of peasant life in India, villagers believe that

the good things of the village are forever fixed in amount, and each person must manipulate constantly to garner a large slice for his own. . . . When one man does achieve a larger slice, he is thereby seen as a threat by those who have been superior in status to him; his rise is interpreted as diminishing them in the all-important social hierarchy. So they cannot usually rest easily until he is somehow diminished (Mandelbaum 1963:x).

Importance of family ties

When it is difficult to place one's trust in others, and yet impossible to operate alone, individuals are likely to put their greatest faith in family and kin. For its part, the peasant family may be seen as a group standing together in the face of a hostile world, although not all peasant communities place the same degree of emphasis on family solidarity. In Mexico, where this cohesive factor is very prominent, Oscar Lewis has noted that "Cooperation within the immedi-

ate family is essential, for without a family the individual stands unprotected and isolated, a prey to every form of aggression, exploitation, and humiliation known in Tepoztlán" (Lewis 1960:54). This reliance on the family, and the assumption that family interests are supreme, has been referred to as "amoral familism" (Banfield 1958).

Obligations of the wealthy

The family may offer some protection, but the successful individual still has to face the burden of success. Even in the poorest villages differences in wealth do exist, and since these differences can cause friction, mechanisms have been developed to reduce

Ostentation is not a characteristic of peasant living even in some of the prosperous rural communities of Western Europe, as is evident from this picture of an austere French peasant household. (Henri Cartier Bresson/Magnum Photos, Inc.)

envy and suspicion. At the simplest level, an individual may take care to play down his money, his business sense, or his good fortune. Wealth often leads to obligation. In Malaya,

the man who works hard in the rubber holding and rice field is praised. But he will meet hostility if his industry is allowed to interfere with his participation in ceremonial events, or with helping his neighbours on these occasions. If he starts, for example, to plant peppers rather than buying them, the neighbours will expect to be supplied free, offering a few cents when they come to ask for peppers, and expecting him to refuse payment. This he will resent, but he will do what is expected of him, give up tending the plant, and when it dies not plant any more. . . . If a man saves and buys land, when he has more than his neighbours they will begin to comment "he wants to own everything." If he has acquired wealth and refuses to spend it lavishly on occasions such as the wedding of his children, and so perhaps halting, if not reversing, his economic advance, they say, "What is the good of all that money, if you won't even let your children taste it?" (Swift 1964:151).

What is demanded of the better-off individual, and who exactly has claims on his wealth, will vary from culture to culture. In many peasant societies, however, the wealthy carry most of the burden of ceremonialism. Writing of the peasants of Zinacantan, a Maya community in southern Mexico, Frank Cancian observes that

the expenditure of great amounts of money in the cargo [ceremonial office] system, especially by the rich, reduces considerably the envy of the rich by the poor. . . . The cargo system assuages this envy very effectively by allowing, and in fact requiring, the rich to make the greatest contribution for community religious observances (Cancian 1965:135).

Economic "leveling" and the consequent reduction of stresses are not the only functions of such systems. They provide "socially controlled modes of personal display" (Nash 1958:69), that is, the wealthy person achieves recognition to the degree that his wealth is put at the service of the community. Prestige comes from redistribution.[3] The consumption of wealth in this manner may act as a restraint on the utilization of capital for nontraditional ends. The wealthy individual is thus given the opportunity to reinforce peasant values, rather than pose a danger to them.

Sense of powerlessness

While peasant communities may include some individuals of considerable means, most peasants are not only poor but tend to regard poverty as a normal and expectable feature of peasant life. Typically, it is assumed that individuals can do very little to control the forces governing their lives and that fate rather than effort dictates human success or failure. The attitude is well rendered in the complaint of an Italian peasant:

Today you think you are going to have at least enough to eat, and all of a sudden something happens. Someone steals your donkey—or God takes him away; a child becomes ill; your wheat doesn't get that last needed drop of rain; a daughter needs a dowry for her marriage. There is always something that keeps you down and in desperate circumstances (Lopreato 1967:245).

Resignation is often reinforced by appropriate religious sentiments: "The Lord giveth and the Lord taketh away"; *"In sha Allah"* [if God wills].

The nature of peasant poverty can be fully understood only when peasants are placed in the perspective of the total cultural and social system of which they form a part. Tribal societies, as we have noted, are often materially "poor" in the absolute sense.

[3]We have noted the importance of redistribution in many tribal societies. In peasant societies, however, there is seldom a central authority that redistributes surpluses.

Nevertheless, tribespeople live, or have lived until recently, in a more or less self-contained world. Politically, they lack the dependence on, and hostility toward, external authority, since all authority is internal and all political questions are resolved within the group. Economically, they do not form part of an external market system they do not control, nor are they forced to compare their limited resources with the wealth of rich governing classes.

In contrast, peasants have for centuries lived in a context where wealth and power are monopolized by local and national upper classes. Consequently, the very notion of autonomy, of control over the determinants of life, may be thoroughly alien to them. All of these circumstances are guaranteed to make the poverty of the peasant more destructive and degrading. Typically, therefore, the peasant condition is one associated with the lower orders of society and can hardly be compared with the material limitations of tribal groups.

It may be asked why, if life is generally so grim, do peasants continue to be peasants? This question is not unlike asking why the poor remain poor in any society. Often there are no other choices, and peasants, like underprivileged people everywhere, simply try to make the best of a bad thing. It is perhaps enough to note that since the middle of the nineteenth century, European peasants (and to some degree peasants in other parts of the world) have moved in large numbers to the cities whenever jobs seemed to be available. Most of the immigrants that came to the United States in the nineteenth and early twentieth centuries were peasants who migrated in search of more secure jobs and a higher standard of living. Given the chance, many peasants—in particular the most exploited and the poorest—are ready enough to "vote with their feet": they will look for a better life elsewhere. However, given the population densities throughout much of the Third World, mass immigration is no longer a reasonable solution.

PEASANTS AND THE EXTERNAL WORLD

In the preceding pages, we have examined a number of interrelated elements that distinguish peasant societies. These traits have a certain cross-cultural validity—they may be encountered in Algeria or India, in Italy or Mexico. Clearly, such a selection accentuates common features in peasant societies and plays down the differences. The characteristics of the national cultures within which peasants necessarily operate are not all of a kind, and since these national cultures encroach on and influence peasant societies, these societies take on a variety of aspects. To a much more limited degree, peasants, as components of the larger culture, exercise some influence on the nation.

The ties of trade Virtually everywhere agriculture is the mainstay of peasant communities and a high degree of economic self-sufficiency is the peasant norm. Nevertheless, in some regions peasants are avid and successful traders. Such trade may be in agricultural produce or peasant-crafted goods. It is always important to those engaged in it but will vary in the extent to which it brings the peasant in close contact with the national culture and its institutions. Thus, many Indian villages in Mexico and Guatemala are centers of craft traditions: pottery making, copper working, weaving, the manufacture of wooden utensils, and the like. These articles are sold, and occasionally exchanged, on regularly scheduled market days. While every village in the system has a designated market day, some strategic localities are especially favored as markets and attract vendors and customers from many miles around. A rather similar system is encountered in Bali, where "in one hamlet almost everyone makes tiles, in the next nearly everyone manufactures musical instruments, or works silver, or manufactures salt, or weaves, or makes pots, or produces coconut oil" (Geertz 1963:89).

Not all peasant craft traditions depend on a high degree of village specialization: a village may constitute its own microeconomic system, sustaining a variety of craft specialties. In one such village, Rani Khera in the Delhi District of India, about 50 percent of the families depend more on craft and ceremonial specialization than on farming (Lewis 1955:151). Such a high percentage of nonagricultural specialists is somewhat exceptional. Flourishing peasant craft systems and related trading networks for the distribution of craft goods are generally found in societies where the impact of factory-produced items is still minimal. With industrialization, both craftsmanship and village markets tend to decline unless the goods in question remain competitive, which is seldom the case. An exception occurs when articles of peasant workmanship are in demand by tourists.

European peasants have for centuries traded their surpluses in regional market towns that have grown up as collecting centers for agricultural produce and as localities where peasants may obtain needed supplies. In such nations, the linkages between the peasant economy and the national economy are firm and of long standing. This is not always the case in other areas—mostly one-time colonial regions—where the life styles of urban and rural populations differ markedly. Even today, many of the nonagricultural items offered for trade in native Mexican markets are bought only by other Indians, and this is true to some degree also of agricultural produce, since Spanish-speaking town dwellers do not eat the same foods as the Indians.

In most instances, however, the disposal of peasant surpluses is a matter of concern not only to peasants but also to the directing classes. While some peasant-produced goods, and even certain agricultural items, may be traded within the limited confines of peasant-operated market systems, typically a substantial portion of the crops not consumed by the agriculturalist ends up in the hands of nonpeasants and may eventually enter the national, and even international, economic system.

This transfer can occur in a variety of ways. Traditional payments and obligations, taxes, shares (as in sharecropping), and other dues and rents skim off the peasant surplus. Depending on the locality and the historical period, demands of this type may be more or less burdensome. In some instances, obligations are fulfilled by labor payments. It is this "rent"—in the form of crops, cash, or labor—that supports the nonpeasant component of pre-industrial and traditional societies. Even the peasant who controls the means of production and is free to dispose of surpluses as he sees fit must still cope with buyers and sellers who are often in a strong position to influence prices and conditions of sale.

Peasants and the wider society

Peasant communities also differ in the extent to which major cultural and religious traditions, what Redfield (1956) has termed "great traditions," influence life at the village level and link the peasant community to the wider society. In East Asia, great traditions have long functioned as mechanisms of religious and cultural integration. In Hindu villages, for example, "great festivals of Sanskritic rationale and nomenclature provide, along with domestic ceremonies, the principal occasions on which most villagers may engage in concerted symbolic activities" (Marriott 1955:193). To some degree, all world religions, all civilizations, have similar goals.

In many instances, however, the penetration of national traditions and institutions is only partial and superficial. Peasants tend to emphasize whatever is of direct concern to them, whether it be local regional identity—the *patria chica* [literally, "little nation"] of Hispanic countries, for example—or the cults of patron saints and deities. As a case in point, peasant religion is often quite distinct from the sophisticated, philosophically inclined theology of city-trained priests. In the religious area, peasants are chiefly concerned with specific problems—

In most peasant societies, the major communal festivities have a folk religious component. These Polish girls are taking part in the Corpus Christi procession. The costumes worn by the participants are now used only on such special occasions. (Sovfoto/Eastfoto)

sickness and suffering, the crops and the weather, the passage of the individual through the sequence of birth, adulthood, marriage, and death. These anxieties contrast with the formulations that commonly concern the specialized religious practitioner. The nominal membership of peasants in a given religious body may in fact obscure considerable resentment toward those in control of established religion. As Pitkin notes for the Italian village of Scrmoneta, "The more the church attempts to embrace its parishioners, the more it alienates many of them" (1959:18). All too often the church, as distinct from the faith, is viewed as just another agent of external authority. In the modern world, religious tradition is being superseded by the contemporary concepts of nationalism and political ideology, but to these the peasant is also likely to react in an ambivalent manner.

In some Western countries, it is possible to find individual peasants, peasant families, and even regional segments of the peasantry that are economically better off than

Barriers to assimilation

some members of the national middle classes. But in terms of life styles, education, and general values, the differences between peasants and middle-class people remain sharp. That this cleavage can be very real is brought out vividly in Laurence Wylie's *Village in the Vaucluse*, a study of a prosperous peasant community in southeastern France. Wylie's informants proved to be extremely suspicious of everything associated with the outside world, especially government, the legal system, and formal education. "The identity of the outside *ils* [they] varies. . . . Usually, however, it refers to the French Government in all its manifestations, for it is the Government which collects taxes, makes war, controls the wine production, and employs impersonal civil servants" (Wylie 1957:206). These are common enough peasant attitudes, but what makes them especially interesting is that Peyrane, the community studied by Wylie, is no impoverished feudal holdover. Its inhabitants own their land and drive automobiles; they sell the produce of their fields and vineyards on the national market and with the proceeds enjoy a standard of living that is well above the French average. According to these criteria, the villagers might be thought of as "middle class," but in terms of identity and attitudes to national institutions and their representatives, they can be recognized as members of peasant subculture.[4] The thresholds that separate the peasantry from the national directing classes may be more or less insurmountable. In some instances, mobility has been relatively easy and the move from peasant to townsperson, from farmer to factory worker, or even into the professions, has been accomplished without too many difficulties. For this transition to occur, though, the society as a whole must undergo significant changes.

Internal factors—traditionalism, suspicion, fear of ridicule—can act as potent brakes on those aspiring to a different class or wishing to change their manner of living. Many of the highest hurdles, however, are external rather than internal. Those in control seldom look with favor on enterprising peasants, since they pose a threat to authority and to the survival of a hierarchical system based on the dominance of the many by the few. A concept complementary to that of the limited good has certainly characterized the attitude of the ruling classes in most of those traditional societies in which peasantry is significant.

A whole complex of social relations and associated patterns of behavior reinforces the social structure of traditional societies. The details vary from country to country and from area to area, but it is possible to distinguish some features that occur with great regularity and are especially germane to our present discussion. We single out what may be termed the institutionalized subservience of the peasant—a role that the peasant is expected to play that in its most

extreme forms combines docility, lack of initiative, and accommodating stupidity. As is true of other social roles, it is backed by a body of custom, belief, and cultural perception that gives credibility to the role. Even in modern societies, myths of peasant dumbness abound and jokes in which peasants are portrayed as basically stupid and out of place in the wider society are a standard element of humor. The American reader may have little personal experience with "peasant jokes," but they rather closely parallel the so-called Polish jokes, jokes about other ethnic minorities, and humor depicting the behavior of various kinds of "hicks," "rednecks," and "hayseeds."

While the peasant certainly resents the role forced upon him and harbors his own less than flattering stereotypes of those in control, the disparity of wealth and power often forces compliance in this role playing. Moreover, certain advantages can accrue to the successful role player: the "childish" and "improvident" Indian can appeal to the paternalism of merchants and landowners; the "stupid" peasant can plead ignorance for failure to comply with demanding orders or inconvenient regulations. However, the price that the peasant pays is often a high level of frustration and a loss of self-esteem—the psychological burden of the underdog in any society.

MOVEMENTS OF PROTEST AND PEASANT REVOLTS

The passivity and traditionalism so often described as features of peasant society may lead one to assume that peasants are incapable of violent action against the agents of the established social order. But the fact is that peasants have not infrequently resorted to acts of protest and insurrection. Revolts of this type, sometimes climaxing in bloody uprisings such as the French *jacquerie* of 1358, occurred long before the development of modern political ideologies. Consequently, to view such rebellions from a

[4]A recent study by Wylie indicates that much has changed since the early 1950s and that a younger generation of peasants is much less suspicious of national institutions and much more involved in them (Wylie 1973).

Throughout history, peasants have occasionally resorted to uprisings in order to stem the erosion of their traditional rights. Like the fourteenth-century French Jacquerie, shown in the illustration, such uprisings were usually quickly suppressed for lack of effective leadership and organization. (Photo Bibliotheque National, Paris)

strictly contemporary perspective—perhaps as ancestral to modern revolutionary struggles—is somewhat misleading. Peasant revolts not only have been ideologically weak but have generally lacked the disciplined organization that gives modern revolutionary movements internal cohesion and a firm leadership structure. In a manner of speaking, peasant revolts are thus prepolitical manifestations, or to use Hobsbawm's (1959) term, "archaic" movements.

Religious fervor

In contrast to weak ideological orientation and poor organization, archaic forms of social protest are characterized by a pervasive religious influence, religious fervor substituting for planning and long-term goals. The new society that peasant rebels strive for is seldom spelled out with any clarity, for it is assumed that a just order will come to pass once the victory of the righteous has been achieved. Any shortcomings in mili-

tary organization, peasants feel, are compensated for by divine help. God, in short, is on the side of the peasants.

Preservation of the traditional social order

Perhaps it is the cruelty and anger, the explosive force of peasant passions, that seem most at variance with the apparent docility of peasant everyday life. But two characteristics of traditional peasant movements make the situation less paradoxical. First, the driving force that impels peasant movements is derived from a highly conservative idealization of society. As Chalmers Johnson has noted:

Both the historic Jacquerie (1358) and subsequent rebellions similar to it were motivated by a belief that the system had been betrayed by its elite; violence was invoked in order to purge the system of its violators and, so to speak, to set it back on the tracks (Johnson 1966:136–137).

Phrased differently, the attack is aimed less at peasant poverty and oppression than at what are regarded as abridgements of established peasant rights. Secondly, regardless of peasant conservatism, hostility toward those in control, perhaps especially such immediate agents as tax collectors, policemen, and landlords, is something of a constant in peasant society. The system as an ideal may not be questioned, but its operation is normally found wanting.

There is no simple relationship between peasant hardship and the development of archaic social movements. Perhaps this is not surprising after all, since such movements are less concerned with abolishing a condition of subordination that with rectifying abuses in the system. The principle of relative deprivation does much to explain the linkage between a peasant's conception of his or her place in society and the violent expression of discontent. It is, thus, not so much the absolute condition of a group that may lead to rural upheavals as that group's perception of what is just and fair. As a case in point, the nineteenth-century Carlist uprisings in Spain—in essence peasant revolts against the encroaching pressures of modernization and governmental centralization—occurred, not in the regions of greatest peasant hardship, but in the northern tier of provinces where a high percentage of the peasants owned their own farms and had for centuries enjoyed some degree of political autonomy and social dignity.

In keeping with much else that is typical of peasant society, hostility is directed at specifics rather than at abstractions and underlying structural conditions. Peasants may be strongly hostile to given individuals and will also resist abridgements of what they consider to be established rights. However, hostility generally does not result in uprisings or even less dramatic overt acts of resistance. Resistance is likely to remain passive—the typical peasant response—until some major dislocation in the workings of society or some radical change in peasant-elite relationships indicates that the directing classes are incapable of exercising their authority or have outrageously overstepped the bounds of this authority.

In the majority of cases it is not a single act but a combination of circumstances, some perhaps of long standing and others more recent, that incites peasants to open revolt. Thus, on the eve of the French Revolution, French peasants had already experienced a spiral of rent increases and a steady erosion of traditional rights. This dual squeeze happened to coincide with a series of natural disasters and political dislocations:

The harvest in the autumn of 1788 was disastrously short. The winter that followed was unusually harsh, while spring brought severe storms and floods. Natural disasters combined with political uncertainties and anxieties by the summer of 1789 to set off a series of panics and peasant uprisings in many parts of France (Moore 1966:75).

By 1789 a good portion of the French peasantry was ripe for revolt. We should note, however, that it took more than discontent, more than generations of drudgery and subordination, to change peasant anger into peasant action.

The bandit mystique A feature closely related to archaic peasant movements is the idealization by peasants of bandits and brigands, whether these are real life figures or folk heroes. Probably every peasant society has a store of songs and tales of the Robin Hood type, myths of bandits who "stole from the rich and gave to the poor." These stories carry a message: the wealthy and, in particular, those who obtain their wealth at the expense of others are not that powerful after all; they can be duped and ill-gotten goods can be redistributed. The same fate awaits the authority of grasping tax collectors and bullying constables—if only the right person comes along to teach them a lesson.

Until modern times the success of peasant movements has always been temporary; and bandits, while they may continue to live in ballads, seldom last very long. The utopias that peasants dream of are never realized and sooner or later order is established and, after punitive measures, the peasant relapses into apparent passivity. By themselves, neither peasant revolts nor bandit groups have the power to undermine the state. However, with the rise of modern political consciousness, peasant expectations of a better life can prove to be a potent force for change.

THE CONTEXT OF CHANGE

We have approached the peasant society as a phenomenon that must be understood in terms of the total society. It follows that change in this wider society is necessary to bring about a transformation in the peasant condition. It is true that some alterations in peasant life are possible even without substantial changes in the society at large. Thus, in many parts of the world where the position of peasants has changed little in generations, one will find that peasants purchase some consumer goods and may even improve agricultural techniques through more efficient tools and higher-yield seeds. It is not that these changes "do not matter"—in the long run they may lead to pressures for social, economic, and political change—but rather that the observer may draw the wrong conclusions. The question one should ask is whether a peasant who has discarded the traditional costume for store-bought clothes or a woman who cooks the family meal in aluminum pots rather than in beaten copper implements is necessarily living a life so very different from his or her grandparents. These could be very superficial, though visible, changes and might not even be indicative of a net improvement in peasant welfare.

How then, it may be asked, is change to occur? The question is not an easy one, for it would seem that there are various kinds of possible changes and that the past gives only some partial answers. There is no question that the life of peasants has altered drastically through the centuries in some parts of the world, and also that some peasant (and national) societies have experienced major transformations in more recent times. Our best information on change in peasant societies comes from Western Europe and some socialist countries.

The European experience

The current position of peasants in Western Europe is the result of several centuries of social, political, and economic developments that, while initially quite disruptive, succeeded in granting to peasants full citizen rights, undermined the dominance of rural aristocracies, and transformed feudal serfs into independent farmers. However, it was not only the peasant sector of society that changed but the whole society.

The industrial revolution set in motion a series of related shifts that changed Western European countries from predominantly rural and agricultural to overwhelmingly urban and industrial. Paralleling industrialization in Europe was the opening up of new overseas territories that attracted masses of former peasants. The United States, Canada, certain Latin American countries, Australia, and New Zealand became new homelands for millions of immigrants, not only from Western Europe but also from central and Eastern Europe. Western European patterns of land tenure had begun to change earlier: as the feudal system broke up, land became just another commodity to be bought and sold. Some peasants became landowners, others were displaced and moved to the cities or overseas. As a result, peasants now constitute a definite minority—seldom more than a quarter of the population, and often much less—in all Western European countries.

Some scholars have predicted an eventual, and not too distant, end of Western European peasantries. It is assumed that the remaining peasants will either become a class of rural businessmen or persist as anachronistic marginal groups in a few out-of-the-way places. In all likelihood, the peasant population of Western Europe will further decline, but it is questionable whether peasants will be reduced to an insignificant remnant or be transformed into farmers who work the land just for profit. It is true that the small family farm is not, strictly speaking, economically competitive with agribusiness, but there are other determinants, other factors, besides profit. Many peasants remain peasants even if they can make more money in other jobs. For some, at least, the life has an appeal that cannot be measured simply in terms of income. Also, with improved communications and the industrialization of the countryside, it is possible for some individuals to be both industrial workers and peasants. Such peasant-workers commute to jobs from their farms but with improved technology and mechanization still manage to work their fields. We should remember that the peasant mode of production is family-based, so that in many instances even if one member of the family holds an outside job, the farm can be kept going as a working concern.

Moonlighting in one form or another is not the only response. Many governments are interested in maintaining peasants as a viable element for social and political reasons. Price support policies and subsidies may be designed to halt further rural exodus and thus alleviate urban pressures and problems. Politically, the established peasants of Western Europe tend to function as a conservative, or at least moderating, force—a factor that governments are well aware of.

Peasants in socialist countries have had a variety of experiences. In the Soviet Union, collectivization has been the official policy since the 1920s. The individual peasant farm was abolished at the cost of much suffering: peasants who would not join collectives were killed or shipped off to Siberia. Those who survived these ruthless measures were transformed into agricultural workers employed by the state. All that remains today of the "private sector" in Soviet agriculture is small plots of land that peasants work in their spare time, the produce of which they are allowed to sell for profit.

A number of postwar socialist countries have not followed the Soviet model of forced collectivization. In Poland and Yugoslavia,

The internationalist orientation of communist Romania and the country's commitment to rapid industrialization of its traditional peasant-based economy go hand in hand with the encouragement of regional folk cultures. A group of costumed pipers perform for an outdoor folk festival in northeast Rumania beneath a banner reading: "Under the leadership of the Communist Party of Romania forward toward the implementation of multilateral development of a socialist society in our fatherland." (Zdenek Salzmann)

where only large estates were expropriated, peasant farmers were permitted to retain their land. As in Western Europe, some peasants have become peasant-workers and others have found employment in the cities.

The European evidence, and not simply that of Western Europe, indicates that peasants are politically pragmatic: they are neither inherently revolutionary nor inherently allied to a given sociopolitical system. What seems to matter is how peasants perceive their position and what kind of support is offered by the government in power—not only direct support for peasant agriculture but also social services, education, and alternative opportunities for part- or full-time employment in nonagricultural sectors of the economy.

However, the European experience, in both capitalist and socialist countries, is only partially relevant to Third World and developing societies. We have to understand that all of Europe, Eastern and Western, and North America, Japan, Australia, New Zealand, and a few other nations, constitute the fortunate countries of the world: lands that are technologically advanced, rich or relatively rich, and not pressed by the major problems of rampaging population growth and antiquated social structures.

It is difficult to generalize for the Third World, for there are Third World nations that seem to be on the threshold of modernization. Certainly, some of the oil-rich countries of the Middle East, some African states, and some Latin American countries have the resources to underwrite programs of modernization potentially of great benefit to peasants. What the future has in store only time can tell, but these too are fortunate countries. There are, however, hundreds of millions of peasants living in societies where the balance between resources and population is most unfavorable.

In only one major country—China—where a generation ago the odds seemed to be stacked against a favorable future has the lot of the average peasant noticeably

The Chinese model

improved. The Chinese case is extremely interesting, although the information available to us is fragmentary. China came out of World War II very badly destroyed, and immediately after the war the country was plunged into a civil war that ended in 1949 with the victory of the communist forces. In 1950 China was predominantly a land of peasants, many of whom were tenants and others landless laborers. Although there were some major urban centers, industrialization was little advanced and many of the industries had suffered from the war and the internal conflict that followed it. The peasantry was discontented and impoverished.

China today remains a land of rural people. Except for the period of The Great Leap Forward, massive industrialization has not been a major priority—in part, no doubt, because it would entail more capital than is available. Instead, the major economic effort has gone into a transformation of the countryside. The values of the communist leadership stress the importance of farming and the peasantry, a peasantry organized into thousands of communes. In fact, many urban people, including teachers, students, government officials, managers, and all manner of professional people, are urged and, where necessary, pressured to work in rural areas for longer or shorter periods. Peasants do not own land (although some of the commune land is put aside for subsistence purposes) and agriculture is highly regimented. This agricultural master plan has not led to upheavals and unrest in the countryside, for it would appear that most peasants view themselves not as exploited but as working for a system that is preferable to the prerevolutionary one.

One reason why the Chinese system works is that it offers peasants not only a secure livelihood (not to be mistaken for affluence) but also the feeling that those in power have the interests of the peasant very much in mind. To dismiss this concern as nothing but propaganda is invalid, for Chinese communist leaders have always shown an awareness of peasants and their needs. To be sure,

these needs are subordinated to the requirements of state policy, but within the system of political and economic coercion peasants are nevertheless perceived as a revolutionary force.

This is in sharp contrast to the European situation, where the urban working class has generally been viewed as the spearhead of revolutionary movements. Yet in underdeveloped countries—and this was the case with China—the urban working class constitutes but a small fraction of the total population. In contrast, the peasantry is large in numbers, and in many instances potentially strong in dedication. Apparently, the revolutionary leadership in China recognized this very early. In 1927 Mao Tse-tung noted that

without the poor peasants there can be no revolution. To reject them is to reject the revolution. To attack them is to attack the

Contemporary Chinese peasants working at a communal agricultural task. In the People's Republic of China not only peasants but also city dwellers are mobilized for agricultural and public works projects. (Marc Riboud/Magnum Photos, Inc.)

revolution. From beginning to end, the general direction they have given the revolution has never been wrong (Mao Tse-tung 1963:184).

These words, at the time, were something of a Marxist heresy, but history proved them to be correct.

The Chinese model of change, involving an emphasis on rural areas, limited industrialization, and the mobilization of the whole society on the basis of communist ideology and semimilitary discipline, may work only in certain contexts. China has a longer history of centralized rule than any other country in the world, which means long-established traditions of government authority and respect for this authority when it governs effectively. These conditions are not present throughout much of the Third World, where even the concept of the state may be very recent.

The type of changes in peasant society that we have been discussing imply a break with traditional society, a shift from a static to a dynamic system. Historians and political scientists, as well as economists, anthropologists, and other students of human societies, often conceptualize these changes in terms of fairly specific events and processes. They speak of the industrial revolution or the French Revolution, the end of feudalism, the rise of the nation-state and the growth of nationalism, the Reformation or the revolution in China. Clearly, these are not developments and events of the same kind, but they do have in common one very important characteristic: the society is transformed and with it the place of peasants within the society.

For the most part we have been considering, however sketchily, events that are in the past or that are already well underway. But what of societies in which the masses of the peasantry remain much as they were centuries or even thousands of years ago? As we noted earlier in this chapter, what occurs in these societies in the years to come is of very special concern to all of us, for we are considering billions of people—the majority of humankind.

The traditional solution to peasant problems, and the problems of global poverty in general, is industrialization. Development, whether on the capitalist or socialist model (China, we noted, is something of an exception), has generally meant industrialization, the establishment of modern political structures, and a shift in population ratios—fewer peasants, more townspeople. It has further meant a greater integration of peasants into the national societies.

Can this work in the future? At this point, the answer is not at all clear. The pressure of people on resources is very real. It is no longer just a question of whether the peasant masses (and the urban masses) of such countries as India and Bangladesh can produce enough to eat—regardless of how much technological aid they may be given by more developed countries—but whether the world as a whole may not have reached the limits

Industrialization and the peasants: future outlook

of growth. True, some authorities expect that with industrialization changes in life style are likely to take place that will lead to a moderation in current levels of population growth. This has been the case historically, but changes of this kind are very gradual and time is very pressing.

The point we wish to make is that in the past, and not necessarily the distant past, the opportunities for economic development made it possible to change systems as a whole (the total national society), and within this context of change, the place of peasants. It now seems highly questionable whether the Third World majority will be able to follow the patterns of the developed countries. But we must leave a more detailed consideration of this subject to a later chapter.

REFERENCES

BANFIELD, EDWARD C.
1958 *The moral basis of a backward society.* Glencoe, Ill.: The Free Press.

BARTH, FREDRIK
1964 Capital, investment and the social structure of a pastoral nomad group in South Persia. In *Capital, saving and credit in peasant societies.* Raymond Firth and B. S. Yamey, eds. Chicago: Aldine. Pp. 69–81.

CANCIAN, FRANK
1965 *Economics and prestige in a Maya community: the religious cargo system in Zinacantan.* Stanford: Stanford University Press.

COHN, NORMAN R.C.
1957 *The pursuit of the millennium.* Fairlawn, N.J.: Essential Books.

FOSTER, GEORGE M.
1965 Peasant society and the image of limited good. *American Anthropologist* 67:293–315.

GEERTZ, CLIFFORD
1963 *Peddlers and princes; social change and economic modernization in two Indonesian towns.* Chicago: The University of Chicago Press.

HOBSBAWM, ERIC. J.
1959 *Primitive rebels; studies in archaic*

forms of social movement in the 19th and 20th centuries. Manchester: Manchester University Press.

JOHNSON, CHALMERS
1966 *Revolutionary change.* Boston: Little, Brown.

LEWIS, OSCAR
1955 Peasant culture in India and Mexico: a comparative analysis. In *Village India: studies in the little community.* McKim Marriott, ed. American Anthropological Association Memoir, no. 83. Pp. 145–170.
1960 *Tepoztlán: village in Mexico.* New York: Holt, Rinehart and Winston.

LOPREATO, JOSEPH
1967 *Peasants no more.* San Francisco: Chandler.

MANDELBAUM, DAVID G.
1963 Foreword. In *Behind mud walls, 1930–1960.* William H. Wiser and Charlotte Viall Wiser. Berkeley and Los Angeles: University of California Press. Pp. v–xii.

MAO TSE-TUNG
1963 Report of an investigation into the peasant movement in Hunan. In *The political thought of Mao Tse-tung.* Stuart R. Schram, ed. New York: Frederick A. Praeger.

MARRIOTT, McKIM
1955 Little communities in an indigenous civilization. In *Village India: studies in the little community.* McKim Marriott, ed. American Anthropological Association Memoir, no. 83. Pp. 171–222.

MOORE, BARRINGTON
1966 *Social origins of dictatorship and democracy; lord and peasant in the making of the modern world.* Boston: Beacon Press.

NASH, MANNING
1958 Political relations in Guatemala. *Social and Economic Studies* 7:65–75.

PITKIN, DONALD S.
1959 The intermediate society: a study in articulation. In *Intermediate societies, social mobility, and communication.* Verne F. Ray, ed. Proceedings of the 1959 Annual Spring Meeting of the American Ethnological Society. Seattle: University of Washington. Pp. 14–19.

REDFIELD, ROBERT
1956 *Peasant society and culture: an anthropological approach to civilization.* Chicago: The University of Chicago Press.

SHANIN, THEODOR
1966 The peasantry as a political factor. *The Sociological Review* 14:5–27.

SWIFT, M. G.
1964 Capital, saving and credit in a Malay peasant economy. In *Capital, saving and credit in peasant societies.* Raymond Firth and B. S. Yamey, eds. Chicago: Aldine. Pp. 133–156.

TAX, SOL
1953 *Penny capitalism; a Guatemalan Indian economy.* Smithsonian Institution, Institute of Social Anthropology Publication no. 16. Washington, D.C.

WISER, WILLIAM H., AND CHARLOTTE VIALL WISER
1963 *Behind mud walls, 1930–1960.* Berkeley and Los Angeles: University of California Press.

WOLF, ERIC R.
1966 *Peasants.* Englewood Cliffs, N.J.: Prentice-Hall.

WYLIE, LAURENCE W.
1957 *Village in the Vaucluse.* Cambridge: Harvard University Press.
1973 The new French village, *hélas. The New York Times Magazine,* November 25. Pp. 62–63, 65, 67, 70, 72, 77, 79, 81–82.

Chapter 10
The anthropology of complex societies

In human history, societies have experienced a number of such major and irreversible transformations that it is necessary to think in terms of new social designs, new organizational structures. These transformations may have been centuries in the making, but even if the pace was slow, the results are revolutionary. In Part Two, we have been following the most critical of these shifts: the emergence of hunting and collecting as the initial form of human subsistence; the establishment of tribal systems; the development within the framework of tribal organization of the first steps towards concentration of power in a limited number of offices and individuals—chiefs, headmen, and the like.

The sequence of cultural development that we traced for the New World in an earlier chapter took us from the first hunters and collectors known from the archaeological record to the empires that flourished in Mesoamerica and Peru at the time of the initial European contacts. An essentially similar succession can be documented for a number of Old World regions such as China, the Middle East, and the Indian subcontinent. We cannot follow these developments in any degree of detail, but no chapter on complex societies would be complete without some examination of the major discontinuities that distinguish complex from tribal societies. When we speak of complex societies, we are discussing state systems or component parts of states.

The study of complex societies

The anthropological study of complex societies is a relatively recent development. Until the early 1900s, anthropologists felt little need to relate their research on far-off peoples to questions touching on their own societies. The "science of man," as it was then understood, was not considered to be directly applicable to such problems as the impact of industrialization on rural communities or even the consequences of colonialism on non-Western peoples. Questions having to do with the rise of civilization, the nature of state systems, and the more recent transformations through which complex societies have passed were left to historians and other students in the traditional humanistic disciplines.

With the new century, anthropological interests began to broaden, although slowly at first. Today one finds much less reluctance in the profession to investigate complex societies, despite the fact that there remains a residual feeling on the part of some anthropologists that such studies are peripheral to major anthropological concerns. These attitudes are linked at least in part to the notion that the proper anthropological "constituency" is the nonliterate band or tribal group. It is pointed out that many fields of knowledge address themselves to some aspect or another of complex societies, whereas anthropology is the only discipline that regularly concerns itself with questions that do not fall within this category.

It is quite true that the study of simple societies falls to anthropologists by virtue of a century-long scholarly tradition, but we would go even further and insist that there is an element of duty in this task. Anthropologists, whatever their shortcomings, have generally recognized that they alone are in a position to champion the rights—sometimes even the existence—of peoples that find themselves threatened by "civilization." The eminent French anthropologist Claude Lévi-Strauss states the situation correctly when he notes that

anthropology is not a dispassionate science like astronomy, which springs from the contemplation of things at a distance. It is the outcome of a historical process which has made the larger part of mankind subservient to the other, and during which millions of innocent human beings have had their resources plundered and their institutions and beliefs destroyed, whilst they themselves were ruthlessly killed, thrown into bondage, and contaminated by diseases they were unable to resist (Lévi-Strauss 1966:126).

There is no incompatibility, however, between a recognition of this situation and a position that gives due weight to the study of complex societies and stresses that the anthropological perspective is universal. Furthermore, the "historical process" that Lévi-Strauss makes reference to also comes into play within the realm of complex societies, as well as in the relationships between the agents of complex societies and simpler societies.

THE INTEGRATION OF COMPLEX SOCIETIES

State rule The state is first and foremost a political structure, a structure for organizing and controlling those spheres of life that belong to the public or civil domain. All societies have a political component including rules of behavior and sanctions against those who break the rules. The concept of an ordered life is thus in no sense limited to states. What distinguishes states from other political structures is that they are designed specifically to govern large numbers of people. In simple societies, political functions are exercised by institutions with more generalized tasks, such as families or lineages. By contrast the state is superimposed on such institutions and acts as the ultimate authority. This authority is used both to maintain internal order and to resist the encroachment of external enemies.

Those of us who live in complex societies tend to take for granted the inevitability of state rule. Possibly we do not approve of a particular form of government, but systems of state control are seldom questioned. As anthropologists are aware, the state is not a universal element in human social organization but is in fact a late development. However, state systems of one type or another have characterized all complex societies, past and present. Aristotle (384–322 B.C.), who initiated the study of sophisticated forms of government, believed that "the good life" was achievable only in the context of a well-ordered state, a point of view that has been echoed by philosophers and political scientists ever since.

This respect shown for state systems is

Soldiers in La Paz, Bolivia, just before dispersing a crowd protesting a rise in electricity rates. In state-level societies the most direct and obvious manifestation of power and authority takes the form of specialists granted the monopoly of officially sanctioned force. (Richard Wilkie)

generally the result of a highly idealized concept of what such systems are capable of doing. The stress is often on the advantages of a regularized and impartial system of law and the protection that the state affords individuals from those who are more powerful or more ruthless than they are. However, there is another side to the picture that has to do with the overwhelming power inherent in a high degree of centralization—an element of coercive force not encountered in more primitive political systems.

The ruling class

In all state systems, authority—real authority—is exercised by a minority, that is, an elite or governing class. A distinction can thus be made between the rulers and the ruled, although those who rule may delegate a greater or a lesser degree of authority and be influenced by the opinions of the governed. Nor should we think that this situation is restricted to despotic forms of government. The state that Aristotle had in mind when he wrote his treatise on politics was founded on rule by the people—the *dēmos*, from which comes our word *democracy*—in the *polis*, or city-state, typical of ancient Greece. The Greek *polis* was a rela-

tively small-scale political entity that, not unlike the New England town meeting, facilitated a high degree of political participation. Equally important, however, is the fact that these ministates consisted not only of citizens but also of a slave underclass that enjoyed no rights of political participation. In the words of a classical scholar:

With little exception, there was no activity, productive or unproductive, public or private, pleasant or unpleasant, which was not performed by slaves at some time and in some places in the Greek world. The major exception was, of course, political: no slave held public office or sat on the deliberative and judicial bodies (Finley 1973:22–23).

While the economies and social systems of many states do not depend on slavery or other forms of involuntary servitude, states are typically much less egalitarian than simpler forms of government and social control. In state systems, access to resources is always restricted, and much the same holds true for political power. In modern democracies, the major problem is the gulf

(left) The power of state authority is often expressed in symbolic forms. The former Ethiopian emperor, Haile Selassie, is shown presiding over a religious and state ceremony. His rank and power are indicated by symbols of office—throne, dais, canopy, and court dignitaries. (United Nations)

(right) Fifty-ninth anniversary celebration of the October Revolution, November 7, 1976. Soviet leaders review the Red Square parade from the stand of the Lenin Mausoleum. Although the forms vary, there are important national days in all state-level societies. (Tass from Sovfoto)

that exists between the ideals of genuine popular rule and the reality of inequality. If this were not the case, issues of civil rights and more equitable distribution of wealth would not loom so large in our own society.

The rise of cities Historically, the emergence of the state is linked to the rise of cities. In fact, it is no exaggeration to view urban life as one of the most distinct characteristics of complex societies. Together with the state, cities appear late in human cultural development. The first Old World cities date back some six thousand years, which from our perspective may seem the distant past but if judged against the backdrop of the hundreds of thousands of years of human existence preceding the first urban centers is relatively recent. Much like today, the cities associated with early civilizations were the seats of government or, more broadly, the locus of political power. Many also functioned as religious and economic centers. Although they contained craftsmen and workers, they were not industrial localities in the modern sense. Basically, the pattern of governmental, religious, and economic centralization remained unchanged from the establishment of the first city-states up to the industrial revolution. This structure of urban life is still discernible in many Old World cities with their government buildings and palaces, courts of law, guildhalls, and markets. With the industrial revolution, the old city centers often became surrounded by new neighborhoods and industrial areas. In fact, many of the old cities that have survived to the present day have become the inner components of a multicity. Such aggregates typically contain the old city (originally surrounded by defensive walls), the developments attributable to industrial and commercial expansion (mostly during the nineteenth century), and more recently, the suburban neighborhoods.

Although the predominant function of the city was and continues to be political, cities were also islands of literacy and sophistication surrounded by villages and hamlets peopled by illiterate peasants. It was the rich and the powerful, concentrated mainly in urban localities, who developed a life style that was distinctly urbane and cosmopolitan—a life style that required some measure of wealth and leisure. We should not forget that the Latin word *civis* ["citizen"], from

Two Bolivian peasant women and a middle-class shopper examine goods in a La Paz store. In many complex societies, urban-rural distinctions follow a variety of cleavage lines—occupation, ethnic group membership, class, dress, and so forth. (Paul Conklin)

which we derive *city*, is shared with the words *civility* and *civilization*, suggesting that sophistication and the higher intellectual achievements flourish in an urban environment.

The ancient cities were essentially economic parasites of the surrounding countryside. They survived on the surpluses produced by peasant or slave labor. For the countryfolk, therefore, the city took on a different meaning. It was their taxes and their agricultural surpluses that maintained kings and officials, prelates and courtiers in positions of privilege. It is probably for these reasons that cities have long been regarded as places of wickedness and waste. This unwholesome quality of city life—as seen from the rural perspective—finds expression in the resentments that countryfolk have long voiced against city life. We find such attitudes reflected in the Bible, as well as in a whole tradition of literature and belief that comes down to our own day. The Lord in his anger does not destroy villages and pastures but descends upon Sodom and Gomorrah with fire and brimstone. Closer to our own time, William Penn (1644–1718) expressed the opinion that "country life is to be preferred, for there we see the works of God, but in cities little else but the works of men." In our own generation, we have witnessed a movement of the young seeking to build new lives in various kinds of counterculture communities located in rural settings. No doubt, the city has always had its attractions but, just as surely, city life generates its discontents and negative reactions.

City life may be ancient, but urbanization on a massive scale is not. Modern cities came into being between 1750 and 1850. As late as 1800 Philadelphia, the largest city in the United States, had a population of less than seventy thousand. However, once started, the pace of city growth was very fast. Today some 70 percent of the citizens of the United States, and a comparable percentage of the inhabitants of other highly industrialized countries, are urban dwellers.

The growth of the cities has been achieved for the most part by drawing on the rural population. But the difference between preindustrial and industrial cities rests not only on the ratio of city to country dwellers and on the greater urban concentrations of modern times but also on the different character of ancient and modern cities.

The modern metropolis

The contemporary city is less the product of slow evolutionary change than of rapid revolutionary developments. These changes are as much qualitative as quantitative. Up to the end of the eighteenth century, city dwellers could hardly escape the realization that they lived surrounded by the countryside. In most cases, the rural world was within walking distance; one stepped through the city gate to find fields and orchards. In contrast, the modern metropolis is a world apart, and those who make a living in it can spend most of their lives in a totally human-built environment of bricks and mortar, concrete and steel.

These large urban conglomerations are the products of several forces. Foremost among these is the industrial revolution and its aftermath. The growth in the size and number of cities reflects the technological advances in agriculture and industry that at one and the same time generated a demand for labor in urban localities and made it possible to grow more food with fewer workers in the countryside. Technology also facilitated mass communications and transportation, improved public health, and in general made it possible for cities to draw on an extensive hinterland for raw materials and labor.

The most distinctive demographic phenomenon of the last 150 years has been the mass movement of rural residents into the burgeoning industrial centers. Never before has there been a comparable realignment of populations; never have so many people changed their occupations, their way of life, within such a short span of time. Urban growth on this scale is undoubtedly responsible for a variety of social ills encountered

A rural family in a Santiago, Chile, slum. The mass movement of peasants to urban areas is seldom an easy solution to rural problems. For this family, there is enough food to get by and four beds to sleep in, but work is scarce and the future unpredictable. (The Rockefeller Foundation)

in many urban settings. The very size of a large city can destroy the close links between individuals found in small social units. In fact, the most persistent accusation leveled against the city (and modern life in general) is that it has dissolved the family and neighborhood ties that existed in small communities.

Granted that urban problems are very real, one should still keep in mind that these problems have to be measured against the conditions of life experienced by those who have decided to make the move from countryside to urban center. Rural poverty is very real also, although not always so visible. The control of peasants by rural elites can be thoroughly dehumanizing. It is necessary to remember that for the rural poor, the situation may look substantially different. To be sure, urban slums are ugly, the jobs available for unskilled immigrants typically pay very low wages, and industrial cities lack fresh air and sun. But the city can also offer opportunity—a release from traditional patterns of exploitation.

COMPLEX SOCIETIES: THE SUBJECT AREA

A rather unsatisfactory approach to a definition of complex societies is to view them as a residual category—that is, all those societies that are clearly not "tribal," "primitive," or "preliterate." This definition does little more than hint at what complex societies are not. A more fruitful approach consists of listing those features that are common to complex societies. Recently Francis L. K. Hsu, an anthropologist who has studied the cultures of India, China, Japan, and the United States, has offered a definition of this type regarding what he terms "literate civilizations":

To begin, by literate I mean just what most people mean—the ability to write a spoken language. I assume that when enough people in a given society have this ability so that a literature is developed, the society can be called literate. . . . I have chosen to use the term civilization because, in contrast to society or culture, it implies an extra increment of scope and elaboration. In this regard the literate civilizations of the world are those which have been literate long enough to have accumulated a wealth of written documents of all sorts and a set of rich intellectual traditions—religious, historical, legal, scientific, and the like. . . . Ancient Egypt, Rome, and Greece, China, India, Islam, Europe, and the United States of America are examples of literate civilizations, while the societies of the Pacific islands, of most of Africa, and the American Indians are not, though many of them are rapidly developing literate traditions (Hsu 1969:1).

In many ways this is a good working definition in that it stresses the extra increment of scope of complex societies and emphasizes the role of literacy and intellectual traditions in providing a common structure to such societies. It would be wrong to assume, however, that most people in such societies necessarily enjoy a high level of education, for until quite recently, even in the West, formal education was beyond the means of most peasants and urban workers, and even today many Third World peasants remain illiterate.

Complex societies fall into two main categories: (1) traditional state systems and (2) modern industrial societies. This division is something of an oversimplification, since many one-time traditional societies are currently undergoing rapid economic change. Differences in economic structure inevitably influence other aspects of life. As we have noted, in traditional societies the mass of the population is made up of rural inhabitants, whereas in modern industrial societies there are relatively few farmers and the population is concentrated in towns and cities.

The complexity of complex societies—ancient, modern, and developing—lies in the overarching organizational and ideological structures that link a multiplicity of communities, classes, castes, ethnic groups, and religious faiths. At the same time, specific features of tribal societies may be just as elaborate as comparable features of complex societies, or even more complex: a technologically very primitive society (such as many an Australian tribe) may have a very rich mythology and an extremely intricate kinship system.

Approaches to the study of complex societies

Given that complex societies are made up of many "parts," it is understandable that a fruitful area of research is the mechanisms by which the various elements are linked. These range all the way from such formal structures as educational systems and political parties (see Figure 10-1) to what are often called *networks*—the relationships between friends, or the links between a city merchant and his peasant client, to cite only two examples. Between such person-to-person relationships and the impersonal bureaucratic structures previously noted, there fall many institutional groups and associations that join people with similar goals and interests. A neighborhood association pressing the city government for better police protection or a snowmobile club are examples of such groups.

It is also important to note that in complex societies, especially modern industrial nations, life tends to be much more compartmentalized than in simpler societies or among peasant groups. As a result, the individual normally lives many parallel "lives" that only partly overlap. For example, although a person may have good friends in his or her place of employment, it is unlikely that those who work together will live in the same urban or suburban neighborhood. Modern patterns of wage labor have also tended to strip the family and other kin aggregates of their function as units of production, although income and resources are typically pooled. These and other structural features of complex societies have dictated a type of research that is very different from that applied to simple societies and small communities in complex societies.

Correspondingly, the anthropological lit-

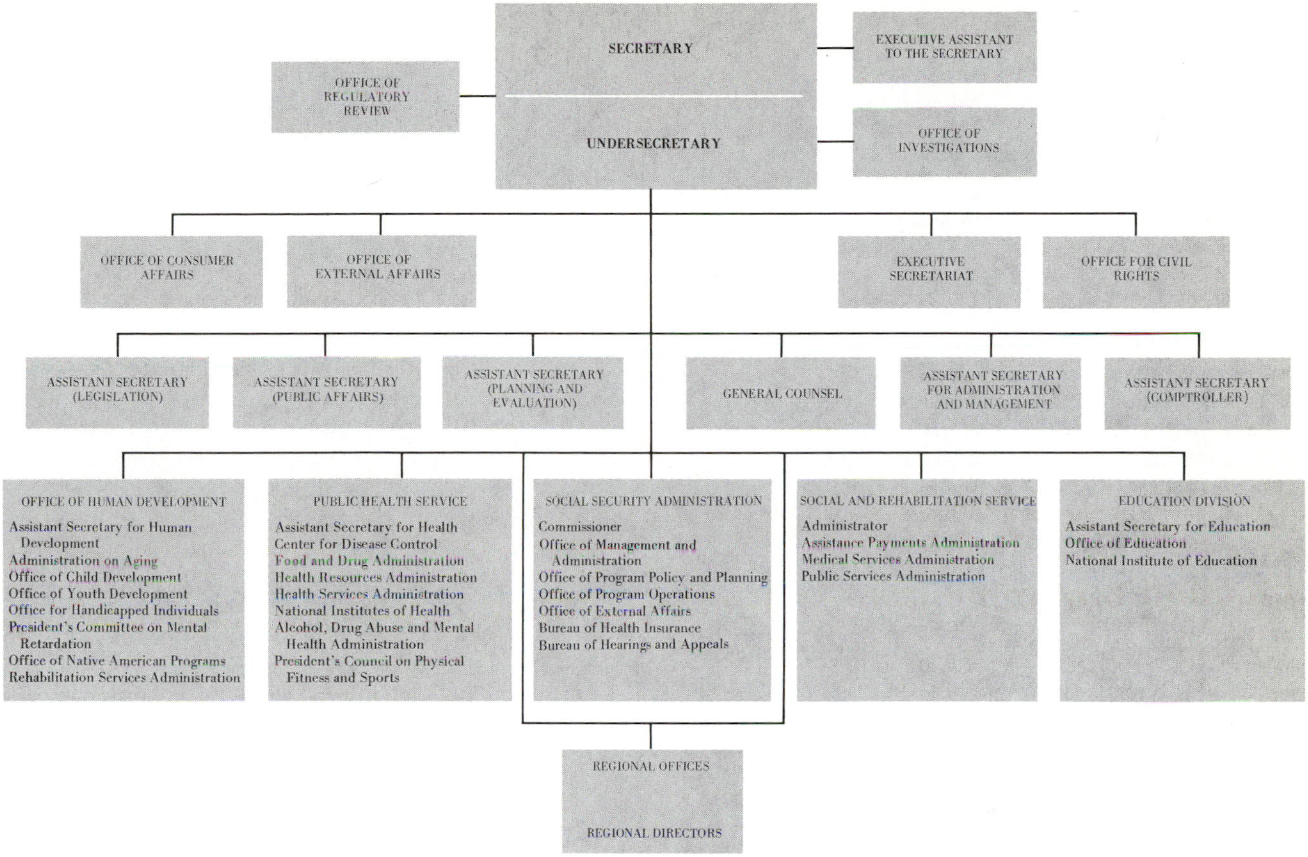
SECRETARY
UNDERSECRETARY
OFFICE OF REGULATORY REVIEW
EXECUTIVE ASSISTANT TO THE SECRETARY
OFFICE OF INVESTIGATIONS
OFFICE OF CONSUMER AFFAIRS
OFFICE OF EXTERNAL AFFAIRS
EXECUTIVE SECRETARIAT
OFFICE FOR CIVIL RIGHTS
ASSISTANT SECRETARY (LEGISLATION)
ASSISTANT SECRETARY (PUBLIC AFFAIRS)
ASSISTANT SECRETARY (PLANNING AND EVALUATION)
GENERAL COUNSEL
ASSISTANT SECRETARY FOR ADMINISTRATION AND MANAGEMENT
ASSISTANT SECRETARY (COMPTROLLER)
OFFICE OF HUMAN DEVELOPMENT
Assistant Secretary for Human Development
Administration on Aging
Office of Child Development
Office of Youth Development
Office for Handicapped Individuals
President's Committee on Mental Retardation
Office of Native American Programs
Rehabilitation Services Administration
PUBLIC HEALTH SERVICE
Assistant Secretary for Health
Center for Disease Control
Food and Drug Administration
Health Resources Administration
Health Services Administration
National Institutes of Health
Alcohol, Drug Abuse and Mental Health Administration
President's Council on Physical Fitness and Sports
SOCIAL SECURITY ADMINISTRATION
Commissioner
Office of Management and Administration
Office of Program Policy and Planning
Office of Program Operations
Office of External Affairs
Bureau of Health Insurance
Bureau of Hearings and Appeals
SOCIAL AND REHABILITATION SERVICE
Administrator
Assistance Payments Administration
Medical Services Administration
Public Services Administration
EDUCATION DIVISION
Assistant Secretary for Education
Office of Education
National Institute of Education
REGIONAL OFFICES
REGIONAL DIRECTORS

Figure 10-1 Department of Health, Education, and Welfare, 1976

The labyrinthine complexity of state agencies in complex societies is reflected in this organizational chart. (Department of Health, Education, and Welfare)

erature now includes studies of religious groups, utopian communes, leisure activities and associations designed to promote them, and even ethnographies of prison populations. A good deal of research has been devoted to examining work situations and occupational groups. Studies of this nature have brought anthropologists into factories, offices, and other highly institutionalized places of employment. A number of the traditional professions, including college teaching, have been examined in substantial detail, as have such sex-linked occupational categories as those of airline hostess, cocktail waitress, professional football player, and pimp. The authors of a recent monograph on cocktail waitressing—one of whom did her field work in a bar—note that the goal of their study "is to see experience through the eyes of these women, to describe their culture in their terms, and to see the larger context in which such behavior occurs" (Spradley and Mann 1975:12). In complex societies, there are many such occupational niches generally filled by individuals falling into sharply defined sex-role categories: women do not command fighting ships; in our society, men usually mix the drinks and women serve them.

COMPONENTS OF
COMPLEX SOCIETIES

Half a century ago, most anthropologists still worked among tribal and band-level societies in the Americas, the Pacific, Africa, and the fringes of Asia. But as the British-Polish anthropologist Bronislaw Malinowski noted, "at the very moment when it [ethnology] begins to put its workshop in order . . . the material of its study melts away with hopeless rapidity" (1922:xv). With simple societies perceived as something of a wasting asset, it is not surprising that anthropologists reached out to communities that, while still small in scale, could in no sense be viewed as primitive self-contained cultures. This shift is reflected in the anthropological literature, which began to lose much of its exoticism as the century progressed. Tribal research did not diminish, but the anthropological bookshelves began to fill with studies of Irish countrymen, European peasants, Latin American *campesinos*, and the inhabitants of New England towns. With the passage of time, it became clearer that research in complex societies was something more than a response to the dilemma of the "disappearing primitive," for it also represented a distinct maturation of the discipline.

These investigations were initially conducted in villages or other localities with small populations and reasonably clear-cut physical and social boundaries demarcating the community from the outside world. Nevertheless, the anthropologist always had to take into account the many links that integrate the community with the larger society. It was soon evident, for example, that institutions regulating the behavior of individuals in the major sectors of social life, such as marriage and the family, economics, politics, and religious and ritual activities, were only in part understandable in terms of local factors.

Once attention was turned to other components of complex society, however, it became much harder to define valid and practical units of investigation. How does one go about studying a city? What is an ethnic group? What are the characteristics of a social class? Entities of this type are not as easily marked out as a peasant village, where one can count the inhabitants and measure the village landholdings.

Also, it is obvious that as one progresses from community to nation there comes a point where it is no longer possible for the investigator to become immersed in the total culture. True, techniques of sampling and such devices as the use of questionnaires allow the anthropologist to obtain information representative of a large number of people, but while such research tools are valuable, something inevitably is lost in the process. Much of what the anthropologist looks for, including the nature of interpersonal relations and the manner in which institutions actually work, is best obtained by intensive observation of a small number of typical cases, rather than through surveys, samples, and other quantitative approaches.

Paradoxically, the very factor that appears to complicate the study of complex societies—their great internal variation—opens certain valuable avenues of research. The fact is that this mosaic of communities, groups, and relationships constitutes a social system, a system in dynamic interaction. The pieces do articulate, they are joined, despite an ever-present potential for tension and conflict.

Networks and institutional groups

Unlike simple societies, where almost everyone knows everyone else, the situation in complex societies is strikingly different. Here we may find an individual is in touch with a number of other people, some of whom know each other, and some of whom do not. It does not follow, for instance, that a person's friends know one another, for an individual makes friends throughout life, in the town where he or she grew up, in school, at work, and in all manner of different contexts. A friendship web of this kind has no defined external boundaries, but it does have a structure. What is true of friendship is true of other relationships built in the same way, and they tell us much about the structure of the sociocultural field within which a given individual operates.

The study of such networks has characterized much recent research on modern complex societies. This concept allows us to understand a wide range of phenomena, including such very practical matters as the workings of political patronage and even the manner in which university professors are hired (the old adage that it is not what you know but whom you know has an element of truth).

Research on complex societies (including modern industrial societies) has also shown that however impersonal we may imagine such societies to be, people still tend to establish and maintain a wide variety of groups. Even such traditional groups as the family (which at one time was thought to lose much of its importance with the spread of urbanization and industrialization) have proved to be remarkably resilient, although often performing somewhat different functions than in simpler societies.

British social anthropologists, in particular, have addressed themselves to the study of what are often termed *institutional groups*. Institutional groups are typically recruited on the basis of conscious membership, common aims, and recognized distinctions between members and nonmembers. The "regulars" of a tavern who meet together every Friday evening to drink beer constitute such a group; so do the members of a bowling club, a woman's liberation group, or a lodge or other fraternal organization.

Concept of the subculture

American anthropologists have for the most part devoted their attention, not so much to groups and networks, but to the study of cultural and subcultural units. This interest is no doubt a reflection of the extensive cultural variety found in the United States. As a case in point, the typical American city reveals a patchwork of what have been called "urban villages," neighborhoods with distinct ethnic, racial, and class memberships. In the nineteenth and early twentieth centuries, immigrants to the United States (themselves often of peasant or small-town backgrounds) tended to cluster in particular parts of the city. Although many of these neighborhoods are currently breaking up (upward mobility and the exodus to the suburbs are chiefly responsible), Little Italies, Chinatowns, and similar ethnic enclaves are still very much in evidence. Not only ethnic, but also racial and/or economic differences divide many towns: "The other side of the tracks" is a shorthand statement of such demarcations.

These components can be approached as subcultures within the larger society. A good deal of confusion may arise, however, unless the culture concept is handled with a degree of care. Perhaps the greatest danger is to see "cultures" everywhere. A New England town, a Puerto Rican neighborhood, an Indian reservation—all are cultural units with distinct attributes. Their residents share a common way of life and subscribe to attitudes and values that have been transmitted over time, and the Puerto Rican neighborhood or the Indian reservation carry the further element of a distinct linguistic tradition. It is harder to come to grips with abstractions such as "black culture" or "middle-class culture," which is not to say that those who are black lack a sense of common heritage and historical experience, or that it is not possible to isolate features especially distinctive of American middle-class life.

What we are saying is that some of the concepts and methods developed earlier by anthropologists are not always readily applicable when such broad categories are under consideration. Is a typist, because she holds a white-collar job, a member of the middle class even though her income is far below that of most blue-collar workers? To what degree do the ghetto youth and the black Harvard graduate share a common black perspective? We pose these questions

The kaleidoscopic nature of modern complex society, with its many components and widely differing life styles, is sampled here in contemporary United States scenes.

A Hare Krishna group chanting on the sidewalk of an American city. A great variety of religious and ideological beliefs and associations characterize the culture of most major Western urban centers. (Charles Gatewood/Magnum Photos, Inc.)

to indicate that the answers are not easy.

In recent years, American anthropologists have tended to resist the temptation of making broad cultural generalizations applicable to complex societies, including their own.[1] In part, we believe, this is a

recognition of a fact that is becoming more generally understood, and not only by anthropologists. Modern national structures may integrate diversity, but seldom have they succeeded in eliminating it. For the American scene, it is evident that the melt-

_____

[1]This observation refers primarily to generalizations having to do with such hard-to-formalize concepts as "national culture," American or otherwise. Few anthropologists would question that the citizens of modern nation-states share some elements of a cultural code, but these cultures are quantitatively and qualitatively different from the cultures that anthropologists have traditionally studied—those of bands, tribes, or chiefdoms. The cement that binds complex societies is much more likely to be the superimposed higher-order structures that we spoke of early in this chapter rather

than internalized cultural patterns applicable to all component groups within the physical boundaries of the state. We should, however, recognize the great power of the state to mobilize opinion, as well as the force of nationalism and similar ideologies, even if in multiethnic states nationalism may well work counter to the goals of state integration. In contrast to the difficulty of using cultural models, a more profitable approach is the analysis of organizational structures operating at the national level. There are many state models, but all states have to meet some common requirements.

(above left) Little League baseball players in an American community. The organizational complexity of modern societies finds expression in highly specialized groups, a phenomenon that is observable in recreation as well as in other activities. (Jan Lukas/Editorial Photocolor Archives)

(below left) Senior citizens play bingo at a club in Westport, Connecticut. Elderly people in many industrialized societies constitute a marginated social component. (Ginger Chih from Peter Arnold)

(below right) Lesbian participants at a gay liberation demonstration in New York City. (Leonard Freed/Magnum Photos, Inc.)

ing pot thesis is a gross simplification: that we are becoming more and more alike is questionable—although there is no denying the cultural influence of mass media, rapid communications, and similar forces.

The fact that complex societies are generally made up of many constituent parts does not mean that all of these components exist as separate cultural or subcultural units. Most anthropologists would probably agree that to speak of a culture peculiar to the young ("youth culture"), the aged, women, homosexuals ("gay culture"), or drinkers ("bar culture") is unwarranted. These are not self-perpetuating entities. In due course the young grow up (and ultimately even grow old); female societies exist only in

Amazonian myths; homosexuality generally affects only one sphere of life; and there also comes a time when the bars close. However, all these and many other variations of life style and social situation do warrant study, as do all major differences occurring within national societies.

TO SUM UP It would seem that anthropologists are especially well equipped to examine many of the constituent units of complex societies. The touchstone of anthropological research has been the ability not only to describe and analyze social and cultural variety but to do so in a manner that is intimate—through information derived from a personal knowledge of informants and their life situation. This is feasible in complex societies, as it is in simpler ones.

THE ANTHROPOLOGY OF POVERTY: AN EXAMPLE IN METHOD AND THEORY

The study of complex societies is a field where many disciplines meet, anthropology and the other social sciences, history, and what are often referred to as the "policy sciences"—public administration, government, and others. Clearly, since this is not an area in which anthropologists work alone, they must be aware of the contributions being made by others working from very different perspectives. While we cannot do justice to all of the research on complex societies, we will examine in some depth one area of ongoing concern in order to bring into focus the kinds of questions that anthropologists ask and some of the methods they apply to answer them.

Those who conduct research on complex societies are keenly conscious of the fact that their work is of more than theoretical importance, for such research is likely to influence the lives of informants in very direct ways. In part, this is so because the subject matter is large-scale literate societies—societies where information is dissemi-

nated rapidly and, in particular, societies with sophisticated administrations and bureaucracies. And in part, it is so because many of the topics that the anthropologist deals with are highly sensitive and open to a variety of interpretations. As a case in point, one of our colleagues who carried out field work in a Gypsy urban ghetto in Mediterranean Europe will not release his research findings for another five years in order to protect his unnamed informants from possible government harassment.

In this section we will be examining the anthropology of poverty. The subject is fitting because poverty in modern societies is in itself something of an apparent contradiction that raises the kind of difficult questions that anthropologists are increasingly confronted with. There is, of course, nothing very novel about poverty, for in some ways it is like an ancient scourge that survives in the midst of plenty. We will be focusing on poverty in America and other developed nations—precisely those lands where its presence is most incongruous.

Poverty: a historical background

For many centuries, poverty was taken for granted; the poor were always there in the background. This attitude slowly changed (in some minds at least) with the breakup of traditional society that accompanied the industrial revolution. We may hypothesize a number of reasons for a growing interest in the condition of poverty, which is something different from the pity, and perhaps guilt, that an individual of comfortable means may feel when confronted with the sight of poverty. First of all, the impact of urban poverty on the senses is far greater than that of rural poverty. Impoverished peasants are tucked away in remote hamlets, but the urban poor are concentrated in great masses and are readily visible. Although the greater visibility of urban poverty may have contributed to a growing concern with the problem, the major motivation behind a new consciousness that one finds in the writings of nineteenth-century social commentators seems to be moral and intellectual.

The directing classes at the time of the industrial revolution believed strongly in rational and moral solutions to social problems: it was a matter of finding the correct answers and applying them. We may take as typical of this approach the solutions proposed by Robert Owen (1771–1858), an English millowner and social reformer:

Train any population rationally, and they will be rational. Furnish honest and useful employments to those so trained, and such employments they will greatly prefer to dishonest or injurious occupations (Owen 1969:129).

This "rational" approach to social ills is interesting in that while the problems are recognized as real, the solution hinges basically on the will of the poor to make the "correct" choices—to work hard and happily at appropriate occupations. One should note that there is no questioning of the economic and social system, no hypothesis that the fault may perhaps lie in a structure of society that makes inevitable great inequalities between millowners and millhands.

From the middle of the nineteenth century to its close there appeared numerous books, reports, and surveys on poverty, including some works like Henry Mayhew's *London Labour and the London Poor* (1851), that were based on a very close observation of the daily life of poor people. Mayhew commented that the reading public "had less knowledge [of the poor] than of the most distant tribes of the earth" (1851:iii), and he probably was not greatly exaggerating. However, by the end of the century, poverty had become a topic not only for social reformers but also for countless novelists and playwrights.

There can be little doubt that with the coming of the twentieth century interest in the poor declined. To the extent that poverty remained a feature of modern societies, it was looked upon as peripheral, a residual social condition that was surely bound to disappear with the march of progress.

Increasingly, it was the problems and lifeways of the middle classes that attracted the attention of both academic and popular writers. In the years following World War II, American authors were especially prolific in recording various aspects of middle-class life—the problems of making it in the corporate world, the loneliness of living in a social system characterized by great social and physical mobility, and, more generally, the emergence of a way of life founded on substantial affluence and patterns of high consumption. In fact, the title of a bestseller of the period, John Kenneth Galbraith's *The Affluent Society* (1958), was adopted as the fashionable label for American society. Apparently, the United States was moving in the direction of a one-class society—the middle class.

Oscar Lewis: culture of poverty

This myth was not to survive the 1960s, for it soon became apparent that poverty was far from eradicated. In fact, the sixties were years of awakening to the magnitude of the problem, and anthropologists can claim some credit for recognizing the situation. Among them, it was Oscar Lewis who pioneered the study of poverty. Writing in 1967, he noted that "it is the anthropologists, traditionally the spokesmen for primitive people in the remote corners of the world, who are increasingly turning their energies to the great peasant and urban masses" (Lewis 1967:480). Today the concept of a culture of poverty has gained some currency, in large measure due to Lewis's books.

Lewis tackled the question of poverty in a manner that reflects his professional background. Trained to study small communities, he selected a unit of investigation—the family—that was manageable in size and permitted direct contact and in-depth involvement with informants. Lewis collected interviews and life histories, many of them on tape, and then wove this information into a series of linked biographies of family members. The results were a cumulative, many-sided, panoramic view of each individual, of the family as a whole, and of life of poverty in general. While Lewis's interpretations of the nature and cause of poverty have not gone unchallenged, his writings offer a remarkably vivid insight on life as the poor live it. The family histories Lewis had gathered came from Mexico, Puerto Rico, and the Puerto Rican neighborhoods of New York.[2] In his view, the poor share not only their poverty, but also a distinct life style, or "culture of poverty," that cuts across national boundaries and even urban-rural differences. What is this culture of the poor? According to Lewis:

> The culture of poverty is both an adaptation and a reaction of the poor to their marginal position in a class-stratified, highly individuated, capitalistic society. It represents an effort to cope with feelings of hopelessness and despair which develop from the realization of the improbability of achieving success in terms of the values and goals of the larger society (Lewis 1966:xliv).

Lewis believed that the culture of poverty was a way of life that tended to perpetuate itself from generation to generation, since children born into poverty would learn only

[2]Toward the end of his life, Lewis was engaged in the reformulation of the culture of poverty concept, in large measure as the result of a visit to Cuba following the Castro revolution. He observed that although the physical appearance of a Havana slum that he knew from previous research had changed very little and the people were still desperately poor, "I found much less of the feelings of despair, apathy, and hopelessness that are so diagnostic of urban slums in the culture of poverty" (1968:14). The other side of the coin is the extreme militarization of Cuban youth. Armed and uniformed youths at the service of the state may not feel hopeless and apathetic, but one should certainly not expect much tolerance from them. Before he was able to do much more than question his original thesis, Lewis died. Readers interested in examining the culture of poverty controversy in some detail are urged to consult Charles A. Valentine's *Culture and Poverty* (1968), and the reviews of fourteen anthropologists and other social scientists of Lewis's major monographs *(The Children of Sánchez, Pedro Martínez, and La Vida)* in *Current Anthropology* (Lewis 1967).

the ways of living under the restrictions, values, and attitudes peculiar to such a condition. His claim, then, was that the culture of poverty—like all cultures—is to some degree a mechanism of adaptation and, as such, provides strategies without which the poor could scarcely carry on. If nothing else, the poor develop ways of coping with pressures from the larger society—officials, the police, the rich, and all institutions and individuals with power and influence.

However, Lewis's descriptions of the culture of poverty tend to stress negative, or dysfunctional, elements: low levels of literacy and education, a lack of participation in the institutions of the larger society, a brittle family structure, a great deal of fighting and conflict, an absence of childhood (a luxury the poor cannot afford), and even a high incidence of, and tolerance for, mental disturbance of all sorts. A rather grim list of traits, to say the least.

A central theme in Lewis's writings is that, regardless of the setting in which it occurs, poverty breeds a distinct style of life, as well as personality characteristics to match. However, some students of poverty feel that the evidence on which this assumption is made—especially the material in the family biographies—hardly constitutes a representative sample of the poor. For instance, one of Lewis's best-known books, *La Vida* (1966), is a study of a prostitute and her family—a way of life and an occupation hardly typical of the poor as a whole. Some of the evidence from other societies is also not in keeping with the theory of a universal culture of poverty. The English poor share many of the same values that one finds in the English middle class, and poverty in Japanese urban slums is apparently not associated with the patterns of sexual behavior and chaotic homelife described by Lewis. Recent research on Irish slum communities in nineteenth-century London indicates that Irish immigrants of that time—living in conditions of crushing poverty—established strong and effective community structures such as clubs and mutual aid societies. While none of these findings disprove that poverty is a great burden carried by the poor, they do raise important questions as to whether the poor respond to poverty in the same way in all societies.

In his writings Lewis periodically recognized that the culture of poverty should more properly be considered a *subculture*, the difference between the two being that while cultures enjoy a substantial degree of autonomy, subcultures are units within a larger cultural whole. This may seem a rather technical question, but it can influence the way in which an investigator approaches the subject to be examined. Regardless of his disclaimers, Lewis is essentially looking at poverty as a culture, or something close to it. The result is that cultural attributes that the poor share with other parts of society are played down and there is little formal examination of the relationships that may exist between ethnicity, social class, and poverty. Since the poor are often minority people (especially in the United States), explanations that fail to take into account the role played by racism in keeping a population subordinate and marginal are likely to be inadequate. The same holds true for social class and economic opportunities. It is not sufficient to attribute poverty to poverty: after all, a major reason why the poor are poor is simply that they seldom can find work that pays decent wages.

Perhaps the major criticism that can be made of Lewis's culture of poverty thesis is that it tends to reinforce popular stereotypes of the poor as dangerous and wicked or, at the very least, as incapable of helping themselves. Given these criticisms, must we conclude that Lewis's contributions to the anthropology of poverty are so skewed as to be of little value? Not at all. Quite apart from his role in focusing attention on a vital problem, the conditions that he records are real enough. His underlying theme is sound: poverty profoundly shapes the lives of people. What is more, Lewis's books are unusu-

Lewis's views examined

ally compelling because the poor are invited to speak for themselves. They do so eloquently, in passages of stark reality and utter grimness.

But the poor are not simply poor. They are the poor of particular societies. This is an important consideration, for it does not automatically follow that poverty and its attendant evils will be perceived by those in positions of power in the same way in all societies.

Societies perceive and tackle poverty in different ways, and the poor themselves do not see their situation in an identical manner. A little before Oscar Lewis began his investigations into the culture of poverty, the Mexican writer Octavio Paz published an interpretive study of modern Mexico, *El laberinto de la soledad* (1950), later issued in English translation as *The Labyrinth of Solitude* (1961). His descriptions of the Mexican poor are in many ways similar to those offered by Lewis. However, the poor as depicted by Paz are both poor and Mexican, and one of the points that he stresses is that this national quality, which includes a strong sense of national identity, is not submerged, but striking.[3]

Poverty: context and cause

What can we learn from the preceding discussion on the anthropology of poverty? Perhaps what comes through most clearly is that poverty means much more than living with very reduced economic resources: the condition of poverty is closely linked to and determined by a particular context. It is not the same to be poor in a large American city as it is to be a member of a low caste in India, which, for all the difficulties its members experience in making a living, will nevertheless have formal caste organizations designed to provide leadership. Historically, there have also been other highly impoverished segments of the population that seem

[3]It is important to note that Paz's subjects are for the most part the socially and economically marginal people of the cities. The Indian population, in many ways "the poorest of the poor," do not identify themselves as Mexican.

The slum district of an Italian city. Extreme poverty and dismal housing conditions continue to be a part of contemporary urban life. While the situation may be more acute in developing societies, it is in no sense limited to such countries and regions. (David Seymour/Magnum Photos, Inc.)

quite distant from the culture of poverty. The Jews of Eastern Europe, for instance, were persecuted and impoverished, but they lived in close-knit clusters rich in communal organization. Furthermore, Eastern European Jewish culture placed great stress on literacy and traditional education.

The poor in modern Western societies are poor of a particular type. Basically, they constitute a culturally and economically disinherited underclass; in this respect they are a different "culture," but it is less a culture of their own choosing than a situation they have been assigned to by a class-structured society. The fact that they are "internal outsiders" to middle-class society makes their lifeways alien to more affluent people. As is usual in such cases, the problems of poverty tend to be perceived by those who form part of the dominant society as due to the poor themselves.

A close reading of Lewis's monographs makes it quite evident that his informants behave and react not only as individuals faced by the crises of poverty, but as people with an awareness of their place in the wider society. In his last study, *A Death in the Sánchez Family*, a bereaved woman—whose aunt has died of overwork and general neglect—offers the following evaluation of what it means to be poor in Mexico:

Life holds no pleasure for me anymore. I expect nothing here in my *tierra*, my own land. Why do we insist on carrying on that absurd masquerade, the gigantic lie that hides the real truth here in this "republic" of Mexico? "We, the Mexicans," amid "this prospering beauty with its politically strong, economically solid foundation. . . ." Oh, yes, we are making progress. We are advancing in technology and science; the steel structures are rising over the corpses. Everyone knows that the peasants and the poor in the cities are being killed by starvation or other means . . . that they are being weakened. An entire generation is disappearing in an unforgivable fashion. I can no longer bear to see how they are humiliated and how they die (Lewis 1969:36).

Current research on poverty raises fundamental questions of policy and of cause. The result has been a good deal of polemics within the social sciences as to what brings poverty about and how best to deal with it. The anthropological contribution has been at a variety of levels. The poor—in their role as informants—have been given a place in the debate. This is not an insignificant consideration, for the human voice has a power to move that cannot be matched by data banks and statistical projections. While there may not be a generally accepted anthropological theory pertinent to questions of poverty, a focus on the subject has helped to clarify the condition of the poor in different sociocultural systems. Perhaps most important of all is the growing recognition that poverty does not explain poverty, that in matters of causation it is necessary to look beyond the bounds of poverty and consider structural factors that take into account the total sociocultural system of which the poor form only one component. This is not an easy task, for it moves the debate from the restricted context of the ghetto to the arena of the wider society.

COMPLEX SOCIETIES:
PROBLEMS OF
EXPLANATION AND
OF SYNTHESIS

Perhaps more than any other students of living cultures, researchers in complex societies are aware of the gap that exists between what they know (from both their own research and that of colleagues) and what there is to be known. This is a paradoxical situation because in many instances anthropologists are studying either their own culture, or a segment of it, or other cultures that share substantial organizational features with it. Knowledge is hampered by a variety of factors, including the scope of the enterprise and the difficulty of establishing some level of objectivity on matters that strike so close to home.

We have mentioned the question of scope earlier in this chapter, but some concrete examples may add focus to the discussion. Some of the anthropology that has been done on simple societies is the result of highly intensive research conducted within a circumscribed frame of reference. Beginning with the 1920s, a number of students of simple societies devoted their total attention to the study of one, or perhaps two, simple societies. This does not mean that they were unaware of the research carried out by their colleagues among other groups, but rather that their own field work was designed to learn everything of relevance about a society made up of a relatively few individuals inhabiting a fixed locality. The results have been some of the most detailed and insightful anthropological writings on record—many of them now "classic" ethnographies. The best of these anthropologists became "marginal natives" in the sense that they felt as much at home in their adopted cultures as in their own, sometimes even more so. However, as outsiders trained in the study of culture, they generally retained the capacity to look at their host cultures with some degree of objectivity, a perspective made easier by cultural distance.

As we have noted, the kind of total immersion possible in the study of small-scale societies is simply not feasible when the subject is complex societies as cultural wholes. Leaving aside for the moment the problems of anthropologists working in their own society, we can consider the difficulties posed by an attempt to come to grips with a complex society such as India. Anthropologists can study an Indian village in the same way they can study a tribe, but a tribe can be conceptualized as a cultural whole, and a peasant village is clearly a small part of a much larger social and cultural universe. But even if it were possible to conduct fifty village studies per year in India—an assumption that presumes levels of funding and personnel that are not realistic at the moment—it would be many decades before a reasonable survey of the thousands of Indian communities could be carried out. It may be argued, and with some validity, that all that is required is a representative sample of Indian village life; but even if this is so, India is a country not only of villages but also of towns and cities, of regions and states. All these units articulate, or fit together, through the agencies of common cultural reference points and institutions that operate at all levels from the village community to the nation-state.

Anthropologists studying complex societies must therefore search for ways to generalize from local-level studies to studies of nations and civilizations. Such generalizing is being done in various ways, and a number of avenues seem especially promising. The study of national institutions and those who direct them is without question a key research area for an understanding of complex societies. Work along these lines is not new, for in their different fashions both sociologists and historians have tackled similar questions. Historians, however, work primarily with documentary evidence of the past, while sociologists emphasize extensive and quantitative rather than intensive research. There are definite problems associated with coming into close contact with elites, not the least being the fact that those in positions of authority have the wealth and power to isolate themselves from the world at large. In all complex societies there is a group of individuals in positions of control, whether we are dealing with the business world, politics, or other national or international institutions. It would be most valuable to have a solid body of information on such entities as the upper bureaucracy of the Vatican or the directors of the top 500 American corporations.

A good deal of the integrative research on complex societies has been conducted not so much with informants as with secondary cultural material such as movies, fiction, and plays. The problems here are in part questions of representation—how accurate or how typical is such material as a picture of the culture in question?—and in part the difficulty of checking out information and following up leads. Perhaps a novel offers a vivid picture of corporate or political life, but there may be many important topics that the novelist (or playwright or screenwriter) does not deal with. It is a situation not unlike that of trying to write an ethnography of a simple society on the basis of myths and other forms of oral literature.

A related approach is the examination of the structural characteristics of a complex society. Complex organizational systems have certain imperatives that lead to cultural and social consequences. Thus, Marvin Harris, an anthropologist who has shown special concern with the ideology and structure of complex societies, notes that

some of the specific forms of inequity and alienation characteristic of industrial society are clearly products of the specific tools and techniques made available by advances in the natural and behavioral sciences (Harris 1974:264).

It is not simply that anthropologists must find ways of synthesizing a potentially vast body of cultural and social information. Studies of simple societies are generally well-rounded, but this is hardly the case with the work that has been conducted to date on complex societies. There are many little-known areas, many gaps, and not only concerning the elites. We need to know much more about middle-class life, and even studies of working-class communities are few and far between. Then, too, there are sectors of the population in modern complex societies that have received very little attention—the young, the old, and women. A generation ago, S. F. Nadel, a British social anthropologist who had worked mainly in Africa, noted that

we [anthropologists] treat a familiar culture as though it were a strange one. . . . We consciously choose this approach so that we may view the culture from a new angle and throw into relief features obscured by other forms of study (Nadel 1951:7).

This is good advice, especially for anthropologists working in their own societies. The perspective that Nadel speaks of is certainly necessary. Equally important are conceptual frames—models for understanding the ways in which complex societies work—that help the researcher in the task of synthesizing an extensive body of information.

REFERENCES

FINLEY, M. I.
1973 Was Greek civilization based on slave labour? In *The slave economies*, vol. I: *Historical and theoretical perspectives*. Eugene D. Genovese, ed. New York: Wiley. Pp. 19–45.

GALBRAITH, JOHN KENNETH
1958 *The affluent society*. Boston: Houghton Mifflin.

HARRIS, MARVIN
1974 *Cows, pigs, wars and witches: the riddles of culture*. New York: Random House.

HSU, FRANCIS L. K.
1969 *The study of literate civilizations*. New York: Holt, Rinehart and Winston.

LÉVI-STRAUSS, CLAUDE
1966 Anthropology: its achievements and future. *Current Anthropology* 7:124–127.

LEWIS, OSCAR
1961 *The children of Sánchez; autobiography of a Mexican family*. New York: Randon House.

1964 *Pedro Martínez; a Mexican peasant and his family*. New York: Random House.

1966 *La vida; a Puerto Rican family in the culture of poverty—San Juan and New York*. New York: Random House.

1967 The children of Sánchez, Pedro Martínez, *and* La Vida. *Current Anthropology* 8:480–500.

1968 *A study of slum culture: backgrounds for* La Vida. New York: Random House.

1969 *A death in the Sánchez family*. New York: Random House.

MALINOWSKI, BRONISLAW
1922 *Argonauts of the western Pacific*. London: G. Routledge.

MAYHEW, HENRY
1851 *London labour and the London poor*, vol. 1. London: C. Griffin.

NADEL, S. F.
1951 *The foundations of social anthropology*. Glencoe, Ill.: The Free Press.

OWEN, ROBERT
1969 *A new view of society* [first published 1813–1814] and *Report to the county of Lanark* [first published 1821]. V. A. C. Gatrell, ed. Baltimore: Penguin Books.

PAZ, OCTAVIO
1950 *El laberinto de la soledad*. México, D.F.: Cuadernos Americanos.

1961 *The labyrinth of solitude; life and thought in Mexico*. Lysander Kemp, trans. New York: Grove Press.

SPRADLEY, JAMES P., AND BRENDA J. MANN
1975 *The cocktail waitress: woman's work in a man's world*. New York: Wiley.

VALENTINE, CHARLES A.
1968 *Culture and poverty; critique and counter-proposals*. Chicago: The University of Chicago Press.

CONCLUSIONS

The broad categories of social and cultural organization examined in Part Two should be viewed as convenient guidelines that allow us to discuss sociocultural systems of roughly the same order and identify the major structural differences among the several levels of social integration. As is usually the case, it is possible to cast a finer net: the societies that we consider "tribal" could further be divided into those with well-developed institutions of chieftainship and those in which power and influence are more diffused. Similarly, the concept of "complex societies" covers a great deal of ground—from the ancient civilizations of the Old and the New Worlds to modern postindustrial states. Although we have arranged our cultural units according to levels, our scheme does not imply that cultures must follow certain predetermined steps from simple to complex.

It is our hope that this survey will serve as a foundation for the study of institutions in Part Three, in which we shift our focus from whole cultures to an emphasis on the major structural principles that charaterize all human societies.

PART THREE

HUMAN SOCIETIES: FRAMEWORKS AND INSTITUTIONS

INTRODUCTION

A general survey of cultural anthropology usually includes an extended discussion of what are often termed social institutions. These institutions, whether kinship structures or forms of political or economic organization, vary greatly from culture to culture but satisfy in each the necessary organizational requirements for a relatively ordered and predictable existence. Thus, all sociocultural systems must find ways to deal with the problems of material survival and the allocation of resources, all regulate marriage and designate a recognized place to the newborn, all define the relationship between their members and the supernatural, and all depend on some regulatory mechanisms for the management of conflict.

Because the potential list of cultural universals or near universals that characterize human societies is long, it is unwise to attempt to isolate a fixed series of key institutions. In the six chapters that follow, we are primarily concerned with broad institutional frames. We begin with individuals and the manner in which they are incorporated into their societies—for although all human beings are born members of a given culture, the meaning of their membership must be learned through both formal and informal instruction. Next we consider the basic bonds of interpersonal relationships, family and kinship in particular. A discussion of sources of authority and the management of conflict is followed by the presentation of the anthropological perspective on economic matters. Finally, two chapters explore the dimensions of art and the role of ideology and religion.

We recognize that the chapter categories used cover related areas of discussion and that it would be equally possible to propose a somewhat different arrangement. For example, although we have chosen to discuss politics and law in conjunction and have included the phenomenon of war within this same chapter, other authors might well have elected to treat these subjects separately.

That there are different ways in which to organize a discussion of sociocultural institutions highlights a very important point: although institutional forms can be treated as if they were distinct and clearly demarcated one from another, such an ap-

proach does not adequately account for and describe the real world. Particularly in simpler societies there is a great deal of what might be termed institutional overlap—kinship influences political forms, political forms reflect differences in power distribution that then are likely to manifest themselves in the realm of economics, and so on. Even art does not exist in a vacuum, for it not only helps to define the values of a culture but also can tell us much about artists and patrons, bringing us once more into contact with economics and politics. In short, while individual approaches to the examination of sociocultural institutions may widely differ, one must not lose sight of the fact that for all humans the many aspects of social and cultural life form a closely integrated whole.

Chapter 11

The individual in society:
freedom and constraints

Let us begin with several generally accepted propositions:

1 Except for identical twins, each human individual is genetically unlike any other individual by virtue of the unique make-up inherited from one's parents.

2 Each individual, too, is unlike any other in terms of the totality of experiences (social or otherwise) that he or she has been subject to since birth, identical twins included.

3 Some individuals are clearly very much like others who have been exposed to the same cultural conventions. For example, members of some societies customarily eat solid food with a knife and fork, others use chopsticks, and still others scoop up food with their fingers or a thin piece of unleavened cornmeal bread; some societies consider the idea of eating pork profoundly repugnant, an attitude reserved by others

for beef, fish, bats, or grubs. (The common belief of members of any society that whereas the patterns of behavior they themselves share are natural and sensible, those of outsiders are deviant if not loathsome is known as *ethnocentrism*.)

4 Every human being is exactly like every other human being in the sense of belonging to one and the same biological genus and species—*Homo sapiens.*

Our concern in this chapter will be with the psychological and sociocultural variables subsumed under the second and third propositions. As an area of anthropological inquiry this subject is commonly referred to as "psychological anthropology" or "culture and personality" (alternatively, also, "personality in culture"). In American anthropology, examination of the individual's role in society goes back to the founder of the discipline, Franz Boas. In a restatement of a view he had put forth on numerous earlier occasions, he stressed the importance of the

problem of the relation of the individual to society, a problem that has to be considered whenever we study the dynamic conditions of change. The activities of the individual are determined to a great extent by his social environment, but in turn his own activities influence the society in which he lives (Boas 1920:316).

The general questions to be addressed in this chapter may be stated as follows: To what extent is the concept of the individual, or of personality, distinct from that of society, and—assuming that there is some dependence between the two—what is the nature of their connection? The second half of the chapter title, "freedom and constraints," points up the dialectic between the individual and society. The concept of individuality carries within it the meaning of separateness and independence, whereas society implies a voluntary subordination to common interests and goals. The dynamic and complex nature of this relationship is reflected in the variety of views anthropologists have taken on the subject. One major approach, prevailing until the 1950s, was to consider the concepts of personality and culture as almost analogous. "Cultures," wrote Ruth Benedict, "are individual psychology thrown large upon the screen, given gigantic proportions and a long time span" (Benedict 1932:24). Today, most anthropologists consider such a view as altogether too simplistic. In the words of Anthony F. C. Wallace:

no population, within a stated cultural boundary, can be *assumed* to be uniform with respect to any variable or pattern. . . . There is no finite list of categories that define personality, nor any specified number or proportion of individuals who must share behavior for it to be called "culture" (Wallace 1961:90–91, 1970:128–129; author's italics).

To borrow Wallace's phrasing, the emphasis on the "replication of uniformity," deriving from the earlier descriptions of small nonliterate groups, needs to give way to stressing the "organization of diversity" if anthropologists are to gain an understanding of modern complex societies and the fast-paced changes that are overtaking them.

THE PROCESS OF GROWING
UP AND THE FORMATION
OF PERSONALITY

Studies of the relationship between culture and personality invariably proceed from the recognition that the perceptions, behavioral tendencies, and internalized values that characterize an individual are determined to a significant degree by those members of the society from whom they have been learned. In a psychocultural sense, a human infant at birth begins with nothing but the most generalized capacity for culture acquisition. Completely free of any learned behavior, it comes into the world endowed with an assortment of biological mechanisms. Some of these serve as important linkages between human nature and culture during the passage from babyhood to adulthood.

The biological equipment of a newborn infant may be assigned to four categories. One group includes species-specific traits, such as the innate tendencies of human babies toward random motor behavior patterns—kicking, "babbling," and others—and the comparatively slow rate of maturation resulting in a prolonged dependence on the adult members of the species, commonly the infant's mother. In a separate category is the wide range of *reflexes*, that is, automatic responses to a variety of stimuli, with which an infant is equipped at birth. Some of these reflexes may eventually come under the individual's control, as in various yoga exercises or in fire-walking (in which pain reflexes appear to be effectively inhibited). A

third class of innate biological characteristics is made up of *drives*, or urges, directed toward satisfying hunger and thirst and relieving other conditions of biophysical deprivation or discomfort. Drives may and do become subject to considerable cultural manipulation, as in forestalling fatigue by a variety of preparations, prolonged fasting, deliberate abstention from sexual activity, and the like. Finally, a child possesses at birth specific potentials inherited genetically from the parents. The extent to which capacities of this sort, ranging from the potential for body size to that for intellectual development, are actually realized depends largely on the nature of the physical and sociocultural environment in which an individual is maturing. We have touched on this subject earlier in our discussion of human biology and human culture.

In the study of personality formation, the principal concern of anthropologists is with

The learning of adult roles and skills is facilitated by situations that permit children to imitate or participate in adult activities. This little Chinese girl cannot contribute much force to the task of grinding, but she is learning cooperation and a valuable peasant skill. (Marc Riboud/ Magnum Photos, Inc.)

The process of socialization

enculturation—the process by which an individual learns the traditional content of a culture and assimilates the bulk of its values and practices. More generally, one may speak of *socialization* if emphasis is placed on the social adjustments required of individuals in all human societies. In common usage, however, the two terms—socialization and enculturation—are often used interchangeably.

While it is evident that fundamental cultural components and patterns are learned during childhood, the manner in which this learning takes place has been subject to various theories and interpretations. A *behaviorist approach* views the newborn child's consciousness as essentially a clean slate. Accordingly, the acquisition of behavior takes place as the individual copes, by trial and error, with basic physical and psychological needs and strives to eliminate or reduce the consequences of a variety of undesirable stimuli. The cumulative effect of positive and negative reinforcements (rewards and punishments) associated with certain responses and of the individual's imitative behavior leads to social conformity. While the behaviorist approach to socialization has been utilized by some anthropologists, the stimulus-response (S-R) formula seems more applicable to the learning of simple commands and the avoidance of negative situations than to the acquisition of a complex cultural code with all its variations and contingencies.

The *Freudian theory* of personality development also suffers from certain disadvantages as an interpretative tool. According to Freudian doctrine, character guidelines are laid down by the age of three. But what a child has learned by this very early age is chiefly the regulation of bodily functions and needs. "Diaper anthropology," as it is sometimes called, may account for some fundamental personality orientations but hardly for the complex and demanding process of culture learning. The Freudian theory of personality further stresses the child's identification with parents and their surrogates through the incorporation of forms and symbols related to these early experiences. Not only is insufficient weight given to experiences gained at a later age, but it would seem that a good deal of Freudian theory is based on a culturally limited range of information: events and activities that may have validity for Western middle-class subcultures may not be in the least characteristic of early childhood in other societies.

Very few anthropologists today accept either behaviorist or Freudian approaches in their starkest form, although both have contributed to our understanding of cultural learning during early childhood. One emerging alternative theory, which takes its cue from recent research concerning language learning, assumes the possibility of discovering some innate predisposition on the part of humans for such cognitive skills as may be necessary for the acquisition of any of the many different cultural ways. If

supporting evidence for such a theory can be developed, the gap between the biological and psychocultural nature of human beings will be significantly narrowed.

An individual typically learns the forms and usages of a culture by being born into a particular society and growing up in it. In a very real sense, human beings become truly "human" by acquiring the cultural orientation of a given group, even though this initial learning does not preclude their adopting the ways of another group at some later time. Since cultural learning, or enculturation, is intimately linked to physical and psychological maturation, it is much harder to repeat the process once an individual has approached or reached adulthood. Consequently, secondary acculturation is not only difficult but seldom completely achieved. Being equally at home in two distinct cultures is rare, as most people, including anthropologists, know from observation or experience.

The degree to which culture may determine behavior is exemplified in this photograph of a Balinese child learning how to enter the state of trance. Trance in Bali is a condition that even children achieve, given the appropriate cultural and psychological stimuli. (Henri Cartier Bresson/ Magnum Photos, Inc.)

In all societies of a certain complexity, informal socialization of children is complemented by the formal institution of the school. The shade of a tree on the outskirts of a village provides such a setting in the mountains of northwestern Pakistan. (Courtesy of Embassy of Pakistan, Washington)

Although speaking of culture in the abstract may be appropriate in certain contexts, one must not forget that any particular culture is "borne" by flesh-and-blood individuals and transmitted by them to other individuals during the long period of cultural apprenticeship that all human beings undergo. By a very early age a child learns to adjust to the society he or she is brought up in and to identify with its members. Initially, they are the people who nurture and protect the child. In band-level groups, which are invariably small in size and relatively homogeneous in their overall socioeconomic structure, institutionalized norms of behavior tend to be limited to a single set, differentiated largely according to sex, age, and kinship. At the other end of the scale, large societies with a high degree of structural complexity are also characterized by normative pluralism along ethnic, economic, religious, and other lines.

The most salient aspect of the socializing process is the acquisition of competence in choosing suitable behavior for dealing with

Social identity and related concepts

other members of a society. Whether particular behavior is judged culturally appropriate or not depends on the social relationship of those who interact with one another. Every individual, whatever the society, possesses at any given time a number of different social identities. Some of these are fixed, outside the individual's control; they are referred to as ascribed. The most common ascribed identities are those based on a person's sex, place among the kin, and age, as in the case of a grandfather. Other social identities are a matter of the individual's choice (girl scout, husband, Republican) or are achieved by the application of personal effort (pianist, schoolteacher, nurse).

The expected behavior associated with a particular social identity—the rights and obligations that accompany it—varies according to the nature of the social relationship between those who interact. It makes a difference whether a teacher is dealing with students, fellow teachers, or school administrators. By the same token, an individual's social identity as teacher will not determine behavior in other settings—for example, at home, with respect to wife or husband or neighbors. In these instances the teacher will assume the social identity of spouse or neighbor. Any matching pair of social identities constitute an identity relationship—for example, teacher-student, teacher-principal, husband-wife, and the like. The reciprocal relations or rights and duties that characterize each such identity relationship define a corresponding status relationship.

In real-life situations, social identities rarely occur singly. For example, in addition to being seen as a teacher, an instructor is usually also identified by students as an elderly male, a young female, and so on. The cluster of identities perceived as relevant in a given interaction constitute the individual's *social persona*. As social personae, individuals typically confine their behavior patterns within appropriate bounds as they enact the role that society assigns to a particular status relationship.

Ward H. Goodenough, on whom we have drawn for the preceding discussion (Goodenough 1951 and 1965), is the source of our example. At the time of Goodenough's field research (1947 and 1948) among the native inhabitants of the atoll of Truk in the Carolines, the dimensions on which status distinctions were made included that of sexual distance. A maturing boy had to learn the exact extent of his duties (or rights), depending on the particular identity relationship. Thus a Trukese man and his "sister"—a term that in Trukese extends to any female blood relative of a male's own generation—if both were past puberty, were forbidden to sleep in the same house or to be seen alone in each other's company, nor was the man allowed to see the woman's exposed breasts, have intercourse with her, or speak to her suggestively in public. At the opposite end of the scale, a set of behaviors characterized the relationship between any man and woman who could call each other by the term corresponding to "my spouse." The women included in this identity relationship were the man's wife's more attractive sisters, some of whom were likely to be married. All of the patterns of behavior forbidden between a man and his "sister" were approved of in the latter identity relationship. Between these two extremes, the measure of avoidance duties (intimacy privileges) varied quite specifically according to the particular categories of the man's kin.

Psychocultural adjustment under crisis

Although in its major aspects socialization is accomplished by about the time individuals, as judged by their societies, are able to assume adult roles, some psychological adjustment continues to take place for the remainder of a person's life. In some societies, ours for example, the adaptive mode in later life may even be marked by a partial "loss" of culture as aged citizens find themselves increasingly marginal with respect to the mainstream activities of the community. This situation contrasts with that in other societies in which age brings high prestige and, often, great power. The subculture of the old in American society exists not so much because older citizens desire to isolate themselves but rather because the culture does not provide a meaningful place for them.

More dramatic, if less common, are the cases in which harsh changes in an individual's physical or psychological environment suddenly place extraordinary stress on internalized behavior patterns and fundamental values. In acute crisis situations, survival may depend on the reaffirmation of one's cultural roots—the resolve that core values must be maintained despite all the pressures that are brought to bear on the individual or the group. Instances of this type of response have been documented in studies based on the lives of prisoners of war and inmates of concentration camps: even under great deprivation morale may remain very high so long as faith is maintained in the validity of the individual's culture and its institutions. The erosion of cultural identity and personal self-image that is sometimes referred to as brainwashing is, fundamentally, a form of deculturation that can beset some individuals unable to resist inordinate physical and psychological stress. However, if a group of prisoners manage to cling to their basic cultural values, they are unlikely to be broken or indoctrinated by their captors.

There are other crisis situations, in particular unforeseen disasters, that may similarly require a temporary restructuring of cultural values. Survival at sea in an open boat — and people have survived for weeks in flimsy lifeboats under extreme weather conditions and with minimal rations — may demand that all individuals be treated equally without respect to rank or position, exceptions being made only for children and the sick. The victims of an air crash in the high Andes who had to cope with freezing temperatures and virtually no food survived by living on the human flesh of their dead companions. The survivors found it possible to rationalize this most extreme breach of the Western cultural code by considering it a form of sacrament: their dead friends would not have wanted them to die when the means of physical survival were at hand (Read 1974).

To believe that the process of cultural learning is rigid would be a mistake. Individuals in any group are not all alike in their abilities and emotional makeup, nor is the training that they receive identical from household to household or from one community to the next. There are always those who manage to cross over the boundaries of what is claimed to be culturally acceptable or desirable, and not infrequently they do so without serious consequences for themselves. This tolerance for individual variability appears to grow directly with the size and complexity of a society. In those societies that advocate and sanction a maximum of personal freedom, the patterns of individual behavior may reach kaleidoscopic proportions. The long-range viability of a society may in fact depend ultimately on how the inherent conflict between individual freedom and societal constraints is resolved.

NATIONAL CHARACTER STUDIES

The temptation to characterize by a few fitting epithets human populations ranging in size from single communities to entire continents is far from limited to early travelers' accounts of the foreign lands that they had visited. In the last revision of his famous *Systema naturae* (the tenth edition published in 1758–1759), the Swedish botanist Carolus Linnaeus (1707–1778) described the native inhabitants of America as "obstinate, merry, free," those of Asia as "severe, haughty, avaricious," Africans as "crafty, indolent, negligent," and Europeans — not surprisingly — as "gentle, acute, inventive" (Slotkin 1965:177–178). Immanuel Kant (1724–1804), the great German philosopher, characterized in his *Anthropologie* (1798) his own countrymen as industrious, tidy, pedantic, obsessed with rank and title, ready to endure difficulties, but tending to submit to rule and accept despotism rather than altering or resisting the established order of authority. Shorthand characterizations of national groups abound to the present day: Americans are said to be "casual" or "extroverted," Italians "excitable," the French "romantic," Spaniards "proud," the English "reserved," and so on.

Although American anthropologists have avoided facile generalizations of this kind, they have engaged in psychologically oriented studies of whole cultures or nations. The assumption underlying their writings was that the common background and institutions that members of any given sociocultural system share from the time of their birth would be reflected in their basic personality structure. These studies were foreshadowed most prominently in Ruth Benedict's *Patterns of Culture* (1934), considered to be one of the most widely influential works in anthropology published in the United States during the first half of the century.

For Ruth Benedict (1887–1948), first a student and later a close associate of Franz Boas at Columbia University, cultures were "coherent organizations of behaviour" and "distinctive . . . configurations that pattern existence and condition the thoughts and emotions of the individuals who participate in [them]" (Benedict 1934:56,55). In her pioneering book, she endeavored to show in some detail that differences between cultures are explainable in much the same way as are personality differences between individual persons.

Benedict's exposition rested on the cultures of the Plains and the Pueblo Indians (especially the Zuñi), and was supplemented by a discussion of the Northwest Coast Indians (the Kwakiutl) and the Dobuans, a Melanesian island people. Drawing on Friedrich Nietzsche's (1844–1900) studies of Greek tragedy, she based her central concept of cultural integration on the contrast between the Dionysian and the Apollonian ethos. The former, named after the Greek god of wine, is characterized by outgoing, self-reliant behavior, given to frequent expressions of individualism and boundless activity. In native North America, such a configuration of character traits was best exemplified by the Indians of the Great Plains. By contrast, the Pueblo Indians, in Benedict's view, displayed an Apollonian ethos—with emphasis on restraint, orderliness, and the subordination of individuality to group interests. The Kwakiutl, in their relentless pursuit of personal prestige and self-glorification bordering on megalomania, were representative of another variety of the Dionysian character. And the Dobuans, ridden with jealousy, suspicion, and given to treacherous and hostile relations among themselves, exhibited a configuration of character traits strongly resembling paranoia.

The position Benedict took, that a single

The configurationist approach

Psychocultural studies of complex societies

psychocultural denominator can serve as the key to understanding a culture as a whole, provided in its time a useful antidote to fragmented and piecemeal cultural descriptions. Today, however, such an approach is seen as overly personal and oversimplified. While there is a great deal of truth in Benedict's generalizations, her selective use of data resulted in conclusions that were overstated.

During World War II and the years immediately following, a considerable number of anthropologists—mostly American—turned their attention to the study of modern complex societies. Their primary purpose was to discover the basic motivations of those allied and enemy nations with which the United States would inevitably be involved in settling the problems of the postwar era. Between 1942 and the mid-1950s, numerous articles and at least a dozen books offered psychocultural analyses of such diverse groups as the Japanese, Germans, Russians, Chinese, and Americans (Benedict 1946; Lowie 1945; Gorer and Rickman 1949; Hsu 1948 and 1953; Gorer 1948; Mead 1942; and others).

While the various writers differed in their approaches, most of the national character studies tended to stress the importance of childhood experiences. Their guiding assumptions may be summarized briefly as follows: (1) Each society goes about caring for and rearing its children in a distinctive, culturally patterned manner. (2) Early experiences, which members of any society may be expected to share, profoundly influence the formation of personality. (3) To the extent to which personality configurations are alike within any given society, one may speak of a particular national character. National character was thus seen as a collective cultural expression of a basic personality type or structure largely determined by common childhood experiences.

Given the nature of the wartime assignments, much of the research on national character had to be carried out at a distance, that is, without the benefit of the customary field work. The limitations imposed by such stay-at-home anthropology helped to stimulate a search for techniques of data gathering and interpretation that were at least in part independent of direct field experience. Since the unit of investigation was the nation-state or one of its major ethnic components, the level of abstraction called for was of a kind not easily derived from community studies. Among the sources of data were films, novels, popular literature, and interviews conducted with resident aliens and refugees.

National character studies: some limitations

Perhaps the best known among these national character studies is Benedict's analysis of the patterns of Japanese culture, *The Chrysanthemum and the Sword* (1946), based on wartime research under the auspices of the Office of War Information. This book—and others that grew out of wartime exigencies—has not escaped deserved criticism. The prime target for critics of the book was its assumption that a limited number of psychological themes can aptly characterize the large population of a complex society. In particular, critics have been skeptical of the kind of psychocultural analysis in which strict toilet training accounts for certain salient features of the Japanese ethos (Benedict 1946) or in which the national character of the Russian people derives in large part from the supposed constraints and frustrations experienced by the swaddled infant—the so-called swaddling hypothesis (Gorer and Rickman 1949). But more fundamental criticisms were raised than those of the somewhat naive uses of psychological models. Margaret Mead, herself a diligent contributor to national character studies, sounded a note of caution when she wrote:

We have studied national character not as the best setting within which to trace the correspondences between political forms and individual character formation—for very possibly a much smaller unit, such as the New England town or the Swiss can-

ton, would be a far better locus for pure research—but because, in today's world, nation-states are of paramount political significance, and a great many activities of individuals and groups . . . are conducted in terms of national values (Mead 1953:660).

More recently, and with greater emphasis, Clifford Geertz has raised much the same question with respect to a culture with which he has become thoroughly familiar through his intensive field research:

Java—which has been civilized longer than England . . . is not easily characterized under a single label or easily pictured in terms of a dominant theme. It is particularly true that in describing the religion of such a complex civilization as the Javanese any simple unitary view is certain to be inadequate (Geertz 1960:7).

From another perspective, the major and inherent flaw of these studies has come from their unabashed association with national political goals. During the 1940s, very few anthropologists questioned the appropriateness of their endeavors—the nation's war effort called for their talents and they were eager to be of help. In the preface of the 1965 edition of *And Keep Your Powder Dry*, Mead evokes the spirit of the war years:

This book was written in 1942 as a social scientist's contribution to winning the war and establishing a just and lasting peace. It was frankly and completely partisan. In writing it, I attempted to use all my experience . . . to present the culture and character of my own people in a way they would find meaningful and useful in meeting the harsh realities of war (Mead 1965:xi).

These limitations notwithstanding, national character studies did much to generate an interest in complex societies. There is no doubt that since World War II anthropology has staked a claim to an area of research that earlier had been considered only peripheral. Thus, psychocultural profiles of whole nations have served their purpose, even if at the same time they were helping anthropologists lose their innocence. Today, studies of national culture and character are in eclipse; clearly, modern technological societies are much too complex to be reducible to the few bold strokes of a single cultural portrait.

SEX ROLES IN CROSS-CULTURAL PERSPECTIVE

That males and females are anatomically differentiated goes without saying. From a biological point of view, the existence of two distinct sexes is the chief source of genetic variation and the mainspring of the evolutionary process, and until quite recently, the division of the sexes was accepted by nearly everyone as a firmly established cultural universal. It seemed a commonplace not only to hold that males and females were biologically different, but to view this difference as

inherently linked to variations in behavior patterns and personality traits, distinct roles, and by extension the differential status and position of women in human society.

On closer examination, the relationship of sex to socially expected behavior patterns is far less straightforward than the conventional wisdom of many centuries would have us believe. While it is true that the socialization of children varies according to sex in every culture we know of, it is equally true that each society follows its own guidelines as to what extent behavioral distinctions between the sexes are to be encouraged and maintained. In other words, the evidence seems clear enough that biology is much less a determinant of individual behavior and a person's place in society than are any of the ways particular groups have organized themselves for social and cultural purposes. And because socialization is above all a process of learning, the personalities of men and women come to be differentiated by their accepting the social roles that conform to traditional cultural standards.

Inasmuch as the great majority of the

The Japanese tea ceremony, a form of traditional etiquette, has been practiced for centuries as a means of developing an aesthetic sense and improving one's spiritual qualities. For this reason it is regarded as an indispensable part of the training of young Japanese girls. (Consulate General of Japan, N.Y.)

members of our society are the products of the Western cultural tradition, one finds it "natural" to associate particular behavior patterns with biological or anatomical differences. For that matter, anthropologists have at times been guilty of the same bias when examining other sociocultural systems. The underlying reasons for such an approach are not hard to find. It is common knowledge, for example, that at maturity men are on the average heavier by about a fifth than women, and stronger physically. Women, on the other hand, have a greater life expectancy—at least in modern industrial societies.[1] Women, not men, bear and are equipped to nurse children: clearly, the early mother-child bond is biologically ordered. But while all these differences are real, the fact remains that they are far from sufficient to account for the striking discrepancies in the roles that men and women play in most of the world's societies. The anthropologist is led to conclude that members of the two sexes behave differently and have different expectations, not because anatomy is destiny (as Freud claimed), but for the simple reason that they are trained to do so.

If biology is not the prime source of the sociocultural differentiation between the sexes, the most likely explanation is that early socialization must be the major factor. For an example of emphasis on sexually determined roles, we may draw on an aspect of child rearing in the Mexican town of Zamora, a community studied by one of the authors:

The selective process starts early. Thus, a little upper-class boy of some two years of

age who hits his mother in a fit of pique, or makes a nuisance of himself by upsetting the routine of female kitchen help, is not rebuked or punished. Rather, his mother, with a show of pride at the antics of the little imp, will turn to those present and smilingly say, "Isn't he growing quickly into a little man?" Guests are expected to agree and add suitable comments about how husky he is becoming. In much the same manner, a little girl who shows the feminine virtues of decorum, shyness, and obedience will be rewarded by the approval of her elders (Pi-Sunyer 1973:52).

What happens in Zamora is not a great deal different from what takes place in thousands of communities in the United States. There are deep-seated traditional concepts of how a "real" boy ought to behave and how a "real" girl should act. Such a boy need not be too concerned about his personal appearance; he is allowed to climb trees and encouraged to hit balls; he should engage in "boy games" like cowboys and Indians; and, until he is a teenager, he is expected to disdain the company of girls. For their part, girls should find particular satisfaction in dressing dolls, making cookies, and the like. Girls who have insisted on playing baseball on local Little League teams have brought turmoil to otherwise tranquil communities; boys who decide to enroll in a ballet class are typically looked at askance by their peers.

Sex roles: a four-way comparison

Once we are willing to grant that sex roles are essentially a matter of cultural training, the question arises whether or not all human societies follow similar patterns of sex-role differentiation. The answer would seem to be in the negative. In her classic book *Sex and Temperament* (1935), Margaret Mead 1901–) compared Western behavior patterns for males and females with those found in three New Guinea tribes. While all three societies recognized male and female roles, these were not necessarily structured along the traditional aggressive-passive dimension characteristic of American and

Sex roles and early socialization

---

[1]There are many other such differences: for example, the incidence of color blindness, hemophilia, harelip, gastric ulcer, heart disease, and stuttering is much greater among males than females. Some of these defects are known to be transmitted by the pair of sex chromosomes, X and Y. Women, on the other hand, are more susceptible than men to diabetes and cancer of reproductive organs.

Margaret Mead holding a Manus, New Guinea, baby during her revisit to the island in the 1950s. Dr. Mead pioneered cross-cultural socialization studies. An important element of her research is that she has retained contact over the generations with her informants. (Wide World Photos)

other Western-derived cultures. Among the Tchambuli people, Mead found the females dominant and aggressive, the males dependent, passive, and given to a variety of artistic pursuits. The Mundugumor defined both sexes as aggressive and life itself as a constant struggle among individuals and between the sexes. For the "gentle Arapesh," passive and compassionate behavior was the norm for both sexes. Schematically, the four different arrangements may be represented as follows:

	BEHAVIORAL NORMS	
	AGGRESSIVENESS DOMINANCE INDEPENDENCE	GENTLENESS SUBMISSIVENESS DEPENDENCE
Western societies	Males	Females
Tchambuli	Females	Males
Mundugumor	Males and females	
Arapesh		Males and females

Mead's study has received some valid criticisms. For example, peace among the Arapesh who, according to her, "see all life as an adventure in growing things. . . . [and who] retire happily in middle age after years well spent in bringing up children" (Mead 1935:14) must in part be attributed to the fact that since early in this century warfare has been kept down by the colonial administrations (Fortune 1939:27). Furthermore, the not infrequent cases that fall outside the norm for a given society are regarded by Mead as instances of "deviant" behavior hardly the most satisfactory explanation (Thurnwald 1936). But even if these criticisms are well taken, they do not invalidate Mead's general thesis that "many, if not all, of the personality traits which we have called masculine or feminine are as lightly linked to sex as are the clothing, the manners, and the form of head-dress that a society at a given period assigns to either sex" (Mead 1935:280).

Ethnocentrism and its parallels, sexism and racism, have had a long history in a great many human societies. At the root of all three forms of unwarranted prejudice has been an emphasis on differences among humans, whether cultural or biological. Anthropology itself has passed through a phase of cultural relativism, during which differences were stressed. Recent tendencies in the profession have been in the opposite direction: the recognition is rapidly growing among anthropologists that all humans are in fact remarkably similar, the superficial variations among them notwithstanding. One of the most important contributions that anthropologists can make is to discredit the many simplistic stereotypes according to which humans are categorized. The myth of biologically based sex roles has especially long roots and many powerful perpetuators.

THE CONCEPT OF DEVIANCE

According to a widespread belief, *deviance* ("social maladjustment" or even "mental disorder") is largely limited to complex societies, occurring in small-scale nonliterate groups only rarely. There is little evidence to support such a claim. Every society includes some individuals whose behavior is so evidently outside the range of what the majority regard as "normal" as to be considered deviant. Such deviant individuals are defined by different societies according to different criteria, and the culture-specific solutions as to what should be done about them vary correspondingly. But even though the conditions that lead to excessive frustration or intolerable stress for certain individuals differ from one group to the next, mental anguish and the disorders that may result are the common lot of human beings everywhere.

Among the Navajo, a general state of depression, described by them as "feeling sick all over," calls for a curing ceremony performed by a specialist known as the singer. In a comparable state of mind, a devout member of a peasant community may look for relief in the confessional, and a well-heeled but distressed urbanite is likely to seek help from a psychiatrist. While the three cases of anxiety may appear similar in their manifestations, their sociocultural contexts differ considerably, as do also the culture-specific methods of treating them.

Social maladjustments and mental disorders fall into two broad categories according to the sources to which they are attributed, although most societies fail to make this distinction. Some disorders are clearly organic, traceable to a variety of physiological causes—for example, a mechanical injury to the brain. The social behavior of individuals so afflicted might be expected to depart from what is considered normal, whatever the culture. A large number of other deviances are lumped together under the labels "functional," or "psychosocial," referring to results of sociocultural stress that some individuals have become incapable of tolerating. The nature of deviant behaviors in this latter category is very complex and bears careful scrutiny.

One may consider, for example, the class of mental disorders known as schizophrenia. If, as evidence suggests, its incidence is partially correlated with genetic predisposition, then the specific sociocultural conditions that help bring it about in certain individuals are only partly responsible. The connection between a particular mental disorder and the sociocultural environment in which it is found may be even more remote, as in the mental disorientation accompanying sleeping sickness, practically indistinguishable in its symptoms from schizophrenia. The incidence of this serious disease, transmitted in much of tropical Africa by the bite of the tsetse fly, is associated with a cluster of factors potentially subject to cultural interference—use of pesticides, control of the nature of land cover, and so on.

The relativity of deviance

Anthropologists recognize not only that the definition of deviance will vary from one culture to the next but that within one and the same group it may change over time.

While enjoying the social approval of the groups to whom they minister, shamans have frequently struck observers from outside the culture, anthropologists included, as individuals who exhibit a degree of psychic disorder. In some societies, deviant behavior may be induced for a limited period of time in order to produce a culturally appropriate experience. Such are the various religious rituals that require individuals to attain a state of trance, a visionary experience, or possession. Once the purpose has been served, individuals are expected to revert to their usual behavior.

Attitudes toward homosexuality and accepted sex role definition provide a particularly good case for the relativity of the concept of deviance. Viewed cross-culturally, they are far from uniform. For example, in the Plains Indian tribes there were *berdaches*—men whose aversion toward having to fulfill the expected aggressive male role was such that they assumed women's dress and habits and not infrequently lived with men. They were fully accepted by their fellow tribespeople, as they would not have been had they retained the external badges of maleness without the concomitant behavioral characteristics expected of males.

In our society, sexual preference for members of one's own sex has long been viewed as a sin, a mental sickness, or as undesirable deviance at best. Beginning in the 1960s, attitudes toward homosexuals rapidly began to change. Though still considering themselves disadvantaged under existing laws, homosexuals have scored some significant gains. For example, in 1973 the board of trustees of the American Psychiatric Association, altering a position held for nearly a century, declared that inasmuch as homosexuality neither regularly caused emotional distress nor was regularly associated with generalized impairment of social functioning, it no longer met the criteria for describing a psychiatric disorder.[2] A subject

[2] For a report, see *The New York Times*, December 16, 1973, pp. 1, 25.

A Crow Indian berdache *of the last century. Among the Plains Indians, men had the option of choosing the life role of a female, thus becoming "women" with respect to cultural behavior and societal expectations. (Photo Courtesy of Museum of the American Indian, Heye Foundation)*

that only a short generation ago would have been unthinkable to see portrayed in films other than by the most subtle allusions is today freely discussed on our television screens even at hours normally given over to family viewing. With gay bars springing up by the hundreds and marriage ceremonies for homosexuals far from rare, behavior that middle-aged Americans may view as deviant is accepted by a growing number of young people as an alternate form of satisfying sexual needs, entitled to full legal recognition.

It is not uncommon for the criteria of deviance to be applied selectively within a society. There is little question, for example, that traditional medical psychology in Western societies has based its standards of behavioral normalcy to a large extent on middle-class conduct. Prostitution and alcoholism are considered deviant forms of social behavior in direct proportion to their public visibility—that is, more so among the poor than among the rich. In other respects, the boundaries between mental health and illness are considerably blurred in modern complex societies, as indicated by the frequent appeals made in cases in which the defendant's mental responsibility for a crime can be a question. Many who dismiss all those who serve time in prison as social misfits (deviants) are just as ready to ignore the fact that the skills of an adroit legal counsel or one's socioeconomic status may well be more decisive than the intrinsic merits of a particular case.

TO SUM UP One taking an anthropological perspective should beware of superficial generalizations concerning behavioral aberrancy. The evidence seems clear that in a large measure the concept of deviance is culturally patterned. It follows that Western psychiatry cannot be applied as a valid tool in differing sociocultural contexts. While the fear of witchcraft may be "real" in many societies, as it was in medieval Europe, a contemporary American suffering from its symptoms would rightly be

regarded as displaying grossly unjustified anxieties. One may therefore define deviance as any persisting form of behavior that a particular group at any given time proscribes among its members as unacceptable or even harmful to its common interests. This is far from implying that, cross-culturally, "anything goes." For example, while the concepts that our culture refers to as "first-degree murder" on the one hand and "justifiable homicide" on the other would have to be redefined for various other societies, no viable community can tolerate indiscriminate killing of its own people if it entertains long-range hopes for survival.[3]

THE INDIVIDUAL
IN SOCIETY

Herodotus, the Greek historian of the fifth century B.C. whom some regard as the "father of anthropology," noted that in the Egypt of his day "custom is king." By this observation he was drawing attention to the fact that in ancient Egypt the life of the individual was narrowly circumscribed by traditional usages and limitations on initiative—at least when compared to the Greek society of the period. His point was well taken, for although definitions of "freedom" and "constraint" are in part a matter of cultural perception, there seems little question that in some societies the individual is faced with greater restrictions than in others.

Turning to a contemporary example, an outside observer is likely to be struck by the differences in play habits and behavior of English and American children, as well as by

[3]One may well argue, and not without some logic, that this is not necessarily so everywhere today when wholesale pollution of the natural environment and of processed foods by proven or potentially pathogenic substances is rampant and continues unchecked. Our best answer would be that sociocultural systems are, typically, self-regulating and, given time, tend to correct what excesses may develop—albeit, at a price.

the more "orderly" nature of British society when compared to the range of behavior acceptable in the United States. Whether children or adults, the English manifest themselves as substantially more rule-conscious and concerned with the fine points of correct conduct. Very early in life, it is impressed on English children that certain things are simply "not done." English rule consciousness shows itself in linguistic usage: a person who deviates from proper conduct is told to "play the game"—life being viewed as something in the nature of a team sport with specific rules and regulations.

While the above observations have validity, the student of cross-cultural behavior should be careful not to put too much stress on superficial indicators of freedom or conformity. The fact that English people, by and large, dress in a more formal manner than Americans—children typically wear school uniforms and businessmen dress in sedate dark clothes—does not automatically imply a high degree of regimentation and a lack of spontaneity. Granted a cultural concern for rules, English society has always been able to tolerate substantial individual eccentricity in some areas of life so long as this eccentricity does not pose a danger to fundamental values.

In this dialectic between cultural constraints and individual autonomy, anthropology has typically focused its attention on the customary, or the cultural, as we would term it. Custom, in its broadest sense, is what is shared by members of a group, and anthropology concerns itself primarily with the study of societies, communities, and other recognizable social units. Consequently, anthropologists look to individuals as representatives of their respective sociocultural aggregates—people who exemplify cultural roles and statuses, and so forth. Yet those who study human aggregates are not unconscious or unmindful of the fact that the units they investigate are constituted of individuals each of whom is to some degree

Cultural constraints and individual freedom

different from his or her cultural co-members. This is more than a "fact" that must be taken into account, for individual variability is itself a major cultural resource—a pool of differentiated talent and varying ideas and emotions. Anthropologists today are far from subscribing to an approach that would perceive the individual as little more than the product of a particular cultural mold. The process of socialization should not be equated with some putative tyranny of custom that shapes interchangeable human beings.

All societies, even those that may appear most restrictive, provide for a certain amount of play in the regulation of the individual's life. Areas of freedom—relative lack of constraints—vary from culture to culture but are always present and allow individual creativity, relaxation, and self-actualization. In traditional Japanese society, the minute observance of forms that characterizes everyday life is counterpoised by situations and events that are much freer from restraints, such as the relaxed atmosphere of the geisha house, an establishment that provides entertainment in an atmosphere not burdened by rules and regulations yet that meets the aesthetic standards that the Japanese prize so highly. In American society, there are ways of "getting away from it all" that take different forms for different individuals—vacations, parties, conventions, and "that cabin in the woods" spatially and psychologically far from the cares and dictates of society. Of course, for all individuals everywhere there is also what might be termed "inner space"—the thoughts, hopes, and expectations in people's minds.

Nevertheless, since we all normally live in company with others, it is necessary that we share a system of beliefs, symbols, and organizational forms. This system relates to the social structure of a society, but underlying it there is something more fundamental—common goals or expectations and an agreement on the means of achieving them. Anthropologists generally

refer to this interlocking complex of ideals as a *value system.* We get along together, most of the time at least, not so much because of formal organizational dictates or traditional social obligations (having to meet a class, pay the telephone bill on time, invite relatives to Thanksgiving dinner, and the like), but because our underlying assumptions regarding what life is and should be are fairly similar. High among these shared assumptions are the culture-specific concepts of right and wrong, of what the "game of life" consists of and the rules by which it should be played. These generally hold true for even the most disparate elements of the same society—note, for example, the insistence of both conservative and radical Americans on freely

Japanese society recognizes quite specific culturally determined areas of personal freedom. The constraints of a highly formal society are not binding within the precincts of a geisha house, an institution that has no exact equivalent in the West. The photograph shows two men being entertained by witty female conversationalists and musicians. (Stern/ Black Star)

expressing their opinions on economic, political, and social issues.

TO SUM UP A value system, which should offer an element of predictability, allows us to speak at a certain level of abstraction of core values distinctive of a culture and its people. By the same token, it is possible to abstract the concept of a basic or modal personality common to a population sharing the same fundamental values. Values, as we have noted, while manifesting themselves in actions, are beliefs concerning key issues, such as how we should relate to others, the symbols we respond to, and our views of ourselves. All this, and more, we learn early in life and incorporate deeply in the process of becoming cultural beings.

REFERENCES

BENEDICT, RUTH

1932 Configurations of culture in North America. *American Anthropologist* 34:1–27.

1934 *Patterns of culture*. Boston and New York: Houghton Mifflin.

1946 *The chrysanthemum and the sword; patterns of Japanese culture*. Boston: Houghton Mifflin.

BOAS, FRANZ

1920 The methods of ethnology. *American Anthropologist* 22:311–321.

FORTUNE, REO F.

1939 Arapesh warfare. *American Anthropologist* 41:22–41.

GEERTZ, CLIFFORD

1960 *The religion of Java*. Glencoe, Ill.: The Free Press.

GOODENOUGH, WARD H.

1951 *Property, kin, and community on Truk*. Yale University Publications in Anthropology, no. 46. New Haven.

1965 Rethinking "status" and "role"; toward a general model of the cultural organization of social relationships. In *The relevance of models for social anthropology*. Michael Banton, ed. London: Tavistock Publications. Pp. 1–24.

GORER, GEOFFREY

1948 *The American people, a study in national character*. New York: W. W. Norton.

GORER, GEOFFREY, AND JOHN RICKMAN

1949 *The people of Great Russia; a psychological study*. London: The Cresset Press.

HSU, FRANCIS L. K.

1948 *Under the ancestors' shadow; Chinese culture and personality*. New York: Columbia University Press.

1953 *Americans and Chinese: two ways of life*. New York: H. Schuman.

LOWIE, ROBERT H.

1945 *The German people, a social portrait to 1914*. New York: Farrar and Rinehart.

MEAD, MARGARET

1935 *Sex and temperament in three primitive societies*. New York: William Morrow.

1942 *And keep your powder dry; an anthropologist looks at America*. New York: William Morrow.

1953 National character. In *Anthropology today: an encyclopedic inventory*. A. L. Kroeber, ed. Chicago: The University of Chicago Press. Pp. 642–667.

1965 *And keep your powder dry; an anthropologist looks at America* (new expanded ed.). New York: William Morrow.

PI-SUNYER, ORIOL

1973 *Zamora: change and continuity in a Mexican town*. New York: Holt, Rinehart and Winston.

READ, PIERS PAUL

1974 *Alive; the story of the Andes survivors*. Philadelphia: J. B. Lippincott.

SLOTKIN, J. S., ED.

1965 *Readings in early anthropology*. Viking Fund Publications in Anthropology, no. 40. New York.

THURNWALD, RICHARD C.

1936 Review of Margaret Mead, Sex and temperament in three primitive societies. *American Anthropologist* 38:663–667.

WALLACE, ANTHONY F. C.

1961 *Culture and personality*. New York: Random House.

1970 *Culture and personality* (2nd ed.). New York: Random House.

Chapter 12
The powerful bond of relationship

Once the basic physical needs have been met, human survival depends on well-regulated social relations. Although these occur on many different levels, the primary and most important are relationships organized around kinship ties. Accordingly, anthropologists, regardless of their theoretical persuasion, have always recognized the necessity of a thorough study of family and kinship.

It may be well to remind ourselves of some of the observations made earlier concerning the different levels of social integration. The exigencies of the subsistence quest among hunters and gatherers are such that their bands are necessarily limited in size and are often quite flexible in composition. With some notable exceptions—especially the Australian aborigines—the social articulation of these bands tends to be correspondingly modest, with the family serving as the principal socioeconomic unit.

As we have already seen, the most elaborately ordered structures of primitive social organization are found in tribal societies. Tribes are large enough to require a mechanism integrating their members beyond the family or the household into groupings based on marriage, common descent, age-grades, sex, and the like. These groupings—whether lineages, clans, or other tribal subdivisions—are characterized by a high degree of personal, face-to-face contact and interaction.

Among the peasantry, the basic residential unit is usually the *household,* which may include in its extended form a sizable number of near relatives. The functioning of the peasant household is affected not only by its relations to other households in the same locality but to a lesser extent by the structure of the larger society of which the peasants are a part. In recent times, the characteristically strong cohesion among the members of peasant households has been steadily eroding as the economic pull of the urban sector becomes harder to resist.

As a social unit the family and its integrity have suffered most in modern complex societies. In the United States, the average household consists at present of less than three persons. Except for two essential functions that still predominate—reproduction and enculturation of the young—the tendency in populous industrial states has been for the family to be supplanted by a network of institutions or interest groups organized along educational, religious, professional, political, recreational, and other lines. But although many of the functions that the family performs in simple or traditional societies have in complex societies been either superseded or partially encroached on by the institutions or organizational structures found in modern states, this erosion is not an unavoidable consequence. The family as a support and reference group continues to be very important in certain segments of complex society. Interestingly enough, these segments tend to cluster at the poles of the class system. Even in the United States, elites remain very family-conscious and, since they control extensive resources, tend to limit access to these resources by preferential patterns of marriage, maintaining wealth and power in a relatively few hands. At the other end of the scale, the family has retained much of its traditional importance for working-class people, some racial minorities, and certain marginal groups, as studies in both the United States and elsewhere have shown. In this latter case, it is a matter of limited resources and a strategy of economic survival—the pooling of incomes from several family members and other techniques of mutual aid.

Although bonds of relationships based on kinship are generally primary and the most lasting, there are other principles according to which members of societies are organized for a variety of purposes held in common. Among the groupings that crosscut the kin-centered networks are age-groups, various voluntary associations, and castes. Because age-groups (age-sets, or age-

grades) are particularly characteristic of tribal societies, their discussion was included in an earlier chapter dealing with the varieties of tribal experience. In addition to, or instead of, being organized according to age, many societies employ the criterion of sex in forging bonds of solidarity among their members. The result is a variety of associations, both open and secret, that restrict their membership to one sex. So-called men's houses, frequently restricted to unmarried males, have worldwide distribution.

Stratification according to socioeconomic class is generally limited to large complex societies, but there are some notable exceptions—the fishers and hunters of the Pacific Northwest coast, for example. When socioeconomic classes are "closed," that is, hereditary and endogamous, they are usually referred to as *castes*. The best-known and most highly developed system of ranked castes persists to the present day on the Indian subcontinent. Although based on religious grounds, today these castes are largely associated with traditional occupations. The economic specialization of Indian castes furthers their mutual interdependence on the local level.

Because of the fundamental importance of kinship ties and groupings based on them, this chapter will be devoted primarily to relationships arising from the bonds based on blood and marriage.

MARRIAGE

The most fundamental relationship between individual human beings, one that serves as the basis for the biological perpetuation of societies, is institutionalized in the form of marriage. In cross-cultural perspective, *marriage* typically involves a close relationship between a man (very rarely more than one) and a woman (in some cases several) that is recognized as appropriate for certain purposes by the society of which

The position and prestige of both the groom's and the bride's families are invariably reflected in the material circumstances surrounding the wedding ceremony. The simple marriage mass in rural Mexico (far right) contrasts with the elaborate costumes of a princely wedding party in northwestern India. ([far right] Wayne Miller/Magnum Photos, Inc.; [right] Henri Cartier Bresson/Magnum Photos, Inc.)

at least one of the parties is a member.[1] As we have already seen in our discussion of tribal societies, marriage fulfills more func-

[1]A definition of "marriage" that would embrace all those relatively rare arrangements that our definition excludes would turn out to be nearly meaningless. Such a definition would have to subsume, for example, an earlier custom of the Nayar in coastal southwestern India of furnishing a girl with a ritual husband but giving her full freedom to become impregnated by any male of suitable caste save a close relative (Gough 1968); one of about a dozen arrangements practiced among the Dahomeans in West Africa whereby a girl's sexual relationship with a designated male is sponsored by a married woman, her "female husband" and "father" of her children (Herskovits 1938:319–322); the stable relationships between homosexual persons in the United States and elsewhere; and several other special cases.

tions than merely sanctioning sexual relations and conferring social legitimacy on the offspring. While children are the most tangible result of a marriage, to view this relationship as concluded chiefly for the benefit of the spouses and their offspring would be a gross mistake. Equally important, marriage is an alliance between two groups and its purpose is broadly economic.

We have to bear in mind that, in a comparative perspective, marriage as practiced in most modern societies is decidedly unusual. Historically, it is a very recent development and the product of a particular social environment that stresses the importance of individual choice (not only in marriage) over the desires of the family or the community. Even in complex Western societies in which

the prime motivation for the overwhelming majority of marriages is the affection and sexual attraction between two people—however fleeting these occasionally turn out to be—other considerations do intrude. Religious affiliation may be important for some, even though a religious ritual is mandatory in only a few modern societies. The consent of parents is generally sought, but it is not essential.

Forms of marriage

Depending on the number of spouses involved, marriage may take one of several forms. The only legal form of marriage in the United States and other countries of the Judeo-Christian tradition is that in which an individual has a single spouse at any given time—a form known as *monogamy*. It may

thus come as a surprise that, as societies of the world go, monogamous marriages are far from the favored arrangement. According to George Peter Murdock (1967), who has surveyed over 850 different societies, those that are strictly monogamous amount to less than one-sixth of the sample whereas those allowing or preferring *polygamy*, in which an individual has two or more spouses at one time, account for all of the rest.[2] Among the

[2]This is a tally according to different human societies; hence it would be wrong to jump to the conclusion that polygamy represents the majority of marriages in terms of overall numbers. All modern complex societies, including those of Europe and America as well as China and Japan, are monogamous. Moreover, monogamy is the stated national policy in most of the Third World countries, as it is often viewed as one of the essential attributes of modernization.

polygamous societies, there are approximately as many of those that in addition to monogamy accept *polygyny*, a marriage with multiple wives, as there are those in which polygyny is the favored form. Of the two other possible arrangements, *polyandry*—with a woman married simultaneously to two or more husbands—is rare, and group marriage, involving plural male and female spouses, has never been customary or common in any society known today.

Each of these major forms of marriage exists in a number of specialized variations. For example, one might view the growing incidence of divorces and remarriages in our own society as a tendency away from the original concept of lifelong monogamy toward what is sometimes referred to as *serial monogamy*—that is, several spouses in succession. In sub-Saharan Africa, where polygyny is a common marriage arrangement, a man may choose his wife's sisters as additional spouses in preference to other women. Such a form of marriage is known as *sororal polygyny* and has some definite advantages over an ordinary polygynous arrangement. Having been reared in the same household,

sisters may be expected to get along with one another more harmoniously than unrelated co-wives.

The explanation for the prevalence of polygyny among the societies of the world is not to be sought in a romantic notion of the male's propensity and natural desire for wider sexual access. The reasons for plural wives are for the most part quite practical. A demographic factor appears to be the imbalanced sex ratio in favor of females in many societies as a result of the occupational hazards to which males are particularly subject, especially warfare and the hunt (Ember 1974). Besides, in many tribal societies polygyny offers the solution to a problem that industrialized nations have largely managed to solve by other means—the need for a smoothly functioning socioeconomic team on the level of the basic kin group. The presence of several wives within one household insures that crucial subsistence tasks (work in the field, for example) are properly and regularly attended to without shortchanging the requirements of nursing infants and dependent children or neglecting other demanding household ac-

This contemporary Mormon polygynous family is composed of a husband and several wives and children. While individual American Mormons continue to practice polygyny, the Mormon church no longer advocates this type of family structure. (Curt Gunther/Camera 5)

tivities. Not infrequently the first-married wife welcomes the additional co-wives, who help lighten the burden of her many domestic chores. The fact that a man under these circumstances appreciates a wife as an important economic asset is evident from the widespread custom of having to pay a *bride price*, or *bride wealth*, for her. In this transaction, very common in African societies, the amount of money or property agreed on is given by the prospective husband, usually with the assistance of his kin, to the family of the bride. The bride price, commonly paid on an installment basis, serves to compensate the bride's relatives for the loss of a productive worker and the children she may bear. As an alternative in part or in full to paying a bride price, some groups require

Bride price is a compensatory payment for the services of the bride that are lost to her family when she marries. This young couple, posing outside their village in North Cameroon, display the goods presented by the husband to the bride's family at the time of marriage. (Kay Lawson/ Rapho, Photo Researchers, Inc.)

the bridegroom to render bride service in the form of labor to the bride's family.

It is all too common to look upon polygyny and bride-wealth payments as customs degrading the wives and reducing them to the status of chattel. Such a view, however, is completely ethnocentric. In his discussion of the African family, Paul Bohannan, an anthropologist known for his extensive research on the African continent, comments on polygyny as follows:

Polygyny has nothing to do with the position of women in society. African women, by and large, have a high social position: legal rights, religious and political responsibility, economic independence. . . .

Women in Africa are not, in short, a deprived group as they were in the nineteenth-century Western world. African men ritualize rather than deny their basic dependence on women.

The next myth that must be banished is that polygyny has anything to do with the concupiscence [sexual desire] of the male. Polygyny is a state into which most African men enter with a certain trepidation. If you think that one wife can henpeck a husband, you should see what three in league can do (Bohannan and Curtin 1971:107–108).

And with respect to the bride price, Bohannan writes:

Initially the husband has to make a bridewealth payment that is tantamount to posting a bond that he will carry out his obligations, thus guarding his new wife's rights. . . . But, in return for his "bond" and his obligations, the husband gets certain rights.

. . . [One of these may be] the right to filiate that woman's children to his kinship group (Bohannan and Curtin 1971:110).

In short, a husband has a considerable investment in cash or kind to protect: if his wife were to return to her parents' home as a consequence of serious ill-treatment received at his hands, he might well forfeit his original payment, in full or at least in part.

The transfer of money, goods, or estate from the bride's family to the groom or his family, known as *dowry*, is much less frequently encountered. The reasons for providing a woman with dowry vary among the societies that employ it. The payment may represent the bride's share of her family's estate, or it may help cement interfamily alliances or enhance the prestige of her former household. In some European countries, dowry also served as compensation to the groom for the costs of maintaining his spouse.

These and similar cases clearly show that marriage in many parts of the world is primarily an economic or political transaction between two family groups. Consequently, except for modern industrial soci-

eties, it is rare for marriage to be considered the concern of the potential marriage partners alone.

FAMILY

Intimately linked to marriage is the family—typically, parents caring for and raising children in a common household. Like marriage, the family may take various forms. Because tracing kinship ties may easily become quite complicated, we shall make use of graphic symbols commonly employed by anthropologists in this context.

To begin with a simple arrangement, a male (▲) may be married to (=) a female (●) in a monogamous union that will serve as a *family of procreation:*

(1) ▲ = ●

In the course of time, the couple are expected to produce one or more children. For the purposes of our illustration, let us assume that there are two offspring descended from (|) this couple, a pair of siblings (⌐‾‾), a boy and a girl. The result is a family consisting of four individuals, the husband and his wife and their two children, a son and a daughter:

(2)

This diagram represents a fairly common form of what is known as the *nuclear family*—a group consisting of husband and wife and their children. From the point of view of the children, this group serves as the *family of orientation*, one in which their initial cultural and social learning takes place.

A particular instance of a polygynous family may be diagrammed as follows:

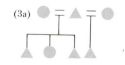

(3a)

Here we have represented a composite, polygynous family consisting of two nuclear families sharing the same husband and father. One of these nuclear families is made up of two sons and a daughter, their mother, and the father who links these four individuals to a second nuclear family, consisting of himself, his wife, and a son:

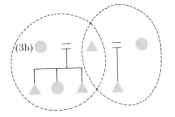

To represent a case of sororal polygyny, mentioned earlier in our discussion of marriage, we would need only to adjust the diagram in the following manner:

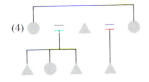

It should be noted that in cases (3) and (4) two generations are involved and the bond

between the two nuclear families is a marital tie (husband-wife relationship).

In the United States, the ideal of middle-class couples is to establish a household separate from either the groom's or the bride's parents, but this is far from the norm in other societies. The result of the co-residence of two or more married couples is the *extended family*, a composite family consisting of "two or more nuclear families affiliated through an extension of the parent-child relationship rather than of the husband-wife relationship" (Murdock 1949:2) or of a household shared by siblings, together with their spouses and children. These two types of an extended family may take a variety of concrete forms, for example,

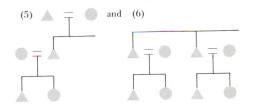

The latter (6), also known as *fraternal joint family*, in contrast to case (5) includes only

A four-generation Hungarian family celebrates the fiftieth anniversary of the founding couple. In some peasant societies, extended kin units of this type constitute an effective and organized pool of labor for working the family holdings. (Sovfoto/Eastfoto)

two generations; however, as against cases (3) and (4), the bond between the two nuclear families is based on blood relationship—that between parent and son (5) and brothers (6).

In a ground-breaking cross-cultural study of social structure, based on an earlier survey of 250 representative human societies, Murdock (1949:2–3) asserted that "the nuclear family is a universal human social grouping" that, in addition to common residence, is characterized by its "distinctive and vital functions—sexual, economic, reproductive, and educational." However, more recent research has once again shown that in anthropology blanket generalizations of this sort have small chance of standing up. For one thing, there are known cases of families in which the attachment of a man to his wife and children is anything but permanent. Then, too, some of the activities of the nuclear family may be so tightly meshed with a larger grouping—as in composite families or in the cases of some communes or kibbutzim—that the nuclear family tends to lose its integrity as a clearly differentiated functioning unit.

THE INCEST TABOO

Every society without exception prohibits marriage and sexual relations between certain kinds of relatives. These are defined quite specifically for that purpose and vary from one society to the next. The practice that forbids marriage between two individuals from within the same local, kin, or status group is referred to as *exogamy*. A coincident, but even more stringent, regulation proscribing sexual relationships between culture-specific categories of kin, and invariably between brother and sister as well as between a parent and child, is known as the *incest taboo*.[3]

[3] The rare cases in which regulations governing incest are known to have been suspended do not seriously invalidate its universality. Best known among these are instances of so-called dynastic

For about a century now, some of the most fertile minds among anthropologists and from outside the discipline have addressed themselves to the intriguing question of how to account for the origin and universality of this taboo. Its ubiquity and persistence through time are uniformly judged to be evidence of its great antiquity, but beyond that there has been little agreement on the ultimate source of the incest taboo despite the many theories that have been put forth to account for it. When considered singly, these theories either are logically inconsistent or do not hold up in the light of the growing empirical data gathered from contemporary human societies.

Theories based on vague or unsupportable claims for the role that mystical or religious notions must have played in limiting sexual access among certain members of the nuclear family are usually dismissed out of hand. Other theories, besides defying available evidence, simply beg the question, as when it is asserted that the avoidance of sexual relations among close relatives is due to a strong disinclination or even an instinctive horror. By and large, such an avoidance does exist, but it is undoubtedly traceable to the training customarily given children who are socialized together. Otherwise, why should marriages between a certain kind of kin be considered incestuous while at the same time marriages between other kin, of comparable relationship, are strongly preferred? And furthermore, if innate revulsion against mating between close relatives should exist, why do children have to be taught something that they innately comprehend?

The claim has been advanced at times that inbreeding among close kin would result in

incest (sibling marriage), which was sanctioned in royal families of highly stratified societies—in ancient (pharaonic) Egypt, precontact Hawaii, and the Inca Empire. The rationalization for this practice was convincing enough: as descendants of the sun, or similar supernatural powers, the royal family could not allow itself to become contaminated by marriage to ordinary mortals.

substandard offspring and a progressive deterioration of the stock. Several arguments can be raised against this theory. Even if inbreeding should be genetically disadvantageous, the understanding of the principles of genetics (incomplete as it still is) goes back only to the beginning of this century. Furthermore, with populations of sound genetic make-up, problems of this nature would not arise. Of one thing there is little doubt—the populations of early hominids were extremely small, and the genetic pool for any given group must have been quite limited in its variation. Some recent findings seem to indicate that "inbreeding among the early hominids would be both highly probable and not dysfunctional from the point of view of the population, and that the origin of incest and exogamy must be sought elsewhere" (Livingstone 1969:46). By the same token, it is generally accepted that inbreeding in large contemporary populations is likely to have minimal genetic consequences, at least in the short run.

Still others have approached the incest taboo from a psychological or sociological vantage point, or from both. One such theory, whose proponents included both Freud and Malinowski, holds that unrestricted sexual access of each member of a family to every other member of the opposite sex would result in rivalries, tensions, and role confusion far too disruptive for the group to survive as the fundamental socioeconomic unit. Another attempt at explanation views the incest prohibition as serving the shared interests of the wider social group: these interests could easily become frustrated if young individuals were permitted to gratify sexual impulses within their families of orientation at the expense of promoting viable connections with other groups outside them. A related, and last, theory to be mentioned here holds that mating outside one's immediate family group has as its effect the establishment of friendly ties with other groups in an area within which cooperation for resources might otherwise easily take an ugly turn under especially dire

circumstances. In this view, incest regulations represent a cultural adaptation with multiple benefits: creating a feeling of potential collectivity among several family or band-level groups for the purposes of mutual aid, economic security, defense against outsiders, and, indirectly, a means of sharing what cultural innovations may be developed in any one group.

The question of the origin and persistence of incest prohibition still awaits solution. But most anthropologists today are probably inclined to look for an answer in the interplay of several factors, along the lines suggested in a report on the results of a work group that met in the spring of 1956 to consider the problem:

In sum, we propose that the adoption of the familial incest taboo was adaptive primarily because of the genetic results of close inbreeding. . . . [common to] intelligent, slow-maturing animals which bear few offspring at a time and which live in family units. The selection of the taboo, however, we hypothesize, occurred through efforts to solve the problem of sexual competition within the family in a cultural animal with an organized family life. . . . [Because] the incest taboo solved this problem and the genetic problem . . . . it had high selective value (Aberle and others 1963:264).

KINSHIP, DESCENT, AND RESIDENCE

In the United States, the scientific study of kinship systems had a brilliant pioneer in Lewis Henry Morgan, who in 1871 published his massive *Systems of Consanguinity and Affinity of the Human Family*. In this comparative study of well over one hundred kinship terminologies from every part of the world, he introduced the idea that the particulars of kinship were indicative of the sociocultural level of a society. Since Morgan's time, the analysis and theory of kinship has become an area of social anthropology receiving concentrated attention. This interest on the part of anthropologists goes back to an early recognition that societies order most social relationships among their members by reference to ties based on kinship and that the nature of these relationships is likely to be reflected in kinship terminologies.

We may begin our discussion by taking a partial look at the terms of reference of the American kinship system. An individual to whom various other persons are shown to be related—so-called *ego*—speaks of his or her parents in a formal or respectful context as *mother* and *father*. Ego's parents' siblings—that is, his or her father's and mother's sisters and brothers—are referred to as *aunts* and *uncles*. All the kin mentioned thus far have been *consanguineal*, or blood, relatives. *Affinal* relatives, those based on marriage, may be brought into the picture by assigning spouses to ego's parents' siblings; they, too, are referred to as *aunts* and *uncles*. While the criterion of sex, which derives from the biological differences between males and females, has been given formal recognition in all of these kinship terms, it happens to be ignored in respect to the children of ego's aunts and uncles, who are called *cousins* regardless of their sex. With a male as ego and the addition of his brother and sister, we may diagrammatically represent all of these relatives and the connections between them as follows:

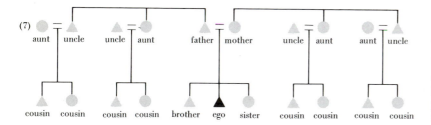

Let us now contrast this portion of a kinship system well known to us all with a similar portion of the kinship system of the

Northern Arapaho Indians of Wyoming (Salzmann 1959):

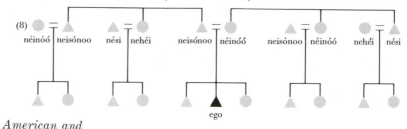

American and Arapaho kinship systems compared

If we compare the two diagrams for egos' parental generation, we observe that while there are two different pairs of kinship terms in each, their distribution is strikingly different. In (7), only ego's biological father, or genitor, is referred to as *father*, and only his biological mother, or genetrix, as *mother*; the other relatives of ego are termed *uncles* and *aunts*. In (8), by contrast, the same kinship term, *neisónoo* (roughly, "my father"), is used to refer not only to ego's biological father (genitor) but also to his father's brothers and to ego's mother's sisters' husbands. Similarly, the term *néinóó* (roughly, "my mother") is used to refer not only to ego's biological mother (genetrix) but also to her sister and to ego's father's brothers' wives. The remaining four individuals represented are referred to as *nési* (ego's mother's brother and father's sister's husband) and *nehéi* (ego's father's sister and mother's brother's wife). The latter two terms, *nési* and *nehéi*, thus roughly correspond to "my uncle" and "my aunt" in English.[4]

It appears, then, that the Arapaho term *neisónoo* includes not only the genitor but several additional kin types whose father-

[4]The Arapaho kinship terms we are dealing with here are even more inclusive: ego's father's parents' siblings' sons are also referred to as *neisónoo* (but their daughters are *nehéi*) and ego's mother's parents' siblings' daughters as *néinóó* (but their sons as *nési*). Furthermore, ego's wife's sister's husband and ego's wife's brother's wife are terminologically lumped together with the other kin of ego's own generation.

hood is defined culturally, or socially, rather than biologically. These relationships parallel exactly those denoted by the term *néinóó*. That ego's mother's sister's husband is also called *neisónoo* (and ego's father's brother's wife *néinóó*) should come as no surprise: since ego's mother's sister is referred to by the same term as his genetrix, this woman's husband would be expected to be designated by the same term as the genetrix's husband (and similarly, ego's father's brother's wife would be referred to by the same term as the genitor's wife, that is, as *néinóó*).

Now let us compare the American and the Arapaho kinship systems for ego's own generation. Whereas we differentiate between siblings (brothers and sisters) and cousins, the Arapaho lump both together, distinguishing instead between those males and females who are older than ego—*nééseh'e* (roughly, "my elder brother") and *nébi* ("my elder sister")—while classifying together all those who are younger than ego under the term *nééhebéhe'* (roughly, "my younger sibling").

To generalize, Arapaho kinship terms are of the classificatory type. Whereas our terminology keeps biological parents apart from uncles and aunts, and siblings from cousins, the Arapaho lump together *lineal* relatives—that is, persons descended in a direct line—with some of the *collateral* relatives, those reckoned in different lines of descent. This practice, which is very common among the societies of the world, is known as *merging*.

If all of the discrepancies between kinship systems went only as far as their respective terminologies, we would be dealing with nothing more than lexical differences between languages. But this is not the case at all. The extension of the Arapaho kinship terms *neisónoo* and *néinóó* from ego's genitor and genetrix to a number of additional relatives—father's brother, mother's sister, and others—is paralleled to a large degree by an extension of ego's behavior patterns from his biological parents to all those who share the same kinship terms with them. All

Arapaho "fathers" and "mothers" have the same duties and obligations toward their "sons" or "daughters," even though opportunities to perform these duties may be limited by circumstances. With the more distant "parents" and "children," between whom interaction may only rarely take place, the emphasis is on the extension of attitudes rather than behavior. Similarly, in Arapaho all children of male ego's "brothers," who in our terms would include not only brothers but male cousins as well, are terminologically classified together with ego's biological sons and daughters. The same linkage between a terminological designation and corresponding behavior patterns and attitudes applies to this and other areas of the Arapaho kinship system.

TO SUM UP   While the biological father (genitor) and mother (genetrix) are recognized as such, each belongs within a more inclusive class of social fathers (any male referred to as *neisónoo*) and social mothers (any female referred to as *néinóó*), and so on. In the American kinship system, a similar situation occurs only in special cases, as when adoptive parents or a stepfather (usually referred to as "father") or a stepmother ("mother") assumes the social obligations of the genitor or genetrix. One should note, however, that these surrogate parents are hardly ever drawn from among the kin of the biological parent(s).

Now it would be a mistake to assume that the few selected particularities of the Arapaho kinship system used here for purposes of illustration are in any sense out of the ordinary as far as societies of the world go. Tightly woven or (from our point of view at least) highly structured systems of relationships among kin are characteristic of most small-scale societies and serve the important function of minimizing the potential conflicts of interest that otherwise might arise in close-knit groups, tribes in particular. There are several principles that codetermine the make-up of households in such societies and the nature and distribution of rights and obligations pertaining to their members. The rules by which these principles are put into effect concern descent, choice of spouse, and residence.

Once again, we begin with the pattern most familiar to us, that of a typical middle-class American family. In this country, as we have said, the decision to marry is usually made by the couple themselves. Initially, they may have met and become acquainted under any one of the widest variety of circumstances—in college, at their place of work, at a party, through mutual friends, while traveling, and the like. Because of the high mobility of Americans, marriages of childhood sweethearts, once fairly frequent, are becoming less and less common. The consent of parents, if sought at all, is asked for only as a matter of form. Once married, and in recent years even before formal marriage in many cases, the couple establishes a residence separate from the households of both sets of parents. The group of kin with which the offspring of the couple affiliate will include relatives on both paternal and maternal sides. Although it is true that the couple's children will be given their father's surname (although here, too, some exceptions are now being made), and that certain family heirlooms of sentimental value (china, a wedding dress, jewelry) are handed down from mother to daughter, in general property is left more or less equally to surviving children, regardless of sex.

While these or closely similar practices are common to most Americans as well as to members of other countries, many societies follow different customs or rules. If a person claims affiliation with a group of kin by tracing descent through both males and females, the rules of descent are said to be *cognatic*. And if such cognatic descent is reckoned evenly along the two lines at each generation, as we have just noted is the case in our own society, anthropologists speak of *bilateral* descent. Alternatively, the tracing of one's membership in a group through both males and females, but not equally and

Descent

simultaneously, constitutes *ambilineal* descent. William Davenport provides an example of such flexible descent reckoning in his description of a Samoan descent group:

> The Samoan ʾaiga sa is a descent group controlling garden land, house sites, and certain ceremonials. It is exogamous, since the incest taboo is extended to all known relatives. . . . Affiliation with a descent group is through either father or mother, and a married couple may affiliate with the groups of either spouse. A person is mainly associated with one group—that with which he lives—but he may participate to some extent in several. Living with and using lands belonging to a particular 'aiga sa, as well as the right to speak at meetings of the group, are dependent upon the consent of its members, and this may be denied if there is doubt about a person's genealogical relationship to the group or if he has failed to fulfill his obligations to it (Davenport 1959:561).

In contrast to the bilateral and ambilineal varieties of cognatic descent, *unilineal* descent is traced consistently through relatives of one sex. The two major kinds of unilineal descent—patrilineal (agnatic) and matrilineal (uterine)—are represented diagrammatically in (9). It should be noted that members of ego's *patrilineal* descent group, the most common kinship organization, trace their relationship exclusively through males, a circumstance that does not, however, prevent female siblings of these males from being counted as members of that group even though they are unable to transmit membership to their offspring. Similarly, in a *matrilineal* descent group, descent is reckoned exclusively through females. Either one of these groups, provided that their members are actually able to trace their descent from a specific ancestor, is known as a lineage. Quite frequently, however, the founder of a group is a legendary or mythological figure, and the distant links between this ancestor and those who claim him (or her) are necessarily only putative. Such a group is invariably much more inclu-

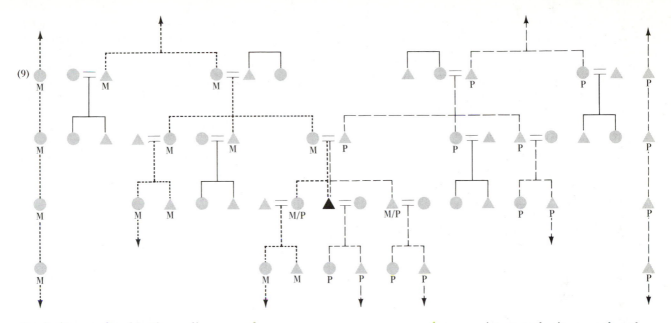

(9)

sive in its membership than a lineage and constitutes a clan.

If an individual traces descent through the male line for certain purposes and through the female line for others, anthropologists speak of *double* descent. An example of such an arrangement may be found among the Afikpo people, who live in southeastern Nigeria in a group of villages sharing a meeting place, one or more public markets, and the same ritual activities. According to Simon Ottenberg (1968), among the major concerns of the Afikpo matrilineal groupings have traditionally been the ownership, use, and protection of farmland, and the inheritance of money and goods. In addition, these groupings are actively engaged in ritual activities associated with the fertility of both the females and the land.

On the other hand, the most prominent features of the Afikpo patrilineal groupings are their residential basis and the major role that they play in the social control of the families of a compound. Furthermore, the patrilineal groupings are the major source of governmental and judicial power.

On the whole, the activities of each type of descent group complement each other. . . . One line of descent does not have consistent authority over the other. The two exist as cooperating equals with defined rights over individuals and over property in specific situations, neither dominating the other in over-all perspective. Conflicts arise between them, mainly over land, . . . but they are not conflicts in which one type of descent grouping is simply trying to gain a dominant position over the other (Ottenberg 1968:250–251).

Even under the conditions of change resulting from Western contact and population increase, the balance between matrilineal and patrilineal activities and functions of the Afikpo is maintained: modification at any one point produces adjustments elsewhere (Ottenberg 1968:262).

Choice of spouse   Just as all societies proscribe marriages between certain categories of close kin, a sizable number of societies consider marital ties between certain specific classes of individuals as highly preferable. One such example is *sister-exchange marriage*, in which the prospective bridegroom is expected to transfer his sister or some other close kin to his bride's family in exchange. This type of arrangement is found in various parts of the world. The case described here is from among the Koman-speaking Gumuz, who live in the valley of the Blue Nile. Sister-exchange marriage is practiced almost without exception and is normally arranged by the elders of the respective patrilineal clans. The most common form is the exchange of a bride for the bridegroom's full sister. However, since this is clearly not feasible in every case, there are a number of alternatives. For example, if a marriage takes the form of an elopement without transfer, the "payment" may have to be deferred until the daughter of the "stolen" woman is old enough to be used to settle the debt. A sisterless bridegroom has to arrange to borrow a girl from a fellow clansman until he can make a replacement with his own daughter, who is pledged even before she is born. The result of these and similar arrangements is that nearly every Gumuz is caught up in an intricate network of exchanges. Because of the mutual obligations that permeate the Gumuz clans, sister-exchange marriage is usually the main source of both interclan feuding and alliances (James 1975).

A very common marriage rule is that marriages should preferably be concluded between two people having a specific kinship relation to each other. Typically, such marriages bind together two first cousins, and accordingly are referred to as *cousin marriages*. For this purpose, two types of cousins are distinguished, parallel and cross-cousins (10). *Cross-cousins* (X) are persons whose parents are siblings of the opposite sex, that is, they are children of ego's father's sister or mother's brother; *parallel cousins* (‖) are persons whose parents are siblings of the same sex.

Of the two kinds of cousin marriages, those between parallel cousins are relatively rare, being largely limited to groups within the Muslim world. These groups are *endogamous*, encouraging or requiring marital ties to be established between members of the same descent group, almost invariably a patrilineage, that is, between a man and his father's brother's daughter. There is no uniformly acceptable answer to how this practice originated and why it should have persisted as long as it apparently has. However, it seems plausible that, given the flexible political organization of those pastoral groups who commonly engage in it, the custom is capable of generating lineage solidarity whenever circumstances demand it.

Cross-cousin marriages are by far the more common. Terminologically, cross-cousins tend to be differentiated from parallel cousins, who are customarily lumped with siblings and ineligible as spouses. There are good reasons why cross-cousin marriages are preferred in many societies over those with nonkin. One is the reduction of potential tensions with in-laws. It will be noted from (11a,b) that if ego were to marry his cross-cousin, it would then be his father's sister (11a) or mother's brother's wife (11b) who would become his mother-in-law. The bride would have an equally good prior acquaintance with her prospective father-in-law. Although either type of cousin marriage will alter somewhat the nature of the social relationship of the individuals involved, their personal rapport would already have been established. More, such marriages will help produce or strengthen social solidarity between two lineages and serve as a way of consolidating property.

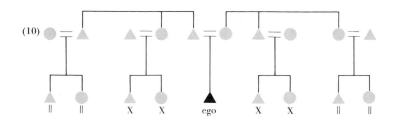

(10)

‖ ‖   X X   ego   X X   ‖ ‖

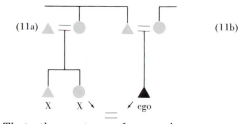

(11a)   X   X   ego

(11b)   ego   X   X

That the custom of marrying cross-cousins may have deep roots in a society is indirectly documented in a discussion of kinship terms among the Indians of Brazil. In the Nambicuara tribe, which permits polygyny, the first marriage commonly takes the cross-cousin form. However, since the chief or shaman periodically withdraws several of the most eligible young women from the regular cycle of marriages, young men on occasion find themselves lacking potential spouses. At such times they rather frequently resort to homosexual relations. The interesting point is that these "homosexual relations occur only between *male cross cousins*" (Lévi-Strauss 1943:400; author's emphasis).

Once a couple marry, they need to establish a residence. In the United States, as we have already mentioned, clearly the most satis-

Postmarital residence

factory solution is to establish a separate household. Most societies, however, practice a different arrangement and follow more or less closely one of several rules, unless special circumstances dictate otherwise. In the following table, we list the most common varieties of expected postmarital residence patterns in the order of their relative frequency:

EXPECTED POSTMARITAL RESIDENCE
OF GROOM AND BRIDE

VARIETY	ARRANGEMENT
1 Patrilocal (virilocal)	With or near the groom's father and his wife
2 Matrilocal (uxorilocal)	With or near the bride's mother and her husband
3 Bilocal	With or near either the groom's or the bride's parents
4 Neolocal	Independent from parents of either spouse
5 Avunculocal	With or near the groom's maternal uncle's family

Why should there exist a postmarital residence pattern according to which a woman joins the groom in his maternal uncle's

A California single-family housing development. Rapid suburban construction has radically altered the landscape—and the way of life—in many American and European localities. In part, suburban expansion reflects the high cultural value placed on individual home ownership; in part, it is also an expression of the flight of the middle classes from the inner cities. (Bill Owens/Magnum Photos, Inc.)

domestic unit? Avunculocal residence, whenever it occurs, is invariably associated with matrilineal kin groups. The fact that men (mother's brothers and sister's sons) constitute the residential core of such descent groups is viewed by some anthropologists as evidence for male dominance: even though the women of a particular society provide the continuity of descent, the interests of males are asserted and protected.

Our discussion of the principles governing the family, marriage, descent, and residence has touched on the most common features of social life as it relates to kinship. But kinship tends to be inextricably bound up with other aspects of society, having to do with production and consumption, social control, mutual aid, and the like. Some of the broader implications and extensions of kinship ties must therefore receive additional consideration.

KINSHIP AND SOCIAL TIES

The basic linkages within kinship groups tend to involve pairs of individuals, or *dyads*, and to be reciprocal. For example, among the Arapaho, a father had the primary responsibility for the training of his sons in the skills of the hunt and other male-oriented activities, while the mother taught her daughters to become proficient in the household duties expected of women, which included the dressing of skins and the putting up and taking down of tepees. In return, the children owed their parents respect and obedience. Behavior between members of various other pairs of kin was similarly defined. Since the custom among the Arapaho was matrilocal residence, a young married man camped with his wife's parents. A mother-in-law and her son-in-law were bound by the highest form of respect for each other: the two were not allowed to speak or to look at each other, or to be present together in the same room (tepee). Any necessary communication between them was transmitted by the man's wife. Diametrically opposed to this type of *avoidance behavior* was the relationship be-

tween siblings-in-law. Termed *joking relationship*, it took the form of teasing, practical jokes, sexual play, and the like. These two extreme forms of obligatory behavior applied to dyadic relationships that were particularly susceptible to serious conflict. In the former case, where the rivalry of mother-daughter and husband-wife relationships posed a constant threat, the potential for conflict was minimized by ritually circumscribing social contact between the two in-laws. In the latter case, the source of possible conflict lay elsewhere. The unmarried brothers of the young woman, under whose protection she had always been, were expected to work closely with her husband, who now claimed control over her. The institution of the obligatory joking relationship channeled potential hostility into socially acceptable behavior.

Dyads are not restricted to kinship ties, as we have seen in the preceding chapter in our discussion of identity relationships. Other dyads are formed in cases of adoption, brotherhoods of various kinds, residential or work groups, and—perhaps most significantly—fictive, or ceremonial, kinship.

Fictive kinship

Fictive kinship is a binding relationship between individuals similar to that of close kin but not based on the bond of birth, marriage, or descent. The best-known example of such a relationship is *compadrazgo*, or godparenthood, widely entered into in Latin American countries. The core of this institution is the assumption by one or several individuals of responsibility approximating that of a father or a mother for a child through the ritual of Catholic baptism. But in addition to the relationship between a child and its sponsor, the godparent, another dyadic relationship develops between the child's parents and the sponsor. In his description of one particular pattern of this institution by the example of the peasant community of Tzintzuntzan in central Mexico, George M. Foster notes that

a godfather and a godmother (rarely, only a godmother) sponsor the baptism of a

A christening in a Swiss village. The god-mother holds the infant, with the god-father on her left; they are flanked by the parents of the baby and the baby's brother. Godparents represent an element of security for a new member of society, and the link is forged in an appropriate symbolic manner. (Dorha Raynor from Leo de Wys, Inc.)

child, thereby becoming spiritual parents. A single godparent of the same sex as the child is named for confirmation and first communion, and a pair of godparents, usually a married couple, is named for weddings. Godparents are responsible for moral advice to their godchildren, and for economic and physical care if necessary. Godchildren, in turn, are expected to show absolute obedience and respect to their godparents, if possible even in greater degree than toward parents. This is an asymmetrical relationship in that in the course of a lifetime godparents have greater tangible obligations toward their godchildren than the latter have toward them. In point of fact, however, the relationship between godparents and godchild's parents . . . is the more important of the two. This is a symmetrical relationship in that the new obligations and expectations usually are between people of equal status and are essentially equal in form and quantity.

Behavior between new compadres [co-parents] becomes more formal. . . . The

compadre relationship in theory is considered to be one of the most sacred of human ties. Compadres must help each other in every possible way, whatever the personal sacrifice and inconvenience may be. The compadrazgo is much like the family in that it has religious sanction, shares the same incest prohibitions, and once established is indissoluble (Foster 1961:1181–1182).

Foster's study of the dyadic contract describes the nature of the various social interactions in which the Tzintzuntzeños traditionally engage. The system of godparenthood is a cultural institution of the wider, social family that depends on reciprocity and acts as "a net in which ego . . . is formally linked to a great many other people" (Foster 1961:1183). Dyadic contracts are established and maintained because both individuals stand to gain from such a relationship. The community of Tzintzuntzan is relatively small, with about

1,800 inhabitants at the time of Foster's research. Its social units and institutions, like those of band-level and most tribal societies, are of manageable proportions and for the most part possess clear-cut boundaries setting them apart from the outside world. In short, almost everyone knows everyone else.

This, patently, is not the case with modern complex societies. While relationships, groups, and institutions constitute the building blocks of all human aggregates regardless of size, complex societies are much more than simple societies multiplied *x* times. The recognition on the part of the anthropologist that social groups and institutions are not bounded and fixed structures — as they were once thought to be — is only part of the solution. Equally challenging is the fact that individuals in a complex modern society find themselves in a vast and intricate maze, very few paths of which they are able to explore during their lifetimes. One method used by anthropologists to cope

Networks

with this maze is *network analysis*. Seen from the point of view of the individual members of a society,

personal networks, when elucidated, provide an inventory of the dyadic roles individuals have accumulated according to the rules, or structures, of their culture and society, and serve to place them in its organization. . . . By tracing personal networks in the field, the structure of a culture can be elucidated and the workings of the society seen in operation. In the case of complex and/or seemingly amorphous societies, or social sectors, this may be the only way in which investigation can proceed (Crissman 1969:80).

Personal networks are thus defined by the specific cultural identities of those whom they encompass and by the links that relate them to the point of reference (ego) (see Figure 12-1). Some portion of a kinship network is almost invariably part of any personal network, but beyond that, there are the thousands upon thousands of

Figure 12-1 Partial personal network of Eve Sheldon, M.D.

The network of Eve Sheldon, physician at the Institute of Family Medicine, Plainsville, includes work-related associations — Dr. Charles Formby, Director, I.F.M.; Harriet (Harriet Sandeman, M.D.), colleague at I.F.M.; William, registered nurse at I.F.M.; and Frances, receptionist at I.F.M. Common work experience does not automatically entail close friendship but is not incompatible with it (e.g., Harriet).

Friendship links exist outside the work setting (Don and Margaret), but professional interests and friendship may coexist (Helena). Some network linkages are established by residence (Mr. Phelps, Mabel), others by recreational interest (George Elliott, owner of Elliott's Marina), or day-to-day activities (Mildred, waitress at Town Square Restaurant). The family links are self-explanatory.

The terms are those used by ego. Three levels of interaction are indicated.

Levels of Interaction

```
————————  high
——————  medium
- - - - - -  low
```

dyadic relationships from among which the individual constructs his own social web. These dyads are of various kinds—patron-client, employer-employee, priest-parishioner, doctor-patient, nurse-patient, doctor-nurse, and so forth, and mutual friends. Those who are involved in legal, political, economic, and administrative affairs and are close to the sources of power, be it Washington, D.C., a state capital, or a corporation headquarters, know how "to go through channels" (the institutional approach), but most of them find it more efficacious at least to try to expedite matters via the friend of a friend who knows so-and-so. These, too, are networks, and very powerful ones at that.[5]

REFERENCES

ABERLE, DAVID F., AND OTHERS
1963 The incest taboo and the mating patterns of animals. *American Anthropologist* 65:253–265.

BARNES, J. A.
1972 *Social networks.* Addison-Wesley Module in Anthropology, no. 26. Pp. 1–29. Reading, Mass.

BOHANNAN, PAUL, AND PHILIP CURTIN
1971 *Africa and Africans* (rev. ed.). Garden City, N.Y.: The Natural History Press.

CRISSMAN, LAWRENCE W.
1969 On networks. *The Cornell Journal of Social Relations* 4:1:72–81.

DAVENPORT, WILLIAM
1959 Nonunilinear descent and descent groups. *American Anthropologist* 61:557–572.

EMBER, MELVIN
1974 Warfare, sex ratio, and polygyny. *Ethnology* 13:197–206.

1975 On the origin and extension of the incest taboo. *Behavior Science Research* 10:249–281.

FOSTER, GEORGE M.
1961 The dyadic contract: a model for the social structure of a Mexican peasant village. *American Anthropologist* 63:1173–1192.

GOUGH, E. KATHLEEN
1968 The Nayars and the definition of marriage. In *Marriage, family and residence.* Paul Bohannan and John Middleton, eds. Garden City, N.Y.: The Natural History Press. Pp. 49–71.

HERSKOVITS, MELVILLE J.
1938 *Dahomey; an ancient West African kingdom,* vol. 1. New York: J. J. Augustin.

JAMES, WENDY
1975 Sister-exchange marriage. *Scientific American* 233:6:84–94 (December).

LÉVI-STRAUSS, CLAUDE
1943 The social use of kinship terms among Brazilian Indians. *American Anthropologist* 45:398–409.

LIVINGSTONE, FRANK B.
1969 Genetics, ecology and the origins of incest and exogamy. *Current Anthropology* 10:45–61.

MORGAN, LEWIS HENRY
1871 *Systems of consanguinity and affinity of the human family.* Washington, D.C.: Smithsonian Institution.

MURDOCK, GEORGE PETER
1949 *Social structure.* New York: Macmillan.
1967 *Ethnographic atlas.* Pittsburgh: University of Pittsburgh Press.

OTTENBERG, SIMON
1968 *Double descent in an African society; the Afikpo village-group.* Seattle: University of Washington Press.

SALZMANN, ZDENEK
1959 Arapaho kinship terms and two related ethnolinguistic observations. *Anthropological Linguistics* 1:9:6–10 (December).

[5]For an informed recent review of the social networks concept, with a selected bibliography, see Barnes 1972.

Chapter 13
Allocation of power and management of conflict

In 1776 Thomas Paine (1737–1809), at that time an unknown English political propagandist, published in Philadelphia his pamphlet *Common Sense*. Its primary aim was to expose the evils of British control over the North American colonies. Paine was certainly not an anthropologist and hardly a student of comparative political systems, but he offered a number of observations that have a direct bearing on this chapter. Ever since Plato (427?–347 B.C.) and Aristotle, (384–322 B.C.), Western philosophers had tended to equate the state, or "government," with society. Aristotle had gone so far as to insist that "the state is by nature clearly prior to the family and to the individual, since the whole is of necessity prior to the part" (1941:1129). Paine made a very different point, essentially that the regulatory institutions of the state should be clearly distinguished from society:

Some writers have so confounded society with government as to leave little or no distinction between them, whereas they are not only different but have different origins. Society is produced by our wants, and government by our wickedness; the former promotes our happiness *positively* by uniting our affections, the latter *negatively* by restraining our vices. The one encourages intercourse, the other creates distinctions. The first is a patron, the last a punisher (Paine 1953:4).

Paine would have made no claim to being a balanced and objective observer of the political conditions of his time; he was, after all, an unabashed publicist for the cause of the American colonists. Nevertheless, if we go beyond the rhetoric, he puts his finger on an unassailable truth: the state should not be confused with society and, further, state systems function in basically coercive ways—in his words, they "punish."

POLITICAL POWER AND LEGAL AUTHORITY

This issue of power and control is critical to any understanding of law and politics. Political organization and the rules of conduct enforced by legitimate[1] social sanctions reflect the realities of power in any society. Political and legal institutions are everywhere closely related and touch on the vital issue of "who gets what, when, and how" which is as good an aphoristic definition of civil society as one is likely to come by (Fried 1967:20).

Both in politics and in law we are dealing with questions of power and authority. In complex societies, power and authority are applied through the formal machinery of

[1]The question of legitimacy is a vexing one, for it is easy to assume that what is legitimate also has the approval of most members of society. In simpler societies legitimacy tends to correlate closely with general assumptions of what is good and proper, but in more complex structures this relationship is not always as evident. Perhaps we can define legitimacy as the obedience given to laws and usages when the majority of the people consider them reasonable. To a greater or a lesser extent, this obedience is given for reasons other than fear of punitive action, but it would be extreme to claim that laws are always validated in the minds of all the people. The use of alcohol during Prohibition is a case in point, and more recently we have the example of marijuana.

(above) In all complex societies, the legal system depends on full-time specialists who interpret the law as a highly formalized structure. This photograph of the Supreme Court of the United States underscores the distinction between "law" and "custom." (The Supreme Court Historical Society)

(right) Adjudication in tribal societies often involves councils charged with the responsibility of aiding the settlement of conflicts. Members of the council of elders surrounding this West African chief are wise in traditional usages and are not solely legal figures. The elders are also important in other domains, such as politics, religion, and economics, for in simpler societies, law is embedded in the total social system. (Peabody Museum, Harvard, photograph by Hillel Burger)

government and legal codes; in simpler societies, they tend to rest on custom and be exercised by corporate entities and individuals whose functions are only partly political and legal. Power may thus have its locus in the political and legal structures of a modern nation-state, the deliberations of a tribal council, or the decisions of a lineage group. Obviously, what falls within the orbit of law and politics will vary from society to society; and within a given society, matters that at one point in history may elicit political or legal action may fail to do so at other times.

In general, though, the more complex a society is, the greater is its degree of control over individuals and, in a legal and political sense, the more residual is the influence of such social components as communities and families. When we speak of complex societies we are in fact referring to a structure of political organization within which power is highly concentrated, the sphere of individual action is limited, and the legal and political influence of groups is severely circumscribed. While there are major differences between complex societies past and present, the state is the great divide between "simple" and "complex" societies, and it largely transcends differences of form and style.

This fundamental distinction between simple and organizationally more complex societies has been recognized for more than a century. In 1861 Sir Henry Maine noted that "the movement of the progressive societies [complex state systems] has hitherto been a movement *from Status to Contract*" (1864:165), that is, a relationship between changes in social affiliation and changes in law and government. Essentially the same point was made by Fustel de Coulanges in his classic study of Greek and Roman law, *The Ancient City* (1874; 1864 in its French original).

These differences are more than a reflection of the greater size of states or their more diversified nature when compared to nonstate systems. Not only do states operate through highly specialized agencies

From custom to law

and structures, but rigid distinctions tend to be drawn between those who govern and those who are ruled, the legal apparatus and those subject to laws and regulations. Administration and law is codified in a body of concrete procedures, generally written down as acts, edicts, and laws. Conversely, the power and influence of customary usages—of "custom" or "tradition"—are restricted to areas that the state regards as of secondary importance.

It is often maintained that formal political structures and statute law grew out of such customary usages. While this assumption is correct in an evolutionary sense, law and politics in complex societies are much more than the codification of earlier practices, for not only do they give rise to specialists in social control, but they also remove the power of sanction and of independent political and legal action from other corporate elements in society.

In many ways, formal political and legal structures are the antithesis of social control established through customary usages: customary rules must be clearly known, for they do not depend directly on organized political force. Conversely, a plethora of ill-understood laws and regulations is often characteristic of complex societies, for laws may always be added to the statute books and, even if highly unpopular, stand a chance of being implemented. In Hitler's Germany laws flourished as never before, backed by the full repressive power of the state. In several chapters of detailed description of Soviet law as a harsh instrument of state authority, Aleksandr I. Solzhenitsyn's *The Gulag Archipelago* (1974) makes the reader painfully aware of the extent to which the legal structure of a repressive political system demolishes traditional institutions rather than builds upon them.[2]

[2]Stanley Diamond (1973) is especially effective in reminding us of the political consequences of the modern state. Every piece of habitable land is now under the jurisdiction of some government claiming the right to tax, conscript, or otherwise control the population. The state with its organized monopoly of force has substituted the "rule of law" for the concensual "order of custom."

(left) This scene from a Vermont town meeting exemplifies a form of political organization that involves the direct participation of citizens in the political process. Grass-roots democracy of this type has inspired political theorists for centuries, but few political organizations operate in this manner. (Chris Maynard/Stock, Boston)

(below) The monumental aspect of official Washington buildings projects an image of government as grandiose and powerful but hardly intimate. Since the style is neoclassical, could one consider these edifices as temples of power? (Thomas Brooks/Stock, Boston)

No doubt, some readers will voice the opinion that dictatorial regimes of whatever political orientation cannot, in all fairness, be taken as representative of modern state systems. The objection is certainly valid, but our point is, not that all states behave in the manner of fascist or Stalinist regimes, but rather that these are extreme examples of a phenomenon common to all modern states, where law is not the cutting edge of custom but a mechanism of control of the many by the few.

Perhaps it will also be objected that in many modern societies the dangers of impersonal "big government" are fully realized and that the electoral process, which assures a periodic and orderly change of those who administer rules, does offer the ordinary citizen some say in political affairs. These are valid points, but they do not go to the heart of the question. Even in the most democratic contemporary societies, a very substantial gap exists between the realities of power and the myths of popular political input. Laura Nader is correct in noting that

a democratic framework implies that citizens should have access to decision-makers, institutions of government, and so on. This implies that citizens need to know something about the major institutions, government or otherwise, that affect their lives.

Most members of complex societies and certainly most Americans do not know enough about, nor do they know how to cope with, the people, institutions, and organizations which most affect their lives (Nader 1972:294).

Not only is grass-roots involvement rare in affairs of government and matters of law, but a reasonable argument can be made that those who manage these institutions are not at all pleased to have ordinary citizens involved in their deliberations. It is certain that the control exercised by modern states contrasts very sharply with the reduced power and authority of higher-level institutions in earlier times. As an illustration, the right of private vengeance was a well-entrenched early European usage, as it continues to be in many simpler societies. Until well into the Middle Ages, individuals not only had the right but the obligation to avenge the killing of a kinsman. A settlement could be made by the perpetrator of the deed by paying a stipulated sum to the family of the victim. The dispute could also be settled by exacting a life for a life, a procedure that was held to be fully legitimate and legal. In such a context a family retained rights of sanction as a corporate entity. By the thirteenth century, however, only the nobility could legally seek redress of this type. According to a medieval commentator writing in 1290:

War, by our custom, cannot take place between bondfolk or between citizens. Therefore, if quarrels or defiance or fightings arise among them, they must be judged according to the misdeed; for they cannot plead the right of war. If so be that one such had killed another's father, and the son, after this misdeed, killed the man who had slain his father, then he would be judged for the manslaughter. . . . For gentlefolk alone can wage war, as we have said above (quoted in Coulton 1925:188).

Our point, lest we be misunderstood, is not that feuds are an ideal way to resolve con-

flicts but that by the end of the thirteenth century the right of blood revenge had been abolished for the ordinary folk and survived only among the aristocracy, who alone enjoyed sufficient independence from the authority of the state and its agencies to exercise this right. Eventually, with the growing power of the state, even "gentlefolk" were made subject to the same laws as other people.[3]

All the anthropological evidence at our disposal indicates that human society can operate only in the matrix of rules specifying the rights and obligations of its constituent members and of recourses for settling disputes and resolving conflicts. We should not mistake these fundamental requirements of social control for "government" as we would normally understand it: as Paine correctly noted, government is a relatively modern accretion to society. Furthermore, modes of social control and conflict resolution tend to correlate fairly closely with the organizational complexity of sociocultural systems.

ORDER IN BAND-LEVEL
SOCIETIES

As we noted in an earlier chapter, the simplest form of social organization is encountered in bands of collectors and hunters. These are genuinely small societies, and yet all cultural functions find expression in units that at the most consist of a few associated bands. What is distinctive in band-level societies is the absence of institutional elaboration. In the economic realm, every able-bodied person collects or hunts. Food distribution is achieved through established reciprocal relations within the kin

[3]Even in some modern nations there remains a residue of this archaic right of personal vengeance. For example, in France, the perpetrator of a crime of passion—typically an individual who attacks an unfaithful spouse or the spouse's lover—is often acquitted on the grounds that the circumstances were overwhelmingly mitigating.

group or residential camp. The economy is thus not a separate sphere of life but a subsistence activity that all engage in. Much the same holds true for what we might term political and legal behavior. It would be hard to identify political or legal machinery, for bands operate without institutionalized leadership, social hierarchies, and legal specialists or institutions. Nevertheless, these are societies with rules and sanctions; and, as in all human aggregates, conflicts occur between individuals and disputes are resolved in culturally approved ways.

Granted this absence of political and legal institutions, how do such societies function? Part of the answer is that many of the needs that these specialized institutions meet (or generate) in more complex societies are absent among hunters and gatherers. This difference is well illustrated by an examination of property and property rights. Not only do band-level societies lack the technological means of accumulating surpluses but, given the nature of the subsistence base, no individual or group of individuals has it within their power to control significantly greater resources than other individuals or groups. As a result, one of the major areas of political and legal considerations in more complex sociocultural systems is severely curtailed.

Furthermore, in all hunter-gatherer societies, an extremely high cultural value is placed on reciprocity. This is a highly adaptive strategy, for only by sharing can the luck of some in the food quest be balanced against the misfortune of others. For an individual not to share poses an evident danger to his own survival and the survival of the group. Food may be relatively plentiful, but security depends on the resources of the group being pooled.

As to control over others, again both the means and the inclination are absent. Not irrelevant here is the observation that no individual need remain a member of the band against his or her will: in most cases, all that the dissatisfied person has to do is to pick up his or her personal gear and move away to join another band. Splitting, generally referred to as flux, or fission, in the ethnographic literature, has clear political implications. It is also a means of conflict resolution, since enemies are not forced to live as members of the same social entity.

The attitude of hunters and collectors toward property is also germane to questions of interpersonal conflict. As Morton H. Fried has noted:

As has long been understood despite occasional statements of denial or ridicule, there is a definite relationship between the concept of individual property and crime. . . . The significant sources of food available to simple societies are not foreclosed to any member of the group and . . . usually are available to outsiders as well. Whatever men and women may fight about in egalitarian societies, it cannot be land (Fried 1967:71–72).

Actually, stealing is extremely rare, and in most reported instances it is treated as a breach of good manners rather than something that poses a danger to the fabric of society. There are, of course, other causes of conflict at the band level, but property is not one of them.

The small size of bands and the interdependence of individuals within them results in a situation where group pressures tend to be very strong. The paradox of band-level societies is that while domination of one individual by another is hard to achieve, it is equally difficult for a person to survive alone for more than a short time. Radcliffe-Brown has noted that in small-scale societies "there is first the sanction of moral coercion as distinguished from physical coercion; the individual who does wrong is subjected to open expressions of reprobation or ridicule by his fellows and thus is shamed" (1940:xvi). While the use of shame as an instrument of social control is amply demonstrated in many cultures, including some highly complex societies, it is refined and highly elaborated among many hunter-gatherer groups.

The effectiveness of such sanctions does not preclude a significant role for leaders. However, leadership as such is not institutionalized and the authority of leaders comes primarily from moral force and their capacity to achieve in themselves the cultural ideals of the group. Hence, any separation from the community at large is eschewed by individuals who aspire to—or, as is more often the case, are forced to perform—leadership functions. The difference between leadership of this kind and the type that one may encounter in tribal societies, where authority is vested not only in the individual but in the post he fills, is well brought out in a discussion by Elman R. Service:

Sometimes a person combines high degrees of skill, courage, good judgment, and experience so that his very versatility in a variety of contexts might give the appearance of authority of full chiefship. But even in such a case, this is not an *office*, a permanent position in the society. Rather, it depends entirely on his personal qualities, real or ascribed—power of the sort usually called *charismatic*. But just because the position is personal rather than a post, he cannot truly command. He can only hold the position so long as people respect him and listen to him; it is a kind of moral influence that he wields (Service 1975:52; author's emphasis).

The attributes of a leader are well illustrated in the case of Toma, a man of influence among the Bushmen. Elizabeth Thomas in describing his case, states:

No Bushman wants prominence, but Toma went further than most in avoiding prominence; he had almost no possessions and gave away everything that came into his hands. He was diplomatic, for in exchange for his self-imposed poverty he won the respect and following of all the people there (Thomas 1959:183).

If we had to look for words in our own vocabulary applicable to such individuals, we would probably come up with something like *chairperson* or *spokesperson*, although even these terms imply institutions and structures that do not exist among the Bushmen. The Eskimo often refer to an important man as "he who thinks," a description that rightly places the stress on wisdom and persuasion.

Can one speak of a legal system in such societies? The answer to this question depends very much on one's definition of the term *law*. In much the same way, and for exactly the same reasons, that band-level societies have no internal political organization, they lack formal legal structures. It is not simply that there are no courts, judges, or policemen, but that one would search in vain for something approaching an inflexible code of conduct. In a practical sense, there are no systematic ways of calling witnesses, presenting evidence, or passing judgment. Cases are not "heard" (in our sense of the word), nor is any individual vested with the power of enforcing legal abstractions.

Management of conflict among the Eskimo

Nevertheless, disputes do take place and the most important ones are settled in the public arena. Each disputant, for it is typically two individuals at odds, attempts to harness public opinion in favor of his or her cause. The methods that are used to achieve this end vary from society to society, but they have much in common with performances and often involve the subtle use of language, wit, and sarcasm. This aspect of conflict resolution is especially well developed among the Eskimo, where song duels are used to dispose of a whole variety of grudges and disputes. In these song contests,

the singing style is highly conventionalized. The successful singer uses the traditional patterns of composition which he attempts to deliver with such finesse as to delight the audience to enthusiastic applause. He who is most highly applauded is "winner" (Hoebel 1954:93).

One such song duel has to do with a dispute over a woman. E—— has married the divorced wife of K——. K—— wants her back but E—— will not give her up, and a song duel ensues:

K——

Now shall I split off words—little, sharp
words
Like the wooden splinters which I hack off
with my ax.
A song from ancient times—a breath of the
ancestors
A song of longing—for my wife.
An impudent, black skinned oaf has stolen
her,
Has tried to belittle her.
A miserable wretch who loves human
flesh—
A cannibal from famine days.

E——, *in his defense, replied:*
Insolence that takes the breath away
Such laughable arrogance and
effrontery.
What a satirical song! Supposed to
place blame on me.
You would drive fear into my heart!
I who care not about death.
Hi! You sing about my woman who
was your wench.
You weren't so loving then—she was
much alone.
You forgot to prize her in song, in
stout, contest songs.
Now she is mine.
And never shall she visit singing,
false lovers.
Betrayer of women in strange
households.[4]

(Hoebel 1954:94–95)

This song duel is of interest on a variety of grounds. It is not only a good example of conflict transferred to the idiom of public performance but pinpoints what seems to be a major area of interpersonal conflict in

band-level societies, jealousy—sexual jealousy and control over women, in particular (Fried 1967:75). Conflict over things, on the other hand, is extremely rare.

The winner of a song duel does not automatically receive restitution. However, he or she does reap considerable public prestige, and this counts for much. Other mechanisms exist, among the Eskimo and in other simple societies, to manage conflict. Even without formal song duels, techniques of shaming and ridicule can be extremely effective. Peter Freuchen, who lived for decades among the Greenland Eskimo, writes that while the Eskimo of the Thule region no longer "have song competitions where the offended one challenges his adversary to the beat of the drum," the basic rule remains "that to improve the one who shames society one must make him appear ludicrous. No Eskimo . . . can bear this. He finds it so utterly horrible that people laugh at him that he promptly tries to improve" (Freuchen 1961:175). A very similar observation is made by a biologist who resided among the Caribou Eskimo of Canada: "A small dose of ostracism usually brings the culprit to an acute awareness of his defects" (Mowat 1952:198).

Homicide and sorcery are other ways in which grudges are worked off in band-level societies, but these are recognized as antisocial acts and sometimes bring death to the offender—an individual is selected to terminate the life of the person responsible for such activities. But even in such cases where the offender is killed, the killing is done more in pity than in anger.

In these ways, band-level societies—without formal political or legal structures—are able to maintain social equilibrium and channel human behavior. Social control is achieved, not by vesting power in specific individuals and discrete institutions, but by making society as a whole the arbiter of correct conduct. This calls for socialization processes that stress shame and internalized guilt. It is not the fear of physical coercion that assures culturally approved behavior

[4]E. Adamson Hoebel, *The Law of Primitive Man; a Study in Comparative Legal Dynamics* (Cambridge, Mass.: Harvard University Press, 1954). © Copyright, 1954, By the President and Fellows of Harvard College. Originally published in Knud Rasmussen, Grønlandsagen (Berlin, 1922), pp. 235–236. Reprinted by permission of Harvard University Press.

but the fear of mockery, ridicule, jokes, and gossip.[5] The aim of such mechanisms of control is not to punish but to make clear the foolishness of deviating from accepted norms of behavior (Foulks 1972:48). In cases where an individual poses a physical and, sometimes, a supernatural threat to the community, the death of the offender may be deemed necessary, but this is seen as a terrible task:

Perhaps three or four men, usually those most closely related to, or most closely concerned with the murderer, meet and speak indirectly of the problem which faces the entire community. One of their number is usually designated as the executioner. But he is not an instrument of justice as we know it, for his task is not to punish, but to release the soul of the madman from a physical life which can only end in agony of the flesh if it is prolonged (Mowat 1952:199–200).

While these words were written with reference to the Eskimo, they have a general applicability to band-level societies, for hunting and collecting groups cherish life and take it only as a last resort.

THE FORMALIZATION OF POWER

In band-level societies it is possible for some individuals to achieve more influence than

[5]Perhaps because of this extreme emphasis on ridicule as a mechanism of social control, some observers are of the opinion that individuals in band-level societies exhibit a high degree of self-consciousness. This has been linked to certain abnormal psychological states—often lumped together as "arctic hysteria"—encountered with some frequency among North American and Siberian groups. In part, these may be understood as a psychological defense countering the overwhelming pressure of group opinion—an escape mechanism. There are, however, other hypotheses that have been brought forward to account for these conditions, including extreme environmental stress and dietary deficiencies among northern hunters. Be this as it may, abnormal psychological states are not universal in band-level societies but are probably a culturally defined response found only in certain regions.

their peers, but potentially any individual can aspire to prominence since talent, broadly defined, is the sole condition for leadership. Furthermore, leadership is ephemeral and lasts only as long as the society—always small, always changing—finds it of practical value. It is easy to understand, therefore, that the fruits of leadership in band-level societies hardly pose much of a temptation and that many individuals are pressed into leadership roles rather than actively seek them.

This situation changes, however, with even relatively simple societies that do not depend on hunting and collecting. The roots of institutionalized allocation of power are solidly bedded in economic imperatives, and it is easy to understand why this should be the case. Only when resources and, in particular, food, can be accumulated beyond the needs of an individual or family, is it possible for a person to establish a superordinate-subordinate relationship with others of the group. This statement might strike some as overly materialistic. Surely, there must be many qualities, many valued attributes, that cannot be reduced to items of consumption? Indeed there are, but this fact does not really contradict our initial statement. If in a given society, titles or genealogies are considered attributes of value, if the right to tell a myth or perform a ceremony are treated as property, or if great prestige accrues to the owner of a ceremonial object, we are witnessing a transference of a concept derived from the treatment of "goods" to other domains of perceived "scarcity."

Among other characteristics, it is this concept of scarcity that one misses in band-level societies. Although there may be times of plenty and times of famine, all bellies will be equally full or equally empty; or if some are emptier than others, it is by individual choice and not by social design. The societies we are concerned with in this section are tribal rather than band-level. Tribes—it will be remembered from an earlier chapter—fall in organizational complexity between bands and states, a range that covers a wide conceptual category from societies that are not much more elaborate than bands, to chiefdoms with political structures integrating thousands of individuals. In virtually all instances, however, tribal societies are dependent on domesticated plants and/or animals, the exception being those very few with especially bountiful hunting or fishing grounds such as the Indians of the Northwest coast.

As with bands, the elementary domestic unit—the household—is important in all spheres of life, including social control. But these units, although enjoying substantial autonomy, are linked through ties of kinship and residence into lineages and communities. We have already noted that the major organizational principle in tribal societies is the lineage system and that, depending on the degree of organizational elaboration, tribal cohesion may be more or less evident.

Headmanship

While not all tribes have an elaborate system of social stratification, positions of prestige are limited in number, if for no other reason than that rank carries obligations (as well as privileges) that not all can aspire to. In this respect, it is useful to examine leadership in some societies without the formal institutions of chieftainship, which typically is a hereditary position. In many small-scale horticultural societies, the local political leaders are better thought of as *headmen,* or—using the term often applied in Melanesia—*big-men*. The authority of such individuals is frequently not much greater than that enjoyed by leaders of bands. For instance, among the Koaka speakers of Guadalcanal, "the headman's only strength lies in his influence over the villagers" (Hogbin 1964:63). While such a leader can be said to persuade rather than rule, the post is one surrounded by considerable dignity:

Usually he is easy to recognize. He is of mature years, over forty, at least; he carries himself with assurance and dignity; he lives in the most solidly built of the houses; he is outstandingly hospitable; on special occasions he may wear strings of shell discs below each knee and bracelets of porpoise teeth; and in former times, he would have had several wives (Hogbin 1964:62).

Clearly, he is not simply a dignified individual but one with considerable resources at his disposal. The two attributes are not unrelated, for the capacity to accumulate surpluses is one of the keys to leadership in this society. How is such wealth acquired? Among the Koaka, as with other neighboring Melanesian and New Guinea societies, the would-be leader first mobilizes his kinfolk to grow vegetable supplies and raise pigs. Pigs eat much the same food as humans, and as the acreage under cultivation grows, so does the size of the pig herd. In due course, this expansion in activities becomes a clear indication that the individual desires to become a man of renown. If with the aid of his relatives, he succeeds in becoming a village leader, he may then decide to compete with headmen from other villages in competitive feasts and sumptuous gift giving. In these enterprises, he will be supported by the village, for all members of the community can then bask in his reflected glory. Economic and political ascendancy is facilitated by numerous wives, since it is women who raise the pigs and do much of the garden work.

Not all simple agricultural societies dispose of their surpluses in the same manner. Even in New Guinea and Melanesia accumulated food supplies are put to a variety of uses—the prestige of headmen, massive communal feasts, and the propitiation of ancestors being some of the variant rationalizations for cycles of accumulation and consumption. The point to keep in mind is that such patterns involve not only the consumption of accumulated surpluses but also the harnessing and organization of much human effort.

This linkage of political and economic domains is brought out very clearly in Roy A. Rappaport's *Pigs for the Ancestors* (1967), a masterly examination of the relationships between ecological constraints, religion, and

politics among the New Guinea Maring, a society with broad similarities to the Koaka speakers. In both groups pork is the luxury food, and pigs are carefully raised to be slaughtered and consumed at great feasts of definite political significance, among the Maring not only as shows of wealth but also to cement war alliances. The general theme in such communities and societies can be paraphrased as "beggar thy neighbor"— force your opponents to concede your greater power and make demands upon rank inferiors within your community (Codere 1950; Newman 1965; Oliver 1955; Sahlins 1962, 1963). In many such exchange relationships, the symbolic importance of the objects is of more consequence than their

The pig feast is a most important event in the ceremonial life of the Dani of West Irian (Indonesian New Guinea). Here a Dani big-man is about to kill one of his pigs, to be distributed and eaten during the forthcoming feast. (Robert Gardner/Film Study Center, Harvard University)

material worth. Philip Newman, noting that the Gururumba of New Guinea may give the impression of being "thing-oriented," comments that "the Gururumba might more accurately be characterized as 'exchange-oriented,'. . . for they appear more concerned with controlling the flow of objects than with the objects themselves" (Newman 1965:52–53).

What we have been sketching out is a fairly rudimentary political system that not only allows but stimulates the concentration of power in the hands of a number of individuals whom we have referred to as *headmen*. Becoming a headman involves the conscious application of strategies of control over material and human resources. With some anthropological license, we may liken this situation to a primitive version of a board game: perhaps not everyone can play, but compared to more elaborate organizational structures, the field is relatively open. Objects and resources flow to successful individuals who then redistribute them to followers, friends, and allies; big-men rise and fall as a result of the pressure of competition and the fortunes of war. There are clear political privileges but, in general, the mechanisms for the transfer of power are poorly developed (the son of a leader does not automatically become a big-man himself); and it is not easy to restrict competition for leadership positions.

Through their manipulative activities, Melanesian big-men manage to amass what Bronislaw Malinowski once termed a "fund of power," much as one might build up a bank account. However, this power is based on personal authority, real enough, but not vested in a clearly determined office. One can contrast this with societies having a much more institutionalized leadership structure in which the officeholder fills an established position of power. For instance, in traditional Polynesian societies, such as those of Samoa, New Zealand, and aboriginal Hawaii, chiefs behaved in ways not unlike Melanesian big-men: they dispensed goods and favors, maintained an appropriate dignity, and mobilized kin and community resources in a manner designed to reflect their rank. The difference was that Polynesian chiefs were, as the saying goes, "to the manner born," for the offices were inherited and the chief's call on human and material resources was never in question.[6]

Chieftainship

Power so firmly entrenched, so sharply demarcated, can come very close to a monarchical system, especially when a hierarchy of

Two chiefs of the Aburi region, Ghana, attending a local harvest ceremony. They are carried on portable thrones and shaded by parasols. Other symbols of chiefly office are in evidence. (UNESCO/Marc Riboud)

[6]We have to distinguish here between the office and the officeholder. It is not the privileges of the office that are in dispute; individual chiefs, however, may well be perceived as overstepping the prerogatives of rank.

lesser and more important chiefs is established. Whether the most evolved chiefdoms can be regarded as primitive states—a term that has been suggested by Service (1975) as applicable to several polities in Africa, Oceania, and native North America—depends on the definition of state. We prefer to use the concept of paramountcy, which recognizes hierarchies of power and yet implies that the position of paramount chiefs is not so supreme that lesser chiefs are not tempted to aspire to them. Even well-organized and established chiefdoms lack the organizational foundations, "the power of the state," that reinforce stability and continuity. In fact, as chiefdoms grow in size, the fissionable tendencies that are present in such political structures become more pronounced (Service 1975:102). Sahlins has described this situation with reference to Polynesian societies:

Advanced Polynesian political systems were overtaxed. In Hawaii and other islands cycles of centralization-decentralization appear in the traditional histories: periodic violent dissolutions of larger into smaller chiefdoms and, by the same means, periodic reconstitution of the great society. . . . The expansion of a chiefdom seems to have entailed a more-than-proportionate expansion of the administrative apparatus and its conspicuous consumption. The ensuing drain on the people's wealth and expectations was eventually expressed in an unrest that destroyed both chief and chiefdom (Sahlins 1968:92–93).

It is very easy for the outside observer or the reader of ethnographic reports and early travel accounts to equate chiefs with kings and chiefdoms with kingdoms in pre-industrial societies. The analogy, however, is incomplete and inaccurate. In part, the difference is technological. The economic base of relatively simple societies contrasts sharply not only with modern states but with archaic civilizations. The surpluses that can be skimmed from primitive agricultural systems are limited, and chiefs lack the specialist administrators—clerks, tax collectors, and the like—who facilitate the day-to-day running of large-scale organizations. Messages and instructions must be relayed by word of mouth and seldom does one find even fairly rudimentary methods of record keeping, not to mention written documents. Basically, chiefdoms are not so much mini-states as tribal societies operating at the limits of efficiency allowed by traditional organizational links, in particular those of kinship.

Authority vested in lineages

As we noted in our discussion of tribal societies, their design can, and does, take a variety of forms, from the politically fragmented Melanesian societies to the ranked lineage systems found in Polynesia, central Asia, and parts of Africa. Lineages, however, do not have to be ranked in order of prestige and importance, and many tribes are composed of loosely related lineages, each operating as an essentially autonomous corporate group without a paramount authority. Such lineages may cooperate in cases of dire necessity, but only for the occasion and in the absence of a permanent superordinate chiefly authority. Typically, lineage heads exercise authority over their descent group, a control that results in the situation of there being "tribes" without "chiefs." Writing of the Tallensi people of the northern Gold Coast (Ghana), M. Fortes noted in 1940:

Twenty-five years ago there was no one who had authority over all the Tallensi; no one who could exact tax, tribute or service from all. They never united for war or self-protection against a common enemy. They had, in short, no "tribal" government or "tribal" citizenship, no centralized State exercising legislative, administrative, juridical and military functions in the interests of the whole society (Fortes 1940: 240–241).

If this is a situation common to many tribal societies, one may well ask how at least the minimal requirements of an ordered life are maintained. Given the rule of exogamy, communities and localities are often made up of a number of unilineal descent groups. This imposes ties that crosscut lineage divisions, and much the same can be said for other links that unite individuals and families, such as trade and ceremonial networks. Thus marriage and other external relationships allow for the establishment of alliances, while common village membership may bring together individuals drawn from a variety of lineage groups. In societies lacking relatively developed political structures, these crosscutting dyads and group relationships bring people from different lineages together for common action. Again, with respect to the Tallensi,

segments bitterly opposed on divergent interests unite vigorously on matters of common interest. Co-members of any unit have a common interest in one another's welfare and in safe-guarding one another's rights. Any of them will take reprisals for a wrong done against another (Fortes 1940:251).

This generalization is illustrated with the specific case of ritual cooperation in another African society, the Ndembu of Zambia:

By establishing ties of co-participation in cults which operate independently of kinship and local linkages, the ritual system compensates to some extent for the limited range of effective political control and for the instability of kinship and affinal ties to which political value is attached (Turner 1957:291).

The societies we have been discussing encompass a wide range of cultural variation and organizational complexity. While it is not feasible to offer broad generalizations concerning dispute settlement and related matters as we have done for band-level societies, there are trends, patterns, and regularities in the juridical process that have special relevance for tribal societies.

Management of conflict on the tribal level

To begin with, many of the same causes of interpersonal conflict found among hunter-gatherers persist in tribal societies and are at least in part dealt with through similar mechanisms. Public pressure is a force in all small-scale societies—an observation that applies not only to tribespeople but also to villagers in peasant communities (Foster 1972).

However, as we move beyond the sphere of the community, the more highly institutionalized the political structure becomes, the more formal, structured, and organized the juridical process is likely to be since both government and law are closely interlinked. The fact that the leaders of tribal societies do not enjoy a monopoly of power and authority is a critically important consideration, for it influences both the aims and the methods of the juridical process. Where power is fragmented and likely to be questioned, it is difficult for even the most firmly established leaders to take upon themselves the full responsibility of adjudication. Tribal chiefs may be garbed in the dignity of office, but they have to rule with the knowledge that in dealing with individuals they are also touching members of politically significant social entities. Hence, in cases of disputes, to rule for one disputant against another may lead to cleavages and factionalism. This is especially the case in segmentary lineage systems where would-be judges are constantly faced with the dilemma of defendants who have kinsmen who are willing to support their interests—by force if necessary.

Typically, this problem is resolved by placing responsibility for the resolution of disputes on individuals or groups that can be said to act for the society as a whole: go-betweens, elders, councils, lineages, and, very often, the supernatural. This is not to say that politically important figures abdicate all responsibility for law enforcement, for their influence is still bound to count. Rather, what we observe is the presence of mechanisms that reduce the stress on the social fabric imposed by disputes.

Under the watchful eyes of the go-between (squatting), an Ifugao of northern Luzon, Philippines, is undergoing an ordeal by boiling water that will determine his guilt or innocence in a case brought against him. (Lowie Museum of Anthropology, University of California, Berkeley)

One way in which this is accomplished is through oaths and ordeals. An *oath* is a formal declaration calling upon the supernatural to witness to the truth or sincerity of what one says: an *ordeal* is a means of determining guilt or innocence by submitting to some dangerous trial or test. Oaths have been incorporated into the legal system of many complex societies as a degree of protection against perjury, but ordeals seem to be linked functionally to political and legal structures intermediate in complexity between bands and states:

. . . ordeals are characteristically associated with higher political integration, but these societies, particularly the African ones, are known for having problems with succession and the maintenance of continuous general authority (Roberts 1965:209).

"Trials" of much the same type, by ordeal or by combat—on the assumption that God supports the innocent—were very much a feature of the legal process in medieval Europe. Their use in Europe reflects a similar structural situation of weak centralized authority, the political importance of kin groups (especially among the aristocracy), and the division of society into strong subunits with a propensity to revolt against the authority of weak state institutions.

A fairly common procedure designed to achieve settlement between contesting parties was described by R. F. Barton (1919) for the Ifugao, who live in northern Luzon, Philippines. If the two parties to a dispute failed to reach a mutually satisfactory solution to their quarrel, a go-between was engaged. The function of this individual was not unlike that of the ombudsman, who is increasingly called upon to act as a mediator in modern complex societies. The go-betweens, persons respected for their skills of negotiation and persuasion, would visit back and forth between the disputants, trying to work out a settlement. In many instances they would be successful, but since they had no power of enforcement, even their good offices were not always able to bring the parties together. In such cases, after a period of compulsory truce, a feud was the only means of redressing wrongs.

It is understandable that the aims of law in tribal societies will contrast substantially with those found in more centralized and impersonal systems of political control and law enforcement. While it may at times prove necessary to decide between the claims of rival disputants, the tendency is to achieve a settlement rather than pronounce one individual guilty and another innocent. Hence, persuasion, argument, protracted debate, and compromise are typical procedures. The goal is to reestablish some degree of harmony between contesting individuals of adversary social units, for in close-knit societies it is more important to maintain social cohesion than to determine questions of guilt.

We have not examined all the varieties of juridical procedures encountered in tribal societies, nor have we posed the question of whether it is valid to speak of "law" in such contexts. The forms vary enormously, from situations in which it would be difficult to abstract a body of practices and usages that could be designated a "legal system" to cases where issues of social control are determined by fairly well-defined institutions. Some of these may indeed closely approximate elaborate court systems, as among the Bantu-speaking and other peoples of equatorial and southern Africa, who have

employed such concepts as witnesses, cross-examination, and the right of appeal.

THE STATE

We began this chapter with a quotation from Thomas Paine that makes the very valid distinction between the state—government—and society and goes on to highlight one of the distinguishing characteristics of state systems: the great concentration of power and authority inherent in the organization of the state. We then made reference to Sir Henry Maine's fundamental distinction between simple and complex societies, the former being characterized by "status" relationships, the latter by those of "contract." Although many other analysts have come forward with variations and refinements pertaining to the nature of the state and the critical differences between organizational types—sacred and secular, folk and urban, traditional and modern, being just a few of the designations—the essential elements of state organization noted by the two authors are not in question and remain the social scientists' dominant view of the matter.

The state is a historical development reflecting the growing complexity of social systems and the increasing authority of those in positions of political management. It did not evolve as a response to the supposed inadequacies of simpler systems of law and government and certainly not, as John Locke (1632–1704) would have us believe, as an attempt to establish "a known authority to which every one of that society may appeal upon any injury received or controversy that may arise" (Locke 1937:58). This is good seventeenth-century rationalism, but states are not established as the result of debates or consultations.

There are, and have been, many forms of the state, more than space allows us to examine. Today, and for some centuries past, the dominant form is usually termed the *nation-state*. It combines a high degree of centralized control, clear territorial demarcation, a nationalistic ethos, sharp distinctions between rulers and ruled, highly institutionalized modes of social control framed in a body of statute law, and a concept of sovereign authority. In its most developed form, this is basically a Western development and has been borrowed and emulated worldwide by emerging nations. There are many forms of the modern state, these different models generally being attuned to variations in ideological orientation. We do not imply that these distinctions are matters of little consequence, for they can have a direct impact on social priorities and on the quality of life of citizens. But in the broad comparative perspective, all state systems have much in common and differ radically from simpler organizational forms.

In modern states, governmental authority is in large measure dependent on the threat or use of force, on law rather than on custom. So long as this authority is not challenged, naked force can be kept in the background. Much more usual is the use of mechanisms of indirect manipulation, a procedure greatly facilitated by the influence of the state on the educational system, communications, and the mass media. To a greater or lesser extent, all modern states are in the business of political indoctrination and the management of opinions.

The very complexity of state systems places the ordinary citizen at a great disadvantage. Long before the world split into the contending camps that most of us have grown up with, the novelist Franz Kafka (1883–1924) described the problems that beset modern individuals as they attempt to deal with the isolation and anxiety that accompany involvement with the impersonal agencies of the state. One of his insights on society is that ordinary citizens are never quite sure what is happening to them as they work their way through bureaucratic mazes. In simpler societies, one may have to fear the malice of others, the tricks and turns of enemies, or the evil

Authority in modern states

disposition of witches. But in modern complex societies, those with power, even the most minor officials, are distant and sanctimonious rather than consciously malicious. As for the direct application of force, the state seldom has to depend on the bayonet or the club; sanctions take the form of laws and regulations that seem sufficient unto themselves—"it is the law." Propriety and decorum are thus maintained, and force is latent rather than manifest.

When the realities of power have to be faced, particularly in societies with democratic institutions, the ordinary citizen is likely to be shocked and angered. This was very much the reaction in the United States as the Watergate investigations revealed the power implicit in the executive. How could our government do such things? The relatively minor figures who faced trial or congressional examination often pleaded a higher authority, or even a higher morality. They were, after all, following the orders of those in direct touch with the highest office in the land; it was as if laws did not pertain to them. It is well to consider that a strange turn of fate has made Adolf Eichmann the best-known apologist for state authority. During his trial in Israel he pleaded that he was simply "following orders" and, furthermore, that in the machinery of Nazi terror he was only a "little sausage."

It is of distinct value, we believe, for people to have some understanding of what life in state societies entails and of the dangers inherent in high concentrations of power. It is equally important to realize, however, that the state is the political unit of the age. This is a truth that has to be lived with. We cannot revert to band-level societies or tribes (all of which now fall within the orbit of some state authority), nor is it realistic to assume that many of us can follow in the footsteps of Henry David Thoreau (1817–1862) and find for ourselves a Walden Pond where we can practice civil disobedience and escape the power of the state. What alternatives we do have are structural and organizational. Our understanding of human social organization suggests that power can be divided between institutions and interest groups, as is done in many tribal societies. While the analogy should not be carried too far, internal diversity is present in all complex societies although it may at times be masked by superordinate authority. At the political level, a functioning pluralism can be aspired to with a system of checks and balances, the test being that the institutions in question actually perform their assigned tasks.

Another observation is that leadership in modern states is much less encumbered by the built-in limitations present in simpler societies. Probably at no time since the inception of the state have political leaders been so well known, or seem to be. Well after the consolidation of modern states, monarchs traveled through their kingdoms on yearly tours to be visible to their subjects, attend celebrations, and receive petitions. Even so, contact was necessarily limited. Today, the media bring presidents, prime ministers, and other heads of government into millions of dwellings. But these links between the leaders and the governed are more apparent than real, for we see and hear only what the leadership wants us to see and hear. Communication in the other direction is notoriously more difficult. The mechanism that is supposed to compensate for this lack of input and influence on the part of the masses is the provision for a regular change of government, usually through election. In this manner, the gap between the individual and society, always much wider in modern states than in less complex structures of government, is presumably narrowed. But the power of the electorate can be weakened or nullified in many ways. It can be coerced into compliance or persuaded to act in a given way by a ruling elite that offers no viable alternatives.

We know that elections in fascist countries are in essence public celebrations rather than acts of power. Similarly, election results in communist countries are designed to show not broad popular support, but

unanimous support. Under certain circumstances, like situations may arise in democratic states. In 1958 a very frightened electorate in France voted overwhelmingly in favor of General Charles de Gaulle and his new constitution.

Authority in traditional non-Western states

We have dealt with some of the problems and some of the characteristics of modern states. As we noted, the pattern is virtually universal today as the result of the spread of Western political ideas. But as with much else that is borrowed, we have to distinguish between the original model and its adaptations. The Western concept of the nation-state assumed that all people were—or should be—ruled by a sovereign authority. As Westerners moved into the non-Western world, they persisted in looking for the political attributes with which they were familiar: agencies and powers with a monopoly of force, sovereign authorities able to negotiate and maintain treaties, fixed territorial boundaries, and formal structures of law and government. It was difficult for Westerners to recognize that not everyone adhered to and felt part of a nation, or that people might be governed other than by an impersonal state.

In due course, it became apparent that many of these concepts were simply not applicable. Nevertheless, the fiction died hard that somewhere, somehow, even if only in rudimentary form, embryonic state institutions could be discovered. Chiefs were assumed to have many of the qualities of monarchs, tribes were treated as nations, and treaties were solemnly entered into with village headmen and clan leaders. There certainly were self-serving aspects involved in these assumptions. For instance, treaties negotiated with native leaders when not carried out in keeping with Western expectations could be used to support the dictum that in "barbaric" societies there was neither "order," "authority," nor "law." The logical conclusion was that where such characteristics were missing, they should be imposed from without.

But Westerners dealt not only with simple societies, but with several types of traditional states that in many instances differed substantially, both in organization and rationale, from the classic European model. Typically, these were also states in decay in which the purported power of the central authority was often more fictive than real. As a case in point, imperial authority in China had been greatly weakened by the middle of the nineteenth century, in part by internal disruptions, in part by the machinations of Western powers. Furthermore, the functions and structures of such states were often of a kind not easily understood by Westerners. In Burma, for instance, the king ruled from the hallowed precincts of the royal palace, which was conceived as the magical-religious center of the universe. According to Lucian W. Pye:

The authority of the king rested clearly
on other-worldly considerations, both
magical and mystical. Within the court
every facet of life reflected awe of
mystical forms and fear of the unpredictable potency of magic. Ceremonies had to
be conducted precisely according to
rituals, and over the years the members
of the court bound and hobbled themselves with an increasingly elaborate code
of manners (Pye 1962:66–67).

For Europeans, even if we grant to them the best intentions, this world must have been difficult to understand. The last independent ruler of Burma owned as his greatest prize a sacred white elephant guarded by no less than a hundred soldiers. This beast lived in a sumptuous palace and was in the keeping of a minister of state whose function it was to provide for its every need— including entertainment by royal dancers and musicians. The elephant was treated regally, but foreign emissaries fared far worse:

Most envoys sent to the Arbiter of Existence [the king of Burma] were treated
very cavalierly in the way of interviews;
not a few in the old days waited long

months without ever seeing the king at all.
All, down to Sir Douglas Forsyth, in 1874,
had to go in shoeless, and sit cross-legged
on the floor, an unaccustomed attitude
which did not tend to render the position
less ridiculous. In other ways they were
treated with every indignity (Yoe
1963:439).

This last quotation is by an Englishman of the period (hardly the most objective observer), but it illustrates admirably the Western impatience with forms of political life that were not in line with the standards of the contemporary nation-state. This aspect of the long history of Western contacts with the rest of the world helps to account for the former Western insistence that where Western concepts of international law and usage were lacking, they should be imposed either by intervention or by annexation of the territories to the then expanding Western empires.

Once incorporation was achieved, Western-style administrative structures were rapidly installed. In due course, both the administrative machinery and the Western concept of the nation-state became entrenched in the non-Western world, even in states that managed to retain their independence. Today the nation-state ideal remains the dominant political model for emerging and recently independent nations. However, underlying Western-derived political concepts are still to be found traditional ideas regarding the nature of the state. The two traditions coexist, though not always harmoniously. As Clifford Geertz has succinctly observed:

As concrete governmental structures,
today's Ghana, today's Indonesia, or
even today's Morocco, have but the most
distant of relations with the institutions of
the Ashanti Confederation, the Javano-
Balinese theatre state, or that motley collection of bodyguards and tax farmers, the
Magrebine Makhzen. But as embodiments
of one or another view of what government and politics are all about, the relation
between traditional states and transitional

ones may be a great deal less distant than the borrowed vocabularies within which third world ideologies are usually stated might lead one to believe (Geertz 1967:13).

The old non-Western states and empires are gone or have been greatly transformed. And although the formal structures of new states and modernized traditional polities are likely to strike the Western observer as close copies of one or another Western state subtype, the assumption that they are in fact the same is not only unwarranted but a potential source of international misunderstanding.

ON WAR

War can be defined as the use of armed force by one society against another or, more broadly, as an instrument of policy used in the resolution of intergroup conflicts. However, what may seem a rather clear-cut concept occasionally becomes somewhat nebulous when one moves from abstractions to specific cases. It is therefore difficult to answer a question that is often posed to anthropologists: Is war a universal feature of human societies?

If the concept of war is restricted to the sanctioned use of force by specialists—warriors or soldiers—serving as agents of society, it is clear that war is the prerogative of political units complex enough to train and maintain such specialists. Many simpler societies, particularly bands and some tribal entities, lack the organizational complexity and material capacity to wage war as so defined.

Such a definition, however, seems unduly limited. Not only does it reflect a range of experience confined to fairly complex societies but it involves the assumption that war can take place only between whole societies. But not all societies are necessarily characterized by internal political cohesion, nor are the political and social boundaries between them always sharp. To get around these

problems, some social scientists differentiate between "primitive warfare" and wars waged by states, whereas others draw the line between conflicts in which one society is pitted against another on the one hand, and such lethal activities as feuds, vendettas, raids, civil wars, and guerrilla wars on the other. These and similar distinctions tend to obscure rather than clarify the concept of war, since they impose a conceptual framework on organized violence instead of examining the nature of this violence. Certainly, such categories resist the test of pragmatic examination, for even if we limit ourselves to nation-states, we have witnessed how "police actions" lead to full-fledged wars.

In many simple societies, armed conflict seldom involves the whole cultural unit, which—as we have indicated—may lack a centralized authority. Much more common is conflict between rival lineages or communities. Even in fairly sophisticated political systems, there may not be an absolute monopoly of force at the disposal of government, as the earlier example from the European Middle Ages shows. The point on which agreement is easy to reach is that the essence of war is organized violence. Although such violence is much more characteristic of some societies than others, its presence or absence does not appear to be directly related to levels of sociocultural complexity. A further characteristic of the violence of war is that it is condoned as "legitimate," at least in the eyes of those who are carrying it out.

Why do people fight wars?

A number of explanations have been put forward to account for war. Some of these can be eliminated as either totally or partially invalid. There is, for example, the very old notion that fundamentally warfare is an irrepressible expression of humankind's innate propensity toward violence—a hypothesis that is once more achieving some vogue through the writings of several well-known students of animal behavior (Ardrey 1961, 1966; Lorenz 1966; Morris 1967). We shall

(right) The Yąnomamö of South America engage in a high level of violence ranging from individual duels to intervillage warfare. The ethos of violence is reinforced by periodic displays in which warriors don appropriate attire and brandish weapons. The Yąnomamö may represent an extreme of bellicosity at the level of conflict possible in societies where the village is the largest political unit. *(Napoleon Chagnon/Anthro-Photo)*

(far right) Warfare as waged by industrial societies is devastating and often impersonal. It requires specialists, elaborate machinery, and "sophisticated" weapons. *(Philip Jones Griffiths/Magnum Photos, Inc.)*

discuss their arguments in the concluding chapter of this book. In the present context, the flaw common to this school of thought is well summed up by Koch:

The concept of aggression as a cause of human warfare differs little from the theological notion of warfare which invokes the devil as the originator of all human mischief. The theory simply cannot explain why people engage in lethal combat, because its main premise (men fight wars because they are aggressive) is tautological (Koch 1974:5).

Compared to theories of instinctive aggression, explanations derived from modern psychology offer an element of insight on individual motivations. For the most part, these theories link war to the release of pent-up frustrations. There is no question that fighting can and does result in the dissipation of frustrations, but to claim that frustrations (or anxieties or tensions) constitute the underlying cause of armed conflict is an altogether different matter. Individually, psychological stress can be dealt with in a variety of ways that may range from getting drunk to committing suicide, from playing practical jokes on authority figures to climbing mountains. On the community level, people may more covertly express aggression by the use of gossip or witchcraft, as among the generally peaceful Pueblo Indians. People fight wars

not because they are frustrated but because they are trained to do so by their culture. There may indeed be psychological satisfactions associated with warfare, but in complex societies at least, boredom rather than excitement is the soldier's usual companion.

If people fight wars because of cultural factors, it is not surprising that some cultures stress warfare more than others and that violence may permeate a society to such an extent that the solution of problems through violent means is part of a generalized behavior pattern. One can be socialized to engage in violence just as one can be socialized to follow the paths of compromise.

War as a
sociocultural
phenomenon

Among the Yąnomamö Indians of southern Venezuela and northern Brazil, who enjoy an anthropological reputation for being fierce, great pride is shown in ferocity, and boys are trained from an early age to behave in the appropriate manner.

The Yąnomamö place a high value on bellicose behavior; all men are obliged to demonstrate their capacity to behave fiercely. This usually takes the form of the stronger pushing the weaker around: threats, intimidation, shouting, chicanery, duels with fists or clubs, and, frequently, just bluffing. Many, however, display their ferocity in the relatively harmless (at least to them) beatings that they administer to their hapless wives (Chagnon 1967:44).

Among the Yąnomamö, violence has become a pivot of interpersonal and intergroup relations, a form of communication. Not only wives and enemies are the potential targets of violent acts but also friends and allies. Chagnon notes that Yąnomamö feasts, which are occasions for cementing alliances, "can potentially end in violence because of the nature of the attitudes the participants hold regarding canons of behavior and obligations to display ferocity" (Chagnon 1968:117). The Yąnomamö case is indeed extreme, but there are other simple societies that place heavy stress on violence as a coercive measure.

The readiness of some groups to resort to war, however, should not obscure the fact that in all instances war is an attempt on the part of some to impose their will on others by the use of force. As such, armed conflict may be viewed as a specialized form of dispute settlement. This may seem to be a contradiction in terms, but only because we associate "settlement" with negotiation and adjudication as ways of resolving disputes. Among the Kapauku Papuans of West New

The extension of a centralized administration into formerly autonomous tribal regions has often been accompanied by recruitment of the local population into military or police units designed to maintain authority and subdue intergroup armed conflict. Shown here are Australian-officered members of the police force of the Trust Territory of Papua New Guinea shortly after World War II. (United Nations from Australian Government)

Guinea (Irian), war is regarded as a necessary evil and is initiated only as a consequence of disputes that cannot be resolved through negotiation:

A war is usually begun by a party injured in an interconfederational dispute. He either tries to secure military support for his cause by pleading with the headman of his political unit, or he may neglect this slow but correct procedure and precipitate a war by starting the fight himself and inducing his relatives and friends to aid him (Pospisil 1963:58).

In state systems, the linkage of diplomacy to war—the continuation of policy by other means—is quite straightforward. In all societies there are rules of war that, although not always obeyed, structure the relationship of disputants. Furthermore, in all societies, wars are concluded and peace is ultimately restored, whether by victory or by negotiation. Disputes that lead to conflict in simple societies are not the disputes that arise between nation-states, but Koch is correct in noting that

Henry A. Kissinger, at that time special White House adviser, shaking hands with Le Duc Tho, the negotiator of the North Vietnamese government, in 1973 following a successful session. These diplomatic negotiations helped pave the way for a termination of the American involvement in the Vietnamese conflict and represent one form of dispute settlement available to contending states. (United Press International)

every social group must cope with conflicts among its members and between itself and other groups. Rather than being something pathological, enmity and disputes are a normal part of social life. A conflict arises when a person or group suffers, or believes to have suffered, an infringement of a right (Koch 1974:13).

Let us make it clear that we are not claiming that war is either natural or inevitable; our point is quite the opposite and has been well stated by Margaret Mead:

. . . we regard warfare as a cultural artifact, which can be used by any human group but is not specifically biologically underwritten. It is a social invention . . . in the same way that the wheel is a social invention, with the probability that it was invented many times by early man, in the course of the development of language, tools, and social organization (Mead 1967:66).

REFERENCES

ARDREY, ROBERT
1961 *African genesis; a personal investigation into the animal origins and nature of man.* New York: Atheneum.
1966 *The territorial imperative; a personal inquiry into the animal origins of property and nations.* New York: Atheneum.

ARISTOTELES
1941 *The basic works of Aristotle.* Richard McKeon, ed. New York: Random House.

BARTON, ROY F.
1919 *Ifugao law.* University of California Publications in American Archaeology and Ethnology, vol. 15, no. 1. Berkeley: University of California Press. Pp. 1–186.

CHAGNON, NAPOLEON A.
1967 Yanomamö social organization and warfare. *Natural History* 76:10:44–48 (December).
1968 *Yanomamö; the fierce people.* New York: Holt, Rinehart and Winston.

CODERE, HELEN
1950 *Fighting with property; a study of Kwakiutl potlatching and warfare, 1792–1930.* New York: J. J. Augustin.

COULTON, GEORGE G.
1925 *The medieval village.* Cambridge: Cambridge University Press.

DIAMOND, STANLEY
1973 The rule of law versus the order of custom. In *The social organization of law.* Donald Black and Maureen Mileski, eds. New York: Seminar Press. Pp. 318–341.

FORTES, M.
1940 The political system of the Tallensi of the Northern Territories of the Gold Coast. In *African political systems.* M. Fortes and E. E. Evans-Pritchard, eds. London: Oxford University Press. Pp. 239–271.

FOSTER, GEORGE M.
1972 The anatomy of envy: a study in symbolic behavior. *Current Anthropology* 13:165–202.

FOULKS, EDWARD F.
1972 *The arctic hysterias of the North Alaskan Eskimo.* Anthropological Studies,

no. 10. Washington, D.C.: American Anthropological Association.

FREUCHEN, PETER
1961 *Book of the Eskimos.* Dagmar Freuchen, ed. Cleveland: World Publishing.

FRIED, MORTON H.
1967 *The evolution of political society; an essay in political anthropology.* New York: Random House.

FUSTEL DE COULANGES, NUMA DENIS
1864 *La cité antique; étude sur le culte, le droit, les institutions de la Grèce et de Rome.* Paris.
1874 *The ancient city: a study on the religion, laws, and institutions of Greece and Rome.* Willard Small, trans. Boston: Lee and Shepard.

GEERTZ, CLIFFORD
1967 Politics past, politics present—some notes on the uses of anthropology in understanding the new states. *European Journal of Sociology* 8:1–14.

HOEBEL, E. ADAMSON
1954 *The law of primitive man; a study in comparative legal dynamics.* Cambridge, Mass.: Harvard University Press.

HOGBIN, IAN
1964 *A Guadalcanal society; the Koaka speakers.* New York: Holt, Rinehart and Winston.

KOCH, KLAUS-FRIEDRICH
1974 *The anthropology of warfare.* Addison-Wesley Module in Anthropology, no. 52. Reading, Mass. Pp. 1–23.

LOCKE, JOHN
1937 *Treatise of civil government* and *A letter concerning toleration.* Charles L. Sherman, ed. New York: Appleton-Century-Crofts.

LORENZ, KONRAD
1966 *On aggression.* Marjorie Kerr Wilson, trans. New York: Harcourt, Brace, and World.

MAINE, SIR HENRY JAMES SUMNER
1864 *Ancient law: its connection with the early history of society, and its relation to modern ideas* (1st Amer., 2nd Engl. ed.). New York: Charles Scribner.

MEAD, MARGARET
1967 Alternatives to war. *Natural History* 76:10:65–69.

MORRIS, DESMOND
1967 *The naked ape; a zoologist's study of the human animal.* New York: McGraw-Hill.

MOWAT, FARLEY
1952 *People of the Deer.* Boston: Little, Brown.

NADER, LAURA
1972 Up the anthropologist—perspectives gained from studying up. In *Reinventing anthropology.* Dell Hymes, ed. New York: Pantheon Books. Pp. 284–311.

NEWMAN, PHILIP L.
1965 *Knowing the Gururumba.* New York: Holt, Rinehart and Winston.

OLIVER, DOUGLAS L.
1955 *A Solomon Island society; kinship and leadership among the Siuai of Bougainville.* Cambridge, Mass.: Harvard University Press.

PAINE, THOMAS
1953 *Common sense, and other political writings.* Nelson F. Adkins, ed. New York: The Liberal Arts Press.

POSPISIL, LEOPOLD
1963 *The Kapauku Papuans of West New Guinea.* New York: Holt, Rinehart and Winston.

PYE, LUCIAN W.
1962 *Politics, personality, and nation building: Burma's search for identity.* New Haven: Yale University Press.

RADCLIFFE-BROWN, A. R.
1940 Preface. In *African political systems.* M. Fortes and E. E. Evans-Pritchard, eds. London: Oxford University Press. Pp. xi–xxiii.

RAPPAPORT, ROY A.
1967 *Pigs for the ancestors; ritual in the ecology of a New Guinea people.* New Haven: Yale University Press.

ROBERTS, JOHN M.
1965 Oaths, autonomic ordeals, and power. In *The ethnography of law.* Laura Nader, ed. *American Anthropologist,* vol. 67, no. 6, pt. 2, Special Publication. Pp. 186–212.

SAHLINS, MARSHALL D.
1962 *Maola; culture and nature on a Fijian island.* Ann Arbor: University of Michigan Press.

1963 Poor man, rich man, big-man, chief: political types in Melanesia and Polynesia. *Comparative Studies in Society and History* 5:285–303.

1968 *Tribesmen.* Englewood Cliffs, N.J.: Prentice-Hall.

SERVICE, ELMAN R.

1975 *Origins of the state and civilization.* New York: W. W. Norton.

SOLZHENITSYN, ALEKSANDR I.

1974 *The Gulag archipelago, 1918–1956; an experiment in literary investigation.* Thomas P. Whitney, trans. New York: Harper and Row.

THOMAS, ELIZABETH MARSHALL

1959 *The harmless people.* New York: Alfred A. Knopf.

TURNER, VICTOR W.

1957 *Schism and continuity in an African society; a study of Ndembu village life.* Manchester: Manchester University Press.

YOE, SHWAY (SIR JAMES GEORGE SCOTT)

1963 *The Burman; his life and notions.* New York: W. W. Norton.

Chapter 14
Economic imperatives

The economic imperatives can be summed up in the message found inside matchbooks advertising home-study courses in meat-cutting: "People must eat." In other words, every society, regardless of its degree of complexity, must find ways of structuring the production, consumption, and exchange of goods and services. When anthropologists look at economics, they see the material support of society and its members not only as the satisfying of utilitarian needs but as a facet of social organization and an integral part of the total culture. This approach does not preclude the identification of regularities in economic systems and the comparison of different modes of production and consumption; it simply asks that economics be analyzed in much the same manner as are other social institutions. With respect to the fundamental issue of subsistence, George Dalton rightly notes that

whatever the human grouping is called, tribe, village, nation, society, it consists of people who must eat to stay alive and

acquire or produce material items and specialist services to sustain social and community life. . . . The acquisition or production of these material items and services necessary for physical and social existence is never left to chance because deprivation means death. All societies therefore have an "economy" of some sort, that is, structured arrangements and enforced rules for the acquisition or production of material items and services (Dalton 1971:31).

Economic theories and simple economies

That all societies have an economic organization in this sense is not questioned by either anthropologists or economists. However, there is far less agreement concerning the nature and function of these arrangements in simple societies. The basic point of contention is the degree to which formal economic theory can be applied to the types of economic organization found in non-Western and nonindustrial societies.

The fact that this argument has been running for a long time (at least since Bronislaw Malinowski wrote about the Trobriand Islands shortly after World War I) without either side convincing the other, would seem to indicate that those involved in it may be speaking at cross-purposes. In part, the lack of consensus has to do with the different meanings attached to the term *economics*. It can be used, of course, to refer to ways of making a living and meeting material needs, but *economics* can also denote quite specific attitudes and organizational principles generally associated with market exchange regulated by price. Notions of price and profit, of sale and purchase, and of credit and debt are part of the vocabulary and conceptual framework of this second meaning. Thus, we are economizing when we scan the shelves of the supermarket and compare unit prices of equivalent goods. By the same token, sellers attempt in various ways to maximize their profits. Ours is a competitive system, an adversary relationship between those who sell and those who buy. We all know that many other factors enter the equation and that it is pure fiction to claim that the market system regulates itself (this was proved in the Great Depression of the 1930s). The point is not how well orthodox economic theory reflects reality but, rather, that it has given rise to certain assumptions and principles that need not be universally valid and applicable to other societies.

Applying Western concepts and categories to simple and traditional societies poses some special problems. Granted that all societies must allocate scarce resources, organizational skills, and human efforts among alternative ends, such allocation may be accomplished in a variety of ways. Eskimo hunters who distribute a newly caught seal in accordance with customary practice (from the moment the animal is killed there are traditional guidelines as to who gets what) are not "marketing" their catch. Furthermore, it may even be that the person primarily responsible for disposing of the animal is not the one who has killed it but an individual who has some culturally recognized claim to it—perhaps the hunter who

struck the first blow, or the owner of the spear or gun that dispatched the seal. In short, the food will be distributed and consumed in a manner that is culturally structured and recognized as legitimate. Robert K. Dentan describes a similar situation among the Semai of Malaya in which a wild pig is killed and brought back to the village, where it is carefully divided into equal portions and distributed to the inhabitants. Rhetorically, he asks:

> The question that immediately occurs to people brought up in a commercial society is, "What does the hunter get out of it?" The answer is that he and his wife get a portion exactly the same size as anyone else gets. No one even says "thanks." In fact . . . saying "thanks" would be very rude (Dentan 1968:49).

Nevertheless, such systems of allocation make eminent sense in band-level societies. It would hardly be practical for the hunter to stuff himself and his immediate family with seal or pig meat and let his kin and fellow band members go hungry; nor, in most instances, would it be possible to store such perishable items for future use. Having been successful, the hunter must perforce share his bounty. These practical considerations, however, do not fully explain the degree to which economic activities form part of a seamless whole with the rest of the culture, or the extreme importance that the exchange of food and other goods has in cementing social relations in simple societies. For these reasons, analogies with Western market systems must be approached with extreme caution. In the examples cited, it is not just food that changes hands but favors and obligations. Although the hunter may appear to go unrewarded for his luck or his good aim, in reality the less he keeps for himself, the more he can count on others and the more he reinforces the cohesion of the group.

Only in hunting and gathering groups are the tasks of production and the benefits of consumption shared equally among the able-bodied. Such simple egalitarian societies are characterized by equally egalitarian economic systems; but in societies with more centralized political control and/or greater differences in social inequality, the forms of distribution and production reflect varying degrees of access to material resources. Throughout this chapter, therefore, our primary concern is what can be termed *political economy*—the economic aspect of social organization.

Since the means of production are closely related to material factors, we shall have occasion to touch on technological variables. Tools and related skills used in the context of a given culture are applied to production tasks, and all technologies and organizational structures have certain potentials and limitations in given environments. Viewed more broadly, all economic systems mediate between society and ecology in the task of providing material support. However, technology is fundamentally a means or an instrument and does not directly determine the distribution of what is produced, for this is guided by social and cultural priorities.

RECIPROCITY

As we have had occasion to note, a distinctive feature of the economic organization of simple societies is the presence of exchange relationships linking individuals and establishing ties between social groups. Anthropologists refer to these mutual exchange relationships as *reciprocity*, and an understanding of the principles underlying this concept is perhaps the chief contribution to comparative economics that anthropologists have made.

What is most striking about reciprocal exchanges is that the individuals involved in activities of this kind do not appear to be preoccupied with either an immediate return or a return that we would normally recognize as of equal value. However, appearances may be deceptive, for they fail to take into account the strong social obliga-

tion that the recipient assumes—namely, to reciprocate in a culturally appropriate manner. Furthermore, to approach reciprocity as a commercial undertaking obscures the fact that there is neither price nor value to primitive exchange in the Western commercial sense. Items or services are not converted into money, nor do the forces of supply and demand play an important role in regulating exchanges.

Reciprocity typically takes the form of gift giving, whether between individuals or such corporate groups as families, lineages, and villages. A gift has the appearance of being voluntary and disinterested but, in actual fact, there is the implicit understanding that it will be returned. The force that compels the recipient to make a return is the full weight of public opinion, made all the stronger by the fact that reciprocal exchanges are only a part of the total exchange network. As Marcel Mauss notes with respect to barter among Polynesians:

Further, what they exchange is not exclusively goods and wealth, real and personal property, and things of economic value. They exchange rather courtesies, entertainments, ritual, military assistance, women, children, dances, and feasts; and fairs in which the market is but one element and the circulation of wealth but one part of a wide and enduring contract (Mauss 1954:3).

Reciprocity in Polynesian societies is elaborate and many-sided, as befits cultures of substantial complexity. Yet the underlying principles governing exchange—that gifts must be offered and received and that such transactions are embedded in the total sociocultural system—find their expression in all societies not regulated by commercial exchange.

In many situations, there is the tendency for partners to over-reciprocate, to return more than was initially received. Writing of the natives of the Andaman Islands, A. R. Radcliffe-Brown observes that the emphasis is placed on generosity that will more than satisfy the debt incurred by the original gift:

The object of the exchange was to produce a friendly feeling between the two persons concerned, and unless it did this it failed of its purpose. It gave great scope for the exercise of tact and courtesy. No one was free to refuse a present that was offered to him. Each man and woman tried to out-do the others in generosity. There was a sort of amiable rivalry as to who could give away the greatest number of presents (Radcliffe-Brown 1922:84).

A crucial factor in the regulation of exchange is that the acceptance of gifts that are not returned debases the recipient and damages the fabric of interpersonal relations. Since gifts are charged with such a strong symbolic meaning, failure to reciprocate can lead to strife. Conversely, the acceptance of a gift is generally taken as a token of peace and friendship. It follows that gift giving that remains unbalanced can be used as a means of achieving political dominance or social prestige. The strategy in such cases is a conscious attempt on the part of the givers to establish themselves as superior to the recipients through the extent of their generosity.

Since gifts carry an implied obligation, and in some societies may even be used as a mechanism marking out inequality, must we conclude that there are no "pure" or "free" gifts? The answer to this question is not simple, for it is necessary to distinguish between the material and nonmaterial aspects of gift giving. A gift is, by definition, a transfer of some scarce material or nonmaterial item, and only by returning a gift of similar significance can the recipient maintain the same relationship with the donor. Only when the roles of donor and recipient are defined as unequal, as that of a child to a parent or a servant to a master, may a gift be considered free. Even so, the gift giver expects something in return, be it affection, or respect, or some other form of recognition.

Some gifts may appear to entail no reciprocity, but on closer examination this is seldom the case. For example, sacrifice (a gift to a supernatural power) is usually made with the expectation of future benefits which are either stipulated as part of a "contractual" arrangement or left to the discretion of the supernatural partner. Charitable gifts are often made to enhance the social position of the giver. However, our point is, not that expectations of reciprocity are selfish or mercenary, but rather that gift giving typically marks a path of close interaction, that it is a kind of social trace element, regardless of the value of the gift or what may be returned for it.

Gifts are thus emotional as well as economic transactions. In our own society gifts have lost most of their economic significance; but in simple societies there is no clear way to differentiate between the ritual, emotional, and symbolic aspects of exchange and those that a Western observer would regard as falling within the domain of economics. For these reasons, primitive exchanges may appear to us to be less than rational. Consider, however, our mutual gift giving at Christmas. If the symbolic value of the tradition is disregarded, exchanging gifts at Christmas can only be considered economically unsound, for it is invariably true that one ends up with presents one has little use for. It would seem much more logical to offer gift certificates or even money to one's friends, for in this way they would be able to buy exactly what they need or want. But how flat these gifts would be, and how much of the quality of Christmas would be lost! Our analogy may be a bit strained, for we do not wish to imply that economic relations in simple societies constitute a string of Christmases. Nevertheless, if it is understood that reciprocity is both a matter of social relationships and a matter of business (and that the former may be more important), the example will have made the point.

One final observation: If the obligation to compensate for a gift is inherent in the

The gifts received at a wedding shower are appreciated not so much for their economic value as for the expression of support and affection for the bride on the part of her relatives and close friends. (Suzanne Szasz)

taking, recipients may find themselves in the difficult position of entering a relationship that is not to their interest. Exchange is cooperation, but cooperation entails friendship. Although gifts mark the paths of close interpersonal links, they can also induce or simulate such links and establish heavy obligations. The intentions behind gift giving are not always benign. In the folklore of many societies we find the phenomenon of the gift given with evil intent, as with the stepmother who presses the poisoned apple on an unsuspecting Snow White. There is more than a little wisdom in this cautionary tale as there is in the adage that parents have for centuries repeated to their children: "Don't take candy from a stranger."

TRADING PARTNERSHIPS

Generalized reciprocity of the type that permeates relationships within band societies and small communities typically takes place between kinfolk or members of closely knit groups. The items exchanged may vary, but the variety of commodities is necessarily limited because the resources of a given area tend to be available to all members of the

society, even if not equally so or at the same time. Hunted food may be exchanged for collected food, or a fisherman may make a gift of part of his catch and at some future date receive in return the products of cultivation.

It is seldom the case, however, that all desirable items are produced by a given small-scale society. Groups without direct access to the sea may still want fish or salt and, conversely, those living by the sea may desire products found exclusively in inland locations—perhaps stone for tools, or forest products. Even if such societies can totally support themselves with food and vital raw materials, goods and wares of external origin may still be in demand.

In situations of this type, where exchange can neither be based on kinship ties nor on common residence, various types of trading arrangements are likely to arise. What is known as *silent trade* is one possibility between groups that have only intermittent contact with one another. Items that one group wishes to trade are left in a designated place and the depositors move to a discreet distance. The would-be partners in this enterprise then inspect the commodities and arrange next to them what they regard

Pygmy women of the Ituri Forest of north-eastern Zaire wearing skirts of cloth and smoking tobacco obtained in trade for their own forest products. (Courtesy of The American Museum of Natural History)

(or hope) are goods of equivalent value. The first group returns and, if satisfied, takes what has been offered in exchange.

Silent trade is generally found in situations where substantial cultural distance separates the participants and more direct interchange is deemed dangerous by one of the two trading groups. It is perhaps first recorded in the writings of the ancient Greek historian Herodotus (fifth century B.C.), who noted that it was practiced by the Carthaginians in their dealings with some African tribal peoples. Since these Mediterranean traders also were in the habit of dealing in slaves, it is not at all surprising that some of their clients were intent upon keeping a safe distance. In recent times, the Pygmies of the Ituri Forest traded in this manner with their much more powerful Bantu neighbors.

The limitations of silent trade are obvious, for in such interchange the security of a binding relationship is replaced by a strategy of distance. Early European trading patterns with simple societies, while not necessarily silent, involved very little communication and in many instances led to conflict and exploitation. Trade of one sort or another is a likely concomitant of all contact situations; and where trade is not structured according to mutually understood patterns, the dividing line between exchange and war is easily crossed. Again and again this gap in understanding is illustrated in the annals of European exploration. For instance, Captain James Cook (1728–1799) on his voyages of discovery recurrently had to cope with natives who assumed that indispensable items of equipment, such as navigational instruments, were subject to trading. These people could not understand why the English captain was unwilling to part with items that appealed to them, regardless of how many pieces of bark cloth, pigs, and other goods they offered in exchange.

The point is that trade between societies without the mediating influence of a commercial market system may easily become difficult and hazardous. One way in which this problem can be resolved is through the establishment of trading partnerships. There are many variations to this arrangement, but basically such partnerships take on many of the symbolic and ritual qualities associated with exchange between kin or community members. Partners stand to one another on a best-friend basis and offer each other protection in their respective home communities. Typically, there is a strong insistence on conducting trade, not for purposes of gain, but simply because exchanging gifts is an honorable thing to do. Such partnerships are started early in an individual's adult career and are maintained throughout the life of those involved. In some instances partnerships may span more than one generation.

The kula ring

The classical description of trading partnerships is contained in Bronislaw Malinowski's account of the trade networks, known as the *kula ring*, that link Trobrianders to other Melanesian communities (see Figure 14-1).

The Kula is a form of exchange, of extensive, inter-tribal character; it is carried on by communities inhabiting a wide ring of islands, which form a closed circuit. . . . Along this route, articles of two kinds . . . are constantly travelling in opposite directions. In the direction of the hands of the clock, moves constantly one of these kinds—long necklaces of red shell, called *soulava*. . . . In the opposite direction moves the other kind—bracelets of white shell called *mwali*. . . . Each of

these articles, as it travels in its own direction on the closed circuit, meets on its way articles of the other class, and is constantly being exchanged for them. Every movement of the Kula articles, every detail of the transactions is fixed and regulated by a set of traditional rules and conventions, and some acts of the Kula are accompanied by an elaborate magic ritual and public ceremonies (Malinowski 1922:81).

It should be noted that each of these two classes of ceremonial trade wares is strictly nonutilitarian. Their importance lies in the fact that they are accorded an arbitrary importance similar to that of heirlooms and jewels in our culture. The owner of a bracelet or a necklace may wear it on special occasions, but otherwise it is kept to be traded to a trading partner at a suitable time in the future. Fundamentally, these are valuable gift items, each with its own history. If this were all that there was to the kula trade, the whole enterprise of trading partners and long voyages in ocean-going canoes would hardly be of major economic significance, however cherished the goods in question. But the kula ring can best be approached as the affective or emotional component of gift

Figure 14-1 The kula ring

A simplified map of the kula ring in which necklaces (*soulava*) travel clockwise and armbands (*mwali*) move counterclockwise. (After Malinowski, 1920)

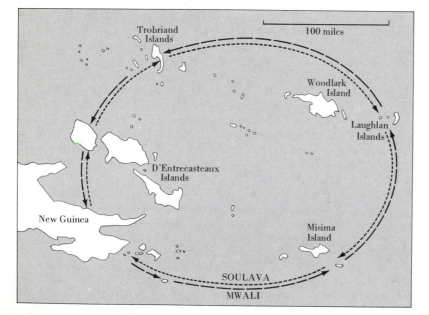

and countergift giving, for the canoes that cross the sea with valuable shells are also freighted with more mundane articles of great practical value—yams, coconuts, pigs, shell knives, and other products of the archipelago. In theory, at least, *soulava* and *mwali* keep circulating forever, but other items of trade are either consumed by those who receive them or in turn passed on by those who acquire them to their trading partners along the kula path. This secondary trade, as Malinowski terms it, entails a good deal of specialization. For instance, the villagers of Gawa Island specialize in the building of ocean-going canoes, which may take from several months to a year and a half to build; ultimately these may end up several hundred miles away, having been exchanged through a chain of trading partners.

In these economic endeavors, the spirit of gift giving and the ideal that it is more honorable to give than to receive are maintained under the umbrella of the ritual exchange of precious shell ornaments. In short, the kula ring with its ceremonial partnerships and circulation of necklaces and bracelets provides the necessary climate of security without which the system could not work.

But the system in question, if we care to look at it in some detail, entails something more than the smooth functioning of individual trading partnerships. While the kula path links individuals who are essentially equal in prestige, some traders are more equal than others. The big traders are the wealthy men of a given community—wealthy because they have bigger gardens with more wives to work them—and their wealth, in turn, permits them to underwrite more extensive expeditions. These expeditions add to their prestige and their local political importance. Since political power facilitates the mobilization of human and material resources, it adds to the trading potential of powerful local men. These different activities constitute a system because they are all interdependent, the function of

each being the part it plays in maintaining the social, political, and economic structure of the society. Kula activities form one feature, and a very important one, of a system that encourages competition for power, wealth, and influence and rewards those who are especially successful. It is not a closed system, except in the sense that only adult males may participate, but it is hardly egalitarian.

TO SUM UP The most significant feature of the kula—and of similar trading arrangements—is that it brings together, through the acceptance of shared values and attitudes, politically autonomous groups. Within the interaction sphere delineated by the kula ring, every type of scarce resource is distributed, not in absolute security, but at least with substantial confidence.

REDISTRIBUTION

In kula exchange and similar forms of trading partnerships items may be diffused over an extensive area, but for all this movement of luxury and utilitarian goods, there is a limit on the control of wealth and resources that even the most successful trader can aspire to. To some degree, this limit is fixed by technological factors. The requirements of subsistence agriculture preclude most individuals from spending uninterrupted periods of time in such activities as canoe building and long trading expeditions. Even more important is the fact that as a pattern of social and economic integration, material exchange links many individuals in horizontal bonds, and consequently no single trader in a given community can come close to controlling the flow of goods and services.

We have already pointed out that in trading partnerships such as those found in Melanesia the individual trader does not work alone, since behind every trader there is a household unit of production. The especially successful trader is likely to be a socially important individual with a number of wives working his gardens, and younger kinsmen associating in his trading enterprises. In general, however, disparities in wealth and social position can be structured much more firmly than in most Melanesian societies, and when this is the case, the major mechanism of social and economic integration is likely to take the form referred to as *redistribution*.

In a sense, redistribution does not represent a radically different form of economic relations; rather, it involves the reorganization of reciprocity to maintain and support the power of locally important individuals. The redistributive principle is based on the upward channeling of goods and services to a king or a chief, who then reallocates them to subordinates or to the community at large. In the majority of cases, redistribution both maintains leaders in the proper style and underwrites the apparatus of government and social control. Sahlins makes a very cogent point in differentiating between reciprocity and redistribution:

Chiefly redistribution is not different in principle from . . . reciprocity. It is, rather, based upon the reciprocity principle, a highly organized form of that principle. Chiefly redistribution is a centralized, formal organization of . . . reciprocities, an extensive social integration of the dues and obligations of leadership. The real ethnographic world does not present us with the abrupt "appearance" of redistribution (Sahlins 1972:209).

Redistributive exchange is usually associated with substantial social stratification, and it is this factor of ranked power positions that gives it its distinctive form. Gifts are still exchanged, but these are not gifts between social equals. Where there is a powerful chieftainship, gifts brought as tribute are rapidly redistributed as rewards and as marks of the chief's generosity. Such a system can help individuals in need—for example, in time of crop failure—and of course every such act of giving on the part of

a chief adds to his renown. According to Audrey Richards, among the Bemba of Zambia,

the prerogatives of a chief consist in rights over the labour of his people, who are required to do a few days' tribute labour each year and to answer sudden calls for help if made; and also claims to tribute in kind, usually paid in the form of an annual present of beer and/or grain, and portions of animals killed in the hunt. It is through this tribute that he is able to pay his advisers, servants, labourers—and soldiers in the old days (Richards 1940:106).

Competitive gift giving

This emphasis on public manifestations of generosity can lead to situations of highly competitive gift giving, best exemplified by the huge feasts sponsored by chiefs of the Northwest Coast tribes. In these *potlatches*, the object was to humble recipients and raise the prestige of hosts. Boasting was not only condoned but expected, and rival chiefs had to throw even bigger affairs or lose face. In fact, the potlatch was a case of a redistributive system run wild, for in order to prove the wealth of the host, vast stocks of valuable items were deliberately destroyed by smashing, burning, or throwing them into the sea.

The ethnographic material from the Northwest Coast (mostly collected toward the end of the last century) can best be understood as the response of a native socioeconomic system to the changes brought about by contact with Western (in this case Canadian) society and institutions. Trade with whites, in particular the Hudson's Bay Company, increased the material goods at the disposal of Northwest Coast Indians just at a time when the Indian population registered a very substantial decline. Moreover, the great natural abundance of the region allowed these groups to devote much of their leisure time to ceremonial activities and the production of a wide array of valuable ritual objects. For some decades, therefore, material abundance characterized the region, even though individual tribes and clans might indeed suffer shortages during any given year.

Although the competitive and destructive character of the potlatch is what most impressed outside observers, including anthropologists, redistribution in the Northwest coast area functioned in much the same way as it did elsewhere. Chiefs had their kinsmen and followers, quantities of goods and supplies were reallocated (not all property was destroyed!), and the political and social position of important personages was reinforced. According to Piddocke:

The potlatch had no one essential function, but several. It redistributed food and wealth. It validated changes in social status. It converted the wealth given by the host into prestige for the host and rank for his numaym [kin group], and so provided motivation for keeping up the cycle of exchanges. The potlatch was, in fact, the linch-pin of the entire system (Piddocke 1965:258).

If the potlatch is viewed as a redistributive feast in essence similar to other such mechanisms found in many tribal societies throughout the world, what requires explanation is not its core features but its destructive aspects. The extreme efforts of chiefs to impress rivals and collect adherents can be linked to the aforementioned decline of population—as a case in point, the Kwakiutl population fell from 23,000 in 1836 to 2,000 in 1886—coupled with the unprecedented amounts of wealth pumped into the potlatch network by foreign settlers and merchants. Remarking on the surfeit of blankets (the famous Hudson's Bay trade blankets exchanged for furs) accumulated by the Kwakiutl of British Columbia, Marvin Harris sums up the situation as follows:

The dwindling population soon found itself with more blankets and other valuables than it could consume. Yet the need to attract followers was greater than ever due to the labor shortage. So the potlatch chiefs ordered the destruction of property in the vain hope that such spectacular demonstrations of wealth would bring the people back to the empty villages. But these were the practices of a dying culture struggling to adapt to a new set of political and economic conditions; they bore little resemblance to the potlatch of aboriginal times (Harris 1974:120).

MONEY AND EXCHANGE

Money as we understand it—a unit of value used for meeting all material obligations—was probably first minted by state authority in ancient Lydia sometime in the seventh century B.C.[1] However, many societies have endowed with value an extraordinary range of objects that fulfill some of the same functions as the dollar in our economy. These items of value take many forms—cacao beans in pre-Hispanic Mexico, cattle in many East African societies, kula shells, potlatch items, and in other societies woodpecker scalps, obsidian blades, pig tusks, tobacco, shark teeth, and dried fish.

Faced with this strange array of moneystuffs, the question is often posed whether, in fact, "primitive money" is really money or something quite different. Phrased in this manner, the question reflects an ethnocentric bias, for the implied standard is a monetary system of an integrated market economy. There is no doubt that such monies differ in both form and origin from francs, dollars, or marks. Still, they do not differ

[1]The invention of coinage is still problematic. However, Lydia, an ancient state of western Asia Minor, seems a good candidate (ancient China is another). We know that the Lydians traded widely with Mesopotamia and that silver and gold were used as a medium of exchange. A controlling authority supervised trade and assured that the silver units in use were of the correct weight and quality (Lloyd 1956:115–118). It would seem, therefore, that at its inception currency was already associated with a fairly sophisticated market structure.

totally, and the variations and similarities are best understood, not in terms of some abstract idea of what money should be, but in the differences in socioeconomic organization of the respective societies.

Definitions of money and its functions in complex societies are based on the assumption of a monetized system of economic relationships. Accordingly, economists would claim that money must be universally acceptable within the society or societies in which it circulates, a concept made explicit in the stipulation carried on American Federal Reserve notes: "This note is legal tender for all debts, public and private." Furthermore, money should be portable, it should be easily dividable into fractional units, and it should not depreciate or appreciate greatly in value. Its issuance is the monopoly of the state and there are restrictions on its supply (we know what happens to individuals who try to print their own bills). Money is thus both stored wealth and a medium of exchange. For a long time, precious metals, because of their universal acceptance, portability, and durability were the preferred materials for coinage in Old World civilizations and modern Western societies. Initially, paper money was backed by gold or silver, although this is no longer the case. If people have faith in paper money—that is, faith in the economy and the government—paper performs all the functions of metal coinage.[2]

If we try to apply these criteria to primitive money, the discrepancies will be obvious. It may be that in a given African society a new bridegroom is expected to pay

[2]Faith in paper money is still far from universal. One of the authors (Pi-Sunyer) worked as an archaeologist on Mexican excavations in the 1950s and, at that time, peasant work crews still insisted on being paid in silver coins. It is also a well-known fact that when the French economy shows signs of distress, the price of gold napoleons (twenty-franc coins) takes a steep rise. Many French peasants (and middle-class people) keep a nest egg of gold coins for emergency use and such obligations as dowry payments. Gold and silver, it is assumed, never lose their value.

a bride price of twenty cows to his parents-in-law, a transaction that in part could be interpreted as the exchange of items of worth for economic services that are now transferred from one kin group to another. But no one—including the people in question—would claim that a healthy adult bovine is identical to a decrepit cow, nor is it feasible to cancel minor obligations with a cow fraction. What is true of cows is also true of most other measures of value used in nonliterate societies, for such "money" lacks the all-purpose qualities of money in state structures.

An examination of the function of money in our own society reveals that it is used in a great many ways. It can buy goods and services, and it may also be given as presents and utilized to pay taxes and parking fines. In some of these functions, money operates in a manner similar to redistributed items in other societies: it is collected by the state and then applied to a variety of purposes. Also, some of the uses of money in our society are in no sense mandatory. For instance, a graduating senior may receive a watch or funds that can be applied in a discretionary manner, perhaps to pay for a vacation trip.

The main difference between money in complex modern societies and "money" in simple societies is that the latter is used for specific and limited ends, such as gifts, exchanges, and traditional payments, in short, for basically noncommercial purposes. It holds significance for a restricted range of functions, including the cementing of interpersonal links, as is the case with the bracelets and necklaces that follow the kula path. The failure to differentiate between the various uses to which money can be put and the commercial mentality that has grown with it in societies such as ours have given rise to much sterile debate on the attributes of primitive money. In George Dalton's words:

To concentrate attention on what all monies have in common is to discard those

Bullion is a form of wealth with a value that is recognized almost universally. However, it is now seldom used in private transactions, although the holding of gold or silver, usually in coinage, is not uncommon. Here precious metals are shown stored in a bank vault. (Elliot Erwitt/ Magnum Photos, Inc.)

A check is a written instruction directing a bank to pay a designated amount of money to an individual or institution. Checks have some of the attributes of currency, but they must (or should) be backed by assets that the check writer holds in the bank. (Charles Harbutt/ Magnum Photos, Inc.)

Despite the modern-type dwelling of the chief in a tradition-oriented village on the Micronesian island of Yap, stone money (circular disks of limestone) have retained their value for ceremonial exchanges to the present day. (Leonard Mason)

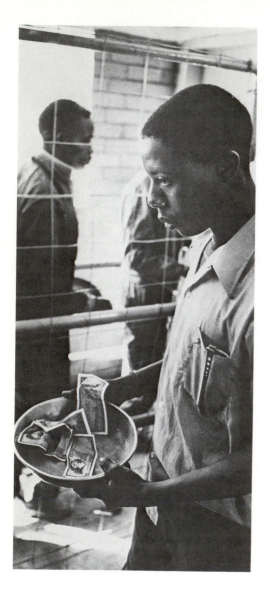

A mine worker in South Africa collects his weekly wage. The economic and social fabric of many nonmonetary societies has been destroyed by stimulating expectations that in the modern world can be met only through wage labor. The man in the picture works in a large gold mine in the Transvaal and probably has his home in a remote black "homeland." (Struan Robertson/Magnum Photos, Inc.)

clues—how monies differ—which are surface expressions of different social and economic organization. . . . Money traits differ where socio-economic organization differs (Dalton 1965:61).

Western societies are so permeated with a price-market mentality that even in situations where no currency is available, a given commodity is likely to take on many of the attributes of money. During World War II, prisoners of war held in Germany soon devised a monetary unit that had universal acceptability in the relatively closed economies of the camps—the cigarette—in terms of which all other exchangeable items could be quoted (a pound of butter at so many cigarettes, and so forth).

In basically subsistence economies, the introduction of Western money not only has displaced primitive money but encourages the fulfillment of traditional obligations with all-purpose money earned in commercial transactions. With the influx of cash and cash-derived goods, the stability of the native system can easily be undermined, as was the case with Northwest Coast peoples who became increasingly enmeshed in the Canadian market economy.

Colonial administrations have seldom looked much beyond the economic and fiscal aspects associated with the introduction of Western money. Efforts to monetize subsistence economies have been rationalized on the grounds that they increase the production of cash crops, make labor available for a variety of uses, and develop a tax base. However, not only do these practices tend to destroy the economic structure of simple societies, but, since economics is so closely linked with social and political organization, they also erode the fabric of social links and generally lessen the prestige and power of local political figures and offices. The chief in a monetized colonial setting is transformed into the paid agent of metropolitan authority.

In such situations, simple societies are also likely to feel the full brunt of market fluctuations beyond their control, for the cash crop that brings a high price one year may be a glut on the market the next. Such uncertainty is bad enough, but the introduction of a cash economy may also have extremely deleterious effects on scarce resources in high demand by the external market. As a case in point, some species of fur-bearing animals, notably the beaver, were virtually exterminated from eastern North America by the end of the eighteenth century, and competition for furs triggered many of the Indian wars of colonial times. Today, the gourmet market for turtle meat has caused a sharp decline in the green turtle population of the Caribbean. The Miskito Indians of Central America who once hunted the turtle for food are now hunting it for sale to processing plants. In the interval, they have been drawn into a cash economy and will remain linked to it regardless of the ultimate fate of what was once their major source of high-quality protein. A village can eat only so much turtle meat, but the outside market is virtually limitless.

MARKETS, STATES,
AND PEASANTS

In primitive economies operating within the framework of a centralized political authority, transactions are seldom limited to local-level exchanges and the redistributive patterns we have previously discussed. Once sufficient political centralization has been achieved, external trade relations are likely to be established between the ruling elites and other societies. Such trade is in part a matter of increased political control and in part a reflection of greater organizational complexity in the society.

Societies at this level of sociocultural integration—often referred to as primitive or archaic states—evidence many of the economic features of chiefdoms in tribal societies. Kings and other potentates receive

*Economies of
archaic states*

goods and services in the form of tribute. These payments support those in control and are in part redistributed downward.

However, powerful elites are in a position to demand something more than subsistence goods. Tribute payments are earmarked to support various types of specialists, such as artisans and courtiers, and to pay for the acquisition of luxury items reserved for elite consumption. While some of these items may be of local derivation, others have to be acquired from beyond the political borders of the state. Such luxuries often came from great distances through an intricate chain of merchants and middlemen.

The historical and archaeological evidence indicates that long-distance trade in archaic states was typically either a government monopoly or was closely regulated by official authority. This is understandable since such trade was designed to meet the needs of the elite sectors of society and reinforce the power of those in political control. Given this subordination of trade to politics and the attainment of social rank, it is invalid to apply economic models that assume the free play of supply and demand. Although one can speak of commerce and of markets (both as trading centers and as population sectors for which goods and services are destined), one must recognize the restricted nature of such trade and its limited impact on the majority of the population.

Early market systems of this type, while limited in scope both in terms of the goods transferred and the class sectors for which these goods are meant, are nevertheless a manifestation of the increased coercive power of political institutions. In various ways, it is the conscripted labor of the village masses and the taxes and other material demands imposed on subsistence agriculturalists that permit economic mobilization to underwrite luxury trade and other activities for the benefit of a ruling class. The same system that transforms the toil of peasants into such items as precious metals, jade, silks, and amber also subordinates the labor force to such tasks as the construction of palaces for living rulers and monumental burial structures for deceased kings. The wealth of the pharaohs hardly indicates that they were crafty entrepreneurs; it does reflect, however, the power and authority inhering in their dynasties.

Early market systems were characterized by the power held over the many by the few. Forms of production, the allocation of labor, and state-supported long-distance trade in prestige goods are but different facets of a socioeconomic framework in which the labor force loses control over the disposition of its time and effort. The concentration of political power is matched by a concentration of economic power that restricts access to land and raw materials. For the societies we have been discussing, the major material resource over which producers lose control is, naturally, land. There are degrees and variations in this alienation of the agriculturalist from the means of production, differences in the coercive power of the institutions of political control. Archaic state systems developed over time and involved a more or less gradual shift in the ownership of vital resources from domestic groups and communities to landowners and the agents of state authority. Furthermore, the state may have the power to extract rent, taxes, and other services, even when agriculturalists retain formal ownership over their agricultural holdings. It is of less economic significance to determine who owns the land than to establish what uses it is put to. In a political and economic system with evolved techniques for diverting productive capacity to satisfy elite needs, food producers can no longer exercise choices and should be thought of as peasants—a class that is politically and economically subordinate. No longer are the processes of production and resource allocation embedded in kinship, as is the case with tribal structures, however prestigious may be the position of a chief. Paralleling these shifts, the political organization is transformed into a class structure with a clear demarcation between those who control property (the elites) and a class of workers who are forced to dispose of their labor according to externally defined priorities.

Peasant economies in the context of the state

The distinguishing feature of peasantries is their clear subordination to the authority of the state and the power of elites. The increasing divergence of interests between rulers and ruled gives rise to corresponding cultural, as well as social, differences. It is therefore possible to speak of lifeways or cultures that are distinctive of peasant populations. Conversely, elite cultures represent a style with little applicability to rural hinterlands.

This stress on cultural distinctions—basically a pluralistic approach—is valid for research oriented to the examination of small communities. However, it tends to obscure the realities of power relations. Peasant societies, it should be remembered, are not simply rural cultures sharing some similarities with other small-scale communities but components of a subordinate class within traditional complex societies. Property, with the power it has to exploit, is the great divide between peasants and elites. This observation remains essentially correct even for peasants in modern states, including those in contemporary socialist countries where higher authority, in the form of the party or bureaucracy, determines such matters as work schedules, quotas of production, and the ultimate allocation of human and material resources.

As a socioeconomic category, the term *peasant* should apply less to what people do (such as grow food or raise cattle) than to where they stand in relation to an asymmetrical distribution of power and resource allocation. It is thus not unlike some terms drawn from the vocabulary of urban-industrial society, such as *hardhat* or *blue-collar* that at one level are occupational designations but socially and economically pertain to the working-class segment of modern American society.

In fact, the work that peasants do differs

little from that of agriculturalists in simple societies. Certainly it differed very little prior to the industrial revolution, when peasants depended on simple technology and organized their labor according to a domestic mode of production, typically the family work team. As we have noted earlier, peasants lived in small communities and produced a relatively narrow range of crops and craft items. While the state and elites extracted "surpluses" from peasant labor, most of the food grown was destined for home consumption. Large-scale market production is either a modern phenomenon or a highly specialized form of agricultural exploitation—the plantation economy in one of its many guises.

It is always difficult to compare the quality of life of different societies, since priorities and values vary enormously between cultures. However, there is little evidence that peasants as a whole fare better materially than tribal peoples. One could, in fact, present a strong case that the opposite might well have been true until relatively recent times. Furthermore, the industrialization of the countryside, which first began to have a major impact on European agriculture during the eighteenth century, led to the transformation of basically subsistence agricultural practices into capital-intensive enterprises requiring a smaller

(above) Sunday market in the central plaza of Chichicastenango, Guatemala. Vendors and customers from surrounding communities meet here to buy and sell the products in which individual villages specialize. In developed capitalist societies, agricultural commodities may be bought and even sold before they are produced. (right) The photograph shows the board in a United States commodities exchange where prices are quoted for futures in live hogs, eggs, and other products. ([above] Oriol Pi-Sunyer; [right] Roger Malloch/Magnum Photos, Inc.)

labor force. The result was the eviction of peasant tenant farmers and the movement of unemployed and unemployable peasants to the cities. The standard of living of many European peasants remained abysmally low during much of the nineteenth century. Improvement in the quality of life of the farmer was attained only with a dramatic thinning down of the rural population. Although the European example cannot be applied without exception to contemporary developing countries, very similar trends are discernible in many parts of the world.

TO SUM UP Peasant society is a socioeconomic category associated with a rudimentary or underdeveloped market organization such as is found in traditional state structures and, historically, pre-industrial Europe. A developed market economy—modern capitalism—is not generally compatible with peasant society, although some peasants have managed to survive either because of geographic marginality—much as have Appalachian mountain people in the United States—or through strategies of adaptation (external employment, commercial truck farming, and the like) that permit viable livelihoods.

PRICE-MARKET ECONOMIES
AND CONTEMPORARY
COMPLEX SOCIETIES

Since the eighteenth century, economic inquiry has centered almost exclusively on the question of markets and market prices. The general assumption has been that supply and demand for goods and services are regulated and mediated by price in open exchange. Economic priorities—the needs of a society—supposedly make themselves apparent in the way in which individuals allocate their resources, not only the money over which they have discretionary use, but also their labor, broadly defined as skills and competencies. Theoretically, such a system of "free enterprise" is self-regulating since a purchaser cannot satisfy all his or her

potential desires and must select from a number of available alternatives, presumably according to some logical criteria.

The majority of modern economists would argue that one cannot apply moral implications to a price-market system any more than one can assign judgmental criteria to the theory of relativity or the second law of thermodynamics: a market is a market. Increasingly, however, some economists are rejecting this assumption of a value-free capitalist economic system. Economic institutions, they maintain, operate in ways that clearly benefit some groups or sectors of society more than they do others, and modern industrial systems perpetuate the differential distribution of power and resources in modern states.

The factors of size and power

To understand why a supposedly open system of exchange is not equally beneficial to all, it is necessary to take into consideration some of the salient characteristics of industrial capitalism. First, and perhaps foremost, is the matter of scale. The economies of developed industrial countries are made up of millions of individuals and thousands of business firms. To these can be added government agencies, such as central banks and treasuries, deeply involved in economic activity and policymaking. The result is a highly complex system generally beyond the comprehension of the ordinary citizen. There is no doubt that the operation of village or tribal economies—the type of economies that anthropologists have generally studied—is far better understood by their participants than the economic system of the United States is understood by the American citizen. Consequently, the market analogy, which assumes knowledge and rational choice, is simply not valid. As buyers, we can, should we wish, apply logical criteria to the purchase of tuna fish or breakfast cereals, but we patently lack the relevant information concerning the workings of highly complex marketing systems.

At the corporate level, businesses are in theory owned by their shareholders; in reality, power in modern corporate structures has long since passed to managers. The goals of managers and boards of directors can be simply stated: to increase profits. Given the power of modern big business, it is fanciful to assume that business and the consumer, or business and the ordinary working person, stand in a relationship of equality. As consumers, we buy not simply what we need; through advertising we are urged to satisfy needs that previously we did not even know existed. Employees, for their part, work within the constraints laid down by an employer. The two are partners only in fiction—there is nothing as dispensable as the working person.

The integration of modern economies through money leads to a situation in which everything has a price, and a price not necessarily fixed by market forces. Although the system is theoretically competitive, businesses much prefer not to compete; hence, the periodic disclosures of cartel arrangements, graft, and political manipulation. It would be unrealistic to see these manifestations as exceptions to the rule; rather, they are standard operational procedures. This linkage of power to economics should come as no surprise to anthropologists, for it is present and overt in small-scale systems in redistribution and the dynamics of trading partnerships. Commercialized systems, and the theories utilized to rationalize them, are neutral only in fiction. Economic theory, as John Kenneth Galbraith has noted, "is the influential and the invaluable ally of those whose exercise of power depends on an acquiescent public" (1973:11).

But this is also a public that finds it exceptionally difficult to make its opinions felt. Government regulatory agencies, supposedly established for the protection of the public, are typically staffed by bureaucrats having much more in common with the corporation staffs they are supposed to supervise than with the citizens they should represent. Public interest groups can and do bring some pressure to bear, but the task is an uphill one.

Fundamentally, the regulation of the economy for the greatest public benefit is not an economic question, but a policy question that should be handled through the institutions of government. In the bid for influence, however, business—organized and powerful—enjoys great advantages, and as a result public policy is often made to suit special interests rather than the preferences of the citizenry. As economist Thomas R. De Gregori notes with respect to transportation:

Did, in fact, our current modes of transportation come to pass simply as a result of private, individual market choices? Obviously not! When Los Angeles, once internationally noted for its system of public transportation, gave cars the right-of-way over trolleys, the shift away from public transportation was begun. The post-World War II building of freeways constituted a subsidy for automobiles and continued the process of decline for public transit. . . . Government at all levels continually has supported the automobile. . . . Today millions of citizens do not have effective choices in commuting to work or other destinations (De Gregori 1974:764).

Power will manifest itself in culturally determined forms, but from what we have learned of state systems it should come as no surprise that in the economies of complex societies, as in their political systems, power is highly concentrated. What we have said of capitalism remains in large measure true of state capitalism, the system found in communist countries. There power resides in the hands of a state bureaucracy and a party elite that allocate resources according to predetermined criteria. Once again, the ordinary citizen plays little part in determining economic policy, although a fiction of popular participation is maintained.

TO SUM UP The economic system will always be a reflection of the broader sociocultural system within which it is positioned. It follows that changes in the economy must come together with changes in the underlying structure of a society.

Even in commercial market-oriented systems, there are no purely economic problems, no strictly economic solutions. It is therefore reasonable to approach all economies, from the simplest to the most complex, as sharing certain attributes.

As with institutions in other societies, the economic systems of modern states validate and rationalize their existence through suitable myths. In communist states, there is the myth of ownership of the means of production by the workers, or the "people"—the absence of an exploiting capitalist class. In capitalist societies, there is the myth of a market easily understandable by the average purchaser, who is constantly confronted with the necessity to allocate his scarce "dollar votes" (or marks, francs, and the like) between competing needs and desires that can never all be satisfied. In reality, however, the system is made up, not of one, but of a number of parallel (and only partly overlapping) economic sectors. We have used the analogy of the supermarket shopper opting for one breakfast cereal over another. But what is available on the shelves is strongly influenced by the policies of supermarket chains, as well as by the policies of giant corporations that have it in their power to stimulate demand through advertising.

The free-market analogy is less than adequate in the analysis of consumer choices, and it fails even more when attention is directed to business enterprises. There are, of course, highly competitive industries, such as restaurants, laundries, clothing stores, and a multiplicity of small manufacturing concerns and service enterprises. At the other end of the scale, there are a relatively few major corporations whose control of the market is so great that competition is hardly present. To place giant conglomerates or multinational corporations in the same category as a barbershop or a diner is clearly invalid. Finally, the government with its immense tax-derived wealth has the power to benefit certain industries, such as the automobile industry through highway building, or defense contractors through arms purchases. It would be hard to maintain that in transactions of this sort, the market is even remotely free.

Our point is that when examining social institutions it is always necessary to distinguish between what they actually do and what they are assumed to do. Members of complex societies live in an economically regulated world in which they are dependent to a great extent on forces beyond their control. High productivity, a generally high material standard of living, and a great variety of goods and services require involvement in higher-order structures that place extreme demands on the individual. To all intents and purposes, the option of independent subsistence is ruled out. The fundamental questions are how well such economic structures satisfy the needs of the citizenry, and at what price. Price, in this sense, is more than monetary cost, for it involves such matters as environmental degradation, "permissible" levels of unemployment, and the exploitation of global resources.

REFERENCES

DALTON, GEORGE
1965 Primitive money. *American Anthropologist* 67:44–65.
1971 *Economic anthropology and development; essays on tribal and peasant economies.* New York: Basic Books.

DE GREGORI, THOMAS R.
1974 Power and illusion in the marketplace: institutions and technology. *Journal of Economic Issues* 8:759–770.

DENTAN, ROBERT K.
1968 *The Semai: a nonviolent people of Malaya.* New York: Holt, Rinehart and Winston.

GALBRAITH, JOHN KENNETH
1973 Power and the useful economist. *American Economic Review* 63:1–11.

HARRIS, MARVIN
1974 *Cows, pigs, wars, and witches; the riddles of culture.* New York: Random House.

LLOYD, SETON
1956 *Early Anatolia; the archaeology of Asia Minor before the Greeks.* Baltimore: Penguin Books.

MALINOWSKI, BRONISLAW
1922 *Argonauts of the western Pacific; an account of native enterprise and adventure in the archipelagoes of Melanesian New Guinea.* New York: E. P. Dutton.

MAUSS, MARCEL
1954 *The gift; forms and functions of exchange in archaic societies.* Ian Cunnison, trans. London: Cohen and West.

PIDDOCKE, STUART
1965 The potlatch system of the Southern Kwakiutl: a new perspective. *Southwestern Journal of Anthropology* 21:244–264.

RADCLIFFE-BROWN, A. R.
1922 *The Andaman islanders.* Cambridge: The University Press.

RICHARDS, AUDREY I.
1940 The political system of the Bemba tribe—north-eastern Rhodesia. In *African political systems.* M. Fortes and E. E. Evans-Pritchard, eds. London: Oxford University Press. Pp. 83–120.

SAHLINS, MARSHALL
1972 *Stone age economics.* Chicago: Aldine-Atherton.

Chapter 15
Not by bread alone: arts and artists

Both Old and New World culture history provides us with abundant evidence that humankind has been producing highly accomplished works of art for many thousands of years. It is also a matter of record that nowhere in the world is there a viable society that does not engage in what can be termed artistic activity. And yet, from an anthropological perspective, a definition of what constitutes art is very difficult to formulate. There are several reasons for this seeming paradox.

What is art?—The traditional view

Until quite recently, criteria for distinguishing art from nonart were fairly well established in complex societies such as ours. According to a traditional view, art is intended for and appreciated by relatively small and sophisticated audiences; and true artistic activities, of whatever kind, are engaged in by a very limited number of uniquely creative individuals recognized as such and judged by highly select groups of specialists or connoisseurs. Today, adherence to such rigid criteria seems altogether too restrictive and elitist: there is clearly no argument against giving Bach or Michelangelo deserved recognition as great artists, but should not the Beatles, a New Guinea carver, or a good peasant storyteller also be accorded appropriate acknowledgment?

Objects of art, in the broadest sense, are created primarily to be seen or heard. In the traditional Western view, they belong to and circulate along a network of their own and are segregated from the multitude of standardized utilitarian objects of manual or industrial production (shoes, refrigerators) or routine activities (jogging, letter writing, lecturing in class). More frequently than not, artists are judged promising or successful according to how strikingly, or "creatively," they manage to break with convention. However, even the most innovative artists work within the aesthetic bounds of their own culture and make use of its idioms. Their creativity consists primarily in redefining the prevailing aesthetic standards. Whenever a reformulation of artistic concepts marks a bold departure from prevailing criteria, art historians speak of a new art style, or "school." For example, around the middle of the nineteenth century the naturalistic (or realistic) style in painting replaced the intensely personal treatment of sensuous or exotic subject matter of the romanticists and was in turn succeeded by impressionism, which stressed the play of light on a scene taken from everyday life rather than painstaking attention to faithful detail. That perennial subject in Western art—the female nude—changed from the mythological Venus of the classicists to the female slave (odalisque) of the romanticists and the wife or model-friend of the realists. The one feature common to elite art of complex societies is that both its production and contemplation tend to be highly specialized and individualized experiences. In short, the cosmopolitan, self-conscious art of societies such as ours is held to exist primarily for its own sake.

Primitive art, so called because it has been attributed to the kind of small, nonliterate societies that used to be called primitive, contrasts markedly in some respects with the sophisticated, or elite, art of complex societies.[1] Typically, it is intended for a relatively large—that is, community-wide—audience, and its production is inextricably tied to ends or purposes extending beyond the specific performance or product. While a measure of innovating on the part of the performer or producer is appreciated, adherence to traditional standards, well understood by everyone in the community or group, is expected and even required.

Besides sophisticated and primitive art, two other categories are frequently identified—folk and popular art. Traditionally,

folk art refers to the products or performances of those members of complex societies who live away from urban centers—particularly peasants and herdsmen. Much like the primitive artists, folk artists tend to be known only to members of their own communities. They make use of everyday skills to create or to perform for the pleasure of it, or for their own needs or those of their families and neighbors. Endowed with a strong sense of the past, they typically work within the bounds of a traditional formula, which may or may not derive from older elite models.

Popular art is characteristic primarily of the urbanized sector of complex societies. Aiming at a broad audience, it has had a profound impact on sizable portions of modern complex societies. Popular music is an especially good example. Aided by the burgeoning recording industry and the ubiquitous outreach of communications media, it has swept not only the countries in which it originates but much of the rest of the world as well. In Nashville, Tennessee, the proportion of persons directly associated with the production of country and western music may well outnumber comparable concentrations of people during any period in history who have derived their livelihood solely from the arts. And as for the sheer size of an audience, such mass happenings as Woodstock's 300,000 spectator-participants in 1969 overshadow even the largest-scale political and sports events. While there are still those who are not willing to consider a rock concert an artistic event, there is no question that popular and elite art performances bear very striking resemblances: highly trained and skilled individuals, valued for their uniquely personal styles, perform for an appreciative audience of connoisseurs.

Primitive, folk, and popular art

A broader view

But even some of these generalizations fail to apply when we reflect on particular cases of what today are unquestionably viewed as artistic activities. For example, if art is meant to give satisfaction to an audience,

[1]The so-called naive art of such painters as Henri Rousseau (1844–1910) or Grandma Moses (1860–1961) has also been called "primitive," the reference being to their lack of formal training and the "childlike" directness and simplicity of their works.

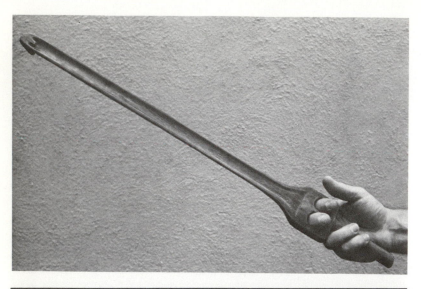

(left) Note the strictly instrumental, or utilitarian, form of a contemporary atlatl (spear-thrower), employed by the fishermen on Lake Patzcuaro (in the state of Michoacan, southwestern Mexico) to propel a three-pronged spear to kill ducks. (Zdenek Salzmann)

(below) By contrast, the well-known fragment of a spear-thrower from the rock shelter of La Madeleine (in the Dordogne region of southwestern France) is finely decorated and skillfully adapted to fit the piece of hard antler from which it was hewn. Representing a bison turning its head to lick its flanks, the piece dates back to the middle of the Upper Paleolithic period, some 15,000 years ago. Reindeer antler; length 4 inches. (Museum of National Antiquities, St. Germain-en-Laye, France)

then what of the exquisite Upper Paleolithic paintings of the Cro-Magnons, which were executed in such dark and remote underground caverns that few could contemplate their beauty? Clearly, they were intended for purposes other than pleasing the groups of hunters responsible for their creation.

The appeal of the visual arts is directed primarily to the sense of sight. With three-dimensional objects, a tactile component is added. Besides meeting specific practical needs, many of these objects evoke an emotional reaction on the part of those who make use of them. Phrased in technical language, the "instrumental form" may be enhanced by features that convey an aesthetic quality, thereby raising the status of such objects to "works of art." Their categories range widely and include architectural structures, furniture, pottery, basketry, and implements of all sorts. While it is virtually impossible to establish the precise boundaries between the finishing of an object and its elaboration beyond the demands of mere utility, no society lacks standards for distinguishing between what is merely commonplace and what evokes an aesthetic response in the viewer or user. These standards differ widely from one society to another and from one period to the next.

In modern Western societies, where art is exhibited or performed in the private homes of wealthy patrons, galleries, museums, concert halls, or spacious outdoor areas, the context in which a work is viewed (heard) or the reputation of its creator(s) may in itself be the decisive criterion. For example, among the five pieces of sculpture Pablo Picasso (1881–1973) sent to the "Liberation Salon" *(Salon d'Automne)* in 1944 was the now famous *Bull's Head*, a bicycle saddle attached to handlebars.[2]

In nonliterate societies, creative activities and their results acquire meaning only when

[2]In a subsequent interview given to André Warnod, Picasso had an interesting comment to make on this piece: "You remember that bull's head I exhibited recently? Out of the handle bars and the bicycle seat I made a bull's head which everybody recognized as a bull's head. Thus a metamorphosis was completed; and now I would like to see another metamorphosis take place in the opposite direction. Suppose my bull's head is thrown on the scrap heap. Perhaps some day a fellow will come along and say: 'Why there's something that would come in very handy for the handlebars of my bicycle . . .' And so a double metamorphosis would have been achieved." (Quoted from Barr 1946:241).

Picasso's now famous Bull's Head *points up the issue of what is "art." The two components of this piece, the handlebars of a bicycle and a bicycle seat, do not independently constitute works of art, as generally understood by the public. Together, however, they constitute a "sculpture" put together from "junk" that is more than the sum of its parts. (Picasso:* Bull's Head, *© S.P.A.D.E.M., Paris, 1976)*

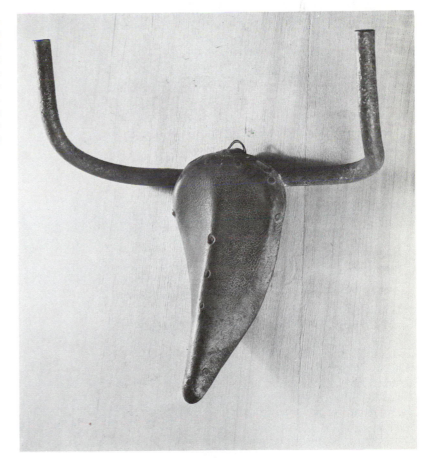

perceived against the total cultural context in which they occur, quite commonly a social or ritual occasion of one kind or another. Thus the term *art* is, in its usual sense, a concept that has gained currency especially among the elite sectors of complex societies. However, the fact that the vocabularies of many societies may lack an equivalent term does not mean that aesthetic experience goes unrecognized; it is simply inseparable from other aspects of their cultures.

The twentieth century has seen a profound change of emphasis in the study of primitive, popular, and folk art. Earlier studies dwelt on the technical, formal, or material aspects of art objects in museum collections, where these works were usually exhibited in isolation, torn out of the context that had given them their real purpose and meaning.

ASPECTS OF ART
AMONG THE NORTHWEST
COAST INDIANS

The culture area of the Northwest Coast affords an example of North American Indian art that is monumental in scope and exceptionally dramatic in its impact.[3] Since the chief medium for the Northwest Coast artwork was wood and the high humidity of the coastal climate does not favor the preservation of wood over long periods of time, many of the surviving objects date from no earlier than the past century.

The Northwest Coast area, extending along the Pacific from southern Alaska to northern California, was unusually rich in natural resources. The Indians of this region derived a plentiful supply of food from the sea and the rivers—salmon in particular—and worked the abundant cedar or redwood timbers with superior skills. They constructed substantial plank houses designed for multifamily use and dugout canoes capable of carrying as many as sixty persons.

[3]For our discussion of the Northwest Coast art we draw primarily on Drucker 1965 and Gunther 1966.

The social and ceremonial life of the Northwest Coast peoples was correspondingly complex and rich. Their societies placed great emphasis on wealth and social rank, and a typical village or lineage included a wealthy chief, hereditary nobles of various ranks, middle-class commoners, and slaves taken in war or obtained in trade with other tribes. The compulsive quest for prestige based on wealth found its expression in competitive potlatches, mentioned earlier in Chapter 6, dealing with Native Americans, and in Chapter 14.

The shamans among these peoples, who rivaled the chiefs in the esteem and fear in which they were held, were called on to carry out or direct impressive cleansing rituals. The major ceremonials of the area were enacted during the winter months by dance societies, whose masked performances were presentations of high drama.

Materials, designs, and forms

The Northwest Coast peoples are known for their expert weaving, fine basket-twining, and painting on wood, but their most remarkable achievements in the arts were the carvings in wood, bone, and horn characteristic of tribes residing north of the Columbia River. Done in relief or in the round, these carvings included objects both the size of a tall tree and small enough to be held in the palm of a hand. The carvers used simple tools—adzes with blades made from several varieties of jade; carving knives of mussel shell, animal teeth, or flint; and various kinds of chisels, gouges, and drills, many fitted with decorative handles of wood or horn. With these tools (later provided with metal blades) the native artists worked a variety of timbers that were carefully chosen to fit the particular purpose they were to serve. The surfaces of small objects were finished to a smooth polish, those of large pieces left with the rippled effect of adzes. Polychrome painting on wood, sometimes used in combination with carving, was applied to house fronts, storage boxes or chests, and totem poles. Before the 1880s, when commercial paints first became available, the colors were limited to blacks, reds, purples, yellows, and greenish blues of natural origin.

The designs of objects made by the Indians of the area were characterized by an unusual combination of forceful vitality and sensitivity. They ranged from portrayals of considerable realism or naturalism, mostly in objects carved in the round, to abstract elements applied to two-dimensional works. Aversion to undecorated spaces resulted in a baroquelike richness of design, demanding of the artists an inventiveness that they were more than equal to. Whether the available space might dictate the reduction or distortion of the subject matter represented or its extravagant elaboration and development, the total effect was invariably one of completeness and unity.

The decorative motifs found on the many objects of native manufacture were strongly influenced by features of the natural environment and closely tied to the various cultures. Representations of animals, which figured prominently in tribal mythologies, served to indicate symbolically the social relationships within the tribes. The names of clans and the principal crests associated with them were invariably taken from the animals native to the area. Among these were the raven, the eagle, and the kingfisher; the wolf, bear, beaver, and the land otter; and the killer whale and the seal. Each was identified by some of its characteristic features: the bear by strong paws and a large mouth with prominent teeth and protruding tongue; the beaver by large incisors and crosshatched tail; and so on. Some, like the mythical thunderbird, were characterized by a blend of features: a beak as long as a raven's but curved like an eagle's.

Richly carved objects played an integral part in both the everyday life and the festivities of these peoples. They included a variety of household utensils and furnishings, hunting and fishing gear, and items of personal apparel and decoration: wooden storage chests and boxes, spoons and ladles from wood or horn, mortars and pestles from wood or stone, fish clubs and fishhooks from wood, baskets and drinking cups from split cedar bark or carefully prepared spruce root, blankets from mountain goat wool, pipes from wood, combs from bone, labrets from ornamental stone, and a variety of bodily ornaments (pendants, earrings, nose rings, bracelets) from shells and other materials. While the execution was admired for the carver's skill, the design was frequently chosen for a particular magical power it was believed to possess. For example, fishhooks were decorated with representations of animals known for their fishing prowess.

If items of daily use were skillfully and delicately embellished, objects used for special ceremonial occasions of the Northwest Coast Indians were truly magnificent. Best-known social occasions were the potlatches, which marked some prominent event in the life of an individual or of a lineage or clan. The potlatch was a most appropriate opportunity for the display of the finest headgear, clothing, and jewelry for both the hosts and the invited guests. Some of the more elaborate hats were carved from wood and decorated with pendants; others were woven like baskets, with basketry disks stacked on the top representing the number of potlatches given by the wearer. There were also massive headdresses consisting of a spectacular frontlet carved from wood, inlaid with abalone shell, and flanked with ermine skins obtained in trade.

Ladle, possibly from the Tlingit tribe, carved from two pieces of mountain sheep horn. The handle is joined to the bowl with eight copper rivets. The figures, serving as emblems of a family or clan, represent from top to bottom: a raven, a man holding a bird, a bear holding a man, a hawk with a frog in its mouth, and a man with his tongue in the frog's mouth and holding the hawk's wings. Abstract faces, carved at the back of the handle, are not visible. Collected in 1864. Length of ladle 21¼ inches; width of bowl 5¾ inches. (Portland Art Museum, Portland, Oregon)

Chief's hat, collected in 1829 near Sitka, Alaska, probably from the Tlingit tribe. Hats such as this one were woven from spruce roots or cedar bark in the same manner as baskets. Patterns were either woven in or painted on the finished surface. The hat here illustrated displays designs of the owner's family crest painted in black, blue, and red paint. The six woven rings at the top indicate high status, signifying the number of potlatches that the owner had given. Spruce roots, black, blue, and red paint; diameter 25 inches. (The Peabody Museum of Salem)

Wooden hat brim from the Tlingit tribe. The opening at the center was provided for the woven rings. The shallow carvings are painted in black, dark brown, blue-green, and red. Diameter 13¼ inches; height 3¾ inches. (Portland Art Museum, Portland, Oregon)

The description below of the work on a wooden hat brim is indicative of the richness achieved by the carvers. According to two informants who offered their interpretations to the collector, the design represented a monster beaver.

The large masks are eyes. The ears are turned down over the forehead for lack of space elsewhere. The forelegs are represented by claws attached by a red curve to the body close to the head. The profile mask back of this with a green wing design adjoining it, bordering the tail, is the hind leg, whose claws . . . are hidden under the end of the tail. The tail has a cross hatched part. . . . At the sides, adjoining the crown of the hat, is the food of the beaver, the root stalks of the yellow lily represented by a peculiar conventional design. The two incisors of the beaver are shown in the broad mouth but inverted (Gunther 1966:96).

Attesting to the versatility of these talented Indian artists are the well-known Chilkat blankets found among the majority of the Northwest Coast tribes during the second half of the last century. Used for a variety of ceremonial occasions, these blankets were another important measure of the wealth and social prestige of the wearer. In order for a man to acquire such a blanket, he first painted the desired pattern on a cedar board. Using this template, his wife began the work by weaving mountain goat wool and shredded cedar bark on a simple loom. Because the elaborate designs made it impossible for the blanket to be woven as a single piece, individual panels had to be made and joined with seams that were then covered with white embroidery.

The uniqueness of these blankets stems not only from the techniques used in making them but also from the treatment of the design motifs. The features of the crest animal, depicted with strict bilateral symmetry, were reorganized in such a manner as to show not only the front but also the side and rear views and occasionally even some of the internal organs. This latter style

Chilkat blanket from the Tlingit tribe, woven completely from mountain goat wool and painted in pale yellow, blue, black, and white. Length, at center and without fringe, 33 inches; width 67½ inches. (Portland Art Museum, Portland, Oregon)

of representation is found only in the Northwest Coast area, Australia, and Melanesia. Symbolic abstractions of the features of the animal's front were displayed in the central portion of the blanket; other views were assigned to the sides.

Besides the ceremonials concerned with the carrying out of social obligations, there were rituals conducted by the dancing societies of a tribe to establish or renew relations with the supernatural world. It was during these winter performances that the powerfully dramatic masks for which the native Northwest Coast is famous were put to use. According to Philip Drucker, one of the most knowledgeable students of the area, the principal performers of the Kwakiutl tribe

relived the ancestral experience and became inspired or possessed by the spirit who had been encountered by the ancestor. The gifts bestowed by the supernatural being thus became hereditary property. They consisted of songs, dances, names, masks, and the like, and the power to perform various magical acts. Use of these privileges was limited to performances of ceremonials. . . .

. . . The plot of each performance called for the novices [principal performers] to go into hiding for some time prior to the public demonstrations. They were said to have been kidnapped by the spirits which were to inspire them. When they reappeared, they were possessed by their particular spirits, bereft of all human qualities. They had to be captured by combinations of force and magical procedures. Public and secret parts of the ceremonial exorcised the monstrous spirits possessing them: calm lucid behavior by the novices alternated with periods of possession during which they ran amuck, out of human control. . . . The public rites terminated with the "taming" of the novices [. . . ,] after which [they] underwent lengthy private purification rites (Drucker 1965:162–163).

The macabre and violent acts of the principal performers were heightened by elaborate stage effects and magnificent masks.

Art in ritual context

Carved, painted, and embellished with feathers, human hair, cedar bark, sheet copper, animal teeth, and pendants from a variety of materials, these masks were made to represent the heads of spirits of the dead (face masks), of animals, or of supernatural characters (sea monsters and others). Many of them had movable parts—eyes or eyelids, jaws, beaks, or fins, some of which could be manipulated with hidden strings to make a clapping sound as a movable part struck a fixed one. Other masks were constructed to present two, three, or even four different faces. The matching halves of each layer were hinged and kept closed until the release of strings attached to them successively revealed the representations concealed behind the outer layer. Quite frequently the layers alternated human and animal forms, corresponding to the transformations common in tribal mythologies.

The effective combination of singing, dancing, and masked appearances characterizing these winter ceremonials was also used by the shamans in their performances. The artistry that went into their paraphernalia corresponded to the wealth and power they held. Among the exquisitely carved pieces that a shaman employed as he worked on a patient were wooden rattles and delicate charms from bone. A most important article of the latter category was the "soulcatcher," a delicate carving made from a hollow bone, designed to recover the patient's straying soul.

Finally, there were the monumental memorial poles (totem poles) found among the northern tribes, some as much as seventy feet tall. Carved from red cedar, these impressive poles represented the hereditary crests of family lineages and often contained references to mythical or historical events. Commissioned to be made by carvers who specialized in such works, the poles were erected by wealthy individuals to enhance the pride and prestige of their families. Like the masks, they made use of native iconography, but their shape commonly invited a complex interlocking vertical composition.

Rather than sampling the wide variety of representational art found among the nonliterate peoples the world over, we have chosen to dwell in some detail on certain aspects of artistic activity in one area of native North America. Our intent has been to show how intimately art was tied to the intense social and ceremonial life of the Northwest Coast peoples with its emphasis on wealth, inheritance, the quest for prestige, and the assertion of privilege.

As we have seen, a great many objects that in our society would unquestionably be assigned to the category of art were a truly functional part of the daily life of these peoples; and a great many individuals were involved in their production and enjoyment, nobles and slaves alike. Although not everyone was a consummate artist, all men were carvers and all women weavers, and each was engaged in producing objects unmistakably his or her own. The scope of their expression was broad, ranging from realistic portraitures of human-faced masks to imaginative and dramatic representations of mythical creatures and the highly stylized symbolic abstractions applied to the Chilkat blankets. It is no wonder that once the institutions of these Indians succumbed to the pressure of the Canadian-American culture, their traditional motivation for artistic activity diminished correspondingly. Recently, attempts have been made to revive the production of traditional arts among the descendants of some of the Northwest Coast peoples. Once again a few talented persons are being commissioned to carve memorial poles or ceremonial masks, and well-to-do individuals are staging modern versions of the potlatch in order to gain or perpetuate social recognition by giving lavish gifts to large numbers of invited guests. However, as with so many old traditions that are being revitalized, the original context is irrevocably gone: the reenactment is an index of a resurgent pride in the past rather than an expression of the continuing viability of traditional institutions.

CURRENT APPROACHES TO
THE STUDY OF VISUAL ARTS

While current research concerning visual arts continues to stress the importance of a broad cultural context, there is a tendency to extend the analysis of art forms beyond the mere consideration of stylistic variation. Like other cultural codes, the visual arts of a society may be approached as the way its members order and categorize cultural experience. In applying this view, behaviors and their products are examined for the meaning they carry—that is, as symbols. Furthermore, there is a great deal of evidence for the assumption that the various domains of culture such as kinship, religion, mythology, and the visual arts all are interlocking. Striving for symbolic perspective should help the anthropologist to reconstruct not only the hidden features of a given social universe, but also the manner in which these features become projected within the subjective experience of those who inhabit that universe.

Some symbols are especially powerful, summing up the deepest human feelings concerning the nature of the world. On occasion, eloquent clues to their meaning may be provided by the members of nonliterate societies themselves. The fundamental and all-pervasive significance of the circle for the Oglala (Sioux) people was

Art as symbolism

effectively described by an Oglala informant:

The Oglala believe the circle to be sacred because the Great Spirit caused everything in nature to be round except stone. Stone is the implement of destruction. The sun and the sky, the earth and the moon are round like a shield, though the sky is deep like a bowl. Everything that breathes is round like the body of a man. Everything that grows from the ground is round like the stem of a tree. Since the Great Spirit has caused everything to be round mankind should look upon the circle as sacred for it is the symbol of all things in nature except stone. It is also the symbol of the circle that marks the edge of the world and therefore of the four winds that travel there. Consequently, it is also the symbol of a year. The day, the night, and the moon go in a circle above the sky. Therefore the circle is a symbol of these divisions of time and hence the symbol of all time.

For these reasons the Oglala make their tipis circular, their camp circle circular, and sit in a circle in all ceremonies. The circle is also the symbol of the tipi and of shelter. If one makes a circle for an ornament and it is not divided in any way, it should be understood as the symbol of the world and of time (Walker 1917:160).

A simple geometric figure, the circle, serves the Oglala as a key to their intuitive grasp of the nature of good and evil (roundness versus nonroundness) and bridges both what comes from the Great Spirit and what is manufactured (the sun, the moon, and other aspects of nature on the one hand, and the shield, the tipi, and other artifacts on the other).

Without the benefit of a similarly incisive native commentary, Nancy D. Munn (1973a, 1973b) has recently attempted to explore the relationship between the visual representations and certain fundamental notions of space, time, and natural philosophy held by the Walbiri people of central Australia. Among the designs commonly drawn in the sand by the Walbiri during storytelling or general discourse, the circle also plays an important role. In different contexts it has different meanings, such as a campsite, a water hole, fire, the place out of which an ancestor emerges and into which he returns, and others. On the one hand, the use of a single graphic element that has a multiplicity of referents reinforces wholeness and continuity in the Walbiri way of thinking about them. On the other, the casual use to which designs are put in the context of daily life serves as a frame for their symbolic significance. Thus, in ritual context and in combination with other graphs, the circle is capable of wide-ranging symbolic force—it stands for the female body or birth—relating the life-giving source both to the ancestral past of the Walbiri and to the features of the particular world in which they live. In Munn's words, "through the circle-line configuration the notions of 'world order' . . . are bound up with manipulative and tactile as well as visual perception, and thus embedded in immediate sense experience . . . [symbolically articulating] the relationship between the individual or microcosm and the macrocosm" (Munn 1973a:216).

While studies such as Munn's are as yet few and exploratory, they seem to indicate that not only is the symbolism of the representational art in a given society systematic (despite the ambiguities it may contain) but the symbols significantly reinforce meanings communicated by other means—ritual dances, the telling of myths, or whatever. The ultimate goal of such case studies is to provide data that will make it possible to investigate symbolic behaviors of all kinds on a more general cross-cultural basis.

Comparative research relating art style to aspects of social organization is by no means new, but recently it has been stimulated by several analyses making use of the statistical method. Suspecting that an artist—regardless of the ostensible contents of his work—unconsciously reflects real or desired social situations of his group, John L.

Art in cross-cultural perspective

Fischer (1961) tested several related hypotheses. Some of them involved the assumption that egalitarian societies are characterized by designs making use of a number of rather simple like elements, a large amount of empty or irrelevant space, symmetry, and unenclosed figures. By contrast, hierarchical societies might be expected to correlate with designs possessing opposite characteristics. In brief, the rationale behind these hypotheses is the fact that in egalitarian societies the equivalence of individual members is stressed, with outsiders being viewed with suspicion, whereas in stratified societies differences and boundaries between individuals of different ranks are stressed, with strangers being readily incorporated into the hierarchy. Fischer's findings show that the hypotheses are supported at statistically significant levels.

In another study, Alvin W. Wolfe (1969) has addressed the question of why some societies produce more art of "high quality" than do others. Noting that a disproportionate number of the twenty nonliterate societies most commonly cited for artistic achievement are characterized by matrilineal kin groups, Wolfe seeks a connection between matriliny and artistic productivity. For the sub-Saharan African societies on which his quantitative analysis is based, Wolfe finds that his results "support the general proposition that art develops in those societies where the men of a local community are divided by important social cleavages [that is, alienation from their local lineage centers]. . . . The data also suggest that the development of art is fostered by a nucleated settlement pattern and fixity of settlement" (Wolfe 1969:14).

These and similar studies have not been received without some valid criticisms, relating both to the nature of the data they deal with (aspects of artistic activity are difficult to define and to classify) and to the analytical techniques applied to them. Their value lies largely in the pioneering of approaches that would supplement the more traditional studies of art done in terms of diffusion, technical evolution of style, and the material limitations imposed upon artwork by the artist's environment. Since the sources of artistic creativity are as yet little understood, but at the same time the importance of the role of art in nonliterate societies is generally accepted, a degree of theoretical and methodological exploration is inevitable.

MUSICAL, VERBAL, AND DRAMATIC ART

Music and culture

Like visual representations, musical expression is a universal of human culture and tends to be bound up with other activities of a society. Among nonliterate groups, it is likely to be employed in a greater variety of situations than in our own society and cannot be so easily abstracted from its cultural context. It has its well-defined uses and functions, whether as entertainment, as symbolic communication, or—on an even more fundamental level—as a means of furthering, maintaining, and validating a group's solidarity.

The study of what has been called primitive music, of music that characterizes the cultures of the Far East and the Middle East, and of folk music has a tradition among anthropologists reaching back almost a century. Since World War II, it has developed into the specialized field of ethnomusicology, or the anthropology of music. According to Alan P. Merriam (1964:45–48), there are at least six areas of inquiry that the study of music from an anthropological perspective should include: the material culture of music—that is, musical instruments and their uses; song texts, both for their relationship to musical sounds and for what they reveal about a society; the categories of musical genres as distinguished by the members of a society themselves; the status and role of a musician in a given society; the uses and functions of music in relation to

other aspects of culture; and, finally, music as a creative cultural activity.

Musical culture of the Flathead

An excellent example of an anthropologically oriented study of music is Merriam's comprehensive account of the musical culture of the Flathead Indians of western Montana (1967). According to the author, the Flathead recognize three sources of songs: individual composition, borrowing from other tribes, and the supernatural, the latter remaining to the present day by far the most important source.

Sometimes in the old days the people would dream about the sweathouse. The dream would tell this person that "tomorrow at such and such a time you build a sweathouse and take a sweat, and you'll be cured if you are sick. If anything comes your way, you'll get out of it." Then certain songs are given in this dream, and you sing them while sweating (Flathead informant quoted in Merriam 1967:6–7).

Although making music has always been a natural part of life for the vast majority of the Flathead, there are musical specialists among them whose ability to sing and to drum is accorded special recognition and whose participation invariably contributes to the success of any event that calls for group singing as an accompaniment to traditional dancing. At the same time, a given song is never valued for its own sake; rather, it is judged by its efficacy—by how well it fits the situation that has occasioned its performance. In short, music for the Flathead is inseparable from the cultural context in which it occurs.

Like other tribal societies, the Flathead have used music on a great variety of occasions. They themselves recognize some forty different kinds of songs, which Merriam has grouped into six major categories: songs of personal power, including shamans' songs, love songs obtained from guardian spirits, and sweathouse songs; songs of the life cycle, sung on the occasion of birth, marriage, and mourning; social songs, such as gift dance songs, owl dance songs, and gambling songs; songs associated with the dances of the former Flathead war complex, including scalp dance songs to celebrate victory; ceremonial songs of religious significance, to accompany prayer or thanksgiving dances; and, finally, miscellaneous songs and dances.

An account of the musical culture of the Flathead would be incomplete without reference to the changes that have occurred in the course of the present century, during which so many of the traditional ways have yielded to the relentless pressure of the encroaching white culture. According to Merriam, many of the young Flathead have recently added a second, Western, style to that of their traditional performances, but the two styles are never mixed. With the steady loss of suitable opportunities for musical performances in their native style, the range of song types has been shrinking rapidly. Nevertheless, what traditional music has survived continues to serve important functions for the Flathead. As one

of the few aspects of their culture that have remained distinctly Indian, music serves as a bridge to the Flathead past. Together with their dances, it further offers an effective means for relieving psychological tensions in the face of a mounting threat to their ethnic identity. And finally, "the occasions for music provide . . . opportunities for self-expression through the mechanism of drawing the Flathead together in one place at one time, thus reinforcing the social integration of the group" (Merriam 1967:158).

Music in comparative perspective

Like the study of unwritten languages, the study of traditional music has been greatly aided by the availability of magnetic recording devices. But just as in transcribing speech, accurate transcription of musical performances requires highly specialized training and involves the employment of additional symbols for such particular features of pitch, rhythm, and performance as are not commonly heard in Western musical styles. Contrary to popular view, which tends to lump much of so-called primitive

Storytelling, combined with a musical performance, is common in the Islamic countries of North Africa. In Fez, a Moroccan entertainer is surrounded by a crowd listening intently and watching the young dancers, who fall into a trance after hours of dancing. (United Nations)

music into one large undifferentiated category, musical styles vary not only from one area of the world to another but within a particular area as well. For example, what once was thought to be the style of all of North American Indian music has been shown by Bruno Nettl (1954) to be a general characteristic of only the Plains-Pueblo area.

Since World War II, the increasing availability of excellent recordings of music from even the remotest societies has made it possible to begin with cross-cultural studies on a worldwide scale. A recent massive contribution toward the comparative anthropology of music is the report on the Cantometrics Project, carried out under the leadership of Alan Lomax. The principal aim of the project was to establish the extent to which "song style symbolizes and reinforces certain important aspects of social structure in all cultures" (Lomax 1968:vii). Inasmuch as song (and dance) is behavior that is learned like the rest of human culture and represents shared social norms, it should, according to Lomax, evoke "the models in terms of which everyday social activities are structured" (1968:305). Rating samples of 10 songs from each of 233 cultures in accordance with 37 variables drawn primarily from performance practice, Lomax and his coworkers have found that song styles tend to vary directly with the socioeconomic complexity of societies, and that song variables such as text load, precision of enunciation, and the degree of embellishment appear to be closely tied to the complexity scale. Some claims are set forth on a fairly specific level—for example, that "relaxed vocalizing not only stands for permissive sexual standards for women, but for another basic source of feminine independence as well— the importance of women in basic subsistence" and that "songs from societies where infant stress is present [are] characterized by wider range [the distance in pitch between the lowest and highest notes of a song] than songs from societies where infant stress is absent" (Lomax 1968:199 and

213). A concomitant study of dance style and culture led members of the project to the conclusion that "dance style varies in a regular way in terms of the level of complexity and the type of subsistence activity of the culture which supports it" (Lomax 1968:xv).

Generalizations that attempt to be global in scope seldom are accepted without reservations, especially those that are advanced in support of specific correlations between such seemingly diverse aspects of human behavior and culture as song styles and patterns of subsistence. Understandably, the observations and findings of the Cantometrics Project staff have been questioned with regard to the size of the samples used and the techniques and methods employed. Even though one may safely assume that future studies stimulated by the project will raise many additional questions and result in various refinements, the contribution of Lomax and his co-workers must be considered a pioneering effort toward a comparative ethnology of music and dance.[4]

Verbal art   Our brief discussion of the arts would be incomplete without mention of verbal art. The recognition that a particular traditional narrative (myth, folktale, or whatever) can be told poorly by some and captivatingly by others has given rise to the conception of verbal art as performance. The skillful employment of such devices as figures of speech, special stylistic and prosodic features (rhymes and intonation patterns, for example), archaic lexical elements, or familiar formulae ("In olden times, when rivers brimmed with milk and their banks were made of porridge . . .") undoubtedly plays an important part in a successful performance. The ultimate proof of the narrator's competence as a verbal artist, however, is the approving reaction of those listening. In

[4]For a general survey of dance ethnology and for a specific description of the ceremonial dancing of an American Indian people (the Iroquoian Seneca), the interested reader may refer to Kurath 1960 and 1964, respectively.

this view, each individual verbal performance is a separate and unique creative act that derives its effectiveness from the narrator's ability to adapt to a given set of circumstances and to maximize his or her hold on the audience.[5]

While they commonly also serve to entertain, verbal performances typically take on the crucial function of inculcating time-honored beliefs and fundamental values in the society's young. This may be accomplished, negatively, by pointing up through ridicule or by other devices the undesirable consequences of culturally proscribed behavior or, positively, by holding up the example of a heroic character whole life style deserves emulation. By institutionalizing appropriate occasions and sanctionable forms for expressing what otherwise is unsayable, the members of a society are able to release harmlessly their feelings of tension or pent-up hostility. At their best and most effective, tribal raconteurs, or storytellers, compare with the literary artists of complex societies, and their short humorous trickster stories and cycles of hero tales compare with our comic strips and novels.

A composite appeal to the senses is achieved in what are sometimes called the mixed arts, which combine music with dance, verbal presentations with the visual components of dramatic enactment and stage setting, and so on. Especially effective in arousing the emotions of the audience, alerting supernatural forces, or mobilizing social action for culturally important ends are dramatic performances in which verbal arts are tied to dance and music. Moreover, in our reference to the winter ceremonials staged by the Indians of the Northwest Coast we have had occasion to note how objects of visual art,

Dramatic art

such as masks, contribute to the multimedia effect of ritual performances. Whether such performances involve general participation under the guidance of the experienced elders of a group or elaborate public presentations by highly trained professionals, they invariably possess a definite structure, and their effectiveness in large part derives from the aesthetic appeal achieved by the application of technical skill to culturally appropriate forms of expression. The powerful impact of a dramatic performance lies in its ability to cast in concrete form the abstract ethical principles underlying human relationships, as in plots involving deceptions, cruel relatives, use of magic powers, and the like.

In his discussion of ethos, world view, and the meaning of sacred symbols, Clifford Geertz, well known for his penetrating analyses of the Indonesian cultural scene, makes this extraordinary claim for a relatively humble variety of dramatic performance:

In a complex civilization such as that of the Javanese—in which Hinduistic, Islamic, and pagan influences all remain very strong—one could choose any of several symbol complexes as revealing one or another aspect of the integration of ethos and world view. But perhaps the clearest and most direct insight into the relation between Javanese values and Javanese metaphysics can be gained through [an] analysis of one of the most deeply rooted and highly developed of their art forms which is at the same time a religious rite: the shadow-puppet play (Geertz 1957:427).

Some of the major characters of the shadow-puppet play are commonly taken to represent the five senses, which the Javanese believe must be brought into union in order for an individual to attain the knowledge of spiritual truth. The puppets and their shadows are identified with human inward life and outward behavior. Various human attributes and emotions are symbolized by the design of the puppets and the

[5]An excellent discussion of a conception of verbal art as performance, with examples, may be found in Bauman 1975. For a comprehensive account of storytelling in a Hungarian peasant community (its "oral folk narratives, their creators and performers, and the participant audience as a complex whole in the expression of culture"), we are indebted to Dégh 1969.

tunes and poems that accompany the play. The performance as a whole, then, serves as a key to the understanding of the many facets of the ordinary Javanese experience.

TO SUM UP   Music, dance, drama, and verbal art are as much a reflection of the culture from which they spring as are the visual arts. And like the visual arts, they furnish valuable clues that lead to a better understanding of aspects of culture that may not be readily accessible through other means. In short, the careful study of performances and their products is indispensable to anthropologists as they search for the symbols that help to define a society's beliefs and values.

As is true of other aspects of culture, the verbal arts may also be borrowed and reinterpreted to fit a given sociocultural context. This is graphically illustrated by Laura Bohannan in her charming paper, "Shakespeare in the Bush," in which she records her efforts to tell the story of Hamlet to a group of Tiv elders. Her West African informants offered a totally different interpretation of Shakespeare's epic, and with a mixture of courtesy and firmness instructed the field worker as follows:

"Sometime," concluded the old man, gathering his ragged toga about him, "you must tell us some more stories of your country. We, who are elders, will instruct you in their true meaning, so that when you return to your own land your elders will see that you have not been sitting in the bush, but among those who know things and who have taught you wisdom" (Bohannan 1966:33).

ART AND SOCIETY

In the introductory section of this chapter we said that in contemporary complex societies art as a rule constitutes an autonomous domain. But this has not always been so, nor is it uniformly true of the present. Medieval Christianity—to use an example from the Western world—found its expression in works of superb artistic achievement not for art's sake but to the greater glory of God. The believers, whether rich or poor, were surrounded on regular occasions of worship with a panoply of art that was notably functional: it was to make them feel both awed and exalted in the presence of their Creator. Soaring cathedrals with their stained-glass windows, magnificent sculpture and paintings, the ritual splendor of church ceremonies—all were charged with a high degree of symbolism that affected every aspect of life in the Age of Faith.

Contemporary societies in which the social control earlier exercised by the church has been assumed by a highly centralized state commonly call on art to perform political and ideological functions. For example, beginning in the 1920s, the Mexican government commissioned some of the country's most renowned painters to cover the walls of public buildings with monumental frescoes that would help both to forge nationalist spirit among the people and to further the revolutionary goals of the society. The results of these efforts are the famous murals of José Clemente Orozco (1883–1949), Diego Rivera (1886–1957), and David Alfaro Siqueiros (1898–1974). Painted in the highly individual styles of their creators, these murals hold a wide appeal for the Mexican people. They portray scenes of the native civilizations that preceded the Conquest, the Conquest itself, the subsequent history of the country, and the Revolution of 1910.

In many contemporary socialist countries, which tend to limit artistic approval to the conception known as socialist realism, artists are urged to control any subjective idiosyncrasies that they as creative individuals happen to possess and to assume responsibility for upholding the official ideology of the state. This applies not only to the visual arts—painting, sculpture, and others—but to literature and even music, as some of the titles of compositions show. Emphasis is on the positive hero—the undaunted engineer or scientist, the diligent

The rising interest in so-called primitive art has stimulated the commercial production of art objects in many parts of the world. Although to some degree based on traditional designs, these items are manufactured primarily for sale to tourists or for export. (UNESCO/Paul Almasy)

industrial worker, the successful collective farmer—and those historical periods or events that hastened the transformation from a feudal or bourgeois society to the new socialist order. In these countries, the artists are rated according to how actively they become engaged in furthering the politico-ideological goals of the state, and their creative efforts are judged correspondingly.

Until the beginning of the twentieth century, what is called primitive art and elite art flourished in totally unlike sociocultural contexts. Since then, the two kinds of societies have been brought into contact with ever-increasing frequency and intensity. Such contacts have generally been more beneficial to Western art than the other way round. It is a well-known fact in the history of modern art that some of the most talented European painters of the early 1900s looked to exotic and "primitive" sculpture for their inspiration. A number of Pablo Picasso's paintings from this period drew on works native to the Ivory Coast and the Congo for their angular masklike faces. The "discovery" of the great tribal sculpture of

black Africa was instrumental in the artists' declaration of independence from nature and helped to usher in cubism and other movements that have so richly contributed to the variety of twentieth-century art.

By contrast, culture contact has generally spelled a decline in the vitality of tribal as well as folk art. Continued exposure to traders and missionaries, foreign armies, and modern technology almost inevitably alters the patterns of traditional culture, with the consequence that the ties between art and the socioceremonial structure of a society become ever more tenuous. And even where attempts have been made to sustain or revitalize traditional production or performance under the changed circumstances—usually for commercial reasons—the results more often than not have been disappointing. With the loss of genuine motivation on the artist's part and of the close integration of his creations with the total culture, what formerly were vibrant expressions of cultural orientation eventually become, at best, instances of competent craftsmanship.

REFERENCES

BARR, ALFRED H., JR.
1946 *Picasso; fifty years of his art.* New York: The Museum of Modern Art.

BAUMAN, RICHARD
1975 Verbal art as performance. *American Anthropologist* 77:290–311.

BOHANNAN, LAURA
1966 Shakespeare in the bush. *Natural History* 75:7:28–33 (August–September).

DÉGH, LINDA
1969 *Folktales and society; story-telling in a Hungarian peasant community.* Emily M. Schossberger, trans. Bloomington, Ind.: Indiana University Press.

DRUCKER, PHILIP
1965 *Cultures of the North Pacific Coast.* San Francisco: Chandler.

FISCHER, JOHN L.
1961   Art styles as cultural cognitive maps. *American Anthropologist* 63:79–93.

GEERTZ, CLIFFORD
1957   Ethos, world-view and the analysis of sacred symbols. *The Antioch Review* 17:421–437.

GUNTHER, ERNA
1966   *Art in the life of the Northwest Coast Indians.* Portland, Oreg.: The Portland Art Museum.

KURATH, GERTRUDE PROKOSCH
1960   Panorama of dance ethnology. *Current Anthropology* 1:233–254.
1964   *Iroquois music and dance: ceremonial arts of two Seneca longhouses.* Bureau of American Ethnology, Bulletin 187. Washington, D.C.: U.S. Government Printing Office.

LOMAX, ALAN, AND OTHERS
1968   *Folk song style and culture.* American Association for the Advancement of Science, Publication 88. Washington, D.C.: American Association for the Advancement of Science.

MERRIAM, ALAN P.
1964   *The anthropology of music.* Evanston, Ill.: Northwestern University Press.

1967   *Ethnomusicology of the Flathead Indians.* Chicago: Aldine.

MUNN, NANCY D.
1973a   The spatial presentation of cosmic order in Walbiri iconography. In *Primitive art and society.* Anthony Forge, ed. London: Oxford University Press. Pp. 193–220.
1973b   *Walbiri iconography; graphic representation and cultural symbolism in a central Australian society.* Ithaca, N.Y.: Cornell University Press.

NETTL, BRUNO
1954   *North American Indian musical styles.* Memoirs of the American Folklore Society, vol. 45. Philadelphia: American Folklore Society.

WALKER, J. R.
1917   *The sun dance and other ceremonies of the Oglala division of the Teton Dakota.* Anthropological Papers of the American Museum of Natural History, vol. 16, pt. II, pp. 51–221. New York.

WOLFE, ALVIN W.
1969   Social structural bases of art. *Current Anthropology* 10:3–44.

Chapter 16

Religion and ideology:
primary questions and
ultimate answers

It is especially difficult for members of complex societies to understand the role of religion in simple and traditional sociocultural systems. That politics and economics fuse with other facets of society into a seamless cultural whole is not, after all, so hard to comprehend: we know from experience that both political and economic considerations touch us all in our day-to-day life. Religious beliefs, institutions, and practices, on the other hand, seem to fall into an entirely different domain—a realm that is sacred and nonmaterial, an area of personal choices and private attitudes with little bearing on the hard realities of making a living.

The role of religion in society

Americans, and in fact Westerners in general, tend to express religious sentiments readily, but almost always as something of an afterthought. Late in the evening, following prime-time television programs, viewers may be reminded that it is a good idea "to worship in the church or temple of your choice," a public service announcement that fits into much the same category as the appeals to support the Community Chest or to give to the Heart Fund—worthy causes, to be sure, but hardly critical issues. Presidents and other important public officials show no disinclination to be photographed leaving places of worship or chatting with religious figures, but usually when religion is the subject of political debate it appears in the context of a disclaimer, such as the pre-electoral statements of John F. Kennedy that his being a Catholic would in no manner influence his policies as president. In 1976, during Jimmy Carter's campaign for the presidency, his strongly held religious beliefs similarly became a matter of some political comment.

The tendency to segregate religion from other facets of existence is at least partly the product of historical circumstances peculiar to the Western tradition. They include such developments as the rise of scientific thought, the emergence of political pluralism, and the industrial revolution. The end result of what in general may be termed

secularization is that in the course of the past two hundred years many traditional institutions have come under question, religious institutions among them. What is more, religion in most modern complex societies has become an area of private discretion, almost a marketplace of alternative beliefs.

Most modern complex societies are not only characterized by religious variety, but by attitudes toward religion—official as well as individual—that indicate a certain ambivalence. Thus, the framers of the American Constitution stipulated that "no religious test shall ever be required as a qualification to any office or public trust under the United States" (Article VI), while the First Amendment reads in part: "Con-

Religion and ideology tend to be closely intertwined. During the recent Lebanese civil war, a Lebanese Christian stands near the firing line next to a tank bearing a picture of St. Theresa and the Infant Jesus. (Philippe Ledru/ Sygma)

gress shall make no law respecting an establishment of religion, or prohibiting the free exercise thereof." Even though this principle of the separation of church and state is not applied without exception—note that generalized religious sentiments are present in oath-taking for testimony in court, on the American coinage ("In God We Trust"), and in the oath of allegiance—we are directed to render unto God the things that are God's and unto Caesar those that are Caesar's. Basically, the same situation is found in other modern states, although not always with the same degree of constitutional formalism. By contrast, in simpler societies religion and other facets of life are closely interwoven. We should note, however, that, as events in Northern Ireland and

Lebanon have shown, under certain circumstances religion continues to be a major political and social force for group identity and a contributory factor in intergroup conflict.

Anthropologists, whose concern it is to study the beliefs and practices of the widest variety of human societies, find the tendency to segregate secular affairs from those considered sacred or supernatural an exception rather than the rule. For the majority of human beings, descriptions of many seemingly practical pursuits are scarcely ever complete without reference to their "religious" dimension. Consider, for example, an account of the cultivation of corn among the present-day Maya:

> . . . the agriculture of the Maya Indians of southeastern Yucatan is not simply a way of securing food. It is also a way of worshiping the gods. Before a man plants, he builds an altar in the field and prays there. He must not speak boisterously in the cornfield; it is a sort of temple. The cornfield is planted as an incident in a perpetual sacred contract between supernatural beings and men. By this agreement, the supernaturals yield part of what is theirs—the riches of the natural environment—to men. In exchange, men are pious and perform the traditional ceremonies in which offerings are made to the supernaturals (Redfield and Warner 1940:989).

How, then, can one define religion in the context of anthropology? Much like definitions of politics, economics, or law, definitions of religion in terms of its attributes are seldom of much help. They either project a culture-bound image of what religion is assumed to be or end up as a laundry list of attributes. As a result, most anthropologists are satisfied with the very broad generalization that *religion* involves the recognition of or belief in some force or power that transcends humans and is capable of assisting or harming them. Beyond this, definitions are applicable to only certain societies and certain religious phenomena.[1]

A more productive approach toward defining religion is to examine it from a functional perspective—asking not what religion is but what religion does. Not only is there greater agreement as to the functions of religion, but the question is posed at the right level, that of society and culture. A critical function of religion is to offer a systematic rationale for human behavior by explaining and validating the place that members of a society occupy within their own sociocultural system and in the universe at large.

What or how much any religion explains varies from one society to the next. In general, all religions tend to provide some answers for otherwise unaccountable phenomena. For the past few centuries in complex societies, science has been steadily taking over the function of explaining natural phenomena, and in the view of some it is the only and ultimate source of explanation, incomplete as our knowledge still is concerning many aspects of the physical universe. Nevertheless, as the mysteries of the material world are unraveled, the questions for which solutions are found are replaced by ever more fundamental questions concerning the ultimate nature and origin of matter, energy, the universe, and so on. Indeed, it would be patently false to claim that the most prestigious scientist-philosophers have

The anthropological approach to the study of religion

[1] A recent book dealing with anthropological approaches to the study of religion may serve as an example. Clifford Geertz, one of its contributors, holds that "what men believe is as various as what they are," with the consequence that "general assessments of the value of religion in either moral or functional terms [are] impossible" (1966:39). In his definition, explicated with some detail in the bulk of the article, religion is "a system of symbols which acts to . . . establish powerful, pervasive, and long-lasting moods and motivations in men by . . . formulating conceptions of a general order of existence . . . clothing these conceptions with such an aura of factuality that . . . the moods and motivations seem uniquely realistic" (Geertz 1966:4).

uniformly come to accept science as the sole source of our comprehension of the universe and humanity's purpose in it. In short, religion may be said to give meaning and provide explanation for otherwise meaningless, contradictory, or inexplicable events.

A second function of religion is to validate or sanction a particular way of life. More specifically, religion customarily provides the basis for group membership and defines the nature and limits of social control to which members are subject. In other words, it significantly contributes to the establishment and maintenance of fundamental values and ethical categories. In the United States, for example, the issues of abortion and capital punishment have been strongly argued against by many on the basis that since life comes from God, it should not be taken by humans except in obvious cases of self-preservation. In some complex societies, the function of validating a lifeway and the ultimate meaning of human existence may be, or at least is supposed to be, performed by such ideologies as socialism, communism, and others. But even in the communist countries of eastern Europe and elsewhere, traditional religious beliefs concerning the purpose of life have persisted, despite the dictates of the state in the realm of personal faith and even when material disadvantages or outright persecution of believers is likely to result.

Religion, like other aspects of culture, is transmitted to the young in both formal and informal ways. In Thailand and other Buddhist countries many boys spend at least part of their lives in a monastery. Prior to attending classes given by teacher-monks, these Thai novices at the Monastery of the Walking Buddha move in procession to greet the rising sun with chanted prayer. (© 1975–Big Blue Marble)

TO SUM UP Belief systems that might be termed "religious" appear to satisfy important needs in all human societies. They explain events or situations that otherwise defy comprehension. They help individuals or groups confront reality and provide comfort in times of stress or anxiety. Equally important, they set guidelines for the culturally proper conduct of human affairs and furnish a sense of common purpose for the members of a social group. In this sense, more frequently than not religion and ideology are inextricably intertwined. Inasmuch as the belief systems of all human societies mediate between the realms of practical experience and inexplicable or unpredictable phenomena, religion, broadly conceived, is a universal phenomenon. It has remained a powerful force even in modern societies, despite the competing forces of rationalism nourished by the scientific achievements of the past several centuries.

ROOTS OF RITUAL
BEHAVIOR: SOME
CLASSIC APPROACHES

There is no question that human belief in forces and beings that from a Western point of view can be termed "supernatural" is of great antiquity. The compelling evidence for magical-religious ritual practices among the Neanderthals was brought out in our discussion of the culture history of the Old World. While most anthropologists would probably link the first glimmerings of "religious" experience with the early stages in the development of human language, there are some who suspect that fear of the unknown, in its most primitive form, may even be precultural, and look for corroborating evidence in the behavior of our closest primate relatives.[2]

[2]To be sure, the evidence is thin for subcultural anticipations of this kind. A. L. Kroeber (1948:66–67) reported on a chimpanzee's reaction somewhat akin to the manifestation of fear or awe when it was presented with the sight of a rude rag animal

Animism

Given the universality and central importance of religious behavior in human culture, there has been no lack of theories during the past hundred years concerning the original source of the concept of the supernatural. While most modern anthropologists consider the search for origins to be futile, some of the older theories are of interest from the point of view of anthropological history. One of the earliest, and the best-known, was put forth by Sir Edward B. Tylor (1832–1917) in his well-documented classic of anthropological writing, *Primitive Culture* (1871). The initial impulse toward developing the notion of a world of spirits was primitive human's attempt to account for the puzzling variety of bodily conditions and states. According to Tylor, there is convincing evidence that the key to the problem was the recognition of an immaterial soul, or spirit, for which the physical body served as dwelling. The soul *(anima)* was thought capable of independent existence. The temporary or permanent departure of the soul from the body occasioned sleep and death, the wanderings of the soul caused dreaming, and the visit of the body by an alien spirit resulted in possession. Since Tylor's speculations concerning the primitive mentality coincided with the period of powerful influence of evolutionary thought, his theory of souls—that he himself termed *animism*—included a developmental scheme. In Tylor's view, early humans extended the concept of the soul to other living organisms (animals and plants) as well as to a variety of inanimate objects (rivers, rocks, and the like). And it was inevitable that in a world populated with spirits of every conceivable sort, human beings would eventually acknowledge some as exerting more powerful influence than

vaguely suggesting a miniature donkey. Jane Goodall (1963) witnessed a frenzied chimpanzee rite that she termed the "rain dance." Adriaan Kortlandt (1962) observed a chimpanzee quietly sitting and watching the sunset for a full fifteen minutes. These and similar observations suggest than chimpanzees at least possess a limited imagination.

others. According to Tylor, the acceptance of one supreme deity as the paramount spirit reigning over the rest marked the transition from polytheism to monotheism.

Tylor's successor at Oxford, Robert R. Marett, found elements of his predecessor's animistic theory well reasoned but not necessarily reflecting the train of thought that early humans would have employed in trying to make sense of the more puzzling aspects of human experience. Searching for a more generalized, "pre-animistic" notion that would have marked the beginnings of human concerns with the supernatural, Marett (1909) came upon the concept of mana, widely documented for the cultures of the Pacific Islanders. *Mana* refers to an impersonal supernatural force that may be concentrated in persons or inanimate objects. Being highly communicable, it is eagerly sought by persons anxious to possess and control as much of it as possible. Success in personal undertakings is due to mana, as are abundant harvests and healthy and fertile domestic animals. In Polynesia, where social standing determines the amount of mana an individual possesses, some persons are believed to be so highly charged as to be dangerous to people of lower ranks, who must be protected from overexposure by a variety of taboos. The concept of mana is thus comparable to high-voltage electricity whose extraordinary potential is matched by the deadly danger it can hold for those not equipped to handle it. While Marett with what he called "animatistic" theory hoped to have identified a form of power behind magical and religious activities that would be even more primitive than Tylor's spirit world, another Englishman, Sir James George Frazer (1854–1941), endeavored to show that any discussion of religious behavior must include the consideration of magical activities and that, in fact, religion evolved from magic (Frazer 1911–1915).

Although the temporal priority that Frazer assigned to magic over religion can never be

The concept of mana

Religion and magic

substantiated, the distinction he drew between the different kinds of magic gained wide acceptance among anthropologists. With respect to the principles on which magic is thought to operate, Frazer's conclusion was that

they will probably be found to resolve themselves into two: first, that like produces like, or that an effect resembles its cause; and, second, that things which have once been in contact with each other continue to act on each other at a distance after the physical contact has been severed. The former principle may be called the Law of Similarity, the latter the Law of Contact or Contagion (Frazer 1922:11).

Of the magic that follows the law of similarity—"imitative magic" in Frazer's term—

perhaps the most familiar application . . . is the attempt which has been made by many peoples in many ages to injure or destroy an enemy by injuring or destroying an image of him, in the belief that, just as the image suffers, so does the man, and that when it perishes he must die (Frazer 1922:12–13).

As for contagious magic,

the most familiar example . . . is the magical sympathy which is supposed to exist between a man and any severed portion of his person, as his hair or nails; so that whoever gets possession of human hair or nails may work his will, at any distance, upon the person from whom they were cut (Frazer 1922:38).

It will be noted from the foregoing examples that *magic* refers to techniques designed to achieve rather specific goals by manipulating the supernatural. According to Frazer, it is this characteristic that helps distinguish magic from religion, which, by contrast, consists in a "propitiation or conciliation of powers superior to man which are believed to direct and control the course of nature and of human life" (Frazer 1922:50).

For some time now, Frazer's contrast

between magic and religion has been seen as seriously overdrawn. Not only do the two occur side by side in many societies and complement each other but, inasmuch as both magical and religious attitudes and practices share a common basis in dealing with the supernatural, they frequently overlap to a considerable extent.

Armed with new insights gained during the early part of the twentieth century from his field work on the coral islands northeast of New Guinea, Bronislaw Malinowski (1884–1942) offered yet another view of the nature of magical and religious beliefs and activities. For him, magic arises to fill a gap in empirical knowledge. It develops at the point where primitive technology no longer produces results and is a practical art engaged in by specialists for very specific ends. Religion, on the other hand, has roots and purposes that are much more complex. It is

not born out of speculation or reflection [as Tylor would have it]. . . but rather out of the real tragedies of human life, out of the conflict between human plans and realities. . . .

The existence of strong personal attachments and the fact of death, which of all human events is the most upsetting . . . are perhaps the main sources of religious belief (Malinowski 1931:641).

Both religious and magical beliefs are greatly aided by the acceptance of myth. Far from being merely

an idle speculation about the origins of things or institutions. . . . [myth] is a statement of primeval reality which lives in the institutions and pursuits of a community. It justifies by precedent the existing order and it supplies a retrospective pattern of moral values . . . and of magical belief (Malinowski 1931:640).

SOCIAL AND SYMBOLIC NATURE OF RITUAL BEHAVIOR

Common to all four approaches, here chosen to illustrate some of the classic contributions

to the anthropology of religion, has been their primary concern with the individual's relationship to the realm of the supernatural. There is, however, another important aspect to religion that must not be neglected—its social nature. The most influential proponent of this approach was the French sociologist Emile Durkheim (1858–1917), who argued that the cognitive roots of religious behavior are anchored in social experience. The main source for his ideas is his classic study of primitive religion, *The Elementary Forms of the Religious Life* (1915; 1912 in its French original).

According to Durkheim, whereas magical activities are essentially an expression of personal, individual pursuits, the tribal mythology is a belief system shared by the entire group, religion itself is the very soul of society. Using as the basis for his analysis accounts of ritual behavior among the Australian aborigines, he saw their clan as filling the function of god. In his discussion of the *totem*—an animal, plant, or other object that gives the clan its collective designation—Durkheim poses the question of what the totem is a symbol or material expression of:

In the first place, it is the outward and visible form of . . . the totemic principle or god. But it is also the symbol of the . . . society called the clan. It is its flag. . . . So if it is at once the symbol of the god and of the society, is that not because the god and the society are only one? (Durkheim 1915:206).

The source of the native Australians' identification of society with all that is sacred, according to Durkheim, is to be sought in their way of life. These aborigines, who commonly wander about through their inhospitable environment in small groups, join together periodically in large ceremonial gatherings. It is on such occasions that primitive people come to realize, however unconsciously, that society is their sole source of strength and survival, and they therefore make its emblem, the totem, the object of their sacred attitude.

While Durkheim's theory of the purely social origin of religion has had its share of justified criticism, his view of religion as a powerful symbolic system, which by expressing and maintaining the value of society makes social life possible, has remained virtually unchallenged. There are, in fact, an increasing number of anthropologists today who have made the study of symbolism in ritual context their major concern. In their view, ritual provides a symbolic connection between the complex system of meanings embedded in a given cultural thought and the level on which social action takes place. A good example of this approach is Victor Turner's account of curing among the Ndembu of northwestern Zambia. Disease among these people is seen as not merely afflicting the sick individual but as having a profound effect on the structural framework of their society:

> It seems that the Ndembu "doctor" sees his task less as curing an individual patient than as remedying the ills of a corporate group. The sickness of a patient is mainly a sign that "something is rotten" in the corporate body. The patient will not get better until all the tensions and aggressions in the group's interrelations have been brought to light and exposed to ritual treatment. . . . Once the various causes of ill feeling against [the patient] and of his ill feeling against others had been "made visible". . . , the doctor . . . was able, [by means of] bloodlettings, confessions, purifications, . . . and build-up of expectations, to transform the ill feeling into well wishing (Turner 1967:392).

In this particular instance, the source of tensions among the members of a group is symbolically identified with the illness of a patient who, in turn, serves as a scapegoat for social disorder. Once the causative agent has been diagnosed, the psychic problems of the patient are symbolically resolved by way of social purification. Interpretations of this kind, far from being limited to the study of curing, have been applied to a variety of ritual contexts—sacrifice, rites of passage, taboo, and others.

TO SUM UP   There are a few anthropologists today who are inclined to reduce the sources of religious behavior to a single set of variables, whether psychological, social, or other. Clifford Geertz was not far from an expression of the modern consensus on the subject when he wrote:

> For an anthropologist, the importance of religion lies in its capacity to serve, for an individual or for a group, as a source of general, yet distinctive conceptions of the world, the self, and the relations between them, on the one hand . . . and of rooted, no less distinctive "mental" dispositions . . . on the other. From these cultural functions flow, in turn, its social and psychological ones (Geertz 1966:40).

RELIGION AMONG HUNTER-GATHERERS

In his book *Religion: An Anthropological View* (1966), Anthony F. C. Wallace sets up four major categories of "religions." Each of these categories is defined in terms of the cult institutions that characterize it (a cult institution is a set of rituals with the same general goal). These institutions range from individualistic—that is, those performed without specialized assistance—to ecclesiastical, involving complex bureaucracies with organized churches and highly professionalized personnel. Between these two extremes are cult institutions whose main feature is the participation of laymen acting on behalf of various social groups or the community as a whole. Starting at the most primitive level, Wallace recognizes the following four types of religions: shamanic religions, comprising only individualistic and shamanistic cult institutions; communal religions, characterized by communal as well as individualistic and shamanistic cult institutions; Olympian religions, adding to those already mentioned a variety of ecclesiastical institutions; and monotheistic religions, possessing all these features and in addition an ecclesiastical system centered on the conception of one supreme deity.

Although a classification of the wide variety of religious practices and beliefs such as that offered by Wallace may seem rather simplified, it correlates surprisingly well with the several levels of sociocultural integration that have provided the overall framework for much of our discussion in this book. There is more than an implicit evolutionary approach in Wallace's scheme. Underlying his sequence of the four main types of religion is a progression from direct manipulation of natural phenomena by individuals, to the formulation of ever more encompassing belief systems serving a collectivity, to an overriding concern with human morality on the one hand and the complex relationship between an elaborate religious apparatus and other cultural institutions on the other.

Wallace's religions of the shamanic type are by and large associated with the band-level societies of hunter-gatherers. Although these peoples are characteristically astute in the understanding of their natural environment and the techniques for exploiting it, in their attempts at controlling nature they commonly employ supernatural means. Any course of events outside the realm of a naturalistic explanation is attributed to spirits that, much as those who believe in them, lack distinct hierarchy. Illness, success or failure in the hunt, and other conditions or situations in the life of members of band-level societies are believed manipulable by establishing contact with the appropriate agency of the spirit world. While access to the supernatural is open to all concerned individuals, shamans are credited with being by far the most adept at gaining it. Because the mode of subsistence of small groups can scarcely justify the maintenance of full-fledged specialists, shamans are invariably part-time practitioners. Usually—but not always—men, they acquire the power to manipulate supernatural forces through a highly personal experience such as a trance or vision or learn their craft from an elder relative.

For the following illustration of the shaman's techniques in dealing with illness we

A Northwest Coast shaman at work. The photograph was taken in 1889, a fact that accounts for its rather posed appearance. It does, however, capture some prime features of the curing ritual and of the doctor-patient relationship: the sick man anxiously undergoing treatment, the curer garbed in the appropriate mask and costume, and the personal attention that is being received by the patient. (Courtesy of The American Museum of Natural History)

are indebted to James F. Downs. His description concerns the Washo Indians, who used to wander through the area near Lake Tahoe in search of plant food, fish, and game:

To affect [sic] a cure, a shaman was called to perform a ceremony over the patient. The cure was felt to be brought about not by the shaman's skill but by his "power". . . . A treatment required that the shaman work for four nights. . . . On each of the nights the shaman prayed to his power to assist him, smoked tobacco . . . and sang special songs. . . . Accompanying his singing with a rattle made of dry cocoons, he passed into a trance and while in this state located the site of the illness and identified the cause. If a ghost was the cause, the shaman would identify the contaminating object and instruct the patient as to whether he should get rid of it or perhaps simply treat it differently. If, on the other hand, an enemy had "shot" a sickness into the patient, the shaman would remove it by sucking, employing an eagle feather and tobacco smoke to make the extraction easier. When the object was removed and shown to the patient and his guests, the shaman would lecture it and then throw it away into the night (Downs 1966:56).

Although the object is invariably produced by skillful sleight of hand, the shaman's purpose is not to deceive but to convince the patient of the magical effectiveness of his power. The patient, placing his confidence in the power of the curer, quite commonly will derive noticeable psychosomatic benefit from such ministrations. If the shaman's treatment fails to produce the desired results, a power more effective than that available to him is held responsible. Conversely, a person who thinks himself threatened by some powerful evil force can become seriously ill and under extreme circumstances may even die as a consequence of his own intense fear.

In band-level societies ritual activities accompanied by the telling of origin myths or by dancing and singing are associated primarily with a change in an individual's social status. Known as *rites of passage*, they mark the critical periods in a person's life, especially the transition from childhood to adulthood (puberty). Typically, those who are initiated into their new social roles are first symbolically separated from the rest of the society (by secluding them in a special hut, for example). Their transition from one state to the next is effected, symbolically again, by a variety of means ranging from genital or facial mutilations to hazing or ceremonial cleansing. Finally, the initiates are reincorporated into the society.

Despite the frequently elaborate nature of these and other rites of passage among hunters and gatherers, their formulations concerning moral and ethical conduct do not appear to be either highly abstract or consistent. Their relationships to one another, as we have already seen, are largely based on the circumstance that any one member of a band must share the fate of the other members in both good times and bad. Their economic, social, and religious activities form a seamless whole.

RELIGION IN TRIBAL AND
PEASANT SOCIETIES
AND ANCIENT EMPIRES

In tribal societies, greater social complexity is customarily accompanied by a corresponding elaboration of religion, evident particularly in community-wide institutions. To be sure, individualistic practices having to do with love magic and other personal matters continue to be employed. Services of medicine men are also widely sought, especially in connection with illness and protection against *sorcery*—a malevolent practice of magic that is learned—and *witchcraft*—an evil power thought to be either intrinsic in certain individuals or acquired as a consequence of association with those already possessing it. Beliefs concerning death and the potential of departed kin to either assist or harm assume significance, and supernatural beings or deities become differentiated according to their powers, function, and rank. Given the usual dependence of tribal economies on food production, and consequently the higher density of their social units, ritual activities–including those of passage–commonly take public, communal form. Our example of a tribal religion is drawn from the culture of the Hopi (Thompson and Joseph 1945 and Titiev 1944).

The tribal pattern: the Hopi

These Indians, close neighbors of the Washo, inhabit about a dozen villages in northeastern Arizona. Most of their pueblos are perched on three high mesas overlooking arid land that averages a scant ten inches of rainfall per year. Although over the centuries the Hopi have acquired remarkable skill as subsistence farmers growing corn and other vegetables, the constant threat of crop failure from lack of moisture has taught them to turn frequently to the supernatural for assistance.

The Hopi tribe lacks centralized tribal government. Each village is an independent entity within which kin and clan ties command first loyalty. Despite an active schedule of elaborate annual ceremonies, there is no formal priesthood among these Indians. Instead, a village chief or other leader assumes responsibility for a given set of rites. Once these have been performed, he resumes his normal round of daily activities. Every Hopi village is organized into a number of secret societies, and each of these in turn comes under the control of a particular clan. As a rule, the clan head is the chief of the group's society and the keeper of its most sacred ceremonial objects. At certain times of the year, usually determined by the position of the sun or moon, each society is expected to carry out the rites entrusted to its care. These observances take place for the most part in the underground chambers, or kivas, owned by the clans. Membership in the secret societies is voluntary but is subject to certain restrictions of age and sex.

A fundamental feature of the Hopi religion is a belief in life after death. The world of the dead is imagined to be much like the world of the living Hopi except that the deceased are immaterial and, as such, are able to float in the air as rain-bringing clouds. Alternatively, the dead are believed to be capable of visiting their people on earth in the form of spirits, known as kachinas, who may also represent animals, heavenly bodies, and a variety of other beings.

The Hopi year is divided by the summer and winter solstices into two halves, each of which is characterized by a series of ritual observances. Because the Hopi stress a close reciprocal relationship between the dead and the living, many rituals are performed twice a year—once in their major form in the upper world of the living while at the same time a minor version is believed to be celebrated among the spirits of the underworld, and conversely, half a year later. The major rituals of the Hopi usually last nine days, with the bulk of the nine-day period devoted to secret observances held in the kivas and accompanied by singing, praying, and other ceremonial activities. On the ninth day, the rituals culminate in public performances staged in the village plaza. For these carefully rehearsed events, known as dances, participants are elaborately costumed.

The main ceremonies emphasize crucial phases in the yearly agricultural cycle: the necessity for the sun to move back into its summer path and bring suitably warm weather for the planting of fields; the importance of fertility and germination of seeds for the approaching planting season; the need for rain to make crops grow; and so on. Best known among the ceremonial events are the so-called homegoing dance and the snake dance. The former, conducted by the Kachina Society in July to mark the return of the kachinas to their home in the San Francisco Peaks (near Flagstaff), symbolically stresses the process of maturing and ripening. For this dance, as for the several other ritual performances of the

The snake dance, celebrated principally as a prayer for rain, continues to be one of the major ceremonials of the Hopi Indians. The photograph was taken in 1897 in the village of Walpi on First Mesa (northeastern Arizona). (Photograph Courtesy History Division, Los Angeles County Museum of Natural History)

kachina cult complex, the kachinas are impersonated by masked men of the village. For the snake dance, thought to have been originally an observance of the Snake clan, members of the Snake and Antelope societies collect numbers of live snakes. According to a myth, snakes are regarded by the Hopi as their ancient kin, endowed with powers to bring rain. On the ninth day of the ritual, after an elaborate dance during which each of the participants holds a snake between his lips, the reptiles are released at designated shrines. Prayers for rain, plentiful corn, and good health conclude the ceremony.

TO SUM UP The Hopi, here representative of tribal societies, possess a definite cosmology and a system of religious behavior that links ancestor worship with both social organiza-

tion and Hopi economic concerns by means of ritual activities of village-wide participation. Although this situation is quite similar to that found in peasant communities, an important difference is that peasant communities are part of a larger society. Consequently, in the words of Eric Wolf:

If [peasant religion] functions to support and balance the peasant ecosystem and social organization, it also constitutes a component in a larger ideological order. Responsive to stimuli which derive both from the peasant sector of society and from the wider social order, religion forges one more link binding the peasantry to that order.

This work of relating the peasant's cognitions of the sacred and his techniques for handling it to the beliefs and techniques of the total society is usually in the hands of religious specialists, much as the work of relating the peasant economically and politically to the larger order becomes the work of political and economic specialists (Wolf 1966:100).

Religion in a peasant community

The manner in which culturally external religious beliefs and practices of the larger society are grafted onto the ancient foundation of a local belief system is well illustrated in the case of the Zinacantecos of southern Mexico (Vogt 1970). Descendants of the ancient Maya, these Indians live in the municipio of Zinacantan in the highlands of Chiapas. The elaborate ceremonial life of the Zinacantecos is a highly integrated system combining Spanish-Catholic elements with others of a basic Mayan character. The world of the Zinacantecos is a large cube whose "navel" marks the middle of their ceremonial center. Above this world, in the Sky, is the domain of the Sun, the Moon, and the Stars. Under the influence of Catholicism the Zinacantecos have come to associate the Sun with God and the Moon with the Virgin Mary. Ancestral gods believed to reside in the surrounding mountains and an assortment of Catholic saints whose images are kept in local churches and chapels are integral parts of the Zinacanteco pantheon and receive essentially the same ritual treatment. There are hundreds of "Calvaries"—elaborate cross shrines—in the area that serve as "ancestral shrines representing units of social structure at various levels, where Zinacantecos go to pray and leave offerings to their ancestral gods who are meeting there and waiting eagerly for the prayers and offerings" (Vogt 1970:13).

Shamans are numerous—at least 160 of them for a population of some 8,000 Indians—and are ranked according to length of service. They are called upon to cure illness, dedicate new houses, perform ceremonies in fields about to be planted with maize, carry out the rain-making ritual, and the like. The ceremonial center of the ancient Maya of the Classic period has taken a new form in contemporary Zinacantan containing a po-litico-religious headquarters, a town hall, and three Catholic churches. The rich ritual life of Zinacantan Center is carried out through a religious hierarchy of 61 positions in 4 levels of a ceremonial ladder. These positions, conceived of as burdens, or *cargoes*, are eagerly sought by Zinacanteco men, whose obligation it is to serve a year at each level at great personal expense for food, drink, and ritual paraphernalia. Great honor and prestige fall to those who are able in the course of time to reach the top of the cargo system. According to Vogt, "a major share of a Zinacanteco's energy and resources in his mature years (from about twenty-five to sixty-five) goes into planning for, serving in, and recovering from the four years of ceremonial duty he puts into performing rituals in the cargo system in Zinacantan Center" (1970:75). The major ceremonies are scheduled in accordance with the Catholic calendar.

The Zinacanteco ritual complex thus represents a *syncretism*—a coalescence of beliefs and practices different in form and origin—characteristic of many peasant communities that have adjusted their native supernaturalism to the context of a superordinate religious tradition. Compared with the communal religion of the tribal societies, there is the additional presence of religious personnel—both the priests from outside the culture who administer the Catholic sacraments in the churches of the Zinacantecos and the hierarchy of native functionaries connected with the cargo system of the local ceremonial center. The situation is somewhat different in European and some other peasant communities where religious practices and beliefs do not derive from the forced imposition of a world religion. Rather, they stem from a long and continuing exposure to Christianity or other organized faith, and are customarily manifested as localized versions of the establishment church.

Religion among the ancient Maya

We have seen how specific features of social organization and economic life in small-scale societies help determine the nature of religious behavior among their members and how peasant communities mesh their religious beliefs and practices with the ecclesiastical institutions of the states in which they are embedded. Linkages of this sort existed between religion and the rest of culture in ancient empires as well. The large populations, high degree of specialization, and social stratification of such societies were invariably reflected both in the professionalization and bureaucratization of their religious personnel and in their members' perception of the supernatural world. Such "Olympian" religions, to use Wallace's terminology, were once found on several continents, most notably in the kingdoms of central Africa, marginal regions of East Asia, and the American high-culture areas of the pre-Conquest Aztecs, Inca, and Maya.

Typically, the social hierarchy of these societies was closely matched by the ranked structure of their pantheon. The gods, or at least the higher ones among them, took active interest in human affairs and gave their sanction to the political institutions of the state. As a source of values and authority, religion reinforced or even represented the power of the state. For example, among the ancient Maya the world was conceived of as consisting, in addition to the earth, of thirteen heavens and nine underworlds, and was populated at all levels by numerous gods who demanded frequent sacrifices, especially of human hearts and blood. Elaborate rituals were conducted in monumental ceremonial centers dominated by temple-topped pyramids, which dotted a sizeable portion of Middle America. Dedicated to the various gods, these centers were served by a hierarchy of full-time priests who were also skilled administrators and made astonishing achievements in mathematics, astronomy, and other fields.

There is little question that members of the priestly class exercised great powers in running the affairs of the theocratic empire of the Maya: very likely they and the nobles must have been closely allied by kinship. In fact, many archaeologists today are inclined to believe that the power of the priests, which was capable of mobilizing vast numbers of people for the construction of a great civilization, eventually brought about its own collapse. According to this theory, the cause of the sudden collapse of the Mayan city-states about a thousand years ago was a virtual civil war between the toiling populace of farmers and the priesthood who held the reins of government. The disintegration of the Mayan centers must have been greatly accelerated in the absence of an effective military force that could have controlled a dispersed farming population once the theocratic rule of the priests had been shaken.

RELIGION, NATIVISM, AND REVITALIZATION

Religion is often viewed as one of the most conservative components of culture. This observation holds true for societies, regardless of their level of complexity, that do not face substantial internal and/or external pressures. In crisis situations, however, belief systems often reflect social turmoil or dangers from without.

A very substantial body of anthropological literature addresses itself to nativistic, revivalistic, or messianic movements sparked by the conquest and subjugation of weak societies by the more powerful—an aftershock of colonialism. These revitalizations, as they are collectively referred to, can be viewed as a religious response to situations that are no longer amenable to physical resistance. In its origins, Christianity was the product of just such circumstances, specifically the distress of the Jewish people following their incorporation into the Roman Empire. That only some Jews followed the teachings of Jesus is typical, for conquest often fragments opposition and gives rise to a variety of leaders espousing different responses to the conquest situation. Typical also is the death of the religious visionary at the hands of the imperial authority and later attempts to dismember the movement.

As we noted earlier, the best-known example of a nativistic movement from the history of American colonization is the emergence of the ghost-dance religion, whose two waves swept the Plains Indian peoples during the latter part of the nineteenth century. By 1890 the only response available to traditional Indian societies was one that stressed supernatural aid in their last-ditch resistance to maintain their cultural integrity and life itself. The cry for help in an Arapaho song is no less poignant today than it was a century ago:

My Father, have pity on me!
I have nothing to eat,
I am dying of thirst—
Everything is gone![3]

(Quoted in Andrist 1964:338)

The infamous slaughter by United States cavalry troops of several hundred Sioux Indians at Wounded Knee finally smashed the ghost dance but did not put an end to revitalization movements. With the new century, Native Americans developed religious forms, such as peyotism, compounded of Christian teachings of love and forgiveness and the long heritage of self-knowledge and cultural pride. Indian groups that for various reasons had not been drawn into the ghost dance, such as the Navajo and the Pueblos, found that their traditional religious usages continued to serve them well. More recently, Indian efforts to resist have added a more strictly political form. "Red power" movements, in particular the American Indian Movement, fight their battles in Washington and the state capitals with the weapons of a minority group in a modern nation-state—litigation, lobbying, and political activism designed to engender pride

in the native heritage and make symbolic statements that will be heard throughout the country and abroad. In these manifestations, the religious element is not lost, for it is the claim of Indian activists that the native way, shaped to modern needs, constitutes a philosophical and religious alternative to destructive materialism.

Elsewhere in the world, especially in New Guinea and on its nearby islands, the exposure over the past hundred years of remote peoples to the wonders of modern technological civilization has stimulated quests for a new identity, one which would draw on both native values and the material abundance most impressively displayed by the United States armed forces during World War II. The central theme of these *cargo cults,* as they are called, is the mystical view that material wealth is destined for native populations but illegitimately kept from them by the whites. Hence their belief in the return—in planes or ships freighted with the products of modern civilization—of ancestors whose arrival will usher in a long-awaited period of prosperity. An interesting example of the practical approach taken toward realizing such hopes was the amassing of a fund of some $80,000 by the people of the island of New Hanover off New Guinea with which to "buy" then President Lyndon Johnson, who as the leader of the world's wealthiest nation would be most privy to the secret of cargo. The failure of this enterprise and of many other attempts to bring about an era of plenty has been variously attributed to interception, theft, or deception by missionaries or government officials from those countries in which the bounty would have originated. The belief in cargo can best be understood in the context of the redistributive economy mentioned in an earlier chapter. As Marvin Harris writes in a chapter of his recent book:

It is easy to dismiss cargo beliefs as the ravings of primitive minds. . . . This would be a cogent theory if there were nothing mysterious about how industrial

[3]From Ralph K. Andrist, *The Long Death; the Last Days of the Plains Indian* (New York: Macmillan, 1964). Copyright © 1964 by Ralph K. Andrist. Reprinted by permission.

wealth gets manufactured and distributed. But in point of fact, it is not easy to explain why some countries are poor and others rich, nor is it easy to say why there are such sharp differences in the distribution of wealth within modern nations. What I'm suggesting is that there really is a cargo mystery, and that the natives are justified in trying to solve it (Harris 1974:136–137).

As we have indicated, revitalization cults are to be found in all manner of societies. Millennial movements, which generally envisage a cataclysmic termination of the established social order, have been part of Christianity almost from its inception. The stress is on a reordered universe that will be brought about by the Second Coming of Christ. The evil will perish, the good will inherit the earth. A fervor of millennialism gripped the Western world with the approach of the year A.D. 1000, and there are some who claim that as the year 2000 draws nearer, the indications of a similar phenomenon are already evident.

Reformist and utopian movements, of a political as well as a religious character, are likely to arise when segments of the population are dissatisfied with current conditions. Religious reformations are often indicative of major power struggles, as was the case in the Thirty Years War, which ravaged much of Europe between 1618 and 1648. Utopian movements attempt to establish societies that are felt to meet more closely the divine ordinances for a righteous life. It was in large measure for this reason that the Puritans settled in New England.

RELIGION IN MODERN SOCIETY

How different will be the new era, when God brings an end to wickedness! Instead of sorrow, sickness and death, there will be happiness, vibrant health and everlasting life! The nightmare of the past will be gone forever. The joy at that time will far outweigh all the agony man has ever experienced (Watchtower Bible and Tract Society 1967:177).

In addition to ministering to the spiritual needs of their members, many churches have begun to take an active stand on contemporary social issues. The photograph shows Dr. Martin Luther King, Jr., accompanied by other clergymen, leading a voter protest march in Selma, Alabama, in 1965. (Wide World Photos)

This quotation is taken from a recent publication of the Watchtower Bible and Tract Society, perhaps better known as Jehovah's Witnesses, a fundamentalist religious group with millions of followers in the United States and other countries. The statement is a prediction, a prophecy, of what the earth will be like once harmony is restored with the Second Coming of Christ: wicked humans and wicked demons will be destroyed by God; perfect peace will reign; and all creatures will live together without conflict.

The attitudes and expectations contained in the passage are remarkably similar to millennial beliefs of centuries ago and, in fact, share a good deal with such nativistic movements as the ghost dance and cargo cults. Must one therefore conclude that religion in the last quarter of the twentieth century is much like religion in the Middle Ages or among the Plains Indians a hundred years ago?

The answer to this question is that while it is impossible to speak of typical religious beliefs in contemporary America (and most other modern complex societies), religious needs have not changed in any fundamental manner. However, these needs are met by a multiplicity of faiths, theologies, and cults catering to different social groups. The appeal of Jehovah's Witnesses is much the same as that of the ghost dance and of popular religious movements in Christian Europe. Many fundamentalist, evangelical, and Pentecostal faiths find a great deal of their support among the poor and the downtrodden, as any observer of inner city storefront churches will verify.

These, of course, are only part of the current religious scene. Another segment of the religious continuum is made up of what may be termed the established churches that, in common with other religions, function to validate and maintain a society's particular way of life. This is in part accomplished by the persistence of rigidly fixed ritual proceedings spanning generation after generation. Such a link with the past offers security in the present and the

Storefront churches are a common feature of many American urban localities. These churches are of different denominations, but typically of dissenting or nonestablishment orientation. Often small in scale and nonhierarchical, they are characterized by a close link between ministers and the communities they serve. (Charles Gatewood)

Chapter 16   Religion and ideology: primary questions and ultimate answers

The structural complexity of world religions is reflected in this perspective of Pope Paul VI presiding over the reopening ceremonies of an ecumenical council in St. Peter's Basilica, the Vatican. The Pope stands in front of the altar while attending cardinals and other churchmen fill the seats on both sides of the aisle. (Wide World Photos)

future, perhaps especially at a time when so much else seems to be in flux. But this sense of continuity may, in fact, run counter to the desires of some—even those in highest authority—to renovate ritual and theology. When in 1962, the Second Vatican Council, called by Pope John XXIII to "bring the Church up to date" and make its teachings more meaningful, authorized the use of local languages in the Mass and other liturgy, the break with long-standing tradition was such that some Catholics have yet to accept it fully. One reaction was that the Church through such innovations was abandoning the people; others felt that the innovations did not go far enough. A similar reaction on the part of Protestants met efforts to translate the Bible when theologians began to sense that the lofty and archaic language of the King James Version had become a formula rather than a living source of the word of God. Even greater cleavages are likely to follow the ordination of women priests in tradition-bound religions, a movement that has already made some headway.

It is apparent, therefore, that religion is not immune to contemporary social currents, but that for some it is the very stability of theology and ritual that is of prime importance. The regular religious services of the Judeo-Christian and Islamic traditions remind believers symbolically of the values by which to live and thus serve essentially the same function as rites of intensification—to emphasize the group's cohesion and its need for unity. On a secular level, these same goals are sought in the various celebrations commemorating the birth of a nation or its founder, the war dead, and the like.

To be sure, the integrative function of religion may be considerably weakened in large pluralistic societies such as the United States, where each of the many faiths tends to reinforce the separate identity of its followers. In other parts of the world, for example on the Indian subcontinent and in Northern Ireland, religious rivalries between Hindus and Moslems, or Catholics and Protestants, have proved to be mur-

derously divisive. We should note, however, that in modern states religious factionalism is seldom a sufficient cause for conflict. The danger of strife becomes imminent when contending factions—of class, ethnicity, or political orientation—make religion their rallying point.

In one way or another, religion must attempt to deal with the critical dilemmas of life. To the standard problems posed by human existence—uncertainty, anxiety, misfortune, and death—modern life brings its own hard questions. We live in a novel world, with few historical precedents, where the lessons of the past seem to have only limited relevance. One response at the religious level is to examine postulates and search for ethical standards congruent with the new situation. Another reaction, a traditional one, is to sever our links with the material world. While most religious traditions contain a mystical and contemplative component, few would claim that this is a dominant feature of modern Judaism and Christianity. Perhaps for these reasons,

(left) Even well-established and hierarchical churches are currently undergoing some major structural shifts. These three women priests of the American Episcopal Church celebrate the Holy Eucharist at New York's Riverside Church. Women have played a significant role in some Western religious organizations, such as the Salvation Army, and the pressure is mounting for the total integration of women in previously male-dominated organizations. (United Press International)

(right) In the modern world, ease of travel and dissemination of information have facilitated the spread of religious beliefs and practices, except in instances where such trends have been hampered by restrictive legislation. Here American Buddhist monks are seen at prayer. (Arthur Tress/Magnum Photos, Inc.)

various oriental religions and sects, some highly demanding in spiritual and intellectual effort, others perhaps more rightly termed "the guru racket," have flourished in the West during the last few decades. There is, of course, a great difference between the teachings of Buddha and the injunctions of self-proclaimed teenage perfect masters— as big a gulf as that which separates the student of Christ's teachings and the individual who "freaks out" with Jesus.

Finally, some mention must be made of the tremendous revival of occult beliefs in the last few years. Indicative of this trend is the vogue in science fantasy books, some of

A Vietnamese Catholic priest celebrates mass in a Hue refugee camp at the height of the Vietnam War. Catholicism has been one of the major religions in Vietnam since its introduction by French missionaries several centuries ago. (Marc Riboud/Magnum Photos, Inc.)

Revival of the occult

which have made the best-seller list for many successive weeks, for example, *The Bermuda Triangle* (Berlitz 1974). Erich von Däniken in his books (1968, 1970) has made many claims that run counter to much hard evidence—that Egyptian pyramids, Easter Island megaliths, and other structures were built by ancient spacemen of a superior race—and he is widely believed. Astrological predictions are printed in syndicated newspaper columns and avidly followed by an increasing number of readers. Covens of witches and warlocks are flourishing in many large cities, and the First World Congress of Sorcery, held in Bogotá, Colombia, in 1975 was reportedly attended by some

30,000 people. "Psychic surgeons" are believed to perform operations without the aid of anesthesia and scalpel, and so on. The reasons for the trend are no doubt multiple—among them the growing anti-intellectual atmosphere, the withdrawal to the mysterious from the increasing complexity of scientific explanation, or simply people's insistence on doing their own thing.

We can bring forward a number of possible explanations for the occult revival and related social/supernatural phenomena that stress the virtues of unreason and the separation of the individual from the complexities of life. Life is, indeed, hard and complex, but it is unlikely to become easier or more manageable if we abdicate reason. We will not broaden our minds, nor add to our spirituality, if we turn away from our brothers and sisters in a drift towards hedonism and "states of consciousness" that satisfy nobody but ourselves. Fear and despair can be managed and in this management religion has played a role, but they can never be eliminated from the human condition. The reality may be that the social structure is fragmented, that the secure foundations of the past are crumbling; but if modern societies are to survive, they will have to be rebuilt. In this respect, it is worth remembering that in contemporary despotisms the new "religion," while secular in form, requires a comparable abdication of the critical faculties.

The growth or revival of occult beliefs in many Western societies may reflect a growing anxiety about the future and a search for "answers" to primordial problems. The photograph shows a section of a university bookstore in the Midwest. (Daniel Brody/Stock Boston)

REFERENCES

ANDRIST, RALPH K.
1964 *The long death; the last days of the Plains Indian.* New York: Macmillan.

BERLITZ, CHARLES FRAMBACH
1974 *The Bermuda Triangle.* Garden City, N.Y.: Doubleday.

DÄNIKEN, ERICH VON
1968 *Chariots of the Gods? Unsolved mysteries of the past.* Michael Heron, trans. New York: Putnam.
1970 *Gods from outer space; return to the stars, or evidence for the impossible.* Michael Heron, trans. New York: Putnam.

DOWNS, JAMES F.
1966 *The two worlds of the Washo, an Indian tribe of California and Nevada.* New York: Holt, Rinehart and Winston.

DURKHEIM, EMILE
1912 *Les formes élémentaires de la vie religieuse, le système totémique en Australie.* Paris: F. Alcan.
1915 *The elementary forms of the religious life.* Joseph Ward Swain, trans. London: George Allen and Unwin.

FRAZER, SIR JAMES GEORGE
1911–1915 *The golden bough; a study in magic and religion* (3rd ed., rev. and enl. 12 vols.). London: Macmillan.
1922 *The golden bough; a study in magic and religion* (one-vol., abridged ed.). London: Macmillan.

GEERTZ, CLIFFORD
1966 Religion as a cultural system. In *Anthropological approaches to the study of religion.* Michael Banton, ed. London: Tavistock. Pp. 1–46.

GOODALL, JANE
1963 My life among wild chimpanzees. *National Geographic* 124:2:272–308 (August).

HARRIS, MARVIN
1974 *Cows, pigs, wars, and witches; the rid-dles of culture.* New York: Random House.

KORTLANDT, ADRIAAN
1962 Chimpanzees in the wild. *Scientific American* 206:5:128–138 (May).

KROEBER, ALFRED L.
1948 *Anthropology: race, language, culture, psychology, prehistory* (new, rev. ed.). New York: Harcourt, Brace.

MALINOWSKI, BRONISLAW
1931 Culture. In *Encyclopaedia of the social sciences.* Edwin R. A. Seligman, ed. New York: Macmillan. Vol. 4, pp. 621–646.

MARETT, ROBERT R.
1909 *The threshold of religion.* London: Methuen.

REDFIELD, ROBERT, AND W. LLOYD WARNER
1940 Cultural anthropology and modern agriculture. In *1940 Yearbook of agriculture: farmers in a changing world.* Washington, D.C.: U.S. Government Printing Office. Pp. 983–993.

THOMPSON, LAURA, AND ALICE JOSEPH
1945 *The Hopi way.* Chicago: The University of Chicago Press.

TITIEV, MISCHA
1944 *Old Oraibi, a study of the Hopi Indians of Third Mesa.* Papers of the Peabody Museum of American Archaeology and Ethnology, Harvard University, vol. 22, no. 1. Cambridge, Mass.

TURNER, VICTOR
1967 *The forest of symbols; aspects of Ndembu ritual.* Ithaca, N.Y.: Cornell University Press.

TYLOR, SIR EDWARD BURNETT
1871 *Primitive culture: researches into the development of mythology, philosophy, religion, art, and custom.* 2 vols. London: J. Murray.

VOGT, EVON Z.
1970 *The Zinacantecos of Mexico; a modern Maya way of life.* New York: Holt, Rinehart and Winston.

WALLACE, ANTHONY F. C.
1966 *Religion; an anthropological view.* New York: Random House.

WATCHTOWER BIBLE AND TRACT SOCIETY
1967 *Did man get here by evolution or by creation?* New York.

WOLF, ERIC R.
1966 *Peasants.* Englewood Cliffs, N.J.: Prentice-Hall.

CONCLUSIONS

In Part Three we have offered a basic framework for an understanding of sociocultural institutions that complements an earlier one that grouped together cultures of similar levels of complexity, from hunter-gatherers to contemporary complex societies. It is against this background that we wish to discuss several important topics in the final section of this book—among them the nature of the ubiquitous and steadily accelerating social and cultural change from which no society is exempt. The foundations that we have laid in this and the preceding parts will help us pose some crucial questions in regard to the uncertain future of humanity that anthropologists, together with other concerned people, must consider and must direct their best efforts to answer.

PART
FOUR

COMMUNICATION:
THE
PIVOT
OF
CULTURE

INTRODUCTION

Concern with language and with communication in general has always been strong in American anthropology. The very nature of ethnographic field work requires that anthropologists learn the languages of the people they study. Moreover, it is generally accepted that the study of speech behavior offers valuable insights into the orientation of particular cultures as well as into the similarities and differences among them. At another level of analysis, an understanding of human communication is indispensable for an understanding of culture in a more fundamental, abstract sense.

An evolutionary perspective calls for the study of human communicative behavior to focus on both the emergence of language and related systems of communication and the development of these systems. Just as in the eighteenth century, when Jean Jacques Rousseau (1712–1778) and other philosophers made serious attempts to explain the origin and development of language, what is understood today about the nature of language plays a significant role in what is understood about the nature of humanity. With respect to the question of language origins, the anthropological approach is unique, combining the study of the biological nature of human beings and their cultural heritage. What is more, anthropology is the only one among the social and behavioral sciences concerned with both language and the other forms of interaction. Anthropologists are thus in a particularly advantageous position to investigate the nature of human communication in the broadest possible context.

The close ties between historical linguistics and anthropology are no less productive, as we attempt to show in the second chapter of Part Four. For a period of some five thousand years, written records have provided archaeologists and culture historians with an invaluable source of information on aspects of past civilizations concerning which material evidence is silent.

In short, language is so firmly lodged within the overall matrix of culture, and speech behavior is so inseparably tied to social behavior, that to study one without the benefit of the other would necessarily result in a one-sided, incomplete understanding of individuals and societies alike. One might convincingly argue that language is humankind's most significant invention—in its absence, the transmission of culture from generation to generation would be so severely impaired as to render the humanizing process impossible.

It is for this reason that the study of language, and of communication in general, deserves careful consideration in any well-balanced investigation of human cultural accomplishments.

Chapter 17

The nature of communication and the structure of language

The concept of communication

Communication between animals is effected whenever one individual receives a signal originating with another. When one gets up from bed to let in a cat who is demanding entry by crying outside the window, this reaction is in response to a simple but effective communicative act.

All communication involves the recognition of signs. When a passenger in the adjacent seat on an airplane sits with eyes fixed on the pages of a book or magazine, it is invariably taken as a sign that he or she does not wish to be interrupted by an attempt at friendly conversation. And when on finishing the book, the person leans back against the seat, eyes closed, one takes it as a sign that he or she wishes to continue to be undisturbed. Not all human behavior, however, is quite so transparent. For example, in the United States loud and sustained whistling during or after a performance carries with it an expression of approval, but in some European countries it means the exact opposite: pointed dissatisfaction or even disgust.

Symbols

Signs of this kind—regarded by cultural convention as representing something else—are referred to as *symbols*. Words are particularly good examples of symbols. Even if sanctioned by time-honored use, they are wholly arbitrary: they bear no inherent relationship to that for which they stand. The unusually long word *hemidemisemiquaver* signifies a sound of the shortest duration in our musical notation; by contrast, the word *sea* gives no indication of the immensity of the concept that it denotes.

Learning the meanings of words from our earliest childhood as effortlessly as we do (and later taking them for granted) prevents us from realizing fully how humanizing is the power of symbols. A unique testimony to the importance of symbols comes from Helen Keller (1880–1968), who at the age of nineteen months was stricken with an illness that left her deaf and blind. In spite of this tremendous handicap, with the help of her teacher, Anne Mansfield Sullivan (Macy), she learned to write and to speak. Miss Keller described the exciting moment when the words that her teacher spelled into her hand stopped being merely signs and became symbols:

We walked down the path to the well-house. . . . Some one was drawing water and my teacher placed my hand under the spout. As the cool stream gushed over one hand she spelled into the other the word *water*, first slowly, then rapidly. I stood still, my whole attention fixed upon the motions of her fingers. Suddenly I felt a misty consciousness as of something forgotten—a thrill of returning thought; and somehow the mystery of language was revealed to me. I knew then that "w-a-t-e-r" meant the wonderful cool something that was flowing over my hand. That living word awakened my soul, gave it light, hope, joy, set it free! There were barriers still, it is true, but barriers that could in time be swept away (Keller 1954:36).

COMMUNICATION AND SPEECH

Any full-fledged process of communication, including human speech, has several essential components. One is the *code*, a system of signals agreed upon by those who wish to engage in some meaningful interaction. Any one of the several thousand languages of the world, whether still spoken or not, represents a special variety of a particular kind of code—the language code. Some nonverbal signals, such as an arrow indicating direction, are readily understood by many people regardless of the language they speak. Words of a language, on the other hand, are arbitrary; they must be learned from scratch.

With some exceptions, such as talking to oneself, communication is a social activity and involves at least two parties. The person who converts a message into code is referred to as the *encoder* (speaker, addresser). The process of encoding consists in selecting appropriate signals of a code (or codes) to be conveyed by one (or more) of the available physical media—the *channel(s)* of communication. In the case of speech, the medium employed is audible sound (and the channel may be said to be acoustic); in this textbook, the channel is visual (or optical) and assumes the form of written characters or illustra-

Components of the communication process

tions. On being received, the signals of the message are identified, or decoded, by the *decoder* (hearer, addressee), and some information has presumably been transmitted. Human languages are bidirectional, that is, everyone is capable of both encoding (transmitting) and decoding (receiving) a message.

But in order for communication through language to be effective, two additional components are needed. One is the setting or context in which a message is placed: it surely makes a difference if one hears the exclamation "Fire!" whether the context is a battlefield or the twentieth floor of a hotel. The other component is *redundancy*, characteristic of the code of all natural languages. Redundancy of a code lies in its unused capacity, that is, in those signals of a message that under ideal circumstances could be eliminated without appreciable loss of essential information. Consider, for example, the written message "Ch.ldr.n .dm.tt.d .nl. wh.n .cc.mp.n..d b. th..r p.r.nts," which is easily intelligible even when all of its letters representing vowels have been eliminated. Were it not for this property, any unwanted signals interfering with a spoken, or written, message could easily make its decoding difficult if not altogether impossible. When in the course of a long-distance telephone conversation one has to resort to frequent requests for repetition, interference (or noise, in the technical sense) has probably exceeded the available redundancy of the code.

Language and its design features

Despite the apparent variety of languages and the differences among them, there are a number of fundamental characteristic features that all human languages share. Charles F. Hockett (1960, 1966) identified over a dozen features of design that languages of the world have in common. Heading the list is the use of the *vocal-auditory channel*, the physical medium employed in audible speech. While this element is perhaps an obvious design feature of human language, it has an immediate advantage:

those who communicate need not be visible to each other. The physical consequences of the production of speech sounds account for the next two features—*broadcast transmission* and *rapid fading*. Whenever we say something, it can be heard within a limited distance all around us (broadcast transmission), and those within these limits generally have little difficulty locating the source of the spoken words. And, unlike a written message, what someone says must be heard at the time it is said (rapid fading) or it is irretrievably lost (an outcome that is occasionally to our advantage).

Another design feature is *feedback*. Any speaker of a language is capable of monitoring everything he or she is saying and making any necessary corrections. Further features of human speech are *semanticity, arbitrariness, displacement,* and *productivity*. Semanticity refers to the fact that we endow most of the vocal sounds we produce with rather definite meanings. On hearing the sentence *Hannibal crossed the Alps with elephants*, we have no difficulty visualizing the event. At the same time, the relationship between words and the things to which words refer is an arbitrary one: what is known as *elephant* in English happens to be referred to with equal effectiveness as *slon* in Czech, *dramblys* in Lithuanian, and *fil* in Turkish. The feature of displacement makes it possible to speak about things remote in both time and space (Hannibal's feat takes us to the Old World over two thousand years ago) and thus extends the universe of human discourse far beyond the immediate situation. Productivity is the capacity for generating and understanding unprecedented utterances, for saying novel things, whether or not they are true or otherwise have any merit.

We conclude with two more features— *discreteness* and *multilevel patterning*. The fundamental nature of language design is said to be discrete rather than continuous, because utterances in languages are encoded and decoded in terms of separate, individually distinct segments of sound even though physically the message may appear to be "continuous." For example, the difference in the meanings of the English utterances *Would you like a piece of roast?* and *Would you like a piece of toast?* is associated with the choice between the discrete sound segments written as *r* and *t*. Multilevel patterning refers to the organization of human language in terms of at least two planes or subsystems: that of a limited number of meaningless but distinctive sound units (for example, *d, e,* and *n*) that are used to represent (or distinguish among) meaningful units (*den, end,* and *Ned*)—as we have just seen above; and that of a vast number of smallest meaningful elements, the analysis of which has traditionally been referred to as grammar ("But Hannibal cross-ed [past tense] the mountain-s [plural] with elephant-s [plural]").

While all of these design features (and a few additional ones not mentioned here) serve very well to characterize and define human language, their usefulness for application to animal communication in general is somewhat offset by two defects. First, they call for yes-or-no, present-or-absent, answers that prevent any consideration of the degree to which a particular feature may be present. Second, they fail to provide a frame of reference that would further a more systematic inquiry into the complex subject of animal communication in general.

A tentative revision of the design-feature approach (Hockett and Altmann 1968) distinguishes among five frameworks. They deal, respectively, with various features concerning the channel(s), social setting, behavioral antecedents and consequences of communicative acts, continuity and change in communication systems, and repertory and messages of specific systems. Provisions are made for indicating the degree to which any particular feature is employed. Thus, in studying a particular communicative transaction or system, one would wish to make inquiries such as the following: What channel or channels are used? What are the number, nature, and location of the participants, and under what circumstances do they exchange messages? What is the range of variations to which a given communication system is subject with respect to such variable factors as sex or age? And finally: What is the structure of specific messages and of the code as a whole? These and additional questions are not only essential to an understanding of subhuman communication; they also serve rather well to outline an area of very recent concern in anthropology—the ethnography of communication.

THE NATURE OF
LANGUAGE ACQUISITION

Let us now consider what has been found out about the human acquisition of language. It is well known that normal children the world over begin to talk during their second year and that by the time they are about five years old their ability to use their primary language is well established (even though the fine points of grammar, the so-called

irregularities, are yet to be mastered and their vocabularies will continue to grow throughout their active lifetimes). This accomplishment appears to be independent of such factors as the degree of intelligence or the nature of the environment in which the child is growing up.

It is also well documented that any child is capable of learning any language at a comparable rate provided the learning takes place under the usual conditions. A baby born to Zulu-speaking parents but adopted shortly after birth by American parents would acquire native control of English as spoken by his or her adoptive parents. And were the situation the reverse, the child born to an American couple but brought up by Zulu parents would master Zulu by the usual age.

It was further observed by Eric H. Lenneberg (1967:139–140) that during the first eighteen months of life, congenitally deaf children go through vocal stages closely resembling those of normal children—cooing, babbling, and producing various sounds associated with their feelings of well-being

A baby learns language as he or she learns culture: by being born into it and by imitating patterned behavior. Primary language learning is acquired not through the tedium of grammatical and lexical instruction but almost unconsciously as the central component of the process of becoming a member of society. (Doug Magee from Editorial Photocolor Archives)

or discontent. These and other kinds of evidence support the view that human capacity for speaking is inborn. What is more, language acquisition seems to be closely related to physical maturation during an individual's early years; and the available evidence indicates not only that this gift of speech is built uniformly into all humankind but also that it is to some extent innately specified. For how else could one explain the fact that *any* normal child can acquire *any* of the innumerable languages with the *same* degree of mastery according to approximately the *same* timetable?

One widely accepted theory, developed to account for the observed propensity of children to acquire language as well as for the similarities shared by all languages, holds that each infant is born with an abstract language model programmed in its brain. Endowed with such a faculty, children are able to apply these innate language patterns and rules to the speech that surrounds them as they learn their particular mother tongue.

APPROACHES TO LINGUISTIC STRUCTURE

The statement made earlier about human languages—that each represents a particular variety of the language code—is another way of saying that languages are systematic, that they are organized according to definite patterns. If they were not, if languages were nothing but haphazard collections of sounds and meanings, how could they serve usefully as effective means of communication?

Responses to patterning in language are in evidence very early in an individual's development. On the basis of such pairs of words as *block, blocks* and *dog, dogs*, a two- or three-year-old child comes up with, by analogy, the forms *foots, mans,* and *sheeps* instead of the correct *feet, men,* and *sheep*. The child has simply applied the expected pattern of English plural formation. Studying grammar in school, whether of a foreign language or one's own, amounts to getting formally acquainted with the plan according to which the particular language code is constructed. For the linguistic anthropologist, however, the conventional, or traditional, grammatical description taught in schools has several serious drawbacks. We shall mention two of them here.

Speech and writing

First, traditional grammar is based almost exclusively on the written language, which is a substitute for oral communication, and the two differ considerably. Moreover, many features of the spoken language—tone of voice, for example—are lost in writing altogether, not to mention signals conveyed by other channels, such as facial expressions. Speaking comes easily; in fact, from early childhood it becomes second nature. But this is not so with writing, and particularly not so with writing in English, a skill that is learned over a long period of time. To begin with, English spelling is notoriously difficult to master. According to George Bernard Shaw, the English word *fish* could as well be spelled *g-h-o-t-i—gh* as in *enough, o* as in *women,* and *ti* as in *nation*. Furthermore, we commonly speak as fast as others are able to follow; but when given a pen and paper, we tend to think carefully about just how to put things down. In short, we tend to express ourselves differently when we are writing. The owner of a rooming house once threw out a student with the words, "Like hell I'm kidding; I've warned you, now get your ass out of here!" But when he wrote to the student's parents about the termination of the lease, the message lost much of its color: "I told him in no uncertain terms that he was no longer welcome here." Finally, while it is true that most of the larger and better-known societies have both a spoken and a written language, many societies have not yet begun to make use of writing as a means of communication.

Description versus prescription

The second serious drawback of traditional school grammars from the point of view of the linguistic anthropologist is that they tend to be *prescriptive grammars*, that is, concerned with laying down rules and giving precise instructions for the use of language rather than studying the various patterns of usage as they actually occur. According to this prescriptive viewpoint, such constructions as *It's me* or *Winston tastes good like a cigarette should* are "bad grammar," or "not good English"; yet the fact remains that most Americans use these forms. Whenever anthropologists include language behavior in their study of a society, they are invariably more interested in how people say what they have to say than in how someone thinks they ought to say it. This is not to deny that in certain circumstances some ways of saying things are more appropriate or strategic than others. "Hey, say that again, Mac!" might easily jeopardize an applicant's chances in an interview for a position, where he would be well advised to phrase his request as "Would you mind repeating the question, please?" Conversely, this polite, formal request would certainly sound out of place if used by one member of a road gang to another. In a sense, then, the different styles, or *functional varieties*, of spoken language are not unlike the different kinds of clothes we choose to wear on various occasions. The anthropologist is interested not only in how people act but also to what extent their behavior represents a strategic choice from among potential alternative ways of acting. Consequently, the anthropologist must study and account for the full range of their speech behavior.

The task of accounting for the structure of a language is by no means simple, nor is there agreement among the specialists on how best to proceed. Two approaches, both drawing on the rich tradition of the past, have a particularly large following: the *descriptivist*, or taxonomic, approach, which dominated the scene until the 1950s, and the *generative* approach, which, although only two decades old, has already made some lasting contributions to linguistic study.

In analyzing a language one must strive to discover the system of rules that estab-lishes the correspondences between the sounds and meanings of that language. But in trying to arrive at a system of rules or a *grammar*, and at the collection of units (sounds, words, and so forth) to which these rules apply, a problem arises: should one operate on the assumption that logically the units are prior and the grammar follows, or is it the other way around? The answer to this question points up one fundamental difference between the descriptivist and the generative approaches.[1]

[1]The literature dealing with the theory and methods of the descriptivist approach is so extensive that it would serve no useful purpose even to attempt to list a fair sample. Instead, the reader is referred to Hockett 1958 and Gleason 1961, whose works are particularly representative.

A good elementary exposition of generative grammar may be found in Langacker 1973. Langacker's text is accompanied by an extensive workbook that is especially helpful to those who wish to try their hand and mind at analyzing specific problems from a wide variety of languages (Langacker 1972). But for the foundations of generative grammar, it is preferable to turn to Noam Chomsky. Among his many writings, of particular interest are his pioneering work on syntactic structures (Chomsky 1957), his major formulation of transformational generative grammar (Chomsky 1965), his contribution to Lenneberg's (1967) book (Chomsky 1967), and his broadly based treatise dealing with language and mind (Chomsky 1972). A detailed analysis of the sound structure of English within the framework of generative grammar may be found in Chomsky and Halle (1968). For an informative exposition of Chomsky's theses, see Lyons (1970).

For a brief introduction to the problem of dealing with unwritten languages, see Gudschinsky 1967.

The reason for neglecting to discuss other contemporary approaches to linguistic descriptions is largely practical: more than likely such a discussion would confuse readers rather than enlighten them. Those who are eager to pursue these other orientations may refer to Lockwood 1972 for the stratificational approach; to Gudschinsky 1967, Longacre 1964, or Pike 1967 for the tagmemic approach; and to Chafe 1970 for a semantic model. Our justification for discussing only the descriptive and the generative approaches is twofold: while most of the past work in linguistic anthropology has been done in terms of the former, the generative approach is bound to have major implications for anthropological theory in the future.

THE DESCRIPTIVIST APPROACH

Let us take as our starting point the fact that any spoken utterance is a succession of speech sounds. Furthermore, each utterance is psychologically as well as physically unique, occurring if not under different circumstances at least at a different point in time. Yet people do not respond to each instance of speech as though it were different from all others. Such utterances as "What is the exact time?" or "Has the mail been delivered yet?" are treated as if they were the same every time they are spoken and regardless of whether they are said by one's husband or daughter or a neighbor whose voice is hoarse from constant smoking.

This fact—that there are so many fundamental likenesses in what is objectively a tremendous variety—makes it possible to represent speech sounds by means of a limited set of written symbols. Just as one can transcribe a piece of music, one can also transcribe a stretch of spoken language. Linguists commonly make a transcription when they wish to obtain a sample of speech and maintain it for analysis. However, instead of using one of the conventional systems of writing, which can be quite incongruous (note, for example, that *wright*, *write*, *right*, and *rite* all sound the same in

Phonetic transcription

The International Phonetic Alphabet. The symbols shown here do not correspond in every detail with those used in this textbook. There is a practical reason for preferring the symbols we use—the special type characters of the IPA are not always available. And because phonetic alphabets are arbitrary, one is just as acceptable as another. Besides, specialists are acquainted with all those most widely used and there is little possibility of confusion. (By courtesy of the International Phonetic Association)

THE INTERNATIONAL PHONETIC ALPHABET.
(Revised to 1951.)

		Bi-labial	Labio-dental	Dental and Alveolar	Retroflex	Palato-alveolar	Alveolo-palatal	Palatal	Velar	Uvular	Pharyngal	Glottal
CONSONANTS	Plosive . . .	p b		t d	ʈ ɖ			c ɟ	k g	q ɢ		ʔ
	Nasal . . .	m	ɱ	n	ɳ			ɲ	ŋ	N		
	Lateral Fricative .			ɬ ɮ								
	Lateral Non-fricative .			l	ɭ			ʎ				
	Rolled . . .			r						R		
	Flapped . . .			ɾ	ɽ					R		
	Fricative . . .	ɸ β	f v	θ ð s z ɹ	ʂ ʐ	ʃ ʒ	ɕ ʑ	ç j	x ɣ	χ ʁ	ħ ʕ	h ɦ
	Frictionless Continuants and Semi-vowels	w ɥ	ʋ	ɹ				j (ɥ)	(w)	ʁ		
VOWELS								Front / Central / Back				
	Close . . .	(y ʉ u)						i y ɨ ʉ ɯ u				
	Half-close . . .	(ø o)						e ø / ə / ɤ o				
	Half-open . . .	(œ ɔ)						ɛ œ / ɜ / ʌ ɔ				
								æ / ɐ				
	Open . . .	(ɒ)						a / ɑ ɒ				

(Secondary articulations are shown by symbols in brackets.)

English, but *lead* ["to guide"] and *lead* ["metallic element"] do not), a linguist makes use of one of the several accepted systems of phonetic symbols. These *phonetic alphabets*, as they are called, have a decided advantage over conventional orthographies. They provide a consistent relationship between speech sounds and the graphemic symbols, or letters, that represent them. Moreover, because most phonetic alphabets are quite comprehensive, they can be used to transcribe the speech sounds of a wide variety of languages and can do so rather effectively whether the language is English, Russian, or Japanese.

Consider now two English words, *pit* and *spit*. If we transcribe them phonetically, we must indicate that the *p* of *spit* is distinguishably different from the *p* in *pit*, which is immediately followed by a puff of air. For those who may not be aware of this, the difference between the two *p*'s can be demonstrated easily. Hold a sheet of ordinary paper vertically between thumb and finger two or three inches from your lips and say the two words. The puff of air or *aspiration* of *pit* will send a ripple through the sheet, whereas saying the word *spit* will leave the sheet motionless. Let us indicate this difference by transcribing *pit* as [p^{c}It] and *spit* as [sp$^=$It], the symbols [p^c] and [p$^=$] representing respectively an aspirated and unaspirated *p*.

If we examine other English words that have a *p* sound in them—for example, *pack, pad, pair, peck, pike* and *space, spade, spare, speck, spike*—we discover that the same difference obtains between the *p* sounds of the first and those of the second group ([p^c] as against [p$^=$]). We may therefore state that in English there are at least two varieties of the *p* sound, the one aspirated and the other unaspirated, and furthermore that the unaspirated one occurs regularly after the sound *s*.

Let us next consider the words *pit, spit,* and *bit*, which we may write phonetically as [p^{c}It], [sp$^=$It], and [bIt]: is the difference between the *p* sound of the first and the *b* sound of the third of the same kind as that

between the [p^c] of the first and the [p$^=$] of the second? Clearly, it is not. It makes a difference whether one says *bit*, [bIt], or *pit* [p^{c}It], because by choosing one or the other initial sound one is distinguishing between two meaningful items of the English word stock, as in *I bit into a pit*. The difference is in a sense just as crucial as if one were to choose between a hammer and a knife to drive a nail into the wall. What about the difference between *pit*, [p^{c}It], and *spit*, [sp$^=$It]? Saying [p$^=$It] or [sp^{c}It], one would no doubt be understood, but the listener is likely to suspect that either English is not the speaker's native language or the speaker is trying to imitate a foreigner. As a matter of fact, native speakers of English never have to choose consciously between [p$^=$] and [p^c]. They employ the first automatically after *s* and the other whenever it occurs at the beginning of a syllable and is followed immediately by a stressed vowel, as in *appear*. In a sense, then, the choice between [p$^=$] and [p^c] in English is much like the choice between a claw hammer and a bricklayer's hammer to drive a nail: either one may accomplish the task adequately but, like the native speaker, the professional user—the builder—will reach for the appropriate one.

Phonemic analysis   In regard to English, linguists consider the *b* sound of *bit* and the *p* sound of *pit* as representing two distinctive sounds, or *phonemes*. They classify the *p* sound of *pit*, [p^c], and the *p* sound of *spit*, [p$^=$], as two variants of one phoneme, or *allophones*, in this case of the phoneme *p*. When the symbol *p* is used to represent the English phoneme /p/, it simply serves as a cover symbol for a class of phonetically similar sounds—[p$^=$], [p^c], and others not mentioned here—whose covariation in actual speech is generally complementary, that is, predictable. (Note the use of slant lines around /p/ to indicate a distinctive element functioning as a part of a specific linguistic system, English.) Similarly, the vowel sounds of *pit*, [I], and *peat*, [i], are phonetically different, and since in English they also function to distinguish between two different words, each has a phonemic status, /I/ and /i/.[2]

Once the investigator has determined what all the significant sounds, or phonemes, of a language are, and in which main variants, or allophones, each phoneme may be found to occur and has presented conclusions in the form of a set of phonemic rules, he or she has accomplished what is known as the *phonemic analysis* of a language. At this point it is no longer necessary to continue recording all the phonetic details, and the investigator may begin to write the language in the simpler *phonemic transcription* (customarily enclosed in slant lines //). Thus, the words *pit* and *spit*, phonetically transcribed as [pᶜIt] and [sp=It], would be phonemically written as /pIt/ and /spIt/. A brief statement to the effect that an English *p* after *s* is never aspirated, whereas syllable-initial *p* followed by a stressed vowel always is, makes a more detailed phonetic reading of the shorthand phonemic record easily possible.

TO SUM UP Phonetic symbols represent a general system of symbols, one that can be used to transcribe the speech sounds of any language. By contrast, phonemic symbols are language-specific: they are used to represent the significant sound units in a particular language.

Besides about three dozen so-called segmental phonemes, there are some additional significant sound features that characterize English utterances. Among them are several phonemic degrees of *stress* (consider, for example, the word *animation* with the strongest stress on its third syllable, a less strong stress on the first, and weak stresses on the second and fourth); the nature of the *transition* at certain points in an utterance (for example, in *a name* or *night rate* contrasted with *an aim* or *nitrate*); and several relative levels of *pitch* that, together with other features, account for the differences in intonations associated with questions, commands, emphasis, surprise, and the like.

The same phonemes do not necessarily characterize every speaker of English. It is common knowledge that British English differs from American English, and that both British English and American English exist in several dialectal varieties, particularly as far as vowels are concerned.

Each language has its own particular system of distinctive sounds, or phonemes, and their allophones. In Spanish, for example, there is a phoneme /i/, the sound of which approximates that represented by the English /i/; phonetically and phonemically, however, there is no Spanish parallel to the English /I/. This and similar differences are the source of the "natural" mispronunciations of Puerto Ricans or Chicanos learning English in American schools, as when they say /mil/ instead of /mIl/ for *mill*, so that it sounds like *meal*. Their Spanish speech habits carry over into a language they are learning or are not familiar with.

To demonstrate the fundamental principle underlying the concept of phonemic analysis we have used English because of its familiarity. But the fairly typical situation that anthropologists face as they analyze and record the speech behavior of the group they are studying is different. Frequently they are among people who do not write and whose language has never before been written by anyone. In such cases, in order to develop a useful orthography based on the phonemic principle, the anthropologist must be able to carry out a phonemic analysis. This includes careful listening for contrasting sounds, repeating of words and utterances and recording them on tape, and a good deal of phonetic transcription in the initial stages of work.

Grammatical analysis

We shift now to another level of analysis, conventionally referred to as grammar. Consider the phrase *ungentlemanly escorts*,

[2]There is by no means uniform agreement about the vowel system of English. In one widely accepted analysis, for example, the vowels of *pit* and *peat* are phonemically represented as /i/ and /iy/, respectively. For our purposes, however, it is enough to note that alternative interpretations do exist.

which can easily and intuitively be analyzed by speakers of English into its constituent words and word elements:

un-, meaning "not, opposite of"

gentle, meaning "kind, given to restraint"

man, meaning "a male human"

-ly, meaning "in the manner of"

escort, meaning "one who accompanies (someone)"

-s, meaning "more than one (plural)."

One may say that the phrase consists of six meaningful segments, none of which is susceptible to further analysis without the loss of meaning. Such linguistic units containing no smaller meaningful parts are called *morphemes*, and the search for such units in a particular language is termed *morphemic analysis*. Morphemes are conventionally placed within braces { }, their meanings in quotations marks " ". One should note that morphemes may coincide with simple words that can occur in isolation (*escort, gentle, man*) or with bound affixes (*un-, -ly*) that normally do not occur by themselves.

A morpheme may be represented on the phonemic level by a single phoneme, as in /s/, one of the phonemic forms of the noun plural morpheme {s}, or by a sequence of two or more phonemes, as in /pɪt/, representing the morpheme {pɪt}. It should be noted that a single morpheme may, in different contexts, have more than one phonemic representation. For instance, let us consider several pairs of words, in phonemic transcription, giving some examples of English noun plural formation:

book /bʊk/ and *books* /bʊks/

box /baks/ and *boxes* /baksəz/

pad /pæd/ and *pads* /pædz/

kibbutz /kɪbʊts/ and *kibbutzim* /kɪbʊtsim/

man /mæn/ and *men* /mɛn/

ox /aks/ and *oxen* /aksən/

fish /fɪš/ and *fish* /fɪš/.

In the order in which the pairs are listed here, the forms marking the plural appear as /-s/, /-əz/, /-z/, /-im/, /æ→ɛ/, /-ən/, and /∅/(zero, the lack of an overt marker). It is evident that the English plural morpheme occurs in several phonemic representations (morphs)—those listed here as well as others not mentioned (for example, in *crises, alumni, alumnae,* and *criteria*). Because all of these forms function alike in English (they are suffixed to nouns), and because they all have the same meaning, namely, of plurality ("more than one"), they are said to be different *allomorphs* of the same morpheme, the morpheme marking the English plural. (Note the parallelism: an allophone is to a phoneme as an allomorph is to a morpheme.)

The distribution of the various allomorphs of the plural morpheme with respect to nouns in English is not quite as random as it may seem. Some of the allomorphs are phonemically conditioned; that is, the occurrence of one or the other depends on the nature of the preceding sound. Thus, /-s/ occurs if the immediately preceding element is /p, t, k, f, θ/; /-əz/ occurs after /s, z, š, ž, č, ž/;[3] and /-z/ after other consonants and all vowels. Of the remaining words in the list, /-ən/ in *oxen* closely resembles the plural ending in *children* and *brethren*; /-im/ in *kibbutzim* parallels a few other words borrowed from Hebrew that have retained their original plural (*seraph* and *cherub*); and the replacement of /æ/ by /ɛ/ in *man* to mark the plural is a specific example of a more general process characteristic of several English common nouns (for example, *woman, foot, goose,* and *louse*). Allomorphs in these and other similar nouns are said to be morphemically conditioned.

Morphology, or the description of how morphemes combine into words and how they are classified, is only one portion of

---

[3]The symbols θ, š, ž, č, and ž represent the final consonants in such words as *pith, sash, rouge, batch,* and *judge,* respectively. The symbol ə, known as *schwa,* is the usual sound of the first and last vowels of *America,* when pronounced by a native speaker of English.

grammar. The other portion, having to do with the manner in which words of a language are strung together into sentences, is *syntax*. The technique common to descriptivist approaches to syntax has generally made use of the concept of *immediate constituents* (ICs), involving the successive breaking up of a sentence into its constituent parts.

TO SUM UP We have begun with units (phonemes, morphemes) and ended with arrangements, or grammar. But a good argument can be made for proceeding the other way around, from the top down, as it were.

GENERATIVE GRAMMAR

Consider now the following pair of sentences: *John is easy to please* and *John is eager to please*. On the surface, both sentences appear to have the same structure, and in an analysis concerned with morphemes and their arrangements they would be treated alike. Yet in the first, *John* is the person who is being pleased (he is the underlying object), while in the second, *John* is the person who is doing the pleasing (he is the underlying subject). The difference between the two sentences becomes readily apparent if they are changed from the active to the passive voice: *John is easily pleased* is acceptable to the native speaker of English, whereas *John is eagerly pleased* is ungrammatical. Similarly, *boiling agent*, *boiling flask*, and *boiling point* appear to be constructed according to a like pattern: the verb stem *boil*, suffixed by *-ing*, and a noun. But in attempting to paraphrase these expressions, one discovers that their apparent similarity is only superficial: *boiling agent* is "agent that causes boiling" or "agent of boiling," *boiling flask* is "flask for boiling (liquids)," and *boiling point* is "point at which boiling occurs." While the superficial, or surface, grammar of both sets of phrases is much the same, there are underlying differences among the members of each set

in what one might call "deep grammar." The mere listing of morphemes and of their sequences is clearly not enough to account for these differences.

Fundamental concepts

These and similar considerations guided Noam Chomsky and his followers in the development of a theory of language that departs strikingly from the descriptivist approach. Chomsky's views may be briefly summarized as follows:

A great many sentences that people produce are novel, that is, they have never been spoken before. Yet they comprise a relatively small fraction among the potential sentences that could be said. (For example, the sentence *The use of denture adhesives was strongly disapproved of by Greek gods who otherwise seemed easy prey to television commercials*, has without question never been produced before and can be infinitely varied with the same effect.) All native speakers of a language know their language in the sense that they are able to understand, utter, or otherwise manipulate a potentially infinite number of sentences. This knowledge, largely unconscious, is referred to as the *competence* of the speaker (or of the listener, for that matter). What the language user actually does with this knowledge constitutes his or her *performance*. The two—competence and performance—are not the same in practice. Thus, while an individual's competence may be expected to remain about the same for a long period of time, performance is likely to suffer noticeably whenever the person is tired, distracted, or otherwise preoccupied.

Sentences may be grammatical (that is, well-formed) and meaningful (*Rosemary's baby was the center of attention*), grammatical but deviant in meaning (*Rosemary's center was the baby of attention*), or ungrammatical (*Rosemary's baby the center of attention was*). The grammar of a language is a definable system that characterizes an infinite set of well-formed sentences. Or, to put it differently, the task of describing a language amounts to specifying the users' (or the listeners') competence—just exactly what they must know in order to know their language.

Whereas the number of sentences that can be said in any particular human language is limitless, the number of rules that generate them is not. Accordingly, generative grammar must also be a finite device capable of generating an infinite number of sentences. If this requirement has a mystical aura about it, an example from everyday experience should help clarify it. Although the rules for multiplication are relatively few and are simple enough to be mastered by young schoolchildren, they can be applied to any two numbers— in fact to an infinity of such combinations.

The aspect of a grammar that consists of a finite system of rules generating an infinite number of sentences is called the *syntactic component*. This component assigns to each sentence an underlying abstract *deep structure* that reveals the logical relationships among the individual elements of the sentence and a concrete *surface structure* that determines its phonetic character—the sentence as one hears it. Thus, there is more than one level of syntactic structure, and the sentence *The apples were eaten* derives from a deep structure that in certain crucial ways resembles some such sentence as *Someone ate the apples*. The fact that these two sentences have different surface structures is readily evident: the sounds, or words, of the first do not exactly match those of the second.

There are two other major components of generative grammar: the *phonological component*, which assigns a phonetic representation to the surface structure of a sentence, and the *semantic component*, which determines the semantic interpretation of the sentence. Taking as a point of departure for any particular language the so-called *base*— a set of rules generally applicable to that language, and its word stock—one may represent the relationships of the various aspects of grammar as shown in Figure 17-1.

The treatment of the phonological compo-

The new view of linguistic structure

nent in the generative approach has also departed in significant ways from the common descriptivist practice. In particular, generative grammarians deny the usefulness of autonomous phonemes (examples of which figured in our discussion of the descriptivist approach). Instead, the phonological component, which is systematically related to the surface syntactic structure, is linked with the phonetic representation by means of rules that operate in a fixed order and yield distinctive phonetic features, such as voicing, syllabicity, tenseness, and nasality.

The semantic interpretation, having to do with the meaning that words acquire as a result of their relations in any given sentence, is still largely uncharted. Initially, the concept of distinctive semantic features, or components, was utilized. For example, the term *bachelor* in its most common sense would be defined as + animate (as against *snowmobile*, − animate), + human (as against *kangaroo*, − human), + adult (as against *child*, − adult), + male (as against *aunt*, − male), and + marriageable (as against *centenarian*, − marriageable). More recently, however, the semantic features approach has been giving way to an analysis making use of highly sophisticated formal logic.

Some scholars have suggested that the semantic component should be taken as basic rather than as interpretive, in which case semantic interpretation would merge with deep structure. Still others have argued for an intermediate position between the two. Some such approach may well turn out to be especially useful for the anthropologist, since the base of language could then be virtually identified with the structure of culture.

Contrasting the descriptivist and generative approaches

Consider the operation of a gas-powered automobile. Like a language, a car that runs is a complex functioning whole. Like a language, too, it consists of many different parts that make up various systems (the drive train, the electric system, the cooling

Figure 17-1 Relationship of the various aspects of grammar according to the generative approach to linguisitc structure

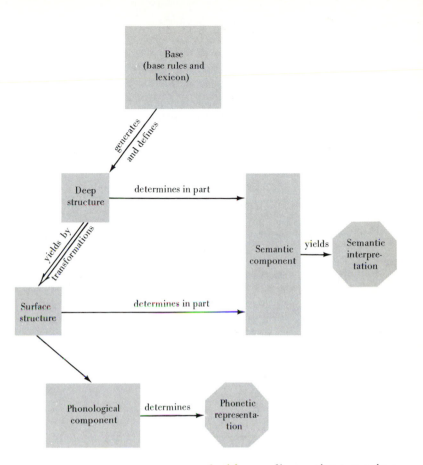

system, and others), each of which operates according to specific principles. Applying the view of Chomsky and his followers to this example, one can liken the descriptivist approach to the skills and operations of a mechanic who is well acquainted with the various automobile parts and their functions but who is not seriously concerned with *how* and *why* a car runs. Very much like the descriptivist linguist, who restricts his or her analysis to surface structures, the mechanic is familiar with the car only superficially, although capable of maintaining it in good running condition.

According to Chomsky, such an approach is not truly scientific because it makes no effort to explain. A real understanding of what makes a car run comes from the comprehension of such fundamental principles as those of combustion, friction, application of force, and the like. Not until these principles are grasped can one say significant things not only about a particular make of car but about cars in general, and about other conveyances that utilize these principles (for example, snowmobiles). Consequently, the fundamental principles, like the rules of grammar, are prior; and the parts and their arrangements, like the linguistic units and their arrangements, assume secondary importance. In Chomsky's view, the fundamental weakness in the descriptivist approach to language—and by extension in the mechanistic conception of the human mind—is "the belief that the mind must be simpler in its structure than any known physical organ and that the most primitive of assumptions must be adequate to explain whatever phenomena can be observed" (Chomsky 1972:25–26). Nevertheless, for the anthropological field worker, who is mainly

concerned with recording native terms in a serviceable phonemic transcription and who rarely possesses intuitive knowledge of the language he or she is dealing with, the descriptivist approach continues to be useful.

FROM LANGUAGE TO CULTURE

Etic versus emic The widely acknowledged rigor of linguistic analysis, regardless of the approach taken, has not been lost on anthropologists of the postwar period. A number of concepts that were originally designed for getting at the structure of language have found their way, with a varying amount of acceptance and success, into cultural anthropology, archaeology, and folklore. One such extension—

known as *componential analysis*—is an adaptation of distinctive features to certain self-contained domains of culture, especially kinship. Another borrowing has been from the method of linguistic reconstruction with the aim of retrieving semantic information about specific domains of prehistoric cultures; an example will be given in the next chapter. The most significant, however, is the extension into cultural anthropology of the *etic-emic* concept, which derives from the distinction between the *phonetic* and the *phonemic* descriptions of linguistic structure.

We have already seen that each particular language utilizes only a highly specific selection of the great many possible speech sounds. For example, both English and Spanish have a *p* sound, but the classes of phonetically distinct allophones that each of the two /p/s subsumes differ. Similarly, English has /i/ and /ɪ/, as in *beat* and *bit*, but Spanish only /i/. Although in the initial transcription of a given language the linguist of descriptivist persuasion draws on a comprehensive, all-inclusive array of sound-types of a phonetic alphabet (an etic grid), his or her goal is to discover and describe the structure of the language in terms of its own distinctive elements and principles of order (an emic description). The underlying assumption of this approach is that each language possesses a unique structure and must be studied individually.

In the late 1950s this premise began to be extended to the study of culture by a group of scholars whose approach has come to be referred to as "ethnoscience," "cognitive anthropology," "new ethnography," or "ethnographic semantics." In their view, just as language is a conceptual code underlying speech behavior, culture is a code underlying social behavior. Accordingly, the primary goal of ethnographic description is a structural statement of the cultural code, or a "cultural grammar." Each individual culture, then, just like each language, must by virtue of its uniqueness be described in terms of its own distinctive elements. The

"New ethnography"

structure of a cultural code is discoverable through the application of systematic procedures to a body of data, derived from what the subjects say about their culture and/or from their behavior (Keesing 1972).

If individual cultures, like different languages, are unique, the question inevitably arises as to what extent, if any at all, cultures can be compared. Of the various critical questions aimed at ethnoscience, this is currently the most serious one. Interestingly enough, this question, too, proceeds from the new developments in linguistics that we have briefly outlined in our discussion of generative, or transformational, grammar. The relativistic approach of "emic" analysis is not readily compatible with the Chomskyan notion that languages of the world represent nothing more than different possible expressions of a single universal language design. There are signs that cultural anthropologists once again are turning to a new linguistic perspective for their model, as they have done in the past. Evidence that an interest is emerging in the exploration of a universal design underlying all of human culture has already come from some of the ethnoscientists themselves. Paul Kay and Brent Berlin have attempted to show that "there is a fixed sequence of evolutionary states through which any language must pass as its basic color vocabulary becomes expanded over time" (Berlin 1970:8). In short, today it is even more important than at any time since World War II that cultural anthropologists keep up with the frontiers of linguistic research. This reminder applies not only to developments in generative semantics but also to the work of those who are making significant advances in the study of speech behavior in its natural social setting.

NONVERBAL SYSTEMS OF COMMUNICATION

While spoken language—speech—is by far the most important means by which humans communicate with one another, it is not the only means employed for that purpose. Some systems, like the various writing systems, are speech surrogates, that is, they are meant to represent spoken words. Other systems, like the Morse code or braille, derive from existing writing systems. Still others, like the sign language of the American Indians, are distinctly independent of speech even though they may occasionally be found used in combination with it. The importance of communication in and for culture and the interest that some of these nonverbal systems enjoy warrant discussion of some of their better-known representatives.

Indian sign language

It may come as a surprise that, although it has frequently been mentioned since the time of the travel accounts of early explorers west of the Mississippi, the sign language of the North American Plains Indians has not yet been thoroughly described despite the rapidly diminishing number of potential informants. For a score of nomadic tribes whose languages were either mutually unintelligible or completely unrelated, sign language appears at one time to have been quite an effective means of communication. It was commonplace for Indians to recount their war exploits or to render a long folktale wholly in terms of signs, and it is a matter of record that the Kiowa Indians gave General Hugh Lenox Scott the account of their sun dance in this manner.

The sign language used by the Plains Indians consisted of a substantial repertory of conventionalized gestures performed with one or both hands. The hands were shaped in a variety of ways and either held stationary at various levels or moved between the extreme positions of just above the ground and over the "speaker's" head. For example, the sign for *whites* was made by holding the right hand, back up, to the left of the face at eye level, the forefinger pointing to the left; the hand was then drawn to the right with the forefinger passing across the face just above the eyes. The sign characterized the whites as people who always wore hats, thus distinguishing them

from the usually bareheaded Indians. To represent *snow* or *snowing*, both hands were extended in front of the face with all ten fingers pointing downward, and then lowered in whirling movements. Abstract notions were conveyed with equal facility. The idea of sadness was rendered by first giving the sign for *heart* and then indicating the heart's low position: the compressed right hand, palm in and fingers pointing down, was brought downward over the heart and then swung out and downward toward the ground with the palm turning up.

Although the bulk of the signs must have been common to the vast area of the Great Plains, there were no doubt "dialectal" differences parallel to those found in widely extended spoken languages. The signs were partly *iconic*—that is, they generally shared more or less recognizable features with the ideas they represented—rather than wholly arbitrary as are the words of spoken languages.

The problem yet to be solved has to do with the nature of these signs. Are they analyzable in terms of two levels, just as spoken languages are analyzable in terms of the significant sounds peculiar to each of them and of the words which these sounds make up? Or are these signs to be analyzed in terms of a single level, with their repertory considered a "vocabulary" of irreducible units?

Speech-derived systems of communication

Whereas the sign language of the Plains Indians in no way derives from any one of their unrelated spoken languages, other special "languages" are not necessarily characterized by such independence. For one example we may refer to the Mazatec Indians living in northern Oaxaca, Mexico. Mazatec is a *tone language*, one in which variations in tone are used to distinguish words of different meanings that otherwise would sound alike. Under special circumstances, as when too great a distance is involved for them to shout, Mazatec males communicate by whistle speech. Since they can represent the four distinctive pitches of their vowels and other reproducible features (glides, length, syllabic units, and pauses) just as well by whistling as by speaking, it is possible for them to carry on an effective conversation concerning a wide range of topics by this unusual means. For a description of the whistled language of the Mazatecs we are indebted to George M. Cowan (1948), who observed the following exchange: a Mazatec standing in front of his hut whistled to another man some distance away on a trail below. After several exchanges in whistle talk, the man on the trail turned around and walked up to the hut with the load of corn leaves he was carrying to market. At the hut, he dumped his load on the ground and received some money from the first man. The entire business transaction, which included the customary bargaining over the price, had been carried on exclusively through whistling.

Even more remarkable is the whistled language of the inhabitants of mountainous La Gomera, one of the Canary Islands lying in the Atlantic off the northwest coast of Africa. Their whistle speech is based on the local dialect of Spanish, which unlike Mazatec is not a tone language. Proficient whistlers are said to use whistle speech over a distance of several miles, with no limitations on the topic of their exchanges. In the whistled language of the islanders, the production of sounds is made to approximate the sounds of the spoken language. As a result, whistled vowels are distinguishable by relative pitch and most of the consonants are heard as modifications of the whistled vowel sounds that come before and after them (Classe 1957).

Other systems of communication that derive from spoken language and employ an acoustic channel include humming, falsetto, and various instrumental devices—for example, horns, lutes, xylophones, gongs, and drums. Among these, the best known and most elaborate is drum signaling in West Africa, practiced by a number of tribes and reportedly effective for a distance of up to fifteen miles. The Jabo of eastern Liberia use both hollow cylindrical wooden "drums"

with a slit (technically speaking, these slit-drums are bells), and to a lesser extent single-headed skin-covered drums, to call meetings to order, summon specific tribespeople who may be working in the fields, introduce warriors or other persons of eminence by their laudatory titles, dismiss meetings, and the like. Just as in the case of the whistle speech of the Mazatecs, drum signaling is made possible by the character of the spoken language whose tone patterns the drummers imitate. In other regions of the African continent drum signaling has achieved such elaboration that unrestricted, fully "productive" conversation can be carried on. That these methods of communicating function as effectively as they evidently do is excellent proof of the high redundancy of natural languages: some of their features can be eliminated without loss of essential information.

Nonverbal channels of communication

Our discussion thus far of individual systems should not obscure the fact that much of human communication operates on several channels simultaneously. In addition to the speech channel, the eyes, facial expressions, body gestures, and use of space serve as important means of communication. Comedians on television are notably adept at slanting or even canceling the meaning of their spoken lines by a well-chosen gesture or grimace of different communicative content, and good mimes are capable of moving an audience without uttering a single word. But speech-related body motions are by no means limited to performers alone—they are an integral part of everyone's daily communicative activity. Ray L. Birdwhistell reports that even when the sound is removed from films recording the speeches of the late New York politician Fiorello La Guardia, it is possible to tell whether he was speaking American English, Italian, or Yiddish, since characteristic body motions were associated with each language (1970:102). Birdwhistell's observations and research of the past two decades have suggested that the information conveyed by human movements and

For complex human communication, language is indispensable. But it is possible to transmit messages by gestures, facial expressions, and other nonverbal means. These two Allied soldiers, American and Soviet, "converse" after the defeat of Nazi Germany in 1945. American and Russian cultures are sufficiently similar to permit communication of this type, but expressive behavior is learned and, hence, not identical everywhere. (Robert Capa/Magnum Photos, Inc.)

A message without words. This scene from a French cafe illustrates that disapproval—and perhaps subcultural distance—can be expressed with no more than a glance. The older woman finds the short dress of the younger woman not to her liking; the younger woman hardly seems concerned. (Henri Cartier Bresson/Magnum Photos, Inc.)

These fans at a sports event are expressing their emotions. The young woman is joyful at the way things have gone at this critical juncture in the game. The young man is urging the team he supports to greater and greater effort. The camera has caught both individuals at the point of rising from their seats, an indicator of both excitement and concern. (Richard Kalvar/Magnum Photos, Inc.)

gestures is coded and patterned differently in different cultures. In order to make these codes amenable to study, by analogy from linguistics he has devised an elaborate system for recording body movements. The work on this aspect of communication, known as *kinesics*, is only in its beginnings.

One additional aspect of communication has to do with the *paralinguistic features* of speech—that is, various optional vocal effects that may communicate some additional meaning when associated with an utterance. For an example of a situation in which expressive (emotive) function dominates over referential function we are indebted to John Boman Adams's description of culture and conflict in an Egyptian village located in the delta region of the Nile:

> Especially important in controlling discussion was that part of the strict code of manners which prescribed not only that discussion should be temperate, but that whatever its content, the voices of the discussants should be moderately pitched, their faces friendly, and their gestures graceful. Any discussant who did not observe these prescriptions would "lose face" and his arguments would be discounted. . . .
> . . . [The villager's] interpretation of what is said depends largely upon his attitude toward the speaker. . . .
> . . . Since the same expressions are always uttered, interpretations of "friendliness" or "enmity" depend upon meanings conveyed by subtle qualities of tone, pitch, and melody. These qualities, in their different modes, are interpretable to one who is acquainted with their culturally defined meanings. Certain melodic patterns connote, e.g., "sincerity," others "irony," "sarcasm," or even "hostility." Certain tones, ways of accenting, abbreviating, or elongating words convey similar meanings (Adams 1957:226).

While the primacy of speech in our cultural transactions will no doubt remain unchallenged, there is no question that our communicative resources are far from lim-

Paralinguistic features of speech

ited to speaking. The wink of an eye or the wave of a hand in face-to-face communication significantly enlivens and supplements the heavy daily diet of words. Moreover, these facial and other nonverbal modes serve to indicate to some extent the obvious continuity with primate communication.

Ingenious as these and other communicative devices may be, however, their importance grows pale when compared with the skill that humankind acquired only in the relatively recent past—the skill of converting the sounds of language into a permanent, visible form.

THE WRITTEN WORD

Viewed in the temporal frame of humankind's cultural evolution, the invention of writing some five thousand years ago is of relatively recent vintage, but its significance has been truly revolutionary and its consequences are comparable to the earlier domestication of plants. Not only is writing a fairly permanent means of encoding messages, which can then be preserved for transmission and receipt over both spatial distances and temporal periods. It also permits very efficient storing of accumulated information far beyond the capacity of individual human memories. In fact, the sheer bulk of printed materials to be kept available in libraries is such that more and more of it must be handled by the less convenient microforms of various types. What once was writing's great asset—the ready availability of the printed page—has today resulted in mammoth problems of storage and retrieval.

The earliest phases in the development of writing are obscure. Rather than springing up at a particular time in a particular place, writing must have been the result of a stream of inventions. On the basis of what little is known about its early beginnings, anthropologists are in general agreement that it was invented independently at least twice: first in the Middle East, and considerably later in Middle America. Some scholars further consider Chinese writing to have been invented separately, whereas others attribute its early use among the Chinese to stimulus diffusion from the Middle East. Whichever the case, there is little doubt that stimulus diffusion played an important role; that is, the idea or general principle of writing, once observed, caught on occasionally even if the specific technique was not fully understood or subsequently employed.

Part of the difficulty in tracing the earliest stages in the history of writing has to do with deciding exactly where to begin. Even if one specifies as the two essential conditions (1) the intent to communicate in the broadest sense (2) by means of some visible signs that are expected to endure, it becomes clear that the discussion must include activities that are antecedent to writing. For example, the Abnaki Indians indicated the direction and distance of a journey, as well as the anticipated absence in days, by means of sticks forced into the ground in a particular manner. Another example is the well-known quipu of the ancient Incas of Peru, a device consisting of a main cord to which smaller variously colored and knotted cords were attached. The opinion of specialists as to the full significance of the quipus differs, but it seems certain that one of their uses was for calculating and record keeping.

There are also the numerous paintings or carvings on rock walls, bones, and a variety of other materials, some going back thousands of years. The intent of many of these was without question magical. Cave paintings of game animals, struck by spears and darts, in all likelihood were made with the hope of achieving success in future hunting forays, a practice based on the assumption that a desired result could be brought about by pictorially enacting it in advance. Broadly seen, then, these were attempts at communication with supernatural forces. The purpose of other pictorial representations was explicitly communicative, as in the

Prewriting stage

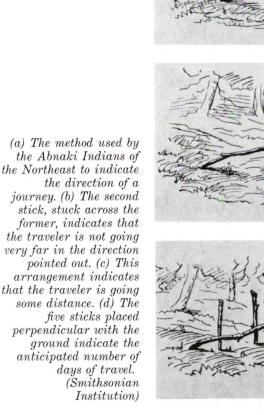

(a) The method used by the Abnaki Indians of the Northeast to indicate the direction of a journey. (b) The second stick, stuck across the former, indicates that the traveler is not going very far in the direction pointed out. (c) This arrangement indicates that the traveler is going some distance. (d) The five sticks placed perpendicular with the ground indicate the anticipated number of days of travel. (Smithsonian Institution)

Chapter 17   The nature of communication and the structure of language case of the various chronicles or autobiographic accounts of bravery executed by North American Indians on bark, buffalo hide, and the like (see Figure 17-2). Yet all of these instances are best assigned to a prewriting stage, for at least two reasons: "reading" them can be independent of any particular language, and their "writer" appears to have enjoyed complete individuality and freedom in executing them.

Strictly speaking, pictographic representations are iconic: the drawing of an eye stands for what it shows—an eye, organ of sight. A more sophisticated use of a picture is made when it is intended to refer also or primarily to some thing or idea associated with the object represented—for instance, in the case of the drawing of an eye, to the faculty of vision or to spying on another person. Any instance of such symbolic representation is known as an *ideogram*. The crucial stage that completed the transformation of picture writing into full-fledged writing must have taken place when pictorial signs came to be associated primarily with the sounds of the words they represented rather than with their meanings.

From ideograms to phonograms

This principle was partially employed in the writing of the Maya (Thompson 1954:165–170). For example, the abstract notion of *count* was rendered by the glyph representing the head of a mythical fish, because the word for *count* and the name of the fish were homophones (*xoc*). To use a modern English example, the word signs, or *logograms*, ⊙ for *eye* and ☾ for *sickle* can be made to assume the function of *phonograms*, together "spelling" the word *icicle*, thus establishing a direct link between the sounds of a particular language and the symbols used to represent them.

The main tendency of the general evolution of the early stages of writing was toward increasing abstraction (picture for an object—picture for a word or an idea—picture for the sounds of a word). The subsequent evolution of writing was characterized by simplification, both structural and formal. The unwieldiness of the most ancient writing systems, in which the typical symbol, a picture, stood for the sounds of a whole word, came to be replaced in some systems by the more efficient syllabic writings, or *syllabaries*. These performed their task of recording the spoken language with a greatly reduced repertory of symbols, each of which represented one of the syllables.

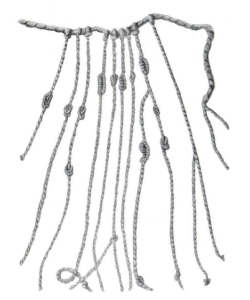

Recent and contemporary writing systems

The logical next step, dictated by the sound structure of those languages to which the syllabic system of writing did not prove particularly suited, was the emergence of alphabetic writing. In this system, for which we are indebted to a long succession of peoples beginning with the Semitic-speaking neighbors of the ancient Egyptians and ending with the ancient Greeks, each significant sound of a language is typically represented by a separate sign, or letter. The effectiveness of the alphabet is best appreciated when one realizes that the hundreds of thousands of English words can all be rendered in terms of no more than twenty-six simple marks.

An account of the general evolution of writing does not apply to any one particular

Drawing of a portion of a quipu. (From G. H. S. Bushnell, Peru. Copyright © Thames and Hudson, London, (1956, p. 127)

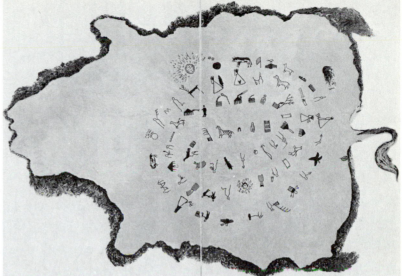

Figure 17-2 An Indian chronicle

A chronicle, or the so-called winter count, painted on buffalo hide by Lone Dog, a Dakota Indian. Read spiralwise from the center, it covers the period from the winter of 1800–1801 to the winter of 1870–1871. The signs for the first three winters (*a* through *c*) and the last three winters (*d* through *f*) are explained below. (Smithsonian Institution)

(a) *Winter of 1800–1801* Thirty Dakota Indians were killed by Crow Indians (the use of black lines to signify dead Dakotas was traditional).

(b) *Winter of 1801–1802* Many Dakotas died of smallpox (represented by red blotches over face and body).

(c) *Winter of 1802–1803* A Dakota stole some horses with shoes on, that is, horses originally belonging to the whites (horses represented by a horseshoe).

(d) *Winter of 1868–1869* Texas cattle were brought to the Dakota country.

(e) *Winter of 1869–1870* An eclipse of the sun occurred (the reference is to the total eclipse observed in the Dakota country on August 7, 1869).

(f) *Winter of 1870–1871* A battle between a group of the Dakotas and the Crows, with bullets flying and the Crows defending their post, pictured in the middle.

Cuneiform writing, which replaced the earlier pictorial writing, derives its name from the wedge-shaped characters impressed into clay with the edge of a special stylus. The earliest known users of the cuneiform were the Sumerians, who in the course of the fourth millennium B.C. developed in Mesopotamia an elaborate urban civilization. The illustration shows one of the few extant early documents, an inscribed brick of Eannatum, king of the ancient Sumerian city of Lagash. (From The Alphabet, by David Diringer, Hutchinson Publishing Group Ltd., 1968, Plate 1.5, p. 23)

Pre-Columbian writing systems of native America are thought to have been invented independent of the Old World. Particularly elaborate among them is Maya writing, much of which has been preserved incised in low relief on stone slabs or pillars (stelae) used for commemorative purposes and dating from c. A.D. 300 to A.D. 900. For the most part, the Maya inscriptions still await satisfactory deciphering. Among the glyphs that can be read are the symbols for time periods used in the intricate Maya calendar. In this illustration, the glyphs represent (a) the day, or kin, (b) the 20-day period, (c) the 360-day period, and so on. (Reprinted from The Ancient Maya, Third Edition by Sylvanus Griswold Morley; revised by George W. Brainerd with permission of the publishers, Stanford University Press. © 1956 by the Board of Trustees of the Leland Stanford Junior University)

A syllabary chart with handwritten Cherokee characters and printed romanizations:

a	e	i	o	u	v
ga	ge	gi	go	gu	gv
ha	he	hi	ho	hu	hv
la	le	li	lo	lu	lv
ma	me	mi	mo	mu	
na	ne	ni	no	nu	nv
gwa	gwe	gwi	gwo	gwu	gwv
sa	se	si	so	su	sv
da	de	di	do	du	dv
dla	dle	dli	dlo	dlu	dlv
dza	dze	dzi	dzo	dzu	dzv
wa	we	wi	wo	wu	wv
ya	ye	yi	yo	yu	yv

Additional column: ka, hna, nah, s, ta, ti, tla

Of special interest to Americans is the Cherokee syllabary, invented about 1821 by Sequoya for use by the Cherokee tribe. The syllabary is an excellent example of stimulus, or idea, diffusion. (From An Introduction to Descriptive Linguistics, *Revised Edition by H. A. Gleason, Jr. Copyright © 1955, 1961 by Holt, Rinehart and Winston, Inc. Reprinted by permission of Holt, Rinehart, and Winston)*

system; it merely traces the likely sequence of the fundamental stages that over a period of several thousand years brought the original invention to its present high efficacy. Nor should one assume that the boundaries between the stages were necessarily sharp: many writing systems of the past and some used to the present day mingle several principles—for example, the syllabic and the alphabetic.

Many hundreds of different writing systems were in use in the course of the last five thousand years, and a surprising variety are in current use today. The study of the evolution of writing is so intricate that the present treatment outlines only the most fundamental landmarks. Anthropologists have always recognized the use of writing as a cultural force of the highest order. Ushered in by the needs of the rising urban civilizations, writing in turn contributed more than its share to their further development and was eventually responsible for humanity's crossing the threshold into historic times.

Today, quite apart from the important function with which we customarily associate it, writing serves as a powerful unifying force for numerous national collectivities. A particularly outstanding example is China, where a number of languages are spoken that, though related, are not mutually intelligible. The writing system of classical Chinese characters, in which the visual symbols essentially represent morphemes regardless of their sounds, facilitates communication across the many linguistic boundaries of that vast nation.

Invention of printing

One invention begets another. For several millennia the art of writing was to be the exclusive skill of a few individuals. By the time the Middle Ages drew to a close in Europe, the demand for copies of many manuscripts had reached such proportions that it was not unusual for an early fifteenth-century Florentine bookseller to employ a score or more copyists in order to satisfy his customers. Although block printing was apparently known in Europe by the beginning of the fifteenth century, it seems not to have threatened the patient work of the copyists. Then, in about 1450, came the invention of printing from movable type, which within a few decades spread over Western Europe like wildfire. This invention customarily is attributed to Johann Gutenberg (1400?–1468?), a German. But even if the invention of printing in Europe was wholly independent of an outside stimulus, it followed several centuries after mechanical reproduction of writing had been invented in China. The oldest extant block-printed book, found in north-central China, bears a publication date equivalent to May 11, 868 on our calendar, and movable type was being used in China as early as the first half of the eleventh century.

Like other great inventions, printing has exacted its price. For while it has helped raise communication to a higher power of efficacy, it has also tended to substitute remote, impersonal messages for face-to-face contact. It is difficult to imagine the growth of civilization without the availability and the permanence of the printed word; but for power, the spoken word remains unsurpassed.

REFERENCES

ADAMS, JOHN BOMAN
1957 Culture and conflict in an Egyptian village. *American Anthropologist* 59:225–235.

BERLIN, BRENT
1970 A universalist-evolutionary approach in ethnographic semantics. In *Current directions in anthropology.* Ann Fischer, ed. Bulletins of the American Anthropological Association, vol. 3, no. 3, part 2 (A Special Issue). Washington, D.C. Pp. 3–18.

BIRDWHISTELL, RAY L.
1970 *Kinesics and context; essays on body motion communication.* Philadelphia: University of Pennsylvania Press.

CHAFE, WALLACE L.
1970 *Meaning and the structure of language.* Chicago: The University of Chicago Press.

CHOMSKY, NOAM
1957 *Syntactic structures.* The Hague: Mouton.
1965 *Aspects of the theory of syntax.* Cambridge, Mass.: The M.I.T. Press.
1967 The formal nature of language. In *Biological foundations of language.* Eric H. Lenneberg (1967). New York: John Wiley. Pp. 397–442.
1972 *Language and mind* (enlarged ed.). New York: Harcourt Brace Jovanovich.

CHOMSKY, NOAM, AND MORRIS HALLE
1968 *The sound pattern of English.* New York: Harper and Row.

CLASSE, ANDRÉ
1957 The whistled language of La Gomera. *Scientific American* 196:4:111–120 (April).

COWAN, GEORGE M.
1948 Mazateco whistle speech. *Language* 24:280–286.

GLEASON, HENRY ALLAN, JR.
1961 *An introduction to descriptive linguistics* (rev. ed.). New York: Holt, Rinehart and Winston.

GUDSCHINSKY, SARAH C.
1967 *How to learn an unwritten language.* New York: Holt, Rinehart and Winston.

HOCKETT, CHARLES F.
1958 *A course in modern linguistics.* New York: Macmillan.
1960 The origin of speech. *Scientific American* 203:3:88–96 (September).
1966 The problem of universals in language. In *Universals of language* (2nd ed.). Joseph H. Greenberg, ed. Cambridge, Mass.: The M.I.T. Press. Pp. 1–29.

HOCKETT, CHARLES F., AND STUART A. ALTMANN
1968 A note on design features. In *Animal communication; techniques of study and results of research.* Thomas A. Sebeok, ed. Bloomington: Indiana University Press. Pp. 61–72.

KEESING, ROGER M.
1972 Paradigms lost: the new ethnography and the new linguistics. *Southwestern Journal of Anthropology* 28:299–332.

KELLER, HELEN
1954 *The story of my life*. Garden City, N.Y.: Doubleday.

LANGACKER, RONALD W.
1972 *Fundamentals of linguistic analysis*. New York: Harcourt Brace Jovanovich.

1973 *Language and its structure; some fundamental linguistic concepts* (2nd ed.). New York: Harcourt Brace Jovanovich.

LENNEBERG, ERIC H.
1967 *Biological foundations of language*. New York: John Wiley.

LOCKWOOD, DAVID G.
1972 *Introduction to stratificational linguistics*. New York: Harcourt Brace Jovanovich.

LONGACRE, ROBERT E.
1964 *Grammar discovery procedures: a field manual*. The Hague: Mouton.

LYONS, JOHN
1970 *Noam Chomsky*. New York: The Viking Press.

PIKE, KENNETH L.
1967 *Language in relation to a unified theory of the structure of human behavior* (2nd, rev. ed.). The Hague: Mouton.

THOMPSON, J. ERIC S.
1954 *The rise and fall of Maya civilization*. Norman: University of Oklahoma Press.

Chapter 18
Language in
time and space

For the most part, the several million-odd years between the simple repertory of calls that must have served our remote ancestors and the full-fledged languages of more recent times constitute a blank page in our knowledge. The absence of firm evidence notwithstanding, hundreds of scholars over the past two centuries have attempted to reconstruct the initial stages in the development of language. Ingenious as some of these reconstructions have been, they must be viewed as strictly hypothetical.

If we take as our point of departure the view that the languages of the world, as we know them today, must have had the same general source or origin, we are at once struck by their apparent diversity. The nature of these differences and how they came about is the subject of this chapter. What is even more important, the study of linguistic prehistory and history holds many clues for the anthropologist who is interested in the cultural past.

THE ORIGINS OF LANGUAGE

In the search for the sources of various facets of human behavior, probably the most intensive activity has occurred in the hunt for language origins. As long ago as 1866 this activity had reached such a fever pitch that the prestigious Linguistic Society of Paris refused to allow at its meetings any further attempt to explore the question. Nevertheless, some of the fanciful theories became so well known that they are listed in *Webster's Third New International Dictionary:* the *bowwow theory,* which sought the origin of language in the imitation of natural sounds; the *dingdong theory,* which assumed a natural correspondence between certain objects and the vocal noises that early humans used in reacting to them; and the *pooh-pooh theory,* which hypothesized that the first words were interjections by means of which people gave vent to pain and other strong sensations.

The probings of recent years have proceeded from sounder positions, resulting in part from the tendency to view the problem in the broader context of human biocultural evolution. One of the by-products of the increasing interest in animal communication has been the theory that human speech has its roots in the communication of lower animals. Pursuing this notion, Charles F. Hockett investigated the extent to which the design features common to the languages of the world could be said to apply to the communicative systems of other animal species. In a paper on the origin of speech, he notes that

the frame of reference [for the investigation of the origin of language] must be . . . such that within it human language as a whole can be compared with the communicative systems of other animals . . . [and] the useful items for this sort of comparison . . . must be the basic features of design that can be present or absent in any communicative system, whether it be a communicative system of humans, of animals or of machines (Hockett 1960:89).

In this paper, he indicates the presence ("yes") or absence ("no") of these design features for several systems, among them the communicative behavior of the bee.

Hockett's feature analysis of the manner in which bees communicate the discovery of an abundant source of food is based on the description of the rhythmic movements, or "tail-wagging" dance, that bees have been observed to perform. In this dance the distance of the food source from the hive appears to be indicated by the tempo, and its location by the direction of the repeated straight waggling runs (von Frisch 1967, 1974). The bees scored an unqualified "yes" on several design features, among them semanticity, displacement, and productivity.

A more important recent attempt to "incorporate the various steps and stages of the

Human speech in the context of animal communication

Origin of speech: a recent theory

evolution of language into the total picture [of the emergence of the first humans from their prehuman ancestors]" is made in Charles F. Hockett and Robert Ascher's essay "The Human Revolution" (1964). The authors begin their account of these evolutionary events with a discussion of East African protohominoid forms (early forms foreshadowing the more recent australopithecines) of about twenty-five million years ago. Drawing on studies of present-day great apes and speculating wherever evidence is scanty or unavailable, they sketch a vivid biosocial profile of these distant precursors of humankind.

The vocal signals that these authors believe the protohominoids may have been capable of employing amounted at best to a call system similar to that of modern gibbons. This very primitive means of communication would most likely have consisted of a handful of signals relating to circumstances vital to survival—the discovery of food, the presence of danger, the feeling of pain, and the like. While particular signals may have varied in their duration and intensity, the calls formed what essentially was a closed system; that is, each call was used to the mutual exclusion of all others, and no two of them were ever fused to indicate situations involving both danger and pain, danger and the simultaneous discovery of a source of food, and so on.

As we have discussed in an earlier chapter, changes in climatic conditions during the Miocene had significantly altered the face of the East African countryside, reducing much of what had been tropical forest to open savanna with only an occasional grove of trees. In some of the protohominoid bands this changed environment forced an adjustment in life style. Those who in the course of time successfully met the problems presented by a changed environment and managed to adapt to existence at ground level were to become our direct, though distant, ancestors.

One of the by-products of bipedalism was that the mouth no longer was needed to grasp, handle, and carry objects—tasks that could be taken over by the hands. In addition to the important biological functions of food and air intake, the mouth was now free to assume a new and vital role in speech production.

According to Hockett and Ascher, the beginning of bipedalism was roughly the stage at which the transformation of the call system into a prelanguage would have occurred. The authors posit two crucial steps for such a transformation. One was the blending of two existing calls into one new one, a development that signified the "opening of the call system." To use a parallel from English—remembering of course that here we are dealing with a fully formed language—*smoke* and *fog* have blended into *smog*, designating a condition characterized by the presence of fog made denser and darker by a noticeable amount of smoke.

Though the process of blending would have somewhat extended the repertory of available calls, the full opening of the system toward its ultimate potential came about only with the progressive discovery that calls consisted of individual sounds. Again, to draw a parallel from English, perception of the spoken word *den* as a sequence of sounds represented by *d*, *e*, and *n*, makes it possible also to say *end* and *Ned*, which are rearrangements of existing sounds rather than combinations of new sounds. (Another parallel offers itself in the physical sciences: the different molecules representing the vast numbers of distinct substances are simply combinations of the relatively few [92] kinds of naturally occurring atoms.) This existence of a limited stock of basic sounds, from which spoken words are formed, is characteristic of any language, past or present.

The discovery of separate sounds would not have come as the result of a conscious effort to make the call system more viable, although it may have been helped along by the necessity of distinguishing between pairs of calls that came to differ in one sound

segment only. Nor should we imagine that the breakthrough came about rapidly and proceeded uniformly in all prehuman bands. One guess for the approximate date of the completion of the process is the beginning of the Pleistocene, put today at about three million years ago, just before a period of prolonged development of the hominid brain. If we accept Hockett and Ascher's hypothesis, the transformation of a closed call system into prelanguage and ultimately language is probably a single development—that is, it occurred only once in one particular part of the world, with revolutionary consequences for the subsequent history of human life.

This account of the origin of language has not been accepted without some criticisms.[1] On the whole, however, these do not substantially detract from what the authors achieved in their provocative essay: the skillful wedding of closely reasoned speculation with what little hard evidence is available.

Studies of chimpanzee communication

At this point mention should be made of the considerable interest taken in the ability, or the potential, to communicate among the subhuman primates. For example, chimpanzees receive signs by way of several channels simultaneously. In fight situations, they may frown or stare at each other while baring their teeth; they express fear by grinning, and enjoyment by a relaxed opening of the mouth; pouting is associated with uncertainty. Some of these emotional expressions are accompanied by particular screams or calls of varying intensity, pitch, and duration. Depending on the situation, they may range from soft grunts or groans to a loud drawn-out roar. Grooming is a significant form of communication by touch.

More than twenty-five years ago an at-

[1]The essay by Hockett and Ascher (1964) is worth reading in full, not only as a good example of a modern quest for origins, but because it is followed by critical comments from no less than twenty-six invited scholars and by replies to them made by the authors.

tempt was made to teach a chimpanzee name Viki to speak, but the results were disappointing. Viki managed to approximate vocally only 3 words, and those poorly; in the reception/decoding process she possessed a somewhat larger vocabulary. A more recent experiment has had to do with teaching an infant chimpanzee, Washoe, the form of sign language used by the deaf in North America. At the time of the first report, near the end of the second year of the project, Washoe had acquired over 30 signs that she was able to use spontaneously and appropriately, both singly and in combinations (Gardner and Gardner 1969). Nor was this the limit of Washoe's capabilities: at the age of five, she was able to make correct use of about 150 hand signs and understood more than double that number. In a sequel to Project Washoe, chimpanzees have been taught American Sign Language from birth by humans who are fluent in the language, including persons who are themselves deaf. The first two subjects, Moja and Pili, began to use signs when they were three months old – at least a year earlier than had Washoe (Gardner and Gardner 1975).

At about the same time that Washoe was being trained to use the gestural language of the deaf, another chimpanzee, Sarah, was being taught to read and write with pieces of plastic of various shapes, colors, and sizes. Each plastic symbol stood for a specific word or concept (for example, *Sarah, apple, Mary; is, give, wash; red, yellow, green; same, different, name of, if–then;* and "interrogative"). A report on Sarah's accomplishments (Premack and Premack 1972) claims a vocabulary of about 130 terms used with a reliability of between 75 and 80 percent. The conditional relation (*if–then*), marked by a single plastic symbol and employed in such clauses as *If Sarah takes a banana, then Mary won't give chocolate to Sarah,* was particularly demanding of the chimpanzee's attention if she was to make the choice that would produce a reward. For a period of time Sarah experienced some frustration, but fi-

Language is an attribute limited to humans and acquired in the process of socialization. However, the use of signs can be learned by some other species, most notably primates. In this photograph Lana, a chimpanzee, is working on a "speech" machine, a panel of signs that can be pressed to give the desired results. (Wide World Photos)

nally she caught on and performed well even when the antecedents and the consequents had been completely changed (Premack 1971).

Interesting as these results are, one must not forget that Washoe's and Sarah's learning has taken place in a highly artificial, human-directed setting. To observe either of the two teaching other chimpanzees what they themselves have learned or, better yet, to find wild chimpanzees making use of symbolic signs, even on a greatly reduced scale, would be of still greater significance.

Human language as a unique development

The expectation that the sources of human ability to communicate by language can best be uncovered by comparative studies of animal communication reflects the powerful legacy of Darwin's doctrine of continuity in the descent of living forms. Those who accept this theory tend to look upon the emergence of human speech as culminating a basically quantitative development, that is, one progressing by degrees rather than one marking a fundamental break with the past. Recently, some strong dissenting voices have been heard. A well-developed argument for considering language as a uniquely human attribute, a brand-new function qualitatively distinct from any sort of animal communication known to us at present, has been put forth by Eric H. Lenneberg. In his criticism of the theory of straight-line evolution of language with only quantitative changes, he observes:

At the root of the idea that human language is merely quantitatively different from animal "language" is the idea that all animals have something that might be called "nonspecific intelligence," but that man has much more of this endowment and that this intellectual potential happens to be useful in the elaboration of a universal biological need for communication. . . .
In man, the ability to acquire language appears to be relatively independent of his own ability to "solve problems," that is, of his type of "nonspecific intelligence." Why should we, therefore, expect that an animal's ability to solve human problems is relevant to his ability to acquire verbal behavior? In most animals the "cognitive strategy" for solving a given problem is quite different from that used by man (Lenneberg 1967:228–230).

As for the theory of straight-line evolution of language by steps, and with missing links (for example, Hockett 1960), Lenneberg's main objections may be summarized as follows:

1 Most instances of communicative behavior among the various representatives of the animal kingdom (insects, fishes, birds) appear to be relatively recent developments peculiar to rather few species. Sporadic as they are, they tend to serve as evidence of gaps in the general evolution of animal behavior (or, at best, of accidental convergence) rather than as direct antecedents of human language.

2 There is no evidence to suggest that human ability to speak is a collection of separate skills that have accrued in the course of evolution. If this development had occurred, one would not expect to find the great apes, the closest relative of humankind, quite as speechless as they actually are.

In short, the fact that certain traits—for example, some sort of communicative behavior—are shared among a variety of animal species cannot be used mechanically to reconstruct their evolutionary histories. According to Lenneberg, we must therefore be content for the present to recognize the unique character of human language and to accept our ignorance of the details of its origin.

Despite this caution, potentially fruitful areas of inquiry still remain. One pertains to the evolutionary changes in the human brain. While in the course of the two or three million years between the australopithecine and the Neanderthal stages brain size increased nearly threefold, there is some evidence that this increase was due primarily to the expansion, coupled with restructuring, of certain cortical regions essential for the primary function that language fills—which is to point to something outside itself. To make this observation is not to suggest returning to the simplistic argument that the emergence of language correlates directly with brain size alone, in the same manner that the bigger the car the more power it has. Rather, it is an invitation to look for the foundation of speech behavior in the human-specific evolutionary development of the central nervous system. Drawing on one of the early theories of the origin of language, Gordon W. Hewes (1973) has suggested that such a neural remodeling may well have been aided by the earlier existence of a fairly effective gestural communication and the subsequent development of mouth-gesturing to accompany it.

There is also the question of timing. Important technological innovations and the corresponding sociocultural advancement associated with the Neanderthals between about ninety thousand and forty thousand years ago suggest that the change from prelanguage to true language may have taken place during this period. However, Philip Lieberman and Edmund S. Crelin (1971) argue from skeletal evidence that the classic Neanderthal did not possess a pharynx sufficiently well developed to produce the full range of modern human speech. On the other hand, there are scholars who believe there is some indication that the Neanderthals may have been right-handed, and hand preference is commonly correlated with the localization of the language function in one side of the brain. Whether or not language had fully developed by the time of the Neanderthals remains a disputed question (Lieberman 1975).

It is beyond reasonable doubt, however, that the Cro-Magnons, who appeared in Europe some thirty-five thousand years ago, had a language or, more likely, languages that in most if not all essentials were much like those spoken today. The confidence with which this statement can be made is based on compelling if circumstantial evidence. The innumerable cave paintings and carvings left behind by the Cro-Magnons attest not only to their intense preoccupation with magical beliefs and activities but also to their exquisite artistry. Moreover, from the thoughtful burials that they accorded their dead it appears certain that they believed in an afterlife. Spiritual and esthetic concerns, then, must have been as important to them as they are to the hunting and gathering peoples of contemporary times. Such a level of development would scarcely have been possible without the use of language. From a linguistic point of view, too, it is difficult to

Language in Homo sapiens

believe that, given the rate of language change, the world's great diversity of languages could have come about in less than about forty thousand years.

TO SUM UP The assumption that human language is unique should not inhibit continuing examination of its relationship to communication in general, that of other animals included. Criteria for distinguishing human language from subhuman forms of communicative behavior are not difficult to cite. Among the most important is the fact that language is readily employed in the absence of external context (Hockett's design feature of displacement) and that it can be used for an unlimited range of topics.

Despite the long and intensive inquiry into the origins of human language, and of communication in general, the question of the exact circumstances and mechanism of this revolutionary development is as open as ever. In modern approaches to this intriguing problem, there has been a significant shift toward stressing the importance of biological considerations. One of the recent theories seeks the roots of human language in the communication of lower animals, a subject that lately has been receiving a great deal of attention. Another respected view holds that the emergence of language represents a genetic development unique to the human genus. Today, there is general agreement that possession of language cannot be viewed merely as a cultural accomplishment. In short, speech seems to be an indisputable part of humanity's biological birthright.

CHANGE IN LANGUAGE

Changes in vocabulary

Cultures, languages included, change constantly. If by *language* one is primarily referring to vocabulary, then the rate and scope of culture change are reflected in language rather faithfully. Even the most trivial and ephemeral fads leave their marks, at least temporarily, in the hundreds of new words introduced each year into the vocabulary of American English (and other languages too, of course). In fact, if the culture of any society were to be totally obliterated except for a record of words its members had used over a period of time, it would be possible to reconstruct with a remarkable degree of accuracy an account of their changing way of life. In the world of fashion, for example, the fast-paced changes in Euro-American garments since 1964 reflect both the continuing influence of couturiers and cultural trends in the direction of more revealing clothes and decreasing differentiation between the sexes. On the one hand, clothes have become more practical; and on the other, their decorative function has been emphasized. Much depends on individual proclivities and situational factors, but the function of clothes as modesty screens has surely declined. These patterns—for more than one tendency is involved—are chronicled in such words as *see-through* or *peekaboo* (garments) and *body-stocking* (1964); *invisible underwear* (1965); *miniskirt* and *shell* (1966); *fun-fur* (1967); *leotites, pantyhose, twofer* (1968); *body shirt, bra-dress, da(i)shiki, unisex* (1969); *bells, longuette, micromini(-)* (1970); *hot pants* (1971); *layered look* (1972); *the string* (1974); and so on. Lest we think that these shifts involve only feminine fashions, it is sufficient to note the increasing use of jewelry and the widespread acceptance of long hair among males, and the general tendency for males to wear much more flamboyant clothes (*the peacock revolution*). The classic gray flannel suit is either dead or resting in mothballs.

To register the introduction of new items of material culture or of new concepts, languages add to their vocabularies either by borrowing words from other languages or by drawing on their own resources. English has been very hospitable to words of foreign origin for well over a millennium and, correspondingly, its lexicon is outstanding for

Word borrowing

its great richness, containing as it does thousands upon thousands of *loanwords*. Thus, *bin* (Old English *binn[e]* "manger, basket") is of Celtic origin; *nun, radish*, and *sock* (Old English *socc*) came from Latin; *skirt* and *steak* from Old Norse; *sausage, pain, prayer*, and *heir* from Old French; and among the more recent borrowings *broccoli, dinghy, moccasin, robot, sauna*, and *slalom* from Italian, Hindi, one of the Algonquian Indian languages, Czech, Finnish, and Norwegian, respectively.

Some languages resist borrowing. The language of the Arapaho, one of the Algonquian-speaking Plains Indians tribes, has been remarkably self-sufficient in its response to cultural pressures from the outside. When the Arapaho Indians first encountered the whites, they extended the meaning of one of their words—*nihʔóóθoo* ("spider")—to include "white man." When later they were introduced to their first monkey in a visiting circus, they named it *bíisnihʔóóθoo* (literally "hairy white man"). They designated the pig as *nihʔóóθouwóx* ("white man's bear") and the chicken as *nihʔóóθouniiʔégii* ("white man's bird"). Along similar lines, the Arapaho managed to coin apt descriptive denominations for items and concepts ranging from the steering wheel or telephone on the one hand to smallpox or Baptists ("he puts you in the water") on the other.

Precisely what it is that makes the speakers of one language hospitable and of the next unreceptive to borrowing is difficult to say, but the nature of the sociocultural contact between the peoples involved seems to play a role. For example, William Bright, in his study of words in the California Indian languages for domestic animals introduced by the whites compares the heavy borrowing of Spanish words with the evident resistance towards loanwords from English. In his opinion, this disparity may well be due to the benevolent though condescending treatment of California Indians under the Spanish mission system and, by contrast, the inhuman treatment received by these Indians from the Anglo-Americans (1960:233–234). But while the lexicon acts as a sensitive index of cultural change, changes in the sounds and grammar of a language proceed much more slowly and bear no direct relationship to the rest of culture.

PROBING THE PAST

It has frequently been said that the birth of modern linguistics dates back to 1786 when Sir William Jones, in a paper read to the Royal Asiatic Society, observed that Sanskrit, Greek, and Latin "have sprung from some common source, which, perhaps, no longer exists [and that] there is a similar reason . . . for supposing that both the *Gothick* and the *Celtick* . . . had the same origin with the *Sanscrit* [and] the old *Persian* might be added to the same family" (Jones 1799). Even those who seek the foundations of linguistics in the still more remote past would agree that Jones' statement was the cornerstone of the *comparative method*—a method characterized by the comparison of languages that have developed divergently from a common origin. In the course of the nineteenth century, scholars demonstrated convincingly that the differences among related languages are far from haphazard. Initially, they showed that sound shifts represent general tendencies. Later, they argued that all sound changes follow certain laws, which operate without exceptions within the same dialect. The nature of sound change has since been the subject of many hypotheses and recently of lively controversy. No doubt several factors contribute to language change in general and sound change in particular. One is the fact that each member of a speech community possesses a repertory of styles or performance standards among which he chooses according to circumstances. Inevitably, complex interplay occurs among the various performance standards in any speech community at any given time. When this interplay results in a modification of the internalized sets of rules concerning sounds, sound changes in languages are regular. Furthermore, structural factors in a particular language may influence the scope of any given change.

Reconstructing linguistic prehistory: Indo-European

Now if changes in the sounds and grammar of a language are changes in the rules of that language, it should be feasible to trace them back as far as available evidence permits. The students of language have done so since the early part of the last century. And in the case of the Indo-European language family—where scholars were particularly fortunate in having the aid of written records in various languages from different periods in history—they were early able to demonstrate that it is possible to reconstruct forms older than those actually attested.

For example, a number of Indo-European languages show a similar word for the kinship term *daughter-in-law:* Sanskrit *snusá̄,* Greek *nuós,* Latin *nurus,* Old Church Slavic *snъkha,* Old English *snoru,* Old High German *snur(a),* Old Icelandic *snør,* Russian *snokhá,* German *Schnur,* Armenian *nu,* and so on. It can readily be seen that the two initial consonants *sn-* of Sanskrit, Slavic, and Germanic correspond to the single initial consonant *n-* of Greek, Latin, and Armenian. On the basis of numerous other correspondences of the same kind among cognate words, and on the reasonable assumption that an original *s* before an *n* was later lost in some languages rather than that a new *s* eventually was added in several languages by chance, it is possible to reconstruct *sn-* as the beginning of the ancestral Indo-European word. Proceeding with the reconstruction of the rest of the word, one arrives at the form **snusós* ("daughter-in-law") (reconstructed forms are conventionally marked with an asterisk). This reconstructed but undocumented Proto–Indo-European, or ancestral Indo-European, word has not been preserved intact in any of the descendant languages. As a result, it is not to be taken as a phonetic representation; rather, it is a hypothetical form, a formula, derived from the rules and sounds for which evidence is found and is only suggestive of how the ancestral word might have sounded.[2]

For most of the Indo-European languages, of course, there is documentary evidence spanning a considerable period of time. But for the other language families of the world such documentation is a rare exception rather than the rule. In principle, however, the comparative method is just as fully applicable to related unwritten languages, provided that reliable sketches of their contemporary grammatical structures have been made. An excellent example is Leonard Bloomfield's (1946) reconstruction of Proto-Algonquian.

The Algonquian language family is one of the largest and most important language groups in North America. In colonial times, it comprised more than a score of different languages and extended—with some interruptions—from Labrador southward to the Great Smoky Mountains and westward to the Great Plains. The Indians encountered in the Northeast by the first settlers were Algonquian speakers, and the earliest recorded information concerning some of their now extinct groups dates back to the seventeenth century. More recently, the surviving Algonquian languages have come to be studied so intensively that among the native languages of the New World the Algonquian family is by far the best known today.

Bloomfield's reconstruction of the sounds and grammar of the ancestral language of the Algonquians is based on four of the so-called Central languages—Fox, Cree, Menomini, and Ojibwa—three of which he became intimately acquainted with through field work. Bloomfield's judgment was that

Reconstructing linguistic prehistory: Algonquian Cultural inferences from linguistic reconstructions

the marked differences found in the three western languages of the family—Arapaho, Cheyenne, and Blackfoot—were of relatively recent date, and that reconstructions based on the four Central languages "will, in the main, fit all the languages and can accordingly be viewed as Proto-Algonquian" (1946:85). Research of the last thirty years has not weakened this assumption.

The great majority of Bloomfield's reconstructions concern the grammar—the different inflected forms of Proto-Algonquian nouns and verbs: *niiyawi* ("my body")—derived from Fox *niiyawi*, Cree *niyaw*, Menomini *neeyaw*, and Ojibwa *niiyaw*; *newaapamaawa* ("I look at him"), *newaapanta* ("I look at it"), *kewaapami* ("you [sg.] look at me"), *kewaapamaawaki* ("you [sg.] look at them"), *waapantamwa* ("he looks at it"), *kewaapamipwa* ("you [pl.] look at me"), and so on.

Wholesale reconstructing of forms, and particularly of meanings, tends to stimulate inferences concerning the culture of speakers of a protolanguage. Thus, there is evidence in Indo-European that ancestral kinship terms for relatives by marriage referred exclusively to in-laws of the bride, not to those of the groom. The inescapable conclusion is that ancient Indo-European society was decidedly centered on the father—one in which at marriage the bride joined the family of her husband. Inferences of this sort can be dangerous if they are made indiscriminately, without additional support. Bloomfield makes this point by reconstructing the Proto-Algonquian terms for "gun," *paaškesikani*, and "whiskey," *eškoteewaapoowi* ("firewater"), on the basis of regular correspondences among whole words of the modern languages. It goes without saying that inasmuch as American Indians of pre-Columbian times fortunately were spared these items of material culture, the fact that words for gun and whiskey are reconstructible must be accounted for in some other way—for example, as a result of a shift in meaning or a loan translation. As

[2]The example of the reconstruction of *snusós* was abbreviated from an excellent discussion by Calvert Watkins of the Proto-Indo-European lexicon and culture appended to *The American Heritage Dictionary of the English Language* (Boston: American Heritage and Houghton Mifflin, 1969).

impressive as the comparative method may be, it is noticeably silent on the time depth of its end product.

DATING THE PAST: GLOTTOCHRONOLOGY

An attempt to gauge time depth—the period of time during which a language or group of languages has been undergoing independent development—was made by Morris Swadesh (1950) in his study of the internal relationships in Salish, an American Indian language family spoken in the Northwest. Strictly speaking, the method that evolved from Swadesh's seminal article would merit the designation *lexicostatistical glottochronology* because it studies time relationships (*chronology*) among related languages (*glott*[*o*]-) by statistical comparison of samples of their lexicons. However, both *lexicostatistics* and *glottochronology* have been used for the sake of brevity, and the latter term will be employed here. In its original application, the method yielded relative dating values, somewhat like those obtained by archaeologists from the stratigraphic record of a site. In the course of the next several years, glottochronology was subject to numerous applications and elaborations, and not a few linguistic anthropologists came to assert that it is capable of yielding absolute dates, comparing it to the carbon-14 method for dating ancient archaeological materials of organic origin.

Briefly, glottochronology operates on the assumption that in all languages there are certain vocabulary items that tend to be replaced at a uniform and relatively constant rate. This *basic core vocabulary* refers to concepts that are likely to be represented in any language and to remain stable regardless of type of culture or environment. There are two widely used test lists, one containing 100 test items, the other, more comprehensive, containing 200. Both lists include the following test items: *I, thou, we, this, that, who?, what?, not, all, many, one,* *two, big, long, small, woman, man, person, fish, bird, dog, louse, tree, seed, leaf, skin, flesh, blood, bone, grease, egg, heart, tail, feather, hair, head, ear, eye, mouth, tooth,* and *tongue*. On the basis of tests made with the 200-item list it was suggested that the rate of replacement, or loss, of the basic core vocabulary averages very nearly 20 percent per thousand years (in other words amounting to a retention rate of just over 80 percent per thousand years). For the 100-item list, the comparable rates are 14 and 86 percent.[3]

The basic assumptions of glottochronology have been subjected to many searching criticisms over the years. Perhaps the most serious question concerns the assumption of a constant rate of change in the basic core vocabulary for all languages regardless of the particular sociocultural context. Even

[3]Let us consider, for example, two languages spoken by Indians living in the Mexican state of Oaxaca—Mazatec and Ixcatec. These languages are related, having derived from an ancestral language common to both (and to others). A comparison of their core vocabularies yields the count of glottochronological sames, that is, true cognates with the same common meaning (for example, Mazatec *ška⁴* and Ixcatec *ška³* ["leaf"] and Mazatec *ni⁴ʔño⁴* and Ixcatec *na²ʔñu²* ["tooth"]) and glottochronological nonsames (for example, Mazatec *ni⁴ma⁴* and Ixcatec *ʔa²ni¹me³e³* ["heart"], because both are undoubtedly recent borrowings from Spanish *anima* rather than descendants of the same ancestral word, and Mazatec *hme¹-ni³* and Ixcatec *nda¹ra²* ["what"]). Let us now assume that out of the 200-item list, 192 word pairs are available for comparison, and that among these, 78 pairs are classified as glottochronological sames and 114 as glottochronological nonsames. Dividing 78 by 192 we obtain a fraction that indicates the proportion of sames within the entire sample—0.406. Substituting in the formula $t = \log c / 2 \log r$, where c stands for the percent of glottochronological sames (here .406) and r for the constant (here .805, based on the slightly more than 80 percent retention rate for the 200-item test list), the equation is solved for t, the time depth of the divergence in millennia for the two languages in question. The result is $t = 2.07$ indicating that, not allowing for the computable range of error, Mazatec and Ixcatec are estimated to have begun to diverge from a common ancestral language about 2.07 millennia (2,070 years) ago, roughly at about 100 B.C. (Gudschinsky 1956).

proponents of the method have come to the conclusion that it is untenable to insist on the acceptance of absolute time references. Instead, the suggestion was made to adopt a relative unit of time depth, the so-called *dip*, for "degree of lexical relationship." To do so, one multiplies the absolute time depth in millennia by 14 (Gudschinsky 1955). Using a figure of 2 millennia for the period of time during which two related languages went their own ways, the length of separation in dips between the two languages would be the product of 2 and 14, or 28 dips.

Two decades of application and examination of the glottochronological method have raised more questions than have been satisfactorily answered: Can a test list be drawn up that is unambiguously applicable to all languages? In view of the changing sociocultural circumstances to which languages are subject, can one assume the rate of retention to be constant from language to language as well as through time? Scholarly opinion is divided between those who dismiss the method out of hand and those who find it useful provided one is aware of its limitations. One possible application may well be in trying to arrive at the successive branching of languages within a language family exposed in recent times to similar cultural influences. But even in such cases one would wish to compare the glottochronological results with other kinds of available evidence.[4]

[4]A good introduction to glottochronology is provided by Gudschinsky 1956. A more advanced discussion of the basis and application of glottochronology and of the uses and strategy of lexicostatistics may be found in Hymes 1960a. Comments by several scholars are appended to this paper and are continued in Hymes 1960b. For a vigorous critique of glottochronology, see Bergsland and Vogt 1962. For an application of lexicostatistics (without going into chronology) to classifying and subgrouping the languages of a whole continent, see Greenberg 1966, and of most of the Pacific islands, see Dyen 1965.

For a major statement concerning the study of linguistic prehistory, see posthumous work of Swadesh 1971.

DISCOVERING THE ANCESTRAL HOMELAND

One question inevitably comes to mind: in the absence of direct evidence, can one infer from linguistic data the approximate location in which the language ancestral to a family was originally spoken? The advances already made in this direction attest once again to the ingenuity of the methods employed by students of linguistic prehistory.

The working assumptions that underlie investigations of this kind can be summarized as follows: the territory occupied at one time by speakers of the ancestral language probably was rather limited in extent when compared with the area in which the descendant languages are (or were) spoken. Unquestionably, too, the vocabulary of the ancestral population included words designating the principal features of the natural environment in which they lived—among them the names for various species of birds, mammals, fish, trees, and the like. The groups that in the course of time wandered off from the parent population to establish new home territories began their independent existence with this ancestral speech, including of course its vocabulary. Eventually the speech habits of these groups began to show the inevitable changes to which all living languages are subject as a result of changing circumstances and the passage of time. The cornerstone of the method for discovering the original homeland is the assumption that the careful comparison of genuine cognates in the descendant languages will reconstruct portions of the ancestral vocabulary that may then help reveal the location of the parent population.

The original home of the Algonquian Indians The demonstration below is based on a study made by Siebert (1967), in which he attempted to locate the original home of the Proto-Algonquian people. Drawing on the available vocabularies of the various languages and their dialects, Siebert succeeded in reconstructing more than fifty Proto-

Algonquian terms referring to features of the natural environment—about a score of both mammalian and bird names, a dozen tree names, and four fish names. However, Siebert's crucial contribution is not his providing us with the assumed ancestral forms but his demonstrating that the modern forms found in the different descendant languages are regularly derivable from the corresponding ancient words of the ancestral vocabulary.

For example, the forms *aˑhkik* from Woodland Cree, *aˑhčok* from the Lake St. John dialect of Montagnais, *aˑskik* from Ojibwa, and *àhkik^w* from the Penobscot dialect of Abnaki, meaning "(harbor) seal," point to an assumed Proto-Algonquian form reconstructed by Siebert as **aˑsk(-ikw-a)*. Similarly, the existence of *mahkwa* in Fox, *maskwa* in both Plains and Woodland Cree, *maškw* in the Lake St. John dialect of Montagnais, *makkwa* in Ojibwa, *mkwa* in Shawnee, *maxkw* in both the Unami and Munsee dialects of Delaware, *masq* in the Natick dialect of Massachuset, and *wóx* in Arapaho serves as firm evidence for an assumed Proto-Algonquian form **maθkwa* ("bear") (the divergent form of the Arapaho word is in fact expectable). Among the vocabulary terms for natural features reconstructible for the ancestral Proto-Algonquian language are the following: golden eagle, raven, kingfisher, nighthawk, blue jay, great horned owl, hawk, and heron or crane; (harbor) seal, raccoon, lynx or bobcat, squirrel, moose, porcupine, skunk, fox, bear, woodchuck, bison, woodland caribou, beaver, and muskrat; white spruce, white ash, conifer or evergreen, elm, alder, sugar maple, beech, and willow; and (smallmouth) black bass, lake trout, northern pike, and brown bullhead. It would appear, then, that the ancestral homeland of the Proto-Algonquians was characterized by the fauna and flora listed above.

But the detective work is far from over. The distribution of individual plant and animal species has changed considerably during the last few centuries as a result of the sweeping resettlement of the continent by immigrants from the Old World. It was therefore necessary for Siebert to engage in equally painstaking research to establish the earlier ranges of these animals and trees. Trees, because they are fixed and their range is governed by soil and long-term patterns of climate, serve as particularly reliable guides. So do fish, since they are largely limited to the environment of the lakes and streams in which they are native. On the other hand, less reliance can be placed on bird species because of their extensive geographic ranges resulting from seasonal migration.

Once the original ranges of those species whose modern Algonquian names appear to have descended from Proto-Algonquian are plotted on a map of the continent, the solution begins to emerge like the outline of a jigsaw puzzle. Of the approximately fifty reconstructible species terms, about a score significantly contribute to the solution of the problem. The earliest homeland of speakers of Proto-Algonquian must have been the territory that all of these significant species shared in common or at least touched. Siebert found that only one area satisfied these requirements—the eastern portion of the Great Lakes region.

The primeval home was a region abounding in lakes and was well supplied with a large variety of fish, waterfowl, and game animals. It lay between the almost strictly coniferous forests to the north and the deciduous woodlands to the south. That the Proto-Algonquians lived in a mixed-forest zone is evident from the frequent use of the two contrasting noun-finals in many tree names, PA **-aˑntakw-* 'evergreen tree, conifer' and **-aˑxkw-* 'wood; hardwood or deciduous tree.' . . .

The original home lay at the southern limit of the woodland caribou. . . .

The raccoon and porcupine lived throughout the entire original Algonquian home. . . .

The harbour seal . . . is the only seal that is common on the eastern coast of the United States. . . . However, in aboriginal times its ascent penetrated much farther into the interior along the upper St. Lawrence River and affluent streams. . . .

. . . The distributions of [the four species of] fishes provide additional reasons for pinpointing the earliest Algonquian residence to southern Ontario rather than to a more western portion of the Great Lakes region (Siebert 1967:36–38).

TO SUM UP According to the author's detailed analysis, the original homeland of the Proto-Algonquian speakers was apparently the region between Lake Huron and Georgian Bay and the middle course of the Ottawa River, bounded on the north by Lake Nipissing and the Mattawa River and on the south by the northern shore of Lake Ontario, the upper course of the Grand River, and the Saugeen River. No other area satisfies the ecological requirements determined by the linguistic evidence.

CONCERNING THE MYTH
OF "PRIMITIVE LANGUAGES"

The fairly widespread belief that the unwritten languages serving small tribal societies are for the most part "primitive" in the sense of "little evolved, closely approximating an early ancestral type," and hence "simple, crude, and substandard" has had a long history and is far from a respectable demise even today. In 1855 a contributor to *The Pioneer: or, California Monthly Magazine* observed of the Indians of northeastern California that "viewed in the most favorable manner, these poor creatures are miserably brutish and degraded. . . . [and] it is said that their entire language contains but about twenty words," and an otherwise sophisticated German explorer of two decades later suggested in all seriousness that the Arapaho Indians were so dependent on sign language to supplement their deficient

vocabulary that for all practical purposes they could say nothing to each other after dark. Still today one hears it said that the Indians speak an (or the) Indian tongue or dialect (as though *language* were too respectable a term to use) and make use of grunts and whines rather than articulate speech (whatever that may mean). Even well-meaning and educated people entertain misconceptions on the subject, somewhat as follows: unwritten languages lack well-defined sounds and grammar and a serviceable vocabulary; not having been forged by generations of poets and philosophers or subjected to the exacting demands of a complex civilization, they are inherently incapable of assuming the functions of English, German, Russian, and other established languages, and in this sense their designation as "primitive" is fitting and justifiable.

But the evidence from linguistic anthropology seems otherwise and rests on careful studies of hundreds of unwritten languages the world over. There are no languages anywhere whose sound systems and grammars are by any imaginable standard underdeveloped or inadequate to the task of communication. To be sure, their sounds and grammars are different from English or Russian and frequently appear inaccessible to those who are unable to escape the mold of their own speech habits. (In regard to grammar, many of these languages are commonly held to be more complicated than English, which is not to say, however, that they are intrinsically more difficult. The matter of difficulty seems to be relative when one considers the fact—already mentioned—that all normal young children will acquire by about the same age any language spoken in their environment.) Quantitative differences among language vocabularies do exist, with technologically advanced societies requiring a high degree of specialized terminology. But ranking vocabularies amounts to examining cultural contents and contributes little if anything to our understanding of languages as such.

Only in one sense is it possible to compare the viability of languages—according to their ability to adjust rapidly and fully to the explosive growth of modern complex civilization (Hymes 1961). It is a matter of common and frequent occurrence that some languages capably serving the various functions of a pre-industrial society are unable to cope with the avalanche of sudden demands made upon them and lose the contest for prestige to the language representing the dominant culture. Such languages stagnate or wither and, quite often following an intermediate stage of bilingualism, go out of use. Their fate is much like that of the small neighborhood grocery stores, more and more of which have to close in the face of the relentless pressure of competition with the much larger supermarkets.

THE WORLD OF LANGUAGES

How many languages are there in the world? A good rough estimate would be

about four thousand—a total that of course does not include the thousands of languages that must have become extinct in the past before there was any opportunity even to establish the mere fact of their existence. All these languages will show a greater or lesser degree of resemblance to one another as the result of shared universal properties, chance convergence, diffusion, or genetic relationship. The different kinds of classification applied to the world's diverse languages reflect these basic factors that cause resemblances (see Figure 18-1).

Structural similarities and diffusion

Typological classifications are based on the comparative study of languages as to structure alone, with no consideration given to their historical relations. When applied in very broad terms, this method of classification has found little acceptance among linguistic anthropologists, doubtless because—

Figure 18-1 World languages

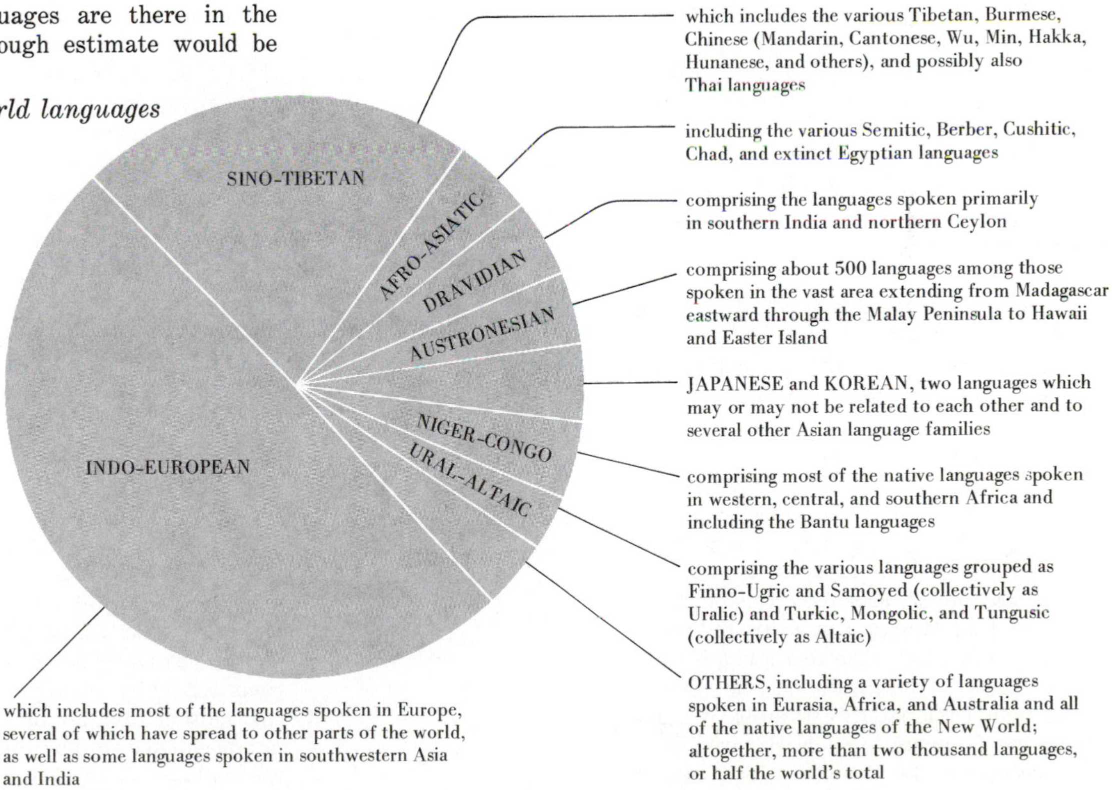

which includes the various Tibetan, Burmese, Chinese (Mandarin, Cantonese, Wu, Min, Hakka, Hunanese, and others), and possibly also Thai languages

including the various Semitic, Berber, Cushitic, Chad, and extinct Egyptian languages

comprising the languages spoken primarily in southern India and northern Ceylon

comprising about 500 languages among those spoken in the vast area extending from Madagascar eastward through the Malay Peninsula to Hawaii and Easter Island

JAPANESE and KOREAN, two languages which may or may not be related to each other and to several other Asian language families

comprising most of the native languages spoken in western, central, and southern Africa and including the Bantu languages

comprising the various languages grouped as Finno-Ugric and Samoyed (collectively as Uralic) and Turkic, Mongolic, and Tungusic (collectively as Altaic)

OTHERS, including a variety of languages spoken in Eurasia, Africa, and Australia and all of the native languages of the New World; altogether, more than two thousand languages, or half the world's total

which includes most of the languages spoken in Europe, several of which have spread to other parts of the world, as well as some languages spoken in southwestern Asia and India

SINO-TIBETAN
AFRO-ASIATIC
DRAVIDIAN
AUSTRONESIAN
NIGER-CONGO
URAL-ALTAIC
INDO-EUROPEAN

in spite of the variety of typologies devised—no connection has yet been demonstrated between the type of linguistic structure and the nature of the associated culture. But the similarities in phonology and grammar between some of the unrelated Indian languages in the Pacific Northwest, or between the Indo-European and Dravidian languages in India, are also of the sort sometimes called *typological*, and these are of considerable interest to the student of culture history. They clearly reflect long periods of linguistic and cultural diffusion.

The importance of resemblances caused by historical connection has always been emphasized and accepted. Culture contact between two unrelated peoples results in their languages coming to resemble each other whenever diffusion or borrowing between the two languages takes place. The language of the Yaqui people of Sonora and southern Arizona has been profoundly influenced by the Spanish culture with which these Indians have been in continuous contact since the early part of the seventeenth century. Not only do the majority of Yaqui words for material objects of recent origin derive from Spanish, but even such a relatively conservative vocabulary domain as kinship terminology has made good use of loanwords.

Resemblances due to common ancestry

The most systematic resemblances among languages, however, are usually those that reflect their descent from a common ancestor, or protolanguage. We then speak of their *genetic relationship* and group them together as members of the same *language family*. We have already seen that the concept of the family implies a common ancestral speech community, which, although too remote in time to be attested by written records, may nevertheless be reconstructible in its general features. But where did these parent languages, or protolanguages, like the Proto-Indo-European or the Proto-Algonquian, come from? Certainly they did not spring from nothing. Each must have represented one of the offshoots from an ancestor even further in the past, an ances-

tor common to languages other than just those belonging to the Indo-European or Algonquian families. The implications of this simple reasoning have engaged the imagination of some of the most brilliant linguistic anthropologists.

The growing boldness in the classification of languages on a continental scale can best be illustrated with reference to the New World. The first comprehensive modern classification of American Indian languages north of Mexico was undertaken by the Bureau of [American] Ethnology and published by its director, Major John Wesley Powell, in 1891. In it Powell listed fifty-eight distinct families, some consisting of a sizable number of member languages, others of a single member, the so-called language isolate. Subsequent work on these languages resulted in successive reductions of Powell's original classification. Most important among these were Sapir's reduction of the number of North American language families to a score and, later, his bold scheme listing only six groups. The latter was based primarily on structural similarities and was admittedly conjectural from the point of view of demonstrable genetic relationship (Sapir 1929).

Pidgins and creoles

Not all languages fit neatly into the genetic model that we have been assuming. Among those that do not are the so-called pidgins and creoles, both of particular interest to the anthropologist because they reflect recent or continuing sociocultural contact. A *pidgin* is a form of speech acquired in addition to a mother tongue and used as an auxiliary language between groups of differing linguistic backgrounds. Even though restricted in vocabulary and simplified in grammar, pidgins possess structures of their own. A *creole*, according to the prevailing view, is a language that, although derived from a pidgin, has assumed the full range of functions served by a language and has become the mother tongue of its speakers. The number of pidgin and creole speakers is in the millions. Creoles center in and around the Caribbean, southern Asia, and West

*Figure 18-2 Development of
black English*

In this diagram, the thickness of the arrows
suggests the weight of influence that earlier
forms of the language(s) have had upon later
ones. (From *English in Black and White* by
Robbins Burling. Copyright © 1973 by Holt,
Rinehart and Winston, Inc. Reprinted by
permission of Holt, Rinehart and Winston.)

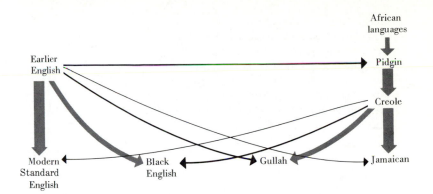

Africa but are also found elsewhere. Creolized French, spoken by dwindling pockets of blacks in Louisiana, and Gullah, once widely spoken by blacks in Georgia and South Carolina and presently surviving mainly on the offshore Sea Islands, are examples of creoles in the continental United States.

A pidgin has mixed ancestry, drawing in part on a local language and in part on an imported model, whether Portuguese, English, French, or some other. Neo-Melanesian, which is an English-based pidgin used in New Guinea and the Solomon Islands, has largely overcome its humble beginnings of more than a century ago and may well be on its way to becoming the official language common to a territory of high linguistic diversity. Not only has the vocabulary of Neo-Melanesian been supplied with thousands of new words, but additions have expanded its syntactic resources, making possible the employment of subordinate clauses and the like. Changes of this kind, marking the process of creolization, have resulted in such pliable and vibrant languages as the French-based Haitian Creole or the English-based Jamaican Creole.[5]

The study of creoles and of creolization has thrown new light on the problem of the

*The sources of
black English*

origin and history of black English. The traditional view, based on our understanding of dialect formation, is that over the course of several centuries and because of the social isolation of its speakers black English diverged from an earlier form of English spoken in the New World.

According to the proponents of a recent hypothesis, however, the source of the features that set black English apart from Standard American English must be sought elsewhere. They believe black English to be derived from an earlier creole stage common also to Gullah and Jamaican.

After having taken into account all of the available evidence, Robbins Burling concludes that

some elements of creolization have probably gone into the formation of all black dialects, but standard English and other forms of non-Creolized English have had long, persistent influence upon black speech as well (1973:121).

Figure 18-2 shows the complex interrelationship among the various forms of speech that are likely to have contributed to black English.

TO SUM UP What we have tried to show is that anthropologists who study the cultural past can significantly profit from the consideration of available evidence that historical linguistics has to offer. For those whose

[5]For a discussion of pidginization and creolization of languages, and pertinent bibliography, see Hymes 1971.

interests have a cross-cultural scope, languages likewise provide a useful index of the nature and depth of culture contacts. The most challenging, however, is the question of the relationships between language and culture or society. The anthropological perspective on this problem is the subject of the next chapter.

REFERENCES

BERGSLAND, KNUT, AND HANS VOGT
1962 On the validity of glottochronology. *Current Anthropology* 3:115–153.

BLOOMFIELD, LEONARD
1946 Algonquian. In *Linguistic structures of native America*. Viking Fund Publications in Anthropology, no. 6. New York. Pp. 85–129.

BRIGHT, WILLIAM
1960 *Animals of acculturation in the California Indian languages*. University of California Publications in Linguistics, vol. 4, no. 4. Berkeley and Los Angeles: University of California Press. Pp. 215–246.

BURLING, ROBBINS
1973 *English in black and white*. New York: Holt, Rinehart and Winston.

DYEN, ISIDORE
1965 *A lexicostatistical classification of the Austronesian languages*. Memoir 19 of the International Journal of American Linguistics (Supplement to vol. 31, no. 1).

FRISCH, KARL VON
1967 *The dance language and orientation of bees*. Leigh E. Chadwick, trans. Cambridge, Mass.: The Belknap Press of Harvard University Press.
1974 Decoding the language of the bee. *Science* 185:663–668 (no. 4152, August 23).

GARDNER, R. ALLEN, AND BEATRICE T. GARDNER
1969 Teaching sign language to a chimpanzee. *Science* 165:664–672 (no. 3894, August 15).

1975 Early signs of language in child and chimpanzee. *Science* 187:752–753 (no. 4178, February 28).

GREENBERG, JOSEPH H.
1966 *The languages of Africa*. Bloomington: Indiana University.

GUDSCHINSKY, SARAH C.
1955 Lexico-statistical skewing from dialect borrowing. *International Journal of American Linguistics* 21:138–149.
1956 The ABC's of lexicostatistics (glottochronology). *Word* 12:175–210.

HEWES, GORDON W.
1973 Primate communication and the gestural origin of language. *Current Anthropology* 14:5–32.

HOCKETT, CHARLES F.
1960 The origin of speech. *Scientific American* 203:3:88–96 (September).

HOCKETT, CHARLES F., AND ROBERT ASCHER
1964 The human revolution. *Current Anthropology* 5:135–168.

HYMES, DELL H.
1960a Lexicostatistics so far. *Current Anthropology* 1:3–44.
1960b More on lexicostatistics. *Current Anthropology* 1:338–345.
1961 Functions of speech: an evolutionary approach. In *Anthropology and education*. Frederick C. Gruber, ed. Philadelphia: University of Pennsylvania Press. Pp. 55–83.

HYMES, DELL H., ED.
1971 *Pidginization and creolization of languages*. Cambridge: Cambridge University Press.

JONES, SIR WILLIAM.
1799 *Works*. Vol. 1. London: G. G. and J. Robinson.

LENNEBERG, ERIC H.
1967 *Biological foundations of language*. New York: John Wiley.

LIEBERMAN, PHILIP
1975 *On the origins of language: an introduction to the evolution of human speech*. New York: Macmillan.

LIEBERMAN, PHILIP, AND EDMUND S. CRELIN
1971 On the speech of Neanderthal man. *Linguistic Inquiry* 2:203–222.

POWELL, JOHN WESLEY
1891 Indian linguistic families of America north of Mexico. In *Seventh Annual Report of the Bureau of Ethnology.* Washington, D.C.: Government Printing Office. Pp. 1–142.

PREMACK, ANN JAMES, AND DAVID PREMACK
1972 Teaching language to an ape. *Scientific American* 227:4:92–99 (October).

PREMACK, DAVID
1971 Language in chimpanzee? *Science* 172:808–822 (no. 3985, May 21).

SAPIR, EDWARD
1929 Central and North American languages. In *Encyclopaedia Britannica* (14th ed.), vol. 5. London and New York. Pp. 138–141.

SIEBERT, FRANK T., JR.
1967 The original home of the Proto-Algonquian people. In *National Museum of Canada, Bulletin 214* (Contributions to Anthropology: Linguistics I). Ottawa. Pp. 13–47.

SWADESH, MORRIS
1950 Salish internal relationships. *International Journal of American Linguistics* 16:157–167.

1971 *The origin and diversification of language.* Chicago: Aldine-Atherton.

Chapter 19
Language in
culture and society

One may argue convincingly that communicating is not an aspect of social behavior but rather that social behavior is the result of communication. After all, whenever two or more people meet, invariably their first attempt is to establish some sort of communication—whether by means of spoken words, gestures, facial expressions, or touch. The manner in which communication between them happens to proceed tends to set the tone of their subsequent behavior. Enemies may meet and talk each other into mutual understanding or even friendship, whereas a stinging exchange between friends can leave lasting scars and lead to actions from which words are conspicuously absent. One is frequently made aware of such a sequence when physical confrontations follow on the heels of what is customarily referred to as a breakdown of communication.

Stressing the key importance of communicative behavior for social interaction should not obscure the effects of positive feedback between speech and culture. There is general agreement among anthropologists that the development of the various aspects of culture was dependent upon the associated development of speech, and that the two reinforced each other. The more complex human culture grew, the more complex became the requisite verbal behavior; and the more serviceable the verbal behavior came to be, the more complex human culture could become. The inquiry into the nature of this relationship is the central concern of the anthropology of language.

LANGUAGE AND CULTURE:
THE CLASSIC VIEW

The nature of the relationship between language and culture or, more precisely, the influence of language on the perception and thought of its speakers, is a question that was raised long before anthropology became a scholarly field in its own right. Wilhelm von Humboldt (1767–1835), a well-known German statesman and scholar who addressed himself to it repeatedly, wrote:

The spiritual traits and the structure of the language of a people are so intimately fused with each other that, given either of the two, one should be able to derive the other from it to the fullest extent. This is so because mental activity and language tolerate and convey only mutually agreeable forms. Language is the outward manifestation of the spirit of peoples: their language is their spirit, and their spirit is their language; it is difficult to imagine any two things more identical.[1]

In the United States, from the beginning of the twentieth century until World War II, anthropological concern with language was primarily associated with the names of Franz Boas, Edward Sapir, and Benjamin Whorf.

With a doctorate in physics and geography from his native Germany, Franz Boas (1858–1942) first became drawn to anthropological questions while serving as a member of a German expedition to Baffin Island in 1883–1884. There among the Eskimos he spent a long arctic winter—an experience that, as he himself recorded, had a profound effect on the course of his future research:

It was with feelings of sorrow and regret that I parted from my Arctic friends. I had seen that they enjoyed life, and a hard life, as we do; that nature is also beautiful to them; that feelings of friendship also root in the Eskimo heart; that, although the character of their life is so rude as compared to civilized life, the Eskimo is a man as we are; that his feelings, his virtues, and his shortcomings are based in human nature, like ours (Boas 1887:402).

The theme of the underlying unity of all humankind that runs through these lines is

Boas: the psychic unity of humankind

Sapir: language as a guide to social reality

found again some twenty-five years later in Boas's 80-page introduction to the first volume of the *Handbook of American Indian Languages*, which marked the beginning of the scientific study of the languages native to North America: ". . . the occurrence of the most fundamental grammatical concepts in all languages must be considered as proof of the unity of fundamental psychological processes" (Boas 1911:71). Seen against the background of Boas's time, when all so-called primitive languages were viewed as fundamentally different from the languages of the civilized world, this was indeed a challenging assertion. In his view, these differences simply reflected the variety among cultures that in turn was the result of adjustments that different groups have made to varying environments and historical circumstances.

Historical problems were a major professional concern when, toward the end of the nineteenth century, anthropology was becoming organized as a scholarly field. Persistent attempts were made to classify the many diverse peoples encountered by an expanding Western civilization, and to understand their relationship to one another. Language, race, and culture were often indiscriminately lumped together. A major task and accomplishment of anthropology was to insist that language, race, and culture were historically separable. In this endeavor, Boas led the way.

While doing graduate work at Columbia University around 1905, Edward Sapir (1884–1939) came to know Boas, whose field experience and breadth of knowledge he found both impressive and inspiring. Before long, the bright student became his former teacher's brilliant equal. Sapir's productivity was enormous and his creativity astounding. During the fifteen years between 1917 and 1931, besides his *Language* (1921) and scores of anthropological articles and reviews, he published over two hundred poems, wrote numerous critical reviews in the arts, and even composed music.

[1]The citation from Humboldt, in our translation, is from *Wilhelm von Humboldts Werke*, Albert Leitzmann, ed., vol. 7, p. 42 (Berlin, 1907).

The study of the relationship between language and culture was one of Sapir's active concerns. While he firmly held to the opinion, just as did Boas before him, "that language and culture are not intrinsically associated [just as language and race are not]," he insisted that "language and our thought-grooves are inextricably interwoven, [and] are, in a sense, one and the same" (Sapir 1921:228, 232). To make this point more explicit: Sapir drew a distinction between the formal structure of a language, or its grammar, on the one hand, and the conceptual content of the language on the other. The intimate connection of the latter with culture was effectively described in a paragraph which fired the imagination of a generation of scholars:

Language is a guide to "social reality." Though language is not ordinarily thought of as of essential interest to the students of social science, it powerfully conditions all our thinking about social problems and processes. Human beings do not live in the objective world alone, nor alone in the world of social activity as ordinarily understood, but are very much at the mercy of the particular language which has become the medium of expression for their society. . . . The fact of the matter is that the "real world" is to a large extent unconsciously built up on the language habits of the group. No two languages are ever sufficiently similar to be considered as representing the same social reality. The worlds in which different societies live are distinct worlds, not merely the same world with different labels attached (Sapir 1929:209).

Sapir: language as a key to the cultural past

The fruitfulness of an inquiry into the relationship between language and culture was convincingly demonstrated by Sapir's *Time Perspective in Aboriginal American Culture* (1916). As the title suggests, the monograph is concerned with the methods that may be utilized in developing cultural chronologies for aboriginal America whenever historical records, native testimony, or archaeological chronology are lacking. The bulk of the work deals with inferential evidence for time perspective, with nearly half of the paper devoted to language.

According to Sapir, language holds several decided advantages over the rest of culture for the reconstruction of the cultural past. Being far more compact and self-contained, languages are better able to resist the many different forces that constantly tend to reshape cultures. Since linguistic changes, which proceed more slowly and uniformly than other cultural changes, are largely free of conscious rationalizations on the part of the language users, probing culture by means of language makes it possible to reach greater time depths and measure them more accurately. The evidence is abundant. One need only think of the major revolutions, violent or nonviolent, that have turned whole societies upside down yet left their languages virtually unscathed except for minor changes in their vocabularies.

One of Sapir's examples is taken from aboriginal California. Mount Shasta was visible to a number of different Indian tribes who at one time lived in northern California, the Hupa and the Yana among them. The Hupa referred to it as *nin-nis-ʔan lak-gai*, a descriptive term meaning "white mountain." The Yana called Mount Shasta *waᶜgaluˑ*, a word that no longer permits analysis or literal translation. Consequently, one is justified in assuming that the Yana were living in the area dominated by the mountain long before the Hupa arrived in the region.

The second example comes from the Northwest Coast culture area. Among the stems of the Nootka language, which characteristically consist of only one syllable, is the three-syllable word *tloˑkwaˑna*, referring to the wolf ceremonial complex of these Indians. The unexpected length of this word suggests that the term, together with the ritual, may have been borrowed from elsewhere. Following up this clue, one discovers among the neighboring Kwakiutl people the existence of a wolf dance, referred to by a Kwakiutl word that clearly appears as the source of the Nootka term (the Kwakiutl word is *dloˑgwala*, from *dloˑgw-* ["to be powerful"] and *-[a]la* ["for a long time"]). These examples show that languages may and do serve as windows to the remote past of the peoples who speak them.

Above all, Sapir conclusively demonstrated in his writings what Boas had maintained earlier—that all human languages without exception can be described within the same theoretical framework. Furthermore, like Boas before him, he brought to bear the findings of the study of diverse unwritten languages on the then existing notions of the general nature of language. As a result, many inadequate concepts were discarded. The empirical approach of Boas's and Sapir's research was a powerful corrective for the prevailing ethnocentrism with which most of humankind had been viewed.

Boas and Sapir made their students and colleagues keenly aware of the many complex issues involving the relation between language and culture. But Benjamin L. Whorf (1897–1941), through his vivid and persuasive writings, brought these issues once and for all to the attention of a wide community of social scientists. A chemical engineer by training, and later a fire-prevention inspector and insurance company executive, Whorf in 1931 came under Sapir's direct influence and, until his untimely death, successfully combined a business career with a consuming interest in linguistics and Mexican antiquities.

Whorf first formulated the hypothesis that "language produces an organization of experience" in a paper read before the Linguistic Society of America in December 1935 and subsequently published in the Society's journal (Whorf 1936). Examples were drawn from Hopi, a Uto-Aztecan language spoken in the pueblos of northeastern Arizona with which Whorf became well acquainted. In his paper Whorf put forth the claim that the Hopi Indians possess a language that is better equipped to deal with the various aspects of vibratory or rotary motions than is our modern scientific terminology. For example, where Hopi uses the form *tïˑrï* to denote a momentary event characterized by a jar, shock, or other disturbance and the regularly derived form *tïrïˑrita* for a rapid succession of such events, English quite commonly has to resort to two different expressions—"he gives a sudden start" and "he is quivering, trembling," respectively. According to Whorf, then, particular features of Hopi grammar coincide with certain principles in the branch of physics known as mechanics, and the result is that English appears deficient by comparison.

Whorf explored these ideas further in a second paper written at about the same time but published posthumously nearly a decade after his death (Whorf 1950). In his view, the common assumption that such seemingly universal notions as time and space receive approximately the same treatment in different languages simply does not hold. For us, the universe is intelligible in terms of the coordinates of space and of time. Space to us

Whorf: language as a shaper of ideas

is a boundless, static, three-dimensional extent, and time is something that flows ("passes") from the past on through the present and into the future. Apparently not so for the Hopi. For them, the grand coordinates of the universe are the manifest, objective experience and the unfolding, subjective realm of human existence.

As Whorf attempted to show by his analysis, Hopi correspondingly has no terms referring to space and time as such and manages quite adequately without verb forms denoting tenses in the customary sense. Here, a cautionary remark is needed. Whorf's account of the Hopi distinction between the objective and the subjective not only represents a very high-level abstraction but has little solid ethnographic foundation. Most likely, Whorf inferred it from what he knew about the Hopi language. His point, then, that the world view of the Hopi may best be seen as an outgrowth of the structure of their language becomes considerably blunted.

Attempting to follow up on a larger scale the hypothesis that a language and the culture of which it is a part mirror each other, Whorf contrasted western European languages with Hopi (Whorf 1941a). A sampling of his findings may be of interest.

In "Standard Average European" (SAE) time is measured in very much the same way in that separate entities are counted, as in *ten days* compared with *ten men*. In Hopi, cardinal numbers followed by a pluralized noun are used only when the members of the assemblage have an objective reality, as in *ten men*. Such concepts as *ten days* are rendered by the Hopi in a different manner, best approximated by the English translation "[they stayed] until the eleventh day" or "[they left] after the tenth day."

Mass nouns, such as *water, sand, butter,* are characteristically not pluralized in SAE and otherwise behave differently from other nouns—compare, for example, the expressions *glass of water, grain of sand, stick of butter.* All Hopi nouns, on the other hand,

Hopi and European languages compared

are treated alike, those corresponding to our mass nouns implying indefiniteness in some contexts and a certain quantity in others.

Phases of cycles, such as *summer, noon, sunset,* are nouns in SAE, and accordingly are employed in constructions in which other nouns occur. In Hopi, these terms correspond roughly to English adverbs.

Whorf next proceeded to show how these and other differences in linguistic structure compare with the habitual thought and behavior of the SAE and Hopi speakers. According to him, the former tend to view the universe largely in terms of things, the latter primarily in terms of events (or "eventing"). Our conception of time as a succession of periods to be filled with some kind of activity goes hand in hand with our preoccupation with schedules, programs, and the keeping of records. In the Hopi culture, on the other hand, stress is on being in accord, through thoughtful participation, with the unfolding forces of nature.

TO SUM UP   One may refer to Whorf's statement of the principle of linguistic relativity:

The background linguistic system (in other words, the grammar) of each language is not merely a reproducing instrument for voicing ideas but rather is itself the shaper of ideas, the program and guide for the individual's mental activity, for his analysis of impressions. . . . We cut nature up, organize it into concepts, and ascribe significances as we do, largely because we are parties to an agreement to organize it in this way—an agreement that holds throughout our speech community and is codified in the patterns of our language. The agreement is, of course, an implicit and unstated one, *but its terms are absolutely obligatory;* we cannot talk at all except by subscribing to the organization and classification of data which the agreement decrees (Whorf 1940:231).

For example, what one might describe in English by saying "It is a dripping spring," would in the language of Apache Indians be cast in a different mold, indicative of another perception of the world about them:

[They erect] the statement on a verb *ga:* "be white (including clear, uncolored, and so on)." With a prefix *nō-* the meaning of downward motion enters: "whiteness moves downward." Then *tó*, meaning both "water" and "spring," is prefixed. The result corresponds to our "dripping spring," but synthetically it is: "as water, or springs, whiteness moves downward." How utterly unlike our way of thinking! (Whorf 1941b:266, 268).

Here again one cannot refrain from a critical comment: the hold of our language or, for that matter, of any language is surely not all that gripping. We can readily invent and learn new terms for use in the sciences, we can transcend the drab, habitual patterns of our daily discourse with poetry, as in

When as in silks my Julia *goes,*
Then, then (me thinks) how sweetly flowes
That liquefaction of her clothes

(Robert Herrick, 1591–1674)

and we can even use logical and mathematical formulations to express relationships that are difficult or impossible in natural languages.

TO SUM UP   Viewed from the perspective of the last three decades, Whorf's contribution to linguistic anthropology lies more in the continuing research interest that his writings have stimulated than in the incisiveness of his methods or the validity of his conclusions. Let us now briefly review the nature of the relationship between language and culture in the light of some of the more recent investigations that have been probing less ambitiously but more carefully and rigorously.[2]

[2]An easily accessible source of Whorf's works concerning the principle of linguistic relativity is the volume of his selected writings (Whorf 1956). For a classic example of this principle, see also Lee 1949.

LANGUAGE AND CULTURE: A RELATIONSHIP RECONSIDERED

First of all, it may be helpful to specify what one means by the term *language*, which is altogether too comprehensive to be used loosely in the context of this discussion. We have already seen that *language* has come to denote what appears to be an inherited set of universally human potentialities for vocal communication, or, to put it less technically, the human gift of speech. As *a language*, the term refers to any of the thousands of particular systems of verbal communication that, although deriving from these potentialities, are just as culture-bound as the customs and value orientations that differentiate one society from another. When using the term in this latter sense, one must distinguish between references made to the vocabulary, or lexicon, of a language and those made to its grammar, or structure.

No less ambiguous, in the present context, is the meaning of the term *culture*. By *culture*, taken comprehensively, anthropologists understand the total pattern of learned human behavior transmitted from one generation to the next. In this sense the phrase *language and culture* is at best awkward because it includes language both explicitly and implicitly. Distinct from *culture* as a universal possession of humanity is *a culture*, any one of its many concrete manifestations. The restricted term *nonverbal culture* subsumes two categories of phenomena: one is behavior, the observable responses of members of a group to the many stimuli of their total environment; the other is the world view ("cognitive map of the universe") that the group shares.

To facilitate probing of the relationship between language and culture, we shall deal below with the problem in terms of language as

language (inborn capacity for speaking),
vocabulary, and
grammar

and in terms of culture as

culture (taken comprehensively),
nonverbal culture,
behavior, and
world view.

If it should be true that all languages, different though they may appear, reflect a set of shared features of universal endowment—that is, if the structure of language, and consequently of all languages, is determined by the structure of the human mind—one certainly could not exclude the possibility of a common organization of experience for all humans. On a deep level, the problem of the relationship between language and culture might then cease to exist.

Vocabulary and culture

That the vocabulary of any language faithfully mirrors the nonverbal culture of its speakers is self-evident. Whenever a new item—be it an artifact or a concept—gains acceptance by a society, the addition is registered in the vocabulary of the language. For example, the invention of the device that sends out ultrahigh-frequency radio waves and picks them up after they have been reflected by a land mass or some other object was accompanied by the creation of the word *radar*, an acronym from "*r*adio *d*etecting *a*nd *r*anging." When one anthropologist concerned with the study of kinship needed a word to include both *nephew* and *niece*, he coined the term *nibling*, modeled on *sibling*.

Because members of unlike societies have different cultural concerns, their vocabularies can scarcely be expected to correspond on a one-to-one basis. The example frequently given to illustrate such a discrepancy is the case of snow, for which Eskimo is said to have multiple words compared to the one available in English (Whorf 1940). Such a difference between the two languages shows nothing more than a difference in emphasis. Snow is of greater consequence for the Eskimos than it is for most speakers of English, and therefore it must be more finely discriminated as to kind. But ski buffs find the term *snow* just as unsatisfactory: the difference between *powder* and *mashed potatoes* can mean the difference between an exhilarating weekend and wasted money. Even for the members of the same society, individual vocabularies do not match, though they certainly overlap. Our bird-watching neighbors are visibly distressed by our lumping together as *birds* all of their different feathered friends, but they are hard to convince that what for them is simply *cheese* represents to us a delightful range of distinctive aromas and flavors, each bearing a separate exotic label. One is not justified in concluding that a lack of exact correspondence between different vocabularies necessarily prevents their users from perceiving and ordering (conceiving of) the world in much the same manner.

Another assumption has been that a literal translation of a foreign phrase may help reveal some features of a differential "perception of the world," as Whorf put it when discussing his Apache example. To lay bare the fallacy of this assumption, we will draw on examples much closer to home. The English word *breakfast* derives historically from *break* and *fast* (abstinence from food); the German equivalent, *Frühstück*, originally referred to a "piece" (*Stück*) of bread eaten "early" (*früh*) in the day; and the Czech equivalent, *snídaně*, at one time was clearly understood to refer to "eating." Yet the underlying, literal meanings of these words are thoroughly remote from the consciousness of their users, for whom they denote simply "the first meal of the day."

Clearly, then, the test of the hypothesis of linguistic relativity must be more stringent than a mere demonstration that languages differ from each other, followed by the assumption that as a consequence their speakers perceive and categorize the world about them in different ways. To establish the hypothesis as valid, one should be able to show that certain features of a language bear directly on the behavior of its speakers.

There have been several attempts to investigate the relationship between selected vocabulary items and the corresponding nonverbal behavior. One of these studies indicated that those colors that can be easily and unambiguously named are the very same colors that are most easily recognized and recalled. This direct dependence of color recognition on codability appears to hold true not only for English but for other languages as well, although extensive cross-cultural data are not as yet available. Another study of this type, conducted by John B. Carroll and Joseph B. Casagrande (1958), will be described in some detail.

Hopi and English: a recent comparison

Many Hopi verbs referring to various physical activities such as breaking, spilling, painting, or pressing cannot be matched with English verbs that would have exactly the same meaning. For example, when talking about what in English would simply be termed *breaking*, the Hopi must choose between two of their verbs to indicate whether only one fission occurred (as in breaking a stick in two) or many fragments resulted (as in breaking a pot into pieces). Similarly, the notion of *spilling*, which for a native speaker of English carries the connotation of an accident, and that of *pouring*, which implies an intent, are both subsumed in Hopi under one verb, while, on the other hand, a Hopi speaker must choose between two slightly different forms of a verb depending on whether he refers to the pouring or spilling of liquids (like water) or of loose solid materials (like sand or grain). However, for the notion of *dropping* (something) there is a separate verb in both English and Hopi. The question Carroll and Casagrande posed in their experiment was: can these and similar differences that exist between the lexical codes of English and Hopi be shown to correspond to features of nonverbal behavior by the speakers of the two languages?

To answer it, the two investigators made use of a series of cards, each with a drawing representing one such diagnostic activity. The cards were then assembled in sets of three. For example, in a particular set one card showed a man pouring out peaches from a basket (intentional action, loose solid material), a second showed a man dropping a small object from the pocket of his pants as he pulled out a handkerchief (accidental action, solid material), and a third depicted a man spilling some water from a jar (accidental action, liquid material). The subjects—both adult Hopi speakers and native-born white Americans—were presented with these cards and asked to choose which two from each set of three pictures belonged together and to state why. As the investigators has supposed, the Hopi tended to pair the first card with the third (the notions both of "pouring" and of "spilling" being expressed in Hopi by the same verb) while the Americans overwhelmingly paired the second and the third (both denoting an accidental, unintentional action). On examining all of the results and statements obtained, and after eliminating several sets of cards that for one reason or another turned out to be less reliable than originally expected, Carroll and Casagrande became encouraged to think that

not only do we have a promising technique for studying the linguistic relativity hypothesis, but we also have an indication that in further and more extensive trials of this method we may obtain greater assurances that language categories influence at least one variety of nonlinguistic behavior (Carroll and Casagrande 1958:26).

Grammar and culture: a Japanese example

Before examining to what extent grammatical structure is able to shape one's behavior or cultural outlook, it might be well to point out some of the salient differences between the vocabulary of a language and its grammar. Within limits, the speaker of any language has relative freedom of choice among various lexical alternatives and exercises this freedom largely on a conscious level. By contrast, the grammatical categories of a language are on the whole rigid, and their employment is generally automatic and unconscious. For example, to describe the distinctive color of some living room bookshelves painted by one of the authors, a variety of expressions could be used in English: "strong reddish orange," "redder and deeper than coral or fire red," "yellower and slightly darker than poppy," "yellower and lighter than Chinese red," "rich and vivid pimiento red," or simply "paprika red." But in the realm of grammar, whether or not a speaker of English is concerned with making a reference to time, he or she is obliged to select one tense or another: "sea anemone is an animal," "dinosaurs were swamploving reptiles," "I have never seen an aardvark," and so on. Then, too, many words change their meanings noticeably within an individual's lifetime, whereas grammar changes rather slowly. One is tempted to suspect that the grammar of a language may have some effect on the cognitive processes of the speakers, and that the effect, although subtle, could even be profound and long lasting. Carefully conceived and controlled studies are as yet very few. One that merits mention here was conducted by Agnes M. Niyekawa-Howard (1968) and deals with Japanese.

The Japanese passive consists of two different constructions. Each derives from a different deep structure and is characterized by a distinct set of syntactic and semantic properties. One construction, the pure passive, is neutral in meaning. The other construction, the so-called adversative passive, implies that the grammatical subject of the sentence is involuntarily subjected to something undesirable. When this adversative passive construction is combined with the causative, the resulting connotation is that the subject of the sentence is not responsible for what happened because he was "caused" to take the action expressed by the main verb. Few native speakers of Japanese are consciously aware of this subtle connotation.

One part of the study consisted in the examination of all the passive constructions in about twenty Japanese short stories translated into English (by native speakers of English) and of twenty English short stories translated into Japanese (by native speakers of Japanese). As expected, the subtle connotation of the undesirable effect of the passive tended to be lost in the translations from Japanese into English, whereas an adversative connotation tended to be read into the English original in the translations from English into Japanese. The second part of the study compared the perception of the Japanese with that of Americans on the basis of their interpretation of cartoons representing situations of interpersonal conflict. The results confirmed the hypothesis that the Japanese may be expected to show a greater tendency than Americans to attribute responsibility for the negative outcome of events to others. However, such an attitude could conceivably derive its support from the traditionally authoritarian Japanese culture rather than primarily from the structure of the Japanese language. For this reason Niyekawa-Howard also tested a sample of Germans, another group with a tradition of authoritarianism; their responses approximated those of the Americans rather than of the Japanese. What this study indicates, then, is that a specific grammatical pattern may not only correlate with a specific perceptual habit or feature of cultural outlook but can also contribute significantly to its reinforcement.

TO SUM UP Few anthropologists would challenge the assumption that the organizing principles of human thought and the cognitive framework that a group shares can be effectively studied by means of linguistic data. Far from exhausting the intricacies of the problem posed by Whorf and others, we have seen that the relationship between language and culture can best be explored in terms of carefully designed and controlled experiments.

LANGUAGE IN SOCIETY

The speech habits of a small tribal society may be expected to be relatively uniform in structure and vocabulary because members of such a population are able to maintain frequent or even constant contact with one another, tend to share closely similar views and concerns, and commonly have an economy that does not permit or encourage much specialization and social differentiation. But no generalization in anthropology is ever completely safe. In the central Northwest Amazon, an area encompassing many tribes, multilingualism is the cultural norm, with almost every individual speaking three or more languages (Sorensen 1967).

On another level, the language of the now extinct Yana Indians of northern California has a great many words with two sets of forms, full and reduced. The full forms (for example, *ba-na* ["deer"] or *dal-la* ["hand"]) were used whenever one male spoke to another. Corresponding reduced forms (*ba^c* and *dal^c*) were employed whenever a verbal exchange involved a female. Women were not prohibited from using the male forms but made use of them only when they had occasion to quote the words spoken between two men. A differentiation into men's (male) and women's (female) speech is actually quite common among languages, but in Yana it was particularly thoroughgoing (Sapir 1949:206–212). In the English vocabulary, a generation or so ago, there were certain words (the so-called four-letter words, in particular) that men used freely among themselves but women almost never used (and, strange as it may now seem, some women did not even know). Today, there are precious few traits that set apart young men and women in our society, and vocabulary is certainly not one of them.

Another type of speech modification found in societies both small and large is used for purposes of entertainment or concealment. The so-called pig Latin of English-speaking children (as in *Ill-bay ent-way ome-hay* for "Bill went home") has numerous parallels elsewhere in the world. Among the Hanunóo, jungle farmers of one of the islands in the central Philippines, marriageable but as yet unmarried youth have no less than a dozen techniques for modifying their speech during courting. These techniques include barely audible whispers used in crowded surroundings; very rapid speech characterized by clipping off words and shortening long vowels; words said while inbreathing instead of while exhaling; and various rearrangements or modifications of individual sounds or whole syllables of the basic utterances (Conklin 1959). The Chiricahua Apache warriors, who began instructing their sons at puberty in various virtues and physical skills, taught them at the same time a special raid and warpath vocabulary that was unknown to Chiricahua women (Opler and Hoijer 1940).

Specialized speech

Ethnography of communication

Even these few examples indicate that in a typical society there are, not one, but several ways of speaking. In the past, ethnographers have generally been silent on this aspect of culture. Currently, however, speech variation and the uses to which speech is put in different contexts and in different societies are receiving heightened attention.

An adequate *ethnography of speaking*, to use Dell Hymes's apt designation, must account for all the significant features of speech use in a particular society.[3] With this assertion, we do not claim that anthropologists can predict exactly what people will say to one another under culturally defined circumstances. But it is clear that the ways of speaking vary with the sociocultural context and are subject to rules.

A full-scale study of speaking involves a multiplicity of vantage points. One point of departure is to trace the role of speech through the various stages in the life cycles of the society's members. For example, in many societies there are special ceremonies concerned with the giving of names to infants. Among the rural Maguzawa (Hausa) of West Africa, the naming ceremony is performed on the morning of the seventh day after the birth of a child. On this occasion, except in the case of a firstborn,

[3]On ethnography of communication and of speaking, see particularly Hymes 1962, 1972, and 1974.

most of the village men gather in the court-yard of the newborn's household, while the women chat with the mother inside. The naming of the child, according to the day of the week, is performed by a Muslim priest who prays silently in Arabic away from the assembled visitors as he slaughters a sacrificial ram. At the same time, a novice priest recites aloud in Arabic three brief prayers in front of the men, who wipe their faces with their hands following each prayer. When the ceremony is over, the men share kola nuts provided by the father and resume conversation in Hausa, their native language.

Another approach to the study of speaking focuses on the codes that a speech community recognizes. According to published reports, the communicative codes used by the West African Ashanti include a variety of nonverbal systems (whistling, drum, horn, and gestures) besides several verbal codes. Among the latter are Twi, a dialect of Akan, their ordinary means of communication; an archaic form of Twi, used by priests and priestesses for ritual purposes; an "animal language," a highly restricted and modified Twi believed to be used by various animals; a "ghost language," thought to be intelligible to unborn babies and infants prior to teething; and a "language of the dead," by which an individual recently deceased may wish to identify the agent responsible for his death through the medium of a young villager.

We have already seen that normal children everywhere acquire general mastery of the code of their native language by about the age of five. But the process of acquisition of verbal skills extends beyond the code itself: an individual needs to know not only when he is expected to speak or to remain silent but also what he may say on particular occasions and what he may not. Visitors from Europe to the United States are commonly astonished to find children doing much of the talking during family meals. For them, such meals clearly belong among those occasions when children should be "seen but not heard," unless of course spe-

cifically addressed by adults. There are many indications from ongoing research that full understanding of *socialization*—the process whereby an individual assimilates the habits, beliefs, and values of his or her society—cannot be achieved without a serious consideration of the role played by speech.

Attitudes toward speech

Of no less concern to an anthropologist are the attitudes toward language and speaking that any particular group fosters among its members. Among urban middle-class members of United States society, verbal facility is highly valued and absence of speech is viewed with great discomfort. Whenever even short periods of silence occur during social gatherings, several participants will usually hurl themselves simultaneously into the void with the most inconsequential remarks. American political leadership, with few exceptions, has been predicated on an adroit use of speech, or at least the use of speech so judged by the voting public. The Old World proverb "Speech is silvern, silence is golden" clearly has little chance of becoming an expression of wisdom in the New World. Attitudes taken toward the various language varieties used in a speech community are frequently of considerable social consequence; and those taken toward other languages, neighboring or otherwise, determine to a large extent how provincial or cosmopolitan a group will be in its outlook.

On the other hand, in the culture of any speech community there are likely to be some situations from which speaking is conspicuously absent. In a number of societies, this is typically the case in the presence of death. Quaker meetings are characterized by prolonged periods of silence because Friends rely more on spiritual guidance received as a result of individual contemplation than through the sermon of a religious specialist ("When I came into the silent assemblies of God's people, I felt a secret power among them, which touched by heart. . . . " [Robert Barclay]). Among the Western Apache, keeping silent is a response to uncertainty and unpredictability in social relations (Basso 1970).

Other situations are characteristically associated with some appropriate speech activity, and still others are underdefined. The case of two strangers finding themselves occupying adjacent seats on an airliner may serve as an example of the last category. While it is customary to acknowledge the presence of one's seat companion by some perfunctory remark, the extent of verbal interaction between the two individuals may range from complete absence of any speech activity to continuous chatting during the entire trip.

Of special interest are those situations that are marked by characteristic speech activity, such as auctioning, confessing to a priest, haggling over a purchase price in a village market, commencement or graduation exercises, wedding ceremonies, lovemaking, demonstrating for peace, and the like. While a linguist is interested above all in the code of verbal transactions—that is, the structure of speech behavior as abstracted from its use—the anthropologist is concerned with the sociocultural context within which verbal transactions take place.

Among the components that help define this context are the setting, the participants, and the purpose toward which a speech activity is directed. Our illustration comes from the culture of the Subanun, a farming people of the southern Philippines (Frake 1964). In the Subanun society, there are formal occasions on which drinking and talking are closely interrelated. The setting for the speech activity here described is a festivity, marked among the Subanun by the consumption of a festive meal (one with a meat side dish) and rice wine, the Subanun equivalent of beer. Once the participants, who invariably include representatives from two or more families, have gathered for the event, the stage is set for individuals, especially adult males, to manipulate their social relationships through the use of speech. The ultimate goal of each partici-

Sociocultural context of verbal behavior: the Subanun example

pant is to improve his standing in the Subanun society.

The first round of drinking is devoted to tasting. Each among those who provide the large jars of rice wine for the festivity invites that person to drink to whom he and his family owe the greatest deference. The person invited then asks the other participants for permission to drink, expressing the social distance between himself and the rest by means of the order in which he addresses them and the terms of address that he employs. The tasting stage thus serves to assign relative role and authority relationships to the participants in the festivity.

Eventually, the drinking becomes competitive. From this point on, the successive drinkers must at least equal the quantity consumed by the individual who initiated the round. At the beginning of this stage, talk ostensibly focuses on the beverage and the drinking behavior, but in fact the participants are looking for signs of encouragement to continue. When the active participants have dwindled to half a dozen or fewer, the talk as a rule moves through gossip to more serious matters, frequently to cases involving a legal dispute and requiring arbitration. Because such cases are decided on the basis of the cogency with which they are argued by the parties concerned, verbal skills are very highly valued.

The final stage, game drinking, is characterized by a display of verbal art, with many of the songs and verses composed on the spot. Those drinking songs that bring the most prestige to the participants involve the skillful handling of a special vocabulary. On occasion, still unsettled legal cases may again be brought up; at this point verbal artistry is judged more decisive than cogent argument. When the festivity ends, there is typically a feeling of well-being or elation on the part of all concerned.

All but the most serious offenses are tried by the Subanun in this fashion. The successful individual is the man who is able to hold

An American president visiting workers at a ship repair yard. The smile, the hard hat, and the handshake are symbolic statements of the essential equality of people, an appropriately democratic message. (Wide World Photos)

his liquor, but above all one who knows how to talk. Far more than merely helping to maintain social control, these festive trials effectively lubricate the links by which the highly independent family groups relate to each other in the larger, peaceful Subanun society.

From the foregoing account several additional components may be singled out: the key in which the drinking talk is carried on—changing from trivial during the gossip phase to intense and considered during litigation or arbitration; the channel—adjusting from spoken words to songs; and the message-form—as prowess in argumentation gives way to purely stylistic considerations.

Whereas among the Subanun drinking-related verbal behavior is unusually elaborate and highly formalized, it is not without some tradition in Western societies. For the wine-loving Athenians, drinking together (*symposion*) after dinner was no less important than the meal itself. In our times, beer drinking among students and blue-collar workers, cocktail parties among middle- and upper-class groups, and toasting on festive occasions or at diplomatic functions present opportunities for friendly banter, socializing, informal business transactions, patching up old enmities, and reinforcing sagging friendships. For better or worse, drink is to the tongue what oil is to the wheel—up to a point, of course.

Social and linguistic variation   A great deal of what lies within the scope of an ethnography of speaking is also the subject matter of *sociolinguistics*. The use of these terms overlaps to such an extent that little would be gained by attempting to draw a sharp distinction between the two. Briefly, sociolinguistics may be defined as the study of the relationship between language varieties and the social characteristics of those who employ them. Some scholars argue that the identification of social functions in a community is a prior and fundamental step before one can hope to

An African potentate being accorded a deferential greeting. The ceremonial style goes together with a linguistic formula that underscores the distance between lord and subject. (George Rodger/Magnum Photos, Inc.)

proceed with the identification and description of its relevant linguistic behavior.

The range of linguistic diversity within speech communities varies widely from near uniformity in small, well-integrated societies to great variety in multilingual nations such as India, Nigeria, or Switzerland. Between the two extremes lie those speech communities whose verbal repertoires include two or more social dialects or those that are characterized by *diglossia*—the existence of two markedly divergent varieties of a language, one colloquial (low) and the other formal (high). Of these two, the colloquial typically is learned first and is used for ordinary conversations with relatives and friends, with servants or workers, in telling traditional narratives, and the like. The formal variety is taught in schools and assumes most of the functions associated with religious, educational, literary, and administrative needs. Good examples of diglossia are found in the Near East where classical Arabic, based on the standards of

the Koran, complements regional dialects of colloquial Arabic, or in Greece, where colloquial Greek is in use side by side with literary Greek derived in large part from its classical ancestor.

Given the repertory of codes in a speech community—two or more different languages, several language varieties, or both—their relations or the rules of code-switching invariably help reveal the community's social texture. Czech and Slovak, the two languages of Czechoslovakia, are mutually intelligible to such a high degree that both spoken and written communication between Czechs and Slovaks can and does proceed without the slightest hindrance. Yet, despite this close proximity of the two languages, translations from one into the other have been on the increase. Clearly, sociocultural differences are given greater weight than are linguistic considerations alone. In this case, explanation must be sought in the history of the sensitive relationship between the two peoples.

Some of the languages of the Far East possess an elaborate system of politeness forms. Speakers of Standard Japanese have traditionally made use of various speech levels, having to choose among the available forms on the basis of their attitude toward the addressee as well as their attitude toward the subject. The principal factors that determine these attitudes are social position, age difference, sex difference, and the presence or absence of some sort of group affiliation shared with the addressee. Furthermore, the politeness forms employed tend to be proportionate to the distance, size, and impersonality of the audience. The trend toward democratization in postwar Japan has rendered many honorific customs obsolescent, particularly among the younger generation. As one would expect, these changes are reflected in current linguistic usage (Martin 1964).

An especially striking example of a wide assortment of socially motivated lexical choices in Javanese was reported by Clifford Geertz (1960). The society that Geertz studied is differentiated into three distinct social groups—the aristocrats, heirs and descendants of the ancient Javanese nobility, at the top; the townspeople, who engage in petty manufacturing or small business, below them; and the peasants, at the bottom. Although all three groups speak Javanese, they customarily indicate their own social affiliation by a corresponding choice of words. In addition, the top and bottom levels of speech may be further embellished, depending on who is speaking to whom. As a result, such a sentence as "Are you going to eat rice and cassava now?" turns out to be almost unrecognizable on the lowest level (*Apa kowé arep mangan sega lan kaspé saiki?*) when compared to its most adorned high-level equivalent (*Menapa pandjenengan baḍé ḍahar sekul kalijan kaspé samenika?*).

It is difficult to overstate the importance of speech in the study of humankind. Speech is the indispensable lubricant for the working of any society, while at the same time differences in language are among the most effective means of establishing and maintaining social distinctness. To quote E. R. Leach, although he wrote of a particular region of the world:

For a man to speak one language rather than another is a ritual act, it is a statement about one's personal status; to speak the same language as one's neighbours expresses solidarity with those neighbours, to speak a different language from one's neighbours expresses social distance or even hostility (Leach 1954:49).

But words are more than just a social badge—they can become weapons as well. The deliberate disregard, in full public view, of long-standing taboos on certain words symbolizes an attack on the social system itself.

There is every indication that the attention anthropologists have recently given to the study of communicative behavior in its social context will steadily increase.

REFERENCES

BASSO, KEITH H.
1970   "To give up on words": silence in Western Apache culture. *Southwestern Journal of Anthropology* 26:213–230.

BOAS, FRANZ
1887   A year among the Eskimo. *Journal of the American Geographical Society of New York* 19:383–402.
1911   Introduction. In *Handbook of American Indian languages*, part 1. Franz Boas, ed. Bureau of American Ethnology, Bulletin 40. Washington, D.C.: Government Printing Office. Pp. 1–83.

CARROLL, JOHN B., AND JOSEPH B. CASAGRANDE
1958   The function of language classifications in behavior. In *Readings in social psychology* (3rd ed.). Eleanor E. Maccoby, Theodore M. Newcomb, and

Eugene L. Hartley, eds. New York: Henry Holt. Pp. 18–31. [Reprinted in Smith, ed., 1966:489–504.]

CONKLIN, HAROLD C.
1959 Linguistic play in its cultural context. *Language* 35:631–636.

FRAKE, CHARLES O.
1964 How to ask for a drink in Subanun. *American Anthropologist* 66:6(2): 127–132.

GEERTZ, CLIFFORD
1960 *The religion of Java.* New York: The Free Press of Glencoe.

HYMES, DELL H.
1962 The ethnography of speaking. In *Anthropology and human behavior.* Thomas Gladwin and William Sturtevant, eds. Washington, D.C.: The Anthropological Society of Washington. Pp. 13–53.
1972 Models of the interaction of language and social life. In *Directions in sociolinguistics: the ethnography of communication.* John J. Gumperz and Dell Hymes, eds. New York: Holt, Rinehart and Winston. Pp. 35–71.
1974 *Foundations in sociolinguistics: an ethnographic approach.* Philadelphia: University of Pennsylvania Press.

LEACH, E. R.
1954 *Political systems of highland Burma: a study of Kachin social structure.* London: London School of Economics and Political Science.

LEE, DOROTHY
1949 Being and value in a primitive culture. *The Journal of Philosophy* 46:401–415.

MARTIN, SAMUEL E.
1964 Speech levels in Japan and Korea. In *Language in culture and society: a reader in linguistics and anthropology.* Dell Hymes, ed. New York: Harper & Row. Pp. 407–415.

NIYEKAWA-HOWARD, AGNES M.
1968 A psycholinguistic study of the Whorfian hypothesis based on the Japanese passive. Mimeographed.

OPLER, MORRIS EDWARD, AND HARRY HOIJER
1940 The raid and war-path language of the Chiricahua Apache. *American Anthropologist* 42:617–634.

SAPIR, EDWARD
1916 *Time perspective in aboriginal American culture: a study in method.* Canada, Department of Mines, Geological Survey, Memoir 90 (Anthropological Series, no. 13). Ottawa: Government Printing Bureau. [Reprinted in Sapir 1949:389–462.]
1921 *Language: an introduction to the study of speech.* New York: Harcourt, Brace.
1929 The status of linguistics as a science. *Language* 5:207–214. [Reprinted in Sapir 1949:160–166.]
1949 *Selected writings of Edward Sapir in language, culture, and personality.* David G. Mandelbaum, ed. Berkeley and Los Angeles: University of California Press.

SMITH, ALFRED G., ED.
1966 *Communication and culture: readings in the codes of human interaction.* New York: Holt, Rinehart and Winston.

SORENSEN, ARTHUR P., JR.
1967 Multilingualism in the Northwest Amazon. *American Anthropologist* 69:670–684.

WHORF, BENJAMIN LEE
1936 The punctual and segmentative aspects of verbs in Hopi. *Language* 12:127–131.
1940 Science and linguistics. *The Technology Review* 42:229–231, 247–248 (April).
1941a The relation of habitual thought and behavior to language. In *Language, culture, and personality: essays in memory of Edward Sapir.* Leslie Spier and others, eds. Menasha, Wis. Pp. 75–93.
1941b Languages and logic. *The Technology Review* 43:250–252, 266, 268, 270, 272 (April).
1950 An American Indian model of the universe. *International Journal of American Linguistics* 16:67–72.
1956 *Language, thought, and reality; selected writings of Benjamin Lee Whorf.* John B. Carroll, ed. Cambridge and New York: The Technology Press of M.I.T. and John Wiley. [Contains the five articles cited here.]

CONCLUSIONS

Concern with language is without question one of the most active areas of current anthropological research. The signs of vitality that the study of language displays are many: its ever broadening scope and integrative approach; its undiminished function as the proving ground for new theories and methodologies; and its growing commitment to social needs.

In the past, anthropology dealt with the languages of peoples who could be defined in terms of the nature of their communicative systems: oral, mainly face-to-face, rather than written and at a distance. Today, these and similar limitations no longer hold true. By focusing increasingly on the problems of the differentiation of linguistic behavior by sex, age, locality, ethnic membership, and socioeconomic class, the socially motivated study of language not only poses questions of appropriate choice and enlightened policy but helps to provide some of the answers as well.

In his editorial introduction to a recently founded journal, Language in Society (1972–), Dell Hymes characterized the study of language in society as an inquiry that "may touch upon almost everything in man's world" and defined its scope as "the means of speech in human communities, and their meanings to those who use them." In a world in which more and more disparate individuals and groups are brought into contact and expected to interact, the study of language in its social context assumes a crucial role.

PART
FIVE

APPROACHES
AND
APPLICATIONS

INTRODUCTION

Anthropologists have been studying humanity for over a century now. Considering the vast scope of their interests and concerns, which encompass more than a million years and range over all the inhabited continents, approaches to collecting, classifying, and interpreting sociocultural data can be expected to vary not only from one period to the next but among individual scholars as well. Some of the theoretical and methodological frames within which anthropological inquiries have been conducted are discussed in Chapter 20. In this chapter, we focus our discussion especially on the years prior to World War II and deal with only the most significant trends of the postwar period. But although we have not attempted to survey the kaleidoscopic array of the many recent methodological and theoretical contributions of our colleagues, we have drawn liberally on their

research and writings in the body of the text.

One important development of the past half century has been the recognition of the rapidly increasing rate and volume of culture contact in both simple and complex societies and the resulting intensity of sociocultural transformations. This topic receives our attention in Chapter 21, which takes up the nature and direction of social and cultural change.

As anthropologists have become increasingly aware of and familiar with the general features of sociocultural change, they have come to appreciate and utilize the potential of the application of anthropological insights. In Chapter 22, titled "Applied Anthropology," we give an account of some of these practical concerns that can be traced from the essentially academic applications of earlier

anthropologists to the recent efforts by some members of the profession to plan and then assist in carrying out programs of directed social and technological development in specific communities.

The problems that today beset small remote peasant villages and crowded urban sectors of metropolitan areas alike cannot be viewed in isolation, any more than the problem of the rational management of economic resources can be divorced from the fact of galloping population growth. Accordingly, in the concluding chapter we consider the prospects that humanity faces. The challenges that lie ahead are indeed formidable. All fields of knowledge must join in a concerted effort to identify the critical issues, establish the necessary priorities in dealing with them, and then strive together toward global solutions.

In anthropology, as in other fields of inquiry, theory and method are interwoven. It is difficult to speak of method apart from the assumptions that guide the procedures employed, and it is equally hard to formulate or test a theory without a body of concrete information. According to the ideal scheme of scientific inquiry, a theoretical position in the form of hypotheses or postulates should precede methodology—the techniques of collecting, classifying, and analyzing data. In practice, however, researchers seldom proceed in this fashion, for they never quite know what they will find in the field (or laboratory). Perhaps the information they gather will reinforce theoretical assumptions, or perhaps the data will radically alter their working hypotheses. It may even happen that something entirely unexpected will come to light, something unrelated to the problem originally chosen for study. There are many cases of anthropologists setting out to examine a given sociocultural phenomenon and returning from the field with information on a different institution or even a different group. This is not necessarily bad anthropology, any more than the accidental discovery of penicillin is poor biology. Rather, it shows flexibility in the use of time and resources and is a recognition that what may appear a critical issue in the library can take on a different light in the field.

THEORY, METHOD, AND FIELD WORK

But this mental versatility in the search for knowledge is not the major issue. The key point is that scientific research involves the integration of both theory and method, and it matters little whether one begins with formulations or with observations. Raoul Naroll and Ronald Cohen have expressed this well in a chapter on the logic of generalization in science:

So scientific research consists of an endless cycle of observation, classification, analysis and theory. But the cycle is a spiral, moving upward. Each turn advances the state of knowledge. Each of us may begin at any point on the spiral he likes. But the value of his work can only be fixed by examining its relevance to the other points (Naroll and Cohen 1970:30).

In many disciplines, especially the natural sciences, theoretical and methodological investigations are often divided among specialists, with some individuals working on theory while others concentrate on practical applications. This type of division of labor is still fairly uncommon in anthropology, for virtually every anthropologist engages in some field research and attempts to relate it to broader theoretical issues. This dual activity is understandable in terms of the constraints and limitations peculiar to the discipline. Although the number of anthropologists has grown dramatically in the course of the last generation or so, anthropology is still a relatively small profession, whereas its subject matter is enormous in scope. Often, the anthropologist has been the only person with direct knowledge of a given society, or group of societies, in some distant part of the world. By necessity, he or she must be a generalist, able to bring back as much information as possible on a remote culture. It may be years before the anthropologist returns to the same locality or before someone else conducts a follow-up study. Furthermore, anthropologists operate on the assumption that cultures are integral wholes and that information on any one aspect of a culture sheds valuable light on other facets of the same culture. As a result, they tend to devote their professional attention not so much to culture in general as to particular cultures of specific societies. It is not at all unusual to find a well-established cultural anthropologist who has been studying the same tribe for twenty years or more. Having learned the language and the customs of a particular group, he or she is unlikely to go through the same

arduous process a second time. Biological anthropologists and archaeologists seldom face comparable problems of entry and establishment, but even in these subdisciplines there is a strong emphasis on experience gained in active field research.

The field-work orientation is still strong and has much to recommend it, but the conditions that gave rise to it are changing. With knowledge of different cultures much more widespread today than it was a generation or two ago, it would seem that the time is ripe for syntheses. Furthermore, an increasing number of anthropologists are working in complex societies side by side with a great many specialists from other fields. At the same time, social scientists other than anthropologists are studying non-Western peoples, so that anthropologists are no longer the only students of such societies. Finally, one should note that there has been a subtle shift in research priorities. For an earlier generation of anthropologists there were excellent philosophical and professional reasons for documenting variability in cultural ways, not only in order to collect a comprehensive base of data on different cultural forms but to support the argument of cultural relativity. We do not claim that ethnocentrism has been put to rest completely, but the case for recognizing the worth of other cultures has been well made and vigorously pressed home. What we are saying, then, is that, although the traditional research orientation of anthropology continues to be relevant, something new needs to be added.

THE FOUNDERS

No science, no body of knowledge, develops outside a given frame of general inquiry. The questions that scholars pose and the solutions they offer reflect the interests and speculations of a particular time and a particular cultural tradition. This need for a matrix is as true of science as it is of philosophy or theology; the difference is that science is based on verifiable information rather than primarily mental constructs. Theory in science is a formalization of more general concerns. Methodology, for its part, depends on the theoretical options and technical conditions at a given time.

Texts on the rise of anthropological theory often organize their material in chronological sequence according to the dominant conceptual frames, or schools, characteristic of particular periods. We shall follow this approach, but with the understanding that while there is some congruence between schools and periods, a number of research orientations may nevertheless coexist during the same period. New theoretical or methodological designs do not automatically invalidate older ones. Furthermore, since anthropology is both a unified field of knowledge and a collection of subfields with distinct, if overlapping, goals, developments in the discipline have seldom proceeded at an equal pace.

Examined historically, anthropology comprises a number of models applicable to an understanding of the human condition that function as frames of reference for the collection and organization of data. As one would expect, each of these models generates a specific kind of information that is then utilized to test assumptions and hypotheses. Evolutionism, diffusionism, and structural functionalism are some of the models we shall be examining. Needless to say, all anthropological theories involve assumptions concerning the nature of culture and the organization of human social systems. We shall attempt to make these assumptions as explicit as possible.

We noted earlier that anthropology is a relatively new discipline with very ancient roots. The prehistory of anthropology, if we may term it so, extends from the observations and speculations of the ancient Greeks to the sixteenth and seventeenth centuries. This very long period is dotted with an array of philosophers, historians, and theologians who probed into the nature of humanity, but the questions they raised were for the most part neither tested nor testable. The first condition for the development of anthropology was the recognition of a field of investigation in which humanity would be approached as a phenomenon in its own right, that is, without reference to such matters as the nature of supernatural designs. The bases for all fields of anthropology were laid in the sixteenth and seventeenth centuries, and by the end of the eighteenth century they had become well established (Slotkin 1965:vii). These configurations of a distinctly anthropological emphasis become sharper during the next century, and the period between 1860 and 1900 can be taken as the first stage of professionalism in anthropology. The dominant theoretical influence at the time was evolution, and its most famous exponents were Herbert Spencer (1820–1903) in the social sciences and Charles Darwin (1809–1882) in biology.

Foundations of evolutionary anthropology: British contributions

The idea of evolution as progressive development preceded the work of these two men and can be documented in the writings of several eighteenth- and early nineteenth-century scholars. In archaeology, the sequential development of Stone, Bronze, and Iron Ages had been established by about 1850. Evolution was therefore very much an idea whose time had come. Darwin's indispensable contribution was to identify the mechanism—natural selection—through which evolution worked. Spencer, for his part, applied the principles of natural selection to human societies, believing social change to be subject to natural evolutionary process from simple forms to complex systems. We concur with T. K. Penniman, who wrote:

[Darwin's] theory then, not only brought order out of chaos in the biological sciences, but also furnished a rational method of studying the origin and development of human institutions and beliefs. It was now possible to bring under one scheme all the variations and developments which would otherwise have remained as unrelated inventories, and to study society as an organism, whose development results from natural and social selection operating in the struggle for existence of the materials of which society is composed (Penniman 1965:20).

Soon after the middle of the nineteenth century, anthropology was established as a field of inquiry, with human origins and primitive societies the main subjects of its concern. The two were seen as not unrelated, since "primitives" were viewed as living examples of earlier stages of societal development. One can easily understand why so much effort was expended in trying to determine the evolution of customs and institutions, since the assumption was that a single formula could be found to explain the historical development of all cultures. Techniques of field work were still very rudimentary and, with few exceptions, anthropologists worked with materials gathered by others—colonial officials, explorers, missionaries, and so forth. As might be expected, much of the data suffered from a lack of objectivity, poor selection, and superficial understanding. Archaeologists, however, had already established a tradition of field work, limited though it was initially. For the greater part of the nineteenth century, archaeology was virtually synonymous with the study of classical antiquity, a circumstance that led students of earlier materials or of remains of nonliterate societies to define themselves as prehistorians.

The dominant theme of evolutionary anthropology was the ordering of ethnographic materials through time. This approach could be applied to whole cultures or to specific cultural institutions. The broadness of Sir Edward Tylor's greatest work, *Primitive Culture* (1871), is indicated by its subtitle, *"Researches into the Development of Mythology, Philosophy, Religion, Art, and*

The most deserving claim to having laid the foundations of modern anthropology belongs to Sir Edward Burnett Tylor (1832–1917). His contemporaries referred to anthropology as "Mr. Tylor's science." (Pitt Rivers Museum)

custom." Other works of the period are more limited in scope. Sir Henry Maine's *Ancient Law* (1861), J. J. Bachofen's study of matriarchy, *Das Mutterrecht* (1861), and J. F. McLennan's *Primitive Marriage* (1865) can be taken as representative of books attempting to trace the development of an institution from its simple origins to more complex forms.

Nineteenth-century evolutionists brought together a vast amount of information, including some of dubious quality, and attempted to force it into a single theoretical frame. The result was that in the majority of cases the cultures or institutions under examination were portrayed as quaint anachronisms—little more than fossilized and lifeless survivals—with scarcely any feeling for how people live and how cultures work. What these accounts offered was largely an array of customs dealing with such matters as the behavior of in-laws, the propitiation of supernaturals, and the punishment of criminals. It may be of interest to know that Aztec deities and the gods of classical

Greece both required somewhat similar attention from humans, but an understanding of this similarity should go beyond the observation that both civilizations fit a conceptual category between animism and the worship of a single supreme god. In the end, the reader is left with a sort of anthropological alphabet soup—a catalogue made up essentially of unrelated bits and pieces torn out of their cultural context.

Evolutionary theory in the nineteenth century thus suffered from a variety of shortcomings, some of which can be attributed to the uneven quality of available ethnographic information. However, the most valid criticism that can be made is that in all the mixing and matching that anthropologists indulged in, the central idea of Darwinian thought—the concept that adaptation is the major mechanism of survival—was generally lost sight of.

Lewis Henry Morgan was the author of League of the Iroquois *(1851), considered to be the earliest complete ethnography based on field work. (Lewis Henry Morgan Papers, University of Rochester Library)*

Evolutionism in the United States: Lewis H. Morgan

In the United States, the evolutionary perspective is best represented in the work of Lewis Henry Morgan (1818–1881). Although Morgan was very much a man of his period in that he subscribed to rigid sequential schemes and attempted to reconstruct the early history of human society on the basis of ethnographic survivals, his contributions nevertheless stand out as especially significant. For one thing, he enjoyed an advantage over most of his contemporaries in having personally experienced life in a tribal society. A resident of upstate New York, Morgan became intimately acquainted with the culture and social organization of the Iroquois Indians, who had maintained their cultural integrity through centuries of contact with the French, British, and Americans. His *League of the Iroquois* (1851) grew out of these experiences. As one of the earliest field-derived ethnographies, it did much to establish the value of field work. More than a century after its publication, it continues to be a major contribution to North American Indian studies. A number of years later, Morgan became interested in the comparative study of kinship systems and published the monumental *Systems of Consanguinity and Affinity of the Human Family* (1871), a work based on his own investigations among several Indian societies and a body of information derived from questionnaires sent to missionaries, consular officials, and others in contact with non-Western peoples. The aim of all this diligent research was to establish appropriate stages for the development of human institutions. Although this goal was doomed to failure, Morgan's work nevertheless initiated the scientific study of social organization and helped to further the concept of problem-oriented research. Morgan carried these goals further in his last major attempt at synthesis, his classic *Ancient Society* (1877).

Nineteenth-century evolutionary theory, especially when applied to cultural and social interpretation, was instrumental in rationalizing contemporary political and ideological beliefs. It was perhaps all too tempting to regard human history as a force inevitably leading to civilization as exemplified by the dominant Western nations. This concept of an iron law of change and displacement was not limited to those who supported the Victorian status quo, for it came to be richly documented in the writings of Karl Marx (1818–1883) and other political philosophers who predicted the inevitable decay of capitalism and its replacement by a more evolved socioeconomic system. In fact, Friedrich Engels (1820–1895) in *The Origin of the Family, Private Property and the State* (1902; 1884 in its German original) provided what was essentially an exposition of Morgan's theories in the light of a materialist view of history.

Evolution constituted the major but not the only attempt at a theoretical synthesis during the second half of the nineteenth century. A geographic, as distinct from a temporal, integration of ethnographic and historical information occupied the interest of several scholars, in particular Friedrich Ratzel (1844–1904) and his colleagues in German universities. The geographic ordering of cultural elements was a first step in the more complex analysis of the influence of environment upon sociocultural systems. Studies conducted during this period often stressed environmental determinism rather than an approach that viewed human society as interdependent with its physical context. Nevertheless, the more modern approach that recognizes society as part of a total ecosystem had its beginnings in the work of Ratzel and other cultural geographers.

Although the impact of Sigmund Freud (1856–1939) on anthropology was indirect and most of what he wrote on anthropological topics has not stood the test of time, a discussion of the significance of his work is imperative for an understanding of modern anthropology. This may seem to be a contradictory statement, but what is at issue is, not Freud as anthropological theorist, but Freud as initiator of lines of inquiry that

Sigmund Freud and anthropology

continue to be important to the present day. As a young man he was strongly influenced by Darwin's contributions to biology. Later he became an avid reader of anthropological materials to support his hypothesis that what once was conscious in primitives had become transformed into what he called the "unconscious" in modern humans.

Among the half dozen of Freud's major studies with significant anthropological content, the one that has generated most interest is *Totem and Taboo* (1918; 1912–1913 in its German original). As the title indicates, the work is a study of totemic phenomena and taboo restrictions, which Freud viewed as complementary facets of a single event or circumstance—the origin of the Oedipus complex. In Freud's reconstruction, the Oedipus complex is derived from a primal patricide in which the son kills the father and marries his own mother.

By the time *Totem and Taboo* was published, many of the assumptions of evolutionary anthropologists were being rightly questioned as inflexible and based on highly fanciful reconstructions of early human society. The assumptions underlying *Totem and Taboo* are as dubious as the anthropological information they depend on, and if the book is read at all today, it is chiefly for its curiosity value.

In what sense, then, is Freud important? Despite all the faulty anthropological interpretations in Freud's writings, he never lost the awareness that individuals live their lives within social and cultural contexts. In his attempt to relate individuals to their time and place, Freud opened avenues that were to be exploited with much greater success by a later generation of scholars. In much the same way that anthropologists would demonstrate that the cultural behavior and institutions of simple societies made sense for the peoples in question (however bizarre they might appear to Westerners), it was Freud's merit to show that in the realm of the individual, both abnormal and normal behavior was amenable to scientific inquiry and explanation. Finally, within his own area of professional competence, psychotherapy, Freud was a pragmatic and compassionate student of the human condition.

It is difficult to evaluate the work of the earliest anthropological thinkers without succumbing to the temptation of easy criticism. They were the first to try to integrate historical and ethnographic information into a unified theory applicable to all human societies. Even though we now recognize the limitations of the biological analogy when used in a heavy-handed manner, it is worth noting that the concept of cultural evolution proved to have real theoretical value once it was stripped of its deterministic meaning. Today, there are many anthropologists who concern themselves with problems of process and change, and their intellectual precursors were the best of the nineteenth-century thinkers: Charles Darwin, to be sure, and such men as Karl Marx, Lewis Henry Morgan, and Sir Henry Maine.

The danger in applying the insights of biological evolution to cultural evolution lay in the fact that biological change was founded on inequality—not all species were equally adapted to a given environment and not all members of a given species were equally endowed. This variation was at the root of natural selection, for without inequality the concept of the survival of the fittest could have no meaning. When such a model is applied to cultural variation, there is a great temptation to think in terms of superior and inferior cultures. Accordingly, in the second half of the nineteenth century both the scientific professions and the general public tended to view humanity in terms of superior and inferior cultures, superior and inferior races, and superior and inferior individuals.

The work of early anthropologists assessed

TURN OF THE CENTURY

Although developments in anthropological theory and methodology do not, of course, fit a century-by-century progression, the final years of the nineteenth century and the early decades of the twentieth do constitute something of a benchmark in the science of humankind. By the turn of the century, some of the founders, while often still active and productive, were being forced to make way for scholars of a somewhat different stamp, individuals more concerned with gathering ethnographic information than with establishing universal classifications of societal evolution. Furthermore, it was becoming apparent that the traditional subjects of anthropological research—simple nonliterate societies—were often faring badly in their confrontation with the representatives of Western nations. It was not simply that a number of groups were vanishing in the unequal contest, but that many others were becoming so changed as a result of contact that traditional styles of life would hardly survive much longer.

The anthropology of the period reflects these orientations and preoccupations: it is an anthropology of urgency devoted to salvaging as much as possible from the impending ruin. The reconstruction of culture history on the basis of ethnographic data was a first-order priority, although the frame of reference was often a somewhat arbitrary *ethnographic present*, defined as the state of a culture prior to major European influence.

While the first anthropological societies, museums, and university professorships were established considerably earlier in the century, the integrated professional training of anthropologists was a later development. By 1900, however, it is reasonable to speak of a clearly distinct anthropological profession in the United States and Europe. In the United States, several graduate schools were producing a small number of Ph.D.'s to staff expanded museum facilities and initiate teaching programs in a number of colleges and universities. Field research was becoming a virtually universal feature of anthropological training, and much of the field data were being published in newly established journals and museum series.

Given the interests and preoccupations of the anthropologists at the time and what can perhaps best be described as the feeling in the profession that theory and method had achieved a new level of sophistication, it is understandable that the first large-scale efforts at coordinated research date from the turn of the century. Between 1898 and 1900, A. C. Haddon directed the research of a group of British anthropologists working in the Torres Straits region between New Guinea and Australia, an area that was virtually unexplored. It was hoped that this research would shed light on the origins of the Australian aborigines and the cultural linkages between the peoples of northern Australia and Melanesian groups on the other side of the straits.

Franz Boas, the dominant figure in American anthropology during the early decades of the twentieth century, was one of the very few scholars whose active contributions ranged across all aspects of the discipline. (Culver Pictures)

Even more enterprising in scope was the Jesup North Pacific Expedition, which brought together investigators from the United States, Russia, and Canada. Organized under the auspices of the American Museum of Natural History, whose president was Morris K. Jesup, the expedition was to investigate possible relationships between the tribes of northeastern Siberia and those of northwestern North America. Specifically, the investigators set out to:

Franz Boas and the Jesup North Pacific Expedition

1 Determine the period of occupancy of the various parts of the coast on both sides of the Pacific and the changes that may have taken place in the culture of the inhabitants.

2 Investigate the languages and cultures of the coastal tribes with particular reference to the diffusion of culture.

3 Trace the geographic distribution of the physical types of peoples along the coasts and the biological relationship of these groups to the inhabitants of more inland areas.

It was hoped that studies of physical anthropology, material culture, linguistics, folklore, and other aspects of culture would help resolve the problem of American Indian

origins as well as secure ethnographic information on rapidly disintegrating tribal societies. The goal was the reconstruction of culture history. It was to be achieved by the diligent gathering of facts and by interpreting them strictly within their cultural contexts. Franz Boas, a German-born American then curator at the American Museum of Natural History in New York, was responsible for coordinating the field work of the individual scientists and establishing overall research strategies.

The reports and papers resulting from the Jesup North Pacific Expedition are voluminous and run to scores of publications and many thousands of printed pages. These vary in quality but include excellent descriptions of tribal life, good studies of language, and many texts of native myths and folktales. Nevertheless, the major aim of the enterprise—the determination of American Indian origins and, more broadly, the establishment of a cultural historical frame for the entire north Pacific region—was never achieved. Fundamentally, the problem as posed could not be resolved by the methodologies that were applied, since even the most careful collection of descriptive information shed only very limited light on the distant past of tribal societies. Techniques of linguistic and archaeological dating were still very much in their infancy. Furthermore, the biological studies were heavily oriented in the direction of bodily measurements, a technique that generated masses of information on the physical proportions of inhabitants but led to disappointing results. Given these shortcomings, it is perhaps understandable why the final planned monograph on conclusions was never published.

We have gone into substantial detail on the Jesup North Pacific Expedition because it illustrates both the accomplishments and limitations of anthropological research of the period. The accomplishments should not be minimized. They include the publication of some first-rate accounts that for many locations continue to be the prime sources on the native cultures of Siberian and North American peoples. The cooperation of scholars from several countries did much to establish a relatively uniform mode of data collection and categorization of cultural traits; in fact, the organization of ethnographic descriptions changed little in the next several decades. Finally, one should not overlook the training function of the expedition and its indirect impact on later generations of anthropologists who would be taught the craft of field work by individuals who had spent long periods of time in other cultures.

On the negative side, there were some limitations to the reconstruction of culture history through comparative ethnography that at the time did not readily become apparent. In particular, the attention given to specific culture histories did little to further a more general understanding of humankind as a whole. Franz Boas and his students continued at the task of deciphering the Native American past for many more decades. This American historical school, as it is usually termed, was destined to be influential until Indian societies had been so substantially changed that few informants were left who could remember what life was like in the traditional culture. Unfortunately, matters that could and should have been examined, in particular the impact of Western society on tribal peoples, were, if at all, considered only in passing.

The influence of French sociology

While Boas and his colleagues were directing their attention to refining the concept of culture, the French sociologist Emile Durkheim (1858–1917) was conducting investigations into the nature of social organization. Durkheim viewed society as an "organic" whole within which groups and individuals are linked in bonds of interdependence. The well-functioning society, he believed, is a collectivity, and alienation ensues when these bonds are severed. He went further and maintained that without social interaction moral life is bound to disappear, since it can no longer have an objective. These ideas are elaborated in several of Durkheim's studies based on original research, including the ground-breaking sociological treatise on suicide (1897). However, his major anthropological, as distinct from sociological, contribution was *Elementary Forms of the Religious Life* (1915; 1912 in its French original), in which he drew on secondary sources, especially anthropological materials from Australia. Unlike many other writers who had attempted to cover the whole spectrum of religious phenomena, he selected a specific case in a specific locality, namely totemism among the Australian aborigines. His major conclusion was that religion was in no sense external to human society, but rather that it functioned to perpetuate behavior necessary for social existence, such as cooperation and restrictions on individual acquisitiveness.

Quite correctly, Durkheim has been hailed as both the first modern sociologist and the founder of the functional approach in anthropology. His influence on French anthropologists is clearly evident in several generations of brilliant scholars, from Marcel Mauss to Claude Lévi-Strauss. There is little doubt that the British structural functionalists, especially Bronislaw Malinowski and A. R. Radcliffe-Brown, who wrote following World War I, were in some measure influenced by Durkheim, who at his death in 1917 was one of the leading social scientists in Europe.

THE PREWAR PERIOD

The first two decades of the twentieth century were said to mark the "Age of Boas" in American anthropology, but Boas's influence continued to be felt until his death, at the age of eighty-four, in 1942. As in the case of any truly great teacher, his conception of what anthropological work involves was firmly impressed upon those who served their apprenticeship under him. The roster of his students at Columbia University included many who would go on to shape the course of American anthropology by their own important contributions—Clark Wissler, A. L. Kroeber, Edward Sapir, Ruth Benedict, Margaret Mead, and numerous others. Boas, as we have seen, was an empiricist: he emphasized the need for careful collecting of data and distrusted any generalizations that were not rigorously supported by facts. His credo was well stated in one of his early papers, in which he deplored the limitations of the comparative method as used by the evolutionists to support their unbridled speculations:

We have another method, which in many respects is much safer. A detailed study of customs in their bearings to the total culture of the tribe practicing them, and in connection with an investigation of their geographical distribution among neighboring tribes, afford us almost always a means of determining with considerable accuracy the historical causes that led to the formation of the customs in question . . . (Boas 1896:905).

Clark Wissler and the concept of the culture area

One important extension of these ideas was made by Clark Wissler (1870–1947), who in 1905 succeeded his teacher as curator at the American Museum of Natural History. Concerned primarily with the native Indian societies of North America, Wissler explicitly formulated two concepts—the culture area and the age area (1917, 1923, and 1926). Both were derived from his experience in the field with the distribution of culture traits and from the practical problems he faced as a museum curator. His initiation into American Indian studies had been gained during the museum's great endeavor to salvage the remains of the ethnology of the Plains area, whose cultures were rapidly collapsing after the elimination of the buffalo from the prairies and the assignment of the once roving tribes to reservations. Later, as curator, Wissler faced the difficult task of attempting to do justice to the rich variety of material culture found among the Indian peoples, given the limitations on the space available for a well-balanced museum display.

The concept of the culture area grew out of the observation that neighboring cultures tend to possess the same or similar traits or that they share a dominant cultural orientation. Ideally, one might picture a culture area as a circle whose center is characterized by a very high frequency of typical traits. The concentration of these traits diminishes as one moves from the center outward until, along the perimeter, the traits are about equally mixed with those of the adjacent culture areas. An associated concept of age area assumed that the center of a culture area was also the place of origin. According to the principle of cultural diffusion, similar to the ripple effect of a stone thrown into water, culture traits at or near the center were to be considered relatively new, whereas those lying farther away were assumed to be progressively older.

While the concept of culture area, for a time at least, proved quite useful not only for arranging museum exhibits but as a way of organizing the mounting store of ethnographic materials, the formula of the age-area concept was too simple to account adequately for the mass of available evidence and failed to explain why some traits are rejected by a society, whereas others are accepted and still others modified. From a later perspective, then, the approach of Wissler and others like him appears too mechanical, treating culture primarily as a collection of isolated traits and trait clusters assembled by the accident of diffusion through time. Even so, the aims of the American culture-historical and diffusionist school were modest in comparison with the efforts by contemporaneous German and Austrian scholars who applied similar methods on a much grander scale. According to this latter school, the cultural development of the entire world could be traced to diffusion from a relatively few centers of invention.

The most outstanding student of Boas was Alfred L. Kroeber (1876–1960), a prodigious scholar whose active career in anthropology spanned more than sixty years. Kroeber, who died while attending a conference at

Alfred L. Kroeber: the whole anthropologist

the age of eighty-four, was—like his teacher—one of the rare anthropologists whose range of interests was encyclopedic in scope. In an effort to refine Wissler's culture-area approach, Kroeber examined the historical and environmental relations of the native cultures of North America in his *Cultural and Natural Areas* (1939), in which he introduced the concepts of cultural intensity and climax in order to emphasize the temporal dimension in the achievements and influence of particular societies within a culture area. Complementing this work was Kroeber's attempt at an anthropological synthesis of the cultural time-and-space continuum on a global scale, published under the title *Configurations of Culture Growth* (1944). Reflecting Boas's caution in enterprises of this scope, Kroeber's intent was "not so much to offer a final explanation as to make the most pertinent data readily available for those who wish to search farther (Kroeber 1944:vii). The task Kroeber set for himself was

an investigation of one of the forms which culture takes. This form is the frequent

Alfred L. Kroeber addressing a group of anthropologists during the 1952 International Symposium on Anthropology. Under Kroeber's chairmanship, over fifty scholars from all over the world engaged in a professional stocktaking of the results of modern anthropological research. (Wenner-Gren Foundation for Anthropological Research)

habit of societies to develop their cultures to their highest levels spasmodically: especially in their intellectual and aesthetic aspects, but also in more material and practical respects. The cultures grow, prosper, and decline. . . . How far they tend to be successful in their several activities simultaneously, or close together, or far apart in time, and how much variation in this regard is of record, is part of the problem (Kroeber 1944:5).

Configurations of Culture Growth drew heavily on Kroeber's comprehension of culture as superorganic, a view which he first committed to print in 1917. To him, culture was a phenomenon in its own right, with its own laws and processes that can be studied apart from the human carriers who sustain it. In this respect he anticipated the later work of those who came to view cultural evolution as an autonomous process governed by its own principles.

However, Kroeber's primary interest lay in American Indian studies, to which he made his greatest overall contribution. Among the thousands of published pages on every aspect of the New World's original inhabitants, his *Handbook of the Indians of California* (1925) has always been the major source on the ethnology of that area.

Other students of Boas also added significantly to anthropological method and theory. The work of German-born Edward Sapir (1884–1939) in language, culture, and personality, and especially in linguistic anthropology, showed great originality. His intuitive insights into the structure of and relationship among American Indian languages, complementing the cultural studies of his contemporaries, have remained a source of stimulation for scholars to the present day. Sapir's famous essay on the anthropological method in historical reconstruction, *Time Perspective in Aboriginal American Culture* (1916), and some of his contributions to our understanding of the relationship between language and culture

The contribution of Boas' students

The functionalist approach of Bronislaw Malinowski

were discussed in an earlier chapter. The pioneering work of Ruth Benedict (1887–1948) in the area of psychological anthropology, most prominently exemplified in her *Patterns of Culture* (1934), received our attention in the chapter concerning the individual in society. It was she, as well as Boas, who in the early 1920s made a profound impression on Margaret Mead (1901–), known not only for her prolific writings but for her lively commentary on and active involvement in social issues during the past several decades.

Despite the new interests that Kroeber, Sapir, Benedict, Mead, and other brilliant students of Boas later developed, one general approach that their teacher had so vigorously pressed for characterized much of their earlier work. This was the view that the foremost task of the anthropologist was to gather ethnographic data without a preconceived theoretical framework; it was to be understood that solutions to theoretical problems would begin to flow once sufficient information became available.

Separated from the towering influence of Boas, British anthropologists in general rejected the historical and diffusionist method and initiated approaches that stood in stark contrast to those of their American colleagues. The two most prominent scholars from the other side of the Atlantic to influence the course of anthropological research were Bronislaw Malinowski and A. R. Radcliffe-Brown.

For Malinowski (1884–1942) and his followers, the only means of understanding a culture was by identifying the functions that its various institutions performed at a given time. A culture, then, was much like a living organism in which all parts are interdependent and supportive of each other. For one who holds this view, comparisons and historical considerations make little if any sense.

Caught by World War I as an enemy alien in Australia, Malinowski succeeded in spending most of the war years among the

Trobriand Islanders off New Guinea. His isolation in the field forced him to immerse himself in the life of the natives as perhaps no anthropologist had ever done before. His was a case of participant observation in the truest sense of the phrase.

Although Malinowski was acquainted with Durkheim's view of society, he was convinced of the necessity to focus on the actual behavior of individual members of a group whose basic physical needs must be culturally met if the society is to survive. As compared with the Boasians, who conceived of the relationship between humanity and culture as one of essentially passive acceptance, Malinowski viewed the people he studied as individuals of flesh and blood, filled with passions and goals.

At the same time, there was more than a touch of elitism in Malinowski, recently confirmed by the posthumous publication (1967) of a revealing personal diary covering the period of his early Melanesian research. In his prewar writings, he did not appear to question the legitimacy of colonial rule and urged anthropologists to engage in "practical" work, which could not but help the administrators and missionaries of the widespread British Empire in the maintenance of colonial administration. Nevertheless, it was Malinowski who set new standards of ethnographic description in his works, many of which continue to be on the basic reading list for the functional approach that they espouse (Malinowski 1922, 1935, 1948).

Structural functionalism of A. R. Radcliffe-Brown

Whereas Malinowski's strictly functionalist approach was centered on the concept of culture, Alfred Reginald Radcliffe-Brown (1881–1955), the chief proponent of structural functionalism, made society his pivotal concern. Widely known for the account of his early field work among the Andaman Islanders and several aboriginal Australian tribes (1922 and 1931), he later turned to teaching and the development of his theoretical position. Heavily influenced by Durkheim, Radcliffe-Brown made structure,

process, and function the three fundamental concepts of his theory. In his view:

The continuity of structure [of a society] is maintained by the process of social life, which consists of the activities and interactions of the individual human beings and of the organized groups into which they are united. The social life of a community . . . [may be] defined as the *functioning* of the social structure. The *function* of any recurrent activity, such as the punishment of a crime, or a funeral ceremony, is the part it plays in the social life as a whole and therefore the contribution it makes to the maintenance of the structural continuity (Radcliffe-Brown 1935:396; authors' emphasis).

In making the object of his research social structure and social relations, he, more than any other anthropologist, was instrumental in developing a modern school of social anthropology, which was to become the dominant research orientation in Great Britain and would have a major impact on American anthropology after World War II.

Humanistic anthropology at midcentury

Of the many anthropologists in the United States whose research extended through the decades both before and after World War II we single out only two in this brief survey, Robert Redfield and Clyde Kluckhohn. The writings of Robert Redfield (1897–1958) helped stimulate the interest of anthropologists working on isolated and "primitive" peoples toward concern with the process of transition to urban life. His *Tepoztlan* (1930) and *Chan Kom* (1934, 1950) were prototypical community studies, dealing with the rural-urban continuum and the complex problem of social and cultural change. A synthesis of this research concerning the values and world view of "great" (elite, urbanite) and "little" (folk, rural) traditions followed in several of his postwar publications. These works were to become the foundation of peasant studies, which are an important aspect of modern anthropology. Clyde Kluckhohn (1905–1960) contributed greatly to the development of culture theory, especially in the field of values and personality. He always claimed, however, that he did not belong to any single theoretical orientation and that the anthropologist should not be bound by narrow conceptual frameworks. In his own scholarly activities, he was as much at home in the cultural analysis of ancient Greek tragedies as in the psychological interpretation of Navajo myths. On the side of ethnography, anthropologists are indebted to Kluckhohn for his penetrating studies of the Navajo Indians, including *Navaho Witchcraft* (1944) and *The Navaho* (1946, with Dorothea Leighton). Both Redfield and Kluckhohn, who excelled as broadly oriented social scientists and as humanists, commanded the highest respect in the larger scholarly community and were sought after for advice by foundations, the government, and many private and public institutions.

By this time, anthropology was an established, mature science at the threshold of a dynamic postwar expansion. Appropriately, too, the time had come for serious stocktaking. This came about in New York during June 1952 in the form of the International Symposium on Anthropology, organized by A. L. Kroeber and supported by the Wenner-Gren Foundation for Anthropological Research. With the theme "A World Survey of the Status of Anthropology," the symposium was based on fifty background papers, each reviewing the current status of knowledge in a particular field and the problems arising therefrom (Kroeber 1953; Tax and others 1953).

WORLD WAR II AND AFTER

The outbreak of World War II halted a great deal of normal anthropological activity. In many cases, field locations were transformed into theaters of war and anthropologists, with their knowledge of distant places and the societies that inhabited them, were mobilized as part of the war effort. While not every anthropologist was engaged in the manner of the late Sir Edward Evans-Pritchard, who led a band of Sudanese tribesmen in guerrilla action against the Italians in occupied Ethiopia, many American and British anthropologists acted as planners and advisers in Europe, Asia, and the Pacific.

In the long run, however, the war was to have less impact on anthropology than the changes brought about in its aftermath. For the Western European powers, the war marked the beginning of the end of their imperial systems, however protracted the termination might be. British anthropologists continued to work in Africa, but now with the sure knowledge that independence was a foregone conclusion. Their American colleagues, in response to the global role that America had acquired, shifted their attention from American Indians to societies in the rest of the world. The onset of the Cold War certainly influenced research priorities and contributed substantially to the involvement of social scientists in programs designed to further the goals of national political and military policies. The ethical questions raised by this association of anthropologists with government agencies will be explored in the final chapter; our main concern here is with the significance of postwar years for anthropological theory and method.

Role and scope of anthropology reassessed

The postwar boom in anthropology makes it difficult to characterize the period in terms of a few clear developments. As often happens during times of intellectual flux and growth, we find both innovation in new fields of research and a concern for keeping the unifying features of the discipline firmly in view. Typical of the current period are attempts to give anthropology an integrative role in the social sciences as a whole, as expressed by Alfred Kroeber in the introduction to *Anthropology Today*, the first major postwar compendium on the scope of the discipline.

It is evident that anthropology—however specific it may often be in dealing with data—aims at being ultimately a co-ordinating science, somewhat as a legitimate holding corporation co-ordinates constituent companies. We anthropologists will never know China as intensively as a Sinologist does, or prices, credit, and banking as well as an economist, or heredity with the fulness of the genetic biologist. But we face what these more intensive scholars only glance at intermittently and tangentially, if at all: to try to understand in some measure how Chinese civilization and economics and human heredity, and some dozens of other highly developed special bodies of knowledge, do indeed inter-relate in being all parts of "man"—flowing out of man, centered in him, products of him (Kroeber 1953:xiv).

Writing as a contributor to the *Handbook of Social Psychology*, Clyde Kluckhohn stressed the same outlook for his colleagues in sister disciplines:

In brief, the anthropological point of view prefers completeness of context to dismembered precision. It distrusts "similarities" that are taken from the investigator's point of view as independent, self-contained elements (Kluckhohn 1954:966).

Although it would probably be fair to say that anthropology has yet to realize its full potential as an integrative and catalytic agent for the behavioral sciences, by the 1950s American cultural anthropologists were becoming increasingly aware of some of the limitations of traditional research. Anthropology as a true science of humanity was seen to be hampered by a focus largely restricted to small-scale remote societies, making broad generalizations difficult. A re-examination of general cultural models and methods of interpretation also began to take place.

Nevertheless, it would be an oversimplification to claim that in contrast to the prewar decades, interest in simple societies slackened. In fact, the number of anthropologists studying small-scale societies actually grew, as many new Ph.D. recipients entered the profession. The shift was one in proportion and in orientation: a more detailed attention to specific events leading to change and a greater overall emphasis on complex societies and on process and cultural evolution. Some of these tendencies were reflected in, and were perhaps partly a response to, new strategies of inquiry and research organization. The war years had given anthropologists the opportunity to work together with other social scientists in specialized research bureaus, and this legacy of research centers was adopted as part of the research infra-structure. Another development of great significance was the increasingly sophisticated use that cultural anthropologists began to make of quantitative methods of data collection and analysis. As with much else, this was not an entirely new departure (we mentioned earlier Morgan's pioneering work on kinship), but a recognition by anthropologists that the information revolution offered an excellent tool for both in-depth and comparative work. In short, the earlier static approach gave way to dynamic interpretations stressing process, social drama, and conflict.

Modern versions of evolutionism

In terms of broad theoretical perspectives, one of the major developments of the postwar era was the re-emergence of cultural evolution. "Neoevolution," as it is often called, achieved significant attention following the publication of Leslie A. White's *The Evolution of Culture* (1959). White felt that the nineteenth-century evolutionists had been unreasonably dismissed as serious theoreticians. Like them, he believed that the evolution of culture followed determinable regularities, but rather than propose a rigid scheme of progress, he stressed the significance of energy. All human societies harness energy, but they do so not only in different ways but to different degrees. This differential energy use, according to White, is associated with distinct forms of social organization. Hunter-gatherer societies can dispose of little energy beyond subsistence needs, but there are progressively higher forms of energy production—pastoralism, different forms of agriculture, and so on—

that are utilized in the maintenance of more elaborate social systems. Basically, White sees culture as a consequence of technology and material production.

White's work on energy production and disposal was but one of the approaches taken by the new evolutionists. Julian Steward, beginning with *Theory of Culture Change* (1955), examined the interrelationships between social systems and ecological constraints and offered a flexible evolutionary model that would help account for changes in the level of sociocultural integration of societies. The innovative work of White and Steward has come in for its share of criticism, mostly from scholars who consider it too materialistic—overly concerned with environmental, technological, and economic determinants of social organization and social change. We would argue that the evolutionary perspective, in modern form, not only gives to social anthropology a necessary dimension of process but facilitates some highly useful generalizations. The organization of Part Two of this book serves as a good example.

It is also fair to note that there is far from complete agreement within the neoevolutionary camp. White and Steward have engaged in some rather polemic arguments whose details need not concern us here; but much of the controversy, we suspect, is due to a failure to recognize that different facets of evolution are worthy of examination. Thus, evolution both creates diversity through cultural modifications that are adaptive—it is "multilinear" in Steward's terminology—and can cause displacement, as more complex forms arise from simpler ones. In a sense, then, evolution is also a general or universal phenomenon, as White would insist. Much depends on the temporal frame of reference that is applied, for one can speak of microevolution and macroevolution (Sahlins and Service 1960).

For the contemporary anthropologist, the re-examination of evolution has proved to be a valuable theoretical insight. It has allowed such scholars as Robert McC. Adams (1966)

to compare the development of early civilizations in the Old and New Worlds, and various students of political anthropology to tackle problems of early state formation in a comparative frame (Fried 1967; Service 1975). It is perhaps in combination with cultural ecology that the neoevolutionist approach has proved to be a theoretical orientation of major value. In one sense or another, virtually all ecologically oriented anthropologists, prehistorians as well as social anthropologists, subscribe to a broad evolutionary viewpoint.

In many ways, the neoevolutionists tap a traditional root in the discipline, that of historical interpretation and general models. The emphasis is on an abstract, comparative treatment of social reality rather than on the intimate examination of a particular cultural experience. In a word, there is a certain distancing from the realities of social relationships and a stress on the structure of ideas ("models").

Structuralist approach of Claude Lévi-Strauss

The same trend is noticeable in the direction given to anthropological interpretation by the French anthropologist Claude Lévi-Strauss. Here the historical dimension is of lesser consequence and the thrust is put on structural analysis. Based on the assumption that all observable phenomena are analyzable in terms of a limited number of underlying general relationships, structuralists are concerned with the comparison of models on a number of conceptual levels. The basic model owes much to linguistic research and stresses communication and reciprocity. Lévi-Strauss's most important work, *The Elementary Structures of Kinship* (1969; 1949 in its French original), a study of cross-cousin marriage in terms of exchange theory, has revolutionized and revitalized kinship studies. But the concerns of this scholar cannot be contained within a single frame of reference; his search is for general principles that should be applicable to all societies. In Lévi-Strauss's view, there are certain codes, certain principles, essential to human organization that are built into the human mind. It is from these "inner structures"—the tendency of the human mind to categorize and handle reality in terms of opposing and complementary elements—that social order and social continuity arise. The approach is sketched out in a recent acceptance speech that Lévi-Strauss offered on the occasion of his investiture into the French Academy (Académie Française), the most prestigious intellectual body in the French-speaking world:

Institutions construct the social order. As a sheet of paper can be folded, opened up and turned inside out to create a certain shape or form, an institution such as yours, gentlemen, gathers up a surface into a volume. It shortens distances and brings together types of minds and individuals in an unexpected manner (Lévi-Strauss 1974).

For Lévi-Strauss, this propensity to reorder and thus "make" culture is distinctly human; it is manifested in all systems of kinship, in ritual, myth, residential patterns, and the organizational principles underlying society everywhere. By creating and recreating orders, institutions bestow form and predictability in human affairs and forge links of reciprocity between individuals and social components.

In some respects, the goals of Lévi-Strauss and other structuralists of the same general orientation are similar to those of a group of American anthropologists known as ethnoscientists. Both are interested in the underlying logical structures of human organization rather than perceived behavior, both draw heavily on linguistic models to analyze culture. There is a difference in scope, however. Ethnoscience, which is far less prone to making generalizations concerning the human condition, views every culture as a logical entity unto itself, with its own cognitive system structuring reality. The primary focus of ethnoscience is the cultural vocabulary (lexicon) of a given people. Ethnoscience has been used to investigate subjects ranging from color catego-

Claude Lévi-Strauss is the leading exponent of structuralism. This French intellectual has had a profound impact, not only on anthropology, but on the humanities and social sciences in general. He perceives the task of the anthropologist as that of interpreting social systems and cultural myths. The models that he elaborates have, in broad measure, applicability to all human sociocultural systems. (Henri Cartier-Bresson/Magnum Photos, Inc.)

Ethnoscience

ries to kinship. The lexicon is viewed, not simply as a system of pigeonholes, but as a complex structure where a large number of terms are closely and functionally interrelated.

For both structuralists and ethnoscientists, the major task of the anthropologist is less explanation than interpretation. Whether the topic under investigation is general or quite specific, the search is for analytical models that go beyond the perceived premises of the investigator. That this is a difficult task goes without saying: even with the best intentions, every observer sees reality as recorded through his own senses and in terms of a prior ideological commitment. The observer remains the major research tool in social anthropology. In other words, it is hard to escape the models in one's own head, although being conscious of them helps greatly. In terms of methodology, ethnoscience has made a contribution by placing importance on the input of native informants (the emic approach), as distinct from the use of models constructed by the outsider (the etic approach).

TO SUM UP   An examination of the trends in cultural anthropology during the course of the past century shows some significant reordering in the relationships between method and theory. The early anthropologists worked with a paucity of data and a minimum of formal methodology. Early evolutionary theories were elaborated at a time when few anthropologists (with some notable exceptions) conducted their own research. In due course, concrete information on simple societies led to the questioning of the classical evolutionary stages and, ultimately, to the virtual abandonment of cultural evolution. With the new century, the primary concern of anthropologists became the collection of data and the development of increasingly refined methodologies. We can think of the period prior to World War I as a time when the tools of research and the research experience dominated anthropological concerns. The expectation was that theory would develop from the data; but it did not, at least not to any significant degree. Prior to World War II, it was already clear that more and more information on different human societies required a new theoretical alignment. This was accomplished in a variety of ways, using models derived from science or history. In the last generation there has occurred not only a growing integration of data and theory but also a search for theoretical models that are consciously based either on the universals of human experience (evolutionary and ecological approaches) or the underlying structures of human societies (ethnoscience and structuralism).

While a new synthesis has yet to be achieved, there is no doubt that communication has increased greatly among all the fields of anthropology, and that anthropologists have been able to integrate insights derived from history and other behavioral sciences. The goal of anthropology as a generalizing discipline with broad humanistic perspectives is still very much alive. The fear, voiced some years ago, that anthropology might fracture along disciplinary lines has proved unwarranted; rather, what we witness is a spectrum of interlocking specialties that grow through mutual dependence. The profession has faced crises of mission and identity, as is true of all intellectual fields in the postcolonial world, but it remains healthy and vigorous and perhaps has never been more receptive to new ideas. Very much in the forefront of these ideas is the vision of anthropology as pertinent to the needs of a changing world. To make ourselves understandable to others, and vice versa, is a valid motivation. If to this objective can be added the role of advocate for those without voice and power, we need hardly fear that our profession will lapse into irrelevance.

REFERENCES

ADAMS, ROBERT McC.
1966 *The evolution of urban society: early Mesopotamia and prehistoric Mexico.* Chicago: Aldine.

BACHOFEN, JOHANN JAKOB
1861 *Das Mutterrecht.* Stuttgart: Krais and Hoffmann.

BENEDICT, RUTH
1934 *Patterns of culture.* Boston: Houghton Mifflin.

BOAS, FRANZ
1896 The limitations of the comparative method of anthropology. *Science* (n.s.) 4:901–908 (no. 103, December 18).

DURKHEIM, EMILE
1897 *Le suicide; étude de sociologie.* Paris: F. Alcan.
1912 *Les formes élémentaires de la vie religieuse, le système totémique en Australie.* Paris: F. Alcan.
1915 *The elementary forms of the religious life.* Joseph Ward Swain, trans. London: George Allen and Unwin.

1951 *Suicide, a study in sociology.* John A. Spaulding and George Simpson, trans. Glencoe, Ill.: Free Press.

ENGELS, FRIEDRICH
1884 *Der Ursprung der Familie, des Privateigenthums und des Staats.* Hottingen-Zürich: Schweizerische Genossenschaftsbuchdruckerei.
1902 *The origin of the family, private property and the state.* Ernest Untermann, trans. Chicago: C. H. Kerr.

FREUD, SIGMUND
1912–1913 Über einige Übereinstimmugen im Seelenleben der Wilden und der Neurotiker. *Imago; Zeitschrift für Anwendung der Psychoanalyse auf die Geisteswissenschaften* 1:17–33, 213–227, 301–333; 2:1–21, 357–408.
1918 *Totem and taboo; resemblances between the psychic lives of savages and neurotics.* A. A. Brill, trans. New York: Moffat, Yard.

FRIED, MORTON H.
1967 *The evolution of political society: an essay in political anthropology.* New York: Random House.

KLUCKHOHN, CLYDE
1944 *Navaho witchcraft.* Papers of the Peabody Museum of Archaeology and Ethnology, Harvard University, vol. 22, no. 2. Cambridge, Mass.
1954 Culture and behavior. In *Handbook of social psychology,* vol. II: *Special fields and applications.* Gardner Lindzey, ed. Cambridge, Mass.: Addison-Wesley. Pp. 921–976.

KLUCKHOHN, CLYDE, AND DOROTHEA LEIGHTON
1946 *The Navaho.* Cambridge, Mass.: Harvard University Press.

KROEBER, ALFRED L.
1917 The superorganic. *American Anthropologist* 19:163–213.
1925 *Handbook of the Indians of California.* Bureau of American Ethnology, Bulletin 78. Washington, D.C.: Government Printing Office.
1939 *Cultural and natural areas of native North America.* University of California Publications in American Archaeology and Ethnology, vol. 38. Berkeley and Los Angeles: University of California Press.

1944 *Configurations of culture growth.* Berkeley and Los Angeles: University of California Press.

KROEBER, A. L., CHAIRMAN
1953 *Anthropology today: an encyclopedic inventory.* Chicago: The University of Chicago Press.

LÉVI-STRAUSS, CLAUDE
1949 *Les structures élémentaires de la parenté.* Paris: Presses universitaires de France.
1969 *The elementary structures of kinship* (rev. ed.). James Harle Bell and others, trans. Boston: Beacon Press.
1974 We are we are you are you are we are you. *New York Times,* September 28, p. 29.

MCLENNAN, JOHN FERGUSON
1865 *Primitive marriage. An inquiry into the origin of the form of capture in marriage ceremonies.* Edinburgh: A. and C. Black.

MAINE, SIR HENRY JAMES SUMNER
1861 *Ancient law: its connection with the early history of society, and its relation to modern ideas.* London: J. Murray.

MALINOWSKI, BRONISLAW
1922 *Argonauts of the western Pacific; an account of native enterprise and adventure in the archipelagoes of Melanesian New Guinea.* New York: E. P. Dutton.
1935 *Coral gardens and their magic; a study of the methods of tilling the soil and of agricultural rites in the Trobriand Islands.* 2 vols. London: George Allen and Unwin.
1948 *Magic, science and religion, and other essays.* Boston: Beacon Press.
1967 *A diary in the strict sense of the term.* Norbert Guterman, trans. New York: Harcourt, Brace and World.

MORGAN, LEWIS HENRY
1851 *League of the Ho-dé-no-sau-nee, or Iroquois.* Rochester: Sage.
1871 *Systems of consanguinity and affinity of the human family.* Washington, D.C.: Smithsonian Institution.
1877 *Ancient society; or, Researches in the lines of human progress from savagery, through barbarism to civilization.* New York: Henry Holt.

NAROLL, RAOUL, AND RONALD COHEN
1970 The logic of generalization. In *A handbook of method in cultural anthropology*. Raoul Naroll and Ronald Cohen, eds. Garden City, N.Y.: The Natural History Press. Pp. 25–50.

PENNIMAN, T. K.
1965 *A hundred years of anthropology* (3rd ed., rev.). London: Gerald Duckworth.

RADCLIFFE-BROWN, A. R.
1922 *The Andaman islanders*. Cambridge: Cambridge University Press.
1931 *The social organization of Australian tribes*. Oceania Monographs, no. 1. Melbourne: Macmillan.
1935 On the concept of function in social science. *American Anthropologist* 37:394–402.

REDFIELD, ROBERT
1930 *Tepoztlan, a Mexican village; a study of folk life*. Chicago: The University of Chicago Press.
1934 *Chan Kom, a Maya village*. Carnegie Institution of Washington Publication, no. 448. Washington, D.C.
1950 *A village that chose progress; Chan Kom revisited*. Chicago: The University of Chicago Press.

SAHLINS, MARSHALL D., AND ELMAN R. SERVICE, EDS.
1960 *Evolution and culture*. Ann Arbor: University of Michigan Press.

SAPIR, EDWARD
1916 *Time perspective in aboriginal American culture: a study in method*. Canada, Department of Mines, Geological Survey, Memoir 90 (Anthropological Series, no. 13). Ottawa: Government Printing Bureau.

SERVICE, ELMAN R.
1975 *Origins of the state and civilization: the process of cultural evolution*. New York: W. W. Norton.

SLOTKIN, J. S., ED.
1965 *Readings in early anthropology*. Viking Fund Publications in Anthropology, no. 40. New York.

STEWARD, JULIAN H.
1955 *Theory of culture change; the methodology of multilinear evolution*. Urbana: University of Illinois Press.

TAX, SOL, AND OTHERS, EDS.
1953 *An appraisal of anthropology today*. Chicago: The University of Chicago Press.

TYLOR, SIR EDWARD BURNETT
1871 *Primitive culture: researches into the development of mythology, philosophy, religion, art, and custom*. London: J. Murray.

WHITE, LESLIE A.
1959 *The evolution of culture; the development of civilization to the fall of Rome*. New York: McGraw-Hill.

WISSLER, CLARK
1917 *The American Indian; an introduction to the anthropology of the New World*. New York: D. C. McMurtrie.
1923 *Man and culture*. New York: Thomas Y. Crowell.
1926 *The relation of nature to man in aboriginal America*. London: Oxford University Press.

Chapter 21
Social and cultural change

In the introductory chapter of this book we examined the concept of culture from a variety of approaches, emphasizing throughout the value of this concept as a key to understanding and explaining what is uniquely human. As we noted, all human beings—and only they—have the capacity to acquire culture. But whereas this potential is universal, culture learning invariably takes place in a given sociocultural setting—the distinctive way of life characteristic of a particular group of people. Accordingly, our emphasis has been on ways of coping that members of any given society have developed and tested over several generations. But if the application of the old and the tried were all that there is to cultures, we would be living in an essentially static world, as we patently are not.

We need to understand that in every culture there is both change and continuity, and that without the element of change flexibility and adaptation would be impossible. We are often reminded that our own culture is continually changing, even though there are many features of it that have survived for centuries. It may be less easy to grasp that change has always been a characteristic of every culture. To be sure, the rate of change varies between cultures and some cultures are much more receptive to change than others, but change is a constant. This seeming paradox of stability and change poses no special dilemma: to recognize the reality of change does not force us to deny the existence of continuity, and conversely.

Understanding historical experience: Polynesian societies

As a case in point, it is much easier to comprehend certain features of Polynesian societies, such as a concern for genealogy and the presence of institutions that are flexible rather than rigid, when adequate consideration is given to the past experiences of these island peoples. Genealogical interests take on relevance as a reflection of the respect and reverence accorded the founder-chiefs who, in generations past, successfully led colonizing expeditions. To trace descent from such individuals continues to be a matter of pride—much as some Americans take pride in tracing their origins to the first settlers who came over on the *Mayflower*.

This respect for distant ancestors is not inconsistent with a substantial degree of social and institutional flexibility in Polynesian societies. There is room for the enterprising individual, and prestige and status can be achieved as well as inherited. This, too, is understandable in terms of past experience, for these intrepid explorers in their seagoing canoes settled an extensive geographical area covering millions of square miles of open ocean dotted with islands varying in size from New Zealand to tiny coral atolls. Given the uncertainties of navigation, a variety of ecological and climatic conditions, and the problems inherent in colonizing a vast territory, there is little question that individual qualities such as leadership, skill, and bravery were bound to play a decisive role. A highly rigid social organization that could not have been adapted to meet the stresses of uncertainty would obviously have been a great hindrance in such a context. The point we are making, then, is, not that a knowledge of the past is indispensable for all manner of sociocultural analysis, but rather that such knowledge should be utilized to the degree that it is available and sheds light on the problems under consideration.

Ongoing changes that on the surface may seem relatively unimportant can take on a special significance when a people's view of themselves and of the universe they live in is involved. The introduction of steel axes among Australian aborigines can be cited as one example of a minor change having major consequences. Unlike the Polynesians, the native Australians lived for centuries in environments that were perceived as basically static. They believed that the entire universe remained much as it had

Selected elements of modern technology may fit the needs of individuals in technologically less developed areas. This is especially likely when the item in question meets an existing need, is easy to maintain, and does not disrupt established economic patterns. In many societies the sewing machine meets these criteria. (The Rockefeller Foundation)

Steel axes for Stone Age Australians: cataclysmic change

been in the beginning, and in the myths of origin that supported this belief there was no place for steel axes. Hence, the introduction of these tools by missionaries and other agents of Western society did much to undermine the fabric of their culture and their perception of an ordered universe. An anthropologist describes the impact of what to us may seem little more than an insignificant technological shift in one Australian society:

The most disturbing effects of the steel axe, operating in conjunction with other elements also being introduced from the white man's several subcultures, developed in the realm of traditional ideas, sentiments, and values. These were undermined at a rapidly mounting rate, without new conceptions being defined to replace them. The result was a mental and moral void which foreshadowed the collapse and destruction of all Yir Yoront culture, if not,

The rapid rate of cultural change experienced by some societies occasionally results in a striking juxtaposition of modern technology and age-old tradition. Shown here leaving a light aircraft chartered by the government administration are two New Guinea natives returning to their home village from an intertribal meeting. (United Nations)

societies as "backward" and thus likely to be helped by "progress"—a position taken by the missionaries in Australia who distributed steel axes to their native clients and converts. Attitudes of this kind can be used to rationalize all manner of policies that are not in the best interests of weaker cultural groups. In its most extreme form, the distinction that is sometimes made between "traditional" and "progressive" societies has helped to legitimize imperialism, war, and other forms of aggression.

TO SUM UP Change—some degree of change—is a feature present in all societies. While neither inherently good or bad, it holds potential dangers for groups that are deprived of the option to make meaningful choices in terms of their culture and their own internal dynamics. It follows that anthropological insight can help to anticipate the difference between success and failure (or even great harm), when new ideas and technologies are introduced in areas of relative cultural isolation.

indeed, the extinction of the biological group itself (Sharp 1952:85–86).

We cite this example to illustrate a number of points:

1 In examining change and the change process one must guard against intuitive judgments as to what is or may be important or critical for a given society.

2 The past experiences of a people—for centuries Australia was effectively isolated from major external contacts—are likely to influence its responses to novel ideas and materials. The previously cited Polynesian case supports this perspective in the sense of past history serving as the source of flexibility.

3 It is incorrect to view cultures as strictly self-regulating: the capacity of societies to adjust to change varies and, in some instances, adjustment may be impossible.

4 One should beware of labeling simple

CHANGE AND TIME

Cultural perceptions

However rapid it may be, all change takes place within the framework of time. In some cultures, there is a greater awareness of time depth than in others, but regardless of how conscious different groups may be of past and present change, the anthropologist must look beyond culturally defined time perspectives. Culturally and psychologically, Americans as well as citizens of most other modern nations tend not only to perceive change as beneficial but also to look toward the future with anticipation and optimism. This, at least, has been the dominant attitude since the advent of the industrial revolution. More often than not, however, our time perception is relatively narrow: we tend to think of influences that are likely to affect our lives and the lives of our children, but seldom do we project our thoughts much further.

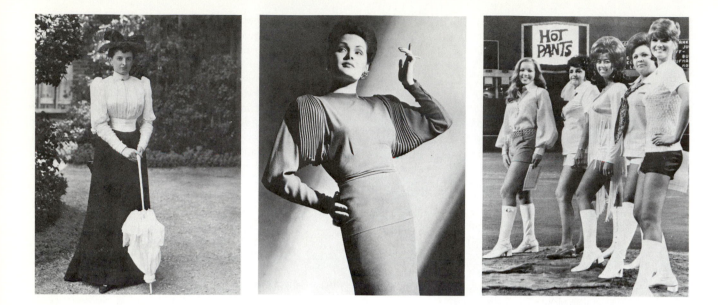

From an anthropological point of view, this is an unduly restricted perspective. The social and cultural changes that we have witnessed in the last generation or so—complex enough to have kept scores of sociologists, historians, economists, anthropologists, and other scholars busy[1]—are different from the long-range changes that have taken place in American society in the course of the past two or three hundred years. In the latter case, there is a shaping of fundamental national institutions in keep-

Long-range and short-range changes

Social attitudes and behavior are often reflected in external attributes such as dress. These photographs illustrate three periods in American women's fashion— around the years 1900, 1945, and 1970. While the fashions depicted should not be taken as the standard dress of most women in the respective periods, they may nevertheless be seen as indicators of changing cultural images over the span of some seventy years. ([left] The Bettmann Archive; [middle] Scaionis Studio/Black Star; [right] United Press International)

[1]The changes that have taken place in American culture in the course of the last few decades include a reinterpretation of the recent past, especially the first half of the twentieth century. We seem to be witnessing a period of nostalgia for a time when life was supposedly less complex but somehow more exciting. The best examples of this "change by reinterpretation" are found in popular entertainment and art forms, as the warm reception given such films as *Summer of '42, Butch Cassidy and the Sundance Kid, The Last Picture Show, The Way We Were, American Graffiti,* and *The Sting* indicates. *The Sting* also played a major role in the rediscovery of Scott Joplin, the ragtime composer from the turn of the century. Perhaps American society is losing some of the future orientation that has long been held to characterize it.

ing with a distinct cultural perspective that can be called "American." Although we associate these institutions with the leaders of the Revolutionary period, this was not the work of one generation, nor was it finished when independence from Britain was achieved. The changes in national society of the past generation are extremely important to us, but in perspective they will be seen as an extension, or a realization, of well-established values in keeping with the requirements of the times.

In their turn, both the long-term and short-term changes in American society have occurred at a pace that is rapid compared with the evolution of the state (some six thousand years ago) or, on an even larger scale, with the biological and cultural transformations that ultimately led to modern *Homo sapiens*. We should recognize, therefore, that changes must be studied within time frames that can vary from several million years to much less than a single lifetime.

We should also be aware that many important changes are best understood as cyclical fluctuations. Such changes are certainly significant and worthy of study, but they are of a periodic nature and seldom drastically alter the sociocultural system. As individuals, we pass through a life cycle from birth to death, each major step associated with different roles and statuses. While these steps differ from culture to culture, they are linked to the biocultural nature of humans and thus find recognition in every human society. Other cyclical changes are related to agriculture and similar seasonal activities. Modern Western economic systems seem prone to a cycle of boom and depression that even economists do not understand very well. These and other repetitive changes take place within certain limits and thus should be viewed as changes internal to a system. While the system, viewed as a whole, may not change drastically, there may well be profound changes in the lives of individual members of the society.

The British anthropologist E. R. Leach has documented how Kachin society in highland Burma oscillates between two forms of political organization over a span of 150 years. In the conclusion to his *Political Systems of Highland Burma*, Leach writes:

My own view is that equilibrium theory in social anthropology was once justified but that it now needs drastic modification. We can no longer be satisfied with attempting to set up a typology of fixed systems. We must recognise that few if any

Cyclical fluctuations

societies which a modern field worker can study show any marked tendency towards stability (Leach 1954:284–285).

While Leach's research dealt with fluctuations operating within a time span of a century and a half, his observation has a more general validity.

Irreversible culture change

Concern for the proper temporal perspective is equally important when the changes to be considered are progressive and irreversible. The problem is relatively simple if one deals with the sociocultural changes that are taking place today or have taken place in the recent past. For example, once industry has moved into a rural community with the consequent changes in life style and work habits, it is generally easy enough to determine when this took place, what life was like beforehand, and how the population responded. Similarly, we can pinpoint without too much difficulty when the impact of Western society first made itself felt on tribal groups and band-level societies. Times and circumstances will vary, of course, but most of the transformations can be linked to fairly specific events—the arrival of missionaries, the imposition of an external political rule, or the penetration of Western economic activities.

However, many changes that can irrevocably alter the fabric of human life proceed at an extremely slow pace and do not manifest themselves by an event or series of events. Such was the case with plant and animal domestication, which archaeological and botanical evidence indicates was the work of thousands of years and scores of generations. At the end of the productive lives of those living at the time there might at best have been very little awareness of change: they may simply have hunted a little less, collected a little more, or tended their crops with somewhat greater care than in their youth. One of the features of such gradual changes is that individuals are given the opportunity to make minor adjustments in their lives without significant disruptions.

But even when change is more rapid, it is not always readily apparent to those who are undergoing it. Changes in population dynamics are a good example of the ways in which social and physical environments impinge on individuals, who are then pressed to make choices that affect not only themselves but, ultimately, the whole society.

Many factors, including birthrates, death rates, family size, and household composition, influence the structure of human populations and the trends that populations are likely to take. We know, for instance, that some band-level societies consciously control birth spacing and the number of children per family. In the majority of cases, these actions are designed to facilitate a nomadic way of life and reduce the burden of having to feed and care for numbers of small children. Population control of this type is an adaptive response to environmental conditions, for in band-level societies it is virtually impossible for a mother to nourish more than a single infant at a time.

However, most societies lack such firm cultural guidelines on questions of population. Even in Western societies, a general awareness of population changes is a relatively recent development, linked to breakthroughs in population control and family planning (much aided by the availability of relatively safe and inexpensive contraceptive devices) and to the spread of knowledge concerning population trends.

The most significant shifts for Western societies occurred in the course of the past two centuries and appear to be linked functionally to the industrial revolution. In the technical literature, the change in Western population dynamics has come to be known as the *demographic transition*. In brief, the change has been characterized by a drop in birthrates, longer life spans, and a reduction in death rates. In some of these societies, the drop in birthrates is associated with a shift toward a later age of marriage for females, in effect shortening their reproductive life. Certainly, in these instances an element of

Awareness of change: the case of population dynamics

Adaptive response to industrialization

The demographic transition

conscious choice was involved—to marry later rather than sooner—but since there was probably little awareness of population trends in the society as a whole, it is difficult to make out a case of overriding cultural guidelines.[2]

It is difficult to come to grips with the demographic transition if one approaches it in terms of single events, the actions of any given individual, or short-run experiences. Matters look somewhat different, however, when we take into account the family units in differing socioeconomic contexts. In traditional agricultural settings, children are often viewed as a positive asset. They are called on to assist in farm chores at an early age and, later on, may be expected to provide security for aged parents. In an industrial urban economy, the advantages of large families are substantially reduced and perhaps even negated. Children enter the labor force later in life, wages replace subsistence agriculture, and pensions and savings may make reliance on children unnecessary.

With the knowledge of family structure, work conditions, and city life now at our disposal, we can recognize the demographic transition as an adaptive response on the part of family units toward the new industrial environment. However, while we have a fair understanding of what happened, it is far less clear how this transformation in population dynamics came about. For instance, delayed age of marriage accounts for only part of the trend, nor was postponing marriage a universal practice in early industrialized countries.

Probably the best way to understand the demographic transition is to approach it from an ecological perspective. All popula-

[2]The lack of such cultural guidelines does not mean that people fail to have some opinions on the ideal number of children. One of the authors, while interviewing Mexican peasants on this subject, often met responses like "Two or three children per family would be nice, but it is really in God's hands."

The crowded housing conditions characterizing the haphazard industrial expansion of the latter part of the nineteenth century are illustrated by these "tunnel-back" houses for factory workers in Birmingham, England. Their miniature gardens were of little use and the housing density per acre frequently reached or exceeded thirty persons. (British Information Services)

tions, human and otherwise, interact with their natural environments and respond to changes in these environments. Adaptations of this nature are only perceptible over time and, important though they may be, are less a matter of conscious change than the cumulative effect of a sufficient number of individuals adopting new positions or ideas.

TO SUM UP   Change cannot be divorced from the temporal context in which it occurs. There are short-range and long-range changes; changes of which members of a society are consciously aware; and changes that affect populations without being registered at the time as social or cultural transformations. The prime cause of demographic changes remains even today somewhat obscure. The best means for understanding a particular change is to view it as a gradual adaptation of traditional society to a system more in keeping with the needs of industrial and urban life.

CHANGE AND CHOICE

Important though it is to understand that changes in culture and social organization

may take place as a consequence of shifts in the broader environmental setting, a great deal of change involves conscious and active reorganization of sociocultural variables. Since the majority of anthropologists work with contemporary populations—people who may be asked questions and observed in their daily lives—most studies of change involve current conditions and responses to such conditions. There are few societies today whose members are not aware of the external and internal pressures that impinge upon them or of the alternatives that are available in a world of increasing contact and interaction.

It is also important to keep in mind that, just as the concept of perfect cultural equilibrium is suspect, no culture is ever totally uniform. Even those sociocultural systems that strike the observer as highly traditional and rigid must contain some built-in flexibility. Viewed from the level of individual behavior and attitudes, all cultures permit and invite a range of thought and action. Such internal flexibility serves to maintain the culture in the face of social and environmental stresses.

Cultural flexibility   Some degree of internal flexibility not only is a highly desirable structural attribute in cultures but is implicit in the primary function of all sociocultural systems, which is to satisfy needs—both those of the group and of the individuals who comprise it. Trying to attain such satisfactions will always involve some selection from among available choices. People constantly attempt to determine what is best for them under a given set of circumstances: whether to fish for an afternoon or work in one's garden, whether to enter the job market or enroll in graduate school. Although the range of choices is far from infinite, every sociocultural system establishes not only central trends but also the limits of permissible variations. These limits are defined by prohibitions and sanctions against unacceptable behavior. Social life is thus a game with rules, but the players can play their hands in a variety of ways.

This concept of alternatives within limits is applicable to all cultural behavior, including mental constructs. Culture, after all, entails much more than the satisfaction of material needs. If cultures are, at the level of the individual, blueprints for living, living covers models for being, for feeling, and for associating with others. While members of a society share a body of common attitudes, it does not follow that every individual harbors identical goals or similar expectations.

The flexibility present in cultural systems makes change not only possible but inevitable. Every society must offer its individual members some measure of satisfaction, but achieving satisfaction takes different forms for different people and different groups within the society. This search includes the chance to test the limits of a cultural system and even to reshape the system in small or significant ways. Needless to say, it would be incorrect to infer that everyone will succeed in maximizing his or her happiness. But the pursuit of greater satisfaction is nonetheless an important force in the service of change.

In no society is an individual's life totally predictable or at the mercy of convention. Moreover, the search for alternatives and variations often has an impact far beyond the configuration of a single life. For we all live within the web of human relations, and what we do invariably affects others—those close to us and, sometimes, people we will never know.

CHANGE AND DIRECTION

Values as a guide to change

While change takes many forms and is brought about by a multiplicity of causes and situations, it is usually a selective rather than random process. Another way of expressing the same idea is that new elements are made to fit the existing profiles of a culture. The values of a given group—its concepts regarding what is right and desirable—function as a selective device in cultural transformation: changes that are perceived as constructive are likely to be adopted, whereas potential changes that might threaten the integrity of a culture will generally be rejected.

Change is often made to fit the existing system by a process of substitution or analogy: the new element replaces an older one or is restructured as an additive component to the culture. What began as a relatively minor addition or substitution can sometimes take on a pivotal importance that was not initially foreseen. When the motorcar ("horseless carriage") was first developed toward the end of the nineteenth century, it entered the scene as a none-too-reliable replacement for the horse, but ultimately it became the single most important element of American material culture. There are few aspects of modern American life, from national economic policies to patterns of dating, that have not been profoundly affected by the automobile.

Institutional change in America

Not only technical change but institutional change as well is guided by value systems, a case in point being the transformation of American secondary education during the course of the twentieth century. Before the passing of compulsory school laws, high schools were mainly upper-middle-class institutions whose major function was to prepare students for college. Their curricula reflected this orientation, with the emphasis placed on classical subjects, while applied and technical fields were poorly represented. Students, parents, and teachers shared common educational goals and expectations.

This picture changed as secondary education was transformed into mass education, offering further schooling to many youngsters who were not destined for college. At this point, traditional American values, including utilitarianism, optimism, and an emphasis on success as a virtue in itself, came into play. Elite education, it seemed to many students and parents, had little relevance. What was desired was an education that would allow the high school graduate to enter the labor market with training in basic skills. Today the proper role of the high school is still a matter of debate. In fact, with the number of college graduates outstripping the available job opportunities in the traditional professions and occupations, universities and colleges are faced with rather similar pressures to provide technical training in fields where there is still a demand for skilled manpower.

This factor of cultural fit, which we have illustrated with the changing role of educational institutions, helps to account for both successful change and resistance to change. An item is functionally integrated into the total culture in terms of the purpose it serves and the degree of utility it has for its users. Since cultures are not static—cultural needs are likely to change—internal shifts and external borrowings will reflect the particular requirements of a given time and situation.

Anthropologists studying the Navajo have long been impressed by the fact that for several centuries these Southwest Indians have been ready borrowers of techniques and material items from their neighbors. Their most recent borrowings include radios, automobiles, and pickup trucks. In fact,

Selective change: the Navajo example

the Navajo have integrated the motorcar into their contemporary life as thoroughly as have other Americans.

An understanding of the Navajo attitude toward the automobile would have to take into account a long prior history of openness to technological change, but more than this, the factor of fit and analogy is especially good since the Navajo place a high value on travel and mobility. Their universe is perceived as in constant motion, with both supernaturals and humans restlessly moving from place to place (Hoijer 1951)—a view that undoubtedly reflects in part the scattered settlement pattern and relatively low population density of the Navajo country. The acquisition of motorcars has necessitated some economic adjustments, such as an increase in wage labor and the purchase of automobiles on time payments, but in some ways, the increased mobility has strengthened a number of traditional cultural patterns. As Evon Z. Vogt notes:

At the same time, the automobile has had a profound integrative and conservative influence upon traditional Navaho culture, and an influence that needs to be emphasized for the benefit of those who tend to think that improved modes of transportation lead mainly to changes in traditional cultures. In the Navaho case, the new mode of transportation has meant an important *increase* in the numbers of Navahos who attend large ceremonials. . . . They gather from more distant points in Navaho country, and, more important still, Navaho families working and living in towns off the Reservation can travel to these ceremonials and return to their jobs the next day or on Monday morning after a week-end. Perhaps even more significant in the long run is the fact that the automobile extends the geographical range of the Navaho singer's practice (Vogt 1960:362; authors' emphasis).

Although the Navajo have proved notably open to the acquisition and integration of material and technological items, their attitude toward foreign religious beliefs and related idea systems is one of distrust and rejection. The Navajo world view—their conception of the universe and their place in it—remains basically unshaken and unlikely to be disturbed by further involvement with the products of modern technology. While alien material culture has always been something to be considered and judged on its merits, foreign elements of a spiritual nature call for the most cautious approach. The Navajo, in fact, have resisted Christian missionaries from the time of their first contact with the Spanish, for Christian religious beliefs run entirely counter to many elements of the native tradition. With such supernatural figures as a protagonist who after three days in the grave was raised again from the dead and another being known as the Holy Ghost, Christianity is hardly a faith likely to gather many converts among the Navajo. One can liken the Navajo attitude toward Christian missions to the reception in a Hindu society that awaits a Christian preacher attempting to teach the virtues of fatherly love on the basis of the Biblical parable of the prodigal son. The Hindus, who consider cows as sa-

cred, would see the slaughter of the fatted calf as anything but a pious act.

Negative analogies

As these examples indicate, negative analogies are likely to be rejected, although the reasons for rejection are often obscure to those who do not understand the values and attitudes of an alien culture. The complexities of rejection are examined by Melville J. Herskovits with the example of the Ashanti response to factory-made cotton goods:

Manchester-made copies of Ashanti cloths, for instance, lay on the shelves of Gold Coast shops for want of buyers, despite the fact that these exact replicas were far less expensive than the native weaves. The reason for their rejection was a puzzle to those who charted their course in terms of economic theory based on concepts of price and value. Prestige and position, however, mean more to the Ashanti than an advantageous price (Herskovits 1948:559).

Among the Ashanti, cloths of the type in question are marks of high rank, and a person not entitled to their use was subject

The case of the Pruitt-Igoe housing complex in St. Louis is a classic example of official shortsightedness in meeting the needs of the poor. This huge development was constructed with such an eye for "economy" that in a few years it had become a dilapidated cluster of high-rise slums. The photograph shows the demolition of the structures (St. Louis Post-Dispatch)

to ridicule. Chiefs, on the other hand, had no need of cheap substitutes, not to mention the fact that the status of a high personage would be damaged by resort to inexpensive imports.

Similar cultural logic accounts for the failure of some otherwise promising programs of directed culture change. A county extension agent of the Department of Agriculture successfully introduced a new strain of hybrid corn among Spanish-American farmers in New Mexico. The corn produced three times the yield of the traditional seed and, at first, the majority of the farmers adopted it. Four years later, however, most of the growers had reverted to the old variety. A follow-up study revealed that the farmers' wives were unhappy with the dough made from the new corn, for it produced tortillas of unacceptable color and taste. Economic rationality was of potential importance in this case, but it did not turn out to be the decisive factor: the housewives were simply unwilling to be associated with a food that did not meet cultural standards (Apodaca 1952). To take another example, in the Assam region of northern India people are fond of pork, and it would thus seem logical that any improvement in the livestock would be readily accepted. Yet, an Englishman trying to improve the food supply by introducing black-and-white Berkshire pigs failed because, according to local belief, the tribal spirits do not like pigs with such markings (Mead 1955:202).

Sometimes changes take place, but not for the reasons expected by those who introduce them. Yellow Cuban corn brought into the lowlands of Bolivia as part of a crop improvement program proved much superior to local strains but, being very hard, was difficult to grind at home. Nevertheless, the corn gained great popularity, for it was found to make excellent corn liquor, a commodity in high demand (Kelly 1960:10–11).

In general, it is much easier to determine why certain items are rejected and others accepted after the events have taken place. Trying to apply the principle of analogy and cultural fit in a predictive fashion, especially for complex situations, is risky. Nevertheless, prediction and planning can be facilitated by an in-depth knowledge of the culture and of the material and social requirements of a people. An article on the plight of Vietnamese refugees living in Fort Chaffee, Arkansas, during much of 1975 pointed out the failure of administrators in helping these luckless people to adjust to the American society:

The one English-language and cultural-orientation program for adults—established by a grant of more than $1 million from the Federal Government—helped not at all, since its directors lacked even the most superficial knowledge of Vietnamese culture. "You'd think we'd learn something, but it's the same thing all over again," another former A.I.D. official concluded. Indeed, it was as if, after all those years of violence, the model had become too indelible to disappear: Fort Chaffee was the replica of all American projects in Vietnam (FitzGerald 1975:32).

In this instance there is little doubt that the program in question would have benefited greatly by the involvement of individuals, not necessarily anthropologists, knowledgeable in Vietnamese culture.

AGENTS OF CHANGE AND
THE CHANGE PROCESS

It is customary in anthropology to distinguish between two major instruments, or agents, of change—invention and borrowing. Invention is often referred to as innovation, cultural borrowing as *acculturation*.

Conscious borrowing and conscious invention, however, are not in themselves sufficient to explain sociocultural change. We have already mentioned the matter of choice and of value-guided selection among available options as well as the fact that new cultural material is integrated through a process of reinterpretation, that is, made to fit the requirements and needs of a culture. But existing sociocultural systems may change also as a consequence of the rearrangement of older elements and not solely because of new inputs. To take a very simple example: it makes no difference whether at a favorite restaurant one orders Boston scrod or chicken Kiev, but if over a period of time no customers order the fish, it will ultimately disappear from the menu.

Internal rearrangements of cultural patterns and contents take place all the time, as some features are stressed while others lose some of their importance. In American society, we can trace a series of steady, if not altogether smooth, changes in the direction of constitutional and legal protection of the civil rights of individuals and groups. The Thirteenth Amendment (1865), while not abolishing discriminatory legislation toward blacks, terminated the existence of slavery in the United States and territories subject to its jurisdiction; state-sanctioned racial discrimination was struck down as unconstitutional in the landmark case of

Brown v. *Board of Education of Topeka* (1954); and the Civil Rights acts of 1957, 1960, and 1964 further reinforced the constitutional and legal position of minorities and individuals. These realignments in American society have encouraged other groups and individuals, including women, to bring their cases before the courts and before Congress. Here we have an egalitarian tradition asserting itself in the face of various forms of prejudice. The original draft of the Constitution, it should be noted, contained a strong antislavery statement that was deleted at the insistence of Southern representatives in the Continental Congress (Blaustein and Zangrando 1970:42–43).

In this photograph of West Point cadets one can spot a young woman undergoing the same rigorous training as her male companions. Sex-specific cultural roles are open to change, but even today the military establishments of some countries continue to be strictly male preserves. (United Press International)

Jomo Kenyatta, who was shortly to become president of Kenya, is shown addressing a rally following independence negotiations with Britain. He is waving a fly whisk, a traditional symbol of chieftainship that became his personal badge of office as a contemporary political leader. (Wide World Photos)

A great deal of cultural and social restructuring takes place very slowly and not as the result of a single or easily identifiable event. Shifts in the social structure often involve realignment of roles and functions rather than the creation of entirely new positions. This characteristic is especially true of many professions and occupations that have evolved in response to the demands of an increasingly complex and specialized social and technological order. Consider, for instance, such relatively new careers as those of astronaut, flight attendant, or marriage counselor. Although these occupations are new, there are pre-existing role-models to fall back upon. Most flight attendants are well aware that they are expected to function as little more than glamorous flying waitresses. Astronauts project a scientific-military image that is

Realignment of roles and functions

easy to recognize, while marriage counselors copy closely the usages and practices of the medical profession—a role their clients can relate to with little difficulty.

Traditional models in changing societies

Anthropologists studying non-Western societies could easily cite a multitude of cases in which new roles and positions have been superimposed on old roles and traditional statuses. This blend of old and new is particularly discernible in politics and political leadership. For example, Jomo Kenyatta, the president of Kenya and an early African graduate of the London School of Economics, is not to be seen without his elaborate fly whisk, a badge of chieftainship in East Africa. Since India's independence, its political leaders have favored attire indicative of a link with the peasantry—the "Congress cap" and homespun cotton two-piece suit.

This symbolic statement was popularized by Jawaharlal Nehru, India's first prime minister, who, like Kenyatta, was greatly influenced by his Western educational experience. In their different ways, both political leaders attempted to forge a symbolic link between the old and the new, between the traditional aspects of the past and the requirements of modern political leadership in emerging states.

It may be claimed that in the cases we have cited style is not as important as content, for just as Kenyatta is much more than a latter-day tribal chief, Indian political leaders should not be confused with members of village *panchayats* (councils). Although this fact cannot be denied, our point is that in the area of political change, a successful strategy often involves continuity with the past that offers people some element of predictability. Of course, the way that political leaders present themselves is only one facet of a much broader picture that includes the incorporation of traditional institutions within the frame of a modernizing society. As Milton Singer has noted for India:

The modern media of film, radio, newspapers, magazines, and books have reinforced the traditional cultural media. . . . Through historical and devotional films, recordings, temple ceremonies, articles, and books on Indian history and archaeology, as well as through Republic Day celebrations, the sense of a shared culture and past seems to grow every day more vivid, making Indian society more "modern" without making it any less "Indian" (Singer 1972:270).

Not every developing society can establish such a link between the past and the present. In some instances, the traditional society was so destroyed or distorted by the experience of colonialism that the new leadership and the new institutions have little linkage with the past. Perhaps the extreme example is Algeria,

Problem of continuity with the past

where the national consciousness, slight to begin with, was trampled out in more than a century of European domination and immigration. The Europeans, who by 1920 formed one-sixth of the population and were a large majority in all urban areas, solidly entrenched themselves as the functioning middle-class element and formed as well a local landed aristocracy. At the same time French intellectual attraction formed, or deformed, most young Algerian thinkers and inevitably ground down the last few traditional avenues of thought that resisted (Silvert 1963:227).

By necessity, the leaders of the Algerian revolution had to be drawn from obscure and almost "classless" sources—former enlisted men in the French army, postal clerks, mechanics, farmers, or simply individuals without professions. Given the impact of French culture in Algeria, this was about the only alternative available, but it is hardly a situation typical of political change in emerging countries.

Innovations

Turning to specific innovations, the romantic notion of an inventor having a flash of inspiration and running to his drawing board or laboratory may make good dramatic copy, but most inventions typically involve improvements on pre-existing devices or ideas. We do not imply that all changes are minor, but rather that a thread of continuity is virtually always present. No major shift in communication or work organization is discernible in the progression of writing instruments from quill pen to felt-tip pen (via steel nib, fountain pen, and ballpoint pen), for all perform essentially the same function in slightly different ways. The typewriter, on the other hand, represents a much more significant invention, whereas the development of movable type and printing (originally a Chinese invention) clearly revolutionized the dissemination of information.

Movable-type printing

The important thing to note is the degree to which major breakthroughs, as distinct from minor improvements, give rise to many analogous developments. Movable-type printing was the first and most important technique in the area of copy-producing devices. It can be seen as the ancestor not only of the photocopier but, by extension, of all instruments that reproduce information, including magnetic tapes and computer memory banks. It is surely not by chance that the first European printing press was established about 1450, when education was just beginning to spread among the new urban classes of merchants and businessmen. To say that the basic technology had been available for some time and simply needed to be refined is not to downplay the significance that the printing press was soon to possess. In passing, it is of interest to note that the first book to be published by this new device was an edition of the Vulgate Bible, another good example of the new dovetailing with the old.

Another instance where a trait or element finds its full potential once conditions are propitious for its use is the development of the lodestone compass. Lodestone is a natural magnetic oxide of iron, and "south-pointing spoons" of this material were used in ancient China for the purposes of divination. In due course, and exactly by what means is still not clear, compasses of the same material were introduced into Europe (Needham 1962; Carlson 1975). It was only with the advent of long-distance sea voyages, themselves the product of a whole gamut of social, technological, and cultural changes, that the compass was transformed from a curiosity into a navigational device, and thus the precursor of all the pointers and dials that we now take so much for granted.

TO SUM UP Social and cultural changes, whatever their ultimate consequences and regardless of whether they represent borrowings, inventions, or rearrangements of existing elements, are seldom totally novel developments. Almost invariably they re-

tain some continuity with the past and display a congruence with existing sociocultural systems. The boundaries are expanded, but the known and the predictable are not jettisoned out of hand. Just as it has always proved difficult to conceptualize and establish totally new societies—even revolutionary regimes base themselves on a body of past experience—there are few significant transformations that cannot in some measure or other be linked to the existing fabric of society and the needs and requirements of the times. Human initiative and even individual genius play their part, but the significance of new ideas, methods, and devices must be judged in terms of their ultimate consequences—their reception and use in a given culture.

Some instances
of discontinuity

The lodestone
compass

To these general observations there are some apparent exceptions. We have noted already that the political leadership in Algeria at the time of its war of independence from France made little use of traditional symbols, nor were revolutionary leaders recruited from the traditional elites. The reason is fairly straightforward: the traditional leadership had long ceased to function and politically conscious individuals had lost their roots in native society. Many, in fact, spoke French much better than Arabic. There are instances of even sharper discontinuity. In 1819 the Polynesians of Hawaii at one stroke discarded their native religion and virtually all became Christians. Chiefs and other political leaders played a leading role in this transformation. In part, this change can be attributed to the very heavy burden of ritual prohibitions, or taboos, to which the native Hawaiians had been subject. Then, too, a system with such extreme constraints made dealing with Europeans difficult at a time when Hawaiians eagerly desired the products and ideas of the West. Since their traditional religion seemed to impede free contact, those in control decided to discard it. Once it became evident that the most prestigious personages could break taboos with impunity, ordinary people were willing to risk following suit.

CONTACTS, CONFLICTS, AND CULTURAL BOUNDARIES

Perhaps because anthropologists have so often witnessed the consequences of the contact of peoples from different cultures, most of the anthropological studies of change, at least until recently, have dealt with acculturation and related phenomena. The fact that cultural elements can be transmitted from one group to another has been recognized by historians since ancient times, and this idea underlies much of the historical reconstruction that was being done by anthropologists around the turn of the century. Anthropological research of

Selective cultural assimilation is shown in this poignant portrayal of an old Native American woman whose traditional jewelry belies her ready-to-eat packaged food consumed on the sidewalk of a reservation town. (Ford Foundation)

this type, however, was largely limited to tracing the distribution of single traits, such as art styles, myths, or techniques of material production, in the light of available evidence (Boas 1896 and 1902). It was assumed, and correctly so, that, whenever different cultural groups met, some interaction took place and these contacts gave rise to the transmission of ideas and materials across cultural boundaries. The emphasis was on the elements themselves rather than on the sociocultural context of the contacts.

Acculturation

In its most simplistic form, the concept of acculturation accounts for change in one society by finding its origins in another. But there is much more to change across sociocultural boundaries than a mechanical diffusion of culture traits; for it is clear that while in any given situation a whole spectrum of borrowable elements may be communicated, only some are adopted and these, generally, after considerable reworking.

One should also be aware that acculturation is a two-way street and that in any sustained contact situation there is both borrowing and receiving, even if such exchanges are not of equal importance for the societies in question. Recognizing that the effects of culture contact are seldom if ever one-directional, some anthropologists prefer to use the term *transculturation* as more descriptive of the nature of mutual influences than the term *acculturation*.

Granted this awareness among anthropologists that all cultures, past and present, have to some degree been open to outside influences, it has been mostly in the course of the twentieth century that culture-contact situations could be carefully studied. Not by chance has the heyday of acculturational studies coincided with the penetration of Western economic and technological systems among hitherto relatively isolated simple societies.

Range of acculturation studies

As acculturational studies appeared with growing frequency during the second quarter of the twentieth century, they were seen

American soldiers were the object of great curiosity in Port Moresby, New Guinea, during World War II. The American troops and their equipment were a powerful source of stimulation for sociocultural change in the immense area of the Pacific. (Peabody Museum of Salem)

to cover a wide variety of situations ranging from such high-impact and accelerated events as the imposition of plantation agriculture on tropical subsistence farmers or the effects of boarding school experience on American Indian children to long-established forms of interaction between populations in contact. Clearly, the concept of acculturation could cover an extremely broad area of inquiry. It also became increasingly evident that in the majority of cases the consequences of culture contact were seldom simple or limited to one sphere of life. Elements of a donor culture might be borrowed or rejected, but change in one part of the cultural fabric typically triggered a whole series of other necessary adjustments. For example, one of the results of colonial control in many Pacific island societies was the introduction of European-operated plantations designed to produce tropical products (copra, palm oil, sugar, and other crops) for distant world markets. These changes involved much more than the imposition of new techniques of work or the cultivation of new crops. A wage economy

was introduced, a demand for Western goods stimulated, and new social and political ideas, as well as new religious concepts, developed as a consequence of the juxtaposition of capitalist business practices and local sociocultural systems. In some instances, the impact on traditional native societies was so powerful that it resulted in the erosion of power of traditional political figures and the abandonment by some groups of such subsistence activities as fishing and agriculture. The result in some communities was extreme dependence on European plantation administrators and the economic system they represented.

Studies of cultural contact also helped to throw light on long-established relations between sociocultural groups outside the effective reach of Western economic and political systems. The type of relationship we have in mind is one in which groups substantially benefit one another, as in the symbiosis between settled agriculturalists and nomads or the relationships between forest Pygmies and their tribal neighbors in the Congo (Lindgren 1938; Putnam 1948;

Lattimore 1962). In such cases, each group maintains its own identity but structures an important aspect of its existence, usually trade or some other exchange, in terms of mutually beneficial association with a traditional partner. For example, nomadic herders may exchange meat and other animal products for grain and the right to graze herds on field stubble following the harvest.

It is against this backdrop of growing interest and information that in the mid-1930s the Social Science Research Council commissioned a study of acculturation aimed at defining the scope of the subject (Redfield, Linton, and Herskovits 1936). In 1953, the council sponsored a follow-up summer seminar whose purpose was to formulate, on the basis of new research, an orderly approach to the study of culture change brought about by culture contact (Barnett and others 1954). As a result of these and subsequent efforts to narrow and refine the concept of acculturation, the term is now generally reserved for relationships between autonomous cultural systems or ethnic groups. It is assumed that such entities are capable of exercising some degree of choice in their rejection or acceptance of external influences and that they also have the capacity to engage in internal cultural adjustments following the acceptance of borrowed cultural items. On the other hand, it is generally considered that relationships between components of the same culture, such as those involving the transmission of ideas from one class to another of the same society, do not fall within the province of acculturation, the assumption being that classes and other components forming part of a cultural system fail to meet the criteria of relative autonomy in selection.

In our opinion, more important than such distinctions between in-culture and out-culture social components and their freedom of choice – a distinction that in today's world is often one of degree – is the fact that the

Acculturation: historical overview

study of acculturation has helped anthropologists to focus attention on cultural boundaries and the mechanisms that sociocultural systems use to maintain and perpetuate separate identities, often in the face of substantial pressures. It is evident that these boundary-maintaining mechanisms function as cultural filters rather than as impermeable walls. Such questions as to how and why cultures change and how and why they perpetuate themselves address the problem that intensely occupies cultural anthropologists at the present – the nature of cultural process. The concern for culture contact and its consequences has greatly increased our understanding of the dynamics of change. We are more aware of the disparities between sociocultural systems, the importance of the relationships established between cultures in contact, and the key role of certain types of individuals in furthering change.

Inventors and adaptors

If we look at change from the perspective of individual actions and motivations, we find that the innovator is a person who gains pleasure and satisfaction from tackling problems that involve unknowns. While problem solving of this nature involves a certain risk, this risk may be controlled by the exercise of abilities, as distinct from the risk of the gambler or the hunch player. Creativity and a degree of freedom from control and restriction appear to be traits closely allied to innovative capacities. Attitudes of the innovator include questioning rather than rejection or rebellion; in fact, the innovator will typically have the support of his own reference group – his family, perhaps his community, or some other social or subcultural entity. We can cite the case of the Puritans in seventeenth-century England, a group with deeply ingrained cultural values stressing initiative and individuality. A minority within English society, the Puritans became the spearhead of political reform, religious innovation, and a series of scientific and technological transformations of major importance. Not surprisingly, they

Cultural boundaries

also founded the first successful English settlement in North America.

The personality of the successful innovator differs little from that of the successful adaptor of foreign ways. Some years ago, Margaret Mead (1956) returned to the island of Manus off the north coast of New Guinea. Thirty years earlier, at the time of her initial study, Manus had scarcely been touched by Western ways. On her return, Mead noticed some startling changes: the islanders had learned to operate machines, had organized local government structures, and, in general, had adopted a wide range of techniques and ideas of European and American derivation. The reasons were not hard to find. Traditional Manus culture placed a great deal of emphasis on independence and initiative. In an environment that was physically dangerous for young children—houses were built on platforms set up on poles over the sea—the response of the islanders was to teach their children to swim at a very early age; in fact, they built small canoes for them and literally taught them to "paddle their own canoes."

This coming to terms with a dangerous aquatic environment was only one manifestation of the emphasis on early independence training. However, it was the catalytic contact with American troops in World War II that allowed the people of Manus Island to experiment with an extensive range of new social and technological forms. Other New Guinea groups, similarly exposed to foreign influence, did not respond half so enthusiastically.

The Manus case may be a rather isolated example of successful acculturation, for seldom does a whole society respond to alien ways in such a positive manner. However, segments of a society may do so when change helps to satisfy deep-felt needs to achieve in ways that are not realizable in terms of the traditional values and institutions. Furthermore, change, which can be potentially destructive to many simpler societies that are forced to cope with the pressures of technologically more advanced nations, may in some instances be welcomed as the avenue of cultural survival. Historically, this technique has been used with success by some formerly traditional state systems. The prime example of rapid transformation as a means of maintaining political—and hence, to a substantial degree, cultural—autonomy is nineteenth-century Japan. From the sixteenth to mid-nineteenth centuries, Japan remained a "forbidden" country, its doors firmly closed to foreign influence. But this policy could not be maintained in the face of growing foreign pressure, and the Japanese leadership opted for a rapid program of industrial development designed to make Japan both economically powerful and militarily strong.

Similarly, around 1860 a Chinese official proposed a program of self-strengthening through selective borrowing:

What we then have to learn from the barbarians is only the one thing, solid ships and effective guns. When Wei Yuan [a Chinese military historian] discussed the control of the barbarians, he said that we should use barbarians to attack barbarians, and use barbarians to negotiate with barbarians. Even regardless of the difficulties of languages and our ignorance of diplomatic usages it is utterly impossible for us outsiders to sow dissension among the closely related barbarians. . . . Only one sentence of Wei Yuan is correct: "Learn the strong techniques of the barbarians in order to control them . . ." (quoted in Têng and Fairbank 1954:53).

In due course, the Chinese did learn such techniques, but successful change involved also the restructuring of Chinese society. This use of alien techniques for the purpose of cultural maintenance is not limited to nation-states but has been used by societies of almost every degree of complexity. What seems necessary in such situations is a clear distinction between cultural goals and the means to achieve them.

Adaptation as cultural survival: Chinese and Japanese responses

TO SUM UP   There are many causes of social and cultural change, some consciously followed, others the result of internal and external pressures that must be adapted to if a society is to survive. Anthropologists have tried to understand the dynamics of change by paying close attention to the conditions that work for cultural continuity as well as those that facilitate transformations. Cultures and social systems are systems in dynamic interaction with their own internal elements and with other sociocultural systems. While it is possible, and easier, to carry on cultural analysis as if cultures were tightly bound isolates, such an approach is unrealistic and leads to the erection of static models that simply are not in accord with the world as it really is. There are no societies that today are entities unto themselves.

REFERENCES

APODACA, ANACLETO
1952 Corn and custom: the introduction of hybrid corn to Spanish American farmers in New Mexico. In *Human problems in technological change.* Edward H. Spicer, ed. New York: Russell Sage Foundation. Pp. 35–39.

BARNETT, H. G., AND OTHERS
1954 Acculturation: an exploratory formulation. The Social Science Research Council Summer Seminar on Acculturation, 1953. *American Anthropologist* 56:973–1002.

BLAUSTEIN, ALBERT P., AND ROBERT L. ZANGRANDO, EDS.
1970 [1968] *Civil rights and the Black American; a documentary history.* New York: Simon and Schuster.

BOAS, FRANZ
1896 The growth of Indian mythologies. *Journal of American Folk-Lore* 9:1–11.
1902 Some problems in North American archaeology. *American Journal of Archaeology* 6:1–6.

CARLSON, JOHN B.
1975 Lodestone compass: Chinese or Olmec primacy? *Science* 189:753–760 (no. 4205, September 5).

FITZGERALD, FRANCES
1975 Punch in! Punch out! Eat quick! *The New York Times Magazine,* December 28, 1975, pp. 8–11, 32–35, 38.

HERSKOVITS, MELVILLE J.
1948 *Man and his works; the science of cultural anthropology.* New York: Alfred A. Knopf.

HOIJER, HARRY
1951 Cultural implications of some Navaho linguistic categories. *Language* 27:111–120.

KELLY, ISABEL
1960 *La antropología, la cultura y la salud pública.* Lima, Peru: Imprenta del SCISP (Ministry of Public Health and Social Welfare).

LATTIMORE, OWEN
1962 *Studies in frontier history; collected papers, 1928–1958.* London: Oxford University Press.

LEACH, EDMUND R.
1954 *Political systems of highland Burma; a study of Kachin social structure.* London: The London School of Economics and Political Science.

LINDGREN, ETHEL JOHN
1938 An example of culture contact without conflict: Reindeer Tungus and Cossacks of northwestern Manchuria. *American Anthropologist* 40:605–621.

MEAD, MARGARET
1956 *New lives for old; cultural transformation—Manus, 1928–1953.* New York: William Morrow.

MEAD, MARGARET, ED.
1955 *Cultural patterns and technical change.* New York: The New American Library.

NEEDHAM, JOSEPH
1962 *Science and civilisation in China,* vol. 4, part 1. Cambridge: Cambridge University Press.

PUTNAM, PATRICK
1948 The Pygmies of the Ituri forest. In *A reader in general anthropology.* Carleton S. Coon, ed. New York: Henry Holt. Pp. 322–342.

REDFIELD, ROBERT, RALPH LINTON, AND
MELVILLE J. HERSKOVITS
1936 Memorandum for the study of acculturation. *American Anthropologist* 38:149–152.

SHARP, LAURISTON
1952 Steel axes for Stone Age Australians. In *Human problems in technological change.* Edward H. Spicer, ed. New York: Russell Sage Foundation. Pp. 69–90.

SILVERT, K. H., ED.
1963 *Expectant peoples; nationalism and development.* New York: Random House.

SINGER, MILTON
1972 *When a great tradition modernizes; an anthropological approach to Indian civilization.* New York: Praeger.

TÊNG, SSŬ-YÜ, AND JOHN K. FAIRBANK
1954 *China's response to the West; a documentary survey, 1839–1923.* Cambridge, Mass.: Harvard University Press.

VOGT, EVON Z.
1960 The automobile in contemporary Navaho culture. In *Men and cultures.* Anthony F. C. Wallace, ed. Philadelphia: University of Pennsylvania Press. Pp. 359–363.

Chapter 22
Applied anthropology

In a narrow sense, applied anthropology is the use of anthropological approaches to achieve some specific policy goal.[1] Typically, the cultural anthropologists work as advisers for agencies concerned with administration or a program involving social or economic change, but in some instances they may even actively participate in planning and administering these programs. This narrow definition of applied anthropology, however, fails to take into account the many applications of academic anthropology that are not directly linked to specific programs of action but nevertheless influence the lives of people.

The general impression both within the discipline and outside it is that, by and large, anthropologists conduct their research and write up their findings for a specialized audience of other anthropologists and professionals in related fields. According to this view, anthropology is something of an esoteric discipline whose main concern is the study of sociocultural phenomena and the formulation of theoretical models of only the most limited practical value.

APPLICATIONS OF ACADEMIC ANTHROPOLOGY

There is enough truth to this perspective of anthropology as self-contained and intellectually elitist to warrant some consideration. Most of our colleagues would agree that the network of professional communication is unduly restricted, with only a relative handful of anthropologists writing for the general public. However, this observation should be balanced by the fact that for at least half a century there have been some anthropologists, often leaders in their pro-

[1]Applied anthropology has also been called *practical anthropology, action anthropology*, and various other terms. While all anthropological research has a potential application, the concept of applied anthropology is generally reserved for programs with a very definite and specific practical goal.

fession, who have recognized that anthropology has broad general appeal. In the United States, Franz Boas in *Anthropology and Modern Life* (1928) insisted that the layperson would find interest and value in what is basically a humanistic enterprise. Ruth Benedict and Clyde Kluckhohn shared this opinion and wrote accordingly. In more recent times, Margaret Mead, in numerous books and magazine articles, has carried the anthropological message to an increasingly wider audience. While competent popularizations may not be considered applied anthropology, lectures, articles, and books that are designed for a nonacademic public help readers to understand both their own society and other cultures with greater clarity and fewer distortions.

In the chapter dealing with method and theory in cultural anthropology we noted the close and mutually reinforcing linkages between theoretical approaches and the methodology of field investigation. Much the same relationship exists between theoretical and applied anthropology, especially once it is recognized that the potential applications of anthropology are many. We should guard against the fallacy that "pure" science somehow develops in advance of its "practical" applications.

Anthropology—many members of the profession would agree—may be more of an art than a science, but if so it is an art with definite applications. At the minimum, it allows us to map out regularities for particular sociocultural systems and to understand how they are ordered. We would go further and insist that there are genuine cross-cultural regularities that can be established. In this sense, all anthropological knowledge has the potential for application. It is true that in certain academic quarters theoretical work carries a higher prestige than applied work, with the resulting tendency to discount practical studies. But this valuation of theory as superior to application is a problem more of institutional contexts than one inherent in the structure of anthropology. The same statement could be made of the natural sciences and of the behavioral sciences in general. More broadly, it is a consequence of Western intellectual tradition in which the practitioner of a discipline has seldom achieved the same renown as the formulator of theories.

Fortunately, there is much in both the anthropological tradition and in those fields of learning of greatest significance for anthropology that helps moderate the dichotomy between theory and practice. Cultural anthropologists, individually and as a group, are constantly exposed to the hard pragmatism of ethnographic research: theory must fit reality, not the other way around. No serious student of medicine would claim that practical, or clinical, medicine is an outgrowth of physiology; on the contrary, theory in the life sciences, from the time of Hippocrates (460?–377? B.C.) to the present, has flourished when grounded in practical and experimental work. The great developments in biology that took place around the middle of the nineteenth century were directly linked to a renewed interest in clinical and experimental work, and we might note that Charles Darwin (1809–1882) was a consummate naturalist—a field worker—as well as the greatest theoretician of his time. Other examples could be drawn from psychology, psychiatry, and sociology.

Practical concerns of early anthropologists Although a great deal of the early anthropology was descriptive and theoretical, its potential practical value was recognized by such founders as Lewis Henry Morgan (1818–1881) and E. B. Tylor (1832–1917). In the last paragraphs of his *Primitive Culture* (1871), Tylor pressed for an applied or practical anthropology and insisted that the science of culture is essentially a reformer's science. Such a humanitarian orientation characterized much of the early anthropology in Europe as well as the United States. Some of the claims put forward for the science of culture were overly optimistic or premature, although perhaps no anthropologist went so far as Auguste Comte (1798–

1857), one of the founders of sociology, who suggested that social scientists should determine and carry out policy, since they alone had the training to understand the inner workings of society.

Initially, anthropological concerns were centered on the welfare of native peoples and, by extension, minorities and the poor. Those we would now call anthropologists were intimately involved in emancipation and antislavery movements. The Ethnological Society of London, founded in 1843, was an offshoot of the Aborigines Protection Society, established several years earlier to further the welfare of the natives of Queensland and Tasmania at a time when settlers in Australia were dispersing the native inhabitants with guns and fire. Similar societies were established in France and Spain at about the same time, primarily to ameliorate the distressing state of simple societies unfortunate enough to be in the way of colonial expansion and white settlement. It is also relevant to note that as early as the mid-1880s, the Women's Anthropological Society of America in Washington, D.C., drew attention to such problems as slum housing and the consequences of extreme poverty on the health of women and children.

In this early period of the discipline, the distinction between academic anthropology and its practical applications had not yet been established. Anthropologists were a varied group of individuals—missionaries, administrators, naturalists, and a good many others interested in so-called primitives—who shared common concerns. By the 1880s, however, a more strictly academic anthropology had developed, with the emphasis turning to descriptive and comparative studies and, of course, to teaching. It was not until the early decades of the present century that the potentials of an applied or practical anthropology were again seriously examined.

In the interval, anthropology had become increasingly associated with academic environments. Typical anthropologists had changed from amateur investigators of "primitive" societies to individuals who spent most of their time in teaching and research work. Understandably, it was (and continues to be) in such contexts that anthropologists have achieved their greatest impact. In literate societies, the functions of formal education involve instruction and socialization—the achievement of academic goals and the formation of minds. The student who takes courses in anthropology, even at a time when curricula are highly flexible, does so with the hope that such courses will prove of value to the maturing mind. Certainly, an exposure to anthropology as part of higher education is often justified on the grounds that it helps students understand the variety of human cultural experience and that such understanding works to reduce ethnocentrism and prejudice.

The value of anthropological perspective

A knowledge of anthropology, however, should do much more than combat parochial attitudes. As educators, anthropologists would insist that an appreciation of the rich variety of human culture and social life is in the best traditions of humanistic instruction. Students learn not only that each people meet the problems that confront them in their own manner and the solutions arrived at are worthy of respect and consideration but, of even greater importance, that what all humans hold in common looms at least as large as what separates them. This perception of humanity was taken for granted by the great thinkers of the Renaissance and the Enlightenment, such as Montaigne, Las Casas, Pascal, and Burke, but unfortunately lost its appeal in an age of industrialism and expansion.

It would probably be fair to say that in both big and little ways we are shifting once more to a relativistic universe with an emphasis on common humanity. We can attribute this change in part to advances in mass communication but in part also to anthropology. Non-Western art—graphic, performing, and literary—is no longer seen as simply quaint, as witness the resounding success of exhibitions of West African bronzes or Chinese archaeological materials, and performances of Indonesian traditional musical dramas in the course of the last few years. Furthermore, these influences have penetrated Western culture to a surprising degree. In the words of Clyde Kluckhohn:

When T. S. Eliot juxtaposes Dante, Heraclitus, and a Sanscrit epic or James Joyce draws words from a dozen languages and folklore from fifty cultures or when Igor Stravinsky and Karl Orff write music that is at once "primitive" and Greek and Oriental, then we are living in an anthropologically sensitive world (Kluckhohn 1957:776).

If it is of value for people to understand that the human mind need not be constrained by the canons of Western art and literature, then an understanding of the diversity of political or legal systems has equally clear implications for the world of practical affairs.

Our examination of applied anthropology centers on specific programs and situations in which anthropologists work to carry out definite policy goals, often those of an official government agency. Such tasks place a heavy responsibility on them and can raise critical moral issues. But to the degree that most anthropologists have the potential of influencing the minds and even lives of others in the classroom or through their publications, the claim that their activities are conducted in an intellectual vacuum, some mythical ivory tower unrelated to the world outside, has little if any merit.

APPLIED ANTHROPOLOGY
AND COLONIALISM

We live in what has been called a postcolonial age. This is not to say that all peoples and nations have achieved political independence, but rather that the vast overseas colonial empires that survived World War II have been almost totally dismantled. It is difficult for those who have come of age in the 1960s and 1970s to realize how much the world has changed in the past three decades. Virtually no one in the West foresaw the rapidity with which colonial peoples were to achieve independence. Immediately after World War II, the mystique of colonialism remained strong, even if progressive political figures in Western countries conceded that colonies must be helped toward eventual independence. Winston Churchill's retort of 1942, "I have not become the King's First Minister in order to preside over the liquidation of the British Empire," would still have found many supporters in the early 1950s. Although *colonialism* is one of those stinging epithets that are exchanged in the United Nations, for the better part of the twentieth century few powers felt it necessary to hide the reality of colonial control.

It is against this background that we must assess the linkage between applied anthropology and colonialism. In a discussion of several papers on applied anthropology, the British social anthropologist S. F. Nadel defined the function and role of the applied anthropologist in the traditional colonial context as follows:

I am going to talk about the applied anthropologist as an employed anthropologist, working as instructed or requested, studying a particular range of problems, so that his employer can then utilize his knowledge and, in a different sense, apply it to practical problems. The employed anthropologist need not work for a salary; he may get a subsidy from the employer or feel a moral obligation toward an employer. The employer is the government—more specifically, the colonial government in the British Commonwealth, mainly in Africa, with some reference to Australia and New Guinea (Nadel 1953:178).

In short, applied anthropology was explicitly related to the tasks of governing dependent peoples. The assumption was that anthropologists had knowledge and insights useful to colonial administrations, while colonial governments were in the position to fund applied research and perhaps general

ethnographic work. In this relationship, anthropologists were typically something more than just colonial administrators. For one thing, they usually worked on a contractual basis and thus enjoyed a degree of autonomy. Nevertheless, what is striking is the extent to which the goals and attitudes underlying colonialism were internalized by so many anthropologists. Fairly representative are the claims for applied anthropology advanced by E. E. Evans-Pritchard.

It will at once be acknowledged that if it is the policy of a colonial government to administer a people through their chiefs it is useful to know who are the chiefs and what are their functions and authority and privileges and obligations. Also, if it is intended to administer a people according to their own laws and customs one has first to discover what these are. It is evident also that if it is intended to change a people's economy, for example to alter their system of land tenure, to encourage them to grow export crops, or to institute markets and a money economy, it is of some advantage to be able to estimate, at any rate roughly, what social effects these changes are likely to bring about (Evans-Pritchard 1951:109–110).

Anthropology and the Bureau of Indian Affairs

We should not assume that only British anthropologists worked as agents of colonial systems. Dutch and French anthropologists obtained support from their respective colonial offices, as did German ethnographers prior to World War I. In the United States, the situation was somewhat different, but the difference was more one of appearance than substance. The United States never controlled a large overseas empire but rather what might be termed a continental empire. For the period under consideration, the Native American population living on reservations (or entering an alien white world) were not in any significant degree different from societies in a colonial empire subject to the jurisdiction and authority of a European metropolitan power. The analogy is not perfect, but close enough: in place of a colonial office there was the Department of the Interior and within it the Bureau of Indian Affairs.

The first deliberate application of anthropological concepts and techniques to administrative problems in the United States occurred in the 1930s when John Collier was Commissioner of Indian Affairs (1933–1945). Collier was an enlightened administrator, as, in fact, were many European colonial officials. He recruited several anthropologists to establish an Applied Anthropology Unit within the bureau. Applied Anthropology Unit members studied the roles and functions of Indian chiefs and headmen and the traditional patterns of tribal governance. Other anthropologists working for the Educational Division of the bureau directed their attention to such matters as the adjustment of Indian boarding school graduates on their return to the reservations or in the wider world of American society. The kinds of problems and topics examined were rather similar to those investigated in British Africa, where anthropologists were faced with the dual task of integrating traditional leadership patterns into a colonial system and coping with the phenomenon of a growing number of natives moving into townships and becoming wage laborers in mines and on plantations.

Applied anthropologists in colonial settings saw their task, at least in part, as adjusting and interpreting legislation in such a way that it would prove less traumatic for dependent peoples. By and large, British social anthropologists believed strongly in the efficacy and essential good sense of a policy of indirect rule that utilized native institutions and leaders. Their American colleagues worked to implement the provisions of the Indian Reorganization Act of 1934, which, in theory at least, was to help establish tribal constitutions that reflected Indian forms of political organization.

One of the fundamental questions raised with respect to these efforts in colonial settings is whether the native peoples significantly benefit from the ministrations of applied anthropologists. There is little doubt

Anthropologists and colonial administration

that colonial officials are better able to understand societies under their control with the aid of anthropological knowledge. Input from anthropology should result in policies that are more realistic and more humane than if they had been planned and implemented without knowledge of the cultural and social attributes of the peoples in question.

Although few anthropologists have exercised important policy-making functions in colonial administrations, it seems reasonable to assume that, on balance, their involvement has resulted in the implementation of policies that have been more palatable to colonial peoples than similar policies carried out without their help. But this judgment is made in terms of two alternatives: colonialism without anthropological input, and colonialism with the aid of applied anthropologists. That dependent peoples might prefer an entirely different option was seldom considered.

It is true that some anthropologists, in particular Americans, developed a degree of ambivalence to the colonial rule. Melville J. Herskovits, an anthropologist intimately acquainted with Africa, observed:

It is in the nature of the case that the anthropologist is best fitted to see the strains and stresses of underprivileged groups, or of natives who no longer control their own lives. He sees these stresses and strains from the less pleasant, under-side of the situations in which they live. He sees the problems of the native as no administrator, however gifted, can possibly see them. Where, then, he is in a position to aid in obtaining for the natives he knows some reinstatement of the human rights they have been deprived of, he customarily welcomes the opportunity (Herskovits 1948:652).

We applaud these sentiments, but it is, of course, in the very nature of colonialism that dependent people are subject to external control and direction and thus do not enjoy the full range of human rights.

APPLIED ANTHROPOLOGY
IN WARTIME

The attack on Pearl Harbor (1941) precipitated the entry of the United States into World War II, an event that was destined to have a substantial effect on American anthropology. Quite apart from the direct employment of anthropologists in theaters of war as individuals with a knowledge of local conditions and native populations, the war marked the beginning of what later would be termed strategic social science. Anthropologists and other social scientists helped to staff government agencies charged with the mission of what could be broadly termed psychological warfare.

One task that we need only touch on here, since it was examined in detail in the chapter on the individual and society, involved the study of cultures at a distance. The cultures in question were primarily the national cultures of the wartime Axis powers, in particular Japan and Germany. The assumption was that a scrutiny of national cultures would facilitate the war effort and the tasks of postwar military government. Anthropologists, for instance, played a significant role in defining the surrender terms for the Japanese. These terms took into account the traditional role of the emperor and the strong feelings of loyalty and obli-

gation that the Japanese servicemen held for Hirohito. It was recognized by the Allies that while the emperor played a critical ceremonial role in Japanese life, he had not initiated Japanese military expansion. Consequently, it was decided that the emperor should not face trial as a war criminal but be allowed to retain the position of a symbolic head of state. The Allies further concluded that it would be wise for the emperor to order the surrender of his troops in order to avoid further bloodshed. There is little question that this policy was a wise one and that an attempt to invade Japan under other circumstances would have cost countless lives, Japanese and Allied. This hypothesis is reinforced by several instances of Japanese soldiers left behind in remote areas of the Pacific who did not learn of the imperial surrender order. In some cases, these soldiers remained in hiding and engaged in sporadic guerrilla warfare for twenty or thirty years after the official cessation of hostilities.

The work of anthropologists in the war against Japan was in part an offshoot of a most deplorable episode involving Japanese and Americans of Japanese descent in the United States. The outbreak of the war triggered all manner of extreme reactions on the West Coast, including some totally unfounded fears of an imminent Japanese

During World War II, a number of American anthropologists worked in these relocation camps in which thousands of West Coast American citizens of Japanese ancestry were interned. (Wide World Photos)

invasion. In response to these anxieties and some deep-seated racial biases the War Relocation Authority was established as a government agency and charged with the management of relocation camps to which West Coast Japanese were dispatched in great haste. These concentration camps, for this is what they were, were used to impound thousands of individuals. Living conditions, at least initially, were miserable and proved highly traumatic for many inmates. In much the same way as applied anthropologists had earlier been employed by the Bureau of Indian Affairs, a number of anthropologists were employed by the War Relocation Authority to facilitate the tasks of administration. The essential injustice of the relocation camps was recognized by some anthropologists, but while a few anthropological reports addressed themselves to the shock of the relocation experience (Spicer 1946), the profession as a whole showed no great sensitivity to the plight of what were ordinary people uprooted from their livelihoods and arbitrarily defined as alien and dangerous.[2]

It is perhaps idealistic to expect anthropologists to show greater sensitivity than other people in times of real or putative national danger. Be this as it may, the evidence strongly indicates that at such times most anthropologists will follow general societal trends. To cite a different and, admittedly, extreme example, few French anthropologists raised their voices against French policies during the long colonial war in Algeria. In the late 1950s, when the French government was pacifying Algeria through military action and extensive relo-

cation schemes, the late Paul Rivet, founder and first director of the world-renowned Musée de l'Homme, was touring Latin American capitals justifying the actions of the French government.

The involvement of American anthropologists in psychological warfare and related matters led to the postwar association of anthropologists with military government branches. Anthropologists, together with other social scientists, participated in the staffing of Civil Affairs Training schools to prepare officers for administrative duties in occupied areas of the Pacific and Asia. As early as 1943, the United States Navy contracted with Yale University for a research program to study Micronesia. Micronesia remained under naval control until 1951, but even when jurisdiction passed to the Department of the Interior, anthropologists continued to work for the administration of the Trust Territory of the Pacific Islands.

It is interesting to note the points of similarity between the anthropologists employed in Micronesia and the tasks of British anthropologists in Africa at an earlier period. In neither case were anthropologists burdened by day-to-day administration. Typically, they worked to facilitate government policies applied to dependent peoples by interpreting these policies to native inhabitants and relaying native attitudes and responses to the appropriate government departments. In short, they acted as intermediaries or what might be termed "culture brokers." The formulation of actual policy fell outside the scope of their assigned duties. The anthropologists involved in the Micronesia project no doubt felt that their participation helped to buffer a series of severe shocks—the experiences of war and life under the rule of military or civilian officials drawn from a very different cultural tradition. Furthermore, the methods, techniques, and experiences gained in the course of such research added to the pool of anthropological knowledge pertinent to Pacific island societies and, more broadly, the intercultural configurations among them.

[2]That the relocation camps were an example of arbitrary power cannot be disputed. The basis of relocation was the declaration of a state of emergency on the West Coast under which various constitutional provisions were suspended. In wartime, most states intern enemy aliens, but the relocation provisions were designed for a specific ethnic/national group. Individuals of German or Italian ancestry were not treated in the same manner as people of Japanese descent, all of whom were interned regardless of whether they were Japanese nationals or American citizens.

Nevertheless, the essential questions having to do with colonial and quasi-colonial relations were just the questions that could not be answered by anthropologists in positions that implicitly supported an asymmetrical political and social order.

APPLIED ANTHROPOLOGY
AND CHANGE

Following World War II, the main thrust of applied anthropology was toward directed, or planned, change. Since we have dealt with some of the specifics of such programs in our discussion of economic anthropology and social and cultural change, this section will be devoted to a general examination of the impact of change on those societies that are forced to experience it. In particular, we wish to draw attention to some of the underlying assumptions—theoretical, ideological, and political—behind such programs.

Although the application of anthropology to promote change in noncolonial regions predates World War II, it was in the aftermath of the war that most such programs were initiated. No doubt, the swift and successful reconstruction of war-ravaged economies in Europe and Japan under the auspices of the Marshall Plan and other recovery programs seemed to offer similar possibilities for countries that were economically underdeveloped. The situations were not comparable, however, for in modern complex societies only the physical infrastructure of factories and communications had been destroyed, whereas in emerging countries the foundation needed for an industrial economy had either never existed or was very rudimentary. Developed countries could count on a pool of technological skills and a well-established industrial tradition, elements missing in traditional societies.

The literature on development shows that this distinction was recognized and that one consequence of this recognition was the planning of projects for less developed countries that were often modest and local in scope:

The societies at this early stage of transition are not ready for comprehensive development programming or the application of large capital sums. They lack political cohesion and the administrative and technical skills to implement and supervise an extended program of investment in capital goods (Millikan and Blackmer 1961:135).

This perspective on traditional societies helps to explain the role of anthropology in development programs. Until very recently, it has been taken for granted that cultural and social anthropologists work in small-scale societies, such as village communities and tribal groups. It would seem to follow, therefore, that if problems of development are to be approached in traditional societies, anthropology should play an important part. Unfortunately, there is a certain fallacy to this seemingly valid inference: programs that aim at general sociocultural transformation cannot be implemented through a multiplicity of village-level changes. But this is only one of the criticisms that have been leveled at applied anthropology. For a variety of reasons that warrant examination, many observers have reached the conclusion that applied anthropology is much more concerned with maintaining sociocultural systems than stimulating substantive changes.

This apparent paradox is for the most part resolved when we examine the premises that most Western applied anthropologists bring to the field and the problems with which they attempt to deal. At the risk of some oversimplification, it would be fair to say that much applied anthropology is characterized by a heavy psychological emphasis in the selection of problems to be studied and the interpretation of research results. In the area of economic change, stress is frequently placed on resistance to change—for instance, finding out why a particular group of peasants fail to use an improved type of seed. In medical studies, anthropologists are likely to search for the native concepts and rationalizations having to do with diseases and their treatment. These areas of research are certainly valid, but however important it may be to understand native ideas, the tendency to interpret social realities in psychological terms is not fully adequate. The fundamental problem in poor countries is poverty, with which one must include such matters as income distribution and patterns of oligarchic control. Questions of this type cannot be approached simply at the level of the peasant village.

Another criticism that can fairly be made of much applied anthropology is that its practitioners distrust rapid change as inherently disorderly and dysfunctional. For this reason, anthropologists tend to promote change that does not disrupt the existing social system and supporting value orientations. It is not far from this position to one that is fundamentally conservative and fearful of all major societal reorganization. Needless to say, such a cautious approach is often in keeping with the vested interests of established power structures in the societies undergoing change. Caution on change is also reinforced by the anthropological tenet of cultural relativity, the belief that it is not the function of anthropologists to make value judgments. Under some circumstances, cultural relativism is a sound position since it works against the imposition of alien systems. Taken to its extremes, however, it invalidates the view that anthropology should be applied to the resolution of human problems.

We have mentioned the matter of community-level orientation in much of applied anthropology. This is more than a question of procedure, for it can lead to a dissipation of efforts to bring about substantive change in the total society—there are enough villages in the Third World to keep legions of anthropologists busy for centuries to come if each village is to be dealt with as an individual case. We can best illustrate the limitations of this approach when we consider the history of the Cornell-Peru Project, an ex-

periment in applied anthropology, admirable for its thoroughness, that simply cannot be replicated in all comparable communities of the developing world.

The Vicos Project The Cornell-Peru Project at Vicos began as a classic research and development enterprise in 1952 when Allan R. Holmberg (1958, 1965), acting for Cornell University and the Peruvian Institute of Indigenous Affairs, assumed the traditional role of *patrón* (landlord-boss) by leasing a Peruvian hacienda called Vicos. This estate was located in the impoverished highland region, where the Quechua-speaking local inhabitants for centuries had been attached to haciendas in a form of bondage similar to serfdom—they worked hacienda lands for whoever owned or leased them.

A number of features of the project are worth remarking on. Initially, the anthropologist-*patrón* formulated the plans for directed change, the assumption being that certain goals, such as participation in the decision-making process and fair sharing of the hacienda's wealth, should be implemented for the good of the entire community. In due course, Indian peasants were moved into positions of leadership and responsibility. We should note that the cost of the enterprise in money and personnel was high. Five years after the initiation of the project, its directors were in a position to hand over the operation of the hacienda to the Vicosiños themselves. However, because of the delaying tactics of local power elites, it took five more years before the title to the property was transferred to the Indian community in 1962. It could be maintained that only the intervention of Holmberg at the national executive level assured the eventual success of the project. Not every village, however, is likely to find such an influential patron or an institution able to devote funds and personnel on a similar scale. Vicos is a community of some 2,000 Quechua Indians, but there are several million Indians in the Andean highlands tied to similar estates. When we consider that even

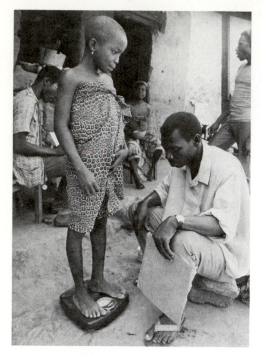

one small project generated intense opposition from the established power structure, it is obvious that change on a national scale would require a totally different approach.

We have examined the Vicos Project in some detail because it illustrates the problems that beset even the most successful efforts in applied anthropology. The dedication of the sponsors cannot be doubted and the project demonstrates that significant and beneficial change can be brought about in the microcosm of a community. But this success—and Vicos is cited again and again in the literature as an example of what applied anthropology can accomplish—should be balanced by the observations of a Mexican anthropologist surveying the whole field of directed change as it has functioned to date:

These are not opportune times to deceive ourselves into thinking that efforts should be limited to the promotion of small changes, shielding ourselves with the fear that radical changes will produce disorganization. On the contrary, we believe that it is the task of the anthropologist to point to the very frequent uselessness of timid development programs, and that it is also his task to demonstrate with scientific rigor the need to carry out radical changes, that is, changes which get to the root of the problems themselves. Sometimes it looks as if those who work along the road of slow evolution intend to achieve only minimal changes, so that the situation continues to be substantially the same; that is, in other words, *to change what is necessary so that things remain the same* (author's emphasis; Bonfil Batalla 1966:92).

The message of the quotation is that much of applied anthropology is still perceived as tinged with colonialist assumptions: health care, education, and technological change are introduced in regulated doses; the recipient societies are "transformed," but never at a rate that would significantly disrupt the established structures of power.

REFERENCES

BOAS, FRANZ
1928 *Anthropology and modern life.* New York: W. W. Norton.

BONFIL BATALLA, GUILLERMO
1966 Conservative thought in applied anthropology: a critique. *Human Organization* 25:89–92.

EVANS-PRITCHARD, E. E.
1951 *Social anthropology.* London: Cohen & West.

HERSKOVITS, MELVILLE J.
1948 *Man and his works; the science of cultural anthropology.* New York: Alfred A. Knopf.

HOLMBERG, ALLAN R.
1958 The research and development approach to the study of change. *Human Organization* 17:12–16.
1965 The changing values and institutions of Vicos in the context of national development. *The American Behavioral Scientist* 8:7:3–8 (March).

KLUCKHOHN, CLYDE
1957 Developments in the field of anthropology in the twentieth century. *Journal of World History* 3:754–777.

MILLIKAN, MAX F., AND DONALD L. M. BLACKMER, EDS.
1961 *The emerging nations: their growth and United States policy.* Boston: Little, Brown.

NADEL, S. F.
1953 Discussant. Problems of application: results (Chapter XI). In *An appraisal of anthropology today.* Sol Tax and others, eds. Chicago: The University of Chicago Press. Pp. 178–190.

SPICER, EDWARD H., AND OTHERS
1946 *Impounded people; Japanese Americans in the relocation centers.* War Relocation Authority Report. Washington, D.C.: Government Printing Office.

TYLOR, SIR EDWARD BURNETT
1871 *Primitive culture: researches into the development of mythology, philosophy, religion, art, and custom.* 2 vols. London: J. Murray.

Chapter 23
Looking toward
the future

In the chapter dealing with the nature of complex societies we discussed some of the approaches that have characterized the anthropological study of contemporary cultural and social systems since the 1940s. Much of this effort has been focused on determining how relatively small social units operate within the fabric of national systems. As a result, a great deal of information has become available on such subject areas as community life, the position of minorities, the place of women, the role of educational systems, and the modalities of socialization in contemporary complex societies.

These are all worthy areas of research and much of what has been learned from it can be applied to practical ends. However, the conceptual models utilized and the questions asked tend to leave out of the picture a whole range of phenomena that are central to an understanding of some very critical problems that confront us today. These problems are global in scope, and the great bulk of

past studies have therefore been altogether too restricted.

Bluntly phrased, disciplinary or subdisciplinary compartmentalization — for example, studies of peasant communities of one country or region, or of the social relations in a city neighborhood — tends to distort reality. Worse, it forces us to look for answers in the wrong place, or on the wrong level.

SOCIAL ASPECTS OF
GLOBAL PROBLEMS

As a case in point — shifting for a moment to the perspective of biology rather than anthropology — the recognition of a growing ecological crisis has focused attention on the role that biologists may play in order to bring ecological problems under control and to find acceptable scientific and technological solutions to coping with an environment in danger. The assumption is that since biologists study organisms, they are in an especially good position to apply their expertise to slowing down and even reversing ecological deterioration.

The question is, not whether biologists can contribute worthwhile suggestions, but rather whether the ecological crisis is in essence a biological or, broadly speaking, a social problem. As Salvador E. Luria, a recent recipient of the Nobel Prize in biology, points out:

If the ecological crisis exists it is a social and political crisis, brought about in part by population increase and urbanization, and in great part, at least in this country, by the unfettered and selfish exploitation of natural resources by industry—aided and abetted by the government. To call on scientists to solve the ecological crisis is but an exercise in buck-passing, as it would be for the board of directors of the Pennsylvania Railroad to ask their train conductors to rescue the railroad from bankruptcy (Luria 1974:27).

In another passage, Luria adds:

It seems clear to me that the central problems are not biological. Neither are they scientific or even technological. They are social, and their solution depends on radical changes in social priorities and on improved machinery to enforce those priorities (Luria 1974:27).

Here, on the part of a renowned scientist, is the recognition that science by itself can no longer come up with the answers—a recognition, no matter how obviously true, that flies in the face of centuries of Western tradition.

The global problems facing humanity today that will become ever more pressing in the years to come are rapidly mounting. Moreover, they are closely interrelated, even if the nature of their connections is not always as clear as one would wish. The problems themselves, however, are hardly a matter of debate: the depletion of critical natural resources; growing population pressures; severe food shortages in many parts of the world; rising levels of pollution and environmental degradation; the specter of nuclear war; a climate of social, economic, religious, and political conflict both within and between nations that is rapidly assuming the status of normalcy. These are matters that know no boundaries, for while they may currently impinge on some nations and societies more than others, no country can consider itself free from danger. Each of these issues has broad implications for the future of humankind; taken together they represent a challenge the likes of which humanity has never before had to face.

As with all highly complex issues, especially when projected into the future, interpretations vary with respect to both the dimensions of a given problem and its possible solution. A variety of scenarios have been suggested by analysts and policy-makers. While these differ in their estimate of the degree of crisis, the reality of crisis is never questioned. Anthropology can play a meaningful role in delimiting the fundamental problems and central questions that loom so large for coming generations, and it should be used to assist in finding effective and responsible solutions. In both instances, what will be required is expanded perspectives—an anthropology for our times. But potential remedies will ultimately rest on the willingness of those in positions of power to implement unpopular policies—unpopular, because they will inevitably expose the limits of strictly scientific-technological solutions and force people everywhere to recognize that in a finite world visions of infinite growth are not only unrealistic but patently suicidal. Such a view, of course, runs counter to virtually every modern ideology; moreover, it calls for a new ethic, whose outlines are as yet barely perceptible.

WORLD RESOURCES AND THEIR ALLOCATION

Historical background   Until the time of the industrial revolution, the presently developed countries were forced to maintain a balance between population and resources. In particular, facilities for the mass storage and transportation of foodstuffs were almost nonexistent. There were regional and, to some degree, national economic structures that allowed the movement of staples over short distances. Long-range trade, however, was limited to goods of high value and little bulk, mostly luxury items. As a result, when crops failed, people died. When the population of a country or region grew beyond the capacity of the local agricultural production to sustain it, there was rarely any escape but death. We often forget that until the end of the eighteenth century, famine was the recurrent lot of most human societies. For instance, between 1200 and 1600 England suffered a famine about once every fifteen years. At the time of the American Revolution, the average European peasant lived on the brink of starvation and in conditions not very different from those of the most hard-pressed inhabitants in some of the Asian and Latin American countries today.

Then two major cultural revolutions, long in the making, burst with full force upon humanity. The first was the modern agricultural revolution. In Western Europe, techniques of agricultural production made possible far higher levels of productivity than had previously been the case. At the same time, very substantial advances were made in the transportation and storage of food and other raw materials. Without these initial developments, the industrial revolution that was shortly to follow might well have been stillborn; for only an expanded food supply could support the inhabitants of the burgeoning industrial cities.

The industrial revolution not only altered the demographic composition of industrializing societies, but multiplied the output per worker many times. Thus, one man or woman or child could produce as much as fifty or a hundred individuals, and for these goods markets had to be found. Industrialization also created vast cities in which masses of workers were crowded into such

(right) In this automobile plant each worker does a highly routine task. The end product is the work of many hands, but individual responsibility is limited to a single facet of the production process. (Stern/Black Star)

(below) Traditional craft activities are different in scale and organization from modern industrial production. Craftsmanship tends to be time- and labor-intensive, low in productivity, and often conducted in the home or in small workshops. This craftsman works his trade in rural Argentina, but even in the most highly industrialized nations, some crafts survive the impact of mass production and standardization. (Richard Wilkie)

slums as the world had never seen. Within a few generations, former agriculturalists were forced to adapt to an entirely new existence ruled by the clock and the machine.

But more than this, the industrial revolution forged an economic system that was global in scope. The countries in the forefront of the industrial revolution, in particular Britain, developed an insatiable appetite for raw materials that could be satisfied only from overseas: wheat, timber, tobacco, cotton, sugar, and eventually minerals. Some of this bounty went to feed and provide for the teeming populations of the industrial lands, but much was transformed into finished goods for export. Soon enough, Britain's industrial primacy was challenged by other European countries. Toward the end of the nineteenth century, the United States moved ahead as a major industrial country, but the fundamental pattern remained the same: to produce and sell, to exploit new material resources, and to develop new markets.

The problem with such an economic structure was that as industrialization became more widespread, competition for available resources and markets steadily increased. We should take note that the danger had been foreseen. In 1798 Thomas Robert Malthus warned in *An Essay on the Principle of Population* that a time was bound to come when finite resources would be outstripped by the demands placed upon them. But he wrote in a climate unlikely to give much credence to his ideas. With the colonization of the New World and other regions, it seemed that resources were nearly infinite in quantity and the time of accounting—should it come—far in the future. Instead of a careful consideration of the consequences of industrialization and rising population levels, what ensued was an attitude that the remedy for national and global ills lay in ever-increasing production. It would not be wrong to define this attitude as a waster's psychology—the mentality of built-in obsolescence.

Hundreds of aircraft await destruction by salvage crews after World War II. War is inherently wasteful. (Wide World Photos)

Prospects for the future

Historically, there is little question that if industrialization had not been linked to the exploitation of new lands and the peoples resident in them, the problems would never have reached their ultimate dimensions. For support of this viewpoint, we do not have to turn to visionaries; it is enough to read the literature published by official agencies. The first paragraph of the 1974 *Annual Report* of the International Monetary Fund could hardly be bleaker:

At mid-1974, the world economy was in the throes of a virulent and widespread inflation, a deceleration of economic growth in reaction to the preceding high rate of expansion, and a massive disequilibrium in international payments. This situation constitutes perhaps the most complex and serious set of economic problems to confront national governments and the international community since the end of World

War II (International Monetary Fund 1974:1).

The *Annual Report* of the World Bank is similar in tone:

The period [July 1, 1973, to June 30, 1974] has been marked by a major upheaval in global economic relationships, the implications of which are still unfolding. Through the resulting confusion and controversy, one point is clear: the prospects for the economic and social progress of a large number of developing countries have been seriously jeopardized (World Bank 1974:5).

The report then proceeds to link the poor economic prospects of developing countries—"per capita incomes will either stagnate or rise very little between now and 1980" (World Bank 1974:6)—to a slowdown of economic growth in industrialized societies.

Economists, planners, and national leaders are understandably distressed at a situation in which economic growth stagnates while population pressures mount, and in which affluent nations feel the pinch while

poor nations find themselves increasingly poorer. But unchecked economic growth, entailing an ever greater depletion of resources, is obviously a cure that in the long run is guaranteed to bring more headaches. In a manner of speaking, the world economic system is like a drug addict who requires higher and higher dosages to maintain some semblance of normalcy. This situation has been recognized by a group of eminent scientists jointly known as The Club of Rome. In their second report, they note that scarcity breeds conflict and that

if the resources were unlimited, there would be a chance to avoid conflict. The very phenomenon of growth on our finite planet, however, implies competition for resources; therefore growth can only create circumstances conducive to conflict (Mesarovic and Pestel 1974:83–84).

Obviously, the depletion of resources is only one factor, albeit a very critical one, influencing the future prospects of humanity; another is the explosive increase of population. The two exacerbate each other, and it is therefore important to recognize that the crises that are currently engulfing the entire globe cannot be dealt with piecemeal. Before we consider some suggestions for amelioration, a series of observations appear to be in order. As we have noted, a feature of industrial development from its very beginning is an asymmetrical relationship between industrial and nonindustrial societies. Some observers would go further and insist that such development is predicated on economic strategies that perpetuate underdevelopment in countries producing raw materials (Frank 1969). The unassailable fact is that developed countries consume a disproportionate amount of the world's resources. Japan currently imports 99 percent of its oil, and it is estimated that the United States will, by the year 2000, depend on imports for over 80 percent of essential raw materials—assuming a projection of current trends (Mesarovic and Pestel 1974:84). We should keep these facts

Wisconsin farmers slaughtering calves in 1974. The farmers were protesting the low prices for livestock and dairy products. (United Press International)

in mind when considering figures on global population, for to the critical data on population size and population growth must be added the variable of per capita resource consumption. The average person living in an industrial society utilizes food, energy, and other resources at a level that would maintain many individuals in less developed countries.

THE POPULATION BOMB

As with the hydrogen bomb, we have lived with the fact of the population explosion for so long that its potential consequences have almost lost their power to shock. But the demographic outlook for the next two or three generations is grim indeed, and careful and reasoned consideration of the problem cannot be avoided.

The bare facts of the population explosion are not in dispute. It took humankind until the mid-nineteenth century to attain its first billion mark. The second billion was reached by 1930, some eighty years later. In 1960, world population stood at 3 billion, and in the short period of only sixteen years, by 1976, yet another billion was added. Of the more than 4 billion people living today, about a third are in areas where population growth has slowed down considerably. These areas include North America, most of Europe, the Soviet Union, Japan, and several other smaller countries. Although not all of these countries are equally industrialized, all are among those with the highest per capita national product in the world. Given current growth trends, it is reasonable to expect that within two or three generations these countries will have achieved zero population growth (ZPG), that is, about 2.1 children per family on the average. This means that, allowing for continued heavy immigration in the future, the United States and Canada will have doubled their populations at the present rates of growth in about 70 to 80 years. The comparable figure for Europe, excluding the Soviet Union, would be approximately 115 years.

Figure 23-1 World population growth

Two projections of world population growth for the next seventy-five years. The solid curve assumes that present trends will continue, while the broken line envisages an early effective program to persuade people to limit the size of their families. (Source: *Britannica Book of the Year 1976* [Chicago: Encyclopaedia Britannica, Inc.] 1976)

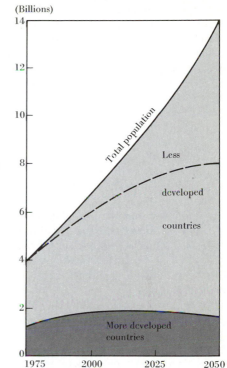

The rest of the world, by contrast, presents a strikingly different picture. If we project from the 1975 figures, Latin America and Africa could double their populations by about the year 2000, while Asia could double its 2.3 billion people some seven to eight years later. In total numbers, then, the world population could be nearing 7 billion by the year 2000, and double this figure by the middle of the twenty-first century. There are, of course, alternative projections of world population growth. The United Nations, for instance, utilizes three different kinds of projections—high, low, and medium—but the picture does not change fundamentally, for even the low reading indicates a dramatic increase. The magnitude of this acceleration is illustrated by noting that at prevailing rates of growth, more people will be added to the world population in one year by the middle of the twenty-first century than during the fifteen hundred years following the birth of Christ (see Figure 23-1).

Despite these demographic projections, staggering in terms of the resources required to sustain even the barest necessities of life, the countries of the world have yet to agree on a concerted course of action to alleviate the growing crisis. Many governments continue to dismiss the danger of population pressures as "neo-Malthusian," as if the logic of Malthus were substantially in error. A somewhat different argument, one that warrants more careful examination, is that poverty in developing countries is due to colonialism, exploitation, and economic deception.

That underdevelopment in the Third World is due to more than high population densities should not be in question. What is happening, however, is that in the population/resources debate, opinions have become polarized: the poor countries blame the rich, while the rich blame the poor. Political leaders in rich countries with relatively stable rates of population growth point to the rapid increase in the population of poor lands as the prime cause of pressure

The specter of poverty and famine

on resources, whereas their counterparts in poor countries focus their attention on high levels of consumption in developed lands. As Lester Brown, a former administrator in the United States Department of Agriculture, points out, both factors are important:

At the global level, the growth in annual consumption of goods and services—about 4 percent per year—is allocated rather equally between population growth and rising individual affluence (Brown 1973:162).

Poverty and overpopulation are certainly interrelated. This assertion does not mean that these burdens are the sole responsibility of less developed countries. We should not forget that, for the most part, it was the impact of the West that drastically altered the stability of populations throughout much of the world. The moral responsibility for past actions—even if the consequences were not foreseen—cannot be avoided. By the same token, countries with galloping population growth should not be reinforced

Because of the high rate of illiteracy in rural India, the dissemination of family planning programs depends largely on pictorial presentations. (United Nations/ILO)

in their illusion that the sole cause of their problems lies in the maldistribution of wealth and resources. Once more, we wish to stress that the problem is global and must be so viewed. Social scientists, not having to profess the official views of their governments, would generally be in agreement with the statement drafted by Margaret Mead on the occasion of the United Nations World Population Conference held in Bucharest, Romania, during the summer of 1974:

The world situation is potentially disastrous. Hundreds of millions are suffering from hunger, poverty, persecution, disease and illiteracy. The unprecedented rate of population growth, doubling population from 3 to 6 billion in a generation, will strain the environment and man's social, political and economic institutions to the breaking point. . . . Some countries consume and waste the earth's resources at a rate that cannot be maintained. Others have densely-settled regions with population growth rates of 2 or 3 percent a year that will exert demands on the international community which may not be met. The urgency of the global crisis must not be ignored nor submerged beneath national ambitions (quoted by Tinker 1975:557).

Hunger is a scourge that has been virtually eliminated in the developed parts of the world. There is no question that there are hungry people even in the United States and that many more suffer malnutrition. But famine in the form of mass starvation is a phenomenon that Americans and Europeans know only at second hand. Hunger is difficult to define, difficult to measure, but certainly starvation and malnutrition still kill millions each year and perhaps as much as a third of the world's population suffers physical and mental impairments as a result of totally inadequate diets.

Food is therefore the issue of first consideration whenever one thinks of population pressures and shrinking resources. Some experts would claim that there is no food problem as such, but rather a problem of

Members of a starving family at a street corner in Dacca, the capital of Bangladesh. The bulk of the country's population of well over eighty million people live under conditions of famine that are sapping the energies of this young nation. (United Nations/Philip Teuscher)

distribution and inadequate agricultural technology in the poorest and most densely populated countries. It is pointed out that world acreage could be doubled, but this suggestion fails to take into account that the potential farmlands are ecologically marginal and/or require heavy capital investment to make them productive. The soils of the Amazon basin, the steppelands of central Asia, and even the deserts of the Middle East could no doubt be made to yield crops— for a time. But agriculture in these and other regions is a chancy matter fraught with the perils of ecological ruin. Some indication of what might be in store is offered by recent events in the Sahel, the sub-Saharan savanna extending from Mauritania to Chad. Here, through overgrazing and the pressures of agriculture, coupled with several years of inadequate rainfall, it is estimated that more than 100,000 people died of starvation and disease between 1972 and 1974. Furthermore, the desert is steadily encroaching on Sahelian territories and it will take more than a few years of good rainfall to correct the damage. The United Nations Food and Agricultural Organization estimates that 250,000 acres of farmland in North Africa are lost to the Sahara each year, while the population has increased sixfold from the beginning of the century.

Is Saharan Africa an isolated case or a portent of things to come? Clearly, the region is especially prone to environmental degradation, as is true of arid lands elsewhere. But land is no longer the only part of the earth's surface where the uphill struggle for food is being waged. In recent years, the nations of the world have begun competing for the last unclaimed natural resource—the sea. Fish catches are dropping in all the great fishing grounds. Many countries have extended their offshore fishing rights to a 200-mile limit, while Britain and Iceland have engaged in periodic confrontations—the "cod wars," as the press refers to them—over North Sea fishing rights. The extensive food reserves that the United States held up to the early 1970s become periodically so depleted that inadequate emergency food supply is available for large-scale famine relief. What all this means is that famine on an immense scale, perhaps within a decade, is a very real possibility.

If we raise visions of global hunger, conflict over resources, and populations outstripping the means to maintain them, we do so because these are the problems that inevitably must be dealt with. We discard as totally unethical the suggestion made by several observers that to continue aid to the poorest and most populous countries simply compounds the problem of population/resource imbalance.[1] On the contrary, what

seems to be called for in the immediate future is programs designed to raise the standard of living of Third World peoples. There are good historical reasons to believe that the first order of priority should be programs designed to assure security in old age, adequate employment, and improved material expectations. The demographer Everett E. Lee makes the telling point that

. . . it can be demonstrated that in India or in almost any other underdeveloped country, the production of children declines as income and education increase. In Ghana the number of children produced by women with no education averages about 5.7, while those with secondary educations have 2.5—approximately the number needed to replace their generation. Ghanaian women with university degrees, however, average only .5 children each (Lee 1975:3–4).

Education and socioeconomic development are, of course, slow processes. Furthermore, as we have already noted, development in the form of industrialization can turn out to be a two-edged sword. It is perhaps valuable at this point to consider the situation in one country, China, where the priorities have been placed, not on industry, but rather on agriculture. Thirty years ago, China was in a chaotic condition of extreme poverty and social and economic disorganization. In this huge country of well over 800 million, a governmental policy of supporting agriculture, limiting migration to the cities, and controlled industrialization has been coupled with public health measures and incentives on birth limitations. Not only has the birthrate in China dropped drastically, but competent observers are agreed that standards of living have been

[1]The solution that has been proposed by some commentators from developed countries is to let the poorest nations fend for themselves—whatever the cost in death and misery. This has been variously termed a "lifeboat" approach (better to save some than swamp the only means of survival) or *triage*, a French word meaning "selection" used in World War I as a euphemism in combat zones when the number of wounded outstripped medical facilities: only the wounded with some chance of survival were given immediate attention; the doubtful cases were a lower priority.

raised, although life is certainly spartan by comparison with Western countries. Perhaps just as important is that China has in large measure eliminated material inequalities, and very few other countries have been able to do so. While the Chinese model may have only limited applicability to other non-Western countries, this should be balanced against the fact that the Chinese have reorganized their society with hardly any external aid.

Having reached this juncture in our discussion, what contributions can we offer toward an understanding of the future and the perils that it may bring? Our comments will center on areas that fall within the province of anthropology and the social sciences, although we are well aware that there is no anthropological solution, only an anthropological perspective. In the problems that lie ahead, there is ample room to draw on all the disciplines, all the competencies.

To begin with, there can be little doubt as to the desirability of a stable world system—stable in terms of conflict, of course, but also stable in terms of growth. The concept of societies in a steady state is not foreign to anthropologists, for many simple groups approach this condition. The idea, however, is quite alien to several centuries of Western thought that viewed societies as either progressing or declining. To the degree that stationary states were considered at all, the concept seemed applicable only to remote peoples beyond the mainstream of world affairs. The current interest in "no-growth economics"—a stationary state by another name—may be indicative of a shift on the part of some concerned scholars, but the implications of what such an equilibrium would entail have not yet been adequately faced.

Learning to live with "no-growth" will involve a major act of mental retooling, in fact, a major shift in values. At the intellectual level, there must come the realization that the process of expansion that has characterized human history since the first

Toward solving global problems

agricultural societies will very shortly terminate. But before we can accept this idea, a new ethic is mandatory. In part, this ethic will require that we view ourselves as an integral component of nature. We do not imply by this a romantic and impractical back-to-nature movement, but simply that our attitudes toward nature must be based on harmony rather than conquest.

In much the same way, we can no longer afford to think in narrow nationalistic and ideological terms, for if, indeed, only global strategies have a chance of confronting global problems, such solutions will require a global consciousness. As anthropologists, we are well aware that it is cooperation rather than competition that resolves problems within the framework of human societies. What has changed is that the unit of human cooperation will have to encompass the entire world. In practical terms, hunger in South Asia must be seen as just as significant to the American citizen as hunger in South Dakota, and conversely.

With respect to resources, people will have to resurrect an old ethic, the virtue of frugality. This should be much more than a personal value—it is not by setting the thermostat down by a few degrees that we will save the universe—and should involve policies of conservation designed to save scarce materials and assure that products are manufactured to give long and reliable service. Furthermore, we need to shift not only our spatial perspectives but also our temporal ones. We cannot take for granted the well-being of future generations. We must learn to think not only of ourselves and our children but their children and their children's children. The lack of consideration for the future, an attitude that each generation will somehow find its own solutions, is a clear invitation to disaster.

Finally, there is a consideration implicit in all that we have said. If sacrifices must be made, and it would seem that they can hardly be avoided, the burdens must be shared equitably. Cutting back on economic growth without at the same time instituting global programs of redistribution will obviously hurt the poor much more than it will the rich. Economic expansion has often been seen by poor people and nations as a means of betterment, the assumption being that while the rich become richer, the poor also benefit to some degree. As a long-run solution to improvements in the standard of living of the poor, the panacea of economic growth will have to be discarded. In its place, there will have to occur a more equitable distribution of the good things of life. It follows that the wealthy will have to contribute their fair share in the form of reduced affluence. There is no denying that this poses very difficult problems, especially in societies that have tended to measure prestige in terms of wealth. But prestige, even in our society, is measured in more than property, and there is a tradition of philanthropy and public consciousness that can be revitalized.

With respect to global relations and programs of aid, the strictest care should be taken that support for poor lands should not end up in the pockets of the local ruling classes but be utilized where it will count most—in direct aid to the people. It is also unrealistic, as well as unfair, to expect a relatively small number of industrial countries to carry the full burden of Third World aid. The rich lands now include a group of countries endowed with a relative abundance of resources, including the oil-producing nations, that are well able to contribute substantially to global welfare. The incomes they derive from the sale of raw materials should certainly be used to better the lot of their citizens, but they also share a responsibility to the world at large. Up to now, much of this new wealth has ended up in personal fortunes, grandiose schemes designed to enhance national prestige, and extensive arms purchases. In these countries, as in all others, military expenditures constitute the most wasteful use of labor, capital, and resources.

These are very general observations, but as we mentioned at the beginning of the chapter, the problems that face us will be resolved through policies that will implement options rather than by science or technology. Options depend, in the last analysis, on moral or ethical guidelines. We do not claim that anthropology holds the key to the solution of the world crisis, but we are convinced that the approach that we have outlined can benefit from the assistance of anthropologists. Their training and outlook emphasize a global perspective, and such a perspective is urgently needed. Also, anthropologists have had increasing professional experience in crisis situations, for much of anthropology records difficult transitions. None will be harder than the changes ahead.

ANTHROPOLOGY AND
CONTEMPORARY
AMERICAN SOCIETY

For a variety of reasons, some of which are easier to recognize than others, there still is a relative dearth of good anthropological information on contemporary American society. In part, no doubt, the disinclination of American anthropologists to address themselves to the issues and problems of their own society has been related to their traditional interest in exotic ways of life. Anthropologists examine the ordinary—the customary—in distant settings, and such distance permits an illusion of objectivity that is much harder to maintain when the society being interpreted is the anthropologist's own. After all, the anthropologist goes to the field and then returns home, but the student of his or her own society can never really "leave."

Traditional ethnographic interpretation is based on highly personal experiences and intense involvement with a restricted number of individuals in small-scale societies. The result is a series of what might be termed "cultural cameos": sharp depictions of events and situations within such fixed boundaries as the village, the lineage, or the tribe. One of the theoretical and methodological problems that face anthropologists working in their own society (or complex societies in general) is moving from such cultural portrayals of small groups to models applicable to the nation or, for that matter, the globe. A series of microscopic analyses cannot do justice to the intricacies and complexities of a world in which all small-scale units are becoming increasingly interdependent.

In an elite American community, the anthropologist lacks the built-in advantages enjoyed by the student of subordinated groups. Furthermore, the anthropologist studying any sector of contemporary American society must cope with the problem of dealing with individuals and institutions that have actual or potential power over him or her. Such situations can be most uncomfortable, if for no other reason than that the researcher may be faced with the dilemma of having to side with either the power structure or those who lack power, a quandary that is seldom as sharp in standard ethnographic situations. Such constraints have acted both to export anthropological

research and to limit home research to the studies of minorities, ethnic groups, and the poor in general. There are hundreds of monographs and articles on Native Americans, but remarkably little effort has been expended in studying the Bureau of Indian Affairs. We have fine accounts of the manipulations of Melanesian big-men but few studies of American corporations, excellent studies of tribal lineage systems but no ethnographies of the Rockefellers or DuPonts. Research in our own society, then, is not only different in degree but different in kind from research conducted among distant or isolated groups. In short, it is a situation that does not permit the luxury of intellectual sanctuary that comes so easily when other societies are the objects of study.

NATIONAL TRENDS, WORLD TRENDS

Not all anthropologists would agree with us on why so few members of the profession have addressed themselves to the study of their own societies. Furthermore, some

The study of the world's peoples has been largely the province of Western anthropologists, American in particular. Valuable new insights will be gained when foreign scholars subject Western culture to anthropological scrutiny. (Jim Scherer)

anthropologists would note, correctly, that there is now an increasing emphasis on such subjects as the anthropology of occupations and the role of women in contemporary institutions. We are aware of these trends and their manifestation in the establishment of specialized journals and the publication of a growing number of monographs on present-day complex societies. Still, these efforts represent but a small fraction of anthropological output, although they may well indicate one of the directions that the discipline will take in the years to come.

Explaining why a profession emphasizes a given range of phenomena and plays down other spheres of possible research is always difficult. It is also notoriously hard to predict the direction that a profession will take in the future. We are on much more solid ground when we turn our attention to actual societal problems and the shape these problems are likely to take in the years ahead. Many of the global problems that we have examined in some detail have special significance for the United States. Obviously, this is the case with resources and their allocation, with factors endangering the environment, and to some degree with population growth. In many instances, however, we can assume with a degree of security that these problems are unlikely to have the same impact on all sectors and groups within the population.

It goes without saying that wealth and position can act to buffer individuals and groups against a general deterioration in the quality of life. For example, those who are most seriously affected by pollution and environmental degradation tend to be the poor and the minorities, especially in the large metropolitan centers, although the problem has its rural variants. As the inner cities become less desirable places to live, those who have the means to do so generally migrate to suburbia or exurbia, leaving behind an urban population made up of a disproportionate number of poor people. The process takes the form of a vicious cycle: deterioration of living conditions in the city

The urban crises

spurs the migration of middle- and upper-class urbanites, and as the urban tax base shrinks, conditions further deteriorate and the movement is accelerated.

It would be wrong, however, to see this as a city problem, for while the problem may be centered in the cities, its causes are national. The fiscal problems of New York, perhaps the urban locality under greatest stress, are an outgrowth of national policies in housing, development, and welfare that place an unfair burden on certain states and municipalities. Hence, what is happening to our cities should not be thought of as some kind of natural process over which society has no control. The fundamental question is not why those who are able to do so leave the city, but rather why the political and social priorities of our times are so ordered as to permit urban breakdown. If current trends follow their course, American cities of tomorrow will be black, Hispanic, and poor white centers surrounded by rings of much more affluent middle-class people—in short, huge ghettos of the poor.

The plight of the cities reflects, at one level, some very general trends in American society, trends toward separation, polarity, and loss of social cohesion. Strains in American society can be documented in politics, group relations, and value orientations. In the political sphere, there are clear indications of a new morality—or lack of morality—in the political process, an ethos that the end justifies the means and that government is not accountable to the people. At the same time, there is a distressing degree of distrust between old and established allies. As a case in point, Jews and blacks have worked together for social justice for many generations and, while it was true that not all Jews were involved in civil rights activities and earlier social and political action, there is no question that a high proportion of them were so involved. Recent years, however, have witnessed a dismaying erosion of the mutual good will that characterized relations between these two groups. This erosion has its origins in a number of developments, including the deterioration of city neighborhoods, traditional fears of anti-Semitism among Jews, and feelings of abandonment among blacks. Other alliances have also suffered, including links between the academic community and liberal political groupings.

For an anthropologist examining the condition of American society, a feature that causes considerable disquiet is the emergence—once again—of theories that purport to examine the biological determinants of human behavior and, by extension, the underpinnings of human society. In the course of the last few years, the concept of sexual equality has been under fire from those who subscribe to the notion that anatomy is destiny. Our reading of the evidence is that sexism has as little claim to scientific legitimacy as racism, that its causes are not unlike those that give support to racial discrimination, and that the problem is in essence cultural and social and not biological. Biology thus becomes a convenient cloak for prejudice.

There is certainly nothing novel about sexism, for it is an ancient prejudice that has survived centuries of Western political and social liberalization. Abigail (Smith) Adams's request to her husband, John Adams, that the patriots of the American Revolution should not "forget the ladies" was roundly rejected; then as later, democracy was viewed as the privilege of males—white males, needless to say. What is disturbing is that after years of legal and political struggle, a very real antifeminist backlash is taking place. As with all complex social phenomena, the causes are multiple, but it surely is not by chance that women (and other highly vulnerable components of the population) are under pressure at a time of economic troubles. When resources and jobs shrink, competition and potential competition from women workers is difficult for those whose own job security is in danger to tolerate; hence, the efforts to re-establish the "correct" role of women as lying primarily in a domestic sphere.

The main focus of the new literature on

Persistence of sexism

sex-based inequality is on animal, and particularly primate, behavior. The titles themselves, for instance, Desmond Morris's *The Naked Ape* (1967), Robert Ardrey's *The Territorial Imperative* (1966), and Lionel Tiger's *Men in Groups* (1969), give more than a clue to content and orientation. We are led to believe that human culture is little more than a refinement of biologically determined drives and biologically structured relationships. Tiger, for example, insists that social organization is everywhere anchored on the phenomenon of "male bonding," defined as "a particular relationship between two or more males such that they react differently to members of their bonding unit as compared to individuals outside of it" (Tiger 1969:19–20). In these arrangements, females are not interchangeable for males, and in fact may endanger the integrity of the male group. The weakness of Tiger's thesis lies not in his claim that many social structures are dominated by males—which is true, although not universal—but that on very dubious evidence, the phenomenon is perceived as biologically based rather than culturally determined. It certainly does not satisfy the cultural anthropologist to be told that "a human male bonding propensity may have been a hominid inheritance from the primates" (Tiger 1969:35), for it does not follow that humans are destined to behave like their primate cousins or their distant fossil ancestors, assuming that it is possible to know with some certainty how our distant ancestors behaved.

That such a theory offers a rationalization for male control and female subjugation should come as no surprise. We are informed that

it is men who dominate the public and private State Councils of the world; men are the Ambassadors, the Linguists (in west Africa); there are few "Spokeswomen". . . . females may simply not release "followership" behaviour. The "look" of them may be wrong for encounters of high state and gravity (Tiger 1969:57).

The theme is repeated in other books of the same genre. Rhetorically, Ardrey asks the reader, "How many men have you known of, in your lifetime, who died for their country?" (1966:6). For Ardrey it is "territoriality" that structures social life, territoriality as the aggressive defense of a group's spatial domain, but again it is men who are the movers and doers. Phrased differently, man is a killer animal, woman the killer's mate. This aggressive image is buttressed with reference to *Homo sapiens*'s long history of hunting, but to equate hunting with aggression is, to say the least, naive.

Even a cursory examination of the ethnographic literature is sufficient to expose the fallacy that simple hunting and gathering societies are structured on the basis of dominance and aggression. If one were to generalize, the weight of evidence would in fact be in the other direction. It is understandable that in small face-to-face groups, where survival depends on a high order of cooperative behavior, no individual would relish the task of passing judgment or administering summary justice; hence the maintenance of internal order is very much a cooperative consensual process. These are also societies that lack the size and the specialized organization for war. The Tasadays of Mindanao, perhaps the simplest of living humans in terms of social organization, have been described as gentle and affectionate;[2] the Bushmen of the Kalahari desert are equally peaceful—a well-known study of Bushman society by Elizabeth Marshall Thomas is

Is violence human destiny?

titled *The Harmless People* (1959); and, finally, a similar lack of aggression is recorded for the Pygmies of the Congo forest. We do not make the exaggerated claim that all simple societies put a premium on gentleness, cooperation, hospitality, and kindness. Instead, we wish to indicate that many groups on the threshold of subsistence place a positive value on a peaceful existence. The hunter of animals should not be mistaken for the hunter of men, nor is it correct to view simple human social organization as life in the "pack," with power and dominance devolving on the strongest and most ruthless.

As against the claim that humans are subject to inborn instinctive forces, the anthropologist feels justified in operating on the assumption that all adult human behavior is thoroughly controlled by custom. This assumption does not deny that some of our habits are annoyingly deep-seated, unfortunately the less desirable ones in particular. Nor does it obviate the fact that humans engage in personal acts of violence and, on behalf of their national collectivities, in bloody and protracted wars. But what the assumption allows, and indeed invites, is the search for the cultural sources of human aggressive behavior, be they in the frustrations induced in one group by another, in the teaching of the doctrine of manifest destiny to a society's youth, or elsewhere. Thus the anthropologist's point of departure not only reflects more adequately what knowledge we possess of human behavior but—and herein lies a substantive difference in approach—it keeps paths open to inquiry, the results of which may yet help to alleviate human aggressiveness.

We have looked into the question of the re-emergence of sexism in scientific guise with reference to a particular body of data—the literature on the purported biological/psychological distinctions between the sexes. That we examine this literature is due to the fact that it falls squarely into the domain of anthropological concern. However, it is only part of a much more general-

[2]Some anthropologists are of the opinion that the Tasadays may represent a deculturated group, one that found refuge in the forests of the interior several decades ago when pressure of the other peoples on them became unbearable. According to this view, the simplicity of their culture is the result of the marginal nature of the new habitat compared to their former socioeconomic mode. However, if such were the case, one would still have to account for the fact that the Tasadays are completely oblivious to the advantages of even the most rudimentary horticultural practices, to which they would have no doubt been exposed in the earlier environment.

ized phenomenon whose manifestations may be found not only in the works cited, but in such endeavors as lobbying against the Equal Rights Amendment and stressing traditional roles for women, such as in the so-called Total Woman movement, which instructs women in the satisfactions to be gained from manipulating males along traditional lines. That women themselves form part of such lobbies and movements is only to be expected since power systems always have the capacity to use some of the oppressed in the tasks of their own oppression.

ANTHROPOLOGISTS
AND ETHICS

Within their own discipline, anthropologists have become increasingly concerned about the roles of the field worker and researcher and the implications of anthropological research. This whole subject area, dealing with explicit and implicit responsibilities and the recognition that the anthropologist is much more than a disinterested observer, is fundamentally a problem of professional ethics. Ethics touches us all, every profession, every person whose activities carry the potential of doing harm to others, and none more so than anthropologists, whose professional life is intricately linked to other individuals, other cultures. Furthermore, anthropologists are often educators and, as such, bear heavy responsibilities to those whom they train. We shall examine some of the major ethical questions with reference to both specific research and general concern as evidenced in the deliberations of anthropologists in their own professional bodies.

In 1972, under the inconspicuous title *The Mountain People*, Colin M. Turnbull published a profoundly disturbing ethnography. His book is a description of the decaying culture of a small African tribe along the northeastern border of Uganda, the Ik, who in the course of a few generations have changed from a group of prosperous hunters to scattered bands of hostile and degraded people. Their only goal, according to the author, is individual survival, at the expense of even the closest kin. Turnbull's account of the Ik was exceptionally well received: "A beautiful and terrifying book of a people who have become monstrous almost beyond belief" (Margaret Mead), "A remarkable book, I recommend it to all who are concerned with human suffering" (Sir Julian Huxley), were two of many comments of praise.

But then came a diametrically opposite view of the work. Writing in *Current Anthropology*, a journal of worldwide circulation, Fredrik Barth of Norway took Turnbull to task for being guilty of, among other things, "poor anthropology" and producing a book that is "emotionally either dishonest or superficial. . . . deeply misleading. . . . [and] grossly irresponsible and harmful to its unwitting objects of study" (Barth 1974:100). The most stinging accusation made by Barth raised the issue of a serious breach of professional anthropological ethics:

So, when [Turnbull was] asked for advice by the Uganda government on relocation of the Ik as a measure against their recurrent famines, this . . . "Friend of the Ik," has his moment of revenge and solemnly develops a final solution, a plan for systematic culturcide [destruction of culture] (Barth 1974:102).

We do not propose to try the case here; fairness would dictate a most careful presentation of evidence (much of the text of Turnbull's book), of Barth's accusations, and of the author's replies.[3] Instead, we turn to the complex issue of ethics in a more general sense as we examine how the recent critical self-examination of the anthropological profession may influence the nature of future field research.

From a changed and still changing global

[3]The encounter between Barth and Turnbull was subsequently joined by several other anthropologists in a later issue of *Current Anthropology* (Wilson and others 1975).

perspective and with the inevitable advantage of hindsight, the attitudes of earlier anthropologists toward the peoples whom they were studying are far from unassailable. While it is true that for a century the intellectual motivation of anthropologists has been to learn about and better understand the remarkable variety in humankind and human culture, the relations between anthropologists and those who were the subject of their study have been grossly asymmetrical. For the most part, the anthropologists were the products and representatives of those Euro-American societies that up until World War I were bent on extending their power over many hundreds of human populations on every continent. It was inevitable, then, that anthropologists, some consciously and others unwittingly, would become instrumental in furthering or maintaining the cultural and politicoeconomic imperialism that marked the relationship between much of the Western world and the pre-industrial societies. For example, the British colonial policy of indirect rule, with its commitment to the use of lower-level native administrators and its acceptance of institutions of local culture for the sake of peaceful and efficient control, drew heavily on the skills of anthropologists. Their reports and advice, especially with respect to sub-Saharan Africa, significantly contributed to the relatively smooth-running machinery of Britain's overseas possessions. American anthropologists, whose work was not done in the colonial context that many of their European colleagues worked in, concentrated largely on the study of Native American cultures trampled on by the rapidly expanding society of their own continent. By adopting the approach of cultural relativism—the doctrine that different societies must be judged on their own terms and that invidious comparisons between cultures are unacceptable—American anthropologists of the first half of the twentieth century did much to eradicate the paternalism that strongly permeated the attitudes of their predeces-

sors toward the so-called primitives. Yet this value-free, neutral stance harbored its own serious failing, for it neglected or did much to obscure the aggressive nature and destructive impact of the Western world on societies not materially equipped to hold their own.

Anthropology in the context of national policies

In the context of our present discussion, the question of where the paramount responsibility of anthropologists lies first began to be posed during World War II. The answer at the time was unequivocal: American anthropologists' first loyalty was to their country, engaged in a just war with an implacable enemy. Soon after the entry of the United States into hostilities, it became evident that anthropologists could contribute much useful information and advice on areas of probable combat operations, especially in the Pacific. Among the organizations aiding the war effort was the Cross-Cultural Survey at Yale University, charged with the preparation of practical handbooks for military government officers in places within the theater of war such as the Marshalls, Carolines, Marianas, Ryukyu, and other islands. Another direct consequence of the war was the concentration on national character studies, as we have already seen in our discussion of the individual in society.

But although the issue of loyalty and professional responsibility seemed transparent during World War II, it rapidly became clouded as a result of the postwar reshaping of the world. Emerging politically and economically as the most powerful country, the United States assumed many far-flung commitments on several continents, particularly in Asia, and our government began to expend sizable amounts of money for social science research in areas particularly susceptible to potential communist influence.

Two projects, both sponsored by the military, became especially notorious. One, known as Project Camelot, came to light in 1965, in an advanced stage of planning. It was designed to investigate, at the cost of about $6 million, the factors promoting social unrest in Chile and other countries and to estimate the political and military potential of counterinsurgency measures. The second, a direct by-product of the tragic military involvement in Southeast Asia, concerned the work of a group of anthropologists in Thailand and also involved research on counterinsurgency. The cumulative effect of these and similar affairs rocked the profession and brought about a period of ethical self-evaluation that dominated several annual meetings of the American Anthropological Association during the early 1970s.

Far from being a tempest in a teapot, the controversy over political and ethical issues touched on a fundamental aspect of the work of anthropologists. More than any other scholarly activity, anthropological research has always been closely identified with the less developed Third World countries and the peoples who inhabit them. To the extent that governments sponsor and make increasing use of the data resulting from anthropological field work, anthropologists have come face to face with the vexing problem of the human consequences of their work and the priorities of their professional obligation. Is there such an enterprise as neutral science? What if the interests of a sponsor—a foundation, government, or whatever—run counter to the socioeconomic or cultural aspirations of a community or a minority group? Is it the proper role of the anthropologist to become an advocate for peoples who are powerless against the forces that dominate them? Is it the duty of the anthropologist not only to describe but also to profess? Or, as a group of activist anthropologists hold, should all field research be so oriented that it assists non-Western peoples to oppose imperialism?

Since anthropologists tend to be highly individualistic, it would be too much to expect agreement from them on questions that cut so deep. It seems, however, that in their majority, they will be guided for some time

Professional ethics: priorities for the future

to come by the "Principles of Professional Responsibility," adopted by the Council of the American Anthropological Association in May 1971. According to this document:

In research, an anthropologist's paramount responsibility is to those he studies. When there is a conflict of interest, these individuals must come first. The anthropologist must do everything within his power to protect their physical, social and psychological welfare and to honor their dignity and privacy (1973:1).

Significantly, in the priorities of responsibility, responsibility to the public comes next, then to the discipline, students, and sponsors, and last of all to one's own government and to host governments. The statement further insists that "no reports should be provided to sponsors that are not also available to the general public and, where practicable, to the population studied" (1973:1).

The nature of complex industrial societies, both Western and communist, is such that the disparities between the world that the anthropologists represent and those whom they study will not be bridged for a long time. As a result, the asymmetrical relationship that we have discussed earlier will, in all likelihood, continue as a feature of the ethnographic and general research picture for some time in the future. Yet, with all due consideration and sensitivity to the issues at stake, we are wary of a solution that a minority of our colleagues defend—that anthropology become a weapon of political radicalism. All ideologies are self-serving in the sense that reality is pressed into preconceived "truths." We strongly believe that the anthropologists' first obligation is to those who accept them in their midst, and that this duty is indivisible. Human concerns must command the first loyalty of anthropologists as they are called upon to act as advocates for a wide variety of cultures and societies. Least of all do we wish to think of those who make it possible for us to practice our profession as pawns on a political chessboard on which dogmatic ideologues, from whatever quarter, make their moves.

This chapter has been devoted more to problems than to solutions, more to questions than to answers. It should not be thought that the future will come as a surprise; for at least some of the writing is on the wall. We see the primary tasks and potential contributions of anthropologists as raising awareness and offering guidelines on the reasonable assumption that informed people have it in their capacity to influence the shape of things to come, in the United States and elsewhere.

REFERENCES

AMERICAN ANTHROPOLOGICAL ASSOCIATION
1973 *Professional ethics; statements and procedures of the American Anthropological Association.* Washington, D.C.

ARDREY, ROBERT
1966 *The territorial imperative; a personal inquiry into the animal origins of property and nations.* New York: Atheneum.

BARTH, FREDRIK
1974 On responsibility and humanity: calling a colleague to account. *Current Anthropology* 15:99–103.

BROWN, LESTER
1973 Rich countries and poor in a finite, interdependent world. *Daedalus; journal of the American Academy of Arts and Sciences*, vol. 102, no. 4, Fall 1973: The no-growth society. Cambridge, Mass. Pp. 153–164.

FRANK, ANDRE GUNDER
1969 *Capitalism and underdevelopment in Latin America; historical studies of Chile and Brazil* (rev. and enl. ed.). New York: Monthly Review Press.

INTERNATIONAL MONETARY FUND
1974 *Annual report of the executive directors for the fiscal year ended April 30, 1974.* Washington, D.C.

LEE, EVERETT S.
1975 Population and scarcity of food. *The Annals of The American Academy of Political and Social Science*, vol. 420, July 1975: Adjusting to scarcity. Philadelphia. Pp. 1–10.

LURIA, SALVADOR E.
1974 What can biologists solve? *The New York Review of Books* 21:1:27–28.

MALTHUS, THOMAS ROBERT
1798 *An essay on the principle of population, as it affects the future improvement of society.* London: J. Johnson.

MESAROVIC, MIHAJLO, AND EDUARD PESTEL
1974 *Mankind at the turning point: the second report to the Club of Rome.* New York: E. P. Dutton.

MORRIS, DESMOND
1967 *The naked ape; a zoologist's study of the human animal.* New York: McGraw-Hill.

THOMAS, ELIZABETH MARSHALL
1959 *The harmless people.* New York: Alfred A. Knopf.

TIGER, LIONEL
1969 *Men in groups.* New York: Random House.

TINKER, JON
1975 World Population Year. In *Britannica Book of the Year 1975*. Chicago: Encyclopaedia Britannica. Pp. 556–557 (Special Report).

TURNBULL, COLIN M.
1972 *The mountain people.* New York: Simon and Schuster.

WILSON, PETER J., AND OTHERS
1975 More thoughts on the Ik and anthropology. *Current Anthropology* 16:343–358.

WORLD BANK
1974 *Annual report 1974.* Washington, D.C.

CONCLUSIONS

The world in which humans live today has become so interdependent that it is no longer reasonable to consider its basic problems in terms narrowly defined by social, environmental, or economic concerns. Nor is there any hope that long-range solutions to such problems can be effectively undertaken on a local or regional scale. Instead, there is urgent need to transcend the limitations of the traditional model of the world and to engender a new comprehension of the global human condition, one in which respect for cultural diversity is balanced by a complementary view of the oneness of all humankind. A peaceful world in which people everywhere are accorded an opportunity for a productive life free from hunger and the scourge of eradicable disease has at last become an attainable material objective. But progress is likely to be hampered by deep-seated prejudices and narrow self-interest, which both individuals and national collectivities find difficult to overcome. A better understanding of the cultural basis of human nature, of humanity's time-tested capacity for adaptation, and of the increasingly fragile relationship between people and the environment in which they live would be at least a promising beginning. In these endeavors, anthropology has a significant role to play.

GLOSSARY

absolute chronology Determination of the actual age of a site or its contents.

acculturation Cultural borrowing or cultural change, usually as a result of the impact of one society upon another.

Acheulean Toolmaking cultural tradition of the Lower Paleolithic associated with *Homo erectus* and most prominently exemplified by hand axes and cleavers.

affinal Pertaining to a relationship based on marriage.

age-grade An institutionalized cultural category of persons based on sex and chronological age.

allomorph One of several variants of a morpheme.

allophone One of several variants of a phoneme.

ambilineal descent Descent that traces membership in a group through both males and females, but not equally and simultaneously.

animism The extension of the concept of the soul to nonhuman organisms and inanimate objects.

anthropology The study of cultural and biological variations in human groups, past and contemporary.

arbitrariness The absence of any intrinsic relationship between a word and the idea that the word symbolizes.

archaeology The study of past cultures through the analysis of their material remains.

Archaic An early developmental stage in the cultural evolution of New World peoples characterized by, among other things, the polishing and grinding of stone tools.

aspiration An *h*-like puff of breath that may follow certain consonants, as in the English *p* in *pit*.

australopithecine A member of, or pertaining to, an extinct genus of early hominids.

avoidance behavior Prohibited or severely restricted social interaction between certain relatives, usually in-laws.

avunculocal residence Residence with or near the groom's maternal uncle's family.

band A loosely organized aggregate of hunter-gatherers, larger than the basic family group, sharing in the performance of economic, social, and ritual activities.

base In generative grammar, a set of basic rules applicable to a language, together with the word stock of the language.

basic core vocabulary In glottochronology, words for concepts likely to be present in any language.

baton technique Percussion flaking by means of a cudgel of wood or bone.

behaviorist approach In the theory of socialization, the view that behavior is explainable as a response to a stimulus.

berdache Among American Indians, a man whose aversion to fulfilling the expected male role causes him to assume female dress and habits.

biface A stone tool prepared by trimming a core on both sides.

bilateral descent Descent reckoned evenly along both the male and the female lines at each generation.

bilocal residence Residence with or near either the groom's or the bride's parents.

biological anthropology The study of human origins and the subsequent development of the human species.

blade An elongated sharp-edged flake struck from a core.

bowwow theory A theory basing the origin of language on the imitation of natural sounds.

bride price (bride wealth) A payment of money or goods to the bride's family by the prospective husband and/or his kin.

broadcast transmission Propagation of sound in all directions.

burin A stone blade with a chisellike point.

carbon-14 dating A method of absolute dating of organic remains by means of the radioactive isotope carbon 14.

cargo cult The mystical view held by many Pacific islanders that material wealth, destined for native populations but illegitimately kept from them by the whites, will at last reach them and usher in a period of prosperity.

caste An endogamous social group whose membership is hereditary.

channel The physical medium by means of which communication is effected.

clan A cluster of lineages claiming a common distant ancestry.

Classic A developmental stage in the civilization of Mesoamerica and Peru characterized by monumental architecture, elaborate art, and the establishment of empires.

classical archaeology The study of ancient urban civilizations of the Old World.

code A system of signals agreed upon by those engaged in communication.

cognatic descent Descent traced through both males and females.

collateral Pertaining to a relationship in which descent is not reckoned in a direct line.

compadrazgo In Spanish-speaking countries, the institution of godparenthood.

comparative method Controlled comparison used by anthropologists in the study of sociocultural systems; comparisons made among languages that have developed from a common origin.

compartmentalization The tendency for indigenous institutions to persist side by side with institutions of foreign derivation.

competence Knowledge of the rules of a language possessed by a native speaker.

componential analysis The study of the structure of a cultural domain by means of its distinctive features.

conical clan A number of lineages organized as a common-descent group on the basis of genealogical seniority.

consanguineal Related by blood.

core tool A tool produced by striking flakes from a stone until the original lump approximates the desired shape and size.

cousin marriage Marriage between two (first) cousins.

creole A language, derived from a pidgin, that has assumed the full range of functions for its speakers.

cross-cousin Child of ego's father's sister or mother's brother.

cross-cousin marriage Marriage between two cross-cousins.

cross dating The comparison of traits between several sites in order to establish their chronology.

cultural anthropology The study of cultural variation in human societies.

cultural crystallization The process of modification that a colonial culture undergoes once it has become established.

culture Patterns of behavior that are learned and shared by a group, as well as the results of such behavior.

culture area An area within which societies share the same dominant cultural orientation.

culture history The description of societies known from the archaeological record and/or documentary evidence.

culture type A concept stressing structural similarities common to a number of distinct cultures.

decoder The hearer or addressee of a message.

deep structure A level of syntactic analysis that reveals the logical relationships among the individual elements of a sentence.

demographic transition The change in Western population dynamics that has occurred in the course of the past two centuries and that appears to be functionally linked to the industrial revolution.

dendrochronology A technique of absolute dating of wood remains by making use of the growth rings of trees.

descriptive approach   In linguistics, the analysis of the structure of a language in terms of minimal units and their combinations.

developmental stage   A stage of evolution based on archaeological and sociocultural evidence from a large variety of archaeological sites.

deviance   Behavior that the majority of a society's members consider outside the range of what is "normal."

diglossia   The coexistence of two markedly different varieties of a language, one formal and the other colloquial.

dingdong theory   A theory basing the origin of language on a natural correspondence between certain objects and the vocal noises they evoked in early humans.

dip   In glottochronology, a degree of lexical relationship amounting to the absolute time depth in thousands of years times 14.

discreteness   A feature of language design whereby utterances are encoded or decoded in terms of separate, individually distinct segments of sound.

displacement   The ability of human languages to refer to ideas remote in both time and space.

double descent   Descent that is traced through the male line for certain purposes and through the female line for others.

dowry   The transfer of money, goods, or estate from the bride's family to the groom or his family.

drive   An innate urge to relieve conditions of biophysical deprivation or discomfort, for example, hunger or thirst.

dyad   A basic linkage, within a kinship group, involving a pair of individuals.

ego   An individual within a kinship system to whom various other persons are shown to be related.

emic   Pertaining to what members of a society perceive as significant and valid.

encoder   One who converts a message into a code; the originator of a message.

encomienda   In Spanish-colonized areas, a form of exploitation analogous to the feudal system of peasant servitude.

enculturation   The process by which a young individual learns the traditional contents of a culture and assimilates the bulk of its values and practices.

endogamy   A practice requiring persons to marry within the group to which they belong.

ethnocentrism   The common assumption of members of any society that their beliefs and patterns of behavior are natural and sensible, those of other societies less worthy or "strange."

ethnographic present   A hypothetical time frame used in describing a culture, usually couched in the present but referring to an earlier time for which reliable information is available.

ethnography   Descriptive study of a culture.

ethnography of speaking   Descriptive study of the features that characterize the use of speech in a society.

ethnology   Comparative and analytical study of cultures.

etic   Pertaining to cultural categories as perceived or employed by an outside observer, usually those categories possessing cross-cultural validity.

exogamy   A practice forbidding marriage between individuals from within the same local, kin, or status group.

extended family   A composite family consisting of two or more nuclear families related to each other.

family of orientation   Family into which ego is born and in which ego is considered a child.

family of procreation   Family in which ego is a parent.

feedback   A design feature of human languages based on the capacity of speakers to monitor their own speech.

fictive kinship   A binding relationship between individuals similar to that of close kin but not based on the bond of birth, marriage, or descent.

folk art   Artistic products and performances of members of complex societies who live away from urban centers, especially peasants.

Formative   A developmental stage in the civilizations of Mesoamerica and Peru characterized by settled village life, integrated agricultural economy, and a complex ceremonialism.

fraternal joint family   A composite family consisting of the nuclear families of two or more brothers.

Freudian theory of personality development   The assumption that character guidelines are established by an early age and that the adult personality is highly influenced by childhood experiences.

functional variety   The existence, in spoken languages, of differing styles from among which speakers choose according to the situation.

generative approach   A method of linguistic analysis striving to account by means of formal rules for all potential utterances in a given language.

genetic relationship   In linguistics, a relationship among languages based on common origin.

ghost dance A nativistic movement among western North American Indians during the last decades of the nineteenth century having as its goal the return of the dead and the restoration of the old ways of life.

glottochronology A method of dating change among related languages by comparing their basic core vocabularies for similarities and divergencies.

hominid Pertaining to modern humans and their direct fossil ancestors.

hominoid Pertaining to a subdivision of the primates comprising both contemporary and extinct humans and apes.

Homo erectus An early, now extinct, species of humans.

Homo habilis An extinct hominid, possibly an advanced australopithecine form.

Homo sapiens neanderthalensis An extinct variety of modern humans.

Homo sapiens sapiens The variety of modern humans to which all contemporary populations belong.

household A basic residential unit, typically made up of persons who live under the same roof and are related.

iconic Pertaining to a sign which bears a formal resemblance to its referent.

ideogram A pictorial representation that refers to a thing or idea associated with the object represented.

immediate constituent Any one of several constituent parts obtained by the successive analysis of a linguistic construction, such as a sentence.

incest taboo The regulation proscribing sexual relations between culture-specific categories of kin.

infanticide The culturally sanctioned practice of killing a newborn child.

institutional group In complex societies, a group of people recruited on the basis of conscious membership and common aims, as for example members of a bowling club or a fraternal organization.

joking relationship An institutionalized form of behavior, particularly among in-laws, characterized by familiarities.

kibbutz A form of agricultural village in Israel characterized by collective ownership and management of resources and communal organization.

kindred A group of bilateral relatives.

kinesics The study of how certain nonlinguistic body motions are used in communication.

kula ring A trading partnership involving ceremonial items exchanged among the islanders north and east of New Guinea.

language family All those languages that can be shown to be genetically related, that is, possessing the same common origin.

Levalloisian technique In stone toolmaking, a method of striking flakes off a stone core.

lexicostatistics A method of dating change among related languages on the basis of statistical comparison of their vocabularies.

lineage A unilineal group of kin who trace their descent from a known common ancestor.

lineal Pertaining to relatives descended in a direct line.

linguistic anthropology The study of human language in both its biological and social contexts.

Lithic The earliest developmental stage in the cultural evolution of the New World, characterized by chipped-stone technology.

loanword A word borrowed from another language.

logogram A sign representing a word.

magic A technique designed to achieve specific goals by manipulating the supernatural.

mana An impersonal supernatural force concentrated in persons or inanimate objects.

marriage Typically, an institutionalized relationship between a man and a woman that a society recognizes as appropriate for the nurturing of offspring; in a more general sense, a close relationship between a man and a woman that is recognized as appropriate for certain purposes by the society of which at least one of the parties is a member.

matrilineage A lineage in which descent is traced through the mother.

matrilocal residence Residence with or near the bride's mother and her husband.

merging A practice in which both lineal and collateral relatives are terminologically lumped together.

Mesolithic The Middle Stone Age.

mestizo In Latin American countries, an individual of mixed American Indian and European—especially Spanish or Portuguese—ancestry.

microlith A small geometric flint flake tool characteristic of the Mesolithic.

monogamy Form of marriage in which an individual has a single spouse at any given time.

morpheme The smallest meaningful unit of speech.

morphemic analysis The determination of the smallest meaningful units of a language and their mutual relationships.

Mousterian A tradition associated with the Neanderthals and characterized by the use of specialized tools fashioned from flakes detached from cores.

multilevel patterning Organization of human language in terms of several levels or subsystems.

nation-state A form of complex political organization under which power and cultural dominance is biased in favor of a given ethnic/national entity, often at the expense of minority cultural elements.

national character study A psychocultural characterization of a whole culture or nation.

Neolithic The New Stone Age.

neolocal residence Residence independent of parents of either spouse.

network analysis The study of the social relationships of individuals, their nature, linkages, and overlap.

nuclear family A family group consisting of a father and mother and their children.

oath A formal declaration calling upon the supernatural to witness to the truth or sincerity of what is to be said.

ordeal A means of determining guilt or innocence by submitting the accused to a dangerous trial or test.

Paleolithic The Old Stone Age.

paralinguistic feature Any one of several optional vocal effects, such as a whisper, that communicate additional meaning.

parallel cousin Child of ego's father's brother or mother's sister.

patrilineage A lineage in which descent is traced through the father.

patrilocality Residence with or near the groom's father and his wife.

percussion flaking The technique of shaping stone tools by using a stone to strike a flake from a core.

performance In linguistic anthropology, the manner in which speakers use the knowledge of a language in concrete situations.

phoneme One of a set of distinctive sounds characteristic of a particular language.

phonemic analysis The study of a language with the aim of determining its distinctive sounds.

phonemic transcription A record of a speech sample written down in terms of the phonemes of the language.

phonetic alphabet A set of symbols used to transcribe speech sounds.

phonogram A sign used to represent a sound or a group of sounds in a language.

phonological component The component of generative grammar that assigns a phonetic representation to the surface structure of a sentence.

pidgin A form of speech acquired in addition to a mother tongue and used as an auxiliary means of communication between groups of differing linguistic backgrounds.

pitch In some languages, distinctive highness or lowness of tone associated with vowels and occasionally with certain consonants.

Pleistocene A recent geological epoch characterized by a succession of glaciations.

political economy The economic aspect of social organization.

polyandry The marriage of a woman to two or more husbands at one time.

polygamy The practice of having two or more spouses at one time.

polygyny The practice of having more than one wife at one time.

pooh-pooh theory A theory of the origin of language according to which the first human words were interjections signifying pain or other strong sensation.

popular art Art characteristic of the urbanized sector of complex societies.

Postclassic The last developmental stage in the civilizations of Mesoamerica and Peru, characterized by the emergence of large-scale, militaristic states.

potassium-argon dating A method of absolute dating by which the age of rocks is determined by measuring the decay of potassium 40 into argon.

potlatch Among the Indians of the Northwest Coast, a ceremonial feast featuring a display of wealth, ostentatious destruction of personal property, and lavish gift giving.

prehistoric archaeology The study of past cultures through the analysis of the material remains of preliterate peoples.

prescriptive grammar A grammar concerned with laying down rules for correct language use.

pressure flaking The technique of forcing off flakes from a stone by applying pressure.

primitive art Artistic activity and output of small-scale nonliterate and usually nonpeasant societies.

productivity The capacity to generate unprecedented utterances, a design feature that all human languages possess.

ramapithecine A member of, or pertaining to, an extinct genus of the earliest hominids.

rapid fading The irrecoverable loss of speech sounds immediately after their utterance.

reciprocity The mutual exchange relationships that characterize the economic organization of most simple societies.

redistribution The upward channeling of goods and services to a powerful local figure who subsequently reallocates them among those who originally provided them.

redundancy Those signals of a message that can be eliminated without appreciable loss of essential information.

reflex An automatic biological response to a stimulus.

relative chronology Determination of the age of a site or its contents relative to another site.

religion The recognition of or belief in supernatural forces or beings.

rite of passage Any ritual activity that marks a critical period in a person's life, such as the transition from childhood to adulthood.

salvage archaeology An effort on the part of archaeologists to obtain as much information as possible from sites threatened by destruction as a result of either natural causes or human activity.

salvage ethnography The study and protection of endangered cultural forms.

semantic component The aspect of generative grammar that determines how the meaning of a sentence is to be interpreted.

semanticity In linguistic anthropology, the definite meanings with which humans endow the vocal sounds they produce.

senilicide The culturally sanctioned practice of killing old people.

serial monogamy The practice of having several successive spouses.

silent trade A practice in which trading parties exchange commodities without coming into face-to-face contact, usually accomplished by leaving goods at a designated place and later returning to collect what was left there in exchange.

Sinanthropus pekinensis The former designation of an extinct variety of *Homo erectus* found near Peking, China.

sister-exchange marriage The practice of transferring the prospective bridegroom's sister or some other close female kin to the bride's family in exchange.

socialization Social adjustments required of individuals as they learn to become members of society.

society A human aggregate, greatly varying in size, that is characterized by common patterns of relationships and shared cultural institutions.

sociolinguistics The study of the relationship between language varieties and the social characteristics of those who employ them.

sorcery The use of magic for malevolent purposes.

sororal polygyny The practice of choosing additional spouses from among the wife's sisters.

stratigraphy The principle that layers of older objects or geological deposits are found beneath more recent ones; archaeological analysis that makes use of this principle.

stress The prominence, or force, that certain syllables customarily receive.

subculture A social group that is a part of a larger cultural whole.

sun dance Among the Indians of the Plains, a tribal ritual characterized by fasting and dancing.

surface structure The outer, concrete form of a sentence.

syllabary A system of writing in which symbols represent syllables.

symbol A sign that has been given an arbitrary meaning.

syncretism A coalescence of religious beliefs and practices differing in form and origin.

syntactic component The aspect of a grammar that consists of a finite system of rules generating an infinite number of sentences.

syntax The manner in which words of a language are strung together into sentences.

tone language A language in which variations in tone are used to distinguish words of different meanings that otherwise would sound alike.

totem An animal, plant, or other object that gives a clan its collective designation.

transculturation Culture change resulting from the influences that societies in contact have upon each other.

transition The way in which adjacent sounds are joined together.

tree-ring dating A technique of absolute dating of wood remains by making use of the growth rings of trees; dendrochronology.

tribe An aggregate of people linked together by social ties, common language, and the recognition of a common cultural heritage.

typological classification The sorting and comparison of languages on the basis of structural criteria alone.

unilineal descent Descent reckoned through one line, either the maternal or the paternal.

value system An interlocking complex of ideals held by members of a society.

varve One of a layered series of annual deposits of silt or clay left behind by retreating ice sheets at the bottom of lakes and ponds.

vision quest Among the Indians of the Plains, a supernatural experience derived from solitary fasting and praying.

vocal-auditory channel   The physical medium employed in audible speech.

war   The use of armed force by one society against another to resolve a conflict between them.

witchcraft   Evil power thought to be either intrinsic in certain individuals or acquired as a consequence of association with those already possessing it.

Index

anthropological approach to, 321
classification of, 326–327
Hawaiian, 441
integrative function of, 336
in Latin America, 111–112
and magic, 324–325
among Maya, 331–332
in Middle America, 112
in modern society, 334–339
Navajo, 436
peasant, 180, 183, 330–331
role of, 319–321
and science, 21, 322
socialization in, 322 (fig.)
social role of, 415
in tribal societies, 328
Research
acculturation, 442–444
in complex societies, 200
implications of, 475
interdisciplinary, 8–9
in linguistics, 8
theory and method, 407–408
wartime, 223–224
Residence, postmarital, 249–250
Resources, world, allocation of, 461–465
Revitalizations, 332–334
Revolt Against civilization, (Stoddard), 35
Richards, Audrey, 288
Rickman, John, 223, 224
Ridicule
and conflict resolution, 262
in Eskimo society, 261
Rites of passage, 168, 169, 326
nature of, 328
in peasant society, 181
Ritual activity
among Australian aborigines, 151 (fig.)
beginnings of, 70
classic approaches to, 323
cooperation, 267
costuming, 112 (fig.)
and cultural reconstruction, 58
ghost dance, 121–123, 122 (fig.)
of *Homo erectus,* 68
marriage ceremony, 236 (fig.), 237,
237 (fig.)
nature of, 325–326
of nonhuman primates, 323n
Rivera, Diego, 316
River systems, 77 (fig.)
Rivet, Paul, 455

Roberts, John M., 268
Robertson, William, 86
Roles
and cultural change, 439
of peasant, 182
See also Sex roles
Rondon, Cândido Mariano da Silva, 113
Rousseau, Henri, 301n
Rousseau, Jean Jaques, 133, 344
Rules
in band-level societies, 259
of grammar, 356
language, 350
in peasant society, 175
Rumania, peasant society of, 186
Russians, wartime research on, 223–224.
See also Soviet Union

Sacrifice
economics of, 283
interpretation of, 326
Sahlins, Marshall D., 88, 163, 164, 264, 266,
288, 422
Salvage archaeology, 6 (fig.), 7
Salvage ethnography, 133
Salzmann, Zdenek, 244
Samoyed, hunting ecology of, 145
Sampling, 200
Sanctions, in band-level societies, 259, 260
Sanders, William T., 97
Sandia points, 88 (fig.), 89
Sapir, Edward, 384, 389–391, 390 (fig.), 397,
416, 418
Savanna, hominid development in, 27
Scarcity, concept of, 262
Science, and religion, 21, 322
Scott, Gen. Hugh Lenox, 359
Scott, Sir James G., 272
Scrapers, of *Homo erectus,* 67, 69
Sculpture
Mayan, 101
Paleolithic, 72, 73 (fig.)
of Upper Paleolithic, 146
See also Art
Sea, competition for, 468
Secularization, 320
Semai, distribution among, 281
Semantic component, of grammar, 356
Semanticity, in speech, 347
Semantics, ethnographic, 358
Senilicide, 144
Senior citizens, 203, 221

Serial monogamy, 238
Service, Elman R., 88, 260, 266, 422
Settlement
and agriculture, 154
of hunter gatherers, 143
patterns of, 58
Sexism
history of, 227–228
persistence of, 473–474
Sex roles, 225, 227
in cross-cultural perspective, 225
and cultural change, 438, 438 (fig.)
and occupation, 199
Sex and Temperament (Mead), 226
Sexual demarcation
and clothing styles, 376
in hunter-gatherer societies, 152
in language, 397
Shamanic religions, 326–338
Shamans
of Northwest coast peoples, 304, 327 (fig.)
in peasant society, 331
role of, 229
Shame, for Social control, 259
Shanidar cave, 71
Shanin, Theodore, 174
Sharecropping, 180
Sharp, Lauriston, 429
Shaw, George Bernard, 349
Sheehan, Bernard W., 114
Siberia, hunter-gatherer societies of, 145
Sickle-cell trait, 30
Sidescrapers, of Neanderthals, 70
Siebert, Frank T. Jr., 380, 381, 382
Sign language
of American Indians, 359
chimpanzee experience, 373
Signs
in communication, 345
iconic, 359, 364
Silent trade, 284
Silvert, K. H., 440
Sinanthropus pekinensis (Peking man), 66
Singer, Milton, 440
Sioux Indians, attachment to homeland of,
169–170
Siqueiros, David Alfaro, 316
Sister-exchange marriage, 247
Siuai tribe, feasts of, 160
Skull
of *Australopithecus,* 26 (fig.)
of human infant, 25, 28

and ethnoscience, 423
  ranking of, 382
Vocal-auditory channel, 346
Vogt, Evon Z., 435
Vogt, Hans, 380n
Voguls, hunting ecology of, 145
von Humboldt, Wilhelm, 389

Waddell, Jack O., 126
Walbiri people, symbolism of, 310–311
Walker, J. R., 310
Walker, Patrick, 82–83
Wallace, Alfred Russel, 23n
Wallace, Anthony F. C., 217, 326–327, 332
War
  applied anthropology during, 454–456
  defined, 273
  explanations for, 273–275
  among hunter-gatherer societies, 151
  and labeling of societies, 429
  psychological, 454
  as sociocultural phenomenon, 275–277
  among tribal societies, 157
  wastefulness of, 463 (fig.)
Ware-jaguar, in pre-Columbian art, 97
Warner, Lloyd W., 321
War party, of Plains Indians, 165
War Relocation Authority, 455
War societies, of Plains Indians, 169
Washburn, Wilcombe E., 121
Washo Indians, shamanic religion of, 328
Watson, O. Michael, 126
Weaving, in Neolithic villages, 76
Wenner-Gren Foundation, 420
Western societies
  art in, 300, 303
  poor in, 208
  See also Europe, United States
Weyer, Edward Moffat, Jr., 142

Wheeler, Sir Mortimer, 40
Wheeler-Howard Act, 124
Whistle speech, of Mazatec Indians, 359
White, Leslie A., 421
Whorf, Benjamin, 389, 391, 393, 394
Willendorf Venus, 72, 73 (fig.)
Willey, Gordon R., 46, 86, 89, 95, 159
Wilson, Jack, 121
Wilson, Peter J., 475n
Winter count, of Dakota Indians, 365 (fig.)
Wiser, Charlotte Viall, 176
Wiser, William H., 176
Wissler, Clark, 106n, 416
Witchcraft
  as alternative to war, 274
  cultural content for, 230
  in Middle American peasant
    tradition, 112
  in tribal religion, 328
Wolf, Eric R., 49, 112, 172, 174, 330–331
Wolfe, Alvin W., 311
Women
  African, 239–240
  conflict over control of, 261
  and cultural change, 438
  as gatherers, 140, 142, 149
  life expectancy of, 226
  Nuer, 168 (fig.)
  as priests, 337 (fig.)
  role of, 472
  and sexism, 473–474
  social movements of, 475
  status of, 225
  Yanomamö, 155 (fig.), 275–276
Women's Anthropological Society of
    America, 450
Woodburn, James, 148
World Bank, 464
World view, 393
  Navajo, 436

peasant, 176
  research on, 419
World War II, influence on anthropology,
    2, 223, 224–225, 314, 420–424,
    454, 476
Wormington, Hannah Marie, 91
Wounded Knee
  massacre at, 122, 123, 123n, 333
  seizure of, 125
Wovoka, 121–122
Writing, 359, 362–368
  in ancient world, 5
  cuneiform, 366 (fig.)
  Mayan, 101
  in Mesoamerica, 86
  in New World, 95, 366 (fig.)
  and urban civilization, 77
Wylie, Laurence, 181, 182n

Xavante people, initiation ceremonies of,
    169 (fig.)

Yana, language of, 391, 397
Yanomamö
  diet of, 155
  warfare of, 274, 274 (fig.), 275–276
Yoe, Shway, 272
Youth culture, 203
Yugoslavia, peasants of, 186–187

Zamora, socialization in, 226
Zangrando, Robert L., 438
Zero population growth (ZPG), 465
Zinacantecos, religion of, 331
Zulu
  age-grade system of, 168
  political organization of, 166
Zuni, character studies of, 223

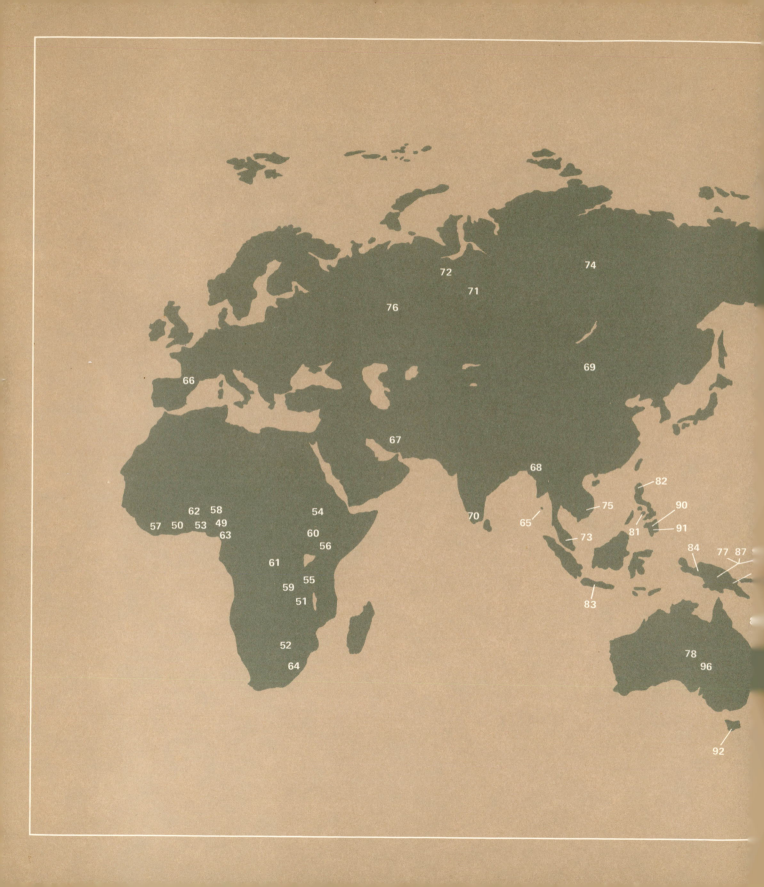